INTERNATIONAL VOLATILTIY AND ECONOMIC GROWTH

The First Ten Years of the International Seminar
on Macroeconomics

INTERNATIONAL VOLATILITY
AND
ECONOMIC GROWTH

The First Ten Years of
The International Seminar on Macroeconomics

Edited by

Georges de Ménil

Maison des Sciences de L'Homme, Paris, France

and

Robert J. Gordon

National Bureau of Economic Research, Cambridge, Massachusetts, USA
Northwestern University, Evanston, Illinois, USA

N·H

1991

North-Holland
AMSTERDAM . LONDON . NEW YORK . TOKYO

ELSEVIER SCIENCE PUBLISHERS B.V.
Sara Burgerhartstraat 25
P.O. Box 211, 1000 AE Amsterdam, The Netherlands

Distributors for the United States and Canada:
ELSEVIER SCIENCE PUBLISHING COMPANY INC.
655 Avenue of the Americas
New York, N.Y. 10010, U.S.A.

Library of Congress Cataloging-in-Publication Data

International Seminar on Macroeconomics.
    International volatility and economic growth: the first ten years of the International
Seminar on Macroeconomics/edited by Georges de Ménil and Robert J. Gordon.
        p.   cm.
    A selection of papers from the International Seminar on Macroeconomics (held annually
since 1978), and originally published only in special issues of the European economic review.
    Includes bibliographical references and index.
    ISBN 0-444-89284-2
    1. Economic policy--Congresses. 2. International economic relations--Congresses. 3. Inter-
national finance--Congresses. 4. Economic histroy--1971--Congresses. I. De Menil, George,
1940-. II. Gordon, Robert J. (Robert James), 1940- . III. European economic review. IV.
Title.
HD87.I56 1991
338.9--dc20   91-33530
                                                                                                      CIP

ISBN 0 444 89284 2

PRINTED IN THE NETHERLANDS

Contents

A decade of debate on international macroeconomic policy

This volume is a collection of papers presented and discussed at the International Seminar on Macroeconomics during its first decade, the decade of the 1980's. The contributors are Europeans, Americans and Japanese; the subject matter is macroeconomic policy.

That focus gives most of the papers an empirical character. Even when the theoretical models used are not readily quantifiable, the emphasis is on their power to clarify concrete policy issues.

The 1980's were marked, more than anything else, by the growing internationalization of economic activity. Markets became both more global and more volatile. Increasing interdependence made national economies more vulnerable to international disturbances and reduced the ability of national governments to control domestic developments. In the global competition of ideas, it became increasingly common to judge national institutional structures by comparing them with their counterparts in other countries and to measure the performance of national economics comparatively.

As a cross-national forum for scientific debate, the International Seminar on Macroeconomics has functioned at the crossroads of the major controversies of the decade. It was formed as the first annual international conference on issues of economic policy to bring together academic economists of the highest quality from Europe, the United States, and Japan, and its achievement of commissioning comparative papers providing an empirical analysis of two or more countries is unique. This volume is a record of the issues, the controversies, the comparative analyses, and the debate. The flavor and perspectives of the times are preserved in the contemporary comments and criticisms of the discussants that are presented here with each contribution.

* * * * * *

The International Seminar on Macroeconomics was launched in 1978 to promote dialogue and scientific exchange on policy issues between Europe and the United States.

Four years after the first oil shock, the United States was still searching for a definition of its role in the post Bretton Woods world. Some American policy makers and economists, mindful of the loss of fixed exchange rates, hoped to recover stability and growth through concerted efforts to convince Germany and Japan to be the 'locomotives' of the new order. Others, lured by the vaunted merits of floating exchange rates, argued that autonomous national policy was optimal, and that market pressures were a more effective means of disciplining national governments than conscious efforts at coordination.

The governments of Europe were, for their part, seeking to compensate for what they perceived to be the volatility and unpredictability of trans-Atlantic relationships by pursuing the construction – economic and political – of the Common Market. France and Germany were on the verge of leading the implementation of a new and strengthened European Monetary System, which was to prove over the ensuing decade to have a determining influence on the policies of its members. At the same time, all of these governments were being obliged to acknowledge that there would not be a rapid return to the rates of expansion of the 1960's – when unemployment was much lower in Europe than in the United States – and were beginning to grapple with the rigidities of 'Eurosclerosis'.

Parallel to the need for dialogue on the substance of policy was a need for scientific exchange between the students of policy. Unaccustomed to the realities of a more interdependent world, American economists too often tended to assume that other nations would be replicas in behavior and structure of the American model. Their analyses sometimes suffered from the absence of an understanding of diversities and assymetries which only first-hand research experience outside of America could provide. European economists, on the other hand, had struggled to recover from the human and intellectual destruction wrought by fascism and World War II. Some of the economic faculties of the Continent were still – though there were many notable exceptions – on the periphery of the dynamic developments in the discipline in the decades following the War. The need there was for exposure to and debate with some of the new methods and concepts.

It was against this background, in conversations in Paris, that Martin Feldstein suggested to Georges de Ménil that an international seminar be organized to promote scientific dialogue about macroeconomic policy issues between Europeans and Americans. The National Bureau of Economic Research – soon to be represented by Robert J. Gordon – was to sponsor and select American participants, and the Maison des Sciences de l'Homme to sponsor and select European participants for an annual meeting. [1]

---

[1] An Advisory Committee was formed to assist de Ménil and Gordon, consisting initially of Giorgio Basevi, William Branson, John Flemming, Heinz König, and Jean Waelbroeck. They were subsequently joined by Jacob Frenkel, Koichi Hamada, Jacques Mairesse, and (for three years) Masaru Yoshitomi.

The nature and style of the International Seminar on Macroeconomics was shaped by a number of important early decisions. The first was the decision to opt for collaborative sponsorship and direction. The reality then was that funding for such initiatives was more readily available in the United States than in Europe, and the course of least resistance would have been to depend exclusively on American sponsorship and financing. The partnership which in fact evolved between the National Bureau of Economic Research and the Maison des Sciences de l'Homme gave European participants the sense that they had an institutional as well as a personal stake in the long-run success of the effort. Their commitment was further reinforced by the choice the organizers made in the programming to emphasize European contributions, reflecting their judgment that this was where the need for communication was the greatest. The pattern which rapidly emerged was that each Seminar had roughly twice as many European papers as American papers, but that the two discussants of each contribution were selected from opposite sides of the Atlantic.

From the start, the Maison conceived of its role as that of an umbrella organization permitting and channeling the contributions of a series of different national European entities. The first few meetings were held at the Maison des Sciences de l'Homme in Paris. But as other institutions proffered support and offered sponsorship, [2] subsequent meetings came to alternate between Paris and other European locations – Oxford University, Universität Mannheim, the conference center of the Banca d'Italia in Perugia, the Ragny conference center of the Banque de France, les Facultés Universitaires Notre Dame de la Paix (Namur, Belgium), and subsequently to the years covered by this volume at the headquarters of the Banque de France and the Centro de Estudios Monetarios y Financieros, Banco de España. In 1989, the European Economic Association – which had not existed when the Seminar was launched, but whose new mission encompassed some of the stated objectives of the Seminar – agreed to join what then became a three-way partnership of sponsors: the NBER, the MSH, and the EEA.

The European–American emphasis which has characterized the Seminar has not been an exclusive one, and, indeed, the organizers have from the beginning elicited Japanese participation. Thanks to the generous financial support of the Foundation for Advanced Information and Research and the Institute of Fiscal and Monetary Policy, Japanese Ministry of Finance, the

---

[2] Financial support of the seminar for the ten conferences covered by this volume (1979–1988) was provided by, in addition to the National Bureau of Economic Research and la Maison des Sciences de l'Homme, the following organizations: Banque de France, Banca d'Italia, Commission of the European Economic Community, Deutsche Forschungs Gemeinschaft, École des Hautes Études en Sciences Sociales, Foundation for Advanced Information and Research (Japan), Institute of Fiscal and Monetary Policy (Japanese Ministry of Finance), National Bank of Belgium, Rock Foundation, Thyssen Foundation, and Universität Mannheim.

first Asian meeting of the Seminar was held at the Ministry of Finance, in Tokyo, in 1988.

The Seminar was fortunate to find early, in the *European Economic Review*, a respected outlet for publication. The *Review* was notably supportive of the organizers' goal of promoting scientific exchange on the highest level. The relationship of the Seminar to the *Review* was renewed and strengthened in 1988 when the *Review* became the official publication of the European Economic Association.

* * *

The papers in this volume were selected from the first ten annual issues of the *European Economic Review* to be dedicated to the International Seminar. The editors and the Advisory Committee chose what they felt was both an excellent and a representative selection. Contributions fell naturally into three broad areas: (1) comparative analyses of the relationship between structure and national macroeconomic performance; (2) the evolving nature of the external constraint, and alternative strategies for managing it; and (3) the consequences of internal and external debt.

The volume is divided into three parts corresponding to these three broad topic areas. We have written an introduction to each part that helps to place each contribution in the perspective of the time when it was written. Each contribution is presented as originally published in the *European Economic Review*, as are the contemporary comments of the conference discussants.

I. STRUCTURE AND PERFORMANCE

Introduction to Part I

One of the striking characteristics of the 1970's – which persisted into the first half of the 1980's – was the divergence of the economic performances of the major industrial democracies. Though the differences within Europe were great, [1] none was perhaps so dramatic as the reversal of the pattern of high unemployment and slow growth in the United States and tight employment and rapid growth in Europe which had characterized much of the previous post-War period.

After the first oil shock, American labor markets and the American economy were able to absorb the additional unemployment, contain the additional inflation, and resume moderate growth. The consequences of the second oil shock were more severe worldwide, but by the mid-1980's, the American economy had again contained its outburst of inflation and was resuming real growth. In Europe, on the other hand, unemployment mounted through most of the 1970's and 1980's, inflation persisted, and growth disappeared. By the middle of the 1980's, many of the nations of Europe had remarkably high unemployment and slow growth.

Even casual observation suggested that it was differences in structure rather than differences in policies that were primarily responsible for these contrasting responses to the oil shocks. All of the industrial economies had, after all, faced essentially the same oil and commodity price increases. Yet some experienced markedly less difficulty with both inflation and unemployment than others. [2]

Both the inflationary nature of the oil shocks and the prevalence of inflationary pressures world-wide in the preceding decade, pointed to the strategic importance of wage–price relationships. Several European economists, notably Herbert Giersch, identified the rigidity of the real wage

[1] See, for example, the differences between France and Germany described and analyzed by Georges de Ménil and Uwe Westphal, 1982, The Transmission of International Disturbances: A French-German Cliometric Analysis, 1972–1980, in the third annual International Seminar volume, European Economic Review, vol. 18, no. 1/2.

[2] The difference between European and American performances in the preceding decades – in that age of innocence when Phillips curves were not yet vertical and supply shocks were unimportant – seems, by contrast, to have been in part a reflection of differences in the willingness on the two sides of the Atlantic to use discretionary Keynesian policies to exploit the ephemeral rewards of moving up the Phillips curve.

– protected by de jure and de facto indexation and by pervasive social pressures – as a central structural impediment to successful adjustment in Europe. William Branson and Julio Rotemberg, inspired by a lecture by Giersch at Princeton in 1978, developed the first model and analytical study of the implications of real wage rigidity for macroeconomic policy in an international setting. The introduction to their paper, 'International Adjustment With Wage Rigidity', which is the lead article in this volume, succinctly summarizes the macroeconomic policy debate between Europe and the United States in the late 1970's, and points to the flexibility of the real wage in the United States – where inflation is relatively free to reduce the purchasing power of contractually fixed nominal wages – as the key to the success of its expansionary policies.

They suggest that real wage rigidity in Europe would cause the same expansionary policies to produce more inflation but not more output. The unstated implication is that the coordination of macroeconomic policies in interdependent countries with differing degrees of real wage rigidity calls for asymmetric combinations of both supply and demand policies.

Even as the policymakers of Europe and the United States struggled with adjustment problems in the 1980s, they never lost sight of the eventual objective of a return to steady growth. A lively interest in the determinants of growth thus persisted on both sides of the Atlantic. In 'Comparing Productivity Growth: An Exploration of French and United States Industrial and Firm Data,' Zvi Griliches and Jacques Mairesse provide an example of the light that careful, comparative econometric analysis of firm data can throw on these issues. The authors examine and ultimately reject a set of 'single-cause' hypotheses proposed by others to explain the productivity slowdown. Their findings are that neither slower growth in the accumulation of either physical capital or research and development (R & D) capital, nor the post-1972 increase in the relative price of raw materials, appears to explain any appreciable share of the productivity slowdown in France and the U.S.

The authors base their findings on an ambitious research project which involved assembling, partly from previously unpublished data, a new set of comparable information on key variables, using consistent definitions, for 15 manufacturing industries and over 500 firms in the two countries over the period 1967–1978. The data for output and input were used to compute growth rates of total factor productivity (TFP) for each firm, industry, and country. TFP growth was higher in France than in the U.S. not only for manufacturing as a whole, but also for each industry separately. In both countries productivity growth slowed hereafter with a somewhat greater slowdown in the U.S.

Much of their paper is devoted to a detailed examination and ultimate rejection of several single-cause explanations. They show no tendency for industries having relatively slow capital accumulation or relatively large increases in energy prices to exhibit relatively large slowdowns in TFP growth. Similarly, R & D does not help, both because there was only a modest slowdown in the ratio of R & D spending to GNP in the U.S., and also because France has an even lower R & D-to-GNP ratio than the U.S. yet achieves faster productivity growth across-the-board. The most positive aspect of this part of the study is the confirmation of previous estimates that the overall gross rate of return to investment in R & D is about 25 percent.

Intractable real wages are not the only structural rigidities that can have an effect on economic performance. The thirst for remedies to Europe's stagnation inspired a resurgence of studies of institutions and policies at the microeconomic level which hinder adaptation. The 1986 meeting of the International Seminar (published in the *European Economic Review* in 1987), was devoted exclusively to supply side impediments to growth. Three of the papers presented then, and reproduced in this volume, give a sense of the varieties of comparative and empirical work which the Seminar has promoted.

In 'Housing Markets, Unemployment and Labour Market Flexibility in the U.K.', Gordon Hughes and Barry McCormick show graphically how housing policies have unwittingly reduced the mobility of workers in that country. They document with micro data the fact that the inevitable queues for public and rent-subsidized housing are a strong disincentive to mobility. In an interesting speculative part of the paper (part 4), they examine the relationship between geographic mobility and the NAIRU, and conjecture further that there may be a relationship between the low level of geographic mobility and aspects of unionism in Britain: 'When mobility is costly, workers have an increased incentive to ... join and be active in unions ... [and] the choices of the unions (for example, whether to strike or not) [tend to foster] ... adversarial ... management–union relations [of the kind which are one] traditional explanation of low U.K. productivity.' [3]

In both Europe and the United States, the reputed flexibility of the Japanese economy has been a recurrent standard of comparison for studies of structural rigidities and macroeconomic performance. In 'Labour Market Flexibility in Japan in Comparison with Europe and the U.S.', Toshiaki Tachibanaki provides an empirical survey of the differences between these labor markets and analyzes their contribution to macroeconomic performance. The array of differences is impressive: the high mobility of labor, the importance of the share of part-time and self-employed labor, the flexibility of hours and wages, the relative weakness of social policy toward labor, etc. Tachibanaki is careful to warn against extrapolating simplistically from Japanese experience to the possible consequences of following the 'Japanese model' in Europe or the United States.

---

[3] *This volume*, Chapter 3 pp. 101–102.

In the last paper in Volume I, we move from econometric studies of markets based on panels of microdata to highly aggregated time-series analysis. In 'Productivity, Wages, and Prices Inside and Outside of Manufacturing in the U.S., Japan, and Europe,' Robert J. Gordon studies for 1964–1984 the comparative dynamic behavior of annual series on prices, wages, output and productivity in the U.S., Japan, and a composite he calls 'Europe' (a fixed-weight aggregate of eleven countries in and out of the EC).

Gordon emphasizes the differences between his results and that of the previous literature on inflation and productivity in Europe. One of the central issues in that literature is the assertion that excessive real wages were a significant cause of the unemployment of the 1970s and 1980s throughout the OECD and particularly in Europe. Bruno and Sachs, for instance, report high and rising values in eight OECD countries during that period of the 'real wage gap' – defined conceptually as the difference between the real product wage and its market-clearing value. [4] This concept is related to the emphasis that Branson and Rotemberg, interpreting Giersch, placed on real wage rigidity and the potential for excessive real wages in Europe.

Gordon points out that much of the earlier evidence is based exclusively on data for real wages and productivity in manufacturing, and does not apply to the larger, nonmanufacturing sector, where data problems are much greater. One of the unique features of his study is its systematic exploitation of published and unpublished data on nonmanufacturing aggregates, and one of his most striking results is the finding that the real wage gap in nonmanufacturing *declines* over the 1970s in both the United States and in his European aggregate. His finding for the wage gap in manufacturing – which rises more in his European countries than in the United States over the 1970s, and then reverses itself – is not inconsistent with other findings. But the decline which he finds in the nonmanufacturing sector is sufficient to leave the economy-wide wage gap unchanged over the period in both Gordon's European aggregate and the United States.

As Gordon points out, this striking result for nonmanufacturing is in part attributable to his inclusion of 100 percent of the income of self-employed persons in his measure of labor compensation in nonmanufacturing. Allocating this volatile series – which includes the incomes (particularly significant in Europe) of farmers, artisans, and shopkeepers – more to capital income and less to labor income would alter the result.

In the econometric section of his paper, Gordon estimates extended Phillips-type wage equations, price equations, and the partial reduced form relating prices to output for both manufacturing and the residual nonmanufacturing sector in the three regions. His direct and indirect estimates of the

---

[4] Michael Bruno and Jeffrey D. Sachs 1985, The Economics of Worldwide Stagflation. (Harvard University Press, Cambridge, MA) Chapters 9 and 10.

reduced-form response of prices to output – a measure of sensitivity of inflation to excess demand – are about the same in the U.S. as in the European aggregate. He concludes that nominal prices and wages have a similarly low degree of sensitivity to excess supply and demand in both regions.

Gordon's paper is not exclusively contrarian. It confirms the consensus of empirical studies in this area on a number of significant points – notably the importance of autonomous wage push episodes in the late 1960s and early 1970s as a source of higher real wages, and hence lower employment, in both Europe and Japan. He finds that the wage explosions of those periods are best captured by highly significant dummy variables, whose indirect effect on employment he then further documents. This result rejoins some of the concerns of Giersch and other European commentators.

European Economic Review 13 (1980). North-Holland

INTERNATIONAL ADJUSTMENT WITH WAGE RIGIDITY*

William H. BRANSON and Julio J. ROTEMBERG

NBER, and Princeton University, Princeton, NJ 08540, USA

1. Background and introduction

Since 1974 the OECD area has seen several attempts at recovery from the 1974–75 recession, but the result has been stagnation. The recovery of 1975–77 in the United States took it well ahead of the rest of the OECD in the business cycle, even though the unemployment rate reached a low of only 5.7 percent. The U.S. recovery led to a massive increase in its current account deficit and the sharp depreciation of the dollar in 1978. The 'balance of payments constraint' on uncoordinated recovery reappeared as an 'exchange-rate constraint'.

In November 1978, U.S. policy shifted sharply toward restraint and support for the dollar; the shift was announced publicly by President Carter. Demand policy has remained tight ever since, especially with monetary policy tightening in West Germany in 1979. The tightening of U.S. policy simply recognizes that the U.S. cannot attempt recovery significantly faster than Europe or Japan. The OECD countries appear to be locked into a system in which economic growth is significantly limited by the growth rate of the slowest major participant. The result of the shift in policy is renewed recession and rising unemployment throughout the OECD area.

The constraining factor in the stagnation since 1974 seems to be the difficulty of recovery, or reluctance to stimulate demand, in Europe and Japan. The question we address is: why is recovery so hard in Europe and Japan? During 1976–77 the OECD policy debate on recovery was mainly the U.S. suggesting (more or less politely) that the countries in 'strong' current account positions, Japan and West Germany, take the lead, and those governments either refusing or reluctantly proposing fairly timid measures. Essentially their position was that rapid demand expansion would lead only to more inflation, with no significant gains in real output.

One popular explanation for the policy difference between the U.S. and,

*Paper presented at the International Seminar on Macroeconomics, Paris, September 10–11, 1979. We wish to thank the participants for helpful comments and the NSF for research support.

mainly, West Germany was that their sensitivity to or expectations of inflation differed. Another could be that the implicit model behind the German view was a textbook 'classical' model with no money illusion and fully flexible wages and prices, while the implicit U.S. model has sticky wages or money illusion. This view of the German economy did not seem realistic.

A more satisfactory model of the European side was presented by Herbert Giersch when he talked in Princeton in March, 1978. Our interpretation of his view was that the German real wage was rigid, at least downward, above its equilibrium value. This model would give the 'classical' results that demand expansion only raises prices with no effect on output, but not in a flexible wage-and-price context. As we see in section 2 below, an assumption of real-wage rigidity of this sort in Europe and Japan plus nominal wage stickiness in the U.S. would make sense of the 1976–77 policy debate.

As an initial check on the empirical plausibility of this model, we perused the time-series data on real wage rates in major OECD countries. If differences between real-wage and nominal-wage rigidities were a major feature of the OECD economies, they should appear in the 1974 recession, with rigid real wages resisting the downturn more than sticky nominal wages. This is especially true with the oil price increase.

The time-series data are summarized in table 1. There we see that the only country with a protracted decline on real wages in the 1973–75 period was the United States. There the real-wage index peaked at 1.042 in 1973:2, and did not pass the level again until 1975:2. In Germany, real-wage growth continued straight through the recession until 1976. In Italy and Japan, there was a pause in 1974, with growth resuming by the beginning of 1975. In the U.K., the real-wage index continued to grow to mid-1976, with pauses in 1974:2 and in mid-1975. These data provide some initial support for the hypothesis, and were the basis for an informal discussion of it at the International Seminar on Macroeconomics in 1978. This paper reports on our continuing theoretical and empirical investigation of demand policy in a series of models with differing types of wage rigidity across countries.

In section 2 of the paper we develop a model of two countries with one commodity and purchasing-power-parity (PPP). Here we obtain the clear-cut Giersch results. Expansion in the country with rigid real wages raises the world price level, increases output in the country with rigid nominal wages, and also reduces that country's trade deficit.

The clarity of these results is blurred in section 3, where we study a model with two commodities and do not assume PPP. This is the same general framework used by Bruno and Sachs (1979) and Argy and Salop (1978). The main differences are that the section 3 model is analytic and focuses on effects of demand policy, while the Bruno–Sachs several-country model is solved by simulation and focuses on analysis of stagflation. Argy and Salop look only at supply-side conditions, while we study demand and supply. As

Table 1

Index of real hourly compensation of employees for selected OECD countries.

Year	Germany	Italy	Japan	U.K.	U.S.
1971:1	1.000	1.000	1.000	1.000	1.000
1971:2	0.997	1.036	1.024	1.025	1.001
1971:3	1.029	1.058	1.053	1.012	1.003
1971:4	1.031	1.049	1.065	1.025	1.003
1972:1	1.057	1.057	1.116	1.037	1.016
1972:2	1.067	1.095	1.116	1.076	1.023
1972:3	1.076	1.111	1.124	1.069	1.027
1972:4	1.086	1.176	1.197	1.072	1.030
1973:1	1.119	1.177	1.142	1.064	1.042
1973:2	1.125	1.236	1.173	1.080	1.036
1973:3	1.139	1.259	1.222	1.088	1.034
1973:4	1.147	1.270	1.307	1.088	1.029
1974:1	1.161	1.255	1.169	1.121	1.018
1974:2	1.196	1.317	1.280	1.120	1.024
1974:3	1.228	1.277	1.305	1.164	1.024
1974:4	1.245	1.293	1.305	1.190	1.032
1975:1	1.262	1.356	1.340	1.204	1.041
1975:2	1.265	1.369	1.311	1.186	1.049
1975:3	1.276	1.414	1.307	1.191	1.047
1975:4	1.282	1.390	1.312	1.203	1.051
1976:1	1.277	1.391	1.312	1.208	1.057
1976:2	1.279	1.407	1.300	1.221	1.072
1976:3	1.294	1.434	1.300	1.217	1.075
1976:4	1.300	1.401	1.313	1.192	1.082
1977:1	1.298	1.391	1.309	1.168	1.085
1977:2	1.318	1.418	1.314	1.150	1.086
1977:3	1.319	1.415	1.324	1.155	1.095
1977:4	1.348	1.423	1.339	1.174	1.103
1978:1	1.331	1.441	1.343	1.195	1.112
1978:2	1.364	1.421	1.345	1.227	1.106
1978:3	1.362	1.421	1.349	1.232	1.109
1978:4	1.385	1.432	1.362	1.248	1.109

we see in table 3, the Bruno–Sachs and Argy–Salop results can be viewed as special cases of ours.

The reason that the clear-cut Giersch results are lost in the two-commodity case is that the relevant prices for workers' and producers' decisions are different (as in Bruno–Sachs and Argy–Salop). Producers look at the price of domestic output; workers look at a CPI with imports in it as well. Thus even if the real wage relative to the CPI is rigid, if a demand expansion at home pulls up the price of domestic output relative to the CPI, employment and output expands. Only if exchange-rate adjustment were immediate and complete, putting us back in the section 2 PPP world, would the difference not appear. The result is that, in section 3, we see that the degree of 'money illusion', or real wage vs. nominal-wage stickiness, is at least as important as actual-wage rigidity for sorting out the effects of demand policy.

In section 4 we report some empirical tests of wage rigidity and money illusion for five major OECD countries (U.S., U.K., Japan, Italy, Germany) on time-series data since 1961. The sample is split at 1971 to see if parameters have changed in the 1970s. An important thing to note about our table 4 regressions is that they report equations for gradual adjustment of wage *levels*, with lagged wages and the *level* of demand as regressors. This formulation follows from the theory of sections 2 and 3, where wage rigidities are stated in terms of the relevant wage level. Bruno and Sachs (1979, p. 16) have the same basic theoretical structure but estimate Phillips-type equations with the wage *change* depending on the *level* of demand.

The empirical results give us a classification as follows. The U.S. stands out as the only country with short-run stickiness of nominal-wage rates. The U.K., Japan, Germany, and Italy all seem to have gradual adjustment of real wages, consistent with effective indexation. In all five countries, response of the relevant wage to demand pressure is much less in the 1970s than over the entire period. These results are consistent with the Giersch hypothesis extended to the OECD.

2. Wage rigidities in the PPP model

In this section we develop the simplest macro model with wage rigidities that yields interesting results for the effects of demand policy. The model has two countries and one commodity (the 'schmoo'), and assumes that the 'law of one price' holds, so that there is one world price, P, for the one commodity.[1] We hold the exchange rate constant at unity; alternatively we could assume two different domestic prices for the commodity, P and P^*, with the exchange rate e defined by $P = eP^*$. We begin with the specification of aggregate supply conditions, then move on to demand in each country

Table 2
Definition of variables.

y = domestic output
P = price index for y
W = nominal-wage rate
w = real-wage rate
K = capital stock
g = exogenous component of demand in real terms
a = real absorption
x = real net exports
$*$ = superscript for the 'foreign' country

[1] See table 2 for definition of variables.

and determination of the equilibrium price level. Next we study the effects of demand policy and the consequences of different forms of wage rigidity.

2.1. Labor market and aggregate supply

On the demand side of the labor market we have a production function and a marginal productivity condition which yields the labor demand function

$$y = y(N, K), \qquad y_N > 0, \quad y_{NN} < 0, \qquad \text{[production function]} \qquad (1)$$

$$y_K > 0, \quad y_{NK} < 0;$$

$$w = W/P = y_N(N, K). \qquad \text{[demand wage]} \qquad (2)$$

In an equilibrium model, we would add a labor-supply function $w = w^s(N)$, and solve for equilibrium w and N. Here we assume that alternately either the nominal wage or the real wage is rigid above its equilibrium value. We assume that with the relevant wage rigid above its equilibrium level, employment is determined along the labor-demand function. This is the familiar minimum condition in non-market-clearing models.[2] Thus if the wage rigidity is effective, labor is constrained in the amount of hours that employers will buy. This is consistent with the specification of the demand side in the next subsection.

In the case of the real-wage rigidity we have $w = \bar{w} > equilibrium$ w, and employment is determined along the labor-demand function

$$w = y_N(N, K). \qquad (3)$$

This gives us N as a function of $\bar{w}$ and the production technology, and through (1) it fixes y from the supply side. This is similar to the textbook 'classical' model [see Branson (1979)] and is illustrated in fig. 1.

With a nominal wage rigidity we have

$$\bar{W} = P \cdot y_N(N, K) \qquad (4)$$

as the labor-market equilibrium (but non-clearing) condition. This is illustrated in fig. 2. The response of employment and aggregate supply to a change in the price level is obtained from total differentiation of (4) and the production function (1),

$$\left. \mathrm{d}N/\mathrm{d}P \right|_{\substack{w=\bar{w} \\ \mathrm{d}K=0}} = -y_N/y_{NN} > 0, \qquad \left. \mathrm{d}y/\mathrm{d}P \right|_{\substack{w=\bar{w} \\ \mathrm{d}K=0}} = y_N(\mathrm{d}N/\mathrm{d}P) > 0. \qquad (5)$$

[2]See Muellbauer and Portes (1979), for example.

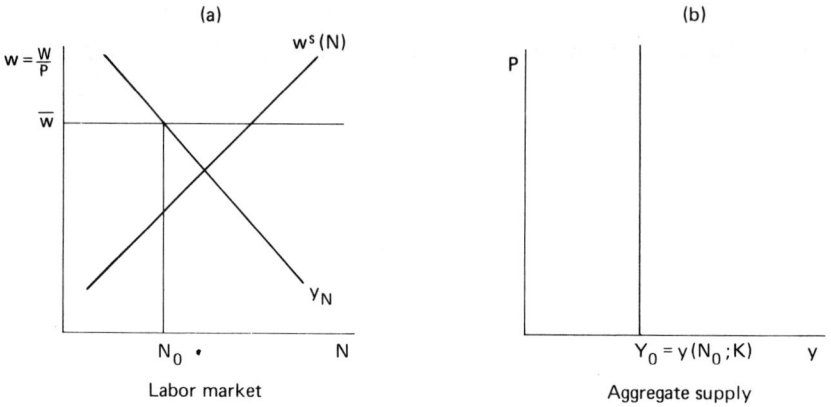

Fig. 1. Real-wage rigidity.

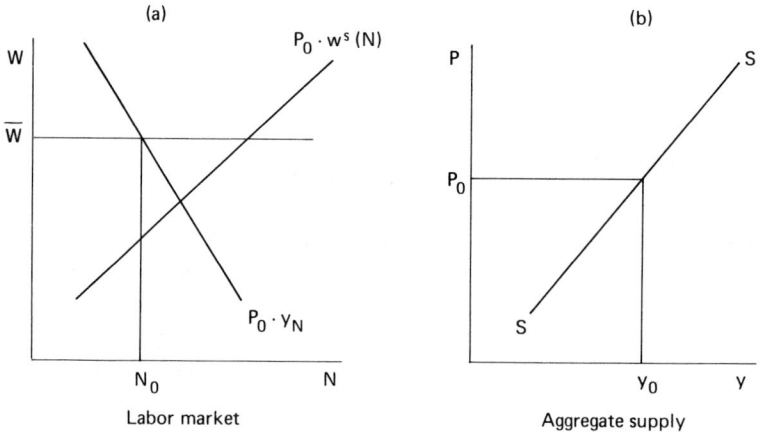

Fig. 2. Nominal-wage rigidity.

The response of aggregate supply to an increase in the capital stock is given by

$$dy/dK\big|_{\substack{w=\bar{w} \\ dP=0}} = -y_N(y_{NK}/y_{NN}) > 0. \tag{6}$$

An increase in the capital stock shifts out the supply curve in figs. 1 and 2. Thus with the rigid nominal wage we can write the aggregate supply function of fig. 2(b) as

$$y = y(P,K), \qquad y_P \gtreqless 0, \quad y_K \gtreqless 0, \tag{7}$$

with a rigid real wage $y_P = 0$; with a rigid nominal wage $y_P > 0$.

In the two-country model we will assume that each country has an aggregate supply function of the form $y = y(P,K)$. The 'home' country will be identified by unstarred variabless; the 'foreign' country by stars. Thus the two aggregate supply functions are

$$y = y(P,K),$$ (8a)

$$y^* = y^*(P,K^*).$$ (8b)

Remember that there is only one world price level.

In the solution for equilibrium and comparative statics below we first assume $y_P > 0$; $y_P^* > 0$ in general. Then when we analyze the effects of differing wage rigidities on the results of demand policy we will assume the 'home' country has a real-wage rigidity so that $y_P = 0$, and the 'foreign' country has a nominal-wage rigidity with $y_P^* > 0$. The effects of changes in investment will come in only when we discuss policy to adjust to a real-wage rigidity, so we omit the K argument in y and y^* until we reach that discussion.

2.2. Demand and equilibrium P

With rigid wages above equilibrium in both countries, real absorption will be a function of income, the price level, and a demand policy variable. Income appears through a Keynesian effective-demand consumption function. The price level represents a real balance effect with predetermined outside money. The demand policy variable can be thought of as the real deficit, or real government purchases with given tax revenue. The income–expenditure equilibrium conditions for the two countries are then

$$y(P) = a(y(P), P, g) + x,$$ (9a)

$$y^*(P) = a^*(y^*(P), P, g^*) - x.$$ (9b)

Here net exports (the current account balance of the home country) x is residually determined by income y less absorption a. With only one good there are no terms-of-trade effects. This simplification will be removed in section 3 below. With two countries, x enters negatively in (9b). The partial derivatives of a are signed $a_y > 0$, $a_p < 0$, $a_g > 0$ ($= 1$), and similarly for a^*.

The equilibrium world price level P is obtained by equating income less absorption at home to absorption less income abroad,

$$y - a = -(y^* - a^*).$$ (10)

Here we sum the excess demand functions in the two countries and find the price level at which world excess demand is zero.

The next step is to derive expressions for the effects of change in demand policy and g and g^* on the price level. The effects on outputs y and y^* will follow immediately from the supply functions. The effects on the current account x can then be solved from (9a) or (9b). Total differentiation of (10) and solution for dP yields

$$dP = \frac{1}{\phi + \phi^*}(dg + dg^*),\tag{11}$$

where

$$\phi = (y_P(1 - a_y) - a_p) > 0 \quad \text{and} \quad \phi^* = (y_P^*(1 - a_{y^*}^*) - a_P^*) > 0.$$

Remember $a_g = 1$. The effect of demand expansion on the price level does not depend on where it originates. The parameters ϕ and ϕ^* are Keynesian-type multipliers.

The effect of demand expansion on net exports can be solved from the total differential of (9a),

$$dx = -\frac{\phi^*}{\phi + \phi^*}dg + \frac{\phi}{\phi + \phi^*}dg^*.\tag{12}$$

An exogenous increase in home demand reduces x; an increase in foreign demand increases x. If both g and g^* rise by the same amount, the effect on x depends on the net absorption coefficients ϕ and ϕ^*. If $\phi > \phi^*$, a balanced expansion increases x since net absorption falls more at home than abroad.

The increase in outputs y and y^* that follows from an increase in g or g^* are simply $dy = y_P dP$ and $dy^* = y_P^* dP$. Thus if the supply curves have positive slopes, both levels of output and employment are increased by a demand expansion in either country.

2.3. The role of wage rigidities

We can now use the one-commodity model to study the effects of differing wage rigidities on response to changes in demand policy. To be specific, let us assume that in the home country the real wage is rigid above equilibrium, while in the foreign country the nominal wage is rigid. Thus $w = \bar{w}$, $W^* = \bar{W}^*$, by assumption. What are the consequences for the effects of a demand expansion?

First, with a real-wage rigidity at home $y_P = 0$ and ϕ in eq. (11) reduces to $-a_p$. When the price level rises, there is an effect on absorption in the real-wage country, but no effect on output. The reaction of the world price level with this pattern of wage rigidities is given by

$$dP = \frac{1}{\phi^* - a_p}(dg + dg^*).$$ (13)

The source of the demand disturbances still does not matter, but the price multiplier is increased from eq. (11) by elimination of the y_P^* output effect. The expression for dx in eq. (12) is also changed by substitution of $-a_p$ for ϕ. It is still the case that $dx/dg < 0$ and $dx/dg^* > 0$, but it is more likely that a balanced increase in g and g^* decreases x because of the zero supply response in the home country.

To summarize, an increase in g in the real-wage country (a) increases P, and by more than in a world with no real-wage rigidity, (b) increases output *only* in the other country, and (c) reduces the trade surplus in the real-wage country. Thus *if* Germany were the real-wage country and the U.S. were the nominal-wage country, a fiscal expansion in Germany would be inflationary and reduce the German trade balance, but all the output and employment effects would appear in the U.S.

This model can be generalized easily to a world of several countries, some with real-wage rigidities, some with nominal-wage rigidities. A demand expansion originating anywhere in the system will raise the price for all, but increase output and employment only where nominal prices are rigid. The trade surplus (deficit) will be reduced (increased) in the area where the demand expansion originated, and a balanced expansion of demand will reduce the trade surplus of the real-wage countries.

2.4. Effect of capital stock expansion

Expansion of the capital stock in one country will increase supply in that country, drive down the world price level, and in general reduce output in the other country. We can see this by putting (8a) and (8b) for y and y^* into the equilibrium conditions (9a) and (9b), inserting these into (10) for the world price level, and totally differentiating with respect to P and K. The result is

$$\frac{dP}{dK} = -\frac{y_K(1 - a_y)}{\phi + \phi^*} < 0.$$

If the home (unstarred) country increases its capital stock, its output rises unambiguously. The expression for dy is

$$dy = y_K\left(1 - \frac{y_P(1 - a_y)}{\phi + \phi^*}\right)dK.$$

Since $y_P(1 - a_y) < \phi$, $dy/dK > 0$.

If the real wage in the home country is rigid above equilibrium, so that y_P $=0$, capital stock expansion can increase output to the point where the wage rigidity is no longer binding on the side of the demand for labor. Thus one policy to escape the wage rigidity is incentives for investment. This was Giersch's conclusion for West Germany. However, by reducing the world price level P, this policy would tend to reduce output abroad unless $y_P^* = 0$.

3. Adjustment with differentiated product bundles

The clear-cut results of section 2 were derived in a framework with only one good and one world price level. The sharpness of these results is reduced when we go to a world of differentiated product bundles with different prices. In reality the industrial countries trade products that can be roughly aggregated into bundles of exportables and importables, with the possibility of terms-of-trade changes between them. To capture the effects of movements in the terms of trade, we turn to a model in which the two countries produce different goods. These can be thought of as different fixed-weight product bundles with their associated price indexes. Introduction of two goods, and two prices, changes fundamentally the characterization of both the supply and demand sides of the model, and makes the signs of the effects of expansionary policy in either country on both outputs depend on particular parameter values.

3.1. The demand side with two commodities

In this section we develop a fairly standard two-country Keynesian model with two goods. The two goods are the home exportable y with a price index P, and the foreign exportable y^* with a price index P^*. In this framework we again study the effects of differing wage rigidities, i.e., aggregate supply specifications, on the effectiveness of demand policy in influencing output.

On the demand side we have the usual absorption equation for an open economy,

$$y = a(y, \hat{P}, g) + x(P/eP^*). \tag{14}$$

The consumer price index entering absorption is a function of the home and foreign prices,

$$\hat{P} = \theta(P, P^*), \qquad \theta_p, \theta_{p^*} \geq 0, \quad \theta_p + \theta_{p^*} = 1. \tag{15}$$

The restriction on the sum of θ_p and θ_{p^*} follows from specification of $\hat{P}$ as a weighted average of P and P^*, and the initial normalization $P = P^* = 1$.

Total differentiation of (14), holding the exchange rate constant at $e=1$, yields

$$dy = \frac{1}{1+a_y} [(a_p\theta_p + x_p)dP + (a_p\theta_{p^*} - x_p)dP^* + dg].$$ (16)

Here $x_p < 0$ is the derivative of x with respect to eP/P^*. From (16) we can write the demand function for y,

$$y = V(P, P^*, g), \qquad V_p < 0, \quad V_{p^*} > 0, \quad V_g > 0.$$ (17)

The partial derivatives of V are the coefficients in eq. (16) above. $V_{p^*} > 0$ assumes that the terms-of-trade effect outweighs the absorption effect when the foreign price level P^* rises. If the home good share in the consumption bundle is at least equal to the import share, $\theta_p \geq \theta_{p^*}$, then $|V_p| > |V_{p^*}|$. This condition is not necessary since x_p enters V_p while $-x_p$ enters V_{p^*}.

3.2. Aggregate supply with two commodities

On the supply side we first develop expressions for labor market supply, demand, and equilibrium, and then show how these are affected by the existence of wage rigidities above equilibrium levels.

The production function is eq. (1) of section 2, where output is the exportable good. The usual demand function for labor is given in eq. (2) above: $W/P = y_N(N)$. As an alternative we also introduce the possibility that producers have market power in both home and foreign markets, and can effectively prevent entry in the short run. In this case, both the home and foreign prices would enter the demand function for labor,

$$W/\tilde{P} = y_N(N),$$ (18)

with $\tilde{P}$ defined by

$$\tilde{P} = \psi(P, P^*), \qquad \psi_p, \psi_{p^*} \geq 0, \quad \psi_p + \psi_{p^*} = 1.$$ (19)

In the competitive case $\tilde{P} = P$, and $\psi_p = 1$. However, (19) provides the price index for a discriminating monopolist producing at home and selling in both markets.[3] In the algebra that follows, the competitive case can be obtained by setting $\psi_p = 1$ and $\psi_{p^*} = 0$.

The labor-supply function makes the real wage demanded a function of the level of employment, with the nominal wage deflated by the consumer price index $\hat{P}$ defined earlier in eq. (15). Thus labor supply is given by

$$W/\hat{P} = g(N), \qquad g_N > 0.$$ (20)

[3]For detailed analysis and proof, see appendix A.

Equilibrium in the labor market equates the nominal supply wage from (20) to the demand wage from (18),

$$\hat{P} \cdot g(N) = \tilde{P} \cdot y_N(N). \tag{21}$$

Total differentiation of (21) plus the production function (1) gives us the expression for changes in y as functions of dP and dP^* on the supply side,

$$\mathrm{d}y = \frac{1}{g_N - y_{NN}} [(\psi_p - \theta_p)\mathrm{d}P + (\psi_{p^*} - \theta_{p^*})\mathrm{d}P^*]. \tag{22}$$

Here we have set all prices at unity initially. It may help to note that this implies also that initial $w = g = y_N = 1$.

From (22) we can write the general form of the supply function for y as

$$y = \Lambda(P, P^*), \qquad \Lambda_p \geq 0, \quad \Lambda_{p^*} \leq 0. \tag{23}$$

The signs of the partial derivatives of (23) are the coefficients of (22), where we assume $\theta_{p^*} > \psi_{p^*}$. This simply says the weight of foreign prices in the worker's CPI is larger than it is in the firms' profits function.

An interesting property of the Λ supply function should be noted here. If workers focus on the real wage, correctly measured, in making the labor-supply decision, then $\theta_p + \theta_{p^*} = 1$. Together with $\psi_p + \psi_{p^*} = 1$, this implies that $\Lambda_p = -\Lambda_{p^*}$; the supply function is symmetric with respect to the two prices.

3.3. The role of wage rigidities

We can now introduce wage rigidities on the supply side as special cases of (22) and (23). Consider first the case in which the real wage is rigid above equilibrium. We interpret this as an infinitely elastic supply curve for labor at the rigid wage $\bar{w}$, so that the supply function (20) becomes

$$W/\hat{P} = \bar{w}, \tag{20^R}$$

and in (22), $g_N = 0$.

This simply removes g_N from (22) and (23), not changing the qualitative slopes of (23). Thus going to a two-good model fundamentally changes the 'classical' effect of the real-wage rigidity. With the two price indexes entering differently in producers' demand for labor and in workers' supply, a change of either price influences output supplied, with $\partial y / \partial P > 0$ and $\partial y / \partial P^* < 0$ even with a real-wage rigidity. This will eliminate some of the sharp results of the one-commodity model.

To impose a nominal-wage rigidity, we re-write (20) as

$$W = \bar{W};\qquad\qquad\qquad (20^{\text{N}})$$

in addition to $g_N = 0$, $\hat{P}$ no longer enters the supply function. This eliminates θ_p and θ_{p*} from (22) and (23). In the usual case of $\psi_p = 1$, this takes us back to the supply function of section 2, eq. (5), with $\partial y / \partial P = -1/y_{NN}$.

With complete wage rigidity, or complete 'money illusion' in labor supply, θ_p and $\theta_{p*} = 0$, since the price level does not enter the labor-supply function as it affects the level of employment. With flexible nominal wages and no money illusion, $\theta_p + \theta_{p*} = 1$. In an intermediate case of partial money illusion, the labor force would 'perceive' a price index with $\theta_p + \theta_{p*} < 1$. The perceived price index could be thought of as the actual CPI raised to a power less than unity: $\hat{P}^\alpha$ with $\alpha < 1$.[4]

To summarize, real-wage rigidity would eliminate g_N from (22) and nominal-wage rigidity would further eliminate θ_p and θ_{p*}. Both types of rigidity would leave us with the supply function (23) with $\Lambda_p > 0$. The sign of Λ_{p*}, the cross-price effect on supply, is less clear. Normally $\Lambda_{p*} < 0$. However, in the case where $\psi_p = 1$, complete nominal-wage rigidity would eliminate P^* from the Λ supply function. If ψ_{p*} is sufficiently large compared to θ_{p*}, then $\Lambda_{p*} > 0$.

3.4. Demand and supply in the 'foreign' country

Eqs. (17) and (23) give demand and supply in the home country as functions of the two price levels. At this level of generality, demand and supply in the foreign country are mirror images. The only point to note especially is that the trade balance at home must equal the deficit abroad. Thus the demand equation in the foreign country is solved from

$$y^* = a^*(y^*, \hat{P}^*, g^*) - x(eP/P^*). \qquad\qquad (24)$$

The foreign demand equation is then

$$y^* = V^*(P, P^*, g^*), \qquad V_p^* > 0, \quad V_{p*}^* < 0, \quad V_{g*}^* > 0. \qquad (25)$$

The supply equation is

$$y^* = \Lambda^*(P, P^*), \qquad \Lambda_p^* \lessgtr 0, \quad \Lambda_{p*}^* \gtrless 0. \qquad (26)$$

The entire discussion for wage rigidities, etc., in the home case applies in the 'foreign' case as well.

Given the values of the two demand policy variables g and g^*, the two demand functions, eqs. (17) and (25), and the supply functions equations,

---

[4]See Branson and Klevorick (1969) for use of this parameterization of money illusion.

eqs. (23) and (26), give us four equations in the variables y, y^*, P, P^*. These already include the restriction that the trade balance x is the same for both countries. Next we study the properties of this equilibrium by considering the effect of a demand increase dg in the home country.

3.5. Expansionary demand policy in one country

We analyze the effect of expansionary demand policy in the home country under a variety of institutional assumptions concerning wage rigidity. It will be apparent that these have impacts on the results for the effectiveness of fiscal policy. The model is summarized in eqs. (17), (23), (25) and (26). Totally differentiating these we obtain the following linear system:

$$
\begin{bmatrix}
1 & 0 & -\Lambda_p & -\Lambda_{p*} \\
0 & 1 & -\Lambda_p^* & -\Lambda_{p*}^* \\
1 & 0 & -V_p & -V_{p*} \\
0 & 1 & -V_p^* & -V_{p*}^*
\end{bmatrix}
\begin{bmatrix}
dy \\
dy^* \\
dP \\
dP^*
\end{bmatrix}
=
\begin{bmatrix}
0 \\
0 \\
V_g \\
0
\end{bmatrix}
dg.
\tag{27}
$$

The determinant is given by

$$
\Delta = (V_p - \Lambda_p)(V_{p*}^* - \Lambda_{p*}^*) - (V_{p*} - \Lambda_{p*})(V_p^* - \Lambda_p^*).
\tag{28}
$$

This is the product of the own effects of price changes less the product of the cross effects. The discussion after eq. (17) led us to notice that the own demand effects are larger than the cross demand effects. Furthermore, in general, the own supply effects are larger than or equal to the cross supply effects. Therefore, Δ can in general be taken to be positive.

The comparative status of the model of eq. (27) following an increase in g are summarized below,

$$
dy/dg = V_g[\Lambda_{p*}(V_p^* - \Lambda_p^*) - \Lambda_p(V_{p*}^* - \Lambda_{p*}^*)]/\Delta,
\tag{29}
$$

$$
dy^*/dg = -V_g[\Lambda_p^* V_{p*}^* - V_p^* \Lambda_{p*}^*]/\Delta,
\tag{30}
$$

$$
dP/dg = -V_g(V_{p*}^* - \Lambda_{p*}^*)/\Delta,
\tag{31}
$$

$$
dP^*/dg = +V_g(V_p^* - \Lambda_p^*)/\Delta.
\tag{32}
$$

The numerator of eq. (29) for dy/dg is essentially V_g times the own price effects less cross-price effects. Therefore in general we expect it to be positive. A major exception would be when home supply is insensitive to prices; then $dy/dg = 0$. The numerator of (30) contains only characteristics of the 'foreign' country. When the foreign supply function is symmetric with respect to the two prices, the sign of dy^*/dg depends on the relative absolute values of the demand effects, and is therefore negative.[5] We return to a detailed analysis of (29) and (30) below.

The condition that $\Delta > 0$ is required to obtain the result that an increase in g will increase both P and P^* in (31) and (32). If $\Delta < 0$, an increase in g will decrease P and P^*. The P, P^* solution for an increase in g is illustrated in fig. 3. There, the PP line is the combination of P and P^* that yields equilibrium in the home market. The equation for this line is

$$(V_p - \Lambda_p)dP = -(V_{p^*} - \Lambda_{p^*})dP^* - V_g dg.$$

For a given g, the slope is $-(V_p - \Lambda_p)/(V_{p^*} - \Lambda\Lambda_{p^*})$. The P^*P^* line is the combination of P and P^* that yields equilibrium in the foreign country. The equation for P^*P^* is

$$(V_p^* - \Lambda_p^*)dP = -(V_{p^*}^* - \Lambda_{p^*}^*)dP^*.$$

If P^*P^* is flatter than PP then Δ is positive and an increase in g raises both prices along P^*P^* as in fig. 3. If P^*P^* were steeper than PP then an increase in g would lower both prices.

3.6. Effects on real output

In analyzing the comparative statics effects on y and y^* of a change in g,

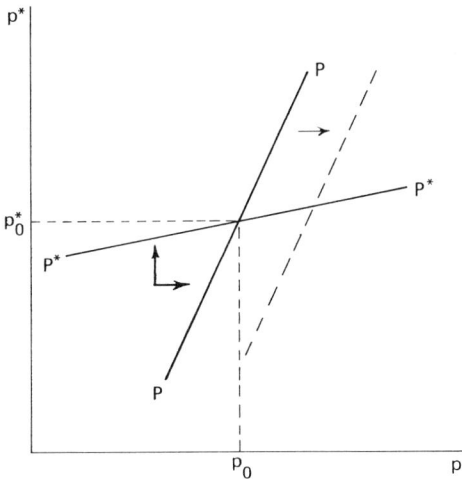

Fig. 3. Increase in g in two-commodity model.

[5]This is the result obtained by Argy and Salop (1978).

we will study the cases in which the 'home' country has no money illusion, so that $\theta_p + \theta_{p*} = 1$. Whether the real wage is rigid will effect only the size of the multipliers, with $g_N \leqq 0$. For the 'foreign' country we will vary the assumptions across several of the differing cases of wage rigidity distinguished earlier. These are

(1) Rigid nominal wages, with $\theta_p^* = \theta_{p*}^* = 0$, and $\psi_{p*} = 1$,

(2) Rigid real wages, with $\theta_{p*}^* \leqq \psi_{p*}^*$,

(3) Rigid real wages, with $\theta_{p*}^* > \psi_{p*}^*$,

(4) Sticky nominal wages, with $\theta_p^* + \theta_{p*}^* < 1$.

Clearly this is only a small subset of the possible combinations of assumptions for wage behavior in both countries, as is obvious from eqs. (29) and (30).

The four cases are summarized in table 3. In the first case, even with no money illusion at home, demand expansion increases home output through the differential effects of P and P^* on home supply. In section 2 with one commodity and corresponding price, $dy/dg = 0$. This may be the proper case to associate with Giersch.

An important thing to note about cases 2 and 3 is that our results are commodity and corresponding price, $dy/dg = 0$. The first case in table 3 may be the proper case to associate with Giersch.

in either country will not affect supply in that country.

If the foreign country (i.e., the one that does not expand) has a fixed real wage while workers are more sensitive to the cross-price than are firms (case 2), the expansion at home is contractionary abroad. This result is the one obtained by Argy and Salop, Sachs, and Bruno and Sachs. However,

Table 3
Effects of demand expansion on output.

Assumptions on wage behavior		Effects on outputs		
Home	Foreign	dy/dg		dy^*/dg
No money illusion $(\theta_p < \psi_p)$	(1) Rigid nominal wage $\theta_p^* = \theta_{p*}^* = 0$ $(\psi_{p*} = 1)$	+	(Giersch case)	+
Same	(2) Rigid real wage $\theta_{p*}^* < \Psi_{p*}^*$	+	(Argy–Salop case)	−
	$\theta_{p*}^* = \psi_{p*}^*$	+	(classical case)	0
Same	(3) Rigid real wage $\theta_{p*}^* > \psi_{p*}^*$	+	(Hong Kong)	+
Same	(4) Sticky money wage $\theta_p^* + \theta_{p*}^* < 1$	+	(Keynesian case)	(+)

there are two caveats to this result. These are shown in cases 3 and 4. Enough money illusion in the foreign country will make the increase in g expansionary there, as in case 4. By 'enough' we mean that

$$\theta_p^* + \theta_{p*}^* < 1 - \frac{(\psi_{p*}^* - \theta_{p*}^*)(V_p^* + V_{p*}^*)}{V_{p*}^*}. \tag{33}$$

In general the right-hand side of (33) will be close to unity since (a) $V_p^* + V_{p*}^*$ is small relative to V_{p*}^*, and (b) $(\psi_{p*}^* - \theta_{p*}^*)$ is between minus one and one. Therefore it takes but a little money illusion to reverse the contractionary effect abroad of an increase in g at home. A final caveat is that if in the foreign-country firms are more sensitive to the cross-price than are workers, a rare case of which Hong Kong may be an example, then our increase in g is expansionary abroad.

4. Empirical results on money illusion and wage rigidity

To test for the existence of money illusion or wage rigidity we begin by specifying a labor-supply equation making the level of the nominal wage dependent on the expected price level and a measure of labor demand. A time trend is added to account for productivity growth and trends in the variables. An estimating form of this static model would be

$$\ln W_t = \alpha_0 + \alpha_1 \ln P_t^e + \alpha_2 \ln D_t + \alpha_3 t + \varepsilon_t. \tag{34}$$

Here P^e represents the expected price level, D is a measure of labor demand, proxied below by real GNP, and the time trend is included to detrend W, P, and D.

If the coefficient α_1 were unity, money illusion would be absent and the real-wage cases of sections 2 and 3 with $\theta_p + \theta_{p*} = 1$ are relevant. If in addition α_2 is insignificant, the real wage would be rigid in the relevant period and $g_N = 0$ in sections 2 and 3. If α_1 were less than unity, money illusion exists $(\theta_p + \theta_{p*} < 1)$, and the extreme case would have $\alpha_1 = 0$.

Estimation of (34) directly would assume that wages adjust within a quarter to changes on their determinants. The literature on wage equations shows clearly that this is not the case. We have estimated equations in the form of (34), and observed generally quite significant serial correlation in the residuals. These equations using instrumental variables for P^e and D, as described in detail below, and the Cochran–Orcutt adjustment for serial correlation, are shown in appendix B. The first-order serial correlation coefficients ρ are generally in the 0.7 to 0.9 range, and the U.K. shows evidence of higher-order correlation. This can be taken as evidence that there is a lagged adjustment process moving wage rates, adjusting the average wage toward the static supply of labor schedule, whatever its slope. This friction could be due to the existence of long-term (more than one quarter) contracts, in nominal or real terms.

In a dynamic context we wish to test whether the adjustment process is in terms of real or nominal wages, and how sensitive it is to demand conditions. Thus the question is whether it is today's *real* wage that depends on past *real* wages and current labor-market conditions or today's *nominal* wage that depends on past *nominal* wages and current labor-market conditions. The former adjustment mechanism (which results for instance from indexed contracts) implies that our model is neutral to fiscal policy in the absence of terms-of-trade effects. The latter corresponds to the presence of 'money illusion'.

Let us reinterpret the static supply of labor function in eq. (34) as giving the target wage W^*,

$$\ln W_t^* = \ln P_t^e + \alpha_1 \ln D_t + \alpha_2 t + \varepsilon_t. \tag{35}$$

We consider only models of the partial adjustment type. Nominal-wage stickiness is given by

$$\ln (W_t/W_{t-1}) = \lambda(\ln W_t^*/W_{t-1}). \tag{36}$$

Real-wage stickiness is given by

$$\ln (W_t/P_t^e) - \ln (W_{t-1}/P_{t-1}) = \mu \cdot [\ln (W_t^*/P_t^e) - \ln (W_{t-1}/P_{t-1})]. \tag{37}$$

These two equations lead to two different short-run supply of labor schedules. Using (35) and (36) we obtain for the nominal case,

$$\ln (W_t/P_t^e) = (\lambda - 1)\ln (P_t^e/W_{t-1}) + \lambda\alpha_1 \ln D_t + \lambda\alpha_2 t + \lambda\varepsilon_t. \tag{38}$$

Using (35) and (37) we obtain for the real-wage case,

$$\ln (W_t/P_t^e) = (1 - \mu)\ln (W_{t-1}/P_{t-1}) + \mu\alpha_1 \ln D_t + \mu\alpha_2 t + \mu\varepsilon_t. \tag{39}$$

These two models are non-nested. We can embed both hypotheses in a more 'general' adjustment mechanism which combines (36) and (37) in the following manner:

$$\ln (W_t/W_{t-1}) = \gamma_1 \ln (W_t^*/W_{t-1}) + \gamma_2 \ln (P_t^e/P_{t-1}). \tag{40}$$

Here if $\gamma_2 = 0$, we have eq. (36) representing nominal-wage adjustment; if $\gamma_2 = 1 - \gamma_1$ we have eq. (37) instead. Substituting (36) for W^* into (40) we obtain the estimating equation

$$\ln(W_t/P_t^e) = (\gamma_1 + \gamma_2 - 1)\ln(P_t^e/W_{t-1}) + \gamma_2 \ln(W_{t-1}/P_{t-1})$$
$$+ \gamma_1 \alpha_1 \ln D_t + \gamma_1 \alpha_2 t + \gamma_1 \varepsilon_t. \tag{41}$$

This is the common alternative hypothesis against which we test (38) and (39). We can compare the three equations directly. If $\gamma_2 = 0$, γ_1 in (41) is equal to λ in (38); if $\gamma_2 = 1 - \gamma_1$, then γ_2 is also equal to $(1 - \mu)$ in eq. (39).

We reject the hypothesis that it is the real wage that adjusts according to eq. (37) if the coefficient on $\ln(P_t^e/W_{t-1})$ is significantly different from zero. On the other hand we reject eq. (36) if the estimate of γ_2 in (41) is significantly different from zero. Of course the models are indistinguishable when the adjustment is instantaneous, i.e., $\gamma_1 = 1$, $\gamma_2 = 0$.

The estimating eq. (41) is derived from specification of an equation for the *level* of the nominal wage, (34) or (35), dependent on the *level* of demand, and a standard adjustment mechanism. This is a different procedure from that followed by Bruno and Sachs (1979),[6] Gordon (1977), and Spitaeller (1976). In particular, their specification assumes that the *level* of demand affects the *rate of change* of wages, while a simple differencing of eq. (41) would put the *change* in demand into the equation for the change in the wage rate. This difference must be kept in mind in interpreting our results below.

In estimating eq. (41) for five major OECD countries, we used price data from the OECD Main Economic Indicators and GNP data from the *International Financial Statistics* published by the IMF. The D_t variable is real GNP for all countries except Italy where it is real GDP. The dependent variable is hourly compensation, provided by the IMF.[7] The price variable is the Consumer Price Index. All variables were seasonally adjusted using the X-11 method.

We estimated all equations using instrumental variable estimates for P^e and GNP. For each country regressions were performed of the CPI and GNP on four lagged values of CPI and GNP plus the current and four lagged values of the money stock. Fitted values from these regressions were used in the wage equation for P^e and GNP. These are denoted as $\hat{P}$ and $G\hat{N}P$ in table 4 below. This procedure can be interpreted econometrically as

---

[6] Bruno and Sachs' specification involves a partial adjustment of the *rate of change* of wages to the equilibrium rate of change of wages which depends on GNP. This leads to an equation similar to (41). We are working on a paper that tests their specification directly against our 'real' and 'nominal' wage adjustment models.

[7] We also estimated the equations using hourly earnings and the hourly wage as dependent variables. The results are virtually identical to those using compensation data and are available upon request.

Table 4

Tests of real- vs. nominal wage adjustment using hourly compensation data: dependent variable $= \ln(W_t/\hat{P}_t)$.

Country	Time period	Explanatory variables					D.W.	R^2	R vs. N
		$\hat{P}/W_{t-1}$	W_{t-1}/P_{t-1}	$G\hat{N}P_t$	Time	C			
U.S.	61:2–78:4	−0.69 (0.15)	−0.06 (0.20)	0.07 (0.02)	0.0011 (0.0002)	−0.06 (0.20)	1.9	0.99	N
	71:1–78:4	−0.74 (0.20)	−0.19 (0.31)	0.07 (0.05)	0.001 (0.0003)	0.01 (0.24)	1.8	0.98	N
U.K.	61:2–78:3	−0.47 (0.24)	0.56 (0.21)	0.10 (0.06)	−0.0007 (0.0006)	−0.34 (0.19)	1.3	0.99	R
	71:1–78:3	−0.50 (0.39)	0.55 (0.31)	0.26 (0.17)	−0.001 (0.001)	−0.85 (0.50)	1.3	0.95	R, N
Japan	61:2–78:4	0.77 (0.42)	1.49 (0.37)	0.14 (0.04)	0.0022 (0.0011)	−1.38 (0.39)	2.7	0.99	R
	71:1–78:4	1.04 (0.71)	1.67 (0.64)	0.0028 (0.18)	0.0040 (0.0024)	0.36 (2.10)	2.6	0.93	R
Italy	61:2–78:3	0.34 (0.36)	1.27 (0.33)	0.16 (0.08)	−0.001 (0.001)	−1.73 (0.83)	2.4	0.99	R
	71:1–78:3	0.43 (0.67)	1.34 (0.65)	−0.12 (0.25)	0.001 (0.002)	1.58 (2.88)	2.6	0.97	R
Germany	61:2–78:4	−0.53 (0.76)	0.35 (0.73)	0.13 (0.05)	0.0003 (0.001)	−0.71 (0.33)	2.2	0.99	N, R
	71:1–78:4	2.27 (1.58)	3.01 (1.49)	−0.05 (0.17)	0.0038 (0.0028)	0.49 (1.18)	2.7	0.98	R

eliminating the simultaneity bias running from the real wage to GNP and the CPI, or as imposition of rational expectations on the wage equation.

We estimated eq. (41) with quarterly observations for two periods, one running from 1961 to 1978, the other from 1971 to 1978. This was done because the latter period exhibits a higher rate of inflation and it is likely that workers are more sensitive to the price level when its increases are larger. Furthermore, the period 1971–78 saw a large increase in oil prices which should have led to a reduction in the equilibrium real wage, therefore making this an ideal period to test the rigidity of the real wage. Equations in Phillips curve form have been estimated for the period 1958–73 quarterly by Gordon, for the period 1957–72 semi-annually by Spitaeller, and for the period 1962–76 annually by Bruno and Sachs.

The estimates of eq. (41) are shown in table 4. In all cases the dependent variable is $W_t/\hat{P}_t$. There are two equations for each country, one for the full period 1961–78, and one for the shorter period 1971–78. The coefficients are presented with their standard errors in parentheses. In the last column of the table we give the result of the test of real- vs. nominal-wage adjustment. R means that the real-wage hypothesis is accepted and the nominal-wage hypothesis is rejected, and vice versa for N. The R, N entries signify that neither hypothesis can be rejected.

The first thing we notice in table 4 is that the coefficient of the demand variable GNP is significantly positive in all countries for the full period, but insignificant for 1971–78. This says that in each of these countries wage movements became less sensitive to demand variation in the 1970s than earlier; in terms of our theoretical model $g_N = 0$.

Turning to the real- vs. nominal-wage issue, we see that the U.S. is the only country where the nominal-wage adjustment model dominates. The coefficient of W_{t-1}/P_{t-1} is effectively zero for both periods, and the estimate of the λ adjustment coefficient in the money wage model is approximately 0.7. This result is consistent with the earlier findings of Bruno and Sachs (1979), Gordon (1977), and Spitaeller (1976). The U.K. regressions yield ambiguous results. The nominal-wage model is rejected over the full period, but neither hypothesis can be rejected in the 1971–78 period. On the presumption that the real-wage model is accepted, the estimate of the μ adjustment coefficient is approximately 0.45 over both periods. This fits the result of Bruno and Sachs, but not Spitaeller.

For Japan and Italy, the nominal-wage model is rejected for both periods. The W_{t-1}/P_{t-1} coefficient is insignificantly different from unity in all four regressions, suggesting a long adjustment process with μ close to zero. These results are roughly consistent with the literature.

For Germany, neither hypothesis can be rejected for the full period, but the nominal-wage model is rejected for 1971–78. As in Italy and Japan, the μ estimate is close to zero. These results are also roughly consistent with the literature. Gordon and Spitaeller found money illusion in earlier data sets ending in 1972 and 1973, respectively, and Bruno and Sachs reject it on data through 1976.

In summary, it seems that sensitivity of wage movements to fluctuations in demand has been reduced sharply in the 1970s relative to the earlier period in all five countries. The U.S. is the only country in which the model of nominal-wage stickiness is supported; in the U.K., Japan, Italy and Germany it is the real wage that adjusts slowly. This is consistent with effective indexation in these countries as compared with the U.S.

In terms of the model in sections 2 and 3, only the U.S. seems to have enough money illusion to bring about an expansion in response to third country increases in demand. On the other hand, money illusion appears to be absent in the U.K., Germany, Italy, and Japan. This means that these countries may have to worry about the effect of expansionary fiscal policy in the other countries.

Appendix A

Consider a discriminating monopolist producing in the home country and selling in two countries. He faces the following problem:

$$\text{Max} \{p(q) \cdot q + p^*(q^*, u)q^* - W \cdot \eta(q + q^*)\},$$

where $p(q)$ and $p^*(q^*)$ are the inverse demand functions, η the employment function with $\eta' > 0$, $\eta'' > 0$ and u a shift parameter such that for a higher u the foreigners are willing to pay more for each quantity q^*. $p_u^* > 0$. We assume further $p_{uq^*}^* = 0$. His first-order conditions are

$$p_q \cdot q + p = W\eta', \qquad p_{q^*}^* q^* + p^* = W\eta'.$$

Totally differentiating with a change in u gives us

$$(p_{qq} q + 2p_q)dq - W\eta''(dq + dq^*) = 0,$$

$$(p_{q^*q^*}^* q^* + 2p_{q^*}^*)dq^* - W\eta''(dq + dq^*) = -p_u^* du.$$

Assuming $p_{qq} = p_{q^*q^*} = 0$, we obtain

$$\begin{bmatrix} 2p_q - W\eta'' & -2p_q \\ -W\eta'' & 2p_{q^*}^* \end{bmatrix} \begin{matrix} (dq + dq^*) \\ (dq^*) \end{matrix} = \begin{bmatrix} 0 \\ -p_u^* du \end{bmatrix},$$

which leads to

$$(dq + dq^*)/du > 0, \qquad dq^*/du > 0.$$

This means that an increase in demand in any one country leads to an increase in demand for labor by the firm. We have written this as a demand-for-labor function that depends on both prices.

Appendix B

Table 5

Estimates of static wage equations; dependent variable $= \ln W_t$.

Country	Time-period	Explanatory variables					D.W.	R^2
		$\hat{P}$	$G\hat{N}P$	T	C	ρ		
U.S.	61:2–78:4	0.90 (0.06)	0.06 (0.07)	0.005 (0.001)	0.62 (0.47)	0.76 (0.08)	2.1	0.99
	71:1–78:4	0.29 (0.16)	−0.13 (0.09)	0.18 (0.003)	1.17 (0.55)	0.81 (0.11)	1.9	0.99
U.K.	61:2–78:3	0.59 (0.12)	0.29 (0.16)	0.019 (0.004)	−0.45 (0.42)	0.95 (0.04)	1.4	0.99
	71:1–78:3	0.50 (0.23)	0.21 (0.29)	0.024 (0.010)	−0.52 (0.77	0.91 (0.08)	1.1	0.99
Japan	61:2–78:4	0.81 (0.25)	0.17 (0.18)	0.018 (0.007)	−1.38 (1.77)	0.91 (0.05)	2.6	0.99
	71:1–78:4	1.99 (0.14)	1.06 (0.18)	−0.24 (0.005)	−9.37 (1.95)	0.14 (0.18)	2.3	0.99
Italy	61:2–78:3	0.80 (0.17)	−0.002 (0.22)	0.020 (0.006)	0.53 (2.38)	0.94 (0.04)	2.3	0.99
	71:1–78:3	0.80 (0.31)	−0.11 (0.32)	0.16 (0.014)	2.09 (3.65)	0.88 (0.09)	2.6	0.99
Germany	61:2–78:4	1.40 (0.22)	0.37 (0.12)	0.006 (0.003)	−1.50 (0.68)	0.83 (0.07)	2.3	0.99
	71:1–78:4	2.10 (0.33)	0.17 (0.27)	−0.003 (0.005)	0.54 (1.60)	0.50 (0.16)	2.1	0.99

References

Argy, Victor and Joanne Salop, 1979, Price and output effects of monetary and fiscal expansion in a two-country world under flexible exchange rates, IMF mimeo.

Branson, William H., 1979, Macroeconomic theory and policy, 2nd ed. (Harper and Row, New York).

Branson, William H. and Alvin K. Klevorick, 1969, Money illusion and the aggregate consumption function, American Economic Review, Dec.

Bruno, Michael and Jeffrey Sachs, 1979, Supply vs. demand approaches to the problem of stagflation, Mimeo.

Gordon, Robert J., 1977, World inflation and monetary accommodation in eight countries, Brookings Papers on Economic Activity, no. 2.

Muellbauer, John and Richard Portes, 1979, Macroeconomics when markets do not clear, in: William Branson, Macroeconomic theory and policy, 2nd ed. (Harper and Row, New York).

Sachs, Jeffrey, 1978, Wage indexation, flexible exchange rates and macroeconomic policy, Quarterly Journal of Economics, forthcoming.

Spitaeller, Erich, 1976, Semi-annual wage equations for the manufacturing sectors in six major industrial countries: 1957(1)–1972(2), Weltwirtschaftliches Archiv 112, no. 2.

European Economic Review 13 (1980). North-Holland

COMMENTS

'International Adjustment with Wage Rigidity' by Branson and Rotemberg

Jeffrey SACHS

National Bureau of Economic Research, Cambridge, MA 02139, USA

In '*International Adjustment with Wage Rigidity*', William Branson and Julio Rotemberg turn our attention to the recent trans-oceanic debate over macro-economic policy. Since 1974, when the industrialized countries entered the 'Great Recession', the U.S. has been urging expansionary monetary and fiscal policy in Japan and the European countries. Most of these countries have been adamant in rejecting the U.S. advice. The different countries' choices reflect more than different tastes for inflation and unemployment in the short run. Branson and Rotemberg share the view of Giersch (1979) and Bruno and Sachs (1979) that the U.S. has chosen expansionary policy because it works in the U.S., while the same policy is likely to cause inflation and little else in the other economies.[1]

As in the earlier papers, Branson and Rotemberg point to the labor market as the source of this difference. In countries with nominal-wage rigidity, expansionary policy can reduce the real wage and thus increase aggregate supply; in rigid real-wage countries, *ipso facto*, it cannot. Their empirical work is devoted to finding which countries are in which category. In all their regressions, the U.S. comes through as a rigid nominal-wage economy.

The spirit of their approach is just right. Their focus on excessive real wages after 1973 is appropriate. I concur in the view that industrialized economies behave differently, and that economists must continue to sort out those differences. However, I suspect that Branson and Rotemberg's empirical work needs more sorting out itself. While they ask the broad questions correctly, they do not specify the narrow empirical questions with

---

[1] In Bruno and Sachs (1979, p. 45) we wrote: 'We suspect that much of the difference in the macro-economic policy recommendations of American and European economists stems from the difference in the behavior of their respective economies reflected in $\hat{\alpha}_2$ [a parameter of nominal-wage rigidity]. In the United States monetary policy *is* effective, while in most European economies, monetary policy probably operates chiefly on prices and not on output.'

sufficient care. And when they try to answer the empirical questions, their results are diminished by econometric difficulties.

The theoretical model in the paper traces out the role of real wages in aggregate supply, along familiar lines. The empirical work seeks to answer two key questions about wage setting. The first is whether real-wage growth can vary fast enough to keep the wage approximately equal to the marginal product of labor at full employment. The second is whether expansionary policy, by raising the price level, can reduce the real wage and expand aggregate output.

On the first question, the authors do not attempt to compare wage movements directly with marginal labor productivity. Rather, they test whether the adjustment of real wages to a target level is rapid, and whether the target itself is a function of aggregate demand. They conclude that real-wage adjustment in Europe and Japan is sluggish, and that the target does *not* depend on aggregate output. In sum, they find that real-wage growth since 1971 is fairly constant. Their findings, I think, are hindered by problems in the empirical work, to which I return. A glance at the data should be enough to dissuade us from their simple rigid real-wage model. In table 1, I show the growth rates of real hourly compensation and real hourly earnings for the seven large industrial countries. The striking aspect of the table for Europe and Japan is not the fixity of real-wage growth, but the opposite. A real-wage explosion hits Europe and Japan during 1969–73, while during the recent recession, real-wage growth falls sharply. In every country outside of North America, high unemployment severely curtails the rise in real hourly compensation after 1975.

Table 1

Annual growth rates of real hourly compensation and real hourly earnings in manufacturing; 1962–78.[a]

Country	Real hourly compensation				Real hourly earnings			
	1962–69	1969–73	1973–75	1975–1977	1962–69	1969–73	1973–75	1975–77
Canada	2.9	3.4	3.8	4.3	2.6	3.6	3.4	4.2
France	4.2	5.9	6.4	4.9	4.1	5.4	4.4	4.8
Germany	5.1	7.9	7.2	4.1	4.8	5.3	3.2	2.8
Italy	6.2	11.7	7.4	2.1	4.4	11.2	5.1	6.4
Japan	7.6	9.5	5.2	0.0	8.0	10.1	4.3	−0.3
U.K.	2.9	4.3	6.0	−1.8	3.1	5.0	2.8	−3.1
U.S.	1.9	1.5	0.8	2.2	1.4	1.4	−1.2	2.1

[a]*Source:* Nominal hourly compensation and hourly earnings from U.S. Department of Labor, Bureau of Labor Statistics, Office of Productivity and Technology, 'Estimated Hourly Compensation of Production Workers in Manufacturing, Ten Countries, 1960, 1965–1978', and other publications of the Office of Productivity and Technology. The consumer price index is from the IFS.

The deceleration in real wages does not vitiate the concern over excessive wage levels, but only the simple test of wage rigidity in the paper. In fact, real-wage growth did not drop fast enough after 1973 to match the slower growth of the full-employment marginal product of labor. Almost all of the industrialized countries faced a severe drop in total productivity growth and an adverse terms-of-trade shift after 1973.[2] These disturbances have required a slowdown in real hourly compensation growth of at least one to two percentage points a year since 1973. In fact, the slowdown in compensation only came with a long lag. Consequently the cyclically adjusted share of labor compensation rose almost everywhere following the oil shock, and profits were squeezed, with the implications for aggregate supply and employment that Branson and Rotemberg describe. In table 2, I show the share of labor compensation. In France, Germany, Japan and the United Kingdom, labor's share rises markedly during 1973–76.

Table 2
Share of labor compensation in manufacturing value-added, cyclically adjusted.[a]

	1962–64	1965–69	1970–73	1974	1975	1976	1977	1978
Canada	0.65	0.68	0.69	0.68	0.66	0.69	n.a.	n.a.
France	0.53	0.52	0.51	0.54	0.53	0.53	0.53	0.52
Germany	0.64	0.62	0.66	0.71	0.72	0.73	0.74	n.a.
Italy	0.64	0.65	0.73	0.73	0.73	0.70	0.68	0.65
Japan	0.52	0.50	0.54	0.58	0.52	0.55	0.58	0.60
U.K.	0.69	0.72	0.75	0.86	0.82	0.80	0.75	n.a.
U.S.	0.77	0.78	0.80	0.81	0.81	0.80	0.80	0.81

[a]*Source:* The share of labor compensation is calculated as the ratio of employee compensation to gross domestic product originating in manufacturing, measured at factor cost. An adjustment is made by multiplying the share by the ratio of output per manhour to potential output per manhour, calculated by Artus (1977), and updated by the IMF. The underlying compensation and GDP data are from the U.S. Bureau of Labor Statistics, Office of Productivity and Technology.

Branson and Rotemberg correctly ask what the role of policy might be in the face of excessive real wages, the second issue raised above. Their model suggests that nominal-wage stickiness gives scope for policy. Again, their empirical specification does not face the question at hand. In their 'static' model (section 4), they test the long-run neutrality of the real wage with respect to the price level; in the dynamic case, it is the neutrality of the real wage with respect to the inflation rate. In both cases, nominal-wage stickiness is made synonymous with a long-run Phillips curve trade-off. But surely the issue of nominal-wage rigidity is a matter of short-run stickiness in

[2]Artus (1975) has estimated a decline in total factor productivity of 2.6% for the large industrial economies. For alternative estimates of the productivity decline, and measures of the terms-of-trade shift, see Sachs (1979).

nominal-wage change, perhaps due to long-term contracts, rather than a proposition about the long-term determination of the real-wage level. Because the Branson–Rotemberg tests of wage sluggishness do not allow for short-run rigidities and long-run inflation neutrality, their conclusions should not be directly compared to the results in Bruno and Sachs (1979).[3]

Why do Branson and Rotemberg find so little effect of demand on real wages in the 1971–78 period, even though high unemployment led to a clear real-wage deceleration after 1975? The answer is not clear, though is probably related to the econometric procedures. First, the authors use GNP (with a time trend) to proxy for labor market activity. This is unwarranted. During a period of stable productivity growth, Okun's law allows us to translate unemployment to GNP, but during a period of declining productivity growth, the GNP variable will indicate looser labor markets than indeed exist.

More importantly, the estimation is subject to biases. How do we know that the regression of wages on output identifies a labor-supply schedule, with a positive coefficient on output, rather than an output-supply schedule, with a negative coefficient? Presumably, the answer is the instrumental variables procedure. But the choice of instruments is suspect. In the first stage of estimation, quarterly GNP data is fit with *thirteen* instruments, including four lags of GNP. The lagged values of GNP are almost surely not valid instruments (serial correlation in the wage equation bars their use), and the over-fitting of the first stage probably contributes to inconsistency. The concern over simultaneous equation bias is not a cavil, since so much of the authors' theory relies on the negative link of wages and output supply. Also, the equation is estimated with a lagged dependent variable, but with no attention to serial correlation. Our concern here is justified. The authors' theory suggests that the coefficient on W_{t-1}/P_{t-1} should lie between zero and one; this is in fact so for only three of the ten regressions. The suspicion of misspecification is heightened by Durbin–Watson statistics generally far from 2.0, and the unexplained instability of the regression coefficients across sub-periods.

I believe that econometric equations will take us only part way in elucidating the differences in wage determination among countries. We should spend more time trying to link observable institutions with wage outcomes. For instance, nominal-wage sluggishness in the U.S. is consistent with the preponderance of long-term overlapping contracts, as shown in the theoretical work of Fisher (1977) and Taylor (1979). The absence of discernible nominal-wage stickiness in Germany, on the other hand, probably

---

[3]In the empirical estimates in Bruno and Sachs (1979), the wage equation is specified so that the real economy is neutral with respect to the steady-state rate of inflation. In Sachs (1979), statistical tests fail to reject the hypothesis of long-run neutrality in the wage equation for the seven large OECD economies.

results from short-term contracts, negotiated at branch levels, in the context of the 'Concerted Action' policy. Similarly, institutional detail can help us to explain the sharp deceleration in real wages after 1975 in countries such as the U.K., where income policies contributed, along with high unemployment, to the real-wage deceleration.

Branson and Rotemberg have shown us why the issue of wage determination is important. I look forward to further empirical application of their model.

References

Artus, Jacques, 1977, Measures of potential output in manufacturing for eight industrial countries, 1955–1978, IMF Staff Papers XXIV, March, 1–35.

Bruno, Michael and Jeffrey Sachs, 1979, Supply versus demand approaches to the problem of stagflation (presented at the 1979 Kiel Conference on Macroeconomic Performance in the 1970's), Weltwirtschaftliches Archiv, forthcoming.

Fischer, Stanley, 1977, Long-term contracts, rational expectations, and the optimal money supply rule, Journal of Political Economy 85, no. 1.

Giersch, Herbert, 1979, Aspects of growth, structural change, and employment — A Schumpeterian perspective (presented at the 1979 Kiel Conference on Macroeconomic Policies for Growth and Stability), Weltwirtschaftliches Archiv, forthcoming.

Sachs, Jeffrey, 1979, Wages, profits, and macroeconomic adjustment in the industrialized economies in the 1970's, Brookings Papers on Economic Activity, forthcoming.

Taylor, John, 1979, Aggregate demand and staggered contracts (Columbia University, New York) in process.

COMMENTS

'International Adjustment with Wage Rigidity' by Branson and Rotemberg

Richard PORTES

Centre d'Economie Quantitative et Comparative, Paris, France
Birkbeck College, University of London, UK

The paper by Branson and Rotemberg is an excellent example of the use of an apparently simple model to throw theoretical light on a complex and controversial policy question, as well as to give guidance for empirical specification. American policy-makers have resented the reluctance of Europe and Japan to adopt expansionary policies since 1974, in part because they have seen no basis for such caution in the face of substantial and growing unemployment throughout the OECD area. Europe and Japan, on the other hand, have resented what they see as American unwillingness to comprehend the obvious, namely that demand expansion would for them raise prices rather than employment and output. Branson and Rotemberg, starting from a suggestion by Giersch, have produced a model which makes sense of these divergent positions, albeit under some fairly strong simplifying assumptions.

The theoretical argument is for the most part quite neat and clear, and it contains a particularly appealing feature, the willingness to apply explicitly the 'minimum condition' from the quantity-rationing models to the labor market. With just a single market in 'disequilibrium', one does get only some of the characteristic responses of this class of models, but they come at a low cost, without much of their complexity. Nevertheless, I think it would be feasible to incorporate some repercussions from the goods market onto the labor market, and I shall return to this below.

In the paper, the labor market is taken as an aggregate (contrast Muellbauer and Winter), and only the case of excess supply is considered as an alternative to equilibrium. The goods market in each country clears through trade as in Dixit's (1978) model of a single small open economy, but here this market clearing comes through price adjustment, whereas in Dixit the domestic wage and price levels are rigid. Thus although he too has 'classical' unemployment, his labor market is unaffected by fiscal policy, which influences only the balance of trade. In both, excess supply in the labor market has only one cause: whether because of rigidity of the money or of the real wage, the real wage in equilibrium is too high, and the marginal productivity condition determines the demand for labor at a level below supply, with no 'spillover' from the goods market.

Here, however, in the two-good case, the marginal productivity condition which determines unemployment involves a different price index from that faced (or perceived — see below) by workers. Thus a wage which is rigid for workers is not rigid for employers. Workers are assumed to put more weight on foreign prices than employers do. While neither of the two economies is 'small', the stress is on their 'openness', the precise extent of which indeed determines the model's properties. The fundamental equation is (22), which very neatly expresses the effects of the differences between the price indices and allows an exceedingly simple incorporation of the 'disequilibrium' features of the model through eqs. (20^N) and (20^R).

I found one confusing point in the specification, in regard to the workers' price index. Initially, in the discussion of the demand for output and eq. (15), this price index is treated as a measured CPI, i.e., as a weighted average of the domestic and foreign prices. In the subsequent discussion of the supply of labor, however, following eq. (20^N), money illusion is represented by reference to the properties of a *perceived* CPI. Moreover, one is tempted to confuse nominal-wage rigidity with money illusion, although it is only their *effects* on the role of this price index which may be represented similarly.

The properties of the model are summarized in table 3, which is somewhat less complicated than it appears. Case 1 (Giersch) is a special case of case 4, and as the text points out, relatively little money-wage rigidity will give an unambiguously positive response of domestic demand expansion on foreign output, so we need not worry much about the special case. The three remaining cases all suppose rigid real wages and differ *only* in the relative sensitivity of workers and firms to domestic and foreign price changes.

In fact, it seems to me that the model suggests testing directly not merely wage rigidity, but perhaps more importantly, these differences in responses to domestic and foreign price changes. This turns out to be the key to the behavior of the model, and it is not immediately obvious for countries like Japan and the U.K. (say) whether the Argy–Salop, the 'classical', or the 'Hong Kong' case would be empirically appropriate.

Finally, it might not be overly complex (especially if one were to focus on just a couple of the cases in table 3) to extend the model to allow the possibility that the goods market might not clear, at least in one of the two countries. We would then have 'Keynesian' as well as 'classical' unemployment [see Malinvaud (1977)]. An economy with the former would normally have a trade surplus, though not enough to absorb all the excess supply of goods. An economy with the latter would normally have a trade deficit, though not so great as to satisfy all the excess demand for goods.

Evidently in this sense the non-clearing goods market in a large open economy is more plausible for the Keynesian than for the classical case.

If the domestic economy is in Keynesian unemployment, expansionary fiscal policy raises wages, prices, employment and output, while reducing net exports. Then if the foreign economy were also in Keynesian unemployment, it would experience expansion all around as well. But if unemployment abroad were classical in character, though its price level and net exports would rise, the effect on output (and hence on employment and goods market conditions) would differ according to the stickiness of money or real wages. It would be very interesting to see how this argument might be modified by the assumption that households and firms face (or perceive) different price indices.

References

Dixit, A., 1978, The balance of trade in a model of temporary equilibrium with rationing, Review of Economic Studies, Oct.
Malinvaud, E., 1977, The theory of unemployment reconsidered (Blackwell, Oxford).

European Economic Review 21 (1983) . North-Holland

COMPARING PRODUCTIVITY GROWTH

An Exploration of French and U.S. Industrial and Firm Data*

Zvi GRILICHES

NBER, and Harvard University, Cambridge, MA 02138, USA

Jacques MAIRESSE

INSEE, and Ecole des Hautes Etudes en Sciences Sociales, 75006 Paris, France

1. Introduction

The United States, France, and many other industrial countries experienced a significant slowdown in the growth of productivity in the recent decade. This slowdown exacerbated inflationary pressures and contributed to the growing pessimism about the prospects for future economic growth. Its causes are still unclear and controversial. It makes a difference from a policy response point of view whether it was caused by insufficient investment, by rising energy and raw materials prices, or by a decline in the fecundity of R&D and the exhaustion of technology opportunities.[1]

In this paper we bring a comparative perspective to the analysis of some of these issues. To accomplish this we had to assemble and construct consistent and comparable data sets for French and United States manufacturing industries and firms. After a discussion of the respective data sets and a description of the extent of the slowdown in productivity growth in the two countries and the great variability in it, we turn to an analysis of the potential causes of such fluctuations. At the industrial level, we focus on the contribution of capital and the rise in material prices to an explanation of the observed productivity slowdown. At the firm level we look also more closely at the potential effect of R&D expenditures on productivity growth. A number of tentative conclusions close the paper.

*This work is part of the National Bureau of Economic Research Program on Productivity and Technical Change Studies. We are indebted to the National Science Foundation (PRA79-13740, PRA81-08635, and SOC78-04279) and to the Centre National de la Recherche Scientifique (ATP 070199) for financial support, to Sumanth Addanki, Phillipe Cuneo, Bronwyn H. Hall and Alan Siu for research assistance and Martin Baily, Michael Bruno, and Robert J. Gordon for comments on the first draft of this paper.

[1]See Denison (1979) and Nordhaus (1982) for a more detailed discussion of some of these issues.

2. Productivity growth at the industry level

2.1. Data and basic facts

In this section we focus on comparing total factor productivity growth rates in manufacturing industries at the approximate 2-digit level in both France and the United States. Our industry breakdown (described in the appendix table A.1) is somewhat unorthodox. It is the result of trying to match the U.S. SIC classification to the French NAP classification, and was chosen primarily on the basis of the availability of the French data, and secondarily because of our interest in R&D (which led us to subdivide several industries). It differs from the usual 2-digit SIC scheme in the U.S. mainly by the separation of drugs and 'parachemicals' from the other chemicals, the aggregation of several minor industries, and the exclusion of the petroleum refining industry from manufacturing so defined.

The French estimates are based on national accounts publications, augmented by various unpublished data from the 'branch' (establishment level) and 'sector' (company level) accounts. The U.S. estimates were aggregated from the 4-digit SIC level detail data base constructed by Fromm et al. (1979) on the basis of the Census Annual Surveys of Manufactures and National Income accounts based detailed deflators. Both data sets yield a gross output measure (shipments adjusted for inventory changes) in constant (1972) prices and divide inputs into three categories: labor (man-hours), capital (gross capital stock in constant prices), and purchased materials (intermediate consumption including energy inputs). With each input and output measure we associate a set of price indexes and cost shares. For each of our fifteen industries, in both countries, we compute Tornquist Divisia total input indexes and use them to construct Total Factor Productivity (T FP) indexes for the 12-year period, 1967–78, and for two sub-periods, 1967–73 and 1973–78. The final results of these rather extensive computations are given in table 1 and illustrated in fig. 1.

For the period as a whole, the rate of growth of total factor productivity was higher in France than in the U.S., and this was also true for *each* industry separately. The median difference was on the order of one percent per year with larger differences occurring in the 'heavy' industries (Primary Metals, Fabricated Metals, Machinery, and Aircraft and Boats). In both countries productivity growth slowed significantly in the second sub-period, though here the results are much more variable across industries. For aggregate manufacturing the deceleration was somewhat larger in the U.S. (by about 0.7 percent).[2]

---

[2]This conclusion depends on the exact choice of time periods. If 1972 is chosen to divide the two time periods instead of 1973, the magnitude of the deceleration is essentially the same in both countries. The U.S. peaked more in 1973.

Table 1

Total factor productivity growth rates in manufacturing industries; France and the United States (percent per year).

Industry	1967–78			1967–73			1973–78			Change		
	FR	US	FR–US	FR	US	FR–US	FR	US	FR–US	FR	US	FR–US
1. Paper and allied products	1.0	0.8	0.2	0.5	1.8	-1.3	1.5	-0.4	2.0	1.0	-2.3	3.3
2. Chemicals (excluding drugs)	1.5	0.3	1.2	1.8	3.7	-2.0	1.1	-3.7	4.8	-0.7	-7.5	6.8
3. Rubber, misc. plastic products	0.9	0.1	0.8	1.0	1.9	-0.9	0.9	-2.0	2.9	-0.1	-4.0	3.9
4. Stone, clay, and glass products	1.5	0.1	1.4	2.3	1.0	1.4	0.5	-0.9	1.4	-1.9	-1.9	0.0
5. Primary metal industries	1.0	-0.7	1.7	1.7	0.2	1.5	0.2	-1.8	2.0	-1.5	-2.0	0.5
6. Fabricated metal products	1.4	-0.4	1.8	1.9	0.5	1.3	0.7	-1.5	2.3	-1.1	-2.0	0.9
7. Machinery and instruments	1.9	0.1	1.8	3.2	1.1	2.1	0.3	-1.2	1.5	-2.9	-2.3	-0.6
8. Electrical equipment	2.6	1.9	0.7	2.9	1.7	1.2	2.3	2.1	0.2	-0.6	0.3	-0.9
9. Automobile and ground transport	1.8	1.1	0.7	2.6	2.1	0.5	0.9	-0.1	1.0	-1.7	-2.1	0.5
10. Aircraft, boats, and space vehicles	3.4	-0.4	3.7	2.7	-0.9	3.6	4.2	0.3	3.9	1.4	1.2	0.2
11. Textiles and apparel	1.4	0.8	0.6	2.0	0.9	1.1	0.7	0.7	0.0	-1.3	-0.2	-1.2
12. Wood, furniture, and misc. products	1.6	0.1	1.5	2.0	0.9	1.1	1.2	-0.8	2.0	-0.8	-1.7	0.9
13. Printing and publishing	0.6	0.3	0.2	-0.4	0.7	-1.1	1.7	-0.1	1.8	2.1	-0.7	2.8
14. Drugs	0.9	0.9	0.1	1.1	1.4	-0.3	0.7	0.3	0.4	-0.4	-1.1	0.7
15. Leather	1.1	-0.2	1.2	1.9	-0.4	2.3	0.1	0.1	0.0	-1.8	0.5	-2.3
Aggregates												
Aggregate manufacturing	1.7	0.4	1.3	2.2	1.2	1.0	1.2	-0.5	1.7	-0.9	-1.6	0.7
Sectors included in micro study	2.0	0.8	1.2	2.5	1.8	0.7	1.4	-0.5	1.8	-1.2	-2.3	1.1
Sectors not included in micro study	1.5	0.2	1.3	1.9	0.8	1.1	1.1	-0.5	1.6	-0.8	-1.4	0.6

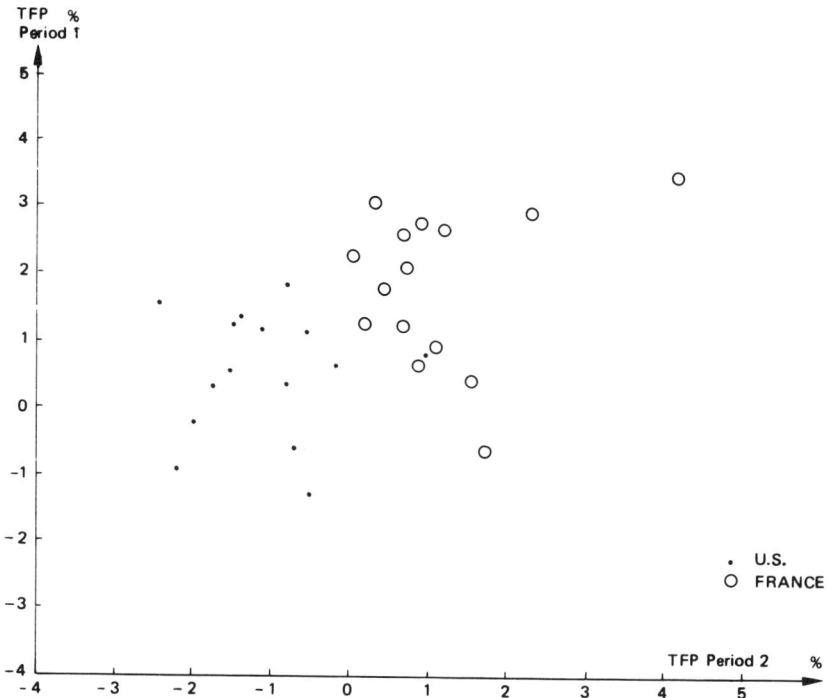

Fig. 1. Total factor productivity; fifteen manufacturing industries in France and the U.S., comparison across periods (1: 1967–72, and 2: 1972–78).

If we divide the periods so that they are equal in length and independently constructed; i.e., if we use 1967 to 1972 as our first period, we can do an analysis of variance on the resulting sixty *TFP* growth numbers, using country, period and industry as classification categories. This yields the following estimates: an average *TFP* growth rate (in both countries across all industries) of 0.8, an average French advantage over the U.S. of 1.5 percent per year, and an average deceleration of 1.0 percent between the two periods. In terms of contribution to the total variance in *TFP* growth, the most important factors are country and period, with computed *F* statistics of 25 and 11, respectively (the 0.05 critical value of the *F* statistic with 1 and 43 degrees of freedom is about 4). Surprisingly, industrial differences contribute relatively little (the computed $F = 1$ contrasted to a critical $F_{0.95}$ (14,43) of about 2), though individually two industries (electrical equipment and aircraft) have significantly above average *TFP* growth rates. This is a rather unfortunate finding from our point of view, since we had hoped to find consistent and significant differences in the rate of productivity growth across industries which might have provided clues to causes of the productivity slowdown. In fact, no consistent industrial differences emerged, either within or across countries.

If we look at the numbers for the more recent sub-period in table 1, the biggest difference between the two countries in *TFP* growth occurs in the chemical (excluding drugs) industry, while the smallest are in textiles, leather, electrical equipment and drugs. It should be noted here that some of these differences may be spurious, the result of errors in the basic data. The biggest potential source of error comes from the price indexes, which could be both erroneous and improperly associated with the relevant industry output. One becomes suspicious of the numbers when one notices that in the U.S. chemical industry capital grew by 5.7 percent per year during 1973–78, materials purchased grew at 9.6 percent, while output went up by only 3.1 percent per year. The other numbers could be wrong, but the suspicion falls on the output number and the associated price index, especially when we note that it had the highest rate of growth of all the industrial price indexes — 13.2 percent per year.[3] At this moment, however, we have no way of checking what are basically ingredients of the national income accounts computations. We do want to warn the reader not to place too much confidence in the various numbers; there may still be quite a bit of error left in them.[4]

Looking at table 2, which lists the components of the *TFP* calculation for aggregate manufacturing, we observe that output growth in France was significantly higher in the 1967–73 period (7 vs. 4 percent), and fell by more in the 1973–78 period than in the U.S., to roughly equivalent levels (about 2 percent per year). Throughout both periods, fixed capital was growing faster in France than in the U.S., at the rate of 1 to 2 percent more per year. The big puzzle is in the behavior of man-hours. In the earlier period their growth is small and roughly parallel but diverges sharply during 1973–78. In France labor use declines at about −2 percent per year, while in the U.S. it rises at over 1 percent per year, in the face of a severe output growth slump.[5] There is also a divergence in the materials use story. Materials use is growing much faster in France during the first period and the drop in the second period is much sharper than in the U.S. (from over 7 to about 1 percent per year versus a drop from 3.5 to only 2.5 in the U.S.).

Looking at the price side, average output price inflation was slightly higher

---

[3]See appendix table A.2 for this detail.

[4]While there is agreement on the general outlines of the slowdown, there remains much disagreement among various sources about its exact magnitude, especially at the more detailed industrial level. *TFP* estimates for manufacturing industries at the 2-digit SIC level have been computed in the U.S. by Gollup and Jorgenson (1980) through 1973, and by Kendrick and Grossman (1980) and APC (1981) through 1979. They vary quite a bit from each other (in the 1967–73 overlap period the correlations between these estimates and between them and ours is only on the order of 0.5). Some of the discrepancies could be explained by the use of different data bases (revised vs. unrevised, Census vs. NIPA) and some by differences in methodology (value added vs. gross output, Divisia vs. fixed weight indexes), but the size of some of them remains a puzzle. Within the confines of this paper we cannot pursue this further, but we hope to return to it in the sequel.

[5]This difference is smaller if we look at employment rather than man-hours.

Table 2

Growth rates of output, inputs and prices, and levels of factor shares; French and U.S. manufacturing industries, 1967–78.[a]

Variable	1967–78			1967–73			1973–78			Change		
	FR	US	FR–US	FR	US	FR–US	FR	US	FR–US	FR	US	FR–US
Output	4.8	3.2	1.6	7.4	4.1	3.3	1.8	2.1	−0.3	−5.6	−2.0	−3.6
Capital	5.5	3.9	1.6	6.1	4.0	2.1	4.7	3.8	0.9	−1.4	−0.2	−1.2
Employees	0.3	0.4	−0.1	1.5	0.4	1.2	−1.1	0.4	−1.5	−2.6	0.0	−2.6
Man-hours	−0.6	1.0	−1.6	0.8	0.8	0.0	−2.2	1.2	−3.4	−3.0	0.4	3.4
Intermediate consumption	4.5	3.1	1.4	7.4	3.5	3.9	1.2	2.6	−1.4	−6.2	−0.9	−7.1
Price of output	7.1	6.0	1.1	4.6	3.5	1.0	10.2	9.0	1.3	5.6	5.5	0.1
Imputed price of capital	4.9	5.1	−0.2	5.9	4.2	1.7	3.8	6.2	−2.4	−2.1	2.0	−4.1
Price of labor (wage)	13.6	7.2	6.3	10.8	6.2	4.6	17.0	8.5	8.5	6.2	2.3	3.9
Price of interm. cons.	7.4	6.6	0.8	4.9	4.2	0.7	10.5	9.6	0.9	5.6	5.4	0.2
Share of capital in output	0.14	0.23	−0.09	0.15	0.23	−0.09	0.13	0.24	−0.10	−0.02	0.01	−0.03
Share of labor	0.31	0.27	0.05	0.31	0.28	0.03	0.31	0.25	0.06	0.00	−0.03	0.03
Share of interm. cons.	0.54	0.50	0.04	0.54	0.49	0.05	0.55	0.51	0.04	0.01	0.02	−0.01
Labor productivity (man-hours)	5.4	2.2	3.2	6.6	3.3	3.3	4.0	0.9	3.1	−2.6	−2.4	−0.2
Total factor productivity	1.7	0.4	1.3	2.2	1.2	1.0	1.2	−0.5	1.7	−1.0	−1.7	0.7

[a]Growth rates shown are percent per year; factor shares are period geometric averages.

in France, by about 1 percent per year, but not strikingly so. This is true also of material prices, which rose slightly faster in France. The big discrepancy, however, is again in labor. Wages appear to have grown much faster in France, accelerating in the second period to a rate *double* that in the U.S. While the real cost of both labor and materials remained roughly constant in the U.S. in the second period (and rose only gradually in the first), in France real labor costs were rising sharply in both periods (at a rate of 6 to 7 percent per year). This may provide a 'push' type explanation for the more rapid productivity growth in France than in the U.S. though the causality is far from clear here.[6]

2.2. Looking for causes of the slowdown: Capital and materials

There are three potential explanations of the productivity slowdown and the shortfall of the U.S. relative to other countries in this regard which we can explore with our data: differences in investment, a differential rise in materials (and energy) prices, and different R&D policies. Those who claim that part of the productivity slowdown can be explained by a shortfall in the rate of capital investment must have in mind a model in which the contribution of capital to output growth exceeds its factor share for some reason or other (disequilibrium, taxation, or the embodiment of technical change).[7] While capital stock was growing somewhat faster in France than in the U.S., the *TFP* calculations take this already into account, to a first order of approximation. One way to check on this is to take apart the *TFP* calculation and ask whether output growth was faster (slower) in sectors which experienced above (below) average growth in capital input.

Define the 'production function' as

$$q = \lambda + \alpha l + \beta c + \gamma m + e,$$

where q, l, c, m and λ denote rates of growth of output, labor, capital, materials and disembodied technical change, respectively; α, β, and γ are the respective input elasticies of output, and e is a disturbance term. Approximating the relevant elasticities by their corresponding factor shares, we estimate

$$q = a_{jt} + b_1(s_l l) + b_2(s_c c) + b_3(s_m m) + e,$$

---

[6]These facts have been noticed before. See, for example, Sachs (1979).

[7]They may be thinking primarily of the behavior of output per man-hour, a measure that does not take into account the contribution of the other inputs. Some of the fluctuations in output per man-hour are due to differential movements in capital and/or materials. The concept of total factor productivity attempts to allow for this by including all the major inputs in its definition of total input, weighting them in proportion to their share in total factor costs.

where the constants (technical change terms) are allowed to differ across countries (i) and periods (t). If the TFP calculations are roughly right, the estimated b's should be around unity. If an input is in some sense 'more important' than that, it should show up with a coefficient significantly above unity.

The results reported in table 3a do not support the capital (or materials) story.[8] Only the labor coefficient exceeds unity significantly and even this result disappears when we exclude the chemical industry with its dubious 1973–78 numbers from the U.S. equation. The capital coefficients are not significantly different from unity, either in the direct production function estimates, or the partial productivity versions, where we first treat labor and then both labor and materials as endogenous variables, constraining their elasticities to equal their factor shares, and subtracting them from the left-hand side.[9] If anything, the coefficient of capital is lower in France than in the U.S., which is exactly the opposite of what would have been needed to provide an explanation for the more rapid productivity growth in France. This is even more obvious when we try to explain cross-country differences in sectoral output growth. There, the estimated capital coefficient actually turns negative, though not significantly so, implying that output was growing faster in France than in the U.S., in industries where the relative capital growth was lower.[10]

As far as materials are concerned, while the direct coefficients are sometimes higher than unity, the differences are not statistically or economically significant. The materials story, suggested especially by Bruno (1981), is based on the notion that in the short-run their elasticity of substitution is less than unity and that a response to a sharp rise in their price is more costly to output growth than is implied by the standard formulae. This can be tested either by looking at the estimated coefficient of materials in the 'production function' framework, or by substituting the real price of materials for the more endogenous materials quantity variable.[11]

[8]To reduce dependence, these regressions are based on a partition of the data into two non-overlapping periods, 1967–72 and 1973–78. The results are similar when other partitionings, 1967–73 or 1972–78, are used instead.

[9]It makes little sense to think of input changes as exogenous in this context of rather aggregate changes over five-year periods. The regressions should be interpreted as a data summary device and not as structural estimates of *the* production function. The partial productivity regressions try to focus on the contribution of specific inputs by constraining the other coefficients to reasonable a priori values.

[10]These results are robust to the exclusion of the chemicals industry with its possibly bad U.S. numbers from these regressions and to the use of slightly different time periods.

[11]One should note that our definition of purchased materials includes also materials purchased from the same and other manufacturing industries and is not a net 'outside' materials concept. The computed materials price changes understate, therefore, the true magnitude of changes in the price of 'outside' materials. But the computed share of all 'materials' overstates their overall importance, with the product of the two being essentially unaffected by this distinction. Let the computed p_m (rate of growth in materials prices) be $p_m = (1-d)p_q + dp_0$, where

Table 3a

Primal productivity regressions: Output, productivity and price growth regressions; fifteen manufacturing industries in the United States and France, 1967–72 and 1973–78.[a]

Dependent variable and country	Coefficients (standard errors) of				Residual standard error
	$s_l l$	$s_c c$	$s_m m$	$[s_m/(1-s_m)]$ $\times (p_m - p_q)$	
I. *Output, q*					
U.S.	2.21	0.93	0.62		1.21
	(0.47)	(0.43)	(0.26)		
U.S.[b]	1.13	0.44	1.23		1.20
	(0.58)	(0.58)	(0.22)		
France	1.36	0.32	1.14		1.18
	(0.52)	(0.54)	(0.21)		
Combined[b]	1.11	1.08	1.37		1.08
	(0.26)	(1.9)	(0.16)		
France–U.S.[b]	1.52	−0.43	1.26		1.24
	(0.60)	(0.47)	(0.29)		
II. *Partial productivity, $q - s_l l$*					
U.S.		0.90	1.11		1.33
		(0.47)	(0.19)		
France		0.46	1.21		1.17
		(0.50)	(0.19)		
France–U.S.		−1.15	1.25		1.49
		(0.56)	(0.17)		
III. *Partial productivity, $q - s_l l - s_m m$*					
U.S.			1.01		1.31
			(0.42)		
France			0.64		1.17
			(0.47)		
IV. *Mixed partial productivity, $q - [s_l/(1-s_m)]l$*					
U.S.		0.92[d]		0.64	1.34
		(0.23)		(0.25)	
France		1.06[d]		0.44	1.46
		(0.28)		(0.14)	
Combined IV[c]		0.87[d]		−0.22	n.c.
		(0.23)		(0.32)	

[a]q, l, c, m and p's are rates of growth of output, labor, capital, materials and of the relevant output and input price indexes $[x = \log X_t - \log X_{t-5})/5]$.

s_k's are the average (beginning and end period) estimated factor shares of the respective inputs.

Combined equations estimated using generalized least squares, allowing a freely correlated disturbance matrix (4×4) between countries and time periods across industries. I.e., four separate equations (2 periods × 2 countries) are estimated, with the relevant coefficients constrained to be the same across equations.

All equations contain separate unconstrained country and period constant terms.

n.c. stands for not computed.

[b]Excludes the chemicals industry.

[c]Combined IV treats $[s_m/(1-s_m)](p_m - p_q)$ as endogenous, using $[s_m/(1-s_m)]p_m$ and $(s_m/(1-s_m))p_l$ as additional instrumental variables.

[d]The variable here is $[s_c/(1-s_m)]c$.

Treating materials as a separate input with an elasticity of substitution $\sigma < 1$ between itself and the aggregate of other inputs (value added, consisting of capital and labor) one can write the equation to be estimated as

$$q - \frac{\alpha}{1-\gamma} l = \frac{\lambda}{1-\lambda} + \frac{\beta}{1-\gamma} c - \frac{\gamma \sigma}{1-\gamma} [p_m - p_q] + e,$$

where, in addition to the symbols defined above, p_m and p_q are the growth rates of materials and output prices, respectively.[12] When such an equation is estimated, it yields invariably the wrong sign for the coefficient of the weighted real price of materials $[(s_m/(1-s_m)](p_m - p_q)$ implying that productivity improved in industries where real material prices rose more rapidly. This could be due to errors in the measurement of industrial output prices, since both the construction of the output variable and the real materials price variable depend on the same output price deflators. An attempt was made to get around this problem by treating $p_m - p_q$ as endogenous and using p_m and p_l (the growth rate of wage rates) as additional instruments. This yielded a negative but not statistically significant coefficient for the real price of materials, with an estimated σ of about 0.2.

Actually, it is not all that surprising that we cannot get much from the materials story since the basic facts go the wrong way.[13] The growth in material use fell more sharply in France than in the U.S. and hence cannot account for the sharper productivity deceleration in the U.S. Nor is there any evidence that real materials prices were rising more rapidly in the U.S. or accelerated more there; if anything, the opposite appears to be the case. Thus, whatever explanation they may provide for the short-term timing of such movements, the rise in material prices cannot explain the persistent and increasing difference between French and U.S. productivity growth.[14]

Another way of looking at the relationships between our variables is to look at the dual price side. Treating output price as dependent, one can write

$$p_q = -\lambda + \alpha p_l + \beta p_c + \gamma p_m + \varepsilon,$$

---

p_q and p_0 are the rates of growth of the industry's own price level and of outside materials prices respectively and d the share of purchases of 'outside' materials in total expenditures on materials. Then the variable we use, $s_m(p_m - p_q) = s_m d(p_0 - p_q) = s_0(p_0 - p_q)$, is the same as if we had used the 'outside' definition of materials. Our conclusions should, therefore, be robust with respect to the exact definition of 'materials' and the boundaries of the various industries. (We are grateful to Michael Bruno for this remark.)

[12] See Bruno (1981, eq. 8).

[13] Moreover, our data are not very powerful in this respect. The real price of materials varies surprisingly little over five-year periods. It appears that most of the materials price changes were passed through to output prices within this length of time.

[14] Most of the evidence presented in Bruno (1981) for the materials story is based on aggregate *annual* time series for different countries. France is not considered explicitly and the results for the U.S. are not as good as for some of the other countries.

where, in addition to the terms defined above, p_l and p_c are rates of growth in labor and capital price indexes, and ε is a disturbance. Table 3b presents the results of such regressions where, as before, factor shares replace α, β and γ, and the estimated coefficients should be on the order one. Estimates of a 'factor price frontier' equation,

$$p_c - p_q = \lambda/\beta - (\alpha/\beta)(p_l - p_q) - \gamma/\beta(p_m - p_q) + \varepsilon,$$

which endogeneize the price of capital (using the real return to capital as the dependent variable), are also reported in this table. In the direct price equations there is a stark contrast between U.S. and France. In the U.S. labor cost and especially material price increases where transmitted to product prices *more* than proportionally, more than could have been predicted by their relative importance in total costs. In France, material price increases appear to have had less than their predicted impact on product prices. When factor price frontier equations are estimated, with the real return to capital as the dependent variable, real material prices invariably come out with the wrong sign. Somehow, the spuriousness introduced by errors in the output price deflators appears to dominate. This is another manifestation of a problem that is endemic to such data — real factor price

Table 3b

Dual price regressions: Output, productivity and price growth regressions; fifteen manufacturing industries in the United States and France, 1967–72 and 1973–78.

	$s_l p_l$ or $(s_l/s_c)(p_m - p_q)$	$s_c p_c$	$s_m p_m$ or $(s_m/s_c)(p_m - p_q)$	Residual standard error
I. *Output price, p_q*				
U.S.	1.36	0.65	1.67	1.13
	(0.49)	(0.26)	(0.24)	
France	0.96	0.56	0.79	1.20
	(0.28)	(0.57)	(0.19)	
II. *Partial price equation, $p_q - s_c p_c$*[a]				
U.S.	2.01		1.55	1.09
	(0.34)		(0.19)	
France	0.82		0.79	1.11
	(0.21)		(0.16)	
III. *Factor price frontier, $p_c - p_q$*[a]				
U.S.	−0.60		0.33	3.99
	(0.69)		(0.54)	
France	0.22		0.04	4.66
	(0.12)		(0.11)	

[a]Estimated jointly using the SUR procedure.

differences are rather small across industries within any one country, small relative to the size of transitory and erroneously measured movements in output prices.

One way of reducing the endogeneity of the right-hand terms in the factor price frontier equation is to solve out both the output price and the endogenous capital return measure from the right-hand side of this equation. This leads to the estimation of 'partial price equations' with $p_q - \beta p_c$ as the dependent variable, i.e.,

$$p_q - \beta p_c = \lambda + \alpha p_l + \gamma p_m + \varepsilon.$$

These equations (listed in the middle of table 3b) also imply an above average transmission of wage and materials price changes to output prices in the U.S. relative to France. If factor prices have had a special role in this story, it has been their differential impact in the two countries. Thus, they cannot provide a unified explanation for the events in both countries.

2.3. The role of R&D

We cannot really analyze the contribution of R&D to productivity growth in any detail in this section because there are no R&D time series at the industry level in France. We do have, however, French data on R&D expenditures and employment by industry for 1975 and we can use similar U.S. data (see appendix table A.3) to investigate whether differences in productivity growth are related to differences in R&D intensity. An earlier study [Griliches and Lichtenberg (1981)] found that one can attribute only very little of the productivity slowdown in the U.S. to the retardation that occurred in the growth of R&D in the late 1960s. This study utilized a more detailed industrial breakdown and showed that the relationship between TFP growth and the R&D to sales ratio did not deteriorate in the 1970s. Moreover, it indicated that the R&D to sales ratios remained relatively stable across industries between the 60s and 70s (r^2 for the correlation of R/S in 1964–68 and 1969–73 across twenty-seven manufacturing industries was 0.97). Assuming a similar stability in France, we may use the 1975 data to proxy also for the unavailable earlier data.

If we combine all of our data for the two countries, two periods, and fifteen industries ($N = C \times T \times I = 60$), and estimate a common R&D coefficient in the two countries, using a seemingly unrelated regression framework, we get the following equation:

$$TFP = 0.23\,DUS1 - 1.02\,DUS2 + 1.49\,DF1 + 0.76\,DF2 + 0.28\,R/S,$$
$$\quad\;\;(0.31)\qquad\;\;(0.37)\qquad\;\;(0.31)\qquad(0.29)\qquad(0.09)$$

$$SEE = 1.10,$$

where *DUS1* is the U.S. constant term (average rate of *TFP* growth) in the first period, and similarly for the other terms, while *R/S* is the ratio of company financed R&D expenditures to total sales in the respective countries.[15] The estimated R&D coefficient implies a 28 percent excess gross rate of return to R&D investment. It is excess because much of the R&D input is already counted once in the construction of labor and capital and it is gross because no allowance has been made for possible depreciation of R&D capital [see Griliches (1979), Schankerman (1981) and Cuneo–Mairesse (1983) for a more detailed interpretation of such coefficients].

When we allow for separate country coefficients we get the following equation instead:

$$TFP = 0.30\,DUS1 - 0.94\,DUS2 + 1.42\,DF1 + 0.68\,DF2$$
$$(0.33)\qquad(0.38)\qquad(0.36)\qquad(0.33)$$

$$+\,0.23\,R/S(US) + 0.33\,R/S(F),\qquad SEE = 1.11.$$
$$(0.12)\qquad\quad(0.14)$$

The difference between the U.S. and French coefficient is substantial but not statistically significant.

The estimated *R/S* coefficient for the U.S. (0.23) is comparable to what we found in the earlier study. If we accept such a rate of return or even if it were twice as high, this still would not account for much of the deceleration of *TFP* in the U.S., since the decline in R&D to sales ratio was in fact rather small.[16] Nor can our estimates account for the differences in *TFP* growth between France and the U.S., since the R&D to sales ratios tend to be lower at the industry level in France than in the U.S. We shall re-examine this conclusion, however, in the next section where the available micro data contain more information on firm R&D expenditures over a longer time period.

---

[15]The OLS estimates, although less precise, are very similar to the SUR estimates. When we use total R&D to sales ratio (or R&D employment to total employment ratio) instead of company R&D to sales ratio, we obtain rather poor and statistically insignificant estimates for the U.S. These are due mainly to one outlier, the U.S. Aircraft, boats and space vehicles industry, which had very low *TFP* growth rates (the lowest in the first period) and the highest total R&D to sales ratio (of which 80 percent is federally funded). When this industry is left out of the sample all estimates become comparable. Earlier work has also shown that productivity growth in the U.S. is more closely related to company R&D expenditures than to the federally financed components of total R&D.

[16]The total R&D to sales ratio in U.S. manufacturing declines from about 4.4 percent in the mid-60s to 3.1 in the mid-70s. The decline is much smaller, however, for company financed R&D, from a peak of 2.2 percent in 1969 to a low of 2.0 in the mid-70s.

3. Productivity growth at the firm level

3.1. Data and basic facts

In this section we examine the growth of productivity at the firm level. Because of our interest in assessing the contribution of R&D to productivity, we have been assembling data on R&D performing firms in both France and the U.S.[17] Data problems and the desire for comparable and adequately sized samples limited the study period to 1973–1978 and to five manufacturing industries for which we had a sufficient number of firms (at least 30) in each of the countries: Drugs, Chemicals (excluding Drugs), Electronics, Electrical Equipment (excluding Computers), and Machinery. The exact definition of these five industries in terms of the two- or three-digit French 'NAP' or U.S. 'SIC' classifications is indicated in table A.4 in the appendix. It differs somewhat from our aggregate industry breakdown. The 'parachemical' firms were brought together with the chemical firms (rather than with the drug firms), and the medical instrument firms were added to the 'drug' industry. The electronics and electrical equipment firms are treated separately, and computer and (non-medical) instrument firms have been excluded, since there were too few of them in France.

Our samples correspond best to the subtotal of the four aggregate industries $(2 + 7 + 8 + 14)$ given separately in table 1 of the previous section. The number of firms is relatively small $(N = 185)$ in the French sample and only somewhat larger $(N = 343)$ in the U.S. one, but these firms do account for about 25 and 85 percent of the total number of employees in these four aggregate industries in France and the U.S., respectively. They are not a representative sample from these industries, however. This occurs, first, because we include only firms which actually perform R&D and, second, because our data cleaning efforts result in additional selection. In particular, firms which grew through major mergers have been excluded.[18]

That the use of similar selection procedures in both countries yields a much lower coverage for the French sample than the U.S. one is rather interesting. Only about a third of the French firms (in terms of the number of employees) in these industries have significant levels of R&D expenditures as against most of the firms in the U.S. This difference in the industrial structure of the two countries also accounts for the observed discrepancy between the R&D to sales ratios at the firm and industry levels in the two countries. (See the data sources appendix for more details.)

In addition to constructing our samples along the same lines for both countries, we also defined and measured our main variables as similarly as

---

[17]See Griliches and Mairesse (1981) and Cuneo and Mairesse (1983) for a description of earlier work and for more detail on these data.

[18]We recognized 'major mergers' by large jumps in the data such as the doubling of gross plant, sales or the number of employees. This eliminated about 50 firms from the French sample and 80 from the U.S. one.

possible. Output is defined as deflated sales. The industrial level of the sales deflators depends on their respective availability in the two countries (eleven different price indices for the French and twenty-five for the U.S. data).[19] Labor is measured by the total number of employees and gross physical capital stock by the book value of gross plant adjusted for inflation (based on a rough estimate of the average age of the capital stock). An R&D capital stock variable is constructed as a weighted sum of past R&D expenditures, using a 15 percent rate of depreciation and all of the pre-1973 information on R&D that we could get for our firms.[20] Because materials purchases and labor costs are not separated for most U.S. firms (they are lumped together in the item 'cost of good sold') it was not possible to treat materials as a separate factor of production and estimate a *TFP* index similar to that computed at the industry level. We focus, therefore, on labor productivity Q/L and on an approximate *TFP* measure $Q/[L^{0.75} C^{0.25}]$, which assumes the proportionality of materials to value added and uses constant labor and physical capital cost shares.[21] We also put more emphasis on econometric estimates of the contribution of physical investment and R&D to labor productivity growth, using a standard Cobb–Douglas production function framework to allow factor elasticities to diverge from their corresponding cost shares.

Table 4 presents means and standard deviations of the growth rates of our main variables between 1973 and 1978 and of their levels as of 1974. It also reports their weighted growth rates and compares them to the corresponding aggregate growth rates.[22] The standard deviations of the rates of growth of labor productivity are 4.9 and 4.2 percent per year in the French and U.S. samples, respectively, and the corresponding interquartile ranges are $[-0.1; 6.0]$ and $[-1.8; 3.4]$. In fact, when one looks at any histogram of individual rates of growth, or any plot of them, the scatters overlap widely across countries. This is illustrated in figs. 2 and 3 which show for both samples the histogram of $q-n$ (labor productivity growth rate) and the plot of $q-n$ against $c-n$ (capital stock per employee growth rate).

[19]For the U.S. sample firm-specific price indices were also computed as weighted averages of sectoral indices, the weights being obtained from the information on sales by different business segments within a company in 1978. Using such firm specific price indices did not alter our results in any significant way.

[20]We were able to use R&D data as far back as 1963 for two-thirds of the French sample, and at least back to 1968 for practically all the firms of the French sample and most of the firms in the U.S. sample. We tried also alternative measures of R&D capital, retrapolating R&D series on the basis of the corresponding industry growth rates instead of using all the firm information whenever possible and adopting a 30 percent rate of depreciation. The means of such different measures differ of course appreciably (and thus the estimates exhibited in table 4 for our main measures are only roughly indicative) but the estimated regression coefficients (elasticities) are practically unchanged.

[21]Using specific country and industry cost shares of labor and physical capital (rather than 0.75 and 0.25) to compute an alternative *TFP* variable did not affect our results significantly.

[22]Table A.4 in the appendix gives similar detail for the five industry sub-samples.

Table 4

Characteristics of the main variables in the French ($N = 185$) and U.S. ($N = 343$) samples.

| Main variables | Rates of growth of variables over 1973–78 (except R/S for which the 1974 level is given) | | | | Levels of variables in 1974[a] | |
| | Unweighted sample means (standard deviations) | | Weighted sample means [corresponding aggregate estimates] | | Unweighted sample means (standard deviations) | |
	FR	US	FR	US	FR	US
Deflated sales per employee, $q - n$	3.2 (4.9)	0.7 (4.2)	3.6 [3.5]	2.2 [1.9]	25.8 (0.4)	33.5 (0.4)
Gross plant adjusted per employee, $c - n$	5.6 (4.9)	5.0 (6.5)	5.5 [6.9]	5.9 [3.3]	9.8 (0.5)	14.6 (0.6)
R&D capital stock per employee, $k - n$	5.9 (6.7)	3.7 (7.9)	5.8	3.6	3.8 (1.0)	3.0 (0.8)
Number of employees,	0.4 (4.4)	2.5 (7.1)	0.8 [−0.4]	0.8 [1.8]	0.9 (1.3)	3.0 (1.7)
Total factor productivity, TFP	1.8 (4.8)	−0.5 (4.1)	2.2 [1.8]	0.8 [1.1]		
R&D to sales ratio in 1971, R/S	4.8 (4.4)	2.6 (2.0)	3.7 [2.6]	2.9 [3.0]		

[a]Levels of deflated sales, gross-plant adjusted, R&D capital stock are in millions of dollars. An approximate rate of 5 francs for 1 dollar has been used to convert the French figures. Levels of numbers of employees are in thousand persons. The sample means are the geometric sample means, while the standard deviations are the log-standard deviations.

Another interesting point is that the dispersion of growth rates, even though quite large in its own terms, is rather small (about a tenth) relative to the dispersion of the corresponding levels. Moreover, growth rates and levels are almost uncorrelated, Gibrat's law of proportionate and independent growth holding also for productivity and not just for the growth in size (number of employees or sales), as it is usually formulated.[23] These two features are reflected in the long period stability of firm rankings by absolute productivity in spite of the great variability in their productivity growth rates.

Looking at the average growth rates of our variables and comparing unweighted to weighted averages, it appears that smaller firms are growing faster than larger ones in the U.S., while no such differential tendency is

[23]For example, the correlation between the 1973–78 growth in labor productivity and its level in 1974 is only −0.05 and −0.07 in the French and U.S. samples, respectively, while the correlation between the growth rate in employment and its level is only −0.02 and −0.15. Gibrat's 'law' asserts that percentage growth rates are independent of both levels and previous growth rates; i.e., the logarithms of levels follow a random walk. See Marris (1979) for references on this and related literature.

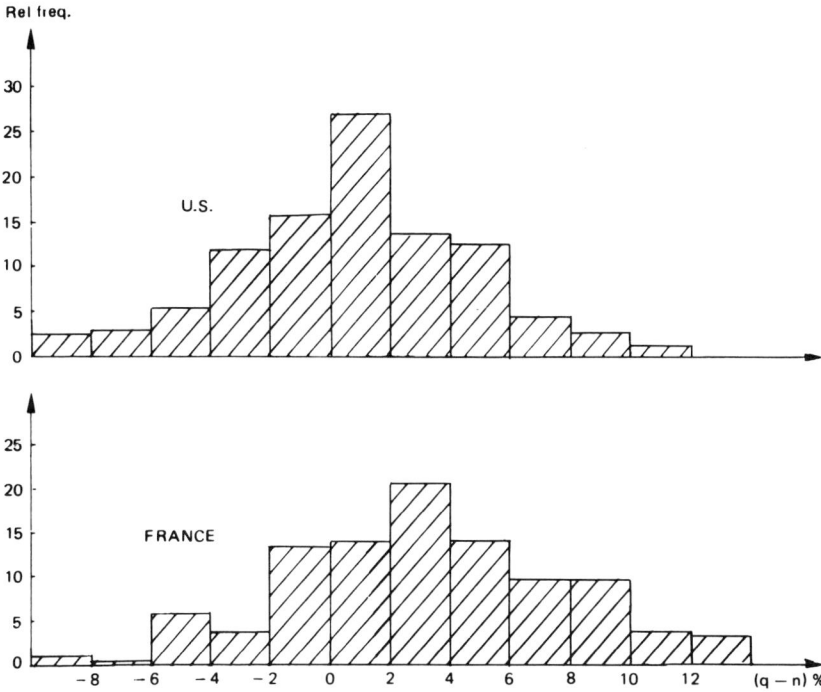

Fig. 2. Frequency distributions of labor productivity growth rates; French and U.S. samples, 1973–78. *France:* Mean = 3.20, standard deviation = 4.85, interquartile range = 6.12; *United States:* Mean = 0.73, standard deviation = 4.17, interquartile range = 5.20.

apparent in France. This is particularly striking when we look at the number of employees, but is also true for the growth in sales and capital. Some of this may be explained by differences in the size (and also in the range of sizes) of French and U.S. firms: the geometric means of the number of employees being 900 in France and 3000 in the U.S.[24]

Given all the discrepancies that could have arisen from the selection of our samples and the measurement of our variables, the agreement between our 'micro' and 'macro' numbers is rather surprising. The weighted sample means and the corresponding four industries aggregates are not that far apart. In France, the growth of R&D firms has been apparently more rapid than that for the corresponding industries as a whole, which is not surprising. Curiously, the reverse seems to be the case for the U.S., R&D firms having a

[24]The arithmetic means of the number of employees are 2,100 and 12,600 in the French and U.S. samples, respectively. While the growth in employment was about the same in France for firms with less than 2,000 employees and for those with more than 2,000 employees, in the U.S. the respective growth rates were 3.6 and 1.7 percent.

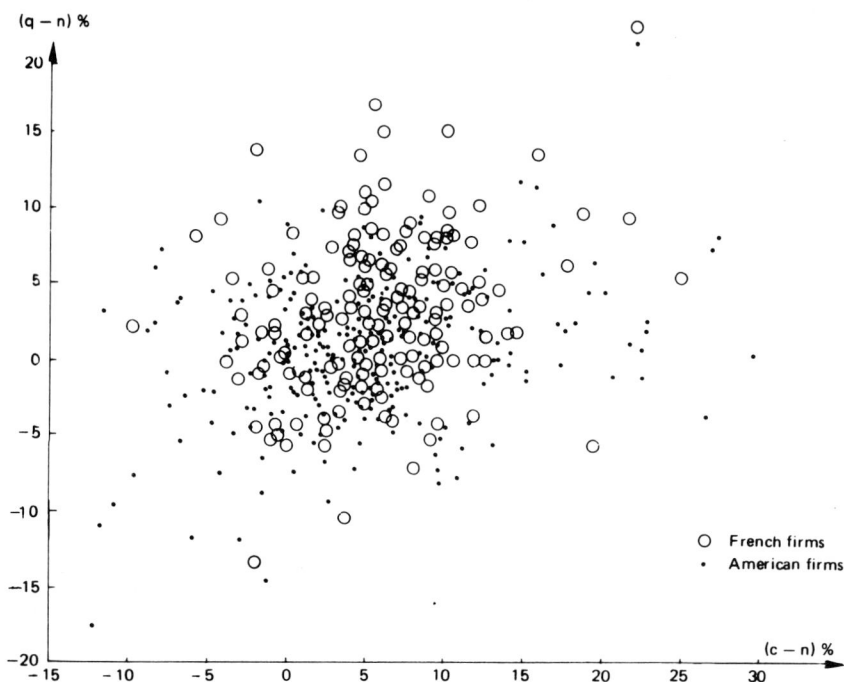

Fig. 3. Plot of labor productivity growth rates against the growth in capital–labor ratios; French and U.S. samples, 1973–78.

somewhat lower growth in employment (although they invested more) and a lower growth of sales than the corresponding industries. We have already noted the remarkable difference between our 'micro' and 'macro' R&D to sales ratios. French firms performing R&D have been investing relatively more in research and development than their U.S. counterparts, but since they constitute a much smaller proportion of the totals the opposite is true for the corresponding industries taken as a whole. The unweighted and weighted average R&D to sales ratios are 4.8 and 3.7 percent, respectively, for the French sample, 2.6 and 2.9 percent for the U.S. sample, while the corresponding industry estimates are 2.6 and 3.0 percent, respectively.[25]

In spite of such differences, a comparison of the 1973–78 productivity growth rates in the two countries yields essentially the same picture as before. Both labor and total factor productivity (based on our rough calculation with a capital share of 0.25) increased much faster in France than in the U.S., by 1.5 to 2.0 percent per year.

[25]The large difference between the unweighted and weighted ratios in France implies a difference in the R&D intensity of small and large firms: 5.1 percent in firms with less than 2,000 employees, 3.8 percent for those with more than 2,000 employees.

We should, finally, remark on the comparison of productivity levels in the two countries given in table 4 using five francs for one dollar as an approximate rate of conversion. Though productivity growth has been more rapid in France, labor productivity levels are still below those in the U.S. by about as much as 25 percent on the average. Part of this gap may be due to differences in physical capital intensity and the scale of enterprises between the two countries.

3.2. Assessing the contribution of R&D to productivity growth

In an attempt to assess the contribution of R&D as well as that of physical capital to productivity growth, we find it convenient to pool the French and U.S. samples together. This is not unreasonable since the standard deviations of our variables and the correlations between them are rather similar in both samples. Among different ways of handling such panel data, we chose to analyze differences in firm growth rates between 1973 and 1978. This has the advantage that the general economic situation in these two years was good in both countries, in contrast to the 1975–1976 recession years. Compared to using year-to-year growth rates, it also has the advantage of reducing biases due to measurement errors in the variables (diminishing the ratio of error to true variance). In doing so, we discard all the cross-sectional information in our data panel, relying only on its time series components. As we know from the literature on the econometrics of panel data and from previous work, cross-sectional estimates often differ from time series estimates. In our earlier studies [see Griliches–Mairesse (1981) and Cuneo–Mairesse (1983)], they actually provide more sensible estimates of the elasticity of output with respect to R&D capital. Despite that, we do not report here on such cross-sectional estimates to keep the analysis parallel to the first section.

Let us denote by $q-n$, $c-n$ and $k-n$ the annual rate of growth between 1973 and 1978 of labor productivity, physical, and R&D capital–labor ratios respectively (dropping for simplicity the firm subscripts i); and by COU, IND, SIZ the appropriate set of dummy variables indicating whether or not firms belong to one of the two countries, one of the five industries, or one of four size groups (which we defined to control for the different range in the number of employees in the French and U.S. samples). The following types of regressions were estimated:

$$(q-n) = \beta \cdot (c-n) + \delta \cdot (k-n) + DUM + e,$$

or

$$(q-n) = \beta \cdot COU \cdot (c-n) + \delta \cdot COU \cdot (k-n) + DUM + e,$$

or

$$(q-n) = \beta \cdot COU \cdot IND \cdot (c-n) + \delta \cdot COU \cdot IND \cdot (k-n) + DUM + e,$$

where the slope coefficients are first constrained to be constant across countries and industries and then free to differ across countries and also across industries, and where *DUM* denotes either the set of dummy variables *COU, IND, IND·COU, SIZ* (thirteen independent ones) or only the sub-set *COU, SIZ* (five independent ones). When the full set of dummy variables is included, the regressions are based only on intra-country and intra-industry growth differences. When the industry dummies and their interactions are excluded, the regressions are based also on inter-industry growth differences and are therefore more similar to those computed in section 2. To relate these regressions even more closely to the previous analysis and because we did not find evidence of a statistically significant contribution of $k-n$ (the growth in R&D capital) to productivity growth, we used also an R&D intensity variable ($R/S74$) instead of the R&D capital measure. We used the R&D to sales ratio as of 1974 instead of a comparable 1973 ratio, so as to avoid any spurious correlation with the 1973–78 growth rate in labor productivity $q-n$. The substitution of R/S for $k-n$ implies a different specification of the production function, one that assumes a constant marginal product for R&D rather than a constant elasticity across firms or industries [see Griliches–Lichtenberg (1982)].

Our main results are summarized in table 5 which gives the estimated parameters of interest for a number of specifications we tested. Starting with the simplest analysis of variance which uses only dummy variables, we find that all the effects are statistically significant. Among the various dummy variables, the country and industry effects are most highly significant while the size effects are less so, implying a slight tendency for faster growth of productivity in larger firms. The country–industry interactions are just on the border of statistical significance.

In addition to such country and industry effects, physical capital growth also contributes significantly to the growth in labor productivity, especially when constrained to have the same average elasticity in all five industries. The evidence is weaker when different industries are considered separately. But the discrepancies in the estimated elasticities by industries and countries are not statistically significant, and we can maintain the hypothesis of a common elasticity. Given the small size of our industry sub-samples, we cannot really discern differences in elasticities across industries.

In contrast to physical capital, growth in R&D capital is not significant at all, even when we impose a constant elasticity across industries. These negative results may be due to our turbulent sample period [see Griliches–Mairesse (1981)] and also to problems of measurement. Double counting of R&D-related employees and R&D-related capital expenditures in our actual measure of labor and physical capital stock may obscure the relation between productivity and R&D investments. In the French sample, where we can correct for some of these problems, we obtain much more sensible

Table 5

Inter- and intra-industry regressions, without and with industry dummies (and possibly separate industry slopes), respectively: Productivity growth differences in pooled French–U.S. sample $(N = 185 + 343 = 528)$.

Different specifications	Coefficients (standard errors) of			Residual standard error
	$c - n$	$k - n$	R/S	
France and U.S. combined				
Inter-industry estimates	0.17 (0.04)	0.02 (0.03)		4.26
	0.17 (0.03)		0.28 (0.06)	4.18
Intra-industry estimates	0.16 (0.03)	0.03 (0.03)		3.99
	0.17 (0.03)		0.12 (0.06)	3.99

	Coefficients (standard errors) of				Residual standard error
	$(c - n)$		R/S		
	FR	US	FR	US	
France and U.S. separately					
Inter-industry estimates	0.19 (0.06)	0.16 (0.04)	0.31 (0.07)	0.19 (0.11)	4.18
Intra-industry estimates, with different industry slopes — Drugs	0.20 (0.09)	0.08 (0.10)	0.27 (0.15)	0.41 (0.23)	
Chemicals	0.40 (0.19)	0.03 (0.09)	0.00 (0.23)	−0.19 (0.36)	3.99
Electronics	−0.04 (0.18)	0.21 (0.06)	0.12 (0.11)	−0.06 (0.19)	
Electrical equipment	0.13 (0.14)	0.15 (0.10)	0.45 (0.24)	−0.44 (0.33)	
Machinery	0.21 (0.13)	0.25 (0.06)	−0.55 (0.38)	0.11 (0.27)	

looking estimates, with an estimated output elasticity of R&D capital δ of about 0.1 [see Cuneo–Mairesse (1983)].

On the other hand, the R&D to sales ratio does turn out to contribute significantly to the explanation of the interindustry differences in productivity growth. When it is restricted, however, to the explanation of intra-industry differences, the contribution of R/S dwindles to insignificance. In the inter-industry regressions, the estimated coefficient of R/S (ρ), which can be interpreted as the marginal product or gross rate of return of R&D, is 0.28, while in the intra-industry regressions (those containing industry dummy variables) it is only 0.12. Part of the discrepancy might be attributable to externalities, the fact that R&D performed by a particular firm may benefit other firms in the same industry. Unfortunately, the evidence of an intra-industry effect becomes especially weak when we relax the constraint that the coefficient ρ be the same in the different industries. Nonetheless, to end on a positive note, it is quite encouraging that the contribution of R&D to productivity growth is confirmed by our analyses at both the industrial and the firm levels. It may even be a bit of luck that the estimated order of magnitude of the overall gross rate of return to investment in R&D comes out so close in both cases: about 0.25, somewhat more perhaps in France and less in the U.S..

4. Conclusions

Analyzing the French and U.S. industrial data we confirmed both the fact of faster productivity growth in France and the pervasiveness of the recent productivity slowdown. Looking at the individual industry experiences did not yield any new clues about its sources, but it did reject some old ones. Three explanations of the slowdown were examined and were found not to bear on the differences in productivity growth across the two countries. It has been alleged by some that the productivity slowdown has resulted from insufficient physical investment and this argument has been also used to justify policies that would subsidize savings and investment. The evidence we examined does not indicate any close relationship between investment and the growth in productivity. industries with above (below) average growth in physical capital did not have an above (below) average growth rate of total factor productivity. The rise in materials and energy prices has also been implicated in the productivity slowdown, working either via a low short-run substitutability of materials for other inputs and/or complementarity between equipment and energy. The evidence we examined at the individual industry level does not support this view. Industries that experienced above average growth in the price of materials and/or had been more materials-intensive, did not appear to have suffered differentially. The notion that the productivity slowdown is associated with the decline in the growth of R&D expenditures has also been quite prevalent and has led to various proposals (and legislation in the U.S.) to subsidize or provide special tax treatment for R&D. While we did find some modest evidence of a positive effect of R&D on productivity, it could account for only very little of the aggregate cross-country differences, since the overall R&D investment intensities were not higher in France than in the U.S.

Looking at the individual firm data did not change these conclusions. The major impression that emerged was one of variance. At the firm level, the estimated output elasticity of physical capital is positive and statistically significant but does not exceed its factor share in either country. Thus, there is no evidence for the notion that investment in fixed assets is more important in accounting for changes in labor productivity than is already implied in the usual total factor productivity calculations. Because a much smaller proportion of firms in an industry do R&D in France than in the U.S., it turns out that the French sample is more research-intensive than our U.S. one, while the reverse is true at the aggregate level for the corresponding industries. Nevertheless, the estimated R&D effects are statistically significant and of comparable magnitude at both the micro- and macro-level; they cannot account, however, for much of the observed differences in productivity growth.

This is our first look at the comparative performance of manufacturing industries and firms in France and the U.S. It is obvious that we have still many unsolved problems and puzzles, both in the quality of the underlying data and in our understanding the substance of what has happened. But we have made a beginning and hope that others will be encouraged to pursue such comparative studies further.

Appendix: Data sources at the industry and the firm level

The French industrial data come from the National Accounts data bases. Gross output, materials (intermediate consumption) and their associated price indexes and the total number of employees by industry are taken from 'Les comptes de l'industrie' [*Les Collections de l'INSEE* no. C55 (1977), C76 (1979), C92 (1981)]. Hours of work are obtained by multiplying the average total number of employees, over the year, by the average number of hours worked per week by production workers in the same years. The latter is taken from the INSEE national accounts data bank. For a description of the methods used in constructing capital stock, see J. Mairesse, 'L'evaluation du capital fixe productif: Methodes et resultats' [*Les Collections de l'INSEE* no. C18–19 (1972)]. The numbers are taken from INSEE national accounts data bank. The share of labor in gross output is computed from the labor share in value added data, available in 'Les comptes d'entreprises par secteurs' [see *Les Collections de l'INSEE* no. C78 (1979)] by multiplying them by $(1 - s_m)$, where s_m is the share of materials in gross output. The estimates from the 'sectoral' national accounts (based on firm's data) are not quite coherent with the other estimates from the 'branch' national accounts (more or less based on establishments data). But at our national level of industrial aggregation and for our purpose of computing *TFP* estimates, the possible discrepancies are negligible.

The U.S. industrial data are aggregated from the 4-digit SIC level data base constructed by the Penn-SRI-Census project [Fromm et al. (1979)] and updated and extended at the NBER by Wayne Gray and Frank Lichtenberg. The basic data come from the *Census Annual Surveys of Manufactures*, while the price series are based on the underlying detailed national income deflators. Labor input (total hours) is computed by dividing total payrolls in operating establishments by the average hourly wage rate of production workers. It can be interpreted as an estimate of total man-hours in production-worker equivalent units. The capital stock data were constructed by Fawcett and Associates for Penn-SRI by perpetual inventory methods from Census sources. Output and input price indexes are based on unpublished detailed National Income deflators and tabulations. The price index of intermediate consumption was revised at the NBER by using the 1972 I–O table and I–O sector level price indexes constructed by the Bureau of Labor Statistics. The total labor costs were revised at the NBER by adding the payrolls of Central and Auxillary Offices for Census years and interpolating in the intercensal years.

One source of discrepancies between the French and U.S. industrial data sets is that the latter are based on Census sources and not on NIPA conventions. In particular, in the U.S. Census, the notion of 'materials' does not include all intermediate consumption, excluding especially purchased services. Since the capital share (s_c) is computed residually, it is somewhat too high in the U.S., perhaps by as much as a third (see the attempt at reconciliation of value added and GNP originating in the *U.S. Census of Manufacturers*, 1977, Vol. 1, p. XXVII).

The French firm sample is the result of matching two different data sources: INSEE provided us with the balance-sheet and current account numbers (from the SUSE files) while the Ministry of Research and Industry provided the R&D numbers (from the annual survey on company R&D expenditures). The U.S. firm sample is built from the information available in the Standard and Poor's Compustat Industrial Tape. These samples are larger than the ones actually used in Griliches–Mairesse (1981) and Cuneo–Mairesse (1983). More details on the construction and cleaning of the samples, as well as on the definition and measurement of the variables can be found in these two studies.

Table A.1

France–U.S. joint classification of manufacturing industries.

Ind.	Niveau 40	Niveau 90 (NAP)	French industries	2–3 digits (SIC)	U.S. industries
1.	T21	50	Papier–Carton	26	Paper and allied products
2.	T11	171, 172, 43	Chimie de base. Fibres synthétiques	28 (excluding 283, 284, 285, 289)	Chemicals (excluding drugs and pharmaceuticals)
3.	T23	52, 53	Caoutchouc—Matières plastiques	30	Rubber, miscellaneous plastic products
4.	T09, T10	14, 15, 16	Matériaux de construction—Verre	32	Stone, clay and glass products
5.	T07, T08	09, 10, 11, 12, 13	Minerais et métaux ferreux et non-ferreux	33	Primary metal industries
6.	T13	20, 21	Fonderie, travail des métaux	34	Fabricated metal products
7.	T14	22, 23, 24, 25, 34	Construction mécanique	35, 38 (less 357)	Machinery and instruments (excluding computers)
8.	T15A, T15B	27, 28, 291, 292, 30	Matériels électriques et életroniques professionnels et equipement menagers	36, 357	Electrical equipment (including computers)
9.	T16	311, 312	Automobile et transport terrestre	37 (less 372, 373, 376)	Automobile and ground transportation equipment
10.	T17	26, 32, 33	Constructions navales et aéronautique, armement	372, 373, 376	Aircraft, boats and space vehicles
11.	T18	441, 442, 443, 47	Textile, habillement	22, 23	Textiles and apparel
12.	T20	48, 49	Bois, meubles, industries diverses	24, 25, 39	Wood, furniture and miscellaneous products
13.	T22	51	Presse, imprimerie, édition	27	Printing and publishing
14.	T12	18, 19	Parachimie, pharmacie	283, 284, 285, 289	Drugs and parachemicals
15.	T19	451, 452, 46	Cuir et chaussures	31	Leather

Table A.2a
Growth rates of output and inputs, and price of output.[a]

	Q				C				L				M				PQ			
	1967–73		1973–78		1967–73		1973–78		1967–73		1973–78		1967–73		1973–78		1967–73		1973–78	
Ind.	FR	US	FR	US	FR	US	FR	US	FR	US	FR	US	FR	US	FR	US	FR	US	FR	US
1.	6.6	4.6	0.9	1.8	6.0	3.7	4.5	3.8	0.7	0.4	-2.9	0.4	8.3	3.3	-0.6	2.3	5.6	3.1	11.8	9.6
2.	10.0	7.3	1.4	3.1	7.3	4.2	1.8	5.7	0.4	0.4	-1.1	2.1	11.8	4.1	0.5	9.6	3.0	0.3	11.8	13.2
3.	9.2	8.8	2.5	2.0	8.2	7.7	3.0	5.6	4.3	4.7	-1.5	3.3	11.0	7.6	3.3	3.6	3.3	2.0	12.4	9.8
4.	7.8	3.7	0.7	1.7	7.6	2.3	4.7	2.5	-0.5	1.5	-3.0	1.0	9.0	3.9	0.8	3.7	5.0	4.7	11.4	9.9
5.	5.1	3.3	0.4	-1.5	4.1	2.7	4.6	1.7	-1.3	0.6	-1.7	-0.8	4.6	4.3	0.1	0.2	6.8	4.6	9.5	11.9
6.	5.2	2.4	-0.2	0.2	6.0	3.9	3.6	3.6	0.7	0.5	-3.0	1.2	4.5	2.0	-0.3	1.1	5.7	4.4	12.1	11.0
7.	8.8	4.5	0.2	2.3	8.5	5.2	7.3	5.2	1.1	1.3	-2.6	3.0	8.2	3.8	-0.3	3.0	4.2	3.5	10.9	9.9
8.	9.6	5.0	6.2	5.3	8.7	6.8	10.2	4.7	3.2	0.6	-0.6	2.0	8.5	3.3	5.1	3.3	2.3	1.8	6.3	5.6
9.	10.3	7.5	3.3	3.0	8.6	3.2	6.9	5.4	4.0	4.2	-0.1	1.3	9.2	6.1	3.0	3.0	4.5	3.3	12.7	8.6
10.	7.9	-4.7	5.9	1.1	2.3	3.2	1.9	0.0	0.3	-6.2	-1.2	0.8	7.7	-4.0	2.5	1.1	3.5	4.0	9.4	9.3
11.	5.1	3.2	-1.9	1.3	2.8	4.2	0.5	2.8	-1.8	0.7	-4.7	-1.2	5.7	2.5	-2.0	0.7	4.5	3.2	9.2	5.3
12.	7.1	4.9	1.6	1.4	5.8	4.1	5.0	4.4	0.5	2.7	-2.2	0.9	7.4	4.6	0.7	1.9	5.5	6.3	8.7	8.4
13.	4.1	2.7	3.0	2.7	6.6	3.1	2.9	1.9	1.4	0.8	-2.0	2.3	6.0	2.4	2.9	3.9	7.4	4.4	10.5	8.3
14.	9.1	5.6	4.1	4.0	8.1	5.3	7.2	3.8	1.6	1.4	0.2	2.2	11.0	4.1	3.8	4.3	2.4	2.2	9.3	7.8
15.	3.1	-2.0	-2.0	-0.2	2.6	1.9	1.7	0.6	-2.0	-2.9	-3.9	-1.2	2.7	-2.4	-1.5	0.0	5.7	5.1	11.9	6.7

[a] Q, C, L and M are output, capital stock, labor input (man-hours) and intermediate consumption, respectively. The rates of growth of these (real) quantities and the rate of growth of PQ — the price of output — are shown.

Table A.2b

Growth rates of input prices and average levels of factor shares.[a]

Ind.	PC 1967–73 FR	US	PC 1973–78 FR	US	PL 1967–73 FR	US	PL 1973–78 FR	US	PM 1967–73 FR	US	PM 1973–78 FR	US	SL 1967–73 FR	US	SL 1973–78 FR	US	SM 1967–73 FR	US	SM 1973–78 FR	US
1.	3.1	5.0	6.3	5.7	11.3	6.8	21.0	9.3	4.8	4.3	11.9	10.6	0.24	0.24	0.26	0.20	0.61	0.53	0.62	0.56
2.	7.0	4.0	5.2	5.4	12.7	6.6	20.1	9.8	1.0	3.1	12.6	10.9	0.23	0.18	0.25	0.14	0.57	0.48	0.56	0.54
3	5.0	5.1	5.8	1.5	9.5	5.5	17.8	7.5	0.5	2.3	12.8	11.1	0.34	0.28	0.35	0.26	0.47	0.46	0.50	0.49
4.	3.5	6.7	4.5	8.3	13.3	6.7	15.9	8.3	5.0	4.3	12.5	9.8	0.34	0.30	0.33	0.27	0.44	0.42	0.47	0.45
5.	9.7	3.3	−5.5	6.1	12.5	7.1	16.4	10.4	7.3	4.5	10.1	11.0	0.20	0.24	0.21	0.22	0.67	0.60	0.68	0.62
6.	5.4	4.1	5.9	6.8	12.0	6.2	17.5	8.2	5.1	4.6	10.9	11.3	0.38	0.31	0.42	0.28	0.46	0.48	0.43	0.49
7.	2.6	3.5	0.7	6.2	10.0	6.1	16.5	8.2	7.5	4.2	10.6	10.4	0.39	0.32	0.39	0.30	0.44	0.42	0.46	0.43
8.	4.0	1.6	−1.8	6.9	8.8	5.7	13.9	8.1	3.0	3.1	8.7	7.8	0.37	0.32	0.36	0.31	0.45	0.43	0.48	0.44
9.	9.2	8.2	7.6	3.4	12.4	7.1	19.7	9.6	4.3	4.3	11.7	9.5	0.29	0.18	0.31	0.18	0.59	0.65	0.56	0.67
10.	1.4	−6.5	18.9	12.5	8.4	6.5	21.0	8.3	6.1	4.1	10.8	9.7	0.29	0.41	0.28	0.39	0.63	0.41	0.64	0.42
11.	8.5	3.9	2.9	3.4	10.2	5.5	15.0	7.6	4.3	3.5	8.7	6.2	0.31	0.26	0.31	0.25	0.57	0.55	0.59	0.56
12.	6.4	9.3	2.5	3.8	10.0	6.4	14.4	8.1	6.4	6.8	9.5	9.0	0.31	0.28	0.29	0.26	0.55	0.50	0.59	0.52
13.	4.5	4.6	7.6	9.4	10.0	6.4	15.6	6.6	5.7	4.2	11.5	8.7	0.33	0.36	0.33	0.34	0.55	0.33	0.56	0.35
14.	−0.7	2.5	4.1	6.4	7.0	6.6	13.2	8.1	3.0	3.6	10.2	10.0	0.27	0.17	0.22	0.16	0.57	0.38	0.66	0.42
15.	6.8	1.3	9.9	6.0	11.0	5.2	18.9	6.9	6.0	5.8	8.0	7.1	0.31	0.31	0.36	0.29	0.58	0.48	0.52	0.50

[a] PC, PL and PM are the price of capital (imputed), labor (the wage rate) and intermediate consumption, respectively. The rates of growth of these prices and the average levels of SL and SM — the shares of L and M in output — are shown.

Table A.3

Various measures of R&D intensity.[a]

Ind.	R&D percent of sales				Company R&D		R&D employees per 1000	
	Total R&D							
	FR	US			FR	US	FR	US
1.	0.1	0.6			0.1	0.6	0.3	0.8
2.	2.9	3.5			2.7	2.9	5.4	3.5
3.	2.0	1.7			2.0	1.1	2.5	1.4
4.	0.6	0.8			0.6	0.8	0.6	0.7
5.	0.5	0.5			0.5	0.5	1.0	0.6
6.	0.2	0.4			0.2	0.4	0.3	0.5
7.	0.8	2.0			0.8	1.2	1.0	1.0
8.	6.4	7.7			3.5	4.9	6.7	4.9
9.	2.2	3.2			2.2	2.7	2.9	2.5
10.	8.0	12.7			4.4	2.8	9.9	7.2
11.	0.1	0.1			0.1	0.1	0.0	0.1
12.	0.0	0.3			0.0	0.3	0.0	0.3
13.	0.0	0.2			0.0	0.2	0.0	0.2
14.	3.1	3.7			3.2	3.7	6.2	4.5
15.	0.0	0.1			0.0	0.1	0.0	0.0

[a]French R&D numbers are estimated from 'Le compte satellite de le recherche, Methodes et series 1970–1976', Les Collections de l'INSEE C85 (1979), and U.S. ones are estimated from NSF79.313, Research and Development in Industries, Detailed Statistical Tables (1979).

Table A.4

1973–78 rates of growth of the main variables by industry in the French and U.S. firm samples (1974 levels for R/S); unweighted means with standard deviations given in parentheses.

	Drugs		Chemicals		Electronics		Electrical equipment		Machinery	
FR: Niveau+90-600 (NAP)	19+1811		17+18		291		28+292+30		22 thru 25+3407	
US: 3–4 digits (SIC)	283+2844+ 3841+3843		28 (−283−2844)		366+367		36 (−366−367)		35 (−357)	
Country	FR	US	FR	US	FR	US	FR	US	FR	US
Subsample size	47	57	30	62	37	65	32	47	39	112
Deflated sales per employee, $q-n$	4.5 (4.8)	0.1 (3.7)	2.2 (5.0)	1.1 (3.5)	5.4 (4.7)	3.0 (4.7)	3.2 (4.3)	0.1 (4.0)	0.3 (3.9)	−0.5 (4.0)
Gross plant adjusted per employee, $c-n$	5.7 (6.2)	3.8 (5.8)	5.6 (3.7)	5.7 (5.8)	6.0 (3.6)	4.3 (8.2)	5.1 (5.0)	5.6 (6.0)	5.3 (4.9)	5.3 (6.2)
Total factor productivity, TFP	3.0 (4.7)	−0.1 (3.7)	0.8 (4.8)	−0.3 (3.7)	3.9 (4.7)	1.9 (4.4)	2.0 (4.3)	−0.1 (4.0)	−1.0 (3.7)	−1.8 (3.6)
R&D capital stock per employee, $k-n$	6.5 (6.5)	3.1 (7.1)	4.4 (5.5)	3.5 (7.2)	6.1 (6.2)	3.0 (7.8)	5.0 (6.0)	4.9 (6.9)	6.9 (8.4)	4.1 (9.1)
Number of employees, n	0.2 (4.4)	5.5 (7.2)	0.5 (3.5)	1.2 (5.9)	1.8 (4.5)	3.4 (8.2)	0.6 (4.6)	−0.0 (6.7)	−1.1 (4.5)	2.4 (6.5)
R&D to sales ratio in 1974, R/S	6.4 (3.9)	3.4 (2.4)	3.6 (3.3)	2.6 (1.5)	7.8 (6.0)	3.5 (2.6)	3.2 (3.0)	2.0 (1.8)	2.0 (1.7)	1.9 (1.4)

Table A.5

Sample comparisons: Numbers of employees (E) in thousands and R&D to sales ratios (R/S) in percent, for the French and U.S. samples, for the corresponding aggregate industries, and also for all 'R&D doing firms' in the two countries.[a]

	Samples (S)		R&D doing firms (R)		Corresponding industries (I)			Coverage	
	E_S	$(R/S)_S$ (%)	E_R	$(R/S)_R$ (%)	E_I	$(R/S)_I$ (%)	$(RT/S)_I$ (%)	E_S/E_I (%)	E_R/E_S (%)
France (1974)	395	3.7	565	4.3	1550	2.6	3.3	25	35
U.S. (1976)	4250	2.9	4500	2.6	4900	2.9	4.1	85	90

[a]The estimates for the samples and the corresponding industries are the ones obtained in this study. The estimates for the 'R&D doing firms' are computed from 'La recherche–developpement dans les entreprises industrielles en 1974' [*Documentation Française*, 1977] and from 'Who does R&D and who patents?' [Bound et al. (1982) NBER working paper]. RT/S refers to the ratio of total R&D performed in the industry (whether company or public financed), while R/S refers only to company-financed R&D. These estimates are only indicative and can be misleading for a number of reasons. First, they are part of the corresponding industries. This explains specifically why $(R/S)_I$ appears to be higher than $(R/S)_S$ and $(R/S)_R$ in the U.S. Second, they are not strictly comparable also due to the conglomerateness and the importance of foreign activities. This results in a severe overestimation of the coverage ratios in the U.S., but is not enough to change the finding that the proportion of R&D doing firms in the industries considered is much less in France than in the U.S. Third, the cutoff point between R&D and non-R&D doing firms seems somewhat higher in France than in the U.S. This is not enough, however, to account for the finding that R&D doing firms appear to do relatively more R&D in proportion to their sales in France than in the U.S. Fourth, the picture differs across industries, the coverage and the R&D sales ratios being both much less for machinery than for drugs and chemicals or for electronics and electrical equipment.

References

APC, 1981, Multiple input productivity indexes, Vol. 1, no. 3 (American Productivity Council, Houston, TX).

Bruno, M., 1981, Raw materials, profits, and the productivity slowdown, NBER working paper no. 660R.

Cuneo, P. and J. Mairesse, 1983, Productivity and R&D at the firm level in French manufacturing, NBER working paper no. 1068.

Denison, E.F., 1979, Accounting for slower economic growth (The Brookings Institution, Washington, DC).

Fromm, G., L.R. Klein, F.C. Ripley and D. Crawford, 1979, Production function estimation of capacity utilization, Unpublished paper.

Gollop, F.M. and D.W. Jorgenson, 1980, U.S. productivity growth by industry, 1947–73, in: J.W. Kendrick and B.N. Vaccara, eds., New developments in productivity: Measurement and analysis, Studies in income and wealth, Vol. 44 (NBER/University of Chicago Press, Chicago, IL).

Griliches, Z., 1979, Issues in assessing the contribution of research and development to productivity growth, Bell Journal of Economics 10, no. 1, 92–116.

Griliches, Z. and F. Lichtenberg, 1981, R&D and productivity growth at the industry level: Is there still a relationship?, NBER working paper no. 850.

Griliches, Z. and J. Mairesse, 1981, Productivity and R&D at the firm level, NBER working paper no. 826.

Kendrick, J.W. and E. Grossman, 1980, Productivity in the U.S.: Trends and cycles (Johns Hopkins University Press, Baltimore, MD).

Marris, R., 1979, The theory and future of the corporate economy and society, Ch. 3 (North-Holland, Amsterdam).

National Science Board, 1980, Science indicators (N.S.B., Washington, DC).

Nordhaus, W.D., 1982, Economic policy in the face of declining productivity growth, European Economic Review 18, no. 1/2, 131–158.

Sachs, J., 1979, Wages, profits, and macroeconomic adjustment: A comparative study, in: Arthur M. Okun and George L. Perry, eds., Brookings papers on economic activity, Vol. 2 (The Brookings Institution, Washington, DC).

Schankerman, M., 1981, The effects of double-counting and expensing on the measured returns to R&D, Review of Economics and Statistics LXIII, no. 3, 454–458.

COMMENTS

'Comparing Productivity Growth: An Exploration of French and U.S.
Industrial and Firm Data'
by Z. Griliches and J. Mairesse

Martin Neil BAILY

The Brookings Institution, Washington, DC 20036, USA

This is a valuable paper. It shoots down several explanations of the productivity growth slowdown. However, it does not leave us with an alternative approach. The paper is in halves: the first is an analysis of two-digit manufacturing industries in the U.S. and France, and the second takes a look at data on individual firms.

The two-digit industry data serves to demolish three popular theories. Griliches and Mairesse show first that neither a decline in physical capital accumulation nor a decline in intangible capital accumulation (R&D capital) can account for the productivity growth slowdown. The third theory to go is the Bruno materials hypothesis. Comparing the U.S. and France, the authors find that the price of material inputs grew no more in the U.S. than in France, while materials use fell more sharply in France. And yet the slowdown was noticeably more severe in the U.S. A variety of regressions fails to show that movements in the price or quantities of materials across different industries can explain why some industries slowed more than others.

The second half of the paper is interesting to read — it gives a flavor of the distribution of productivity growth across firms. But there are not a lot of hard results in it. The authors do find an association between rapid productivity growth and both rapid capital accumulation and high R&D to sales ratios. That is worth knowing, although it may simply follow from the fact that successful firms have money to spend on investment and R&D. In particular, I do not really understand a production function in which the R&D to sales ratio determines productivity growth. Their measure of the stock of R&D capital is not associated with rapid productivity growth.

Further, I have a couple of problems with the methods used in the paper. First, I am skeptical about the use of a gross output production function. The example of the motor vehicle industry can illustrate. In the U.S. in 1972, gross output of industry 371 (motor vehicles and equipment) was $65.2

billion. Purchased materials were $43.8 billion, leaving only $21.4 billion for value added. Does it make sense to think of these materials as a factor of production working along with capital and labor to produce gross output? The materials purchased by this industry are not, for the most part, raw materials. Eighty-three percent of them are purchased from other manufacturing establishments and 33 percent are even purchased from other establishments within the same industry! This means that 22 percent of gross output also appears on the other side of the production function as part of material purchases. The gross output of industry 371 includes not only finished automobiles, but also double counts the clutches and air conditioners that went into those automobiles. Even for purchases from other industries, it is odd to talk about substituting capital and labor for materials (or vice versa) when most of the value of material purchases consists of the capital and labor they embody.

The second problem is that there is no adjustment made for demand variations. Presumably Griliches and Mairesse believe that 1967, 1973, and 1978 are all years of similar aggregate demand. But even if that is equally true in both countries, there are industry-specific demand cycles that may be distorting the results quite a bit.

Despite these two doubts, it is unlikely that the authors' conclusions about the three possible causes of the slowdown will be overturned. The data are good enough to say that there has been a slowdown and to show that capital accumulation cannot explain it. The Bruno materials hypothesis should be framed in terms of raw materials, but it does not do any better in these terms than in Griliches–Mairesse. The price of energy has indeed risen, and this may have contributed to the productivity slowdown, but it cannot account for much of it because energy is such a small share of total costs. The producer price index for non-energy crude materials in the U.S. has actually fallen relative to finished goods prices since 1967. Manufacturers are not substituting capital and labor for non-energy raw materials.

The bottom line, therefore, is to drive one to look for possible causes of deterioration in the quality of capital or labor, and to wonder whether the flow of new ideas or technologies has been temporarily or permanently depleted. Quite possibly there has been some decline in both the rate of technical change and in the quality of the labor input (or in work effort), but I want to talk about capital and the way the capital input is measured.

There is a long history of debate about the nature of capital and how it can be measured. That debate went off the rails by getting into the empirically irrelevant issue of re-switching. But the right idea to come out of the debate is that the physical capital stock may be only loosely related to the economic value of capital in producing output. Technological choices have been embodied in past investment decisions, so that if there are sharp changes in factor prices or in the product mix or in the regulatory environment, then the existing capital stock is reduced in economic value. Capital goods are scrapped sooner, utilized less or must be rebuilt. Because of several kinds of sharp structural changes in the 1970's, it may be that the ratio of the effective capital input to the measured capital stock has declined.

One sign of the difficulty of measuring capital is the very wide dispersion of estimates of the contribution of capital to growth. In the Griliches–Mairesse study, the industry data indicate that capital goes the wrong way as an explanation of the slowdown. The firm data finds capital to be a major contributor to growth. Cross-country comparisons made in other studies seem to show that capital contributes more to growth than is indicated by its income share. The reason for this dispersion of results is the endogeneity of investment. In countries with rapid growth there were many factors favorable to growth. These were 'good news' countries. The generally favorable conditions stimulated capital formation even as capital formation contributed to growth.

Under certain circumstances, however, 'bad news' that hurts productivity can also stimulate investment. A rise in the price of energy or a new regulation are two such examples. If various kinds of bad news have hit the industries in the Griliches–Mairesse sample, that could explain why productivity slowed even as capital accumulation speeded up.

European Economic Review 21 (1983) . North-Holland

COMMENTS

'Comparing Productivity Growth: An Exploration of French and U.S. Industrial and Firm Data' by Z. Griliches and J. Mairesse

Michael BRUNO

NBER, and The Hebrew University, Jerusalem, Israel

Comparative productivity studies are important not only for their own sake, namely to learn about the reasons for basic differences in productivity performance between countries. They can also throw possible light upon common reasons for a productivity slowdown that has affected several countries at the same time. Griliches and Mairesse should be commended for pooling their expertise in an attempt to look simultaneously at the recent French and U.S. experience. This paper represents one phase in an ongoing project.

The Griliches–Mairesse paper falls roughly into two parts. One looks at the more aggregated industry data to search for reasons for the pervasiveness of the productivity slowdown in both countries. The other takes more disaggregated 'micro' data to look in greater detail at the role of R&D in both countries' industries. I will confine my remarks to the first topic not only because their analysis relates to some of my own recent work. I believe quite firmly that, while R&D may be a very important factor in explaining the differences among industries or countries (though in the present paper the conclusions on that are still very tentative), it is unlikely to be an important factor in the explanation of the sharp slowdown that has taken place after 1973.

In the first part of their paper Griliches and Mairesse try to account for what looks like a sharper slowdown in productivity in U.S. manufacturing. They use a fifteen industry cross-section regression of changes between 1967–72 and 1973–78 growth and conclude that neither capital or R&D growth nor the rise in raw material prices can explain the productivity slowdown itself or the difference in performance between the two countries. I would raise several questions and reservations about their negative findings. My first question concerns their aggregate data which seem to differ in at least one major item from other published sources. According to the Bureau of

Labour Statistics regularly published data, the average rate of growth of manhours in U.S. manufacturing was 0.6 in 1967–73 and −0.4 in 1973–78. The aggregate implied by the data used in Griliches–Mairesse (see their table 2) implies a very similar number for the first period (0.8), but a substantially different one for the second (+0.4). If we are to believe the BLS on the aggregates this in itself may make the U.S. slowdown look almost the same as the French one (about 1% drop in the total productivity growth rate). Why do their regressions show only mild evidence, if at all, for the effect of the material input price increase? I can see two reasons for that. One has to do with the decision to confine the regressions to averages over non-overlapping periods (1967–72, 1973–78). It so happens that by leaving out the 'notch', i.e., the change from 1972 to 1973, one loses most, if not all, of the action in the raw material price index (according to the aggregate indices that I have been using, the total rate of change over the period 1967 to 1978 has been less than the rate of change in the one single year 1973). Another reason for getting insignificant results may come from the limited variability of factor price changes across different sectors within a single economy.

To get a fair test of the role of raw material prices one has to look at either disaggregated time-series data by industry or at cross-sections of more countries to increase variability in the observations. It so turns out that either one of such experiments, yields much more significant results. I will confine myself here to the second.

Table 1

Selected regressions of average factor productivity growth in manufacturing: Ten OECD countries, change in rates of growth from 1955–73 to 1974–80.

	(1)	(2)[a]	(3)	(4)	(5)	(6)[a]
Constant	−1.18 (0.60)	−0.96 (0.49)	−0.76 (0.65)	−0.56 (0.63)	−(0)	(0)
Input prices[b]	−0.17 (0.09)	−0.18 (0.08)	−0.17 (0.08)	−0.16 (0.08)	−0.21 (0.06)	−0.26 (0.04)
Public consumption	—	—	0.27 (0.20)	—	—	0.31 (0.14)
Total domestic absorption	—	—	—	0.24 (0.13)	0.31 (0.11)	—
Statistics						
$\bar{R}^2$	0.19	0.37	0.27	0.37	0.39	0.43
SE	0.70	0.57	0.67	0.62	0.61	0.54
No. of observations	10	9	10	10	10	9

[a]Excluding Japan (Japan had a much larger than average drop in aggregate demand growth).
[b]Difference in rates of change of material input prices deflated by output prices, lagged one year (i.e., from 1954–72 to 1972–79).

The enclosed table lists a set of cross-section regressions for the manufacturing sector in ten major OECD countries which also include the U.S. and France (the other countries are U.K., Germany, Belgium, Italy, Netherlands, Sweden, Canada, and Japan). The dependent variables in these regressions is the change in average productivity growth per labour and capital from the 1955–73 to the 1973–80 period. The independent variable in the first two regressions is the change in the rate of growth of relative raw material input prices. This shows a coefficient of 0.17–0.18 which implies an elasticity of substitution of 0.35 for materials. The negative intercept indicates that raw materials alone do not provide a full explanation for the slowdown. Subsequent regressions (3 to 6) incorporate aggregate demand proxies which seem to eliminate the negative intercept without substantially changing the estimated coefficient for the raw material price. The last two regressions (with and without Japan) go through the origin.

These regressions imply that approximately half of the slowdown can be attributed to the direct role of the raw material price shock, while the rest can be attributed to the role of the demand squeeze which followed in the wake of the price shock.[1] Neither the U.S. nor France show any substantial deviations from the regression lines.

What such experiment suggests is that for an explanation of the productivity slowdown one may very well want to look explicitly at the macro-economic phenomena that have taken place in and around 1973 (and repeated again in 1979–80). Thus R&D expenditure differences may be very important for investigation across industries, but their change over time, if at all, is too slow a process to account for the type of watershed that has actually taken place in the 1970s. All of this should not in the least detract from the need to look at micro-firm-data on R&D and other factors in order to tell purely technological stories either for productivity comparisons or for long-term processes of technical change. For these the approach suggested in the Griliches–Mairesse study should be very valuable and their present paper has opened up quite a few important questions for further study.

---

[1]For more details, see my paper 'World Shocks, Macro-Economic Response and the Productivity Puzzle', forthcoming in *Slow Growth in the Western World*, edited by R.C.O. Mathews (Heinemann, London, 1982).

European Economic Review 31 . North-Holland

HOUSING MARKETS, UNEMPLOYMENT AND LABOUR MARKET FLEXIBILITY IN THE UK*

Gordon HUGHES

University of Edinburgh, Edinburgh EH8 9JY, UK

Barry McCORMICK

University of Southampton, Southampton SO9 5NH, UK and
Cornell University, Ithaca, NY 14850, USA

1. Introduction

Since the recent dramatic rise of unemployment levels in Europe, and the comparatively high level of employment growth achieved in Japan and in the U.S., increasing emphasis has been placed upon the 'inflexibility' of European labour markets. The observation that a market is 'inflexible' may not, of course, be a useful indicator of its efficiency, but we can be confident that inflexibilities arising as an unanticipated consequence of government policies reflect efficiency losses and not optimizing behaviour. Our purpose in this paper is to consider one such welfare-reducing barrier to efficient labour mobility.

British policy-makers have intervened extensively in the housing market since the turn of the century in ways which appear likely to influence the functioning of the labour market. Unfortunately, these influences were almost entirely unintended side-effects of housing policies, rather than the second-best consequences of a unified view of the likely outcomes for both markets. While the cost of this myopic approach can be mis-stated and exaggerated, it remains an outstanding example of the need to consider the ramifications of policy beyond the market which is directly affected. The purpose of this essay will be to draw together our understanding of these spillovers paying particular attention to any implications for macro-economic modeling of labour markets. In keeping with this objective, and in order to address

*We are grateful to the discussants and participants at the seminar and to Vic Possen for helpful comments on earlier drafts of this paper. We are also grateful to the U.K. Office of Population Censuses and Surveys and the ESRC Data Archive who provided the survey data used in our work. Barry McCormick would like to acknowledge financial support from the ESRC under project F00230102 on Labour Market Flows and Unemployment. We are solely responsible for the interpretation of the data and for other views expressed in this paper.

questions concerning labour market flexibility, we shall distinguish the following indicators by which economists might view flexibility to have been influenced by a micro policy or market structure.

(1)   The nature of the short-run wage/employment response to an aggregate demand shock, and the period of time required to adjust to the long-run equilibrium.
(2)   The short and long run response to a change either in the composition of demand or a 'supply shock'.
(3)   The value of the equilibrium (NAIRU) rate of unemployment and its regional distribution.

The rest of the paper is organized as follows. In section 2, we discuss how housing market policies have affected inter-regional migration and, since our ultimate concern is largely with unemployment, the relationship between unemployment and migration. This theme is extended in section 3 by examining the links between job mobility and housing movement in order to establish the importance of the apparent constraints imposed by the U.K. housing system on labour mobility. In section 4 we discuss how this evidence may be of value in understanding the patterns of inflexibility and unemployment that is observed in the U.K. Section 5 concludes the paper with a discussion of policies which might ameliorate the worst side-effects of U.K. housing policies.

2. Housing and unemployment: Implications for geographic mobility

The implications of housing market policies for geographic labour mobility can be largely explained in terms of the consequences of these policies for the pattern of house tenure in the U.K. Three major policies have influenced the evolution of house tenure patterns in the U.K.: that of constructing and retaining in public ownership a large amount of primarily blue-collar rental accommodation (council housing); the application of rent controls to large proportions of the private sector; and tax relief on loans to house-purchasers. These policies have all served to squeeze the private rental sector, so that, whereas seventy years ago about 90% of households lived in private rental accommodation, less than 12% presently do so. About 28% of British households live in publicly owned accommodation and over 60% are owner-occupiers.

The dramatic contraction of the size of the private rental sector and the remaining excess demand for its services have almost totally undermined that sector's familiar function of supplying short-term housing for migrants into an area. This has amplified the weaknesses in the operation of the council housing system which itself discourages migration by its tenants. Having little access to private rental housing, council tenants wishing to migrate who are unable or unwilling to purchase a dwelling must obtain council housing in their destination region. To locate suitable accommodation council tenants are expected to rely upon council house exchanges/transfers; if there are unequal number of households seeking to enter and leave an area some workers will be 'rationed' out of an exchange. Such an imbalance is inevitable given the asymmetry of the U.K. labour market: the largest stocks of council housing are located in regions of high unemployment, from where workers are likely to want to migrate.

There are, therefore, clear arguments as to why the linkage between tenure and migration is likely to be quite different in the U.K. from that in the U.S. The large majority of rental tenants are likely to find the costs of migration both greater and more uncertain than is normally associated with the rental market. However, the tenure-migration linkage is complicated by the simultaneous influence of migration plans on tenure choice. We believe this to be unimportant in the U.K. for all but relatively few households; the following simple model explains the basis for this view.

Assume that individuals reside in one of three tenures: owner-occupation (OO), unfurnished rental (UR) – which is rent-controlled and includes council housing (CH) – and furnished rental (FR), which is not fully controlled. Initially, let us assume that households do not intend to migrate. There is rationing of both OO housing – in the sense that households may not borrow freely at going interest rates – and UR housing. Empirically it is also reasonable to assume that in the absence of rationing, all households will choose to occupy either OO or UR housing, with the choice between these tenures depending upon rents, interest rates and household characteristics. FR accommodation would then only be occupied by households rationed out of one or both of the primary tenures.

Now, suppose that some households take account of the gains from migration net of the costs of moving house when choosing tenure. Moving into or out of a dwelling in the rental sector is relatively *inexpensive*, but movement into or out of OO housing is relatively *expensive*. Thus, any household that in the absence of migration opportunities would enter OO might in the presence of such opportunities decide not to do so prior to migrating; conversely a household that in the absence of migration opportunities would move out of OO would not be (much) affected by migration possibilities. Tenants in FR considering moving into OO would have to balance the financial savings from changing tenure against the additional expected costs of migrating from OO. Likewise tenants in UR who because of changed personal circumstances now prefer OO must balance the utility so gained against the higher cost of migration from OO. Still, the importance of this influence is substantially attenuated by (i) the considerable financial incentives to move from FR to OO and (ii) the small number of moves from UR to OO.

To capture the effect of (i) in a simple manner we may suppose that the intention to migrate will only discourage a household's move from FR to OO if it intends to migrate within h months. The value of h will increase with (a) the costs of buying and selling OO houses, and (b) the expected relative price of OO housing services relative to FR housing services. Our estimates yielded values of h in the range 12–14 months for most households in the early 1970s and the relative movements of rents, interest rates and house prices during the subsequent decade tended to reduce rather than increase the value of h. As a comparison Shelton (1968) suggested that h was of the order of $3\frac{1}{2}$ years in his analysis of the comparative costs of owner-occupation and rental in the United States. Thus, while we are not entirely justified in treating tenure as an exogenous variable in our estimates, it would appear that the existence of rationing, together with the financial advantages of owner-occupation and unfurnished rental vis-a-vis furnished rental, will greatly limit the influence of migration plans on the choice of household tenure prior to migration.

This analysis suggests that, as a result of ignoring this selection bias, OO should be found to be associated with less migration, and both FR and UR with more migration, than would be the case if the bias was removed. Thus, comparisons made below between council tenancy and owner-occupation may, if anything, *overstate* the migration rates of council and private tenants relative to those of owner-occupiers.

2.1. Evidence

The definitions of mobility used in the evidence discussed here are largely determined by the data sets which collect sufficient information about current and past circumstances to perform the necessary estimations. For Britain we rely upon the General Household Survey (GHS) for 1973 and 1974 and the Labour Force Survey (LFS) for 1983 which are made available to researchers with individuals identifiable only in terms of the following regions: North, North-West, Yorks/Humber, East Midlands, West Midlands, East Anglia, Greater London, South-East, South-West, Wales, Scotland – Northern Ireland is not covered by the GHS and has been excluded from our analysis of the LFS data. We shall describe a *migrating* household as one in which the current address is in a different region to that one year previously. Unfortunately, the LFS does not distinguish between Greater London and the rest of the South East in recording the previous residence of the household, so that in some of the tables our definition of migration excludes moves between these two (sub)regions. In such cases comparisons with the GHS data have been performed on a consistent basis. A *moving* household is one moving house in the past year to any destination. For comparative purposes we have used data from the family data tape of the

Michigan Panel Survey of Income Dynamics (PSID) for 1980. The nature of this data means that our figures will refer to migration/movement rates for heads of households who are members of the labour force. For Britain gross migration/movement rates for workers who are not heads of households are very similar to those for heads of households, so little seems to be lost as a result of this restriction. In order to limit the impact of migration/movement associated with the beginning and end of working lives we have restricted our attention to those aged between 21 and 64 years.

It is often conjectured that British workers are less likely than workers in other countries to migrate between regions, so it is interesting to begin our empirical analysis with some basic statistics concerning this point. We are not aware of any detailed comparative study of this proposition based upon cross-section data and, in any case, comparisons between geographically different countries are not easy to make. In table 1 we give migration and movement rates calculated from our three datasets for all heads of households, for 'young' (age <35) heads of households, and for heads of households split between those engaged in non-manual and manual occupations. In the case of the GHS data for the U.K. and the PSID data for the U.S. it is possible to distinguish between those who reported that they migrated/moved for job-related reasons and those migrating/moving for other reasons. The U.K. figures on migration exclude moves between London and the South East. We regard inter-state migration in the U.S. as providing the most appropriate comparison for inter-regional migration in the U.K., since the numbers of geographical units relative to population are similar with some being large in population and/or area and some quite small. It is also interesting to compare moves across a county line with all movement in the U.S., since inter-county movement is the closest approximation to moves from one local authority district to another in the U.K. for which data is not available.

The table shows that movement and migration rates are much lower in the U.K. than in the U.S. Even when we use whichever is largest of the figures for the two British datasets, gross movement and migration rates in the U.S. are between two and three times those in the U.K. For job-related migration the ratio lies in the same range but the job-related movement rate in the U.S. is over 3.5 times that in the U.K. The pattern of the movement and migration rates for young heads of households in the two countries is similar to that for all heads of households but with somewhat higher U.K. migration rates relative to U.S. rates, especially for job-related reasons. In the U.S. the rates of movement across a county line for both young and all heads of households are typically twice the corresponding migration rates. Thus, about one-half of 'non-local' moves, most of which involve a shift from one local labour market area to another, take the form of longer distance migration, but in total these represent only about one-quarter of all changes in residence.

Table 1

Migration and movement rates for the U.K. and the U.S. (percent of heads of households in the labour force).

	Movement/migration rates (%)			
	All	HOH aged < 35 yrs	HOH occupation	
			Non-manual	Manual
(A) UK – General Household Survey 1973–74				
Movement				
All	7.74	17.42	9.30	6.57
Job-related	0.99	2.12	1.80	0.39
Migration between regions				
All	1.14	2.52	1.83	0.62
Job-related	0.45	1.12	0.93	0.10
(B) UK – Labour Force Survey 1983				
Movement	11.65	19.02	12.57	10.62
Migration between regions	1.01	1.87	1.35	0.62
(C) US – Panel Survey of Income Dynamics 1980				
Movement				
All	26.03	43.94	26.62	25.37
Job-related	3.52	6.05	2.68	4.44
Movement across a county line				
All	6.55	11.8ᴜ	5.96	7.21
Job-related	1.84	3.33	1.16	2.60
Migration across a state line				
All	3.09	5.56	2.67	3.56
Job-related	1.16	2.12	0.59	1.80

Sources: UK – General household surveys 1973, 1974 and Labour force survey 1983. US – Michigan panel survey of income dynamics family tape 1980.

The most striking feature of the figures in table 1 concerns the great difference between the ratios of U.S to U.K. migration rates for non-manual and manual heads of households. For non-manual workers the U.S. migration rate is only 46% higher than the U.K. rate and when we focus on job-related migration the U.S. rate is less than the U.K. rate. On the other hand, for manual workers the U.S. rate for all migration is over 5.7 times the U.K. rate while for job-related migration this ratio is 18, largely because the British rate is so low. In the U.S. both all and job-related migration rates are substantially higher for manual than for non-manual workers, but in the U.K. this pattern is reversed with much higher migration rates for non-manual than for manual workers. Note also that in the U.S. the proportional gap between the two groups increases with the distance moved and is larger for job-related migration/movement than for all migration/movement. These figures provide quite strong *prima facie* evidence for the view that council housing has an important effect in reducing migration rates in the U.K., since it is the major institutional difference between the two countries which is specific to manual workers as few British non-manual workers are council tenants.

In order to identify the influence of council tenancy on regional migration and house movement, we have used individual data from the 1973–74 GHS to examine both migration intentions and actual migration behaviour – see Hughes and McCormick (1981, 1985). We found that migration rates for owner-occupiers are, *ceteris paribus*, approximately 4 times higher than for council tenants, even though differences in transactions costs would lead one to expect higher migration rates for tenants than for owner-occupiers. Of the 3658 heads of household in the 1973 GHS who had been council tenants one year earlier, only 7 had an address in a different region in the following year, and 5 of these had been living in Greater London. Whereas council tenants outside London comprised 30% of household heads in 1973 they provided only about 3% of total migrants. Owner-occupiers comprised about 55% of household heads outside London while 53% of the migrants were owner-occupiers.

One possible objection to this finding is that council tenants are a self-selected group who are less likely to move even after factors such as age, education, industry, occupation and region are allowed for. It is noteworthy therefore that when total house movement is studied, making no distinction according to whether a regional boundary is crossed, council tenants have a movement rate which is about 60% higher, *ceteris paribus*, than for owner-occupiers. Thus, within local areas the council exchange system seems to work well. It is perhaps even more interesting that if *intended* migration is studied, council tenants are no less likely than owner-occupiers to wish to migrate, merely less successful in fulfilling their intentions. The difficulties arise where house exchanges are sought *between* labour market areas so that (a) the cost of collecting information may be high, and (b) there may be a substantial imbalance in the numbers of intended movers in each direction.

Figures which illustrate the separate importance of tenure as an influence upon migration rates are given in table 2. The diagonal elements in the table give the predicted average migration rate for households in each tenure category. The off-diagonal elements give the predicted *average* migration rates on the assumption that the households which have non-housing characteristics of those in the column tenure category behave as if they were in the row tenure category. Thus, the average migration rates of council tenants in column 2 are predicted to increase from 1.0 to 3.9 per 1000 should they become owner-occupiers. It is particularly striking to compare the figures in row 2 of the table with those in rows 3 and 4, as these highlight

Table 2

The impact of tenure on migration rates in the U.K.[a]

Alternative Tenure	Predicted migration rates per 1000 households currently in tenure group			
	Owners (1)	Council tenants (2)	Furnished tenants (3)	Unfurnished private tenants (4)
(1) Owners	9.4	3.9	16.7	6.7
(2) Council tenants	2.5	1.0	4.5	1.8
(3) Furnished tenants	35.8	15.8	60.2	25.8
(4) Unfurnished private tenants	17.0	7.2	29.7	12.2

[a]This table is read by considering a sample of households with non-housing character-istics similar to those in the column tenure category and then imagining that these households move between house tenure categories.

Source: Calculated using migration equations from Hughes and McCormick (1985) and households in 1974 GHS.

the differences between the three tenancy categories in their effect on the migration rates of specific populations. In all cases furnished tenancy implies a migration rate over 10 times as large as that for council tenancy, while the rate for unfurnished tenancy is over 6 times that for council tenancy. Since unfurnished private tenants benefit from low controlled rents and have security of tenure, it cannot merely be the availability of rent subsidies which leads to the low migration rates for council tenancy. Note also that migration rates for owners are low by comparison with those for private tenants. This is further confirmation that it is the nature of council tenancy which depresses migration, since the relative migration rates of owners and private tenants correspond to the pattern of their relative movement rates and to what one would expect on *a priori* grounds given the relative transactions costs for each tenure.

We can use the results of these studies to examine how far the difference between U.K. and U.S. rates of (a) migration and (b) house movement can be explained by the U.K. house tenure system. To do this we will examine predicted U.K. migration rates on the assumption that the aggregate tenure pattern is similar to that in the U.S. while holding the tenure influence on migration constant. The tenure composition of U.S. households is approxi-mately: 65% owner-occupiers, 32% private tenants and 4% tenants in public housing, whereas for our U.K. 1973–74 sample the composition was: 53.5% owner-occupiers, 31.5% council tenants, 7.5% private furnished tenants and 7.5% private unfurnished tenants. Thus, our experiment involves a hypo-thetical redistribution of households out of public housing (council tenancy) to owner-occupation and private tenancy in order to match the U.S. tenure pattern. This has been done by assuming that, randomly, 36% of council tenants become owner-occupiers, and 26% each become private unfurnished and furnished tenants – this latter split replicates the division of U.K. private tenants between furnished and unfurnished accommodation since we have no comparable data for the U.S.

The impact of this change may be seen by comparing the first two rows of table 3. Despite the apparently large dampening effect of tenure on migration this hypothetical switch from council tenancy (which has the lowest migration rates of all four tenures) to other tenures increases overall predicted migration rates by less than one-quarter. The effect is even less for young workers than for all workers since a smaller proportion of them are council tenants. The principal reason for the relatively small impact of this tenure redistribution is that the other socio-economic characteristics of the population of council tenants, who are predominantly manual workers with few educational qualifications and are older on average than the whole population, mean their migration and movement rates are low relative to those for households in other tenure categories even after controlling for the influence of tenure. This point may be understood by comparing the figures in column 2 of table 2 with the other columns.

Another major difference between the two countries lies in the proportion

Table 3

The impact of U.S. tenure/education patterns on U.K. migration/movement rates

	Predicted migration/movement rates per 1000 households for			
	All workers		Young workers[a]	
	Migration	Movement	Migration	Movement
(1) U.K. population characteristics	10.6	56.6	21.8	121.8
(2) Adjusting for U.S. tenure pattern[b]	12.7	69.2	25.5	141.9
(3) Adjusting for U.S. college education pattern[c]	12.5	66.5	26.0	145.0
(4) Adjusting for both U.S. tenure and college education patterns	14.7	79.3	29.8	165.6

[a]Households with head aged <35 years.

[b]Based on assumption that the tenure pattern is: owners 65%, council tenants 3%, private tenants 32% (of which 51% are unfurnished).

[c]Based on assumption that 23% of heads of households have a higher educational qualification instead of 8%.

Source: Calculating using migration/movement equations from Hughes and McCormick (1985) and households in 1974.

of the population who have attended college or have undertaken some equivalent form of higher education or training. This is important because our analysis of migration behaviour suggests that households whose heads have acquired some kind of higher educational qualification are, *ceteris paribus*, more likely to migrate than are those without such a qualification. There are obvious difficulties in calculating comparable figures for the proportion of households in each country headed by someone with a higher educational qualification because of the very different character and traditions of the educational and professional training systems in the two countries. However, on a crude basis the 1981 U.K. Census figures show that 7.9% of males aged 25 or more have a degree or an equivalent professional qualification, while 23% of males in the same age group in the 1980 U.S. Census had completed 4 years of college education.

In this case the comparison with the U.S. is carried out by assuming that all of those heads of household with 'A' levels or similar qualifications (equivalent to the baccalaureat or abitur in Europe) have a college education as also do 45% of those with 'O' levels (the public examination taken at age 16). The impact of these educational changes in our hypothetical population on migration/movement rates is shown in the third row of table 3. It is quite similar to that of the changes in the tenure pattern, slightly larger for young workers, who are better educated already than the average, and slightly lower for the whole population.

Putting the joint effects of tenure and college education together yields the final row of table 3. This gives predicted migration rates which are about 38% higher than for current tenure and educational patterns. It follows that, after allowing for these two major differences between the U.K. and the U.S., British inter-regional migration rates are still only one-half the level of the American inter-state migration rate for comparable households. For all house movement – which, given the difficulty of making geographic comparisons, is a less ambiguous measure of comparative mobility rates – the impact of the combined tenure and educational changes is very similar to that for migration – an increase of 40% for all workers – which might raise the predicted U.K. rate of house movement to 16.3% p.a. if we use the 1983 LFS figures as our base. This is much lower than the comparable U.S. rate of 26% p.a., so that much of the difference between the two countries in both migration and movement rates remains unexplained.

Since our ultimate concern in this paper is with labour market flexibility and unemployment, we will now outline what is known about whether unemployment in the U.K. is a stimulant to migration between geographic labour markets. Interestingly, the two basic findings here are broadly similar to those for the U.S. – see DaVanzo (1978). Our investigations of U.K. migration (Hughes and McCormick, 1981, 1985) have shown that

(*a*) living in a high unemployment rate region does not exercise the

expected positive effect on actual or planned migration (and there is some evidence of a negative effect),
(b)   an unemployed individual is more likely to plan to migrate (U.K.) and to actually migrate (U.S.).

An important qualification should be made to the U.K. finding concerning the migration behaviour of unemployed individuals: while there is clear evidence that being unemployed increases the intended migration rates of *non-manual* workers, we have been unable to detect any influence upon the intended migration rates of *manual* workers. Thus, if council housing has all but ended migration for the representative manual worker, there appears to be no need to qualify this for the unemployed. In a two region model of the U.K., with two types of labour, one could realistically treat one type of labour as immobile for the purposes of macro-economic analysis. This is not to rule out the possibility that depressed regions experience net total outflows of labour – probably primarily because the depressed conditions deter immigration of non-manuals rather than by encouraging emigration.

Table 4 draws upon the 1983 Labour Force Survey to illustrate the pattern of recent inter-regional labour flows and their relationship to unemployment rates. The distinction between manual and non-manual workers is crucial because of the completely different unemployment situation for the two groups. Unemployment rates are low and vary little across regions for non-manual workers whereas they are much higher and show a high

Table 4

Regional composition of unemployment and migration in the U.K.

Region	% Unemployment Rate		% Composition by region of HOHs who are					
			In labour force		In-migrants		Out-migrants	
	Non-manual	Manual	Non-manual	Manual	Non-manual	Manual	Non-manual	Manual
North	4.7	17.5	4.7	6.5	6.0	4.8	4.5	6.0
Yorks/Humber	5.0	14.6	8.4	10.1	10.2	9.5	9.9	7.1
North West	5.5	17.7	10.6	11.7	9.0	6.6	10.5	8.9
East Midlands	3.2	9.6	6.7	8.0	12.4	11.9	8.1	11.3
West Midlands	5.5	17.3	8.4	10.9	6.9	7.7	11.1	9.5
East Anglia	4.2	9.2	3.3	3.9	6.0	10.1	6.0	4.8
London	4.8	12.8	13.8	10.1	8.4	7.7 }	27.4	32.7
South East	3.2	9.2	22.7	15.7	17.5	12.5 }		
South West	3.8	9.6	8.3	8.0	16.6	17.3	10.8	10.7
Wales	3.8	17.1	4.0	5.3	2.4	5.4	6.0	4.8
Scotland	4.1	15.1	9.1	9.6	4.5	6.6	5.4	4.2
Total sample			21 633	25 856	332	168	332	168

Source: Labour Force Survey 1983.

degree of regional variation for manual workers. Migration rates – which, as explained above, exclude moves between London and the South East in this source – are low for both groups but the non-manual rate of 1.5% is over twice the manual rate of 0.65%. There is no significant relationship between net migration and unemployment rates for either group. London and the South East together experienced net out-migration of both non-manual and manual workers – especially the latter – despite relatively low unemployment rates while regions such as Yorks/Humber, Wales and Scotland experienced a net inflow of manual workers despite relatively high unemployment rates. The major systematic patterns seem to be

(a) the movement of both manual and non-manual households to the South West (Britain's sunbelt!),
(b) an eastward movement out of the North West and the West Midlands to Yorks/Humber, East Midlands and – for manual workers – East Anglia.

3. Job mobility and house movement

The evidence presented in the previous section indicates that the restraints on migration associated with British council housing tend to reduce the overall level of migration by a significant amount, though this does not account for the large difference between British and American aggregate migration rates. However, this does not demonstrate conclusively that barriers to housing mobility inhibit job flexibility, since it is possible that potential job changers are more successful than other council tenants in achieving council house transfers – either because they are more persistent or because they are treated more favourably by local authority housing administrators. To investigate this point and related issues concerning the link between housing and labour mobility we have estimated a number of models.

The principal work to be discussed here examines the effect of house tenure on the probability that a household will migrate/move for *job-related* reasons. This analysis may be carried out by estimating logit equations for the probabilities that a household actually migrated/moved (past migration/ movement) or is seeking to do so (potential migration/movement) for job-related reasons on two bases

(a) comparing these households with *all* other households,
(b) comparing these households with other households which migrated/ moved or are seeking to migrate/move for any reason.

In all cases the identification of a household as a past/potential migrant/mover for job-related reasons is based on a question which asked all actual/potential movers to specify their primary reason for moving from a list of possible responses. Apart from job-related reasons, which comprised a single response category, the other reasons given were (in PSID parlance) consumption reasons, i.e., to obtain better/different housing, or family reasons, i.e., to move closer to relatives.

The coefficients on housing tenure in logit equations for these two sets of probabilities are given in table 5. As well as tenure categories the equations included dummy variables for socio-economic groups, for educational qualifications, for employment in the service sector, for living in a depressed region, for not being married and for having an occupational pension. Age, age squared and length of residence in the household's current/previous home were the continuous independent variables. These independent variables were included on a priori grounds as a result of our previous work on housing movement and on job mobility. We have made no attempt to obtain the most parsimonious model in each case since the role of the non-tenure variables in this context is to control for the influence of extraneous factors which may be correlated with tenure. For all of the equations reported in this paper the sample consists of heads of households who are

Table 5

Tenure coefficients in logit equations for job-related movement/migration.[a]

	Migration		Movement	
	Potential	Actual	Potential	Actual
(A) Job-related migration/movement for all households				
Council tenant	0.00	−0.91	−0.10	−0.87
	(0.00)	(1.67)	(0.52)	(0.82)
Furnished tenant	0.37	1.50	1.04	1.54
	(1.04)	(5.01)	(5.91)	(3.45)
Private unfurnished tenant	1.05	0.69	0.31	1.40
	(3.09)	(1.71)	(1.26)	(2.73
(B) Job-related migration/movement conditional upon migration/movement				
Council tenant	−0.63	0.67	−0.66	−1.60
	(1.63)	(0.36)	(3.39)	(2.81)
Furnished tenant	−0.44	0.10	0.21	−0.26
	(1.01)	(0.14)	(1.13)	(0.72)
Private unfurnished tenant	0.48	1.82	−0.60	−0.61
	(1.04)	(1.73)	(2.32)	(1.37)
No of positive responses	97	38	282	77
Sample size: A	7239	8067	15120	8067
B	380	74	2326	446

[a]See text for details of other variables included in the equations. The figures in brackets are the asymptotic t-ratios of the coefficients. Owner-occupiers are the control tenure category.

Source: Estimated from GHS 1973/74 data.

members of the labour force. In analysing migration/movement we are interested in labour force behaviour so that moves as a result of marriage, marital breakdown, etc. are excluded by restricting the sample to households with the same head before and after a previous move or in which the head of household was thinking of moving.

Section A of table 5 provides estimates of the coefficients on tenure in logit equations for the probability that a household migrated/moved for job-related reasons in the past year or is considering migrating/moving for similar reasons. In this case the sample consists of all households satisfying the criteria specified above. The default tenure category is owner-occupation so that the coefficients in the table reflect differences between the influence of the tenure concerned and owner-occupation on the probability investigated. Section B of the table gives the tenure coefficients in logit equations for the probability of past/potential migration/movement for job-related reasons *conditional* on migration/movement. In other words, column 1 of section B is estimated from a sample of households who were considering migration for any reason and the coefficients relate to the probability that households among this group were considering movement for job-related rather than other reasons. Similarly, column 2 of this section of the table is extracted from the equation for the probability that a household which migrated in the previous year did so for job-related rather than other reasons, while columns 3 and 4 provide the same coefficients for the probabilities of job-related movement conditional on movement.

In effect section A replicates our earlier work except that the focus is on migration/movement for *job-related* rather than for all reasons. The first column confirms that council tenants are as likely as owner-occupiers to *seek* to migrate for job-related reasons, while the second column shows that they are much less likely actually to migrate for job-related reasons. The coefficient on council tenancy is significantly less than zero on a one-tailed test, but the level of significance is low because of the very small total number of actual migrants for job-related reasons. Thus, the relative absence of job-related migrants from council tenancy, which is the source of the negative coefficient, is less significant in a statistical sense than in our previous study. In view of the results of our previous work we believe that these results reinforce the general conclusion that council tenants experience much greater difficulty than owner-occupiers in actually fulfilling their migration intentions for job-related as well as for other reasons. This is not true for tenants in general since both furnished and private unfurnished tenants are more likely to migrate for job-related reasons than are owner-occupiers. With respect to house movement, our previous investigations showed that, ceteris paribus, council tenants were more likely to move than were owner-occupiers which conforms with the predicted pattern given the differences in the costs of moving for each tenure. However, the coefficient on council tenancy in column 4 implies that this does not hold for job-related movement, though council tenants are similar to owner-occupiers in the probability that they are considering movement for job-related reasons. This means that the higher rate of house movement, *ceteris paribus*, among council tenants is associated with moves to better or more suitable accommodation rather than to more appropriate jobs. It seems, therefore, that it is not only migration which is discouraged by council housing but all forms of job-related movement. Again the contrast between council tenants and other tenants is very marked since the coefficients on furnished and private unfurnished tenancy in this equation are both significantly greater than zero. Our explanation for this pattern is that moves for consumption reasons tend to take place within a limited geographical area and, so long as council tenants remain within the district covered by a single local housing authority, council house exchanges or moves are quite easy to arrange. On the other hand, a move for job-related reasons will typically involve a move to a different local authority district and thus will encounter similar difficulties to those affecting migration over a longer distance.

Since the costs of moving for tenants are much lower than for owner-occupiers, which comprise the default tenure group in the estimated equations, one would expect that tenants would be more prone to move for non-job-related reasons than would owner-occupiers. This would imply negative coefficients on the tenancy dummy variables in the equations for job-related movement (or search) *conditional* on movement. However, there is no inherent reason why movement should be more or less expensive for a public tenant than for a private tenant, so that differences between the three types of tenancy are likely to reflect the way in which these tenures are restricted or controlled.

As expected there are significant negative coefficients on council tenancy and private unfurnished tenancy in the logit equations (columns 3 and 4 of table 5B) for job-related movement conditional on movement – both for potential and past movement – though in this respect there is little difference between owner-occupiers and furnished tenants. However, both types of controlled tenants are more likely to have migrated in the past for job-related reasons than are are owner-occupiers, which indicates the difficulty of 'casual' migration when there are rent or other controls affecting the availability of rented housing. The small number of migrants in this equation means that neither coefficient is statistically significant. The differences between the coefficients for these two tenures, which one would expect to be very similar in an unrestricted environment, are striking and they imply that council tenants are systematically less likely to migrate or move for job-related reasons than are private unfurnished tenants, though in the case of movement there is little difference between them in their propensity to search.

To provide quantitative indicators of the importance of these tenure effects tables 6 and 7 follow tables 2 and 3 but with specific reference to job-related migration and movement only. Since we are primarily interested in the impact of council housing on job-related mobility table 6 focuses on the predicted values of migration and movement rates per 1000 council tenants either in their own tenure (column 2) or in the three alternative tenures – i.e., the rows in this table correspond to column 2 in table 2. In addition to predicted mobility rates we have used the methods described in Hughes and McCormick (1985) to calculate two measures of the likelihood that someone who embarks on search to migrate/move will be successful. The first measure (z_i) is the probability that the search is successful within a fixed period and the second measure (t_i) is the length of time spent searching in order to achieve a fixed probability of success. Both measures are calculated using the

Table 6

Differences between council housing and other tenures in job-related migration/movement.

	Predicted values per 1000 council tenants in alternative tenure group[c]			
	Owners (1)	Council tenants (2)	Furnished tenants (3)	Unfurnished private tenants (4)
(A) Mobility Rates				
Migration	1.1 (3.9)	0.5 (1.0)	5.1 (15.8)	4.5 (7.2)
Movement	4.3 (23.1)	1.8 (39.9)	18.7 (155.9)	8.6 (91.3)
(B) Probabilities of Successful Search[a]				
Migration	16.3 (6.6)	6.8 (1.9)	52.3 (17.3)	23.2 (7.6)
Movement	35.1 (17.3)	15.6 (20.1)	56.0 (61.8)	51.5 (30.4)
(C) Relative Lengths of Search for Uniform Success[b]				
Migration	3.5 (11.8)	8.5 (40.8)	1.1 (4.5)	2.5 (10.3)
Movement	0.8 (1.8)	1.8 (1.6)	0.5 (0.5)	0.6 (1.0)

[a]Defined as z_i in Hughes and McCormick (1985).
[b]Defined as t_i in Hughes and McCormick (1985).
[c]Figures in brackets are the equivalent values for all migration/movement.
Source: Calculated from logit equations in table 4 using 1974 sample of council tenants.

estimated equations for past migration/movement and for migration/movement search. Higher values of the probability of successful search and lower values of the relative length of search indicate that the tenure group finds it less costly or encounters less barriers to fulfilling an intention to migrate/move for job-related reasons.

The differences between council tenants and owner-occupiers in their predicted rates of job-related *migration* are smaller than for all migration since the hypothetical shift from council tenancy to owner-occupation doubles the rate of job-related migration for council tenants whereas this ratio is approximately 4 for all migration. The same is true for furnished tenancy when compared with council tenants, whereas the difference between unfurnished private tenants and council tenants is similar for job-related and all migration. For job-related *movement* the pattern is dramatically different because, as the figures for all migration/movement in brackets show, council tenants have a predicted rate of all movement which is nearly twice that of owner-occupiers whereas this relationship is reversed for job-related movement.

In most cases the probability of success in fulfilling an intention to make a job-related migration or movement is higher than for all migration/movement – for migration by council tenants it is over three times higher – but again for council tenants the probability of successful search for job-related movement is lower than for all movement. The same is true for furnished tenants though the success rates are both much higher and relatively closer together.

With respect to our interest in labour market flexibility the figures in table 6 imply that households find it substantially easier to fulfil an intention to migrate for job-related reasons than for other types of migration. The difference between council tenants and other tenure groups with respect to job-related migration rates is less than for all migration. On the other hand council tenants seem to experience substantial difficulty in organising local moves for job reasons. For example, the probability of successful search for an owner-occupier who wants to move for job-related reasons is over double the equivalent probability for a council tenant, whereas the probability of successful search to move for all reasons is slightly higher for council tenants than that for owner-occupiers. This is particularly notable in view of the higher success rate of private unfurnished tenants for job-related moves relative to all moves. Again this casts doubt on any simple interpretation of the influence of council tenancy relying upon the effect of rent subsidies.

Turning to the aggregate impact of tenure and education on job-related migration/movement the figures in table 7 show that the overall adjustments to aggregate job-related migration/movement rates due to tenure and college education differences between the U.K. and the U.S. are very similar to those for all migration/movement. They are a little smaller for young workers and

Table 7

The impact of U.S. tenure/education patterns on U.K. job-related migration/movement.[a]

	Predicted migration/movement rates per 1000 households for			
	All workers		All workers	
	Migration	Movement	Migration	Movement
(1) U.K. population characteristics	4.8	9.6	10.6	20.8
(2) Adjusting for U.S. tenure pattern	5.7	12.0	12.2	25.0
(3) Adjusting for U.S. college education pattern	5.7	11.1	12.5	24.2
(4) Adjusting for both U.S. tenure and college education patterns	6.6	13.7	14.3	28.7

[a]See notes to table 2.

Source: Calculated using migration/movement equations in table 4 and households in 1974.

a little higher for movement by all workers, but the earlier conclusions about differences between the U.K. and the U.S. apply equally to job-related movement. For job-related migration, especially by young workers, the proportional gap between the two countries is somewhat smaller than for all migration, so that after the adjustments in table 7 have been applied the hypothetical rate of job-related migration for young workers rises to about 70% of the U.S. rate.

To establish whether it is the labour market or the housing market which imposes the binding constraint on household decisions involves tricky problems of econometric modelling and, ideally, requires fuller data than we have available at present. We have attempted to investigate this issue in some incomplete work using techniques of simultaneous and recursive bivariate probit analysis. Estimation of these models is very expensive with large datasets and, unfortunately, we have not been able to obtain clear-cut results concerning the nature of the link between decisions concerning job mobility and house movement. Inferences which do appear to be valid are as follows

(*a*) For all households, housing search is conditioned upon job search, i.e. the probability that a household will be observed searching for a new residence is increased if the head of household is also thinking of changing his or her job, whereas the reverse is not the case.

(*b*) For council tenants, past house movement and job changes appear to be independently determined, which is only possible if the job moves take place within the household's local labour market area.

(*c*) For owner-occupiers, the direction of causality for past decisions is the reverse of that for search. Thus, past house movement seems to increase the probability of a job change but not vice-versa. This means that the housing market may, in practice, be a constraint on labour market decisions made by owner-occupiers as well as for council tenants.

Overall, this evidence suggests that the housing market does constrain labour market flexibility, but the links involved are quite difficult to disentangle.

4. Labour market flexibility and unemployment

In the previous section we summarized evidence concerning housing and labour mobility in the U.K. In this section we examine how these relationships might affect various measures of the flexibility of the labour market and the pattern of unemployment.

4.1. Wage fixing and adjustment to demand shocks

Of the three parts of this section, our comments here are necessarily the most speculative. Nevertheless, the potential implications of geographic immobility for the nature of wage contracts deserve attention, and we shall discuss three ideas. First, geographic immobility may have influenced the size of the union sector. Second, game-theoretic analysis of wage determination in the context of a declining industry, as recently discussed by Lawrence and Lawrence (1985), is perhaps of heightened interest. Third, low migration rates have increased the need for differential regional wage adjustment to remove regional labour market imbalances, which may increase the difficulty of coordinating a wage policy during a depression. We now consider these points in turn.

To adopt Hirschman's terminology, trade unions provide a means for the expression of 'voice' when an issue of concern to the workforce arises. Workers may alternatively respond to the source of concern by seeking work elsewhere – the 'exit' option. When mobility is costly, workers have an increased incentive to exercise the 'voice' option and to join and be active in unions. Adopting a more traditional argument, where labour turnover is high and substitute labour can easily move into the area, the difficulties confronting a labour organiser are greater and, if a union is formed, it will have more difficulty enforcing its preferences. Thus the high unionization rate in the U.K. may partially reflect the factors contributing to geographic immobility, particularly amongst manual workers. Furthermore, the choices of unions (for example, whether to strike or not) and the adversarial character of management–union relations – the traditional explanation for low U.K. productivity – may also reflect the costliness of exercising the 'exit' option for many British workers. There is interesting work in this area by Freeman (1980) who considers the effects of unions on workplace turnover, but further empirical work unscrambling the related roles of geographic and workplace turnover on which firms bargain with unions would appear to offer the possibility of a richer understanding of the simultaneous determination of both workplace turnover and the size of the union sector. This leads naturally to our second point.

An interesting analysis of wage adjustment in the context of shocks to the demand for labour is provided by Lawrence and Lawrence (1985). In this model an adverse demand shock may push the firm into an optimal policy regime in which investment is terminated. Because the capital stock is no longer sensitive to the real wage, the elasticity of demand for labour declines. This reduced elasticity may prompt the union to *increase* the wage in the declining industry: the earnings of the firm, net of variable inputs, have become pure rents that an attentive union may sequestrate in the drawn-out decline of the firm. A policy which increases the costs of migrating between regions reduces the elasticity of supply of the labour force. This increases the incentive for the firm to engage in bargaining games to secure locational rent, and while the analogy is not exact, increases the likelihood that models of the sort studied by Lawrence and Lawrence offer an insight into how wages and employment respond to a demand shock.

Third, geographic immobility increases the importance of regional wage adjustment to clear markets, and the coordination of a deflationary wage policy in the fact of a depression is made more difficult for labour contract negotiators to reach if there exists an imbalance of excess supplies for labour across regions. Such an imbalance may not prevent an appropriate nationally agreed wage policy, but given that union representatives and firms will experience different regional circumstances, it may (a) make its need more difficult to perceive, and/or (b) increase the difficulty of achieving majority support amongst the union or firms' representatives.

4.2. Adjustment to supply shocks and changes in the composition of demand

Both supply shocks and changes in the pattern of demand will generally alter the equilibrium allocation of resources between regions. Barriers to geographic mobility can be expected to increase the period of disequilibrium, and perhaps also the nature of the eventual equilibrium. The higher unemployment associated with any given pattern of shocks can be expected to reduce aggregate demand because of either lower consumption or the crowding out effect of financing unemployment compensation, so that structural change exercises a larger adverse effect on aggregate demand.

Thus, both directly and indirectly – through its effects on aggregate demand – geographic immobility is likely to increase the amplitude of employment cycles associated with these sorts of shocks.

Geographic immobility is also likely to increase the level of *long-term* unemployment associated with a given pattern of shocks. This may facilitate circumstances in which the NAIRU is likely to increase if the actual rate is perturbed above its previous equilibrium. That is, the 'hysteresis' or path-dependency effect may be particularly powerful in economies with geographic immobility where the ability to reabsorb redundant workers into employment is considerably reduced – see Blanchard et al. (1985), Hargreaves-Heap (1980).

Many of those becoming redundant following the recent U.K. shocks are older workers, whose incentive to migrate is already low, so that the hysteresis effect is likely to be further reinforced. If there is a tendency for seniority to be a less important criterion for deciding upon layoffs in Britain and other European countries than it is in the U.S., then the resulting consequences for the extent of long term unemployment and the force of the hysteresis effect may be important. We believe that further analysis of the effects of geographic immobility upon the tendency of workers to withdraw from job search, and of the comparative lay-off behaviours of U.S. and European firms, would be of particular value.

There is a further issue, connected with the hysteresis argument, which is relevant for the U.K. We suggested in section 2 that the evidence that labour flows out of regions of high unemployment, so that regional labour reallocations occur, is not strong. Unemployed individuals in a depressed area do not seem to have either higher actual or higher intended migration rates (and the evidence points to lower actual migration rates). The only link that has been established using individual data between unemployment levels and migration is that unemployed white collar workers are more likely to *intend* to migrate. (We are currently investigating the relationship between unemployment and actual migration rates). Thus, an economy with two regions which are identical except for their unemployment rates may experience a small net inflow of white collar labour into the low unemployment rate region, as a consequence of higher gross flows from the high unemployment region. Detailed evidence is not yet available concerning whether depressed regions experience lower *inflows*, which would certainly offer the possibility of providing a more balanced means of regional adjustment including manual workers. For this reason the consequence of high regional unemployment for the level and nature of U.K. regional *inflows*, must be considered a priority research topic.

We feel obliged to end these remarks with a note of caution. In view of the evidence that only white collar workers migrate from depressed areas it is presently far from apparent that, even if a net migratory adjustment is prompted by unemployment, it would help restore to equal prosperity the various regional labour markets. For example, consider a model in which the regional demand for labour is influenced by the entrepreneurial quality of its local labour force. Now suppose that entrepreneurship is more likely to develop amongst more able workers. If more able workers tend to be white-collar workers, whom we know to be most likely to migrate, then the adjustment process may involve a higher outflow of potential entrepreneurs/employers, the 'seed-corn' of future businesses providing the demand for labour, than of future employees. It is more usual in regional analyses to assume that the location of a firm's owner is irrelevant to the location of capital, but this may be inappropriate for small businesses and thus most of the high-growth businesses.

4.3. The level and the regional distribution of the NAIRU

In section 2 we discussed how the housing system influences geographic mobility, and in sections 4.1. and 4.2. how the system may also affect the nature of adjustment to shocks to the level or composition of demand or supply. Now we consider other arguments concerning the effect of housing policies on the distribution of unemployment and labour shortages in the U.K. – perhaps because they cause unemployment to accumulate in areas with a high density of council housing – and on individual incentives to be unemployed. The origins of these arguments were various pieces of evidence concerning high unemployment amongst council tenants. We shall briefly consider the arguments and then interpret the direct evidence linking unemployment and tenancy.

Towns and regions with a high density of council housing are likely to experience an excess of tenants seeking to migrate out of the area over those trying to enter it. This inhibits the migration of council tenants, who will not wish to give up their location-specific housing subsidy. In contrast, the major subsidy to house purchasers is not location-specific and thus it does not frustrate migration. Over time there will be a tendency for areas with more council housing – and thus with more location-specific subsidies – to retain a larger labour stock than those with less council housing. (The argument is similar to the wage-compensating principle used by Hall (1972) where all workers in an area receive the location-specific subsidy.) While the pattern of council house construction may in this way change the spatial allocation of the labour force, it will only affect unemployment if wages are not locally flexible.

Alternatively, there are various reasons why, apart from considerations arising from geographic immobility, unemployment may systematically differ between house tenure groups. For example, the replacement-ratio for social security benefits is affected because of the different ways in which tenants and owners – with and without mortgages – are treated under the social security system. An argument we would emphasize concerns the role of wealth in labour supply decisions. A large proportion of the typical U.K. household's wealth is invested in housing – either in the form of an equity stake or in terms of the present value of a dependable rental subsidy. A tenant in good accommodation might well consider himself more wealthy than certain owner-occupiers with a small amount of realizable capital after allowing for house selling costs. Unfortunately, the U.K. data sets do not allow a direct investigation of how far wealth affects the length of job search but it seems possible that this factor may directly influence the relationship between house tenure and unemployment. Council tenants may also differ in unemployment behaviour in so far as they are a self-selected group with certain unobserved characteristics that influence various aspects of behaviour including unemployment.

What evidence relates house tenure and unemployment? In work based on a sample of manual workers from the 1973–74 GHS McCormick (1983) found that there was a strong correlation between tenure and the probability of being unemployed. After controlling for other observable characteristics and for regional unemployment he found that council tenants are about 3 times more likely to be unemployed than are owner-occupiers. We have re-examined this relationship using data from the 1983 LFS and again find a very strong link between unemployment and tenure with the ratio of the adjusted unemployment rates for council tenants and owner-occupiers being even larger than ten years earlier. In view of the arguments that council tenants are self selected and that unemployment may reflect inherent ability, it is interesting that the model can be applied to *skilled* manual workers on their own with the same outcome. Similarly, the finding cannot be explained by higher job turnover amongst tenants: job turnover is only 40% higher among tenants than among owner-occupiers.

The argument that something other than self-selection is at work suggests that areas with more council housing will have higher unemployment – this cannot be true with self-selection unless the additional assumption is invoked that some towns have more workers with the unobserved unemployment-inducing personal characteristics. Again, models of the unemployment rate in large towns in England and Wales, controlling for socio-economic composition and demand shocks, show that the proportion of controlled rental housing (council and private) has a strong positive effect on local unemployment rates though less than in individual data. (This cannot be readily explained by the argument that council housing was constructed in areas that at the time of construction were depressed: heavy building in the Midlands and North West, and relatively little in Wales are the counterexamples – see McCormick (1983) for further details.)

What may be inferred from these findings? While the tendency of council tenancy to inhibit migration may explain why certain regions experience labour shortages and others unemployment, we doubt for two reasons that this accounts for the higher unemployment rates of tenants found in individual data, both before and after controlling for socio-economic characteristics, unobserved heterogeneity, and regional unemployment. First, the parameters on the various tenure categories in a model of unemployment probabilities always indicate identical behaviour for tenants of private and council controlled housing, and yet only council housing reduces migration. Second, since it is never possible to reject the hypothesis that owners without mortgages have similar unemployment probabilities to the controlled rental groups, the most appropriate distinction is between owner-occupiers with mortgages and the rest. This leads us tentatively to favour the view that the wealth/incentive package for mortgages may substantially affect unemployment patterns in addition to the usual socio-economic and demand variables. Thus, if council housing can be assumed to have replaced private rental accommodation that was squeezed out by rent controls, we would argue that the individual equilibrium, and therefore the NAIRU rate of aggregate unemployment, may not have been substantially affected. At the same time, it seems entirely plausible that the pattern of relatively high unemployment rates in the depressed regions of the U.K. combined with persistent labour shortages in southern England has been aggravated by a council housing system which significantly limits the ability of manual workers to relocate from the sites of declining traditional industries in the north towards southern areas.

5. Policy response

There are two levels on which policy might be developed. In our view the appropriate response is not to attempt to patch up the existing system by implementing ad hoc reforms focused upon the issue of mobility but to consider the broader framework of taxation, housing finance and rent control legislation. The nature of housing finance leads to excessive investment in owner-occupied housing which involves high transaction costs and low mobility for individuals who could be expected to prefer good quality rental accommodation were there incentives to make it available. Again, a coherent policy determining local authority rents, building levels and migration arrangements, thereby providing our largest nationalized industry with a framework respecting overall national needs and not local interests would be especially advantageous. Finally, a policy of gradually removing rent controls would be especially beneficial for young mobile workers.

On a more ad hoc level there are just two points we would make regarding the management of council housing in the present framework. First, the central government should insist that local authorities fix the share of new lettings available to migrants at no less than a certain minimal level. Local authorities acting individually do not have the appropriate incentives to choose this variable at a socially optimal level. Second, we favour the establishment of a central unit to coordinate the location of new council housing, for at any given level of council house building local incentives in both the North and the South are likely to lead to the share of new council house construction occurring in southern England to be below the optimal level.

More generally it seems that job-related migration is low in the U.K. – at least by comparison with the U.S. though not perhaps by comparison with other countries in Northern Europe – even after we have adjusted for the major effects of tenure and education. If migration is seen as an important means of encouraging greater labour market flexibility, then the government will probably need to take action to reduce the costs of migration borne by the individual. Much job-related migration is sponsored in the sense that it arises because firms transfer workers from one part of the country to another – either as a succession of career moves or as a result of the relocation of office or production facilities. For the U.S. Bartel reports that such migration represents approximately one-third of all migration by workers, whereas the share of sponsored migration is much higher in the U.K. – in the 1973–74 and 1983 surveys about 60% of workers who had migrated in the past year and were employed a year ago were still working for the same employer. In these cases the costs of migration are usually defrayed by the firm and are tax-deductible in computing the firm's tax liability and – so long as any expenses paid are 'reasonable' – are not taxed in the hands of the migrant. On the other hand public sector employers and many firms are unwilling to meet the full relocation costs of new employees. In the U.S. such un-reimbursed expenses, which are essentially an investment yielding a higher employment income flow, may be tax-deductible under the personal income tax code, whereas they are not in the U.K. A change in this direction deserves serious consideration. The reluctance of the tax authorities to create further tax expenditures – even small ones in a worthy cause – may rule out action in this direction.

The present system seems to bear hardest on manual workers. In part this is because regional wage differences are surprisingly small in money terms, and for owner-occupiers real wages are highest in areas of high unemployment where house prices are low. Thus, either an increase in regional wage differentials will be required to stimulate greater migration or a reduction in regional differentials in housing costs (both rents and house prices). Regional wage differentials seem to be much larger in the U.S. than in the U.K., which goes some way to explaining the difference in migration rates between the two countries. However, this is clearly not a complete explanation as we have seen that differences in migration rates are mirrored by similar differences in local movement rates, especially job-related movement by manual workers, which cannot plausibly be ascribed to the influence of differential wage rates. The regional pattern of wages seems to have been remarkably stable despite major changes in the composition and level of unemployment, so it is clear that there is very strong institutional inertia resisting the realignment of local wage rates in response to the pressure of demand in local labour markets.

Whatever happens to regional wage differentials, any attempt to increase geographic labour mobility in the U.K. must involve a much higher rate of new housebuilding suitable for manual workers in low unemployment areas – particularly in the South East. This runs directly counter to the interests of existing residents of these areas who are benefitting from the capital gains resulting from the limited supply of housing and who also object to new building on the grounds that it will reduce the environmental benefits which they currently enjoy. Such conflicts over zoning have, of course, been a feature of Californian growth but in Britain they are given a special twist by the existence of strong planning controls combined with 'green belts' designed to stop urban sprawl in the immediate post-war period but which are now tending to strangle residential development in much of southern England. In essence U.S. zoning controls tend to be local in character whereas British ones have a much wider regional impact.

Finally, we should note that in a variety of measures the British government has attempted to encourage migration on a limited scale and there are even schemes which provide subsidies to migrating workers. The money available for such schemes is small and, in general, there seems to be little public or government support for migration as a remedy for regional unemployment differentials.

Overall, our conclusions concerning the contribution of geographic labour mobility to achieving a greater degree of flexibility in the labour market are not optimistic. The empirical work discussed above provides convincing evidence that the council housing system represents a substantial barrier to job-related local movement as well as to migration. However, even if this barrier to geographic mobility was suddenly removed so that council tenants were able to move as easily as other tenants or owner-occupiers, there would still be very large differences between U.S. and British rates of job-related migration/movement. Focusing specifically on manual workers, who are most severely affected by the operation of the council housing system, the removal of all tenure constraints on geographic mobility would increase job-related migration and movement rates by less than 75%. American rates of job-related migration and movement for manual workers are over 10 times as large as comparable British rates, so that much more than a change in tenure arrangements would be required to close this gap. Since it is unemployment rates for manual workers which display large regional disparities, there seems little prospect that these will be significantly reduced as a result of geographic labour mobility in the absence of major social and institutional changes affecting both the incentive for and willingness of households to migrate/move for job-related reasons. Nonetheless, there are strong equity and efficiency arguments for removing artificial barriers to geographic mobility by manual workers, so that reforms in housing policy which contribute to this goal are clearly desirable.

References

Bartel, A.P., 1979, The migration decision: What role does job mobility play?, American Economic Review 69, 775–786.

Blanchard, O., et al., 1985, Employment and growth in Europe: A two-handed approach (Centre for European Policy Studies, Brussels).

DaVanzo, J., 1978, Does unemployment affect migration? – Evidence from micro data, Review of Economics and Statistics 60, 504–514.

Freeman, R.B., 1980, An exit-voice trade-off in the labour market: Unionism, job tenure, quits and separations, Quarterly Journal of Economics 94, 643–673.

Hall, R.E., 1972, Turnover in the labour force, Brookings Papers on Economic Activity 3, 709–756.

Hargreaves-Heap, S.P., 1980, Choosing the wrong 'natural' rate: Accelerating inflation or decelerating employment and growth?, Economic Journal 90, 611–620.

Hughes, G.A. and B. McCormick, 1981, Do council housing policies reduce migration between regions?, Economic Journal 91, 919–937.

Hughes, G.A. and B. McCormick, 1985, Migration intentions in the U.K.: Which households want to migrate and which succeed?, Economic Journal 95, Conference supplement, 76–95.

Lawrence, D. and R. Lawrence, 1985, Manufacturing wage dispersion: An end-game interpretation, Brookings Papers on Economic Activity 1, 47–116.

McCormick, B., 1983, Housing and unemployment in the U.K., Oxford Economic Papers 35, 283–305.

Shelton, J.P., 1968, The cost of renting versus owning a home, Land Economics 44, 59–73.

COMMENTS

'Housing Markets, Unemployment and Labour Market Flexibility in the UK' by G. Hughes and B. McCormick

Martin N. BAILY

Gordon Hughes and Barry McCormick have written a first-rate paper exploring the extent to which public housing (council housing) in the United Kingdom is a barrier to migration, and hence an obstacle to labor market adjustment. They draw on their own prior work and present some new results to make a convincing case that council housing does discourage migration, but that the elimination of this mobility barrier would not help much in reducing overall unemployment.

The authors begin with a comparison of migration and movement in the United States and the United Kingdom. Migration in the United Kingdom means a move across a regional boundary, while in the United States it is across a state boundary. Movement means any address change. The validity of their migration comparison can be questioned, because states and regions are different concepts. Moving across a state line can be as large as from New York to California or as trivial as from the New York suburbs of New York City to the New Jersey suburbs of the same city. Many migration studies of the United States try to track in more detail the nature of the move – how far, or whether it was rural to urban, and so on.

Despite this reservation, the relatively high propensity of Americans to both move and migrate comes through clearly in the data. Even if Britons had the same pattern of house tenure and education as Americans, they would move less. Most Americans are immigrants or have recent ancestors who are immigrants, so a high propensity to move is hardly surprising.

Now that Europe is facing severe long-term unemployment, the flexibility of the U.S. labor market looks attractive. But it was only a few years ago that economists were explaining why unemployment in the United States was so much higher than in Europe. The high turnover rate in the United States was often cited as a cause of high frictional unemployment and a high NAIRU. This may show that labor market institutions or patterns that work badly in one situation may work well in another. At the least it should make us hesitate to advocate social engineering.

The bulk of the Hughes–McCormick paper explores the evidence for the impact of council housing on migration. And the case is overwhelming. Council house tenants make up nearly a third of United Kingdom households and most of these households are headed by manual workers. They do move often from one council house to another in the same locality, so they are not just families that stay put. However, they very rarely leave a locality. Of the 3658 household heads in the 1973 survey, only 7 changed regions in a year, and 5 of these had lived in London.

The main question about results such as these, of course, is whether council house tenancy is a proxy for some unobserved characteristics of the individuals. Do people who want to stay put choose council housing? To some extent this must be true. If all the council housing were suddenly sold to the private sector and market rents levied on tenants, it is doubtful if the tenants would immediately migrate at the rate predicted by the authors' equations. But the impact would certainly be substantial. Moreover, in one respect their results understate the impact of council housing because many of those now living in private rental accommodation are on waiting lists for council housing, and may be just as reluctant to move as existing tenants.[1]

[1]This point was made by Martin S. Feldstein.

Given that council housing reduces migration, does that make it a significant barrier to equilibrating job mobility? The authors look at reasons for migration and at the impact of unemployment on it. The results are very discouraging for anyone hoping to use housing policy to aid the labor market. Blue-collar workers do not seem to respond to differences in job opportunities as reflected in unemployment rate differences. When a region becomes depressed, the professional and white-collar workers do migrate out. But the blue-collar workers remain behind, living in council housing and being supported by unemployment compensation and other family members. The power of mobility to equilibrate the labor market in Britain is apparently very limited.

The authors raise an interesting implication of their findings about low mobility. Labor unions are stronger and more militant in the United Kingdom than in the United States. That fits, because U.S. workers are more likely to vote with their feet by moving, whereas U.K. workers do not see migration as an option and use group action in the form of a union. Strategic end-game wage bargaining is probably more common in the United Kingdom than in the United States.

The final issues remain: what should be done about housing policy in Britain and, indeed, what should be done about unemployment? It is clear that current housing policy in Britain is not optimal. It inhibits migration, for whatever reason, and is not an efficient form of income redistribution. The program to sell off council housing is apparently not working and, in any case, drastic policy changes would create upheaval. A gradual move to raise rents towards market-clearing levels seems indicated, combined with specific steps to open up council housing to in-migrants, as the authors suggest. It should be noted, however, that describing a fully efficient housing market is not easy. When a region becomes depressed, this imposes large capital losses on the owners of housing capital and infrastructure capital, whether these owners are in the private sector or public sector. A high level of migration by workers does not necessarily indicate an efficient market. Flexible regional wage rates that encourage new business investment to replace the plants that have closed may be more efficient. Unfortunately, such flexibility is apparently less in Britain than in the United States, exactly the opposite of what one would expect from the low U.K. migration rate.

The blue-collar work-force in Britain has suffered for over five years from a massive shortfall of jobs and the solution to this problem is one of doubtful feasibility. It is to combine forceful expansionary macroeconomic policies with limits on union power and a reorientation of the tax and transfer system to provide greater rewards to work. Housing policy is probably not a big player in this story.

COMMENTS

'Housing Markets, Unemployment and Labour Market Flexibility in the UK' by G. Hughes and B. McCormick

Takenori INOKI

This paper provides convincing evidence that the council housing system in U.K. significantly limits job-related local house movement as well as labor migration. Since it is asserted in conventional economic theory that labor mobility that shifts human resources between geographic areas is of central importance to the efficient operation of labor market, the problem dealt with in this paper is highly relevant to the analysis of economic adjustment, particularly when we are concerned with the actual contents and cause of unemployment in relation to the concept of NAIRU. The points argued as well as statistical techniques employed in this paper are quite solid, and their limitations and qualifications are carefully noted. So the paper is basically self-contained and is not vulnerable to substantial criticism.

My first comment concerns the method to evaluate labor market 'flexibility' adopted by Hughes and McCormick. Job mobility and migration are usually considered to be a favorable indicator to detect the efficient operation of labor market, but the other side of the coin of mobile labor is high labor turnover which generally tends to reduce the workers' skill and productivity due to the change of their specific work place. Indeed Freeman's 'voice-exit hypothesis' focuses on such an aspect of 'exit' solution which increases recruitment and training costs of job movers and their loss of skill in the workshop. It will be interesting to know to what extent Freeman's conclusion that unions have positive effects on productivity turns out to be valid in U.K.'s industrial scene. The welfare implication of labor immobility may be a little more complex than is assumed in this paper.

Secondly, the link between employment levels and migration that was established in this paper by using individual data is that unemployed white collar workers are more likely to *intend* to migrate across regions. If, as the authors put it, more educated workers tend to be white-collar workers, we need some theory which explains the difference in migration behavior between the more educated and the less educated. One possible theory is given by Schwartz (1976) which was tested to be valid for the case of Japan (Inoki and Suruga (1981)), i.e., the more educated are found to be less deterred by an increase in distance. (Smaller distance elasticities of migration are observed for more educated persons.) In the U.K. case which was examined by Hughes and McCormick, it also seems that the fixity of blue collar workers due to the public housing system makes a contrast to the relatively (compared to the U.S. case) high migration rate of non-manual workers.

Finally, I would like to add one technical point concerning simultaneity or endogeneity of migration decision and house tenure choice. Since I have no good alternative to correct the bias, my comment will be brief and only touches on the point related to my second comment. If it is the labor market, and not the housing market, which imposes the constraints upon household decisions about migration, the reason why the area of search of manual workers tends to be narrower (hence less manual workers cross regions) should be explored more thoroughly. I surmise that here we will have to partly rely upon human capital theory and upon the concept of skill-specificity.

References

Inoki, T. and T. Suruga, 1981, Migration, age and education: A cross-sectional analysis of geographic labor mobility in Japan, Journal of Regional Science 21, no. 4.

Schwartz, A., 1976, Migration, age and education, Journal of Political Economy 84, 701–719.

European Economic Review 31 (1987) . North-Holland

LABOUR MARKET FLEXIBILITY IN JAPAN IN COMPARISON WITH EUROPE AND THE U.S.*

Toshiaki TACHIBANAKI

Kyoto University, Sakyo-ku, Kyoto 606, Japan

1. Introduction

There is a common understanding outside of Japan that the Japanese labour market is more flexible than those of the other industrialized nations, and that this flexibility has facilitated to lower the rate of unemployment and to provide a better performance of the macroeconomy in general. Fig. 1 is presented to show that the rate of unemployment in Japan has not changed at all despite a big drop in the GDP in comparison with the other industrialized countries. The reduction in employment also was not so great. Almost all other countries show that a drop in GDP is accompanied by a drop in employment and thus by an increase in unemployment, although the degrees are varied by countries. These results in Japan are somewhat mysterious but deserve a serious investigation. This paper attempts to examine, on the basis of studies by both Japanese and non-Japanese, whether flexibility is the real story. The paper also attempts to seek the reasons for this flexibility, if any, with particular emphasis on a comparison between the Japanese economy and the economies of other industrialized nations, and the reasons for the very minor change in the rate of employment.

Obviously, it is impossible to cover all the dimensions of labour market flexibility. This paper concentrates on a few subjects such as (1) labour adjustment, (2) wages and labour demand, (3) labour cost, (4) labour supply, (5) labour mobility, (6) seriousness of unemployment, and others.

It might be useful to summarize the reasons for the relatively better performance in the Japanese labour market (especially the low rate of unemployment) during the 1970s and the early 1980s. First, there was no strong pressure of labour supply by young people and female workers. The

*An earlier version of this paper benefited much from extremely useful and constructive advices given by two discussants at the International Seminar on Macroeconomics, held at Namur in Belgium, Richard Layard and Jacques Mairesse. The author is very grateful to them who improved the quality of this paper substantially. Other participants, namely Martin Baily, William Branson, Martin Feldstein, Robert Gordon, Lawrence Summers and Jean Waelbroek gave me useful comments. Comments by Masahiko Aoki, Tatsuo Hatta, Yoko Sano and Hirofumi Uzawa were helpful. The author is responsible for any shortcomings in this paper.

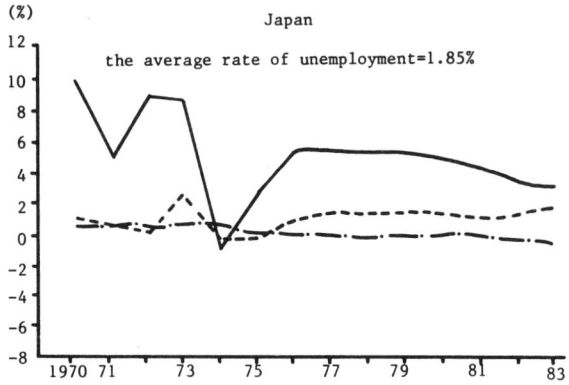

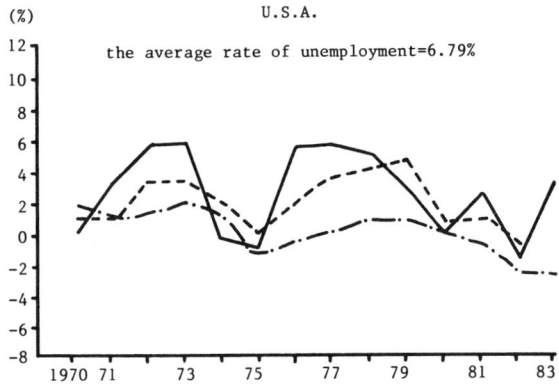

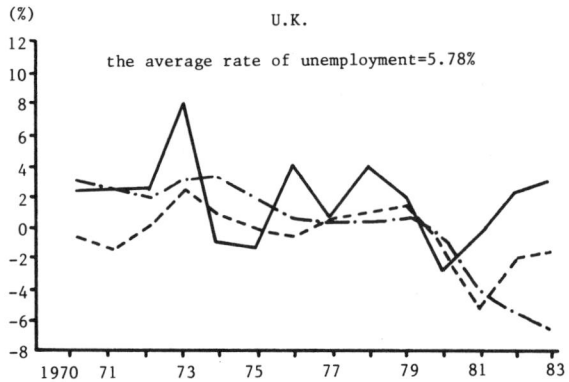

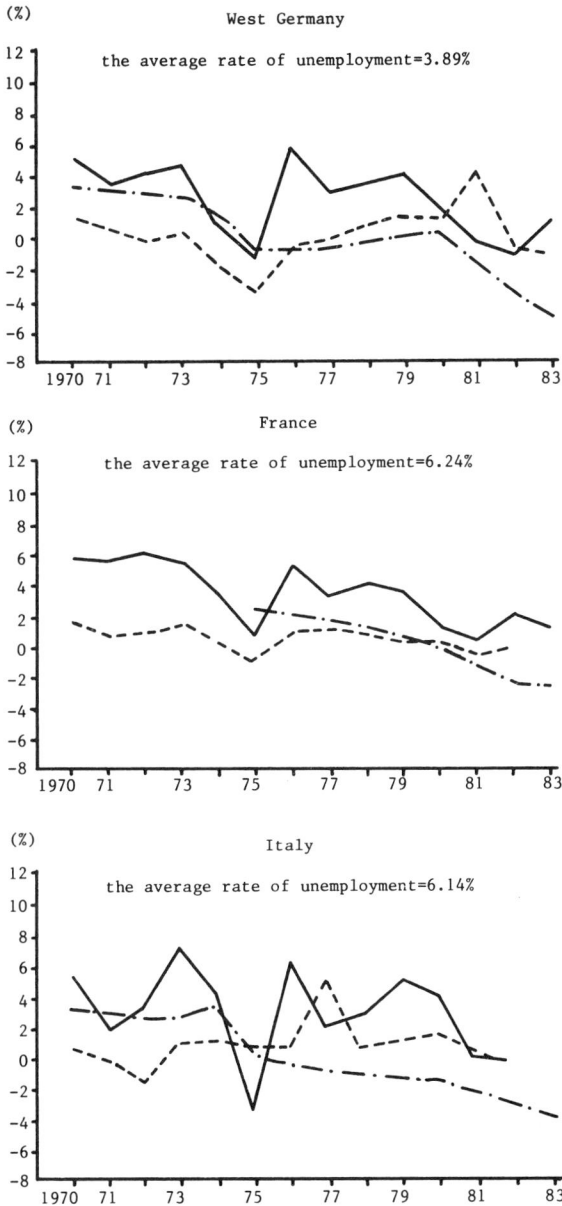

Fig. 1. The movement of GDP, the number of employed people and the rate of unemployment, where ——— = GDP, –––– = the number of employed people and ——–– = the rate of unemployment. The movement of GDP and the number of employed people is measured by the annual rate of change. The movement of the rate of unemployment is measured by the difference between the average rate of unemployment in the sample and the respective year's rate of unemployment. When the rate of unemployment in this graph moves in a parallel motion with GDP or the number of employment, it implies that when GDP or employment increases (or decreases), unemployment decreases (or increases). *Source*: Higuchi, Seike and Hayami (1986) (Original Source: *International Statistics*, Bank of Japan).

proportion of the working population of youth has been somewhat declining due largely to both a decrease in the youth population and an increase in the enrollment rate for higher education. The female labour force participation rate had been in a decreasing trend for a long time, although quite recently it is somewhat increasing. Secondly, the pressure of foreign workers was almost negligible, unlike the U.S. and Europe where internationally immigrated workers became one of the main sources for unemployment, especially in Europe. Thirdly, the growth rate of unemployment in the tertiary sector was considerably high, and it absorbed a large number of the work-force in contrast to a minor decrease in employment in manufacturing industries. During the past period of rapid economic growth, the manufacturing sector had absorbed an incredibly large number of workers from the rural areas, where people were predominantly engaged in agriculture. It is no exaggeration to say that the regional and industrial mobility of workers was extremely high. Fourth, the proportion of temporary employees such as part-time workers, employment with fixed durations and others (a very rough estimate is about 30 percent of the total non-agricultural labour force) and of self-employed workers including family workers (about 30 percent) has been considerably high. As a result, the proportion of permanent employees has been about 40 percent. The high share of temporary employees suggests that employment may fluctuate rather easily, while the high share of self-employed workers implies that those people are rarely unemployed unless they change their labour force status. Fifth, the effect of discouraged workers contributed significantly. Sixth, the movement of labour productivity, working hours and wages was quite flexible. This point was emphasized by Gordon (1982), Hamada and Kurosaka (1986), and others. Seventh, union power and 'search intensity' in terms of both the generosity of unemployment compensation and strictness of the unemployment protection laws were weak. See Gordon (1982) about conflict avoidance as a social norm and the Shuntō (the annual spring offensive) in union power, and Shimada, Hosokawa and Seike (1981) and Tachibanaki (1984b) who found a minor disincentive effect of unemployment compensation. See also Layard and Nickell (1986) about its quantitative assessment. Eighth, several forms of labour adjustment to minimize the number of discharges (or layoffs) are adopted by Japanese firms and encouraged by the government. Ninth, the share of non-wage labour costs within the total labour cost has been relatively small. This is related to the relatively poor social security system in Japan at least in comparison with Europe. Several of the above arguments are examined carefully in this paper.

2. Labour adjustment

This section intends to investigate how firms adjust employment. A considerable number of efforts have been made in Japan to estimate the labour demand functions, in particular the labour adjustment functions. The main purpose of these studies is to estimate the degree of responsiveness or the speed of adjustment to labour demand. Some of the results are reviewed in comparison with the other countries.

A relatively simple labour demand function (1) is a starting point, which was originated by Brechling (1965), Ball and Cyr (1966), Nadiri (1968) and others.

$$\ln N_t - \ln N_{t-1} = \lambda(\ln N_t^* - \ln N_{t-1}), \tag{1}$$

where N_t is the employment at time t, N_t^* is the desired level of employment and λ is the adjustment coefficient. This is a partial adjustment model. When we take account of adjustment costs such as hiring, training and firing costs, which were considered by Rosen (1968), Ehrenberg (1971) and Nadiri and Rosen (1974), the adjustment model with fixed costs is obtained.

Let us summarize the estimated speed of adjustment in employment briefly. In the United States those coefficients are 0.5–0.6 by Soligo (1966), 0.59 by Brechling and O'Brien (1967), 0.643 by Nadiri (1968) and 0.4 by Shinozuka and Ishihara (1977), respectively. In the United Kingdom the coefficients are 0.307 by Brechling (1965), 0.185 by Ball and Cyr (1966) and 0.22 by Brechling and Cyr (1967), respectively. The Japanese coefficients are 0.1 by Muramatsu (1983) and 0.04–0.08 by Shinozuka and Ishihara (1977), respectively. It is found that the Japanese speed of adjustment is considerably slower than those in the U.K. or the U.S. Thus, it may be concluded that the Japanese response to labour demand is very slow by the international standard.

Why has the Japanese speed of adjustment been slower? Labour input has been regarded as a quasi-fixed factor of production. This may be interpreted by the notion of specific human capital and of hiring and training fixed costs. A firm invests in a worker's human capital in order to achieve a higher expected marginal value product over his expected future working lifetime in the firm. The higher such an investment is, the less adjustment there is in labour.

When the labour inputs are distinguished between employment and man-hours (employment times working hours), the speed of adjustment is considerably different between them. As Hamermesh (1965) concludes, in general the adjustment of employment is slower than that of working hours, although there are minor exceptions such as Hart and McGregor (1982) for West Germany and Briscoe and Peel (1975) for the U.K. Japan is not an exception to this general rule, as Muramatsu (1983) and Shinozuka (1980) have shown. Shinozuka (1980), for example, found that the speed of adjustment of employment was 0.10 for firms with more than 30 employees and 0.30 for firms with 5–29 employees, while the speed of adjustment of hours was 0.37 for firms with more than 30 employees and 0.49 for firms with 5–29 employees. Shinozuka (1986) confirmed those findings. They attribute this to the following factors: first, higher fixed costs of hiring, training and discharge than those of overtime premiums associated with a change in working hours are normal. In fact, it is no exaggeration to say that most of the labour adjustments in Japan were made through the change in working hours and the cut in new hires to a lesser extent, as will be shown later. Secondly, Japanese firms prefer internal work forces rather than external work forces when they adjust labour input. For example, re-allocation or transfer of workers to other establishments within a firm or re-to other sections within an establishment are frequently used, and also labour hoarding is quite common. In other words, the internal labour market dominates the external labour market.

Several supplementary notes are provided about labour adjustment in Japan. First, there is a considerable gap between men and women with respect to the speed of adjustment. Nakamura (1983, 1984) finds that the coefficient for women is much higher than that for men when the speed of adjustment in employment is investigated. Shinozuka (1980) obtained a similar result to Nakamura's, but proposed another valuable finding: when the speed of adjustment in employment is estimated for large firms and small firms separately, the female coefficient is higher than the male coefficient at large firms, while the opposite result is observed at small firms. When we combine the two sexes, the speed is quicker at small firms than large firms. She suggests, then, that the first instrument is adjustment by working hours, the second is the use (or discharge) of temporary or part-time female workers, the third is separation of female regular employees and the final is discharge of male regular workers as the order of priority when labour adjustment at large firms takes place. Results for small firms are less clear in determining such an order since almost the same values of the adjustment coefficients were obtained when man-hours were used instead of employment.

Secondly, a non-negligible difference is observed by industries in Japan, unlike the U.S. [See Hamermesh (1976) for the U.S.] Seike (1985), Muramatsu (1986) and others conclude that the speed of adjustment in light industries was quicker than in heavy industries. One of the reasons is that technology in heavy industries is more capital intensive, and thus the fixity of labour input is higher.

Thirdly, labour adjustment in employment is made through a cut (or an increase) in new hires rather than a change in current stock (discharge or layoff) of workers. Fig. 2 shows that a considerable rate of fluctuation in new hires is observed. This is in particular true in manufacturing industries. This does not necessarily imply, of course, that there are no discharges or layoffs. For example, Muramatsu (1986) finds that when a firm has to reduce more

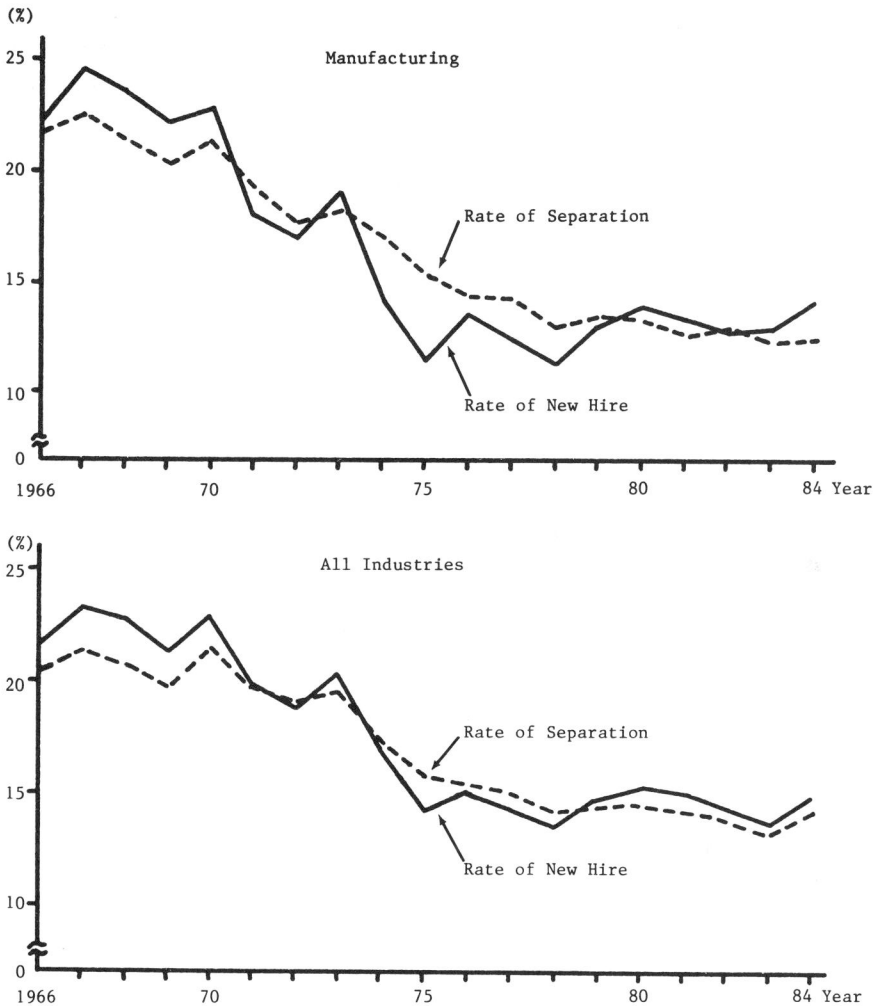

Fig. 2. Time series change in the rate of new hires and separations.
Source: *Employment Trend*, Ministry of labour.

than ten percent of its man-hours in response to a fall in demand or output, the probability of adopting discharge is positive. A dismissal of workers by designation is the final step, probably because no rule, such as for example seniority rule, for determining who is dismissed is prepared. The first step is to send workers (normally older workers) to subsidiary companies or to firms in the same group (say in the ex-zaibatsu Mitsubishi group, for example). The second step is to call voluntary quits by offering some premiums. Finally, dismissals come.

Finally, many studies suggest that the speed of labour adjustment by employment has been increasing in the past years, especially after the two oil crises. One reason is that Japanese firms do not have high expectations for the recurrence of a rapid growth of the economy as in the past. In other words, they are somewhat pessimistic about the future. Thus, they tend to minimize the number of employees as much as possible. Secondly, it may be possible that both employers and employees do not have strong hesitations in applying a drastic method such as adjustment by employment in recent years.

Tables 1 and 2 are presented to confirm some of the above propositions from a different angle. The estimated standard deviations in table 1 suggest that Japan shows the highest deviation in working hours and the lowest in employment among the major industrialized nations. Working hours are much more flexible than employment.

Moreover, it should be emphasized that the change in total working hours is strongly affected by the change in overtime hours. Table 2 shows a decomposition of the change in total working hours into the change in regular hours and the change in overtime hours. The table clearly indicates that the contribution of overtime hours is as strong as the contribution of

Table 1

Estimated standard deviations of output, employment, working hours and real wage per hour.[a]

		Labour input			Real wage per hour
	Production	Employment	Hours	Man-hours	
(A)					
Japan	6.509	2.089	1.903		
U.S.	6.963	4.376	1.447		
U.K.	4.635	2.409	1.508		
W. Germany	4.014	2.325	1.509		
France	5.368	–	0.728		
(B)					
Japan	0.147			0.048 (0.048)	0.111 (0.343)
U.S.	0.062			0.052 (0.050)	0.038 (0.045)
U.K.	0.045			0.056 (0.159)	0.052 (0.121)
W. Germany	0.070			0.062 (0.089)	0.057 (0.192)
France	0.069			0.037 (0.083)	0.036 (0.231)

[a]*(A)* signifies that the standard deviations are calculated for the rate of change in each index of the variable for 1970–83, while *(B)* signifies that standard deviations are calculated for log-transformed variables which are de-trended for 1964–83. The numbers in parentheses are the values for non-trended variables. Thus, *(A)* and *(B)* are not comparable.
Source: Higuchi, Seike and Hayami (1986) and Ohtake (1986) (Original sources: *International Statistics*, Bank of Japan and *Main Economic Indicators*, OECD).

Table 2

Decomposition of the change in total working hours into the change in regular hours and the change in overtime hours (% per year).

	Total hours	Regular hours	Overtime hours
1955–1960	0.9	0.3	0.5
1960–1965	−1.1	−0.5	−0.5
1965–1970	−0.5	−0.7	0.1
1970–1973	−0.8	−0.6	−0.2
1973–1976	−1.3	−0.6	−0.7
1976–1980	0.2	−0.1	0.3
1980–1985	−0.1	−0.2	0.1

Source: Monthly Labour Statistics, annual series, Ministry of Labour.

regular hours. The overtime premium is 25 percent in Japan as well as the U.K. and West Germany, while it is 50 percent in the U.S. Thus, Japan does not provide firms with an extra incentive to utilize overtime hours by the international standard. The mutual interests of both employers (coping with a fluctuation in demand and output smoothly) and employees (the desire to obtain higher wages by overtime hours and corporate loyalty to firms) may be another reason.

It is important to add the cost factor. The Ministry of Labour (1986) conducted a valuable study which compared the cost between a new hire and overtime hours by a currently employed person. It concluded that the cost to a firm for an additional new hire would be the same as the cost for overtime hours by a currently employed person if the overtime premium rate were 62.9 percent. In view of the current premium 25 percent, no firms would hire new employees instead of utilizing overtime hours. Interestingly, the break-even premium rate is 74.4 percent for larger firms (more than 500 employees), 61.0 percent for medium-size firms (100–499 employees) and 47.4 percent for smaller firms (30–99 employees), respectively. This is due largely to the fact that the fixed cost is higher in larger firms than in smaller firms. This is one of the primary reasons why larger firms are inclined to use flexible overtime hours rather than changing the numer of employment in comparison with smaller firms which tend to use flexible employment.

Let us conduct a brief international comparison with respect to the level of working hours. The total annual working hours and overtime hours in 1983 were 2,152 and 202 (the rate of overtime hours to total hours, 9.39 percent) in Japan, 1,898 and 156 (8.22 percent) in the U.S., 1,938 and 140 (7.22 percent) in the U.K., 1,622 and 45 (2.77 percent) in Italy, 1,613 and 78 (4.84 percent) in West Germany and 1,657 and 78 (4.71 percent) in France. Both the total working hours and the overtime hours (including the rate of overtime hours) are the longest in Japan among the six countries. The importance of overtime hours in Japan is recognized further by this international comparison.

A higher fluctuation in working hours is confirmed internationally by table 1. As noted before, Japan shows the highest standard deviation in working hours and the lowest in employment among the major industrial nations despite very high fluctuations in output. When we use the total man-hours, the story is considerably different since Japan shows the lowest fluctuation. In sum, a very high adjustment by working hours and a low adjustment by employment are the Japanese ways of labour adjustment. The U.S. is the other extreme, namely a high adjustment by employment and a low adjustment by working hours. Europe stays between the two extremes.

Which is more desirable as an adjustment policy? If a national consensus that to keep the rate of unemployment as low as possible as the first national goal of the economic policy is supported universally, the Japanese way of labour adjustment is certainly desirable. However, non-negligible costs such as, for example, inflation, inefficient management of firms due to excess employment, profit squeeze or foreign trade conflict must be paid to achieve this goal. I do not believe, therefore, that the Japanese way of labour adjustment can be recommended to the other industrialized nations easily. I evaluate the U.S. temporary layoffs positively, as will be argued later. Each country has its own preference which must be assessed highly.

3. Flexible wage rates and labour demand

There is a common understanding internationally that Japanese wages (both nominal and real) are flexible, and that this flexibility has helped the Japanese economy to perform relatively well. This section intends to re-examine this issue based on a large number of studies.

Japanese economists were ignorant of this aspect, namely flexibility of wages. It is ironic that foreign observers opened Japanese economists' eyes to this issue. Representatively, we can name Sacks (1979, 1983), Branson and Rotemberg (1980), Gordon (1982), Grubb, Jackman and Layard (1983), and others. Many studies, except for perhaps Sacks, support the observation that flexibility of real wages in Japan is considerably high, and thus it has helped to lead to a better performance. It is important to consider two issues separately. The first is to investigatee whether the real wage is flexible, statistically speaking. Secondly, provided that this flexibility is supported empirically, is it possible to propose that this flexibility has raised labour demand, and thus lowered unemployment?

3.1. Statistical wage flexibility

Since the seminal articles by Sacks (1979) and Gordon (1982) appeared, a lot of investigations were performed to re-examine whether real wages in Japan are flexible. Many studies such as Yoshitomi (1981), Shinkai (1982), Komiya and Yasui (1984), Mizuno (1985), OCED (1985), Hashimoto and Raisian (1985), Koshiro (1986), except for perhaps Ohtake (1986), support Gordon's view, namely that the Japanese real wages are more flexible than the other industrialized nations, although various reasons are provided by different authors to support it.

Gordon (1982) basically attributed the flexibility to 'bonus' payments paid twice a year. Mizuno (1985), however, emphasizes that not only bonus payments but also basic wages (total wage earnings minus bonus payments) are flexible. His point is that the proportion of bonus payments to total wage earnings is at most 25 percent, and it is declining constantly. Thus, if flexibility of total wage payments is observed statistically, its main cause is not flexibility of the bonuses but of the monthly wages. He actually estimated that the relative contribution of flexibility of the bonus payments to the flexibility of the total wage payments was about 10 percent during the period of 1960–83. The main source for the big contribution of the fluctuation of monthly wages is wage payments by overtime hours, due partly to overtime premiums.

Bonuses are explained very briefly. In 1983, 97.9 percent of firms paid bonuses, and 99.3 percent of all employees received some amount of bonuses. Thus, they are well-established and systematic payments. About 32.0 percent of all firms say that they determine the total amount of bonus payments on the basis of firms' performances such as sales, value-added, and profits. Smaller firms stress the consideration of performances and profits more than larger firms. The majority of Japanese firms, especially larger firms, regard bonuses as quasi-regular wage payments rather than as profit-sharing. Koshiro (1986) supports this view in his econometric work. Thus, although the bonus payments in Japan have a profit-sharing aspect in terms of Weitzman (1984), it is not a pure profit-sharing scheme. This does not necessarily imply, however, that the amount of bonuses is fixed. It is fairly varied in response to the firms' business conditions, as many authors suggested. See Hashimoto (1979), Tachibanaki (1982) and Freeman and Weitzman (1986).

An interesting aspect about bonuses is how to allocate the total amount of bonus payments to individual employees. About 70 percent of firms say that they take account of the individual employee's performance. Only about 30 percent of firms pay the equal amount (say, two or three months' regular wages) to all employees regardless of the employee's performance. What are the criteria for determining each person's performance? The rate of absence, contribution to a firm, skill, responsibility and leadership as a supervisor, tenure at a firm, and etc. Thus, bonuses are used by firms as an incentive payment to a certain extent. This, however, depends upon industries, and the incentive aspect should not be overemphasized since the amount determined by it is considerably small.

Another method for estimating the degree of flexibility of wage payment is to rely upon the Phillips curve approach, which Grubb, Jackman and Layard (1983) have adopted. If a change in the wage rate was sensitive to the labour market condition (say, the rate of unemployment), it would be concluded that flexibility of the wage determination is high. This method is likely to overestimate the degree of flexibility if an economy does not have a sizeable movement in the rate of unemployment. It is possible that the Japanese flexibility has been somewhat overestimated because of the almost constant rate of unemployment. Thus, the OECD study (1985) which showed that Japanese real wage rigidity was the lowest among the OECD countries is somewhat dubious. The method utilized a change in the unemployment rate as well as a change in the consumer prices. Related to this, it is noted that the work by Hamada and Kurosaka (1984), who estimated the Okun's coefficient ten times higher in Japan than in the U.S., was accepted unfavourably not only by a non-Japanese, Mairesse (1984), but also by several Japanese economists. An unbiased estimation of the Okun's coefficient requires a certain degree of fluctuation in the rate of unemployment. In sum, a method for estimating the flexibility of wages which utilizes a change in the rate of unemployment in estimating wage or price equations (say, the Phillips curve approach) needs careful interpretations when the rate of unemployment does not fluctuate sufficiently, like Japan's case.

It is possible to conclude based on a large number of studies, in particular pure statistical studies which do not use the Phillips curve approach, that wages (both nominal and real) in Japan are considerably flexible. One important exception is Ohtake (1986) who found less flexibility when he considered the de-trended wage figures. He also examined real wages which are standardized by a change in output. He proposes that a shock in output (say, the two oil crises) which gives an excessive impact on a change in wages must be eliminated. Since his argument has a point, it is necessary to examine it further. However, he does not deny that real wages in Japan are variable, at least based on the purely statistical evidence.

It is necessary to argue why real wages are flexible. Several economic and institutional factors, in addition to the bonus payments and flexible working hours examined before, are suggested here, but a serious discussion is avoided. (i) Wage contracts are determined largely on a yearly basis in the framework of the Shuntō, unlike the three-year contract in the U.S. The past performance of productivity movement, inflation rate, macroeconomic conditions and others, is taken fully into account by both employers and trade unions at the Shuntō. (ii) Several studies, Yoshitomi (1981), Shinaki (1982), Komiya and Yasui (1984) and others, propose that a change in wages is strongly affected by a change in terms of trade and productivity. (iii) Trade unions are concerned with the assurance of the employment of their members. When the utility function of trade unions was estimated by Hayami (1986), a stronger preference of employment rather than wage increase was found. Thus, it is likely that trade unions are willing to make the sacrifice of wages in exchange for the assurance of employment. This is a big contrast with the European experience, especially in the U.K. where the impact of union powers on wages is fairly strong, as shown by Minford (1983) and Nickell and Andrews (1983).

Furthermore, the rate of unionization in Japan is fairly low (about 30 percent) by the international standard, and more importantly, the rate is under a constant decline. For example, see Hamada and Kurosaka (1986). Not only weak preferences of wage increases by trade unions but also the low rate of unionization contributed to some of the flexibility of wages. It is an irony but interesting that both Japan and the U.S., where macroeconomic performances are relatively better than the European countries, have lower unionization rates. I argue that the labour side should be able to demand higher wage payments in view of the fact that the properly measured labour share within the national income in Japan has declined constantly, and that some increases in wages in boom industries will encourage a higher domestic consumption which has a positive effect on reducing the current huge trade surplus. Labour market flexibility in terms of a cooperative behavior of trade unions vis-à-vis managements may be regarded as one of the causes for the current foreign trade surplus. This gives one example of the fact that labour market flexibility cannot be evaluated always positively.

3.2. Wages and labour demand

A second important issue is the relationship between wages and the demand for labour. Specifically, is it possible to propose that a flexible wage system increases employment? The U.S. result was surveyed by Hamermesh (1976), and a consensus, namely stable and robust wage effects on the demand for labour, was obtained at least up to 1976. However, some recent papers by Hall (1975, 1980) have presented unresponsive wages, and Bell and Freeman (1985) find that flexible wages by industries in the U.S. have not contributed to employment growth. Thus, even in the U.S., the recent story may be different from the past. In Europe the result was inconclusive as surveyed by Nickell (1982). The recent studies, however, tend to support that there are some clear real wage effects on the demand for labour when relative material/fuel prices are accounted for. See Nickell (1984) and Symons (1985). See also Symons and Layard (1984) about a rigorous international comparison.

What is the situation in Japan? Muramatsu (1985) gave a useful survey on the estimation of the real wage elasticities with respect to labour demand.

His main conclusion, on the basis of about ten studies in Japan, suggests that the real wage elasticities are considerably lower than the U.S. elasticities surveyed by Hamermesh (1976). Under the constant assumption of capital cost and output, the average elasticities are at most -0.03 for total industries and -0.15 for manufacturing industries. The effect is smaller in Japan than in the U.S. Incidentally, the output elasticities in Japan are on the average 0.24 for total industries and 0.44 for manufacturing industries, even after two years' lag. Those values are smaller than the U.S. values, which are about 0.75–1.00. In sum, it is possible to proclaim that the real wage effects on the demand for labour in Japan are weak.

Let us summarize this section. Although it is true that the real wage flexibility is considerably high in Japan, it has not helped to increase the number of employment. The role of wages as an adjusting factor has been quite limited. The growth of employment, if any, should be explained by reasons other than the real wage effect. It should, however, be pointed out that flexibility prevented current employment from falling to a certain extent, because the firm's cost condition was saved considerably.

3.3. Other aspects of flexibility related to wages and labour costs

3.3.1. Nenko wages and equality

Japanese wage determination is characterized by the 'nenko' wage system: the wage rate is determined largely by employees' tenures and ages. See Tachibanaki (1975, 1982). Every country has a similar system. The only difference is that the Japanese case is much more apparent than in the other countries. See fig. 3 which shows a steeper age-earnings profile in Japan. Several implications of the system for the performance of the labour market are considered.

First, since the growth rate of wages by tenure and age is high, the wage level of younger prople is low while it is high among older people. This is, incidentally, the main reason for the higher unemployment rate by older people (ages over 55), 4.3 percent in recent years. Curiously, the rate of unemployment by younger people (ages 15–24) is not so low (about 4.5 percent). This is due largely to factors that arise from the supply side, as shown by Tachibanaki (1984).

Secondly, the wage distribution among the *same* age group is quite equal because of the 'nenko' system, although the wage distribution of total employees may be quite unequal, because samples of both younger and older workers are included in the total number of employees. This is obvious because the wage level of nearly all employees is proportional to their tenures and ages. It is also found that education and occupation are minor variables to differentiate the wage rate of employees. See Tachibanaki

(1975, 1982) and Atoda and Tachibanaki (1986) about it. Those features provide employees with a feeling of equal treatment by employers. This equal treatment gives incentives for corporate loyalty and hard-working to employees, especially workers with lower educational and occupational attainment. I believe that this is one of the reasons why labour productivity has been high in general.

There must be several questions about this interpretation. For example, how is the incentive of educated and skilled workers evaluated? The American literature emphasizes the incentive of qualified and supervisory workers who should receive higher wages. See Calvo and Wellisz (1979), and Rosen (1982), for example. Incentives for qualified workers are not provided by monetary rewards at least currently in Japan. There is an incentive by bonus payments, as noted previously. This is still minor, and does not have a strong impact.

One important problem remains. Does productivity of workers increase in proportion to the workers' tenure at a firm? Since the 'nenko' system implicitly assumes that the above is true, it is important to investigate whether it is empirically supported. Otherwise, firms and/or workers may be

Japan and the U.K. (1975-76)

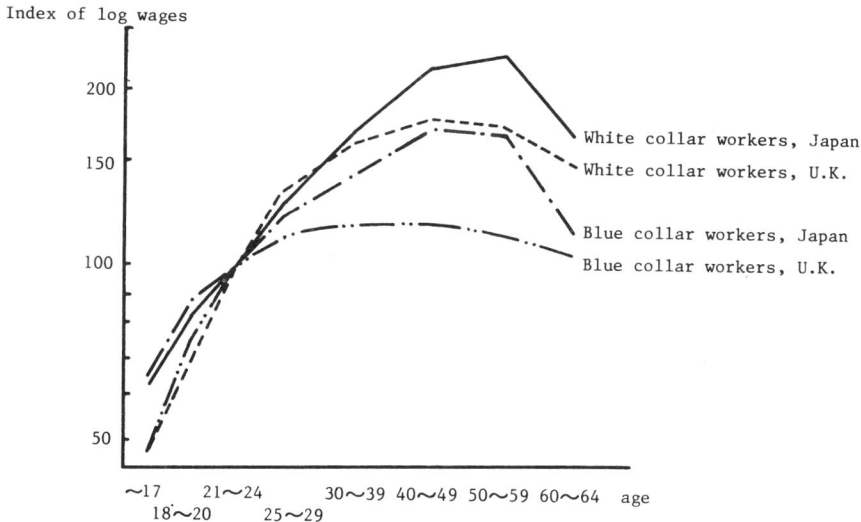

Fig. 3A. Wage growth by age: Japan and the U.K. This graph shows the index of log wages in comparison with the wage level at age = 21–24. *Source:* Koike (1981), *Skill Formation in Japan*, Yuhikaku, Tokyo (in Japanese) (original sources: Japan, *Wage Structure Survey, 1976*, Ministry of Labour, U.K., *New Earnings Survey, 1975*, Department of Employment).

Japan and the U.S. (1966–67)

Wage index

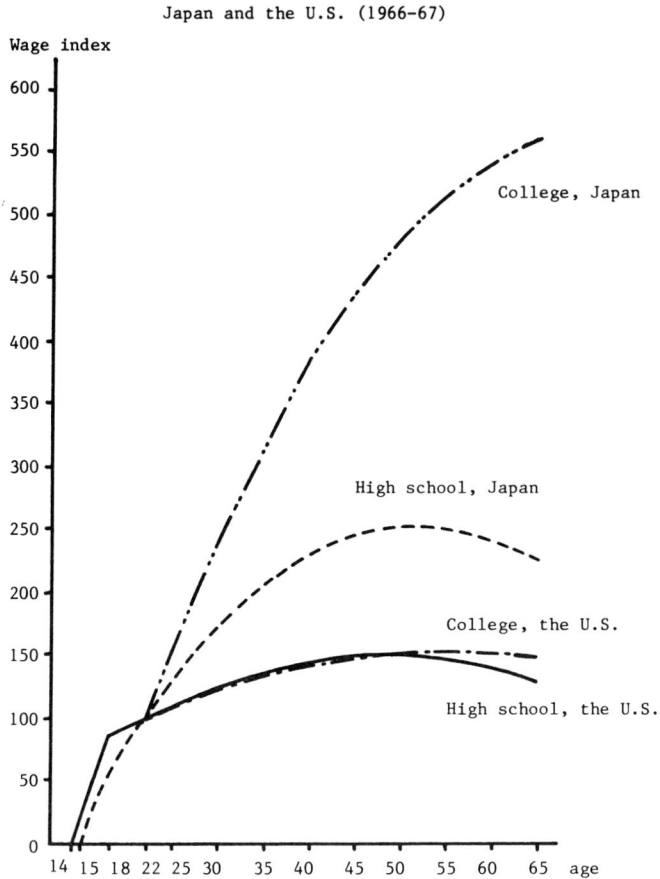

Fig. 3B. Wage growth by age: Japan and the U.S. The wage indexes are given in comparison with the wage level at age=22 where the index value is equal to 100. Those wage indexes are not the actual wages earned at each wage, but merely show the growth of wages by age. The graph does not show that the wage levels of college graduates and high school graduates in the U.S. are the same. It indicates that the growth of wages is almost the same in comparison with the wage at the age 22 between college graduates and high school graduates. *Source:* Shimada (1981), *Earnings Structure and Human Investment*, Kogakusha, Tokyo (original sources: Japan, *Wage Structure Survey, 1967*, Ministry of Labour, U.S.A., *Survey of Economic Opportunity, 1966*).

paying higher wages than requirements, or receiving lower wages than contributions. Unfortunately, there are no rigorous studies which have investigated the relationship between wages and marginal productivities in relation to the 'nenko' system. Flexibility due to the 'nenko' system may be evaluated precisely only when the relationship is made clear empirically.

Another question may be posed: several studies, for example Klau and Mittelstadt (1985), show that the average inter-industry wage differential is the highest in Japan among the OECD countries. They evaluate this as flexibility of the wage structure. This may be inconsistent with the equal wage distribution as proposed previously. I find that a part of the large inter-industry wage differentials should be explained by the difference in age and sex compositions of employees in each industry. Thus, the highest inter-industry wage differentials ought to be discounted to a certain extent. I do not deny, however, that some degree of inter-industry wage differentials due to the difference in productivities in industries contributes to the flexibility of wage payments to a limited extent in Japan.

3.3.2. Minimum wage law

Minimum wage law specifies that the minimum wage should be determined by each prefecture. Since the economic condition is considerably different by regions, such a decentralized system can be evaluated positively as flexibility. Moreover, the minimum wage law is not obeyed strictly by employers, and the penalty is almost non-existent. In sum, it is hard to believe that the minimum wage law has been an obstacle to hire new employees. This is contrary to American or European experiences in which some adverse effects are often mentioned.

3.3.3. Male–female wage differentials

Wage differentials between men and women are reviewed. Several studies, for example Tachibanaki (1975), and Kawashima and Tachibanaki (1986), conclude that the most eminent variable which explains wage differentials is sex (male–female differences). A large part of male–female wage differentials are discriminations against women in wage payment and promotion. They are not receiving the payments that correspond to their contributions to firms. About one-third of the labour force is women currently. Firms have benefited from lower wage payment for women considerably since it has saved labour costs. Although this is not flexibility, it is an important element which has helped Japanese firms in cost performance. It is anticipated that the recently enforced equal employment and treatment act for men and women will help women, but hurt firms to a certain extent.

3.3.4. Non-wage labour costs

It is well documented that Europe suffers from a heavy burden of non-wage labour costs, in particular statutory social security contributions to health and pension programmes. This heavy burden has induced labour cost rigidity to firms, and is supposed to be one of the most important reasons for the high unemployment rate in Europe. This issue must be argued in relation to various aspects such as the problem of the incidence of the employer's contribution to social security schemes, fixed labour costs and others. We find several through discussions elsewhere. See Hart (1984) for example.

Here, only a brief comment on Japan is made with respect to non-wage labour costs.

It is said that Japan and the U.S. are two countries among the industrialized nations where the low rate of non-wage labour costs has contributed to a better performance of employment. I understand that the U.S. has a national consensus that services such as medical care and pension programmes should be arranged privately. Statutory social security programmes organized by public authorities do not have a great share. This is the main reason why the U.S. shows a low rate of non-wage labour costs.

Japan is somewhat different. In principle, Japan wanted to adopt the welfare state in the European sense about twenty years ago. The government modified the social security system completely, by raising the amount of public pension payment and medical expenditure considerably. It was proud of having achieved the European standard with respect to the amount of per capita pension and medical payment. This achievement, however, was not supported by a rigorous budgetary background. The aggregate pension and medical payment was very low because the proportion of retirees to the total population was quite low at the time. Since the growth rate of the economy was quite high, huge revenues from both general taxes and social security contributions could be collected without necessarily assigning high rates of social security contribution both to employers and employees. In sum, the government wanted to introduce the notion of a welfare state only on the payment side without a sound budgetary or actuarial calculation. This was a mistake some twenty years ago. Thus, firms were not asked to pay a sufficient amount of social security contributions in the past. This is the main reason why the statutory employer's contribution had been lower in Japan. Although sympathy for the government is possible because of the unanticipated stagflations after the two oil crises, the mistake is serious. It is no longer possible to enjoy such low non-wage labour costs in the future since the share of non-wage labour costs is in an increasing trend.

4. Labour supply

There is a widespread belief that flexible labour force participation is quite effective in adjusting labour supply. Specifically, the labour supply is increased when an economy is in boom, while it is decreased in a recession. Ono (1981) and Hamada and Kurosaka (1986) are the representative examples who propose that this flexibility helped to lower the number of unemployed people. This notion had been already recognized by many writers in Japan, and those workers are called 'discouraged workers', who lose their desire to seek jobs and are forced to retire from the labour market. A large number of female married employees are likely targets. Discouraged workers are sometimes called 'added workers', 'secondary workers' or 'marginal workers'. Nurkse (1953) called it 'disguised unemployment'. Although the exact meanings are different, they all indicate the discouraged effect.

Three methodologies are possible to verify the existence of discouraged workers. First, the number of discouraged workers may be estimated directly through various published labour force surveys. Secondly, average flow rates and transition probabilities among three states, namely (i) employment, (ii) unemployment and (iii) not-in-labour force, may be examined and compared with the movement of business cycles. Thirdly, the rate of labour force participation can be examined for time-series data. The representative studies are as follows. Ono (1981) for the first method, Mizuno (1983) for the second, and Shimada and Higuchi (1985) for the third.

Ono (1981) conducted an interesting comparative work between Japan and the U.S. in which he estimated the number of discouraged workers. 8.9 percent were discouraged among people who were not in the labour force in Japan in 1978, while only 1.4 percent were discouraged in the U.S. The official unemployment rate was 2.2 percent in Japan, while it was 6.0 percent in the U.S. in the same year. The result suggests that it is quite misleading to rely on the official rate of unemployment to argue the labour market condition, at least in Japan, in view of the large number of discouraged workers.

Higuchi, Seike and Hayami (1986) performed a valuable comparative study of the average flow rates and transition probabilities between Japan and the U.S. from 1970 to 1982. They concluded that several transition probabilities such as from not-in-labour force to unemployment, from unemployment to employment and from employment to unemployment are much more sensitive to business cycles in the U.S. than in Japan. In other words, the several American transition probabilities fluctuate more significantly than the Japanese ones, as Fig. 4 shows. It is noted, however, some transition probabilities such as from employment to not-in-labour force have similar movements in both Japan and the U.S.

Shimada and Higuchi (1985) presented a very high rate of decrease in the labour force participation rates by female workers during a fall in labour demand until the early 1970s, by estimating the labour force participation equation econometrically. This again suggests clear evidence of the discouraged worker effect until the early 1970s.

Although these studies mentioned above support a view that the effect of discouraged workers has been considerable, and that this is in particular serious among female workers, some of the studies suggest that the effect is becoming weaker and weaker quite recently, and a new phenomenon, 'involuntary' part-time workers, has appeared.

One of the most important findings based on the study of Higuchi, Seike and Hayami (1986) is that the rate of staying in the labout force after being

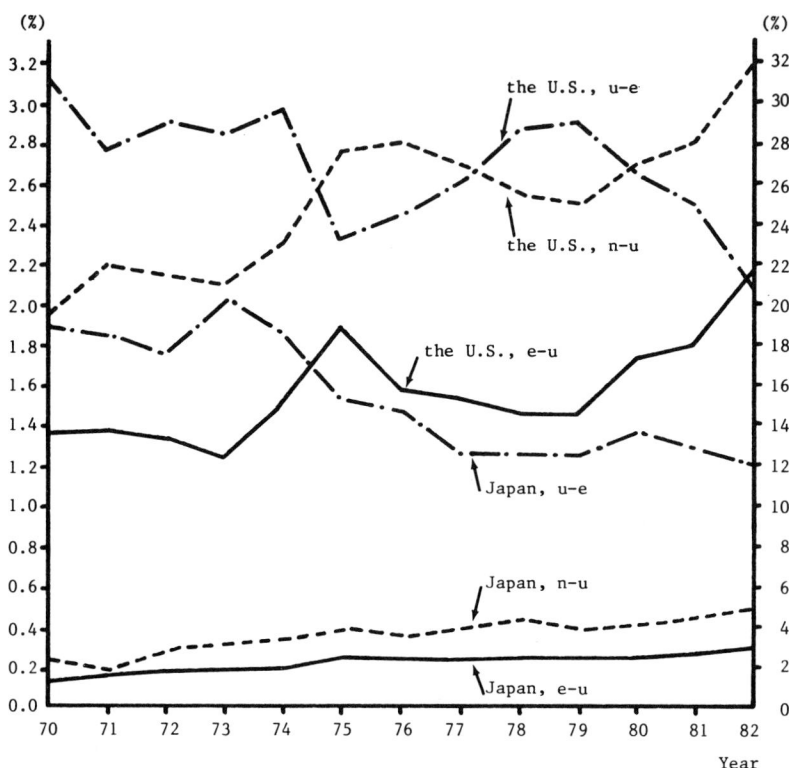

Fig. 4. Time series movements of several transition probabilities in Japan and the U.S.
(1) 'e' stands for employment, 'u' for unemployment and 'n' for not-in-labour force. Thus, the solid line shows, for example, the transition from e (employment) to u (unemployment).
(2) The left-hand vertical axis shows an index for e–u and n–u, while the right-hand shows an index for u–e.
(3) The other transition probabilities such as e–n, n–e, and u–n are not written here since both Japan and the U.S. show similar movements. It is noted, however, that all the probabilities in the U.S. are higher than those in Japan, as is true for the case of e–u, n–u and u–e.
Source: Higuchi, Seike and Hayami (1986). (original sources: *Labour Force Survey*, in Japan and *Current Population Survey*, in the U.S.).

unemployed has been increasing since 1975 both in Japan and the U.S. among female workers. In other words, the importance of discouraged workers has declined recently in the two countries, and its decline is greater in Japan.

Wakisaka (1986) made an important contribution by adopting the first approach. He found that although it is true that the number of discouraged female workers had increased until 1977, it has decreased considerably after 1977. The implication is that despite a fall in labour demand a large number of unemployed females do not leave the labour market, but stay on. What do they do? One group obviously continues to be unemployed, and seeks new employment. This is one of the reasons why the rate of unemployment has increased marginally in recent years.

Why do they stay unemployed recently? Several reasons may be raised. First, as Higuchi (1982) pointed out, there has been an increasing trend in the preference of working rather than not-working among women. Higuchi estimated several parameters of a utility function which consist of leisure and income, and obtained a strong preference of working by women. Married women to supplement incomes of a family since the growth rate of their husbands' income is low recently. Women tend to stay in the labour market in order to seek an alternative job even if the job prospect is not bright. Secondly, the effect of unemployment compensation must be considered. The Japanese unemployment compensation system had been fairly generous, since the financial condition has been healthy due to the lower rate of unemployment. As Tachibanaki (1984b) showed, a limited amount of prolongation of the duration of unemployment was observed due mainly to generous support by the unemployment compensation. This certainly encourages females to stay in the labour market for a while even if they are going to retire from the market later.

Another group can find employment not as full-time workers but as part-time workers unwillingly. An increase in part-time workers, in particular female part-timers, is a world-wide trend in many industrialized countries, as the OECD study (1983) shows. Japan is not an exception to this trend. A crucial result in Japan is that a large number of part-time workers are 'involuntary' rather than voluntary.

Wakisaka (1986) estimated the number of female involuntary part-time workers by examining various statistical sources. The definition of part-time working is given as either (1) the total annual working days are less than 200, or (2) the weekly working hours are less than 35; the definition of involuntary part-time workers is part-time workers who are seeking full-time jobs, additional hours, or alternative jobs. Table 3 presents such figures. The most important finding based on the two sources is that the growth rate of involuntary part-time workers is very high, although some differences in numbers are observed between the two sources. Currently, Japanese workers, in particular female workers, are obliged to work as part-time employees despite their desire to work on a full-time basis.

In summary, it is true that the effect of discouraged workers is still observed. The important difference, however, from the past experience, which pushed a large number of the work force out of the labour market, must be emphasized: a large number of involuntary part-time workers are being produced recently. Needless to say, those two effects have contributed to lower the rate of unemployment.

Is it possible to say that those two effects can be regarded as labour

Table 3

Estimated numbers of involuntary part-time workers (ten thousands).[a]

(1) Employment Status Survey (Female only)					
Year	1968	71	74	77	79	82
	16.1	20.3	22.1	33.5	42.4	67.0
(2) Labour Force Survey (Male and Female)					
Year	1979	80	81	82	83	84
Male	16	17	20	20	22	18
Female	29	33	32	38	45	46

[a]Employment Status Survey (every three years normally) and Labour Force Survey (every year) are different in sampling method and especially in the definition of an involuntary part-time worker. Employment Status Survey defines it as a worker who has either less than two hundred working days per year, or less than thirty-five working hours per week on the average even if a person worked for more than two hundred days a year, and who wants to have an additional employment (or hours), or wants to change employers. Labour Force Survey defines it as a worker who has less than thirty-five working hours per week in a specific week (i.e., the last week of March), and who wants to have an additional employment (or hours), or wants to change employers. In other words, Employment Status Survey asks the usual status in a whole year, while Labour Force Survey asks the status of a specific week. In view of these definitions some differences appear between them with respect to the estimated figures. Source: Wakisaka (1986).

market flexibility which is desirable? Some economists believe that those effects cannot be blamed for the following reasons. First, it it highly desirable and probably a top priority to have a lower rate of unemployment even if some other harmful effects are accompanied simultaneously. Secondly, those discouraged workers are normally secondary workers whose economic conditions are not severely penalized. The majority of discouraged people are married women who can be supported by their husbands. I personally do not share with those opinions. Thus, I do not evaluate the 'discouraged effect' positively as flexibility. The dispute, however, has not been settled yet.

5. Labour mobility

It is widely believed that the Japanese labour market stands out as providing the longest duration of tenure and less frequent job mobility among the OECD countries. Table 4 supports such a view. Japan has a longer job tenure by about three or five years compared with the other industrialized nations. As to labour turnover rates (including quits and

Table 4

Average current job tenures (years) and labour turnover rates (annual number of accessions (A) and separations (S) per 100 employees, and annual quits (Q) and layoffs (L) per 100 employees).[a]

	Job tenures				Labour turnover rates				
	Year	All	Male	Female	Year	A	S	Q	L
Austria					(1982)			27	13
Canada	(1983)	7.5	8.6	5.8					
France	(1978)	8.8	9.7	7.2	(1981)	16	17		
W. Germany	(1972)	8.5	8.9	5.7	(1982)	25	25		
Italy	(1972)	7.1	7.4	6.6	(1981)	9	15	11*	3*
Japan	(1982)	11.7	13.5	8.8	(1983)	20	20	10	2
Sweden					(1982)			15*	5*
U.K.	(1979)	8.6	9.6	6.4	(1984)	19	21		
U.S.	(1983)	7.2	8.4	5.6	(1981)	39	41	24	17(6)

[a]Accessions and separations include turnovers at establishment level.

Quits and layoffs with asterisks are manual workers only, and Italy, Sweden and the U.S. include mobility between establishments.

Quits and layoffs are for manufacturing industries.

The figure in parenthesis in the U.S. is layoff rate less the rate of recall of laid-off workers.

Source: OECD, *Employment Outlook 1984, and Technical Report MAS (85)25*.

layoffs), only the U.S. has a high degree of labour turnover. Europe and Japan have almost the same rate of labour turnover.

It is sometimes said that the duration of jobs is the longest in Japan because Japanese firms provide their employees with lifetime employent contracts. This is not true. First, there is no official commitment of lifetime employment by both an employer and its employees. Only an implicit understanding is operative between them. 'Desirable' is a proper word that describes how both employers and employees feel about lifetime employment. The effect of this implicit contract in terms of Baily (1974), Azariadis (1975) or Okun (1981), or the agency theory in terms of Lazear (1981) may have a great effect on the working of the labour market. It should be noted, however, that we observe a lot of discharges (or separations initiated by employers' even in Japan despite this implicit understanding. Secondly, the coverage of the lifetime employment as 'desirable' is rather limited; only about 30 percent of employees are covered by this understanding. Moreover, in fact, a much lower rate than 30 percent of workers commit themselves to lifetime employment according to the statistics. See Cole (1979) or Tachibanaki (1984a) about this. Incidentally, the bigger a firm is or the higher the educational and occupational attainment of the workers, the higher the probability of lifetime employment. Female workers have been virtually excluded from it. Thirdly, it should be emphasized that Japan is not unique in having longer duration jobs. Hall (1982) suggested that near lifetime jobs are common even in the U.S., after workers experience a high frequency of short spells of employment during their younger ages. In sum, it is unreasonable to emphasize the importance of lifetime jobs in interpreting the working of the Japanese labour market.

The relationship between labour mobility (turnover) and unemployment is briefly mentioned. More than 90 percent of labour turnovers in Japan are held without having a status of unemployment, as Mizuno (1983) has stated. Most Japanese employees do not experience unemployment when they change employers. Although a smaller frequency of labour turnover makes the rate of unemployment lower in general, the net effect in Japan is very minor for the reason mentioned above.

How should we evaluate the high degree of labour turnover in the U.S.? Although there are several merits and demerits, I find that this is not a harmful phenomenon. For example, since more than 50 percent of workers who are laid-off are recalled and return to their original employers, temporary layoffs can be evaluated as buffers to cope with a fall in demand, and can be regarded as a risk-sharing device by both employers and employees. We showed that Japanese employers and employees used not only flexible working hours as a risk-sharing device but also other practices. If the system of unemployment compensation is prepared well, workers do not necessarily worry about their economic hardships during temporary layoffs. See Feldstein (1975, 1976, 1978), Baily (1977) and Lilien (1980). Of course, the adverse effect of the compensation system must be eliminated. As Medoff (1979) has shown, it is possible to conjecture that unions in the U.S. prefer temporary layoffs to more fluctuations in working hours and wage payments. When a rigorous principle, like the seniority rule, is agreed upon, the cost of the conflict due to temporary layoffs is minimized.

It must be noted, however, that the importance of short-spells of unemployment has been challenged by several studies. For example, Clark and Summers (1979) conclude that only a minor proportion of the aggregate unemployment rate is explained by short spells of unemployment in the U.S. Many countries in Europe also show that the proportion of the long-term unemployed has increased in recent years. Thus, even in the U.S. my positive evaluation of temporary layoffs may no longer be possible.

A troublesome aspect is voluntary quits and working at a different firm. The traditional job search theory suggests that a worker will move to another firm when he (or she) finds a job with a higher wage payment than his (or her) reservation wage. A large number of American studies such as Pencavel (1972), Stoikov and Raimon (1968), Bartel and Borjas (1981), Mincer and Javanovic (1981), and many job search studies suggest that the wage rate is one of the most important factors to explain quits, and that the wage gain from quitting is positive although the gain becomes smaller for older workers and frequent movers. Japanese studies suggest, however, that more than 50 percent of voluntary quits had to accept lower wage payments than their current wages, and that the great majority of them do not receive higher wage payments than their 'reservation' wages, as shown by Tachibanaki (1984b) and (1986). Ono (1981) presented an econometric study, proposing a very minor effect of wages on voluntary quits. Japanese employees do not change their employers to gain a possible increase in wage earnings but for non-monetary incentives. In sum, there is an interesting contrast between the U.S. and Japan with respect to the motivations of voluntary separations. It is hard, however, to argue about which motivation is more flexible or rational with respect to the performance of the labour market.

The most serious demerit of voluntary quits is a loss of specific human capital, as Parsons (1972) pointed out. The quasi-rent shared by a firm, represented by the difference between the worker's marginal value product and the wage, must be lost by a quit. Although deferred payment such as a private pension scheme or seniority wage payment can be considered as a device to prevent such a loss, the loss may be bigger in the U.S. than in Japan in view of more frequent quits in the U.S. as shown by table 4. Probably, Japan shows the steepest age (seniority)-earning profile among the OECD countries. See fig. 3 the age-earning profiles in Japan, the U.K. and the U.S. Perhaps, Japan's having the steepest growth rate of the wage by seniority has contributed to preventing workers from voluntary separations, as several theories of incentives to work or not to shirk, or of a reduction in the uncertainty of future incomes of risk-averse workers proposed by Lazear (1981), Stiglitz and Weiss (1983), and Ioannides and Pissarides (1985) suggest. See Collier and Knight (1985) about a useful first step to initiate serious empirical investigations.

Finally, it is noted that some degree of mobility (or turnover) is desirable because it allocates the work-forces efficiently. In other words, human resources are allocated smoothly, if the labour market has an environment of flexible mobility. For example, one of the reasons for the big difference by regions in the rate of unemployment in the U.K. is regional immobility of workers. With respect to this, the American labour mobility, not only job mobility but also regional mobility, can be evaluated positively. Also, such an environment enables firms to adjust labour input easily, and thus contributes to a better functioning of the labour market. It is not an easy task, however, to define the optimal level of labour mobility.

6. Seriousness of Unemployment

There have been several attempts to estimate the degree of seriousness of the rate of unemployment in Japan. Some believe that the official rate of unemployment does not take account of the heterogeneity of the unemployed people, and that it does not indicate the seriousness of unemployment properly. The argument is that it is necessary to assign some weights when the degree of seriousness is estimated. For example, a middle-aged married man with several children cannot be compared on a common basis with a young unmarried man who is living with his parents even if those two persons are unemployed. The literature on this is reviewed briefly.

There are two types of approaches for estimating the degree of seriousness of unemployment. The first is to examine a particular group of workers (or unemployed people) who are supposed to be much affected by unemployment. The second is to estimate the overall rate of unemployment by assigning various weights to particular groups.

The first type is discussed. First, married men with several children may be regarded as more serious compared with the other groups. Secondly, when we focus on the reasons for becoming unemployed, job losers (i.e., unemployment due to involuntary separation) may be more serious compared with the other motivations, for example voluntarily separated unemployed. Thirdly, if skilled workers (experienced workers) are unemployed, the loss of human resources at the national level may be greater in comparison to the case of less-skilled workers. Fourth, an unemployed person with a longer duration of unemployment may be suffering more compared with an unemployed with a shorter duration. The above examples suggest that a particular aspect such as (1) age, marriage or family status, (2) the reason for becoming unemployed, (3) skill, or (4) duration of unemployment may be applied to examine the seriousness of unemployment. Several economists have investigated this problem by picking up one or two of the aspects mentioned above.

Yashiro (1983) presented his view, by using the first aspect, that since the rate of unemployment by married adult male full-time workers (who may be called 'core workers') was very low even during the stagflation and did not fluctuate much, the seriousness of unemployment can be almost dismissed. He implicitly assumed that an increasing trend in the rate of unemployment of married women might not be serious since they are supported economically by their husbands, and that it would be sufficient if the policy authority paid attention to only the movement of unemployment by the 'core workers'. This opinion was criticized by the public, in particular several activists of women's movements. In view of the fact that Japan adopted an equal employment act between men and women quite recently, the majority of people would accept an equal weight of unemployment between men and women nowadays.

Koike (1984, 1986) made important contributions to the second and third aspects, both focusing on unemployment due to involuntary separations and skill differentials. He found two observations. First, there is a strong negative correlation between a change in the number of unemployed people due to involuntary separations and a change in the labour demand (the number of job vacancies). This is more obvious for males than females. In this regard, a change in the number of unemployed people due to involuntary separations has a time lag of one quarter behind a change in business cycles. Secondly, the majority of involuntary separations (mainly discharges) are middle-aged or older workers in Japan, unlike in the U.K. and U.S. where the strict seniority rule (the less tenured, the more likely discharged or laid-off, or last-in first-out) is held. See Meadoff (1979), and Oswald (1982). The loss of per capita human resources is greater in Japan than the other nations at least with respect to involuntarily separated persons because workers with longer tenures have more skills in general. Thus, so long as a loss of human resources is concerned, the Japanese practice is less flexible than the British or American practice. The seniority rule prevents the loss of skills of workers accumulated at the firm, while the Japanese system encourages the loss of more skills. This does not necessarily imply that the actual aggregate loss of human resources in Japan is greater than in the U.K. or the U.S., since the actual rate of involuntary separations in Japan is lower.

Going back to the story of the seriousness of unemployment, the second type is reviewed. Several attempts have been made to estimate the real rate of unemployment by calculating the weighted average of unemployment by many groups. The second type includes all groups of workers, and calculates the weighted average. A controversy involved is how to choose the base of the weight. Several candidates are (1) income lost during unemployment, (2), working hours lost, (3) the duration of unemployment, (4) heads of households or not, (5) skill lost, etc. In other fields, several attempts which consider not only unemployment but also other aspects of the labour market such as a change in employment, separation and others have been made. Ohashi (1986), Tomita (1986), and Wakisaka (1986) contributed to this issue.

Two important observations were obtained by those studies. First, the seriousness of unemployment calculated by the weighted average of all unemployed people shows more fluctuations than the commonly used rate of unemployment in the time-series data. Secondly, several labour market indexes which are constructed by taking account of a large number of variables such as unemployment, employment, separation, vacancy and others present closer correspondences with the change in the GDP. We found before that no change in the rate of unemployment was observed despite a dramatic fluctuation in the GDP. Thus, it may be concluded that even the Japanese labour market would be sensitive to a change in the output, if the labour market condition was measured properly. In other words, the observed rate of unemployment is a poor indicator of the labour market condition at least in Japan.

7. Concluding remarks

This article examined various aspects of labour market flexibility in Japan, Europe and the U.S. with particular emphasis on Japan. Labour adjustment, wages and labour demand, labour cost, labour supply, labour mobility, seriousness of unemployment and other aspects were examined, and then compared between Japan and the Euro-American countries. It was found that Japan has flexibility in some areas, while rigidity also is observed in other areas. In some cases, flexibility does not contribute to a better performance of the labour market. Also, some sacrifices or costs are paid occasionally in order to achieve flexibility in those areas. Thus, it is not possible to propose that labour market flexibility is always evaluated positively. We have to be careful about introducing labour market flexibility from one country to another country without examining the impact on the labour market and macroeconomy since it may hurt a better aspect in another country. Incidentally, I believe that the main reason for the better performance of the Japanese macroeconomy, if any, is due not to labour market flexibility but to elements other than the working of the labour market, although I have not argued this point at all. I do not deny, however, that labour market flexibility, especially flexible working hours due mainly to overtime hours and the other flexibilities, was effective in minimizing the fluctuation of the rate of unemployment.

Finally, it is noted that the rate of unemployment is a poor indicator of the labour market condition in Japan for the following reasons. First, the rate of unemployment is considerably underestimated because of the existence of discouraged workers. And secondly, a considerable degree of fluctuation is observed in response to a change in output when the index for the labour market condition is measured appropriately, unlike the rate of unemployment.

References

Atoda, N. and T. Tachibanaki, 1986, Earnings distribution and inequality over time: Education vs. relative position and cohorts, unpublished manuscript.

Azariadis, C., 1975, Implicit contracts and unemployment equilibria, Journal of Political Economy 83, no. 6, Dec. 1183–1202.

Baily, M., 1974, Wages and employment under uncertain demand, Review of Economic Studies 41, no. 125, Jan. 37–50.

Baily, M., 1977, On the theory of layoffs and unemployment, Econometrica 45, 1043–1063.

Ball, R.J. and St. Cyr, 1966, Short term employment functions in British manufacturing industry, Review of Economic Studies 33, 179–207.

Bartel, A.P. and G.J. Borjas, 1981, Wage growth and job turnover: An empirical analysis, in: S. Rosen, ed, Studies in Labor Market (The University of Chicago Press), 65–90.

Bell, L.A. and R.B. Freeman, 1985, Does a flexible industry wage structure increase employment?: The U.S. experience, N.B.E.R. working paper, no. 1604.

Branson, W.H. and J.J. Rotemberg, 1980, International adjustment with wage rigidity, European Economic Review 13, 309–332.

Briscoe, G. and D.A. Peel, 1975, The specification of the short-run employment function, Bulletin of the Oxford Institute of Economics and Statistics 37, 115–142.

Brechling, F.P.R., 1965, The relationship between output and employment in British manufacturing industries, Review of Economic Studies 32, 187–216.

Brechling, F.P.R. and P. O'Brien, 1967, Short-run employment functions in manufacturing industries: An international comparison, Review of Economics and Statistics 49, July, 277–287.

Calvo, A.C. and S. Wellisz, 1979, Hierarchy, ability and income distribution, Journal of Political Economy 87, no. 5, Oct., 991–1010.

Clark, K.B. and L.H. Summers, 1979, Labor market dynamics and unemployment: A reconsideration, Brookings Papers on Economic Activities 1, 13–61.

Cole, R.E., 1979, Work, mobility and participation: A comparative study of American and Japanese industry (University of California Press).

Collier, P. and J.B. Knight, 1985, Seniority payments, quit rates and internal labour markets in Britain and Japan, Oxford Bulletin of Economics and Statistics 47, no. 1, Feb., 19–32.

Ehrenberg, R.G., 1971, Fringe benefits and overtime behavior (D.C. Heath & Co.., Massachusetts).

Feldstein, M.S., 1975, The importance of temporary layoffs: An empirical analysis, Brookings Papers on Economic Activities 6, 725–744.

Feldstein, M.S., 1976, Temporary layoffs in the theory of unemployment, Journal of Political Economy 84, 937–957.

Feldstein, M.S., 1978, The effect of unemployment insurance on temporary layoff unemployment, American Economic Review 68, 834–846.

Freeman, R.B. and M.L. Weitzman, 1986, Bonuses and employment in Japan, NBER Working Paper, no. 1878.

Gordon, R.J., 1982, Why U.S. wage and employment behaviour differs from that in Britain and Japan, Economic Journal 92, March, 13–44.

Grubb, D., R. Jackman and R. Layard, 1983, Wage rigidities and unemployment in OECD countries, European Economic Review 21, 11–39.

Hall, R., 1975, The rigidity of wages and the persistence of unemployment, Brookings Papers on Economic Activity 2, 301–350.

Hall, R., 1980, Employment fluctuations and wage rigidities, Brookings Papers on Economic Activity 3, 91–142.

Hall, R., 1982, The importance of lifetime jobs in the U.S. economy, American Economic Review 72, Sept., 716–724.

Hamada, K. and Y. Kurosaka, 1984, The relationship between production and unemployment in Japan: Okun's law in comparative perspective, European Economic Review 25, 71–94.

Hamada, K. and Y. Kurosaka, 1986, Trends in unemployment, wages and productivity: The case of Japan (Conference on the Rise in Unemployment, Sussex, U.K.).

Hamermesh, D.S., 1976, Econometric studies of labor demand and their application to policy analysis, Journal of Human Resources 2, Summer, 310–329.

Hamermesh, D.S., 1985, Job security policy and labour demand: Theory and evidence (A Report to the OECD).

Hart, R.A., 1984, The economics of non-wage labour costs (George Allen & Unwin).

Hart, R.A. and P.G. McGregor, 1982, The returns to labour services in West German manufacturing industry (International Institute of Management, Berlin).

Hashimoto, M., 1979, Bonus payments, on-the-job training and lifetime employment in Japan, Journal of Political Economy 87, Oct., 1086–1104.

Hashimoto, M. and J. Raisin, 1985, Wage flexibility in the United States and Japan, Unpublished manuscript.

Hayami, H., 1986, Wage determination in Japan under changing conditions in world economy, The Monthly Journal of The Japan Institute of Labour 28, June, 16–26 (in Japanese).

Higuchi, Y., 1982, Labour supply behaviour of married women: An analysis of cross-section, time-series and pooled data, Mita Shogaku Kenkyu 25, no. 4, 28–59 (in Japanese).

Higuchi, Y., A. Seike and H. Hayami, 1986, Recent trend in labour mobility in Japan, forthcoming in Economic Policies since World War II in Japan (University of Tokyo Press) (in Japanese).

Ioannides, Y.M. and C.A. Pissarides, 1983, Wages and employment with firm specific seniority, Bell Journal of Economics 14, no. 2, Autumn, 573–580.

Kawashima, Y. and T. Tachibanaki, 1986, The effect of discrimination and of industry segmentation on Japanese wage differentials in relation to education, International Journal of Industrial Organization 4, no. 1, 43–68.

Klau, F. and A. Mittelstadt, 1985, Labour market flexibility and external prime shocks, OECD Working Papers no. 24.

Koike, K., 1981, Skill formation in Japan, Yuhikaku (in Japanese).

Koike, K., 1984, How is unemployment worsened? in, K. Koike, ed. Contemporary Unemployment, Dobunkan (in Japanese).

Koike, K., 1986, Implications of involuntary separations, in: A Report to the Ministry of Labour (in Japanese).

Komiya, R. and K. Yasui, 1984, Japan's macroeconomic performance since the first oil crisis: Review and appraisal, Carnegie-Rochester Conference Series on Public Policy 20, 69–114.

Koshiro, K., 1986, Labor market flexibility in Japan—With special reference to wage flexibility, The Center for International Trade Studies, Yokohama National University, Discussion Paper no. 86–2.

Layard, P.R.G. and S.J. Nickell, 1985, Unemployment, real wages and aggregate demand in Europe, Japan and the U.S., Center for Labour Economics, LSE, Discussion Paper no. 214.

Lazear, E.P., 1981, Agency, earnings profiles, productivity, and hours restrictions, American Economic Review 71, 606–620.

Lilien, D.M., 1980, The cyclical pattern of temporary layoffs in the United States manufacturing, Review of Economics and Statistics 62, Feb., 24–31.

Mairesse, J., 1984, Comments on K. Hamada and Y. Kurosaka, European Economic Review 25, 99–105.

Medoff, J.L., 1979, Layoffs and alternatives under trade unions in U.S. manufacturing, American Economic Review 69, June, 380–395.

Mincer, J. and B. Janovic, 1981, Labour mobility and wages, in: S. Rosen, ed, Studies in labor market (The University of Chicago Press, Chicago, IL) 21–64.

Minford, P., 1983, The labour market in an open economy, Oxford Economic Papers 35, Nov., 531–568.

Ministry of Labour (1986), Annual White Paper on the Labour Market (in Japanese).

Mizuno, A., 1983, Dynamics of Employment and Unemployment, Keizaigaku-Ronso 24, 37–61 (in Japanese).

Mizuno, A., 1985, Wage flexibility and employment fluctuation, in: R. Nakamura, S. Nishikawa and Y. Kosai, eds., Economic system in contemporary Japan, 50–73 (in Japanese).

Muramatsu, K., 1983, Labour market analysis in Japan: Internal labour market, Hakuto-shobo (in Japanese).

Muramatsu, K., 1985, The impact of wages on employment: A survey, Academia 871, July, 1–25 (in Japanese).

Muramatsu, K., 1986, Discharge and its alternatives, in: M. Mizuno, T. Matsugi and Th. Dams, eds., Mechanization and employment: A comparison between Japan and West Germany (Nagoya University Press), 133–164 (in Japanese).

Nadiri, M., 1968, The effects of relative prices and capacity on the demand for labor in the U.S. manufacturing sector, Review of Economic Studies 35, July, 273–288.

Nadiri, M. and S. Rosen, 1974, A disequilibrium model of demand for factors of production, NBER.

Nakamura, J., 1983, The role of the labour market for solving the problem of stagflation, Economic Studies Quarterly XXXIV, Aug., 147–155 (in Japanese).

Nakamura, J., 1984, Macroeconomic policy and employment–unemployment, in: K. Koike, ed., Contemporary unemployment, Dobunkan, 175–200 (in Japanese).

Nickell, S., 1982, Research into unemployment; A partial view of the economic literature, Center for Labour Economics, LSE, Disucssion Paper no. 131.

Nickell, S. and M. Andrews, 1983, Unions, real wages and employment in Britain, 1951–79, Oxford Economic Papers, Nov., 507–530.

Nickell, S. and M. Andrews, 1984, An investigation of the determinants of manufacturing employment in the United Kingdom, Review of Economic Studies LI, no. 4, Oct., 529–558.

Nurkse, R., 1953, Problems of capital formation in underdeveloped countries (Blackwell, Oxford).

OECD, 1983, Employment Outlook 1983, 1984.

Ohashi, I., 1986, Searching for the index of the seriousness of unemployment, in: A Report to the Ministry of Labour (in Japanese).

Ohtake, F., 1986, On flexibility of real wages, in: A Report to the Ministry of Labour (in Japanese).

Okun, A.M., 1981, Prices and quantities, (Blackwell, Oxford).

Ono, A., 1981, Japanese labour market: Function and structure of external labour market, Toyokeizai-shimposha (in Japanese).

Osward, A.J., 1982, The microeconomic theory of the trade union, Economic Journal 92, 576–595.

Parsons, D.O., 1972, Specific human capital: An application to quits rates and layoff rates, Journal of Political Economy 80, Nov./Dec., 1120–1143.

Pencavel, J.H., 1972, Wages, specific training, and labour turnover in U.S. manufacturing industries, International Economic Review 13, Feb., 53–64.

Rosen, S., 1968, Short-run employment variation on Class-I railroads in the U.S., 1947–63, Econometrica 36, 511–529.

Rosen, S., 1982, Authority, control, and the distribution of earnings, The Bell Journal of Economics and Management 13, no. 2, Autumn, 311–323.

Sacks, J., 1979, Wages, profits and macroeconomic adjustment: A comparative study, Brookings Papers on Economic Activity 2, 269–319.

Sacks, J., 1983, Real wages and unemployment in the OECD countries, Brookings Papers on Economic Activity 1, 255–304.

Seike, A., 1985, The employment adjustment in Japanese manufacturing industries in the 1970s, Keio Business Review 22, no. 3.

Shimada, H., T. Hosokawa and A. Seike, 1981, A study on labour market structure, Economic Planning Agency (in Japanese).

Shimada, H., 1981, Earnings structure and human investment: A comparison between the United States and Japan, Kogakusha.

Shimada, H. and Y. Higuchi, 1985, An analysis of trends in female labor force participation in Japan, Journal of Labour Economics 3, no. 1, part 2, S355–S374.

Shinkai, Y., 1982, Anatomy of contemporary macroeconomic problems, Toyokeisai-shimposha (in Japanese).

Shinozuka, E. and E. Ishihara, 1977, Employment adjustment after the oil crisis: A comparison of four countries and firm–size differentials, Japanese Economic Studies (Nihon Keizai Kenkyu) 6, August (in Japanese).

Shinozuka, E. and E. Ishihara, 1980, Recent employment adjustment by firm--size differentials, R. Nakamura and S. Nishikawa, ed., Contemporary labour market analysis, Sogorodo-kenkyu-sho (in Japanese).

Shinozuka, E. and E. Ishihara, 1977, Employment adjustment in Japanese manufacturing industries: 1971–83, Japanese Economic Studies (Nihon Keizai Kenkyu), no. 15, March, 61–72 (in Japanese).

Soligo, R., 1966, The short-run relationship between employment and output, Yale Economic Essays 6, Spring, 161–215.

Stiglitz, J.E. and A. Weiss, 1983, Incentive effects of terminations: Applications to the credit and labour markets, American Economic Review 73, no. 5, Dec., 912–927.

Stoikov, V. and R.L. Raimon, 1968, Determinants of differences in quit rate among industries, American Economic Review, Dec., 1281–1298.

Symons, J., 1985, Relative prices and the demand for labour in British manufacturing, Economica 52, 205, Feb., 37–50.

Symons, J. and R. Layard, 1984, Neoclassical demand for labour functions for six major economies, Economic Journal 94, Dec., 788–799.

Tachibanaki, T., 1975, Wage determinations in Japanese manufacturing industries: Structural change and wage differentials, International Economic Review 16, no. 3, Oct., 562–586.

Tachibanaki, T., 1982, Further results on Japanese wage differentials: Nenko wages, hierarchical position, bonuses and working hours, International Eeconomic Review 23, no. 2, June, 447–461.

Tachibanaki, T., 1984a, Labor mobility and job tenure, in: M. Aoki, ed. The economic analysis of the Japanese firm (North-Holland, Amsterdam).

Tachibanaki, T., 1984b, Measurement of unemployment, international comparisons and the effect of unemployment compensation on the duration of unemployment, in: K. Koike, ed., Contemporary unemployment, 89–115 (in Japanese).

Tachibanaki, T., 1984, Unemployment problem of the youth, The Monthly Journal of The Japan Institute of Labour 26, Dec., 12–22 (in Japanese).

Tachibanaki, T., 1986, Subjective satisfaction and objective economic and social background in labour turnover, unpublished manuscript.

Tomita, Y., 1986, Seriousness of unemployment on the basis of employment statistics, in: A Report to the Ministry of Labour (in Japanese).

Wakisaka, A., 1986, Seriousness of female unemployment: A study of employment status survey, in: A Report to the Ministry of Labour (in Japanese).

Weitzman, M.L., 1984, The share economy (Harvard University Press, Cambridge, MA).

Yashiro, N., 1982, An economic analysis of women workers: Another subtle revaluation, Toyokeizai-shimposha (in Japanese).

Yoshitomi, M., 1981, Japanese economy, Toyokeizai-shimposha (in Japanese).

COMMENTS

'Labour Market Flexibility in Japan in Comparison with Europe and the U.S.' by T. Tachibanaki

Richard LAYARD

I am not an expert on Japan, so I will base my remarks on some of the stylised facts which emerge from this interesting and informative paper. There seem to me to be three major questions.

(1) Why does unemployment fluctuate so little in Japan?
(2) Why is unemployment so low in Japan?
(3) How serious is unemployment in Japan?

Low fluctuations in unemployment

In comparison with other countries, Japan seems to rank as follows, in terms of the variability of

output	high
worker-hours	average
hours per worker	high
employment	low
unemployment	very low
real earnings	high

These remarks relate to the standard deviation of the detrended logarithm of each variable, and are based on table 1, as well as Gordon (1982) and Wadhwani (1985).

The first finding, on output, is important because it casts doubt on Weitzman's thesis that it is profit-sharing which is stabilising employment. In a pure profit-sharing economy, output would be stable as well as employment [Wadhwani (1987)]. The reason why Japanese employment is stable is not that shocks have no effect on output. As Wadhwani shows, they do, as much as elsewhere. The difference is that in Japan the fluctuation in output is mainly absorbed by fluctuation in hours per worker. This must be due to implicit contracts, which are felt to be more important in Japan and are reflected in longer job durations. The less generous availability of social security may be another reason why lay-offs are avoided. So we get high fluctuation of hours per worker. When hours per worker vary there are high returns to scale (Feldstein, 1968), and this 'explains' how output can be so variable relative to worker-hours. Finally, unemployment varies less than employment due to the fact that the labour force is pro-cyclical, with discouraged secondary and temporary workers leaving in recessions.

As regards real earnings, these vary a lot; and this is the mechanism which helps to stabilise employment. After an adverse productivity shock (or an import price rise) employment has only to fall a little to generate a big fall in real wages. This is enough to restore employment. This process was outlined at an earlier ISOM meeting (Grubb, Jackman and Layard (1983) and has since been beautifully displayed in Newell and Symons (1985).

The author however questions the Phillips curve relation underlying this interpretation. He implies that, if unemployment varies little and real wages a lot, one is bound to get the impression that small changes in employment cause large changes in real wages, even if they do not. The argument is wrong. If the variance of unemployment is low, it is all the more impressive that one can detect its influence with a significant t-statistic in a Phillips curve. There is further evidence that we are measuring a genuine response of wages to the labour market. If in the Phillips curve the independent variable is log vacancies (rather than unemployment), its effect is twice as high in Japan as anywhere else and highly significant [Johnson and Layard (1986)].

Thus Japanese unemployment fluctuates little for three reasons: due to implicit contracts hours fluctuate a lot; the labour force moves with employment; and wages respond a lot.

Low level of unemployment

The low *level* of Japanese unemployment is a different issue (except to the extent that the effect of shocks are perpetuated by hysteresis). What institutional features could explain the low Japanese NAIRU?

A starting point is the observation in the paper that employment is roughly

permanent employees	40 per cent
temporary employees	30 per cent
self-employed	30 per cent

For temporary employees we have a labour market which roughly clears. So the problems which arise from institutional wage pressure are confined to 40 per cent of the market. In addition, lay-offs are not by inverse seniority, so that those who control the union are not themselves immune from the employment effects of the wage bargain. Moreover the percentage unionised in Japan is low by world standards. So we have an economy where institutional wage pressure is a less all-absorbing problem, with a big self-employed sector providing an alternative outlet for those who might be unemployed in a pure wage-system. In addition the self-employed sector is a source of additional labour and thus prevents overheating when the modern sector expands, just as in Europe in the 1950s and 1960s workers moved from agriculture to the towns and prevented overheating of the urban labour market.

Social security too may play a role. Benefits run out after a year for long-term workers and much quicker for those with shorter work histories. This helps to prevent the build-up of long-term unemployment. Finally, there has been, until recently, the high rate of productivity growth, which is a wonderful oiler of the wheels and mollifier of the struggle for income shares. It will be very interesting to see whether Japanese unemployment remain so low, as productivity growth abates.

How serious is Japanese unemployment?

The author speculates about how serious Japanese unemployment is. My own view is that relative to other countries it is no more serious than appears from the crude (and amazingly low) figures. The author suggests otherwise. He suggests that there are large numbers of discouraged workers, and others who are rationed to part-time rather than full-time work. Both these facts matter but they do not matter anything like as much as people who are actively looking for full-time work and have none.

To measure the cost of unemployment to an individual one should evaluate the welfare triangle that (s)he losses by not being able to work as many annual hours as (s)he would choose. The cost (relative to annual income) is approximately proportional to d^2/η, where d is the fraction of desired hours for which unemployed and η is the elasticity of supply of annual hours [Layard (1981)]. Since the amount of unemployment the individual experiences is measured by d, the average seriousness of each unit of unemployment is proportional to d/η. It is worse the lower the supply elasticity and the longer the duration. Discouraged workers must have high supply elasticities, as have some married women seeking work. Most married men have low supply elasticities, which is why their unemployment is particularly inefficient. It is good that Japan has so little of it. It is also excellent that Japanese unemployment is so relatively short. Youth unemployment of 4.5 percent is not so good, since that has effects on the supply of skill and work attitudes. But Japanese economists need not lean over backwards to disparage their own garden. Everything there may not be perfect, but most of us would willingly change it for our own.

References

Feldstein, M., 1968, Specification of the labour input in the aggregate production function, Review of Economic Studies 34, no. 4, Oct.

Gordon, R.J., 1982, Why U.S. wage and employment behaviour differs from that in Britain and Japan, Economic Journal 92, no. 365, March, 13–45.

Grubb, D., R. Jackman and R. Layard, 1983, Wage rigidity and unemployment in OECD countries, European Economic Review 21, 11–39.

Johnson, G. and R. Layard, 1986, The natural rate of unemployment: Explanation and policy, in: O. Ashenfelter and R. Layard eds., Handbook of labor economics (North-Holland, Amsterdam).

Layard, R., 1981, Measuring the duration of unemployment: A note, Scottish Journal of Political Economy, Nov.

Newell, A. and J. Symons, 1985, Wages and employment in the OECD countries, Discussion paper no. 219 (Centre for Labour Economics, London School of Economics).

Wadhwani, S., 1987, The macroeconomic implications of profit-sharing: Some empiricial evidence, Economic Journal, Suppl., March.

COMMENTS

'Labour Market Flexibility in Japan in Comparison with Europe and the U.S.' by T. Tachibanaki

Jacques MAIRESSE

Toshiaki Tachibanaki's survey paper is an effort to analyse the various dimensions of 'labour market flexibility' in Japan in a comparative perspective. It is particularly interesting and valuable since he has direct access to the recent booming literature by Japanese economists (in Japanese) on this topic. The issue of labour market flexibility, however, raises various definitional problems and there are many aspects to it. For a short survey the subject may be in fact too wide. Given this large scope of his topic, Tachibanaki has done a good job, and one, who is not an expert on either Japan or labour markets, learns a great deal from reading his paper.

I shall restrict my comments to giving a general feeling and underlying observations, and I shall end on a couple of more specific econometric considerations.

Like other Japanese economists, it seems that Tachibanaki is inclined to somehow minimize or downplay the differences between the Japanese economy and the European and U.S. economies. A priori I am sympathetic to his attitude, and I am quite willing to believe that a number of such differences are not well established or very important, and that they have been overstressed. However, in reading his paper, I have the strong feeling that even if the Japanese economy does not differ in many respects from the western economies more than they do between themselves, the society at large (i.e., the social environment, the behavioural rules and values) is indeed very different. To the extent that there is a definite westernization process of the cultural attitudes and beliefs of the Japanese people (as Tachibanaki suggests in some ways) there seems to be still a very long way to go.

At a general level, the issue of labour market flexibility can be viewed as one of a compromise (or a trade off) between social and economic targets (or social and economic constraints). Enforcing social guaranties and rights for the workers imposes restrictions and rigidities for the operation and management of the firms. Conversely trying to improve the flexibility and efficiency of the labour market, in order to accommodate economic pressures and to cope with economic crises, leads to the loosening or abandonment of social advantages. In this respect, one finds in Tachibanaki's paper an impressive list of more or less socially rooted differences between Japan and most European countries and between Japan and the U.S. Let us go over this list rapidly.

(*1*) The extreme flexibility of labour force participation or the existence of a large number of discouraged workers, mainly women. On this point, one may remember the startling figure given in the Hamada and Kurosaka paper presented in this conference three years ago.[1] In Japan between 1973 and 1975, after the first oil shock, the number of men and women who were discouraged and went out of the 'labour force' increased by 350,000 and 840,000 respectively, while the number of those who stayed as officially unemployed increased only by 220,000 and 100,000 respectively. The estimates cited in the present paper give a similar picture. While the official unemployment rate was 2.2 percent in Japan in 1978 as against 6.0 percent in the U.S., 8.9 percent of workers (among those out of the 'labour force') were discouraged in Japan as against 1.4 percent only in the U.S. If we assume that the proportion of discouraged workers was the same in Japan as in the U.S. (and if we take the average rate of labour force participation to be 0.65 in Japan[2]), the rate of unemployment would also be about the same

---

[1]Hamada and Kurosaka (1984). Reference given by Tachibanaki.
[2]OECD Economic Studies, 'Japan', 1986 (Table 25).

in the two countries. Even if the importance of discouraged workers has been declining recently in Japan, there is still a striking difference with the U.S. and I think with most European countries.

(*2*) The existence of an increasing number of involuntary part-time workers, mainly women. Apparently these are taking the place of discouraged workers in recent years.

(*3*) The relative importance of lay offs of middle aged or older workers, or their relegations to subsidiaries companies, in spite of (or in part because of) the Nenko seniority wage system, and in spite of the existence of lifetime employment implicit contracts for the more qualified fraction of the labor force in the large firms.

(*4*) The fact that half of the workers who are said to quit voluntarily their positions had to accept lower wages in their new jobs.

(*5*) The high level of total annual working hours in Japan relative to the western countries: 2,152 hours in 1983 as against 1,898 in the U.S. and 1,657 in France.

(*6*) The relative weakness of labour unions as compared to Europe.

(*7*) The low level of unemployment compensation.

(*8*) The general fact that employment protection laws are less stringent than in Europe.

(*9*) The fact that minimum wages vary widely by regions, and are not well enforced.

(*10*) The fact also that the 'Equal Employment and Treatment Act' is recent in Japan and has no penalty provisions.

(*11*) The low cost of the social security (health and pensions programs) for the Japanese firms, until now, as compared to their European counterparts.

One must admit that taken together this list of differences is impressive. Of course the problem for us is whether these differences matter much for the working of the economy as a whole, and to what extent they can explain the remarkable Japanese economic performances, specially in the last decade, in comparison to the other industrial countries? More specifically the question is how are these differences reflected in the main equations of our simple macro-models?

My econometric remarks concern precisely the specification of the wage and labour demand equations in such a model. I quite agree with Tachibanaki's criticism about the estimation of the 'Phillips curve' in Japan, and for the same reasons about that of the 'Okun's law'. Since the official rate of unemployment varies very little, due mainly to the existence of a pool of 'discouraged workers', one has to deal with a particular type of errors in variables problem. One way to go about it is to adopt an unofficial rate of unemployment, adding back the discouraged workers, or a fraction of them, to the officially unemployed workers. With such a correction, we can expect that the estimated elasticity of the wage relative to unemployment or that of the output gap (Okun's coefficient) would go down for Japan and would fall closer in line with the orders of magnitude found for the other countries.

A similar problem arises with the estimation of the elasticity of labour relative to output, either in terms of the number of employees or in terms of total hours of work. Output fluctuations, even after detrending, are much larger in Japan than in the other countries (see Tachibanaki, table 1, panel B). A great part of these fluctuations, however, may be transitory, while in a proper specification of labour demand equations the permanent or expected changes of output should be the main determinants. If this specification problem is not taken into account, the labour elasticities will be under-estimated. Besides the various explanations given by Tachibanaki, this may be one important reason why the adjustment of employment appears to be relatively slow and rigid in Japan.

European Economic Review 31 (1987) . North-Holland

PRODUCTIVITY, WAGES, AND PRICES INSIDE AND OUTSIDE OF MANUFACTURING IN THE U.S., JAPAN, AND EUROPE*

Robert J. GORDON

Northwestern University, Evanston, IL 60201, USA
National Bureau of Economic Research, Washington, DC, USA

1. Introduction

1.1. The issues

On the eastern side of the Atlantic only one great economic puzzle of the 1980s is acknowledged: persistently high unemployment in Europe. Faced with an unwillingness of policymakers to reduce unemployment by expanding aggregate demand, many economists and commentators have retreated into cataloguing a litany of European supply-side maladies. To construct this list of ills, Europeans often cast envious glances toward America and Japan to reveal those aspects of European economic institutions that are different, and hence 'worse'.

Based on a new data set and a methodology that differs from most past research on comparative macroeconomic behavior, this paper argues that, whatever other differences between Europe and the U.S. may exist, any differences in the cyclical dynamics of productivity, wage, and price behavior have been greatly exaggerated. There is little evidence to support previous claims that, in comparison with the U.S., Europe exhibits (a) classical short-run diminishing returns in the relationship between output and labor input, (b) greater 'rigidity' of real wage behavior, or (c) greater 'flexibility' of nominal wage and price behavior. The absence of a case supporting a unique set of cyclical aggregate supply responses in Europe undermines the case against policies that expand the growth rate of nominal aggregate demand in order to raise output and reduce unemployment in Europe. The main emphasis in this paper is on comparisons between Europe and the U.S.;

*This research has been supported by the National Science Foundation and the German Marshall Fund. I am grateful to Jacques Artus for contributing segments of the data, to Daniel Shiman for creating the data bank, and for helpful comments to William Branson, Heinz Konig, and participants in workshops at the Institut fur Weltwirtschaft, Kiel and the Centre for Labour Economics, London School of Economics. I owe special thanks to Clarissa Compaq and Ronald Rats for helping me with the estimation, and to Wanda Wordperfect for impeccable secretarial assistance.

however, evidence for Japan is also presented that confirms important differences between Japan and both Europe and the U.S.

1.2. The central role of the real wage

Evaluations of the European unemployment problem often center around a distinction between Keynesian and classical unemployment, in which the real wage plays a central role. Evidence for classical unemployment is provided by a demonstration that growth in European real wages has been excessive, and that employment responds negatively to an increase in the real wage. A widely discussed summary measure of the excess component of the real wage, popularized by Bruno and Sachs (1981, 1985) and Sachs (1979, 1983), is the 'wage gap', an index of the ratio of the real wage to labor's average product, which amounts simply to an index of labor's share in national income. In their analyses of European unemployment and stagflation, Bruno and Sachs have exhibited wage gap indexes that increase much more in Europe than in the U.S., and they, together with numerous other authors [especially Layard and Nickell (1984), Bean, Layard and Nickell (1985), and Newell and Symons (1985)] have shown that employment and labor hours exhibit a strong negative elasticity to changes in the real wage.

But the case for an excessive real wage as the crux of the European unemployment has been carried too far. The European problem of declining employment and rising unemployment is centered in the manufacturing sector, yet the European wage gap index for manufacturing has fallen steadily since the late 1970s and is now well below the value of the same index for U.S. manufacturing. Even more inconvenient is the enormous rise in the Japanese wage gap, which dwarfs anything experienced in Europe, without any slowdown in the growth of labor input.

So much has been said about the evil of higher real wages that the benefits of higher real wages, enjoyed throughout history, seem to have been forgotten. The *negative* response of labor hours to an increase in the real wage implies a *positive* response of output per hour to the same increase. Indeed, substitution away from labor in response to an inexorable rise in the real wage has been at the heart of the economic growth process for centuries. In a statistical decomposition, we show below that a substantial component of accelerations and decelerations of productivity growth in Europe, Japan, and even in the U.S. can be attributed to the behavior of the wage gap.

The response of employment to changes in the real wage constitutes only half of the circle linking the two. The Phillips curve can be interpreted as postulating a positive response in the *growth* of the real wage to the level of detrended employment. Thus a stimulus to aggregate demand provides not only the direct benefit of raising output and employment, but also the indirect benefit of raising the real wage and creating substitution away from labor that boosts productivity and, if sustained, the nation's standard of living. With this dual benefit obtainable from demand expansion, the case against demand stimulation must rest with convincing evidence that such policies would create an unacceptable acceleration of inflation.

1.3. The research agenda in this paper

This paper is a comprehensive study of the interrelationships among productivity, wages, and prices in the U.S., Japan, and Europe. New statistical evidence is provided on the four major issues introduced above, (1) the behavior of an index of the wage gap (labor's share), corrected for a major conceptual error in past measures of this concept, (2) the response of employment and productivity to changes in the real wage and the wage gap, (3) the 'Phillips-curve' response of real wages to economic slack, and (4) the division of a nominal demand change between inflation and real output growth. While each of these four issues has been studied by numerous authors, the research undertaken here is unique in its data base, distinction between manufacturing and non-manufacturing, and econometric specification.

Almost all previous studies in this area have used data that are inconsistent by sector, leading to regressions in which the wage rate in the manufacturing sector is related to employment or unemployment in the aggregate economy. Yet in 1984 manufacturing value added was only 24 percent of total output in the U.S. and 29 percent in Europe. In contrast, this study is based on a consistent data base in which time series for 14 countries over the 1961–84 interval have been developed for the aggregate economy, for the manufacturing sector, and for the non-manufacturing (residual) sector. The data series available for all three sectors in each of the 14 countries include such variables as real value added, the value added deflator, compensation per hour, employment, and hours per employee.[1] As we shall see, this distinction between sectors is important, for the interpretion of the productivity growth slowdown, as well as constructed 'wage gap' measures, display quite different time series behavior inside and outside of manufacturing.

A further innovation in the data base corrects an error in previous measures of the wage gap or 'labor's share'. While employment and person-hours data include not only employees but also the self-employed, the income of the self-employed is included in the official OECD national accounting system as part of capital's 'operating surplus' rather than as part

---

[1]The 14 countries are (in the order listed in table 1) U.S., Canada, Japan, Austria, Belgium, Denmark, France, Germany, Italy, Netherlands, Norway, Sweden, Switzerland, and U.K. Countries included in the L.S.E. Centre for Labour Economics data bank, but excluded here, are Australia, Finland, Ireland, New Zealand, and Spain.

of the income of labor. When the income of the self-employed, which the OECD calls 'household entrepreneurial income' is added to the compensation of employees and treated as part of labor's income share, the secular increase in labor's share in Europe and Japan, to which Bruno and Sachs have previously called attention, disappears almost entirely. Rather than criticizing the concept of the wage gap upon which previous investigators have based their claim that European unemployment is 'classical', this paper shows that the properly measured wage gap shows little if any secular increase not just in the U.S., but also in Europe and Japan.

To take advantage of the new information contained in the data base, all regression equations describing the behavior of productivity, wage, and price changes are estimated separately for the three sectors (aggregate, manufacturing, and non-manufacturing). To limit the scope and length of the paper, which would otherwise be unmanageable, results for the 11 European countries are not reported separately. Instead, an aggregate for 'Europe' has been constructed. Thus all results are presented in groups of nine, three sectors for three 'countries' (U.S., Japan, and Europe).[2]

The econometric specification builds on my own past research for the U.S. and hence differs markedly from most other work on these issues. Since unemployment rates by sector are conceptually meaningless, the measure of cyclical variability that enters the productivity, wage, and price equations is detrended sectoral output rather than the level of unemployment. All equations are estimated in first differences rather than levels in order to avoid spurious correlations among variables (especially productivity and the real wage) that display common changes in trend. Special attention is given to the response of real wage changes to the productivity growth slowdown that has occurred everywhere, an issue that is ignored in the majority of studies that include only a single constant term in equations explaining wage changes, and yet is essential in testing the hypothesis that real wage growth in Europe was too 'rigid' to respond to the post-1973 productivity growth slowdown. Wage and price equations are based on an explicit model of disequilibrium labor market adjustment, in contrast to some work [especially Newell and Symons (1985)] based on a market-clearing interpretation.

1.4. Themes that emerge

The results cast doubt on some of the contrasts between the U.S. and Europe that have received heavy emphasis in previous research. While we confirm the real-wage elasticity of labor input stressed in papers by Layard and Nickell and Newell and Symons, we find that the response of labor input and labor productivity to changes in the real wage is roughly similar in

---

[2]Canada is also omitted, since we saw no point in constructing a 'North American' aggregate that would be totally dominated by the U.S.

the three countries, rather than being especially high in Europe. There is absolutely no evidence to support Sachs' (1983) claim that productivity in Europe is 'classical', varying countercyclically, in contrast to procyclical movements in the U.S.

The apparent consensus that European real wages are excessive is simplistic; in 1984 the European wage gap was lower than the U.S. wage gap in manufacturing but higher in non-manufacturing, creating problems for classical interpretations of unemployment in Europe where the great bulk of the employment decline has occurred in manufacturing. The high wage gaps in the non-manufacturing sector in Europe and Japan are shown to result almost entirely from the omission of self-employment income as part of labor's share in national income.

The wage and price equations estimated in the paper address the common distinction between real wage rigidity in Europe and nominal wage rigidity in the U.S. [see especially Branson and Rotemberg (1980)]. We find that the bulge in the wage gaps of Europe and Japan in the 1970s is not due primarily to a failure of real wages to decelerate in response to the post-1973 productivity growth slowdown, but rather results in large part from episodes of autonomous 'wage push' in Europe in the late 1960s and in Japan during 1973–74. In this sense, real wages in Europe and Japan were too *flexible*, rather than too *rigid*.

The nominal wage rigidity part of the Branson and Rotemberg dichotomy receives only partial support. Some specifications indicate roughly similar cyclical responsiveness of nominal wage rates in Europe and the U.S. for the aggregate economy, leaving only the manufacturing sector to support Branson and Rotemberg on the grounds that there is almost complete nominal rigidity for U.S. manufacturing. Yet what matters is the aggregate economy, and here the differences among the U.S., Japan, and Europe are minimal. Responses of the nominal wage rate to the output ratio are of roughly the same order of magnitude in the three aggregate economies, The sectoral division between manufacturing and non-manufacturing displays the expected result that there is little cyclical responsiveness of wage rates in U.S. manufacturing, but the unexpected result that there is also less cyclical responsiveness in Japanese manufacturing than in Europe, and more cyclical responsiveness in both the U.S. and European non-manufacturing sectors than in Japan. These results suggest that the emphasis in my own past research (1982, 1983) on the greater nominal wage rigidity in the U.S. than in Japan may be limited in applicability to the manufacturing sector, and that differences in nominal wage flexibility in the aggregate economy (and in the nonmanufacturing sector) may be much less than is commonly supposed.

2. A disequilibrium wage and price adjustment model

This section develops an explicit model of disequilibrium wage and price adjustment in the labor market.[3] The approach is based on the assumption that the nominal wage rate adjusts in response to any change in the size of the gap between labor demand and supply. The advantage of the formulation is that the influence of supply shocks, of the post-1973 productivity slow-down, and of tax changes on wage and price behavior can be motivated concretely in the model. This section concludes by using the model to develop definitions of the much-discussed concepts of real and nominal wage stickiness, the output gap, and the natural rate of unemployment.

2.1. The static labor market model

The exposition begins with a production function in which output (Q_t) is written as a function of labor input (N_t) and a multiplicative factor Θ_t that incorporates the effects of capital and materials inputs and of technological change

$$Q_t = \Theta_t Q(N_t), \qquad Q' > 0. \tag{1}$$

The real product wage, which is set equal to the marginal product of labor, is expressed as the ratio of the actual wage rate, W_t, to the expected product price, P_t^e, adjusted for the influence of indirect taxes, T_t^1. Payroll taxes do not enter into the expression for the real product wage, because the wage concept in our data (W_t) is measured gross of all payroll taxes paid by employers and employees

$$\frac{W_t T_t^1}{P_t^e} = \Theta_t Q'(N_t). \tag{2}$$

Here the expression T^1 represents an indirect tax factor, defined as

$$T^1 = \left[\frac{1}{1 - \tau^1} \right],$$

where τ^1 is the indirect tax rate.

Eq. (2), inverted, expresses the demand for labor as a function of the real expected product wage, adjusted for the tax term, T_t^1, and the productivity shift factor, Θ_t

$$N_t^d = N^d \left[\frac{W_t T_t^1}{\Theta_t P_t^e} \right], \qquad N'^d < 0. \tag{3}$$

---

[3]This model was first developed in Gordon (1977b) and was recently applied to the U.S. economy in Gordon (1985). The version set out here uses a different definition of the wage rate (gross of all employment taxes) and also solves out the consumer price index term that appears in previous versions of the model.

The supply of labor is a positively sloped function of the real wage stated in terms of the expected consumer price index, C_t^e, with an adjustment for a personal tax factor, $T_t^P = [1/(1 - \tau_t^P)] \cdot [1/(1 - \tau_t^S)]$, where τ_t^P is the personal tax rate and τ_t^S is the total payroll tax rate on both employers and employees, included in our measure of the wage rate (W_t)

$$N_t^s = N^s\left[\frac{W_t}{R_t T_t^P C_t^e}\right], \qquad N'^s > 0. \tag{4}$$

In eq. (4) the factor R_t is the 'aspiration' real wage that workers compare with the tax-adjusted real expected wage.

The excess demand for labor, X_t, can be expressed as the ratio of labor demand to labor supply

$$X_t = N_t^d/N_t^s, \tag{5}$$

so that in equilibrium $X_t = 1$ and $\log X_t = 0$. This expression can be converted into a relationship between the proportional rates of growth of the demand for and supply of labor by substituting eqs. (3) and (4) into eq. (5), taking time derivatives of the log version of (5), and rearranging

$$x_t = -(a+b)(w - \theta - p^e)_t + b(r - \theta + c^e - p^e + t^P)_t - at_t^l. \tag{6}$$

Here lowercase letters indicate rates of change $(w = d \log W/dt)$, and a and b are, respectively, the real-wage elasticities of labor demand and supply.

2.2. The Phillips curve wage equation

The Phillips curve adjustment hypothesis is that the nominal wage rate moves in the direction needed to eliminate the excess demand for labor at a rate that depends on the size of the gap between demand and supply

$$x_t = -g \log(X_t), \tag{7}$$

where once again lowercase letters represent proportional rates of change. Thus in equilibrium $x_t = \log(X_t) = 0$. When the right-hand sides of eqs. (6) and (7) are set equal to each other and solved for the rate of change of real unit labor cost, the result is the augmented Phillips curve wage change equation

$$w_t - \theta_t - p_t^e = \frac{1}{a+b}[b(r - \theta + c^e - p^e + t^P)_t - at_t^l + g \log(X_t)]. \tag{8}$$

Our subsequent reduced form equation is simplified if at this stage we eliminate the expected change in the consumer price index (c_t^e) from (8) by assuming that the only difference between the changes in the consumer and producer price indexes ($c-p$) is due to the difference between the change in import (p_t^F) and export (p_t^X) prices

$$c_t = p_t + j(p_t^F - p_t^X), \tag{9}$$

where we apply the same weight (j) to import and export prices on the assumption of balanced trade. If the rate of change of import and export prices is the same, then the $c-p$ term drops out. We shall make the alternative simplifying assumption that the growth rate of export prices is the same as that of domestic producer prices, so that

$$(c-p)_t = j(p_t^F - p_t). \tag{10}$$

When (10) is substituted into (8), we obtain the modified augmented Phillips curve wage change equation

$$w_t - \theta_t - p_t^e = \frac{1}{a+b}\{b[r - \theta + j(p^F - p) + t^P]_t - at_t^l + g\log(X_t)\}, \tag{11}$$

where the distinction between the actual and expected change in the real import price term has been dropped.

2.3. Price equations: Markup and reduced-form

Eq. (11) describes the time series behavior of the rate of change in the nominal wage rate and in the wage gap ($w_t - \theta_t - p_t$). To determine the cyclical behavior of the inflation rate to changes in demand or supply, (11) must be supplemented by an explicit hypothesis regarding the determination of prices. We assume that the product price is set as a weighted average of domestic unit labor cost adjusted for the indirect tax factor T_t^l introduced in eq. (2), and the import price P_t^F, with a variable markup, M, that depends on excess demand (V_t) in the commodity market

$$P_t = T_t^l M(V_t)(W_t/\Theta_t)^h (P_t^F)^{1-h}. \tag{12}$$

Although imports are excluded from the domestic value-added price index (P), nevertheless the prices of foreign goods can influence domestic value-added prices through their effect on import substitutes. The weight h incorporates this effect, and h would be expected to differ from the import share j that appears above in eq. (10).

By taking the time derivative of the logarithmic version of (12), we obtain an expression that relates the current inflation rate to the current rates of change of unit labor cost, foreign prices, excess commodity demand, and the indirect tax factor

$$p_t = h(w_t - \theta_t) + (1 - h)p_t^F + t_t^I + m(v_t). \tag{13}$$

Now, substituting the wage change eq. (11) into the price change equation (13), it is possible to obtain a reduced-form expression for the inflation rate that does not directly involve the wage rate

$$p_t = p_t^e + m(v_t) + \frac{hg \log(X_t)}{a + b}$$

$$+ \left[(1 - h) + \frac{hbj}{a + b} \right](p^F - p)_t + \frac{1}{a + b}\{hb(r - \theta + t^P)_t + [b + a(1 - h)]t_t^I\}. \tag{14}$$

To interpret eq. (14), it helps to combine all of the terms on the second line into a single 'cost-push' or 'supply-shift' term z_t, where

$$z_t = [(a + b)(1 - h) + hbj](p^F - p)_t + \{hb(r - \theta + t^P)_t + [b + a(1 - h)]t_t^I\}. \tag{15}$$

This definition allows us to write a more compact version of the reduced-form inflation equation as

$$p_t = p_t^e + m(v_t) + \frac{1}{a + b}[hg \log(X_t) + z_t]. \tag{16}$$

This expression (16) is an expectational Phillips curve relating the actual inflation rate to the expected inflation rate and the growth (v) and level ($\log X$) of excess demand. When the economy is operating at a fixed *level* of excess demand, with $v_t = 0$, inflation accelerates ($p_t > p_t^e$) when the level of $\log(X_t)$ is positive and decelerates when $\log(X_t)$ is negative.

2.4. Alternative interpretations of the natural rate hypothesis and the wage gap

The presence of the cost–push term (z_t) in (16) requires that we identify two concepts of the natural rate of unemployment. The 'conventional' or 'no-shock' natural rate of unemployment (U_t^*) is that which is consistent with zero excess demand in the labor market when the supply shock terms net out to zero ($z_t = 0$). With z_t and v_t set at zero in (16), then a steady rate of inflation, with $p_t = p_t^e$, is achieved whenever $\log(X_t) = 0$. This situation also defines the natural unemployment rate (U_t^*) as that which is consistent with zero excess demand in the labor market

$$U_t^* = U_t + \log(X_t), \tag{17}$$

where U_t is the actual unemployment rate.

However, when the supply shock terms in (15) do not net out to zero $(z_t \neq 0)$, then the alternative 'shock' natural rate concept (U_t^S) indicates the unemployment rate consistent with steady inflation

$$U_t^S = U_t^* + \frac{z_t}{gh}. \tag{18}$$

The cost–push or supply–shock factors appearing in (15) that may set the z_t term at a non-zero value can be a cause of inflation, unemployment, or both. If the monetary authority accommodates the shocks by attempting to set $X_t = 0$, then inflation will accelerate when $z_t > 0$. If the authority extinguishes the shocks by attempting to maintain $p_t = p_t^e$, then unemployment will rise above U_t^* by the amount shown in eq. (18). Thus the three components of z_t in (15) can be interpreted as causes of inflation, unemployment, or both, depending on the degree of monetary accommodation provided by the monetary authority

(1) There can be an increase in the real price of foreign goods expressed in domestic currency $(p^F - p)$.
(2) There can be an excess in the growth rate (r_t) of the 'aspiration' real wage relevant for labor supply over the growth rate of productivity (θ_t) that is relevant for price setting.
(3) There can be an increase in either of the two tax factors, personal or indirect.

2.5. Interpretations of real and nominal wage rigidity

Eqs. (15) and (18) help us gain insight into the interrelationship between real and nominal wage rigidity. The usual interpretation of real wage rigidity is an excess of workers' aspirations for real wage increases relative to the rate of productivity growth, i.e., that the term $(r_t - \theta_t)$ is positive in (15), presumably because of a failure of the rate of real wage increase to adjust downwards in response to a slowdown in productivity growth, such as that which occurred after 1973. Clearly, real wage flexibility in the sense that r_t always stays equal to θ_t is necessary but not sufficient for an avoidance of classical unemployment, since the other terms on the right-hand side of (15) that comprise z_t could have a positive sum. Conversely, real wage rigidity in the sense of an inflexible r_t is not necessary for classical unemployment to occur, because real wage *flexibility* can be as serious a problem if there is an autonomous jump in r_t while θ_t remains constant. Below we present evidence supporting the interpretation that an 'autonomous wage push' occurred in Europe in the late 1960s and in Japan in 1973–74.

Second, if all of the terms in (15) sum to zero, so that the supply shock term z_t is zero, nominal wage rigidity in the sense of a small adjustment parameter g in (18) is irrelevant to inflation and unemployment, as long as the economy begins in equilibrium with $\log(X_t) = 0$ and matters only by raising the amount of employment or output that must be sacrificed to reduce the inflation rate from some initial value (thus there should be a direct correlation across countries between high values of g and low sacrifice ratios).

Third, the effects of excess wage growth in the sense that $r_t > \theta_t$ cannot be separated from those of nominal wage rigidity, since in (18) the value of U_t^S required to maintain a constant value of the inflation rate depends both on the amount by which r_t exceeds θ_t and on the nominal adjustment parameter g. If g is quite small, then excess real wage growth can cause a large amount of unemployment when the monetary authority acts to prevent inflation from accelerating. More generally, the amount of unemployment that results from any positive component of the supply-shift z_t term depends inversely on the size of the nominal wage adjustment parameter g.

3. The data base and issues in econometric specification

3.1. The data base for manufacturing and non-manufacturing

Most comparative econometric studies of wage and employment equations have indiscriminately mixed data on the hourly wage rate for the manufacturing sector with economy-wide data on unemployment and/or output.[4] The work of Artus (1984) is almost unique in developing a consistent data base for manufacturing, and this paper builds on his research by developing an analogous data base for the aggregate economy, as well as the manufacturing and non-manufacturing (residual) sectors.

The aim of the data compilation is to develop consistent series on value added, the value added deflator, compensation, employment, and hours per employee. These series allow the calculation of all the variables that matter for a study of productivity, wage, and price behavior. Average labor produc-

---

[4]The LSE data base, as described by Grubb (1986), contains hourly earnings only for manufacturing, and not always on a consistent base. Data for Australia and Norway are for males only, data for the U.S. include production workers only, data for Austria, Belgium, Denmark, and Sweden include mining, data for Belgium include transport, and data for Spain include all industries.

tivity is real value added per labor hour, the wage rate is compensation per labor hour, and the wage gap is the nominal wage rate, divided by the value added deflator, divided by average labor productivity. Because the real product wage relevant for the hiring decisions of business firms is expressed at factor cost, i.e., net of indirect taxes, special care has been taken to achieve a consistent set of net-of-tax product price deflators at factor cost.

A unique feature of this study is the symmetric attention to the manufacturing and non-manufacturing sectors. Data for the latter are created as a residual, from data on the absolute values of output, compensation, and labor input for the aggregate economy and for manufacturing. The manufacturing data come from the IMF quarterly data base derived from original national accounts sources, and the aggregate data are developed here from published OECD series, together with a crucial unpublished series on aggregate hours per employee.[5]

Another unique feature of the data base is the explicit treatment of self-employment income. Previous studies have included in indexes of labor's income share and the 'wage gap' only the compensation of employees. But the income of the self-employed, consists mainly of labor income, should also be included rather than being hidden, as at present, in the OECD's umbrella capital income measure called 'the operating surplus'. This is particularly important in this study, which measures the wage rate as compensation per hour. Since measures of employment and total hours include the self-employed, so should the measure of compensation. Thus our measure of total compensation adds the OECD measure of 'household entrepreneurial income' to employee compensation. We assume that most of this entrepreneurial income is earned in the agricultural, trade, and service sector, and so include it in the aggregate and in non-manuufacturing, but make no adjustment in the manufacturing sector. Below we display the effects of the entrepreneurial income adjustment on indexes of the 'wage gap'.

Because regression results are presented below for all three sectors, it is not possible to follow the usual format in such studies by providing separate regression estimates for each of the 14 countries covered in the data base. Instead, a 'Europe' aggregate for the 11 European countries has been compiled, using 1972 GNP weights expressed in dollars, and this allows the

---

[5]This unpublished series was provided by John Martin of the OECD. All other series for the aggregate sector were obtained from an OECD PC data diskette. The manufacturing data were transcribed manually from printouts provided by the IMF in May 1985 and include manufacturing value-added deflators, output, compensation, employment, and hours for the fourteen countries identified in footnote 2. The compilation of the manufacturing data is described in the data appendix of Artus (1984). A critical step in the development of the data base was the location of data on the absolute value of each variable (particularly nominal output, nominal compensation, and labor hours) for each aggregate economy in 1972, in order to allow subtraction of manufacturing values from aggregate values to obtain the needed residual values.

subsequent research to be carried out for three countries, the U.S., Japan, and 'Europe'.

Potential defects in these procedures are obvious and may be enumerated briefly. The use of compensation per hour to represent the wage rate has the advantage that separate wage rate series can be developed for the aggregate, manufacturing, and non-manufacturing sectors, but has the disadvantage that any compensation per hour series displays cyclical fluctuations created by changes in the fraction of hours paying overtime rates, and by changes in the interindustry mix between high and low wage activities, in addition to changes in the 'pure' wage rate itself. While my past work on U.S. wage behavior has been based on an hourly earnings index adjusted for shifts in overtime and the interindustry employment mix, such indexes are not available for other countries, and thus the need for consistency requires use of an unadjusted compensation per hour series for each country and each sector. The addition of self-employment income to employee compensation also raises issues that require further research, including the true breakdown between manufacturing and non-manufacturing, and the more difficult issue of separating the labor and capital components of entrepreneurial income.

Another limitation of our approach is the requirement that detrended output rather than the official or standardized unemployment rate be used as the basic measure of cyclical variability, simply because unemployment rate series are available only for the aggregate economy and are meaningless for sub-sectors. While the regressions presented below for the aggregate sector of the U.S., Japanese, and European economies could be reestimated with the unemployment rate replacing the detrended output series, this task would expand the scope of the paper and is deferred for future research.

3.2. Converting the theoretical equations into an econometric specification

The aim of the econometric research is to estimate equations for wage change (11), price change within a markup framework (13), and price change within a reduced-form framework (14). Decisions required to convert theoretical ideas into an explicit econometric specification are discussed here.

(1) Basic format. All equations take the form of (11), (13), and (14), by expressing all variables (other than the cyclical Phillips curve variable) as first differences of logs.

(2) Expected price change. The p_t^e term in eqs. (11) and (14) is proxied by two lags on the annual change in the value-added deflator. Two lags appear to be sufficient to explain the wage changes without including a third or further lags, while the 'zero' lag (current price change) is excluded to avoid simultaneity and identify the wage and price equations (i.e., the current

change in unit labor cost is entered into the price markup equations, but the current change in price is not entered into the wage equations). This treatment reflects the (structural) assumption that wages can influence prices within the current year more than prices can influence wages, and the high degree of simultaneity between annual changes in wages and prices is attributed to the price-setting process.[6] Note that the wage equation (11) calls for the expected price change term to enter with a unitary coefficient; the wage equations are estimated below with the sum of coefficients on the two lagged price change terms both estimated freely and also constrained to equal unity.

(3) Demand pressure variables. It has been customary in previous studies to designate the unemployment rate or its inverse as the sole demand pressure variable. However, in theory it is not the level of the unemployment rate that matters, but rather the excess demand for labor, which should be measured as the *deviation* of the actual from the natural unemployment rate. If the natural unemployment rate has risen, as seems to have occurred in most countries, the use of the unemployment rate to measure excess demand introduces measurement error. The procedure used here is to take advantage of the regular 'Okun's Law' relationship observed in many countries [Gordon (1984), Hamada and Kurosaka (1983)] in the form of a high negative correlation between the log ratio of actual to 'natural' output ($\log Q - \log Q^*$) and the deviation of the actual from the natural unemployment rate. The required natural output series consists of exponential trends running between the benchmark years of 1961, 1972, and 1979, with the 1972–79 trend extended to 1984 on the assumption that most countries were operating below natural output after 1979 and hence that no benchmark year is available for the 1980s.[7]

The standardized unemployment rates for each country are shown in table 1 for the benchmark years 1961, 1972, and 1979, and also for 1984. While the U.S. in 1979 seems to have been operating close to natural output (Gordon, 1985), the choice of 1979 as a benchmark year is subject to debate for some of the other countries. The unemployment rate for Europe (the fourth line in table 1) rose from 2.7 percent in 1972 to 4.9 percent in 1979, suggesting the possibility that setting natural output equal to actual output in 1979 for Europe may lead to an understatement of natural output and overstatement of the log output ratio for the entire post-1972 period.

---

[6]For a discussion of alternative methods of imposing structure on wage and price equations within this context, see Blanchard (1986). In some of his quarterly wage equations Blanchard imposes the structural assumption that the coefficient on the current price change in the wage equation cannot be higher than a specified amount, e.g., 0.3.

[7]Exceptions to this procedure are that 1984 is used as a benchmark year for Japan to take account of highly different growth rates of output during 1979–84 in manufacturing versus nonmanufacturing. Also, since 1961 was a recession year in North America, the first benchmark is 1964 in Canada and the U.S., and also in France. The 1961–64 growth rate of natural output for these countries is assumed to be equal to the observed 1964–72 growth rate.

Table 1

Standardized unemployment rates, selected years.

	1961	1972	1979	1984
U.S.	6.4	5.5	5.8	7.4
Canada	6.5	6.2	7.4	11.2
Japan	1.2	1.4	2.1	2.7
Eleven European Countries	1.7	2.7	4.9	9.6
Austria	1.9	1.2	2.1	4.1
Belgium	2.1	2.7	8.2	14.0
Denmark	2.0	0.9	6.1	10.1
France	1.4	2.7	6.0	9.7
Germany	0.3	0.8	3.2	8.6
Italy	5.1	6.3	7.5	10.2
Netherlands	0.5	2.2	5.4	14.0
Norway	1.8	1.7	2.0	3.0
Sweden	1.4	2.7	2.1	3.1
Switzerland	0.0	0.0	0.4	1.1
U.K.	2.2	4.3	5.6	13.2

Source: Switzerland and Denmark, 1972 and 1979 from *OECD Labor Force Statistics*, 1984: OECD *Economic Outlook*, December 1985, p. 28.
Other countries for 1972, 1979, and 1984: *OECD Economic Outlook*, June 1985, table R12.
All countries for 1961: *Yearbook of Labor Statistics*, 1971, table 10, linked to OECD Series in 1964.

(4) Tax rates. There are insufficient degrees of freedom to include both tax change terms (t^I and t^P) in annual equations for the short 1964–84 interval. Instead, the rate of change of the total indirect, payroll, and personal tax rates is entered as a single variable. The change in the total tax rate (t^T) is calculated at an annual rate over two years, rather than one year, to allow for lags without using up an extra degree of freedom.

(5) Productivity growth. The wage change equation (11) contains a term $(r - \theta)$ to allow for the possibility that the 'aspiration' real wage rate rises more rapidly than the rate of productivity growth (θ) relevant for price setting; this could reflect either real wage stickiness in response to a slowdown in productivity growth, or an autonomous episode of 'wage push' that is not captured by the other terms in the wage equation. The productivity growth concept assumed to be relevant for price setting is trend productivity growth (θ^*) rather than actual productivity growth (θ).[8] Separate values of θ^* are

---

[8] The price change equations I have estimated for the U.S. over the years, as in Gordon (1965), include a productivity deviation ($\theta - \theta^*$) term to measure the proportion of price setting behavior based on actual as opposed to trend productivity growth. The estimated proportion is usually in the range of 0.15 to 0.20. This productivity deviation term is not included in the price equations estimated in this paper, thus imposing the restriction that price changes depend only on trend productivity growth with no role for actual productivity growth.

estimated before and after 1972, as discussed in section 4, and are subtracted from the rate of wage change to form the dependent variable of the wage equation ($w_t - \theta_t^*$, i.e., the change in trend unit labor cost).

The real-wage rigidity or wage push effect ($r - \theta$), which we can call the 'excess change' in the real wage, is measured by a set of dummy variables. The first is simply a constant term for the full sample period. Since the specification in (11) contains no constant term, a significant positive value for the constant term would indicate that, on average over the sample period, the change in the real wage rate is larger than the trend growth rate of productivity, after taking account of the effect of the other variables in the equation (the log output ratio, the change in the two tax rates, and the relative import price change). Additional dummy variables are also entered for the 1973–84 and 1980–84 periods to test for the excess change in the real wage during different intervals of the sample period. The sum of the constant and the 1973–84 dummy indicates for the 1973–79 period the excess change in the real wage (measured as an annual rate of change), while the sum of the constant, the 1973–84 dummy, and the 1980–84 dummy indicates the excess change for the 1980–84 interval. This interpretation of the excess change in the real wage requires that the coefficients on the lagged product price change terms (p_{t-1} and p_{t-2}) are constrained to sum to unity. The wage equations are estimated both with and without the set of constants and dummy variables.

In previous research on European wage setting behavior Nordhaus (1972) identified a 'wage explosion' in the late 1960s, and this episode of autonomous wage push was confirmed later by Perry (1975) and Gordon (1977a). To isolate this episode, an additional dummy variable is included in the European wage equations, defined as 1.0 for the years 1968–70 and zero otherwise. While there have been no wage explosions in the U.S., allowance for the Nixon wage and price controls period in 1971–72 and subsequent rebound in 1974–75 needs to be made, and this is handled by a single dummy variable defined as 1.0 in 1971–72, -1.0 in 1974–75, and zero otherwise. The fit of the Japanese wage equations is markedly improved when the period 1973–74 is treated as a period of wage explosion in that country, captured by a dummy variable equal to 1.0 for 1973–74 and zero otherwise.

3.3. Summary of the specification of the wage and price equations

The preceding discussion suggests the following wage equation, in which the dependent variable is the rate of change of trend unit labor cost

$$w_t - \theta_t^* = \alpha_{11}p_{t-1} + \alpha_{12}p_{t-2} + \alpha_{20}\hat{Q}_t + \alpha_{21}\hat{Q}_{t-1} + \alpha_3(p^F - p)_t$$

$$+ \alpha_4(t^T)_t + \alpha_5 D_t^{WP} + \delta_0 D_{0t} + \delta_1 D_{1t} + \delta_2 D_{2t}. \tag{19}$$

Here $\hat{Q}_t$ is the log output ratio, t_t^T is the change in the total tax rate, D_t^{WP} is the wage push or controls dummy (1968–70 for Europe, 1973–74 for Japan, and 1971–72 reversed in 1974–75 for the U.S.), and the dummy variables designated D_{it} measure the presence of excess real wage change for the periods 1964–84, 1972–84, and 1980–84. The inclusion of the lagged as well as current output ratio term allows the effect of aggregate demand to enter either as a level effect, rate of change effect, or both. In table 5 this specification of the wage change equation is estimated first with the D_{it} terms omitted and with the coefficients on the lagged price terms freely estimated, and then a second time with the D_{it} terms included and the constraint imposed that $\alpha_{11} + \alpha_{12} = 1.0$.

The wage change equation is supplemented by an equation that explains changes in the value-added deflator, as in (13), which can be estimated in the straightforward form

$$p_t = \beta_{10}(w - \theta^*)_t + \beta_{11}(w - \theta^*)_{t-1} + \beta_{20}\hat{Q}_t + \beta_{21}\hat{Q}_{t-1}$$

$$+ \beta_3(p^F - p)_t + \beta_4 t_t^T + \beta_5 D_t^{WP}. \tag{20}$$

The wage-push/controls dummy variables are entered exactly as in the wage equations. In the case of Europe and Japan, the coefficient β_5 might be negative if an autonomous wage push squeezed profit margins, while in the U.S. the 1971–72 controls program applied to price markups as well as wage rates.

The final equation to be estimated is the reduced-form that results when (19) is substituted into (20). To simplify the presentation of the reduced form, the complex set of lagged coefficients is relabelled (e.g., $\gamma_{11} = \beta_{10}\alpha_{11}$), and several lagged terms that are indicated by the substitution are dropped to save degrees of freedom

$$p_t = \gamma_{11}p_{t-1} + \gamma_{12}p_{t-2} + \gamma_{20}\hat{Q}_t + \gamma_{21}\hat{Q}_{t-1} + \gamma_3(p^F - p)_t$$

$$+ \gamma_4 t_t^T + \gamma_5 D_t^{WP} + \delta_0 D_{0t} + \delta_1 D_{1t} + \delta_2 D_{2t}. \tag{21}$$

Notice that the productivity trend term (θ_t^*) drops out of the reduced-form, but included are the three dummy variables (D_{it}) that measure the presence of excess real wage change for the periods 1964–84, 1972–84, and 1980–84. The reduced-form price change equation (21) is estimated first with the D_{it} terms omitted and with the coefficients on the lagged price terms freely estimated, and then a second time with the D_{it} terms included and the constraint imposed that $\gamma_{11} + \gamma_{12} = 1.0$. If any of the three δ_i coefficients are significantly positive, this would indicate that excess real wage change created an acceleration of inflation, and indirectly an increase in the natural rate of unemployment.

4. Productivity growth and the real wage

The specification of the wage and price mark-up equations contains a productivity trend growth term (θ^*) which must be estimated, in order to disentangle cyclical movements in productivity from trend movements. The cyclical productivity regressions developed in this section also allow us to assess the effect of real wage movements on the demand for labor and on labor's average product. A subsidiary purpose of this section is to assess the claim by Sachs that 'in Europe (but not in Japan) the overall effect of a sustained rise in unemployment is to raise productivity relative to trend' (1983, p. 281). His claim that labor productivity varies countercyclically in Europe contrasts with the standard assumption in the U.S. that productivity varies procyclically.

4.1. Specification of the productivity equations

The basic specification relates the log ratio of hours to trend output $(N_t - Q_t^*)$ to the log output ratio $(Q_t - Q_t^*)$, representing the cyclical effect of output on hiring decisions; to the real wage rate defined relative to the underlying productivity trend $[(W_t - P_t) - \Theta^* t]$, which could differ from zero as a result of excess growth in the real wage; and to the productivity trend itself (Θ_t^*). Taking this opportunity to redefine all upper-case letters as logs of levels, we can write

$$(N_t - Q_t^*) = A + \phi(Q_t - Q_t^*) - \sigma(W_t - P_t - \Theta_t^*) - \Theta^* t, \tag{22}$$

where A is a constant. Note that (22) is consistent with the labor demand function in (3), simply adding the cyclical effect to the normal static labor demand function in which labor hours depend on the real wage and labor-augmenting technical progress. As in (3), the trend in (22) picks up the effects of growth in the capital–labor ratio and of changes in other inputs.

When (22) is rewritten as an equation for the average product of labor (Q/N), we can interpret the parameter ϕ as indicating the effect of cyclical movements in the output ratio on labor productivity

$$(Q_t - N_t) = -A + (1 - \phi)(Q_t - Q_t^*) + \sigma(W_t - P_t - \Theta^* t) + \Theta^* t. \tag{23}$$

If the parameter ϕ is unity, then a permanent increase in the output ratio has no impact on actual labor productivity, whereas a value of ϕ below unity implies a permanent productivity gain ('short-run increasing returns') and a value of ϕ above unity implies a permanent productivity loss ('short-run diminishing returns'). Thus the Sachs phenomenon of countercyclical productivity movements in Europe requires an estimated value of $\phi > 1.0$.

4.2. Theoretical and actual wage gap indexes

We note that (23) allows us to define a wage gap concept adjusted not just for cyclical effects but for the endogenous response of productivity growth to excess growth in the real wage. The actual wage gap index (WG_t) is $W - P - \Theta$ and the adjusted wage gap index (WG_t^*) is $W - P - \Theta^* t$. Using these definitions, we can rearrange (23) to obtain

$$WG_t = A - (1 - \phi)(Q_t - Q_t^*) + (1 - \sigma)(WG_t^*). \tag{24}$$

This expression places an interesting perspective on the interrelationships between real wage behavior, productivity growth, and the wage gap index. If the elasticity of labor input with respect to the excess real wage (σ) in (22) is unity, then (24) shows that the excess real wage growth 'pays for itself' by boosting *actual* productivity enough to keep the actual wage gap index $(WG_t = W_t - P_t - \Theta_t)$ unaffected. Only if the elasticity (σ) is less than unity is excess real wage growth manifested in an increase in the observed actual wage gap index.

The actual wage gap index (WG_t) for each of the three sectors in the U.S., Japan, and Europe *without* any adjustment for self-employment income is displayed in fig. 1. Because the actual wage gap is defined as the real product wage divided by labor's average product, the data displayed in fig. 1 can be interpreted simply as an index $(1972 = 1.0)$ of the share of employee compensation in value added. Three interesting features are worthy of notice in fig. 1. First, in Europe the wage gap index increases relative to that in the U.S., and this feature of the data has been stressed by those authors who have advocated the hypothesis of classical unemployment in Europe. Second, this contrast between Europe and the U.S. is reversed after 1981 in the manufacturing sector; by 1984 the European manufacturing wage gap index had declined back to 1.0, in contrast to a value of 1.07 for U.S. manufacturing Third, in each of the three sectors the wage gap index increased far more in Japan than in either Europe or the U.S., raising a question as to how an increase in the wage gap could be a sign of classical unemployment in

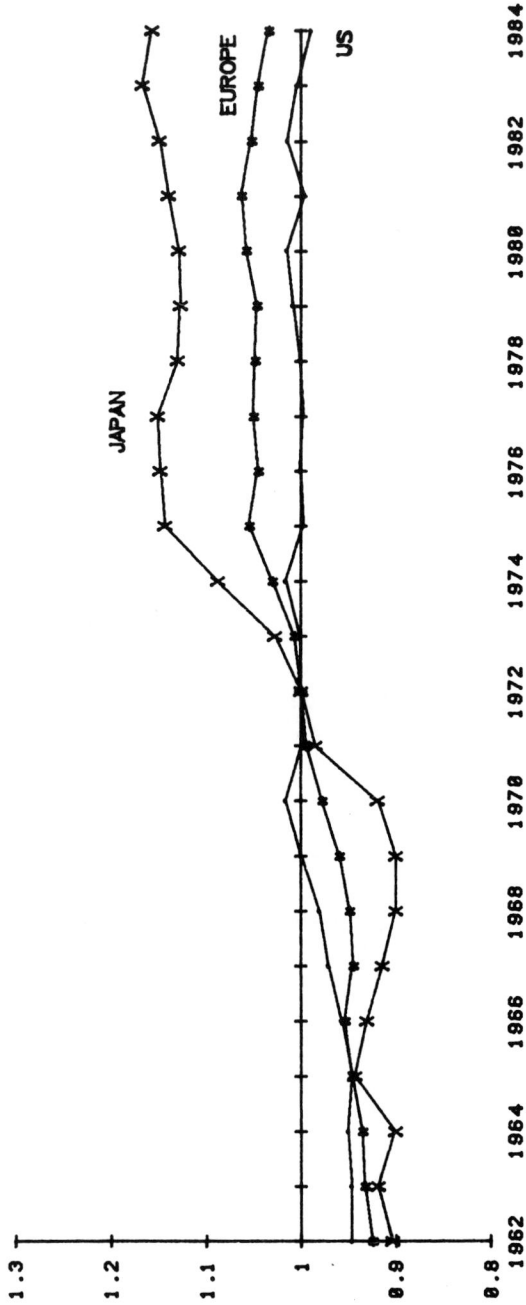

Fig. 1a. Actual wage gap, aggregate economy.

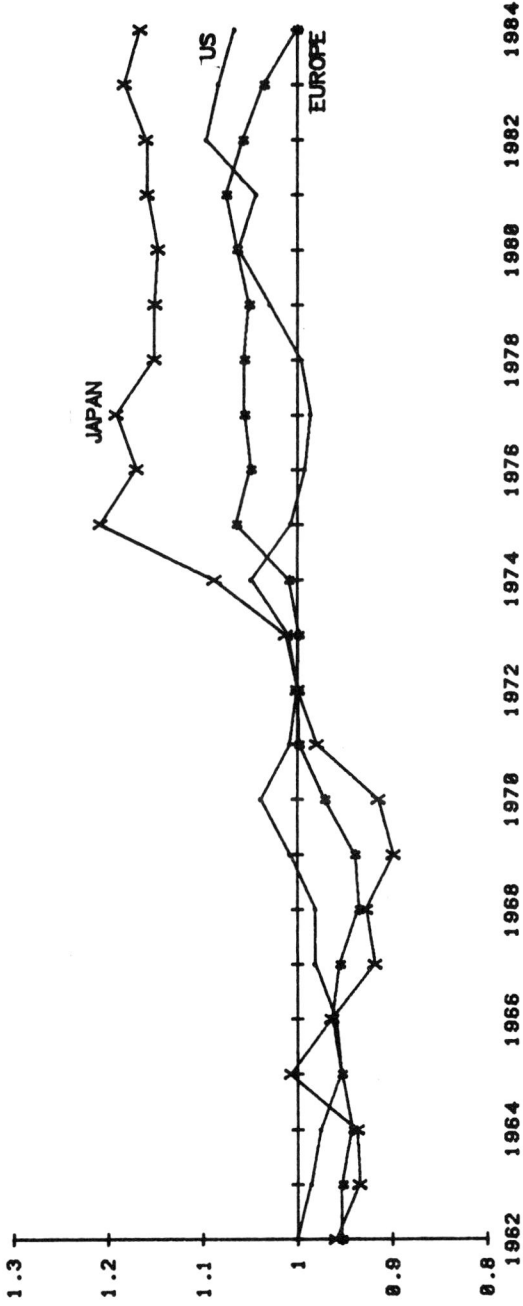

Fig. 1b. Actual wage gap, manufacturing.

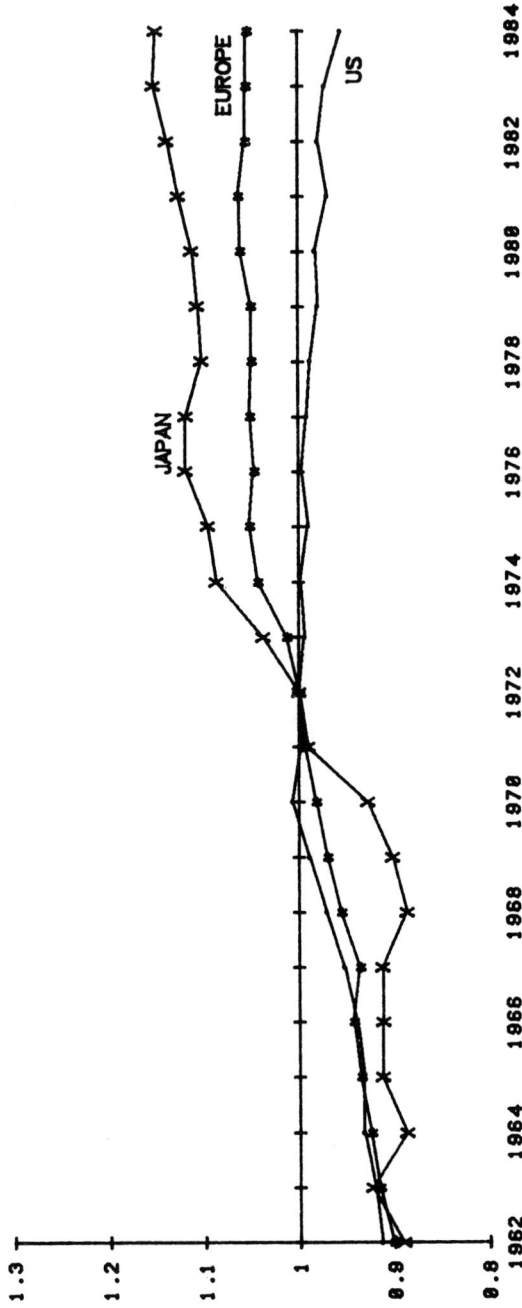

Fig. 1c. Actual wage gap, non-manufacturing.

Europe, whereas an even larger increase in the wage gap in Japan did not cause the same phenomenon.[9]

The Japanese puzzle, as well as most of the contrast between Europe and the U.S., is eliminated by our inclusion of household entrepreneurial income with employee compensation as part of labor's income share. The difference made by the entrepreneurial income adjustment is displayed in fig. 2, where there is one frame for the aggregate sector in each of the three economies. While the difference made by the adjustment is small in the U.S., it makes a substantial difference for Europe and an even greater difference for Japan. With the adjustment, the values of the actual wage gap index for selected years are as in the table.

	U.S.	Japan	Europe
1964	98.0	101.0	98.5
1972	100.0	100.0	100.0
1975	98.7	107.6	102.8
1979	99.3	104.5	100.2
1984	94.9	100.7	97.0

It is hard to see how the minor differences in these indexes could be responsible for the substantial differences among the three economies in the evolution of unemployment rates since the 1960s. Comparing 1964, 1972, and 1979, the U.S. and European wage gap indexes were basically identical, and the 1979–84 decline of 4.4 percent in the U.S. was only slightly greater than the 3.2 percent decline in Europe. The Japanese story seems to have been one of a jump in the wage gap index as a result of the 1973–74 wage push, followed by moderation that returned the index to its 1972 value by the early 1980s.

4.3. Estimation of the labor input equations

(22) could be estimated either in levels or in growth rates. Initial testing indicated that the growth rate specification is superior, avoiding the serial correlation that occurs with the level specification for some sectors. Allowing for lags and a post-1972 break in the productivity growth trend, (22) becomes

$$(n - q^*)_t = \sum_{j=0}^{1} \phi_j (q - q_*)_{t-j} - \sum_{k=0}^{1} \sigma_k \left(w - p - \sum_{i=0}^{1} \theta_i^* \right)_{t-k} - \sum_{i=0}^{1} \theta_i^*, \qquad (25)$$

[9]The Japanese anomaly cannot be explained away by disguised unemployment, since the annual growth rate of labor hours in the aggregate Japanese economy actually accelerated after 1979 when the wage gap index was at its highest (annual growth rates were 0.43 percent during 1960–72, 0.29 percent during 1972–79, and 0.86 percent during 1979–84).

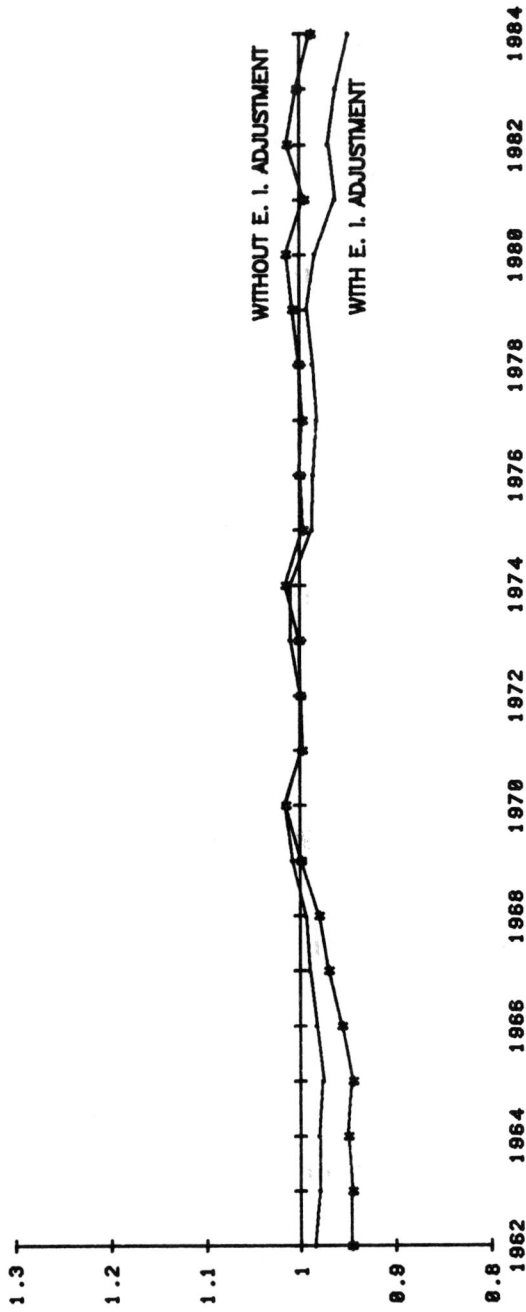

Fig. 2a. Actual wage gap, U.S. aggregate economy.

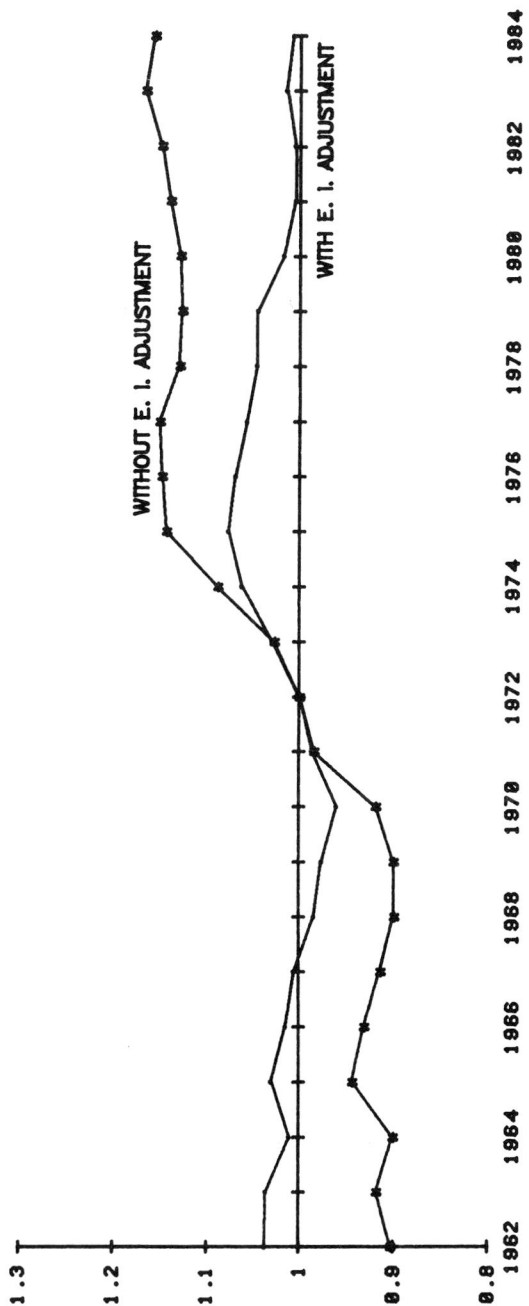

Fig. 2b. Actual wage gap, Japan aggregate economy.

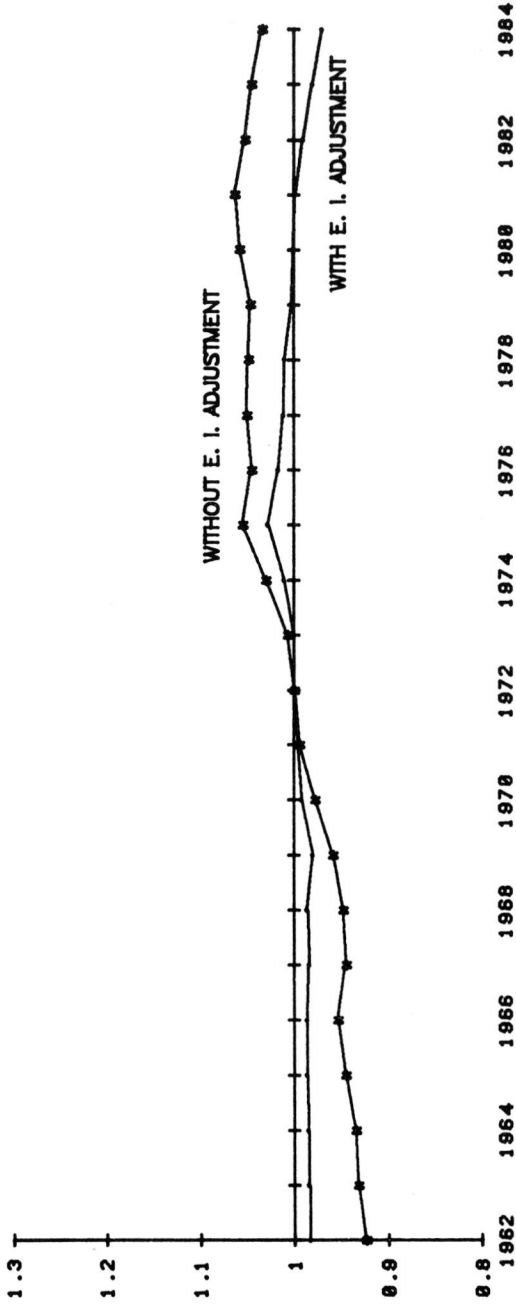

Fig. 2c. Actual wage gap, Europe aggregate economy.

where θ_0^* is the 1964–72 productivity trend and θ_1^* is the 1973–84 productivity trend. To unscramble the productivity trends from the estimated regression, run

$$(n-q^*)_t = \sum_{j=0}^{1} \phi_j (q-q_*)_{t-j} - \sum_{k=0}^{1} \sigma_k (w-p)_{t-k} - \sum_{i=0}^{1} \alpha_i + \varepsilon_t, \qquad (26)$$

where α_0 is the constant term ($=1.0$ 1964–84) and α_1 is a dummy variable ($=0$ 1964–72 and $=1.0$ 1973–84). Then the productivity trend terms are defined as

$$\theta_0^* = \frac{-\alpha_0}{1 - \sum_k \sigma_k}, \qquad \theta_1^* = \frac{-(\alpha_0 - \alpha_1)}{1 - \sum_k \sigma_k}. \qquad (27)$$

In preliminary tests an additional productivity term ($\alpha_2 = 1.0$ during 1980–84) was entered to test for the significance of a second growth slowdown after 1979, but this term was uniformly insignificant in the presence of the real wage variable. With the real wage variable omitted, α_2 was significant for the European aggregate and non-manufacturing sectors, as discussed below in connection with table 4.

4.4. Estimated productivity equations

Results are presented in table 2 for the three sectors within the U.S., Japan, and Europe. All sums of coefficients on the output ratio are between zero and unity, indicating uniformly procyclical behavior of productivity, with U.S. manufacturing and European non-manufacturing closest to a neutral effect, and the Japanese aggregate indicating the greatest degree of labor hoarding (i.e., procyclical productivity response). An interesting result is that the labor hoarding phenomenon is more important in European non-manufacturing than in U.S. non-manufacturing.

The real wage elasticities are about one half in the non-manufacturing sectors of each country but are markedly lower in manufacturing, with a significant negative coefficient within manufacturing only for Europe. The aggregate real wage elasticity is about one-half in Japan and Europe and about one-third in the U.S. (although the U.S. coefficient is statistically insignificant). The productivity trend terms indicate extremely rapid rates of productivity growth in Japan prior to 1973 and very large slowdowns in the productivity growth trend in 1973–84, particularly in the aggregate and non-manufacturing. The U.S. productivity trend growth rates are so low as to be insignificantly different from zero in the aggregate and in non-manufacturing, and the U.S. post-1973 slowdown terms are insignificant in all three sectors. Europe is notable for having a post-1972 productivity trend in

Table 2

Equations explaining annual change in hours relative to output growth $(n_t - q_t^*)$, 1964–84.

	Sum of coefficients on current and one lagged change in		Constant (trend) terms				
	Output ratio (1)	Real wage (2)	1964 –1984 (3)	1973 –1984 (4)	$\bar{R}^2$ (5)	S.E.E. (6)	D.–W. (7)
United States							
Aggregate	0.91[b]	−0.33	−2.02	0.98	0.82	0.78	2.21
Manufacturing	1.00[b]	−0.36	−2.66[a]	0.77	0.92	1.40	2.40
Non-manufacturing	0.79[b]	−0.53[a]	−1.42	0.02	0.66	0.73	1.82
Japan							
Aggregate	0.35[a]	−0.48[b]	−8.76[b]	5.30[b]	0.90	0.92	2.35
Manufacturing	0.53[b]	−0.14	−9.78[b]	3.21[a]	0.71	1.95	2.21
Non-manufacturing	0.56[b]	−0.66[b]	−7.66[a]	6.80[a]	0.85	1.62	2.25
Europe							
Aggregate	0.82[b]	−0.54[b]	−4.83[b]	1.33[a]	0.89	0.43	2.11
Manufacturing	0.85[b]	−0.26[a]	−5.42[b]	1.18[a]	0.83	0.88	1.54
Non-manufacturing	0.93[b]	−0.68[b]	−3.85	0.91	0.83	0.49	1.44

[a]Significant at 5 percent.
[b]Significant at 1 percent.

non-manufacturing higher than in both the U.S. and Japan, and in having a relatively slight slowdown in all three sectors.

Table 3 decomposes the change in productivity growth over three intervals among the effects of the estimated trend, the real wage, and cyclical movements in the output ratio. The total shown in columns (4), (8), and (12) refers is for the fitted value of the equations from table 2. Recall that the post-1972 trend effect is the sum of columns (3) and (4) in table 2, with the signs reversed, as written out in eq. (27).

A novel aspect of these results concerns the non-manufacturing sectors of the U.S. and Japan. The U.S. displays *no* slowdown in trend productivity growth after 1972 in non-manufacturing, despite the slowdown evident in the raw data. This occurs because the equation explains almost all of the post-1973 productivity growth slowdown as a response to a shift from positive excess real wage growth during 1964–72 to negative excess real wage growth in both periods after 1972. This effect of the time path of the real wage on U.S. productivity growth has received remarkably little discussion in the fruitless U.S. literature on the productivity slowdown puzzle. A similar phenomenon occurs in Japan, where real wage moderation after 1979 in non-manufacturing has the effect of cancelling out the positive post-1972 trend, leaving the fitted rate of productivity growth in non-manufacturing exactly zero for 1979–84.

Table 3

Contribution to fitted values of productivity growth of trends, real wage effect, and cyclical output ratio effect, selected intervals, 1964–84.

	1964–72				1972–79				1979–84			
	Trend	Real wage	Output ratio	Total	Trend	Real wage	Output ratio	Total	Trend	Real wage	Output ratio	Total
	(1)	(2)	(3)	(4)	(5)	(6)	(7)	(8)	(9)	(10)	(11)	(12)
United States												
Aggregate	2.02	0.11	0.01	2.14	1.04	−0.09	−0.04	0.91	1.04	−0.43	0.03	0.64
Manufacturing	2.66	−0.02	−0.05	2.49	1.89	0.26	0.01	2.16	1.89	0.53	0.32	2.74
Non-manufacturing	1.42	0.50	0.02	1.94	1.40	−0.74	0.00	0.66	1.40	−1.31	−0.22	−0.13
Japan												
Aggregate	8.76	−0.36	−0.14	8.26	3.46	0.49	−0.03	3.92	3.46	−0.56	0.00	2.90
Manufacturing	9.78	0.19	0.29	10.26	6.57	1.15	−0.04	7.68	6.57	0.16	0.00	6.73
Non-manufacturing	7.66	−0.21	−0.07	7.38	0.86	1.24	0.00	2.10	0.86	−0.84	0.00	0.02
Europe												
Aggregate	4.83	0.25	−0.05	5.03	3.50	−0.05	0.02	3.48	3.50	−1.18	−0.36	1.96
Manufacturing	5.42	0.25	−0.14	5.53	4.24	0.18	0.05	4.47	4.24	−0.43	−0.34	3.47
Non-manufacturing	3.85	0.91	−0.01	4.75	2.94	0.02	0.00	2.96	2.94	−1.29	−0.14	1.51

This approach attributes all of the slowdown in European productivity growth after 1979 to the real wage and cyclical effects, in roughly equal proportions in manufacturing, and with a larger role for real wage moderation in the aggregate and non-manufacturing sectors. The contrast between European and U.S. manufacturing during the 1979–84 period is particularly striking, with U.S. manufacturing managing to achieve above-trend productivity growth as a result of excess real wage growth and a transitory cyclical effect (due to rapid output growth in 1983–4), while in European manufacturing actual productivity growth was below trend as a result of real wage moderation and a negative cyclical effect.

4.5. Trends in output, productivity, and hours

Table 4 brings together the assumed trend growth rates of output (based on the benchmark years 1961, 1972, and 1979, as explained in section 3.2) with the estimated trend growth in productivity. Unlike those in table 3, the productivity trends in table 4 are obtained from estimates of eq. (26) in which the real wage effects are omitted. These trends can be interpreted as incorporating a cyclical adjustment but no decomposition of the portion of the productivity trend attributable to real wage movements. When (26) is re-estimated without the real wage variable, the third dummy variable representing the post-1979 slowdown becomes significant for the aggregate and non-manufacturing sectors of Europe (these regression results are omitted to save space).

The purpose of table 4 is to shed some light on the sources of the divergent movements of European unemployment rate from the unemployment rates of the U.S. and Japan. The counterpart of rising unemployment is, of course, slow or negative growth in labor hours. Obviously some part of the European unemployment problem results from output falling below trend, with log output ratios in Europe for 1984 of -8.5 percent for the aggregate, -11.1 percent for manufacturing, and -7.8 percent for non-manufacturing.

But it is also possible to look at the implications for labor hours of the underlying trends in output and productivity. Taken together, the output and productivity growth trends imply trends for labor input, shown in columns (3), (6), and (9) of table 4. Aggregate European trend hours fell in both periods before 1979 and actually rose slightly in the 1980s, but at a much slower rate than in the U.S. or Japan. However, the European aggregate disguises sharply divergent hours trends in manufacturing and non-manufacturing. The real European problem is low growth in manufacturing output in relation to a much higher rate of productivity growth. In non-manufacturing European trend hours growth on average since 1972 has been about equal to that in Japan.

Table 4

Growth rates in trend output, output per hour, and hours selected intervals, 1962–84.

	1962–72			1972–79			1979–84		
	Output (1)	Output per hour (2)	Hours (3)	Output (4)	Output per hour (5)	Hours (6)	Output (7)	Output per hour (8)	Hours (9)
United States									
Aggregate	3.73	2.14	1.59	3.05	0.88	2.17	3.05	0.88	2.17
Manufacturing	3.80	2.77	1.03	3.27	2.25	1.02	3.27	2.25	1.02
Non-manufacturing	3.70	1.77	1.59	2.97	0.54	2.43	2.97	0.54	2.43
Japan									
Aggregate	9.37	8.46	0.91	4.20	3.51	0.69	4.00	3.51	0.49
Manufacturing	12.24	10.06	2.18	6.34	6.77	-0.43	8.48	6.77	0.71
Non-manufacturing	8.13	7.49	0.64	2.96	1.29	1.67	0.56	1.29	-0.73
Europe									
Aggregate	4.36	5.01	-0.65	2.75	3.73	-0.98	2.75	2.54	0.21
Manufacturing	5.08	5.66	-0.58	1.35	4.30	-2.95	1.35	4.30	-2.95
Non-manufacturing	4.02	4.72	-0.70	2.87	3.37	-0.50	2.87	2.06	0.81

Table 4 places an interesting perspective on the U.S. phenomenon of rapid hours growth. Part of the U.S. difference from Europe stems from a lower decline in hours per employee (at a rate of about -0.25 percent per year as contrasted with -0.9 percent per year since 1972). However, most stems from faster employment growth. One can view the U.S. success in achieving rapid employment growth, however, as the counterpart of its dismal productivity record. One can calculate that if the U.S. had achieved the existing growth rate of output in 1979–84 but had combined it with European trend productivity growth, the U.S. would have had 8 percent fewer hours of labor input, or *9 million additional unemployed* (ignoring effects on labor force participation and hours per employee).

5. Estimated wage and price equations

5.1. Equations for wage change

We now turn to estimates of the equation for wage change, specified as in (19) above in section 3.3. For variables where a string of lagged values is entered, only the sum of coefficients is exhibited in table 5, as in table 2 above. Notes designate the significance of coefficients or sums of coefficients.

Two estimates of the wage equation are presented in table 5 for each sector within each country. The first omits the 'excess real wage growth' dummy variables and freely estimates the coefficients on lagged price change. The second includes the dummy variables and constrains the sum of coefficients on lagged price change to be unity, so the dependent variable is in the form of real wage growth adjusted for the estimated productivity trend.

We discuss first the results of the first version of the wage equation, presented as the first line of each pair. Some of the coefficients on lagged inflation are below unity and some are above. If 'excess real wage growth' occurs but no dummies are included, then the excess growth in the nominal wage rate relative to price change is likely to be picked up by a coefficient of greater than unity on the price change variable. This occurs in the U.S. aggregate and non-manufacturing, and in all three sectors for Europe.

The coefficients on the output ratio are generally positive and highly significant, supporting the Phillips curve hypothesis of a relation between the change in the wage rate and the level of a cyclical variable. Note that, because the current and one lagged output ratio term are included, the specification could reveal either a 'level effect' (a positive sum of coefficients) or a 'rate of change effect' (a positive current coefficient followed by an equal and negative lagged coefficient, with a zero sum of coefficients). Only in U.S. manufacturing and Japanese non-manufacturing is the sum of coefficients insignificant in both versions of the wage equation, and in neither case does an insignificant sum of coefficients disguise a rate of change effect.

Table 5

Equations for annual change in trend unit labor cost $(w_t - \theta_t^*)$, 1964–84.

| | Sum of coefficients | | | | Constant (trend) terms | | | Control and wage push dummies (8) | $\bar{R}^2$ (9) | S.E.E. (10) | D.–W. (11) |
	Inflation (1)	Output ratio (2)	$p^F - p$ (3)	t^T (4)	1964–1984 (5)	1973–1984 (6)	1980–1984 (7)				
U.S. aggregate	1.11[b]	0.57[b]	0.03	-0.10	-	-	-	-2.60[a]	0.67	0.98	2.45
	1.00	0.64[b]	0.02	-0.41	0.60	0.55	0.39	-2.43[a]	0.69	0.96	2.79
U.S. manufacturing	0.66[b]	-0.06	0.20[b]	1.31[a]	-	-	-	-1.65	0.74	1.41	2.02
	1.00	0.05	0.21[b]	-0.18	1.13	-2.10	1.90	-5.16	0.68	1.58	2.65
U.S. non-manufacturing	1.06[b]	1.07[b]	-0.02	0.01	-	-	-	-1.88	0.20	1.33	1.81
	1.00	1.02[b]	-0.03	-0.40	1.06	-0.12	-0.74	-2.33	0.28	1.27	2.21
Japan aggregate	0.77[b]	0.49[b]	-0.01	-0.84[a]	-	-	-	13.33[b]	0.96	1.13	3.04
	1.00[b]	0.43[a]	0.00	-0.52	-0.99	-1.60	1.34	14.46[b]	0.93	1.44	2.50
Japan manufacturing	0.78[b]	0.25[a]	-0.05	1.56	-	-	-	14.16[b]	0.82	2.47	1.58
	1.00	0.27	-0.04	1.94	0.93	-3.45[a]	1.85	15.87[b]	0.85	2.36	2.29
Japan non-manufacturing	0.87[b]	0.27	-0.01	-1.53	-	-	-	14.45[b]	0.87	1.99	1.39
	1.00	0.21	0.02	-1.71	0.88	-2.58	0.80	14.57[b]	0.87	1.95	1.45
Europe aggregate	1.11[b]	0.71[b]	0.05	-1.05[a]	-	-	-	3.66[b]	0.78	1.20	1.75
	1.00	0.74[b]	0.07	-1.12[a]	0.41	0.76	0.02	3.60[b]	0.77	1.24	1.54
Europe manufacturing	1.18[b]	0.48[b]	0.13[a]	-0.95	-	-	-	3.32[a]	0.69	1.82	1.70
	1.00	0.29[b]	0.13[b]	-1.15	0.04	1.02	0.64	3.58[b]	0.74	1.45	2.27
Europe non-manufacturing	1.19[b]	0.98[b]	0.01	-0.95	-	-	-	5.20[b]	0.63	1.31	1.38
	1.00	0.83[b]	0.04	-1.30[a]	2.09[b]	-0.19	-0.93	4.12[b]	0.75	1.08	2.02

[a]Significant at 5 percent.
[b]Significant at 1 percent.

The sum of coefficients on the output ratio is an important indicator of nominal wage rigidity. The theme in the literature supporting a greater degree of wage rigidity in the U.S. than in Europe or Japan is supported here only for manufacturing. In non-manufacturing the output response of wage rates is actually greater in the U.S. than in either Japan or Europe, resulting in an aggregate response that is not appreciably smaller than in Europe and a bit greater than in Japan.

The wage equations also include the change in the real import price and in the total tax rate. The import price terms have the correct positive sign but are generally insignificant, except in U.S. and European manufacturing. The tax terms almost always have the incorrect (negative) sign, with a significant positive coefficient only in U.S. manufacturing, and significant negative coefficients in the Japanese and European aggregate equations. Thus these results deny the existence of a significant 'tax push' effect that is responsible for driving up real wage rates and in this sense conflict with the hypothesis advanced by Tullio (1987) in this volume and with results of Knoester and van der Windt (1985).

Turning now to the coefficients displayed in column (8) of table 5, the wage push dummy variables for Japan and Europe have large and significant coefficients. As an example, the coefficient for the Japanese aggregate economy indicates that in 1973–74 wage rates increased 13 percent more *per year* than can be explained by the other variables, and for Europe in 1968–70 wage rates increased 3.6 percent more per year than the other variables can explain. The wage controls dummy variables are significant for the U.S. aggregate economy, but not for manufacturing and non-manufacturing separately.

The second line of each pair of results displays a version of the wage equation in which the sum of coefficients on lagged inflation is constrained to be unity, and the 'excess real wage growth' dummy variables are included [see columns (5), (6), and (7)]. These coefficients are almost all insignificant, except for a large negative coefficient in Japanese manufacturing after 1972, and a positive coefficient in European non-manufacturing for the entire period. Of particular importance are the small and uniformly insignificant set of excess real wage growth dummy variables for the European aggregate economy and for the manufacturing sector, denying the importance of real wage rigidity, and calling attention instead to the wage push during 1968–70 (column 8) as the sole source of a 'real wage problem' in Europe. Also important for the interpretation of the European unemployment problem is the absence of a significantly positive coefficient for 1980–84, as would be required to confirm the hypothesis that high unemployment in Europe did not hold down wage changes as much as would have been predicted from pre-1980 behavior. The interpretation of the 1980–84 period receives more attention in our discussion of the 'hysteresis' hypothesis below.

5.2. Mark-up price equations

To complete the estimation of the wage-price model, table 6 reports estimates of the price mark-up equation in the form (20) above. To review, the mark-up equation is specified in first difference form. The inflation rate is regressed on the change in trend unit labor cost (current and one lag), the output ·ratio (current and one lag), the current rate of change of relative import prices, the two-year change in the total tax rate, and the single dummy variable for wage push or controls. To validate the original theoretical specification in (13), the output ratio should enter as a first difference, that is, the coefficient on the current output ratio should be positive and on the lagged output ratio should be equal in absolute value and negative in sign.

The results appear to contradict the hypothesis of a procyclical price markup. Of the nine lines in table 6, seven indicate a *negative* sum of coefficients on the output ratio (with four of the seven sums significant), indicating a perverse Phillips curve phenomenon that offsets part of the positive Phillips curve effect in the wage change equations. This can be interpreted as suggesting that in an open economy in which competition from abroad limits the short-run flexibility of prices, a demand expansion that raises the output ratio and the rate of wage change is reflected only partly in price change, resulting in a positive growth rate of the real wage. Such a result implies procyclical rather than countercyclical real wage behavior, but refers to the rate of change of the real wage rather than its level. Five sums of coefficients in column (2) of table 6 are insigificantly different from zero, and in no case does this reflect any significant zig-zag from a positive to a negative coefficient, as would be implied by a rate-of-change effect of the business cycle on the *change* in the markup.

The other coefficients in table 6 imply that the elasticity of price change to the change in trend unit labor cost is close to unity within the current and subsequent year. Import price changes are insignificant, except in the nonmanufacturing sector for the U.S. A positive and significant tax push effect occurs only for the Japanese aggregate economy. Finally, the wage-push and controls dummies are uniformly insignificant, indicating that for Japan and Europe the wage-push episodes raised wages but did not squeeze profits, leaving the markup unaffected.

5.3. Reduced-form inflation equations

Together the wage and price mark-up equations imply the reduced-form equation for price change written above as (21). This relates the current inflation rate to two lags of the inflation rate, the current and lagged output ratio, the current change in the import price, the two-year change in the tax

Table 6

Mark-up equations for annual change in prices (p_t).

	Sum of coefficients on current and one lagged change in				Control and wage push dummies	$\bar{R}^2$	S.E.E.	D.-W.
	Trend unit labor cost	Output ratio	$p^F - p$	t^T				
	(1)	(2)	(3)	(4)	(5)	(6)	(7)	(8)
U.S. aggregate								
Aggregate	0.99[b]	-0.17[b]	0.04	-0.05	0.31	0.92	0.63	2.11
Manufacturing	1.20[b]	0.16	-0.09	-1.35	-3.81	0.71	1.72	2.21
Non-manufacturing	0.94[b]	-0.54[b]	0.09[a]	0.53	1.47	0.80	0.99	1.00
Japan								
Aggregate	0.89[b]	-0.04	0.00	1.34[b]	-2.42	0.85	1.51	2.14
Manufacturing	0.53[b]	-0.06	-0.03	-0.25	4.22	0.73	2.43	2.43
Non-manufacturing	0.87[b]	0.02	0.01	1.26	-1.80	0.79	1.72	2.46
Europe								
Aggregate	1.01[b]	-0.32[b]	0.03	0.11	-0.63	0.86	0.96	1.47
Manufacturing	0.88[b]	-0.26[b]	0.07	-0.14	0.94	0.83	1.16	1.76
Non-manufacturing	0.93[b]	-0.36	0.01	0.21	-2.40	0.85	1.02	1.31

[a]Significant at 5 percent.
[b]Significant at 1 percent.

rate, and the same wage-push and control dummies discussed before. Table 7 presents the results of estimating (21).

The reduced-form equation is critical for determining the overall nominal flexibility of an economy. Flexibility in the form of a high positive coefficient on the output ratio in the wage change equation means little if it is offset by a high negative coefficient on the output ratio in the price mark-up equation. Column (2) of table 7 indicates that there are significant Phillips curve effects of the level of the output ratio in the reduced-form inflation equation in six of the nine sectors. Only in U.S. manufacturing and in both Japanese disaggregated sectors is there no significant Phillips curve effect. At the aggregate level the sum of coefficients on the output ratio is significant for all three economies in the relatively narrow range of 0.30 for the U.S., 0.37 for Europe, and 0.45 for Japan. Thus table 7 conflicts with previous claims that Europe exhibits significantly greater nominal flexibility than the U.S. Table 7 confirms the verdict of table 5 that nominal rigidity is limited to U.S. manufacturing, but nominal flexibility in U.S. non-manufacturing is almost as great as in European non-manufacturing.

The other coefficients displayed in table 7 can be compared with the parallel coefficients in table 5 for the wage change equations. The coefficients on the relative import price change term are all significantly positive for the aggregate and manufacturing sectors of the U.S. and Europe and are of plausible magnitudes. The insignificance of the import price coefficients for Japan may reflect the much-discussed absence of manufactured imports and of an import-competing sector.

The estimated controls coefficients in column (8) for the U.S. aggregate economy are similar to but less significant than those in my recent paper (1985) on the behavior of the U.S. inflation rate in quarterly data. For Japan the 1973–74 wage-push phenomenon was almost entirely reflected in faster inflation in the manufacturing sector, while in non-manufacturing about one-quarter of the 'push' was not reflected in faster inflation but rather (implicitly) in a profit squeeze. As for Europe, the reduced-form coefficients imply a significant acceleration of inflation in 1968–70 which was roughly equal to the magnitude of the wage-push effect in the wage equation.

5.4. The output sacrifice ratio

A useful measure of an economy's nominal rigidity is its 'output sacrifice ratio', a concept originally applied to a hypothetical reduction in nominal GNP growth intended permanently to slow the rate of inflation. The ratio is defined as the cumulative output loss (expressed as a percent of one year's GNP) following a hypothetical nominal GNP deceleration, divided by the permanent reduction in the inflation rate which is achieved. For instance, the U.S. disinflation of the 1980s can be described as involving (roughly) a five

Table 7

Equations for annual change in value-added deflator (p_l), 1964–84.

	Sum of coefficients				Constant (trend) terms			Control and wage push dummies (8)	$\bar{R}^2$ (9)	S.E.E. (10)	D.–W. (11)
	Infla-tion (1)	Output ratio (2)	$p^F - p$ (3)	t^T (4)	1964–1984 (5)	1973–1984 (6)	1980–1984 (7)				
U.S. aggregate	1.07[b]	0.30[a]	0.07[a]	-0.15	-	-	-	-1.67	0.84	0.91	2.51
	1.00	0.36[b]	0.07	-0.37	0.41	0.28	0.54	-1.68	0.83	0.92	2.72
U.S. manufacturing	0.67[b]	-0.01	0.15[a]	0.50	-	-	-	-4.93	0.65	1.56	2.31
	1.00	0.08	0.15	-1.41	2.09	-2.65	1.44	-9.38[a]	0.40	2.48	2.63
U.S. non-manufacturing	1.04[b]	0.46[a]	0.06	0.26	-	-	-	-0.43	0.76	1.10	2.06
	1.00	0.65[b]	0.02	-0.20	0.04	1.61	-0.59	0.13	0.78	1.04	2.18
Japan aggregate	0.70[b]	0.45[a]	0.00	0.43	-	-	-	12.52[b]	0.81	1.70	1.99
	1.00	0.13	0.01	1.01	-0.39	-4.06[a]	2.46	12.52[b]	0.75	1.96	1.99
Japan manufacturing	0.27	0.07	-0.05	0.62	-	-	-	12.78[b]	0.56	3.10	1.87
	1.00	-0.01	-0.08	3.47	-2.47	-4.75[a]	3.48	18.58[b]	0.28	3.98	2.04
Japan non-manufacturing	0.81[b]	0.22	0.02	-0.19	-	-	-	8.54[b]	0.58	2.47	1.69
	1.00	-0.13	0.05	0.26	1.11	-4.70[a]	3.36	10.18[b]	0.65	2.23	1.96
Europe aggregate	1.10[b]	0.37[b]	0.10[a]	-0.94[a]	-	-	-	3.11[b]	0.82	1.07	2.55
	1.00	0.62[b]	0.04[b]	-0.85[b]	-0.01	1.02	1.46	3.06[b]	0.85	0.98	2.08
Europe manufacturing	1.07[b]	0.20[a]	0.18[b]	-1.01	-	-	-	3.66[b]	0.73	1.46	2.53
	1.00	0.29	0.13	-1.15	0.04	1.02	0.64	3.58[b]	0.74	1.45	2.27
Europe non-manufacturing	1.13[b]	0.60[a]	0.03	-0.92	-	-	-	3.14[a]	0.58	1.50	2.39
	1.00	0.75	0.03	-0.92[a]	0.81[b]	0.90	0.38	3.10[a]	0.68	1.48	2.40

[a] Significant at 5 percent.
[b] Significant at 1 percent.

percent permanent reduction in nominal GNP growth, a five percent permanent reduction of the inflation rate, and a cumulative output loss equal to 30 percent of a year's GNP, for an output sacrifice ratio of 6.0 ($=30/5$).

Of course the sacrifice ratio concept can be applied in reverse to the issue of reflation. Starting from a situation of a low output ratio and low inflation, how much output would be gained from an acceleration of nominal GNP growth, and at what cost in the form of permanently higher inflation? The wage–price model developed in this paper can be simulated to calculate the sacrifice ratio implied by the estimated coefficients. When the reduced-form equations of table 7 are used, the simulations are particularly straightforward, consisting of a two-equation model. The first equation is the reduced-form equation relating inflation to lagged inflation and the current and lagged output ratio (the relative import price change, tax change, and wage-push dummy variables are all set to zero). The sum of coefficients on lagged inflation is constrained to sum to unity, and no other dummy variables or constants are included. The second equation is the identity that defines this year's log output ratio as equal to last year's ratio, plus the current growth rate of nominal GNP, minus the current inflation rate, minus the growth rate of natural (i.e., trend) real GNP.

The simulations are calculated for the 20-year period from 1985 to 2004. The growth rate of nominal GNP is initially set at the growth rate of natural real GNP plus the 1984 inflation rate, and the two-equation model is simulated to determine the output ratio and inflation rate over the 20-year period when the growth rate of nominal GNP is set permanently at this initial level. Then an alternative simulation is run in which growth rate of nominal GNP is set permanently at a rate 5 percent higher than the initial level.

Table 8 exhibits the average inflation rates over the 20 year period in each simulation, the cumulative values of the output ratio, and the implied output sacrifice ratio. The line labelled 'reduced form' describes the experiment described above, and the line labelled 'wage-price model' describes the analogous experiment using a three-equation model consisting of the wage equation from table 5, the price mark-up equation from table 6, and the identity defining the current output ratio.

It is important to note that these simulations maintain at zero the changes in the relative import price terms that enter into the wage and price equations. Thus the expansion of nominal GNP growth is implicitly assumed to take the form of a mixed monetary and fiscal policy stimulus that maintains the value of the real exchange rate. Sacrifice ratios calculated for a monetary expansion with the exchange rate endogenous tend to yield a smaller output sacrifice, since the exchange rate depreciation resulting from a monetary stimulus would tend to accelerate inflation faster and reduce the remaining amount of the extra nominal GNP growth available to support real output growth.

Table 8

Output sacrifice ratios based on a permanent acceleration of nominal GNP by 5.0 percent compared to a 'before' simulation.

	Averages, 1985–2004		Cumulative output ratio to 2004		Output sacrifice ratio (5)
	Inflation 'Before' (1)	Inflation 'After' (2)	'Before' (3)	'After' (4)	
U.S.					
Reduced-form	3.2	8.0	0.1	31.5	6.5
Wage-price model	3.2	8.0	−1.2	30.9	6.6
Japan					
Reduced-form	0.6	5.6	−0.1	11.4	2.3
Wage-price model	0.6	5.6	0.1	11.5	2.3
Europe					
Reduced-form	4.7	10.1	24.6	50.3	4.8
Wage-price model	2.6	7.9	−11.5	60.2	13.5

The sacrifice ratios displayed in table 8 for the U.S. are 6.5 for the reduced-form inflation equation and 6.6 for the separate wage and markup equations. These compare to sacrifice ratios in Gordon (1985) of about 8 with no import price feedback, and of about 4.5 with an endogenous foreign price feedback. As might be expected, the sacrifice ratios for Japan are much smaller than for the U.S. Finally, the sacrifice ratio implied by the reduced form equation for Europe is 4.8, only moderately below that for the U.S., and for the separate wage and markup equations is actually 13.5, much higher than that for the U.S.[10]

5.5. The 'hysteresis' hypothesis

The last topic of the paper is the 'hysteresis' hypothesis, which states that the natural rate of unemployment is 'path dependent', that is, is not independent of the evolution of the actual unemployment rate but rather responds with a lag to the path fo the actual unemployment rate. In this paper, which focusses on the equivalent concepts of the natural level of output and the log output ratio, the hysteresis hypothesis states that the natural level of output evolves not along a log-linear trend but with a lagged response to the actual path of output. If valid, this hypothesis would have

[10]The wage-markup model for Europe is prone to oscillations, due to the fact that virtually the entire positive cyclical effect of the output ratio on the rate of wage change occurs with a one-year lag. The results displayed in table 8 were obtained by constraining the current and one-year lagged coefficients on the output ratio to be equal. This constraint reduces the sum of coefficients on the output ratio only from 0.62 to 0.56 and raises the standard error of the estimated equation only from 1.25 to 1.28.

the important policy implication that the output slump in Europe in the 1980s has reduced the natural level of output, gradually eliminating slack to the point that there is no longer any further downward pressure on wage changes.[11]

Out test of the hysteresis approach can be illustrated in a simplified version of the wage equation included here for expository purposes only

$$w_t - p_{t-1} = \alpha_0 + \alpha_{11}(Q_1 - Q_t^*) + \alpha_{12}(Q_{t-1} - Q_{t-1}^*),$$

$$= \alpha_0 + \alpha_{11}\Delta(Q_t - Q_t^*) + (\alpha_{11} + \alpha_{12})(Q_{t-1} - Q_{t-1}^*), \tag{28}$$

where once again upper-case letters designate logs of levels, and both the current and one lagged value of the output ratio are included in the wage equation to accord with our basic specification reported in table 5. The second line of (28) restates the role of the output ratio as entering through the current difference (Δ) and the lagged level.

Let us assume that the unobservable natural output level (Q_t^*) is some unknown weighted average of the linear trends of table 3 (Q_t^T) and a hysteresis term (Q_t^H) equal to a three-year moving average of actual output

$$Q_t^* = \Psi Q_t^H + (1 - \Psi)Q_t^T. \tag{29}$$

To identify the Ψ parameter, we substitute (29) into the *lagged level* term (28), while assuming that in the difference term $Q_t^* = Q_t^T$. Rearranging, we obtain

$$w_t - p_{t-1} = \alpha_0 + \alpha_{11}\Delta(Q_t - Q_t^T) + (\alpha_{11} + \alpha_{12})(Q_{t-1} - Q_{t-1}^T)$$

$$- (\alpha_{11} + \alpha_{12})\Psi(Q_{t-1}^H - Q_{t-1}^T). \tag{30}$$

The hysteresis coefficients (Ψ) listed in table 9 are obtained by running the wage change equations from table 5 and the reduced-form change equations from table 7 again with the addition of the lagged ($Q_t^H - Q_t^T$) term, where Q_t^H is defined as a trend-adjusted three-year moving average

$$Q_t^H = [Q_t + (1 + q_{t-1}^T)(Q_{t-1} + (1 + 2q_{t-2}^T)Q_{t-1}]/3, \tag{31}$$

where a lower-case q^T refers to the growth rate of the output trend for the year in question. The most important finding in table 9 is that the hysteresis coefficients are insignificant for the wage change equation, except in U.S. and

---

[11]Empirical evidence supporting the hysteresis hypothesis for Europe is presented by Blanchard and Summers (1986) and for France by Sachs and Wyplosz (1985). Policy implications are analyzed by Sachs (1986).

Table 9
'Hysteresis' coefficients in reduced-form price equation and in wage equation.

	Wage equation		Reduced-form price equation	
	Ψ Coefficient	[t ratio]	ΨCoefficient	[t ratio]
U.S.				
Aggregate	0.40	[1.50]	0.51	[1.09]
Manufacturing	2.66	[1.98]	1.38	[0.96]
Non-manufacturing	0.30	[0.99]	0.88	[2.56]
Japan				
Aggregate	0.11	[0.30]	0.80	[2.11]
Manufacturing	0.79	[3.41]	1.16	[1.65]
Non-manufacturing	0.33	[0.54]	0.92	[1.80]
Europe				
Aggregate	−0.12	[−0.11]	0.81	[1.13]
Manufacturing	−0.15	[−0.16]	−0.77	[−0.30]
Non-manufacturing	0.53	[−0.67]	0.94	[1.06]

Japanese manufacturing, and in the reduced-form price change equation except in U.S. non-manufacturing and the Japanese aggregate sectors. In Europe, where the problem of high unemployment stimulated the development of the hysteresis hypothesis, the Ψ coefficients are uniformly insignificant.

Because the statistical insignificance of the hysteresis effect for Europe conflicts with most of the recent literature, particularly Blanchard and Summers (1986) and Sachs (1986), we have conducted further tests to assess its importance. First, we display four time series for the European aggregate covering the period 1979–84, including the log output ratio defined alternatively relative to the 1072–84 trend $(Q_t - Q_t^T)$ and relative to the hysteresis concept of the natural rate $(Q_t - Q_t^H)$, as well as the dependent variables of the price change (p_t) and wage change $(w_t - \theta_t)$ equations.

	$Q_t - Q_t^T$	$Q_t - Q_t^H$	p_t	$w_t - \theta_t$
1979	0.09	0.64	7.77	6.44
1980	−1.40	−0.68	10.31	7.97
1981	−4.24	−2.34	9.10	7.62
1982	−6.50	−2.41	8.87	6.47
1983	−7.91	−1.64	6.76	4.71
1984	−8.51	−0.81	5.28	2.60

Thus the hysteresis version of the log output ratio in the second column indicates that slack in Europe had almost disappeared by 1984, in contrast to the GNP gap of 8.5 percent implied by the output ratio measured relative to the 1972–84 trend.

Since the estimated hysteresis coefficients in table 9 do not provide a statistically significant measure of the hysteresis coefficient (Ψ) for Europe, another alternative is to estimate separate wage change and reduced-form price equations using the two concepts of the log output ratio ($Q_t - Q_t^T$ and $Q_t - Q_t^H$) as alternatives. The standard errors for the alternative equations for the European aggregate economy are

	p_t	$w_t - \theta_t$
Using $Q_t - Q_t^T$	1.07	1.20
Using $Q_t - Q_t^H$	1.03	1.56

The first line corresponds precisely to the unconstrained results for the European aggregate economy in tables 7 and 5, respectively. The second line uses the alternative hysteresis concept of the output ratio ($Q_t - Q_t^H$ in place of $Q_t - Q_t^T$) for the full 1964–84 period. The results indicate a mixed verdict. The hysteresis version fo the log output ratio performs slightly better in the reduced-form price change equation but much worse in the wage change equation. Since most theoretical justifications of the hysteresis concept are based on labor market behavior and the presumed failure of wage rates to adjust to labor market slack, these results raise serious questions about the validity of the hysteresis hypothesis for Europe in the 1980s.[12]

What is the implied natural rate of unemployment for Europe predicted by our concept of the log output ratio based on the 1972–84 output trend? To calculate this implication of the results, an Okun's Law equation was estimated for 1964–79 which regresses the unemployment gap (defined relative to an assumed natural rate of unemployment series linearly interpolated between the actual values of 1961, 1972, and 1979) on the current and one lagged value of the log output ratio. The forecast values of the unemployment gap for 1980–84, given the actual values of the output ratio, allow us to calculate the implied natural rate of unemployment as the actual value of the unemployment rate minus the forecast unemployment gap.

	Actual U	Forecast U gap	Implied Natural rate
1979	5.0	0.0	5.0
1980	5.3	0.4	4.9
1981	7.0	1.4	5.6
1982	8.3	2.4	5.9
1983	9.3	3.1	6.2
1984	9.9	3.5	6.4

[12]In the sub-sectors the results are also mixed. In the manufacturing sector, which has previously been the primary focus of proponents of the hysteresis hypothesis, the use of the alternative $Q_t - Q_t^H$ concept of the output ratio unambiguously worsens the fit of the wage

The natural rate of unemployment series implied by our log output ratio thus does not remain fixed at the 1979 level, but rather rises from 5.0 percent in 1979 to 6.4 percent in 1984. Nevertheless, based on the Okun's law relationship of unemployment and output gaps in Europe prior to 1980, the 1984 output gap of -8.5 percent implies an unemployment gap of 3.5 percent. Further, the estimated 1984 natural rate of unemployment for Europe, 6.4 percent, is roughly the same as the 6.0 percent rate for the U.S. estimated in Gordon (1985).

6. Conclusion

The primary theme of the paper is that the previous literature has greatly exaggerated the contrast between the cyclical behavior of labor productivity, wage rates, and price deflators in the U.S. and Europe. Most important, the evidence that the U.S. exhibits more nominal rigidity than Europe is confined to manufacturing. In the aggregate economy and in non-manufacturing the coefficients on the output ratio in the wage equations for the U.S. and Europe are roughly similar. The same similarity arises in the reduced-form inflation equations for the U.S. and Europe. In Japan the familiar result of greater nominal flexibility appears only in the aggregate reduced-form price equation, but not for the two sub-sectors or for the wage equations. Calculated output sacrifice ratios confirm the conclusion that nominal wage rigidity in the U.S. is greater than in Japan, but no greater than in Europe, at least for the aggregate economy. Thus these results undermine the case frequently made against demand expansion in Europe on the ground that a uniquely vertical European aggregate supply curve would cause such an expansion to cause only extra inflation with no bonus of extra output. The sacrifice ratio calculation indicates that substantial extra output would be generated by a nominal demand expansion, albeit with an acceleration of inflation (just as would occur in the U.S. with a similar demand expansion).

The behavior of real wages also receives a new interpretation in this paper. Perhaps most important, the symmetric treatment of the self-employed, with both their income and their labor hours included in measures of labor compensation, labor's share, and the 'wage gap' index, completely eliminates the secular uptrend in the wage gap indexes for Japan and Europe that have been so evident in previous research. Further, the frequent claim that real wages are more rigid in Europe than in the U.S. now requires reinterpretation. In 1984 the European wage gap was lower than the U.S. wage gap in

---

equation (standard error of estimate rises from 1.82 to 2.28) and of the reduced-form price equation (standard error rises from 1.46 to 1.94). In the non-manufacturing sector, however, the hysteresis concept $Q_t - Q_t^H$ reduces the standard errors from 1.50 to 1.36 and 1.31 to 1.10, respectively.

manufacturing (but higher in non-manufacturing), creating problems for classical interpretations of unemployment in Europe where most of the observed decline in employment has occurred in manufacturing. If anything, real wages in Europe and Japan were too flexible rather than too rigid, in the sense that much of the increase in the wage gap indexes in Europe during 1968–70 and in Japan during 1973–74 can be interpreted as autonomous wage push. The component of the higher wage gap that can be attributed to the failure of real wages to adjust to the post-1972 productivity growth slowdown is relatively small.

Finally, the paper contains new results on productivity behavior that are of independent interest, outside of the context of the controversy over real and/or nominal rigidity. The paper confirms the real-wage elasticity of labor input emphasized in several recent papers, but shows that the response of labor input and labor productivity to changes in the real wage is roughly similar in the three countries, rather than being especially high in Europe. The results have the interesting implication that a substantial component of the slowdown in productivity growth, especially after 1972 in U.S. non-manufacturing and after 1979 in Japan and Europe, can be attributed to a shift from excessive to moderate real wage growth. Finally, the paper finds no evidence to support those who have claimed that productivity exhibits a countercyclical response in Europe in contrast to a procyclical response in the U.S. There is a slight procyclical response of productivity to changes in the output ratio that is almost identical in the U.S. and Europe, in contrast to a more marked procyclical response in Japan.

Data appendix

A.1. Data for the aggregate economy

This listing refers to the methods used to compile data for all fourteen countries, which are the United States, Japan, Canada, Austria, Belgium, Denmark, France, West Germany, Italy, Netherlands, Norway, Sweden, Switzerland, and the United Kingdom, except where mentioned otherwise.

Real output (Q)
    Real gross domestic product from *OECD Statistics Paris: 1985* (PC data diskette, 1985).

Nominal output (Y)
    Nominal gross domestic output from *OECD Statistics Paris: 1985*.

Compensation of employees
    Total compensation of employees from *OECD Statistics Paris: 1985*.

Operating surplus
From *OECD Statistics Paris: 1985*.

Indirect taxes
From *OECD Statistics Paris: 1985*.

Import price deflator
The import price deflator is from the *International Financial Statistics*, series 75, various issues.

Unemployment rate
Standardized unemployment rate, from the *OECD Economic Outlook*, table R12. See notes to table 1.

Hours worked
Aggregate hours worked per employee per year, from John P. Martin, at the OECD, covering the period through 1982 or 1983, depending on the country. Updated to 1984 using the *Yearbook of Labour Statistics, 1985* published by the ILO, using the growth rate of weekly hours worked, except for Canada, Germany, Netherlands, and Norway, where it was not needed. No change was assumed for Italy. Since no data were available for Austria, Switzerland and Denmark, the hours for Germany were used for Austria and Switzerland, and hours for Norway were used for Denmark.

Employment
Total employment, taken from *Labour Force Statistics, 1963–83* (OECD). Updated to 1984 using for most countries from *Quarterly Labour Force Statistics, No. 4 1985* (OECD) country pages, except for Denmark and Netherlands, for which we used the Yearbook of Labour Statistics, 1985 (ILO), and Belgium, which was guessed to have 1% growth from the *OECD Economic Outlook* description in December 1984.

Entrepreneurial income
Taken from the *National Accounts, Vol. II* (OECD), various issues, from the old table 6, line 4.1, through 1981, and from the new table 8, line 5, after 1981.

Employment tax
Employment tax rate paid by firms, from Andrew Newell, Centre for Labour Economics, Working Paper 781, series T1.

Income tax
Average rate of income tax paid, from Andrew Newell, Centre for Labour Economics, Working Paper 781, series T2.

Natural real GDP

Geometric interpolation between the benchmark years 1960, 1972, and 1979, with post-1979 using the same growth rate as for 1972–79. For Japan we used the benchmark years 1960, 1972, 1979, and 1984. For the U.S., Canada and France, where output was at or near a cyclical trough in 1960, we used the years 1964, 1972, and 1979, with the growth rate for 1964–72 used to extrapolate natural real GNP backwards from 1964 to 1960.

A.2. The manufacturing sector

All data were taken from an IMF unpublished quarterly data printout. Sources and methods are given in the appendix of Artus (1984).

Real output

Real domestic manufacturing output.

Wages

Hourly compensation in manufacturing.

Total hours

Total hours in manufacturing.

Employment

Total number of employees in manufacturing.

Value added deflator

The value added deflator for manufacturing.

A.3. The non-manufacturing sector

Variables for the non-manufacturing sector were calculated by taking the absolute magnitudes of the series for the aggregate economy and subtracting the corresponding absolute figure for the manufacturing sector. Since the manufacturing series were all in index form, the real magnitudes for manufacturing had to be determined from various sources for a particular base year (1972 was used throughout except where specified):

Manufacturing output in current dollars

Manufacturing output as a percentage of GDP was taken from *Historical Statistics 1960–83* (OECD), p. 59, table 5.3. Since this number was not available for Switzerland, the manufacturing output ratio was taken to be equal to the proportion of civilian employment involved in manufacturing, from the same source, p. 37, table 2.11.

Manufacturing employment

Total civilian manufacturing employment was taken from *Labour Force Statistics, 1963–83* (OECD) in the country tables for Breakdown by Activities. The series for France, Italy and the Netherlands were obtained from the *Yearbook of Labor Statistics, 1980* (ILO) in the series Employment in Manufacturing.

Total manufacturing hours

This was calculated by taking hours per employee per year for the aggregate sector in 1972, and then modifying it to obtain manufacturing hours per employee per year by multiplying it by the ratio of manufacturing hours per week divided by non-agricultural hours per week for 1970, obtained from the *Compendium of Social Statistics: 1977* (United Nations). This was then multiplied by 1972 manufacturing employment (determined above) to obtain total hours for manufacturing in 1972. This number is then multiplied by the index series of total manufacturing hours to obtain a series for nominal manufacturing manhours. Subtracting this series from absolute aggregate hours yields absolute non-manufacturing hours.

Manufacturing compensation

To determine the absolute level of total compensation for the manufacturing sector for Belgium, Canada, Denmark, France, Germany, Japan, the United Kingdom, and the United States, the labor share of value added in manufacturing was obtained from Bruno and Sachs (1985, p. 162). For Austria, Italy, the Netherlands, Norway, Sweden, and Switzerland the labor share of value added in the aggregate economy was used as a proxy.

References

Artus, Jacques A., 1984, The disequilibrium real wage hypothesis: An empirical evaluation, IMF Staff Papers 31, no. 2, June, 249–302.

Bean, C.R., P.R.G. Layard and S.J. Nickell, 1985, The rise in unemployment: A multi-country study, Working paper no. 795, Nov. (Centre for Labour Economics, London School of Economics, London).

Blanchard, Olivier J., 1986, Empirical structural evidence on wages, prices, and employment in the U.S., Working paper, May (MIT, Cambridge, MA).

Blanchard, Olivier J. and Lawrence H. Summers, 1986, Hysteresis and the European unemployment problem, NBER working paper no. 1950, June.

Branson, William H. and Julio Rotemberg, 1980, International adjustment with wage rigidity, European Economic Review 13, May, 309–332.

Bruno, Michael and Sachs, Jeffrey, 1981, Supply versus demand approaches to the problem of stagflation, in: H. Giersch, ed., Macroeconomic policies for growth and stability (Institut fur Weltwirtschaft, Universität Kiel).

Bruno, Michael and Sachs Jeffrey, 1985, The economics of worldwide stagflation (Harvard University Press, Cambridge, MA).

Gordon, Robert J., 1977a, World inflation and monetary accommodation in eight countries, Brookings Papers on Economic Activity 8, no. 2, 409–468.

Gordon, Robert J., 1977b, Interrelations between domestic and international theories of inflation, in: R. Aliber, ed., The political economy of monetary reform (Macmillan, London) 126–154.

Gordon, Robert J., 1982, Why U.S. wage and employment behavior differs from that in Britain and Japan, Economic Journal 92, March, 13–44.

Gordon, Robert J., 1983, A century of evidence on wage and price stickiness in the United States, United Kingdom, and Japan, in: J. Tobin, ed., Macroeconomics, prices, and quantitities (Brookings Institution, Washington, DC) 85–121.

Gordon, Robert J., 1984, Unemployment and potential output in the 1980s, Brookings Papers on Economic Activity 15, no. 2, 537–564.

Gordon, Robert J., 1985, Understanding inflation in the 1980s, Brookings Papers on Economic Activity 16, no. 1, 263–299.

Grubb, David, 1986, Topics in the OECD Phillips curve, Economic Journal 96, 55–79, March.

Hamada, Koichi and Kurosaka, Yoshio, 1984, The relationship between production and employment in Japan: Okun's law in comparative perspective, European Economic Review 21, no. 1/2, 71–94, June.

Knoester, A. and N. van der Windt, 1985, Real wages and taxation in ten OECD countries, Erasmus University discussion paper 8501/GM, Rotterdam.

Layard, P.R.G. and S.J. Nickell, 1984, Unemployment and real wages in Europe, Japan, and the U.S., Centre for Labour Economics, London School of Economics, London, Paper no. 677, October.

Newell, A. and J.S.V. Symons, 1985, Wages and employment in the OECD countries, University College, London, Department of Political Economy, Discussion paper 85-24, Sept.

Nordhaus, William, 1972, The worldwide wage explosion, Brookings Papers on Economic Activity 3, no. 2, 431–464.

Perry, George L., 1975, Determinants of wage inflation around the world, Brookings Papers on Economic Activity 6, no. 2, 403–435.

Sachs, Jeffrey, 1979, Wages, profits, and macroeconomic adjustment: A comparative study, Brookings Papers on Economic Activity 10, no. 2, 269–319.

Sachs, Jeffrey, 1983, Real wages and unemployment in the OECD countries, Brookings Papers on Economic Activity 14, no. 1, 255–289.

Sachs, Jeffrey, 1986, High unemployment in Europe: Diagnosis and policy implications, NBER working paper no. 1830, Feb.

Sachs, Jeffrey and Charles Wyplosz, 1986, The economic consequences of President Mitterand, Economic Policy 1, 261–306, April.

Tullio, Giuseppe, 1987, Long-run implications of the increase in taxation and public debt for employment and economic growth in Europe, European Economic Review, this issue.

COMMENTS

'Productivity, Wages, and Prices Inside and Outside Manufacturing in the U.S., Japan, and Europe' by Robert J. Gordon

William H. BRANSON

This paper marks (by the 1987 publication date) seventeen years of Robert Gordon's research on wage and price equations. In 1970, he published an important paper on the acceleration of inflation in the U.S. The wage equation (2) there had essentially the same form as equation (19) in this paper, and the price equation (1) of 1970 looks much like equation (20) here.

One principal difference is the addition of terms representing prices of traded goods and estimation across countries, representing Gordon's recognition of the importance of international effects and the value of comparative results. A second principal difference is the increase in the coefficient of expected inflation in the wage equation from around 0.5 in 1970 (p. 17) to around unity here in table 5. This represents the verticalization of the long-run 'Phillips curve since 1970. So in this paper and Gordon (1970) we have a comparison that shows the evolution of our views of wage and price equations since the beginning of the inflation cycle in the late 1960s.

In my discussion of the paper I will begin with a few points on the theoretical model of wage and price formation, and then discuss the transition from theory to estimating equations. A brief discussion of econometric results will come next. I will conclude with a few general points that return to the theme of wage rigidity.

At the outset, I should remind readers that Gordon does an important aggregation before moving to estimation. Using GNP weights, he creates a 'Europe' aggregate to compare to the U.S. and Japan. This gives us a view of wage and price behavior in Europe *on average*, not necessarily in Europe *in common*. If behavior in Europe is diverse, then the European average tells us little about any particular European country. The average is descriptive if the European economies' wage and price behavior has much in common. So the value of the 'European' results here depends on the degree of dispersion vs. similarity of European wage and price behavior.

The theoretical model begins with labor demand, eq. (3), which includes a productivity term, and labor supply, eq. (4), which includes a wage 'aspiration' term. Eq. (5) is an expression for excess demand, and eq. (6) gives its rate of change, which depends on the rate of growth of wages, etc. The twist that Gordon puts into the theory is to derive a Phillips curve by hypothesizing that the nominal wage moves to eliminate excess demand at a rate proportional to its level. This is stated in eq. (7). Since the growth rate of excess demand x_t in (6) depends on wage growth, the hypothesis implies that wage growth depends on the level of excess demand ($\log X_t$). This gives the Phillips curve expressions in eqs. (8) and (11).

As in the 1970 model, the specification here implies that an increase in productivity growth θ will increase the level of excess demand in the labor market that is consistent with steady deflation. From eq. (14), with $p = p^e$ and v constant, we get $dX/d\theta = b/g > 0$. This is reflected in Gordon's eq. (18) for the 'shock' natural rate concept. It seems to me an open question whether we believe that a change in the growth rate of productivity should influence the natural rate of unemployment.

Turning to the transition from theory to estimating equations, it is constructive to compare directly eqs. (13) and (20) for p_t. This comparison shows that the coefficient of ($p^F - p$) in eq. (20) is an estimate of ($1 - h$) in

(13). And the sum of coefficients on $\hat{Q}$ in (20) is the estimate of the coefficient of $m(v_t)$ in (13).

The estimates of eq. (20) are shown in table 6. The coefficients of $(p^F - p)$ in (20) say that the effect of import prices on the value-added deflator is virtually zero. This can make sense in economies where imports are both final goods and intermediate imports such as oil. An increase in world prices of traded goods, represented by import prices, would raise both competitive output prices and imported input prices. The direct effect on the value-added deflator is not clear.

More surprising are the coefficients of the output ratio in table 6. As Gordon notes, seven of nine coefficients are negative, indicating a fall in the mark-up as demand rises. But the explanation of this result in the paper is not satisfactory. Consider an economy with two sectors, producing traded and non-traded goods, respectively. These would roughly correspond to manufacturing and non-manufacturing in Gordon's sectorization. Suppose the nominal wage rate follows an average of the prices of the two sectors, with perhaps CPI weights. Then an increase in demand, raising the output ratio, should raise the price of non-traded goods. The price of traded goods remains fixed by the world market. Wages rise by an intermediate value. So in this open-economy model the non-traded good price would be highly pro-cyclical, as opposed to Gordon's story. I take the table 6 results as rejecting the mark-up model.

An intriguing aspect of the estimates in tables 2, 5, 6, and 7 is the frequency with which the estimated coefficient for the aggregate economy is outside the range provided by the coefficients for the two sectors in the equations for Japan. For example, in table 7, the aggregate output ratio coefficient is 0.45, while those for manufacturing and non-manufacturing are 0.07 and 0.22 respectively. One suspects that Ms. Compaq or Mr. Rats may have slipped up here.

Finally, a natural comparison to make is between the reduced form estimates in table 7 and the structural equations of tables 5 and 6. The estimates of coefficients in the latter two tables should combine to give something close to table 7. I did these calculations for the coefficient of the output ratio in the price equation, and found a surprising consistency. The structural and reduced-form estimates fit together very nicely.

On the question of relative wage stickiness, Gordon shows in table 5 that pronounced stickiness of the nominal wage is confined to the U.S. manufacturing sector. This is consistent with my understanding of previous results. Unions and nominal multi-year contracts are more prevalent in U.S. manufacturing than in any other country sectors considered here. In this sense, Gordon's results confirm earlier studies on nominal wage stickness.

On the other hand, I see no test here of real wage rigidity. We have no clear regression that shows the speed of adjustment of real wages to the output gap. In fact, flexible nominal wages in non-U.S. manufacturing could be consistent with sticky real wages. Gordon discusses real wage rigidity and classical unemployment in the context of his analysis of movements in labor shares, shown in fig. 2. The most striking result there is the rising share of labor in Japan since 1962. This could be a normal result of development; the labor share is typically lower in a developing country than in the OECD. I would not be surprised if the rising Japanese labor share in the two decades since 1962 simply follows from capital deepening and industrial development. In any event, the labor share is an endogenous variable. As Gordon suggests in his discussion of eq. (24), the effect of an exogenous push in wages on the labor share is ambiguous. So I find movements of the latter unconvincing as evidence for or against real wage rigidity. The issue remains an open one for Europe.

One final question came to my mind as I read the paper. Where are the effects of the big movement in the real exchange rate of the dollar against the EMS and the yen after 1980 on output and employment in manufacturing in this paper? The 1971–84 increase in the trend in Japanese manufacturing output in table 4 may reflect the real depreciation of the yen. I see no effect in the U.S. or Europe equations. For the U.S., Branson and Love (1986) estimate an elasticity of around -0.2 for the effect of real dollar appreciation on manufacturing employment. I have seen no estimates for Europe. The point here is that the swing in real exchange rates must have altered the relationship between manufacturing output and wage and price inflation in ways that do not come through in the small $(p^F - p)$ coefficients in tables 5–7. Robert Gordon has advanced our understanding of wage and price behavior in the OECD in this paper, but he has left a few puzzles yet to be solved.

References

Branson, W.H. and J.P. Love, 1986, Dollar appreciation and manufacturing employment and output, National Bureau and Economic Research working paper no. 1972, July.
Gordon, R.J., 1970, The recent acceleration of inflation and its lessons for the future, Brookings Papers on Economic Activity 1, 8–41.

COMMENTS

'Productivity, Wages, and Prices Inside and Outside of Manufacturing in the U.S., Japan, and Europe' by Robert J. Gordon

Heinz KÖNIG

Since the early 70s Robert J. Gordon promotes in a series of studies his ideas about the role of wages and prices for unemployment. The present paper picks up the theoretical framework developed in Gordon (1985), the novelty being (a) the distinction between manufacturing and non-manufacturing sectors, (b) a correction of labor's income share by adding the income of self-employed to labor income, and (c) a comparison of the role of productivity growth, nominal wage rigidity, the real wage gap and hysteresis effects for the three economic areas. Before turning to some critical comments let me stress that I, in principle, sympathize with Gordon's findings that 'the case for an excessive wage rate as the crux of the European unemployment has been carried too far'. However, a candidate for the explanation of the low responsiveness of employment to real wage rate reduction seems less the average wage rate but, as has been shown elsewhere for Germany [Franz and König (1986)], changes in the wage structure exhibiting a relative gain of less-qualified labor during the past two decades. Labor Office statistics reveal that particularly these groups share most of the burden of unemployment.

In the following I will focus on three aspects: (i) some ingredients of the theoretical model, (ii) some problems related to data construction and econometric methodology, and (iii) some 'minor' issues concerning aggregation across countries with differences in labor market legislation, participation rates, wage indexation, regulation, and institutional set-up.

(*i*)   As usual in macroeconomics the model posits homogenous labor. Non-economists may argue that, in fact, heterogeneous labor would be more appropriate for the explanation of the unemployment problem. But, as a macroeconomist, I dismiss this argument. However, one may ask whether the neoclassical framework as used in this paper is adequate for both the manufacturing and non-manufacturing sectors. Since Ehrenberg's work (1971) we have learned that especially in manufacturing deviations of demand from its long-term trend are smoothed by variations in utilization rates of labor, i.e., by overtime or short-time work. In 1983, overtime work ranged from roughly 5 percent in both France and Germany to 8.9 and 10.4 percent of normal working hours in the U.S. and Japan, respectively. May be that differences in the renumeration of overtime work explain the 'expected result that there is little cyclical responsiveness of wage rates in U.S. manufacturing, but the unexpected result that there is also less cyclical responsiveness in Japanese manufacturing than in Europe'. In any case it would be preferable to model working hours and persons employed as separate inputs. Recent studies show that nonlinear cost constraints due to overtime or short-time work may have serious implications with respect to the reactions of effective working hours and employment caused by wage rate and/or demand variations. Second, already R. Hall (1985) has questioned the hypothesis of mark-up pricing in particular with respect to international markets. For the non-manufacturing sector in Europe, at least, there exist additional doubts. Agricultural prices are fixed by the EC, prices for transportation, electricity, public services are more or less regulated according to rules whatsoever. Naturally, there are important differences between countries in the cyclical response of prices to labor productivity, as has been shown by de Ménil and Westphal (1985).

(*ii*)   As far as the econometrics are concerned one is somewhat troubled by simultaneity biases and autocorrelations of residuals indicating misspecification. Simultaneity not only causes a bias in the direct coefficient but also a bias in the constant term which – in the context of the productivity equation – with regard to the wage coefficient determines the productivity trend variable. Much more important, however, than econometric refinements are the problems related to the correction of labor income's share. As Gordon shows adding the compensation of household entreprenerial income to the compensation of employees has the effect that the secular increase in labor's share in Europe and Japan dissappears almost entirely. The question arises if this is a correct approach. Calculations for Germany, for instance, based upon the assumption that wage income of self-employed corresponds to wage income of identical (or similar) occupational groups of employed persons indicate still an increase of labor's share in the past decades. Finally, I still have some trouble to deduce reduced form coefficients by substituting wage equations estimates into the price equations. Quite substantial differences emerge which may be due to the strategy to save on degrees of freedom but which may be also a result of misspecification.

(*iii*)   Although I have been instructed by a well-known participant of the seminar that poodles look like poodles and that only they themselves know the differences, I still think that some thought on aggregation across countries might be useful with respect to the interpretation of the results. It is ample to state that European countries despite of the EC differ in many ways: 'Ordnungspolitik', labor legislation, institutional framework, policy goals and performance, demographic developments, participation rates and so on. Labor unions play different roles and wage bargaining may be firm and occuaption specific in one country but covering industrial sectors and regional areas in another. Differences in the sectoral composition – shares of agriculture, public services – are evident. Aggregation, therefore, may wipe out important differences in the structure, and hence, in reactions of economic agents. Poodles may look like poodles but behave quite different.

Nevertheless, in spite of this criticism expected from a discussant, I am convinced that Gordon's results with respect to the European wage gap in manufacturing and non-manufacturing offer not only new insights but also a puzzle to those who still believe that real wages are solely responsible for unemployment.

References

De Ménil, G. and U. Westphal, 1985, Stabilization policy in France and the Federal Republic of Germany (North-Holland, Amsterdam).

Ehrenberg, R.G., 1971, Fringe benefits and overtime behavior (Lexington).

Franz, W. and H. König, 1986, The nature and causes of unemployment in the Federal Republic of Germany since the 1970s: An empirical investigation, Economica 53, Suppl., 219–244.

Gordon, R.J., 1985, Understanding inflation in the 1980s, Brookings Papers on Economic Activity 16, 263–299.

Hall, R.E., 1985, Comment, Brookings Papers on Economic Activity 16, 300 ff.

II. THE EXTERNAL CONSTRAINT AND THE EXCHANGE RATE REGIME

Introduction to Part II

The International Seminar was established in 1978, early enough to catch the first wave of academic research stimulated by the breakdown of the Bretton Woods system in 1971 and the shift in early 1973 to a flexible exchange rate system. The point of departure for much of this research was the distinction between a fixed exchange rate system like Bretton Woods, in which inflation is transmitted from a large country like the U.S. to other nations that are forced to import inflation unwillingly, and a flexible exchange rate system that allows individual nations to uncouple their inflation rates and pursue independent monetary policies. In the paradigm presented by such longtime advocates of flexible exchange rates as Milton Friedman, nations with different degrees of aversion to inflation could go their separate ways, and the exchange rates of the inflation-prone countries would steadily and smoothly depreciate relative to the currencies of the inflation-averse nations. And, while nominal exchange rates would change to reflect inflation differentials between countries, real exchange rates would remain stable and real trade would proceed unhampered by the jarring one-step devaluations forced on inflation-prone countries that ran out of international reserves under the Bretton Woods system.

However, the first few years after 1973 exposed a reality that contrasted sharply with the paradigm of the flexible rate advocates. Exchange rates turned out to be highly volatile, and since nominal exchange rates varied far more than the inflation differential between countries, real exchange rates were volatile as well. Far from insulating real trade flows and domestic real activity from international monetary disturbances, the flexible exchange rate system proved to be highly disruptive. The U.S. economy overheated in 1978–1979, partly in response to the weak dollar, while the 50 percent real appreciation of the dollar between 1980 and early 1985 decimated U.S. exports and U.S. manufacturing output, leading to the popular evocation of the American industrial heartland as the 'rust belt'. Following 1985 the dollar returned roughly to its 1980 level, and the cycle of expansion in exports and manufacturing was repeated.

The volatility of real exchange rate movements provides the central theme for Part II of this volume, as well as the setting for three other subsidiary themes. First, the disruptive effects of real exchange rate volatility has led to a search for intermediate exchange rate systems that combine the best features of fixed and floating rates. Second, partly in response to the role of U.S. fiscal deficits in the 1980–1985 appreciation of the dollar, the volatility of real exchange rates has led to interest in using international policy coordination as a substitute for, or as a part of, an intermediate exchange rate system. Third, within Europe the formation in 1979 of the European Monetary System (EMS) combined an ongoing political process toward economic and monetary unification with a desire to move away from volatile exchange rates at least part of the way toward the ultimate objective of a common currency.

The first paper in Part II, 'The Collapse of Purchasing Power Parities during the 1970s' by Jacob Frenkel, has become a classic statement of the breakdown of the ideal Friedman paradigm in which exchange rate movements would mainly reflect differential inflation rates. Frenkel calls attention to the surprisingly loose relationship between price levels and exchange rates during the first decade of floating. Not only did short-run changes in exchange rates bear little relationship to short-run differentials in national inflation rates, but also divergences from purchasing-power parities (PPP) were cumulative.

Frenkel's empirical work contrasts the experience of the 1920s and 1970s for the bilateral exchange rates between the dollar and the British pound, French franc, and German mark (and also for various cross-rates among the pound, franc, and mark). He finds that PPP held up relatively well in the 1921–1925 period and that policies which affected the trend of domestic relative to foreign prices also changed the exchange rate in the appropriate direction by roughly one-to-one. The results for 1973–1979 differ completely – the slope coefficients relating exchange rate movements to inflation differentials are often insignificant or wrong-signed, and the equations are unstable across variations in specification.

To explain these results, Frenkel argues that exchange rates, like other asset prices, have been much more volatile than national price levels because they are more sensitive to expectations about the future. Exchange rates are forward looking, while national price levels are backward looking, due to the sluggish adjustment of wages and prices. Thus, during periods that are dominated by events that alter expectations, departures from PPP are likely to be the rule rather than the exception. To explain the greater divergences from PPP in the 1970s than in the 1920s, he points to the large number of shocks that caused sharp changes in expectations, including the oil embargo, supply shocks, commodity booms and shortages, shifts in the demand for money, and differential productivity growth. In drawing policy implications from his analysis Frenkel opposes policies of intervention in foreign exchange markets that attempt to force exchange rates to conform to PPP levels, and instead favors actions to minimize costly and unnecessary variations in exchange rates through the adoption of more stable and predictable policies.

Theoretical work has pointed to exchange rate 'overshooting' as an important component of real exchange rate volatility. Part of this theoretical contribution is provided by Willem Buiter and Marcus Miller in the next paper, 'Real Exchange Rate Overshooting and the Output Cost of Bringing Down Inflation.' To understand the overshooting phenomenon, imagine that country A and B initially have the same real interest rate, say 3 percent. Now A shifts to a tighter monetary policy, boosting its interest rate to 6 percent. With international capital mobility, why would anyone hold the securities of country B? This would occur only if the currency of A were expected to depreciate by 3 percent per annum in the future. To achieve this, the A currency must appreciate instantly at the time of the monetary tightening by enough to achieve the expected depreciation in the future. If the 3 percent depreciation were expected to last for 10 years, for instance, the currency of A would appreciate by 30 percent at the time of the policy shift, thus overshooting its value based only on fundamentals like inflation differentials (which are assumed to be zero in this example).

Buiter and Miller examine the implications of overshooting for the effects of deflationary monetary policy, using the 1979–1981 strategy of the Thatcher government as their main example. They stress that any appreciation of the home currency subsequent to an announced reduction in monetary growth is essentially due to the presence of non-classical rigidities in price and wage determination. In the long run, the real exchange rate is independent of the rate of monetary growth, that is, PPP holds. Any short-run appreciation thus constitutes overshooting, and would not occur if prices and wages adjusted instantaneously to the announced change in policy.

The link between the two parts of the Buiter–Miller paper, overshooting and the output cost of bringing down inflation, comes about because an exchange appreciation reduces the relative price of imports, and this acts to reduce the inflation rate and raise the growth rate of real output for any given growth rate of nominal output (just as would a beneficial supply shock like a bountiful harvest or reduction in the relative price of oil). However the authors then provide a demonstration, which they support with rough quantitative calculations based on U.K. parameters, that the additional reduction in inflation obtained by a managed appreciation of the home currency is only a transitory benefit. If it initially rises above its equilibrium level, the real exchange rate must eventually return to that level, causing inflation to be higher later than it otherwise would have been. The cumulative tradeoff between inflation reduction and output loss is thus unaffected by the path of the exchange rate. In all except timing, a stringent monetary policy so designed as to leave the real exchange rate unaffected would have results equivalent to those of a more dramatic unilateral policy.

Following the Frenkel analysis of the causes of real exchange rate volatility, and the Buiter–Miller study of some of its effects, we turn to two types of remedies, and these are intermediate exchange rate systems viewed from a global perspective, and the specific workings and effects of the European Monetary System. The third paper in this section by Marcus Miller and John Williamson, 'The International Monetary System: An Analysis of Alternative Regimes,' examines the relative implications for global price and output stability of three systems. These are free floating, specific agreements to stabilize *nominal* exchange rates (a proposal advocated by Ronald McKinnon), and agreements to stabilize *real* exchange rates (as advocated by John Williamson).

The analysis is conducted in the context of a simple Dornbusch-type, symmetric, two-country world model. McKinnon's proposal is represented as the fixing of nominal exchange rates and the targeting of the global price level. Williamson's proposal is represented as fixing real exchange rates and the use in each country of fiscal policy to target nominal income growth. In both proposals the targeting of something other than the money supply is aimed at the avoidance of shocks to velocity while retaining the monetarist principle of controlling a nominal variable in order to avoid an acceleration of inflation. Both stochastic disturbances are assumed, and the authors analyze the steady-state variances of global prices and global output under alternative systems. They make assumptions regarding the values of the half-dozen parameters of the model and proceed to make numerical calculations of the resulting variances.

These calculations, summarized in Table 5 of their concluding section, show that the effectiveness of the proposals depends on the nature of the shocks. In the case of demand shocks the two proposals 'trade off' the variances of prices and output, as the targeting of the price level by the McKinnon proposal reduces the variance of the price level at the cost of a higher output variance. The authors also show that a regime of free floating with a money-supply target can closely approximate the price and output variances of the McKinnon proposal. Obviously the latter conclusion depends on the amount of overshooting that occurs with the particular model in a free-floating regime; here the authors assume a minimal amount of overshooting.

In the next paper, 'The Advantage of Tying One's Hands: EMS Discipline and Central Bank Credibility,' Francesco Giavazzi and Marco Pagano examine the effects on central bank behavior of a specific exchange-rate regime, the fixed-rate European Monetary System (EMS). They set the stage for their study by noting an asymmetry of the EMS, in which inflation-prone countries periodically realign their currencies in order to counter the loss of competitiveness caused by their high inflation rates. While one would expect in this system movements of the real exchange rate between realignments, and then a return of the real exchange rate to equilibrium upon realignment, in fact the inflation-prone countries have not devalued sufficiently to restore the initial real exchange rate. Why, then, would an inflation-prone country join the EMS if it is likely to imply a trend of real appreciation over time? The authors argue that the answer must be the effect of the EMS on the 'incentive to inflate' of the monetary authority, which now must face the consequences of a trend real appreciation that would not exist under freely floating rates.

Giavazzi and Pagano treat the EMS exclusively as a form of precommitment about macroeconomic policy. Adherence implies that the new entrant agrees to raise inescapably the cost to itself of inflationary surprises by denying itself the possibility of offsetting through currency depreciation the loss of competitiveness which they imply. When the country is outside the EMS on its own its monetary authority has an ill-starred incentive to reduce the value of the public debt and raise output via unanticipated inflation. This incentive is ill-starred, because the public knows it and therefore thwarts it and also systematically raises its long-run expectation of inflation. By accepting in advance to bear an additional cost of unanticipated inflation, the monetary authority offsets this distortion, enhances its credibility, and thereby lowers the effective cost of inflation reduction. The conditions under which that calculus is favorable to joining the System are worked out in a small model in which the monetary authority maximizes an objective function of inflation and output, subject to the typical macroeconomic constraints of an open economy. The authors find that the result is often favorable to 'tying one's hands.'

At the background of most theoretical explanations of exchange rate volatility and overshooting is the assumption of perfect capital mobility. In the final paper in this section Martin S. Feldstein in "Domestic Saving and International Capital Movements in the Long Run and Short Run" raises questions about the interplay between international capital mobility and the autonomy of national macroeconomic policy. Are national capital markets so thoroughly permeable that they can be regarded as indistinguishable sources and uses of funds in a world market in which rates of return are systematically equalized internationally? Or, on the contrary, is the flow of capital as it moves across national boundaries sufficiently viscous for changes in national supply and demand to have persistent effects on national real interest rates?

Feldstein's paper emphasizes the long-run aspects of the question and examines the implications of international capital mobility for medium-term policies. If international capital flows were infinitely elastic, authorities in small- and medium-sized coutnries could not increase the supply of funds for national investment by any independent actions of their own. Only global agreements in which all parties acted in concert could effectively increase the supply of funds available for investment. In contrast, from the perspective of a large country like the United States, perfect capital mobility acts as less of a constraint on longrun policy, because its sources and uses of funds are such a large share of the total world supply and demand that, even acting alone, it could substantially alter global market conditions. Perfect capital mobility would nonetheless have important consequences for the United Sates, for it would imply that national policies pursued by U.S. authorities have major, direct consequences for the rest of the world and that feedback from the rest of the world influences the way in which these policies bear their fruit.

In this paper Feldstein presents an array of tests of the hypothesis of perfect international capital mobility based on cross-country differences of national rates of saving and investment in seventeen OECD countries. He develops a simple model of domestic saving, domestic investment, and net foreign investment in an open economy in the long run, and shows that, under certain circumstances, perfect capital mobility would imply zero correlation across countries between national rates of saving and investment. Using data on five-, ten- and twenty-year averages of these rates between 1960 and 1979, he then demonstrates that this correlation is closer to one than to zero. Feldstein concludes that the evidence rejects the hypothesis of perfect capital mobility and suggests that, in the post-OPEC period, a dollar of sustained increase in domestic saving increased domestic investment in the average OECD country by roughly 85 cents. The implication is that autonomous changes in domestic policy matter, and, for instance, a move toward a fiscal surplus directly increases the supply of national saving available for investment and does not entirely spill over abroad in the form of a reduction in foreign borrowing (or increase in foreign lending). [1]

[1] The Feldstein approach is controversial, and his finding of minimal capital mobility from evidence of highly correlated saving and investment rates seems to conflict with the widespread belief that capital mobility is high and has been growing. For a set of references on more recent work on this controversy, and an approach which measures the extent of capital mobility from forward exchange rate data, see another ISOM paper not included in this volume by Jeffrey A. Frankel and Alan T. MacArthur, 'Political vs. Currency Premia in International Real Interest Differentials: A Study of Forward Rates for 24 Countries, "European Economic Review, Vol. 32, no. 5 (June 1988), pp. 1083–1114.

European Economic Review 16 (1981). North-Holland

THE COLLAPSE OF PURCHASING POWER PARITIES DURING THE 1970's*

Jacob A. FRENKEL**

NBER, and The University of Chicago, IL 60637, USA

1. Introduction

One of the striking facts concerning the relationship between prices and exchange rates during the 1970's has been the dismal performance of the predictions of the simple versions of the purchasing power parity doctrine (PPP). That doctrine in its 'absolute version' states that the equilibrium exchange rate between domestic and foreign currencies equals the ratio of domestic to foreign price levels. The 'relative version' of the doctrine relates equilibrium changes in exchange rates to changes in the ratio of domestic to foreign prices. During the 1970's short-run changes in exchange rates bore little relationship to short-run differentials in national inflation rates and, frequently, divergences from purchasing power parities have been cumulative.

This paper reviews and analyzes the empirical record of exchange rates and prices during the 1970's and the analysis is based on the experience of the Dollar/Pound, the Dollar/French Franc and the Dollar/DM exchange rates. Section 2 presents the evidence on PPP during the 1970's and contrasts it with the evidence from the 1920's — a period during which the doctrine held up reasonably well. This analysis is relevant for assessing whether the flexible exchange rate system was successful in providing national economies with an added degree of insulation from foreign shocks, and whether it provided policymakers with an added instrument for the conduct of macroeconomic policy. The evidence regarding deviations from purchasing power parities is also relevant for determining whether there is a case for managed float. Section 3 attempts to explain what went wrong with

*An earlier version of this paper was presented at the International Seminar in Macroeconomics, Oxford, June 22–24, 1980, and sponsored by the National Bureau of Economic Research, Inc. and the Maison des Sciences de l'Homme, Paris.

**I am indebted to Lauren J. Feinstone for helpful suggestions and efficient research assistance and to Robert J. Gordon for many useful suggestions which stimulated this version of the paper. I also wish to acknowledge a National Science Foundation grant, SOC 78-14480, for financial support. This research is part of the NBER's Program in International Studies. The views expressed are those of the author and not necessarily those of the NBER.

the performance of the doctrine during the 1970's. It examines the hypothesis that the departures from PPP are a U.S. phenomenon, as well as the hypothesis that the departures are due to large changes in inter-sectoral relative price changes within the various economies. Given that the predictions of the simple versions of PPP do not hold up, section 4 proceeds in examining the question of whether national price levels have been independent of each other. Section 5 addresses the question of whether exchange rates and national price levels are comparable and whether in principle one should have expected them to be closely linked to each other. The main point that is being emphasized is that there is an important intrinsic difference between exchange rates and national price levels which stems from the 'asset market theory' of exchange rate determination. This theory implies that the exchange rate, like the prices of other assets, is much more sensitive to expectations concerning future events than national price levels and as a result, in periods which are dominated by 'news' which alter expectations, exchange rates are likely to be much more volatile than national price levels and departures from PPP are likely to be the rule rather than the exception. Finally, section 6 concludes the paper with some policy implications.

2. Purchasing power parities: The evidence

The relationship between exchange rates and prices that is summarized by the PPP doctrine is one of the oldest and the most controversial relationships in the theory of exchange rates. The intellectual origins of the doctrine [which are analyzed in Frenkel (1978)] can be traced back to the writings of Wheatley and Ricardo in the early part of the 19th century and its more recent revival owes much to Cassel's writings mainly during the 1920's. Much of the controversy concerning the usefulness of the PPP doctrine is due to the fact that it does not specify the precise mechanism by which exchange rates are linked to prices nor does it specify the precise conditions that must be satisfied for the doctrine to be correct. Rather, the PPP doctrine may be viewed as a short-cut; it specifies a relationship between two variables without providing the details of the process which brings about such a relationship and, therefore, it should not be viewed as a theory of exchange rate determination.

2.1. Empirical framework

The PPP relationship can be written as

$$\ln S_t = a + b \ln (P/P^*)_t + u_t, \tag{1}$$

where S_t and $(P/P^*)_t$ denote, respectively, the exchange rate (defined as the price of foreign exchange in terms of domestic currency), and the ratio of domestic to foreign price indices (with an asterisk denoting quantities pertaining to the foreign country) and where u_t denotes an error term. The formulation in eq. (1) corresponds to the absolute version of PPP. The corresponding relative version of PPP can be written as

$$\Delta \ln S_t = b \, \Delta \ln (P/P^*)_t + v_t, \tag{2}$$

where Δ denotes the first difference operator and where v_t denotes an error term.

From the empirical viewpoint several issues may be raised: (i) What price index should be used in eqs. (1)–(2)? (ii) Are the data consistent with the hypothesis that $b = 1$? (iii) Is the constant term in the relative version of PPP zero as implied by eq. (2)? Further refinements would also examine whether the coefficients on domestic and foreign prices are equal to each other (in absolute value) as implied by the specification of eqs. (1)–(2). These questions are examined below using monthly data for the U.S., the U.K., France and Germany. To allow for a simultaneous determination of prices and exchange rates, eqs. (1)–(2) are estimated using a two-stage least squares estimation procedure.

2.2. The evidence from the 1920's

In order to fix ideas and to provide perspective for the evaluation of the empirical record of the 1970's, it is useful to start with a brief review of the performance of PPP during the flexible exchange rates period of the 1920's. The experience with flexible exchange rates during the 1920's (which was terminated with the return of Britain to gold in mid-1925) has proven to be extremely important in shaping current thinking about a variety of issues concerning the economics of flexible exchange rates and has been critical for the growth of popularity of the PPP doctrine. That period included experiences under hyperinflationary conditions (the German hyperinflation) as well as under 'normal' conditions (based on the experience of Britain, the U.S. and France).

Estimates of eq. (1) for the 1920's using alternative price indices are reported in table 1.[1] These estimates indicate that in most cases the data are consistent with the hypothesis that the elasticity of the exchange rate with respect to the price ratio is about unity.[2] In assessing these results it is

[1] This paragraph draws on Frenkel (1980).
[2] In applying eq. (2) to the hyperinflation period it was assumed that the variations in P/P^* were completely dominated by variations in German prices so that the foreign price could be viewed as being fixed. For further evidence and tests and for the data sources, see Frenkel (1980).

Table 1

Purchasing power parities: instrumental variables, monthly data during the 1920's (standard errors in parentheses).[a]

Dependent variable ln S_t	Price index	Constant	ln (P/P^*)	s.e.	D.W.	ρ
Mark/Pound (Feb. 1921–Aug. 1923)	Wholesale	−1.676 (0.178)	1.026 (0.017)	0.221	2.01	0.24
	Cost of living	−1.575 (0.423)	1.084 (0.041)	0.367	2.06	0.50
Franc/Pound (Feb. 1921–May 1925)	Wholesale	0.562 (0.207)	1.141 (0.064)	0.044	1.82	0.53
	Material	0.613 (0.180)	1.081 (0.054)	0.042	2.18	0.48
Dollar/Pound (Feb. 1921–May 1925)	Wholesale	−0.118 (0.482)	0.897 (0.267)	0.019	1.99	0.85
	Material	−0.073 (0.453)	0.847 (0.245)	0.022	1.83	0.80
Franc/Dollar (Feb. 1921–May 1925)	Wholesale	1.183 (0.157)	1.091 (0.109)	0.054	1.70	0.58
	Material	1.243 (0.130)	0.992 (0.085)	0.050	1.74	0.54

[a] ln S_t denotes the logarithm of the spot exchange rate. ρ is the final value of the autocorrelation coefficient; an iterative Cochrane–Orcutt technique with two-stage least squares estimation method was used; the instruments are a constant, time, time squared, and lagged values of the dependent and independent variables. s.e. is the standard error of the equation.

important to recall that the estimates are based on monthly data and that short-run deviations from PPP may reflect the fact that not all markets adjust at the same speed. On the whole the results illustrate the main usefulness of the PPP doctrine. It provides a guide to the general trend of exchange rates and prices and it emphasizes that, as a first approximation, policies which affect the trend of domestic (relative to foreign) prices, are likely to affect the exchange rate in the same manner.

2.3. The evidence from the 1970's

In a recent paper dealing with inflation and unemployment, Gordon (1976), analyzed the reactions of a hypothetical modern-day Rip van Winkle who had become well acquainted with the earlier literature but who only recently awoke from a decade-long nap. It is interesting to examine the results of an analogous experiment in the context of PPP. Suppose that Rip van Winkle, who was well acquainted with the data reported in the previous section, went to sleep in 1925 to be awoken in the 1970's. Would his human capital of the 1920's vintage be obsolete? This question is of special interest since world capital markets have become much more integrated, the role of 'real' shocks and 'surprises' in the 1970's have become much more important, views about the role of government in the conduct of macroeconomic policies have changed, the roles of tariff and non-tariff barriers to trade as well as the degree of exchange rate management have been altered and finally, the International Monetary Fund has been created.

Table 2

Purchasing power parities: instrumental variables, monthly data: June 1973–July 1979 (standard errors in parentheses).[a]

Dependent variable ln S_t	Constant	ln (P_w/P_w^*)	ln (P_c/P_c^*)	s.e.	D.W.	ρ
Dollar/Pound	0.712 (0.149)	0.165 (0.507)		0.027	1.63	0.963
	2.982 (2.978)		1.070 (0.897)	0.029	1.66	0.998
Dollar/Franc	−1.521 (0.027)	0.184 (0.374)		0.029	2.26	0.863
	−1.570 (0.047)		−1.070 (0.817)	0.029	2.30	0.901
Dollar/DM	−0.900 (0.018)	1.786 (0.230)		0.034	1.69	0.739
	−0.908 (0.175)		2.217 (0.263)	0.031	1.96	0.759

[a]ln S_t denotes the logarithm of the spot exchange rate; ln (P_w/P_w^*) and ln (P_c/P_c^*) denote, respectively, the logarithms of the ratios of the wholesale price indices and the cost of living indices. Cochrane–Orcutt iterative technique with two-stage least squares estimation method was used; the instruments are a constant, time, time squared, and lagged values of the dependent and independent variables. s.e. is the standard error of the equation.

Tables 2 and 3 report the estimates of eqs. (1) and (2) for the monthly Dollar/Pound, the Dollar/French Franc and the Dollar/German Mark exchange rates using wholesale and cost of living price indices. As may be seen the results are extremely poor and the estimates are extremely imprecise. For the absolute version of PPP (table 2) the coefficients on the price ratios are significant only in the equations pertaining to the Dollar/DM exchange rate, and for the relative version of PPP (table 3) the slope coefficient is again insignificant. It is noteworthy, however, that (as expected) the constant terms in that table do not differ significantly from zero. The poor performance of these versions of PPP during the 1970's is augmented by the fact that in some cases the estimates do not remain stable over the sample period. This instability is especially exhibited in the Dollar/Pound regressions. Table 4 contains estimates of the Dollar/Pound equations for the

Table 3

Relative purchasing power parities: instrumental variables, monthly data: June 1973–July 1979 (standard errors in parentheses).[a]

Dependent variable $\Delta \ln S_t$	Constant	$\Delta \ln (P_w/P_w^*)$	$\Delta \ln (P_c/P_c^*)$	s.e.	D.W.
Dollar/Pound	0.009 (0.007)	1.827 (1.034)		0.036	1.53
	0.010 (0.007)		2.071 (1.084)	0.034	1.59
Dollar/Franc	−0.001 (0.004)	0.967 (0.722)		0.031	2.35
	−0.001 (0.006)		−0.030 (2.800)	0.030	2.36
Dollar/DM	0.004 (0.007)	−0.261 (1.703)		0.032	2.17
	−0.002 (0.008)		1.919 (2.305)	0.034	2.08

[a] $\Delta \ln S_t$ denotes the percentage change in the spot exchange rate; $\Delta \ln (P_w/P_w^*)$ and $\Delta \ln (P_c/P_c^*)$ denote, respectively, percentage changes in the ratios of the wholesale price indices and cost of living indices. s.e. is the standard error of the equation. Two-stage least squares estimation method is used; the instruments are a constant, time, time squared, and lagged values of the dependent and independent variables.

Table 4

Purchasing power parities for the Dollar/Pound: instrumental variables, monthly data: June 1973–February 1979 (standard errors in parentheses).[a]

Price index	Dependent variable	Constant	$\ln (P/P^*)$	$\Delta \ln (P/P^*)$	s.e.	D.W.	ρ
Wholesale price index	$\ln S_t$	0.726 (0.076)	0.424 (0.338)		0.027	1.74	0.938
	$\Delta \ln S_t$	0.003 (0.006)		1.032 (0.712)	0.030	1.71	—
Cost of living index	$\ln S_t$	0.727 (0.071)	0.544 (0.394)		0.026	1.83	0.935
	$\Delta \ln S_t$	0.005 (0.006)		1.637 (0.832)	0.030	1.87	—

[a] $\ln S_t$ and $\ln (P/P^*)$ denote, respectively, the logarithms of the spot exchange rate and price ratios; Δ denotes the first difference of these variables. s.e. denotes the standard error of the equation. Two-stage least squares estimation method was used; the instruments are a constant, time, time squared, and lagged values of the dependent and independent variables. Cochrane–Orcutt iterative technique was used with the levels.

period up to February 1979 instead of July 1979. The comparison of these estimates with those in tables 2 and 3 illustrates the extent of the instability.[3]

3. What went wrong?

From the comparison of the evidence from the 1920's with those from the 1970's it is obvious that if Rip van Winkle were to predict the results of table 2 from those of table 1 his predictions would have failed dramatically. What is responsible for this failure?

3.1. Are the departures from PPP a U.S. phenomenon?

In starting to account for the collapse of PPP in the 1970's it is first relevant to note that all the regressions in tables 2, 3 and 4 involve the U.S. dollar exchange rate and the U.S. price index. In order to examine whether this fact plays an important role in yielding the poor results, the PPP equations were re-estimated for the various exchange rates which do not involve the U.S. dollar or the U.S. price level, i.e., for the Pound/DM and the Franc/DM exchange rates. These results are reported in table 5. As may be seen the results here are much superior. Except for the wholesale price indices in the Franc/DM regression, all the coefficients are highly significant

Table 5

Purchasing power parities: instrumental variables, monthly data: June 1973–July 1979 (standard errors in parentheses).[a]

Dependent variable ln S_t	Constant	ln (P_w/P_w^*)	ln (P_c/P_c^*)	s.e.	D.W.	ρ
Pound/DM	−1.668 (0.041)	0.821 (0.144)		0.027	1.60	0.895
	−1.666 (0.048)		0.965 (0.197)	0.027	1.57	0.909
Franc/DM	0.863 (0.143)	−0.026 (0.487)		0.020	1.61	0.981
	0.602 (0.048)		1.180 (0.327)	0.019	1.48	0.929

[a]ln S_t denotes the logarithm of the spot exchange rate; ln (P_w/P_w^*) and ln (P_c/P_c^*) denote, respectively, the logarithms of the ratios of the wholesale price indices and the cost of living indices. Cochrane–Orcott iterative technique with two-stage least squares estimation method was used; the instruments are a constant, time, time squared, and lagged values of the dependent and independent variables. s.e. is the standard error of the equation.

[3]Further evidence on the empirical record of the PPP doctrine can be found in the various papers in the May issue of the *Journal of International Economics* 8, no. 2, 1978; and for surveys, see Officer (1976) and Katseli–Papaefstratiou (1979).

and the elasticities of the exchange rate with respect to the various price indices do not differ significantly from unity.

What accounts for the vast difference in the performance of PPP among the various currencies? One explanation can be made in terms of the general presumption that due to transport cost, PPP is expected to hold better among the neighboring European countries than among each of these countries and the U.S. A second explanation can be made in terms of changes in commercial policies and non-tariff barriers to trade which have been more stable within Europe than between Europe and the U.S. A third argument, which was put forward in another context by Gordon (1977), emphasizes the unique effects of the various phases of the U.S. price controls and their gradual removal during the first half of the 1970's. A fourth argument could be made in terms of the effects of institutional agreements like the snake and later on like the European Monetary System on the degree of the intra-European flexibility of exchange rates.

3.2. Changes in relative prices

The formulation of the PPP doctrine in eqs. (1) and (2) did not specify which price index should be used in the computation. Of course, when the structure of *relative* prices in the economy remains stable, as is likely to be the case when most of the shocks are of a monetary origin, the choice of the price index is immaterial. On the other hand, when there are real shocks which alter relative prices, the choice of the price index becomes crucial.

To illustrate, suppose that the domestic and the foreign aggregate price levels are a linear homogeneous (Cobb–Douglas) function of the prices of non-traded goods, P_N, and of traded goods, P_T, like in eqs. (3)–(4),

$$P = P_N^\beta P_T^{1-\beta}, \tag{3}$$

$$P^* = P_N^{*\beta^*} P_T^{*1-\beta^*}, \tag{4}$$

where β and β^* denote domestic and foreign expenditure shares on non-traded goods. From (3) and (4) the ratio of the prices of traded goods can be written as

$$\frac{P_T}{P_T^*} = \frac{(P_T/P_N)^\beta}{(P_T^*/P_N^*)^{\beta^*}} \frac{P}{P^*}. \tag{5}$$

Eq. (5) links the relative price of traded goods to the ratio of the price levels through terms which summarize the internal price structures in the two economies. Suppose now that the formulation of purchasing power parities in eqs. (1) and (2) applies only to *traded* goods [so that S equals (P_T/P_T^*)

plus an error term]. Using eq. (5) and adding a constant term yields

$$\ln S_t = a + \beta \ln (P_T/P_N)_t - \beta^* \ln (P_T^*/P_N^*)_t + \ln (P/P^*)_t + u_t, \tag{6}$$

or, assuming for expository purposes that $\beta = \beta^*$, this becomes

$$\ln S_t = a + \beta \ln \left(\frac{P_T/P_N}{P_T^*/P_N^*}\right)_t + \ln (P/P^*)_t + u_t. \tag{7}$$

A comparison of eq. (7) with (1) reveals that when the internal relative price structure remains stable, its neglect would not affect the relationship between the exchange rate and the ratio of *aggregate* price indices and its only influence would be confined to the estimate of the constant term. If, however, relative price structures do vary, then it is crucial to incorporate them explicitly into the PPP equations, and their omission introduces a specification bias.

Since the estimates in the previous tables were obtained from regressions employing aggregate price indices, it is important to examine whether relative price structures remained stable during the sample period. To examine this question it is first noted that the cost of living index contains relatively more non-traded commodities than the wholesale price index. It is likely therefore that when there are large changes in internal relative prices, these changes would be reflected in changes in the ratio of the cost of living to the wholesale price index.

Table 6 reports the estimates of regressions of cost of living indices on the wholesale price indices (as well as regressions of their rates of change) for the U.S., the U.K., France and Germany. As may be seen in all cases the elasticity of the cost of living *inflation* with respect to the wholesale price inflation is statistically significant but smaller than unity, while the elasticity of the *level* of the cost of living with respect to the wholesale price level is about unity in the U.S. and the U.K., is somewhat higher than unity in Germany and is about zero in France. These results indicate that the internal relative prices — as measured by the relationship between the cost of living and the wholesale price indices — have not changed much in the U.S. and the U.K., they have changed somewhat in Germany and have changed dramatically in France. This last observation may account for the poor performance of the PPP equation which related the Franc/DM exchange rate to the ratio of the wholesale price indices in table 5.

The general pattern of the internal price ratios is described in figs. 1–4 which show a scatter of monthly observations of the two price indices for the U.S., the U.K., Germany and France. As is evident from the first two scatter diagrams the changes in relative prices have not been pronounced; the scatter for Germany reveals some degree of relative price variations while the

Table 6

Cost-of-living and wholesale price indices: instrumental variables, monthly data: June 1973–July 1979 (standard errors in parentheses).[a]

Country	Dependent variable	Constant	$\ln P_w$	$\Delta \ln P_w$	s.e.	D.W.	ρ
U.S.	$\ln P_c$	−0.085 (0.220)	1.019 (0.047)		0.008	1.57	0.828
	$\Delta \ln P_c$	0.003 (0.002)		0.558 (0.206)	0.004	1.64	0.035
U.K.	$\ln P_c$	0.091 (0.200)	0.976 (0.041)		0.007	1.23	0.924
	$\Delta \ln P_c$	0.005 (0.005)		0.601 (0.339)	0.007	1.73	0.353
France	$\ln P_c$	4.655 (0.248)	0.077 (0.050)		0.004	0.50	0.980
	$\Delta \ln P_c$	0.007 (0.001)		0.287 (0.087)	0.003	1.85	0.659
Germany	$\ln P_c$	−1.434 (0.675)	1.310 (0.145)		0.006	1.12	0.905
	$\Delta \ln P_c$	0.002 (0.001)		0.414 (0.154)	0.003	1.97	0.373

[a] $\ln P_w$ and $\ln P_c$ denote, respectively, the logarithms of the wholesale price and cost-of-living indices; Δ denotes the first difference of these variables. Cochrane–Orcutt iterative technique with two-stage least squares estimation method was used; the instruments are a constant, time, time squared, and lagged values of the dependent and independent variables. s.e. is the standard error of the equation.

scatter for France shows an extraordinary degree of fluctuations in the internal relative prices. Since these fluctuations have been so large, the information of fig. 4 is supplemented by fig. 5 which presents a time series of the two price indices. In view of these large changes in the internal relative prices the collapse of PPP which was reported in section 2 is much less surprising.

4. Are national price trends independent of each other?

The two versions of the PPP doctrine relate the exchange rate to the ratio of national price levels and changes in the exchange rate to inflationary differentials. As was argued above these relationships are likely to hold when the internal relative price structures remain relatively stable, as would be the case when the predominant source of shocks is of a monetary origin. If, however, relative prices do change — as they should when the predominant source of shocks is of a real origin — then the simple PPP versions which use aggregate price levels are not likely to hold. It is possible, however, that

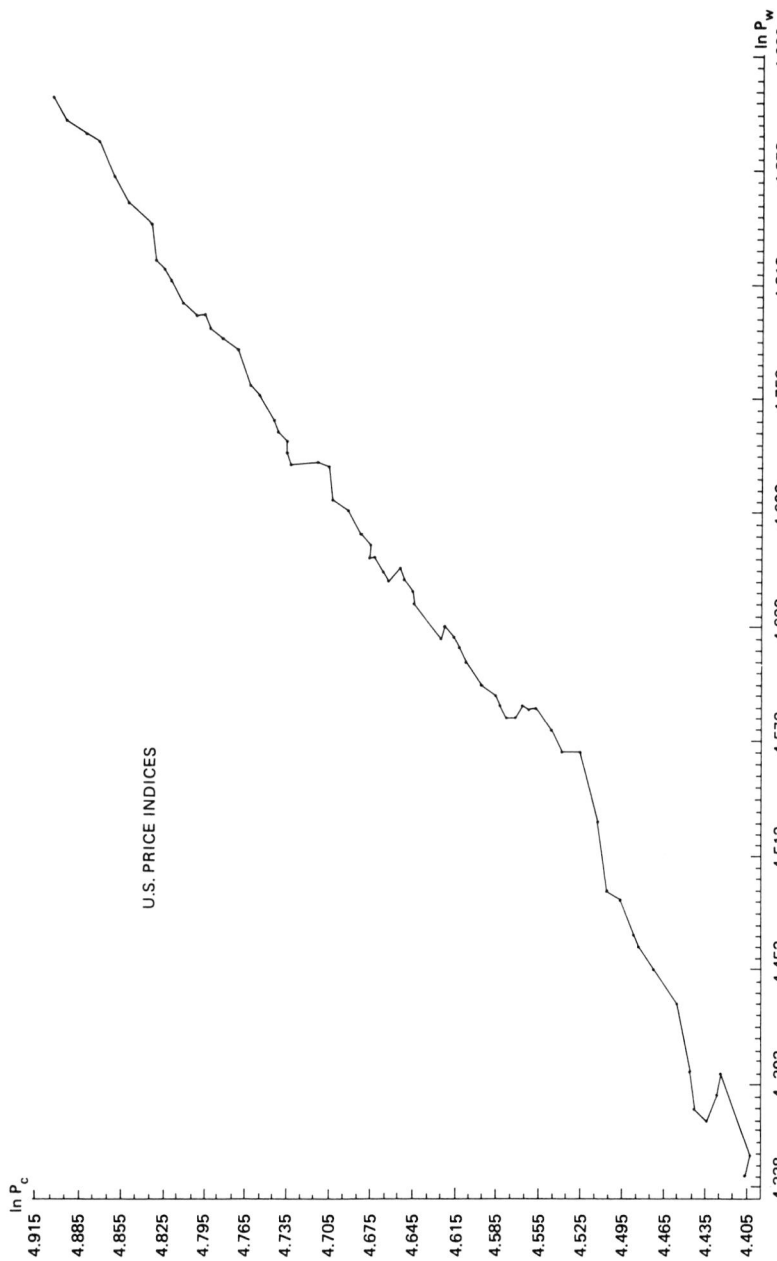

Fig. 1. A scatter diagram of monthly observations of the logarithm of the U.S. cost-of-living (P_c) and wholesale (P_w) price indices.

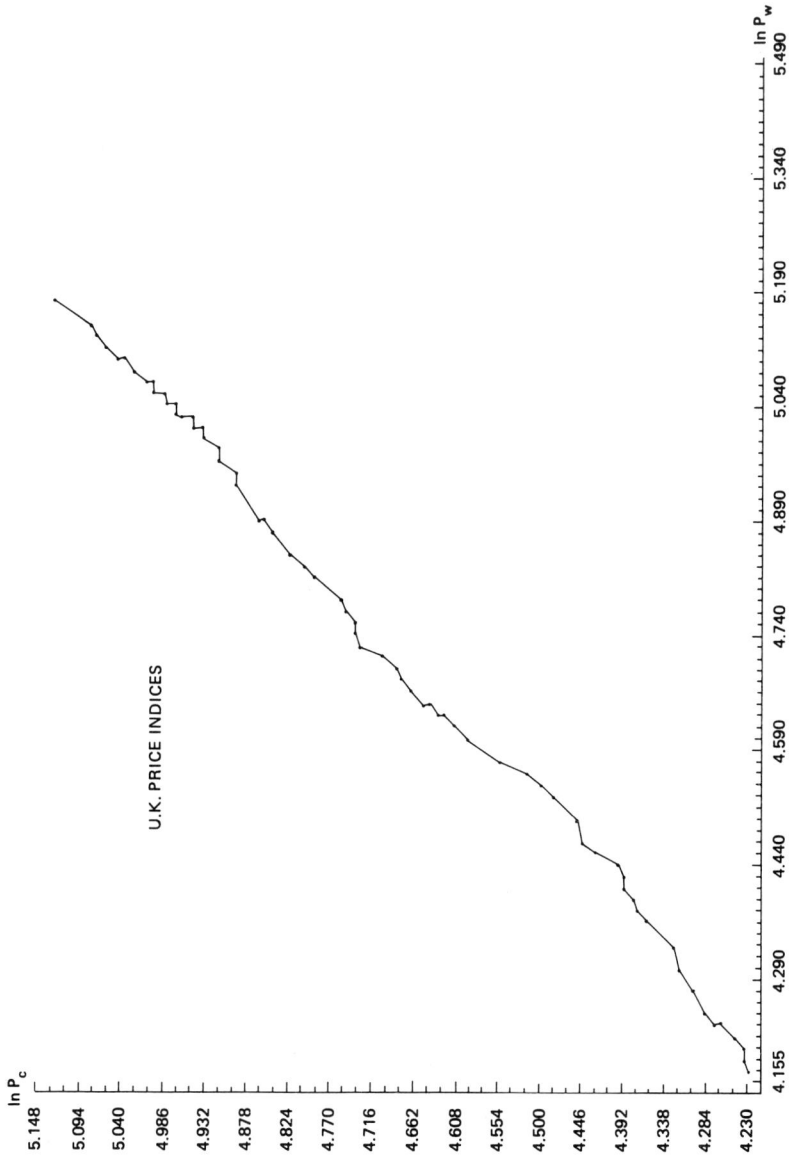

Fig. 2. A scatter diagram of monthly observations of the logarithm of the U.K. cost-of-living (P_c) and wholesale (P_w) price indices.

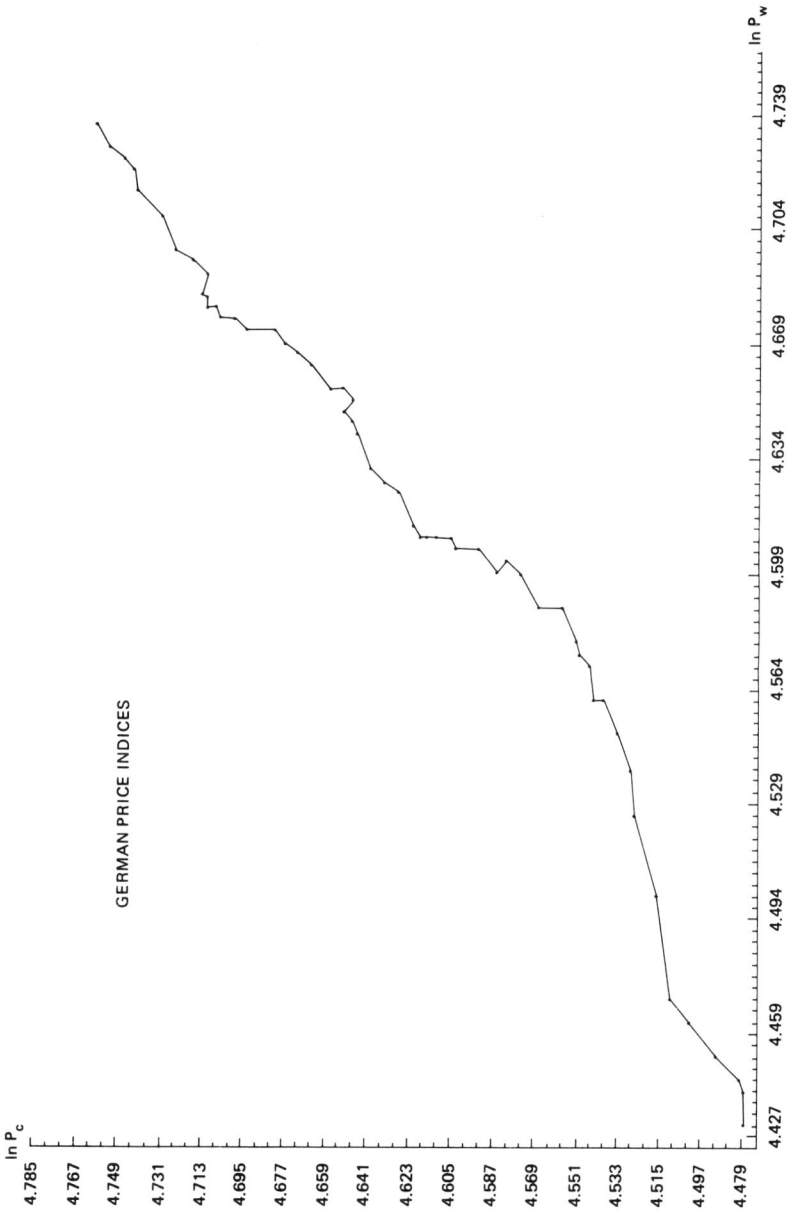

Fig. 3. A scatter diagram of monthly observations of the logarithm of German cost-of-living (P_c) and wholesale (P_w) price indices.

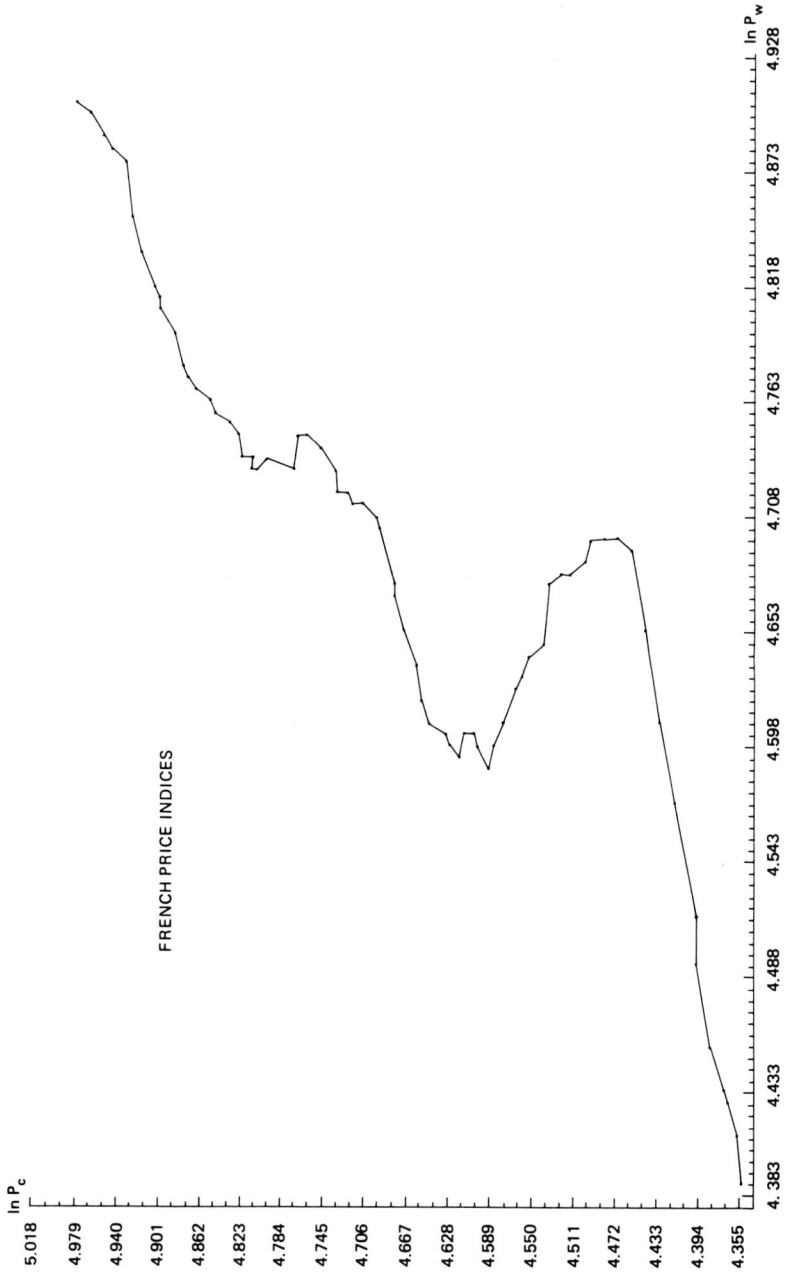

Fig. 4. A scatter diagram of monthly observations of the logarithm of French cost-of-living (P_c) and wholesale (P_w) price indices.

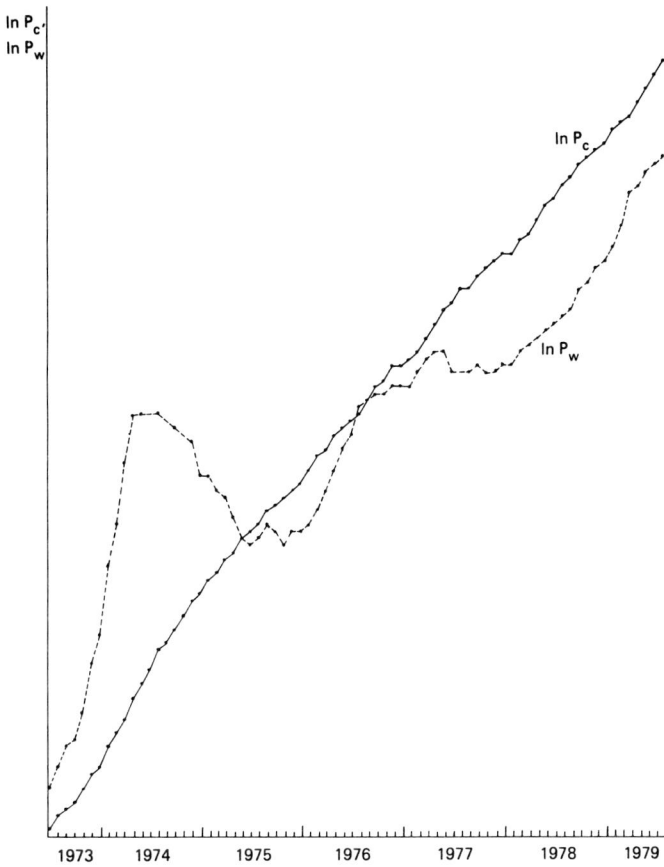

Fig. 5. Monthly observations of the logarithm of the French cost-of-living (P_c) and wholesale (P_w) price indices: June 1973–July 1979.

even though the exchange rate does not move in full conformity with the ratio of national price levels and changes in the exchange rate do not conform fully with inflationary differentials, the two national price levels *expressed in terms of the same currency* do move in conformity with each other. This is an alternative test of the PPP doctrine.

Eq. (8) formulates this idea which has been suggested by Bilson (1980),

$$\ln P_t = \alpha + \beta \ln (SP^*)_t + \varepsilon_t, \tag{8}$$

where the variable SP^* converts the foreign price index P^* to domestic currency units. While the traditional formulation may fail due to changes in *relative* prices, these changes in relative prices may be less important in determining the trends of national price levels (expressed in common currency units) which are dominated by monetary conditions. This distinction may be potentially important for the applications of monetary models of exchange rates [e.g., the models described in Frenkel and Johnson (1978)] since in many of these models SP^* is frequently substituted for P.

Table 7 reports estimates of eq. (8) for the various national price levels (converted to common currency units) using the cost-of-living and the wholesale price indices. The comparison between these results and the corresponding traditional PPP estimates of table 2 is interesting. In table 7 all the coefficients (except for the U.S./France wholesale price index) are highly significant, and analogous to the results in table 5 the link between the price levels within Europe is stronger than the link between the price levels of the U.S. and the European countries (for which the slope coefficients in table 7 are smaller than unity).

Table 7

Domestic and foreign price levels: instrumental variables, monthly data: June 1973–July 1979 (standard errors in parentheses), $\ln P = \alpha + \beta \ln (SP^*) + \varepsilon.$[a]

Domestic country/ foreign country	Constant	$\ln (SP_w^*)$	$\ln (SP_c^*)$	s.e.	D.W.	ρ
U.S./U.K.	2.602 (0.377)	0.383 (0.068)		0.014	1.57	0.919
	3.647 (0.267)		0.213 (0.046)	0.007	1.72	0.971
U.S./France	4.809 (0.309)	0.027 (0.091)		0.010	1.42	0.972
	2.724 (0.197)		0.616 (0.061)	0.018	2.24	0.833
U.S./Germany	2.110 (0.264)	0.675 (0.069)		0.023	1.84	0.793
	2.272 (0.230)		0.633 (0.060)	0.019	2.05	0.812
U.K./Germany	1.070 (0.550)	1.201 (0.174)		0.033	1.60	0.896
	1.498 (0.529)		1.055 (0.166)	0.029	1.57	0.910
France/Germany	2.066 (0.548)	0.500 (0.102)		0.011	1.02	0.913
	−0.293 (0.932)		0.939 (0.172)	0.018	1.50	0.927

[a]$\ln S_t$ denotes the logarithm of the spot exchange rate; P_c and P_w denote, respectively, the cost-of-living and wholesale price indices with an asterisk denoting foreign prices. Foreign prices are converted to domestic currency units by the corresponding exchange rate. Cochrane–Orcutt iterative technique with two-stage least squares estimation method was used; the instruments are a constant, time, time squared, and lagged values of the dependent and independent variables. s.e. is the standard error of the equation.

5. Exchange rates and national price levels are not comparable

The analysis in the previous sections presumed that when inter-sectoral relative price structures remain stable and when there are no significant changes in tariffs and non-tariff barriers to trade and in the degree of capital market integration, the purchasing power parity doctrine should hold even for the short run. The major point that is being made in this section is that the modern approach to the analysis of exchange rates implies that there is a fundamental difference between the characteristics of exchange rates and those of national price levels. This difference yields a presumption that, at least in the short run, exchange rate fluctuations would not be matched by corresponding fluctuations of aggregate price levels.

The central insight of the modern approach to the analysis of exchange rates is the notion that the exchange rate, being the relative price of two durable assets (monies), can be best analyzed within a framework that is appropriate for the analysis of asset prices. A key characteristic of the price of an asset is its strong dependence on expectations concerning the future. In an efficient market for assets, new information concerning the future is reflected immediately in current prices and thus precluding unexploited profit opportunities from arbitrage. The strong dependence of current prices on expectations about the future is unique to the determination of durable asset prices which are traded in organized exchange; it does not characterize to the same extent the determination of prices of non-durable commodities (like fresh fish). The strong dependence of asset prices on expectations also implies that during periods that are dominated by 'news' which induce frequent changes in expectations, asset prices exhibit large fluctuations. Since exchange rates are viewed as asset prices, they will also exhibit a relatively large degree of volatility during periods that are dominated by 'news' which alter expectations. Since by definition the 'news' cannot be predicted on the basis of past information, it is clear that by and large the fluctuations of exchange rates are unpredictable.

In contrast to these characteristics of exchange rates, aggregate price indices are not expected to reveal such a degree of volatility since they reflect the prices of goods and services which are less durable and therefore are likely to be less sensitive to the 'news' which alter expectations about the future.

This distinction between commodity prices and asset prices is fundamental for interpreting the deviations from PPP. As is well-known, changes in commodity prices are serially correlated while changes in exchange rates are not. The 'stickiness' exhibited by commodity prices need not reflect any market imperfection but rather it may reflect the cost of price adjustment which results in finite nominal contracts. Likewise it may reflect the results of a confusion between nominal and real shocks or between permanent and transitory shocks. This, in addition to the fact that commodity price indices are less sensitive to changes in expectations imply that when there are frequent and significant changes in expectations as was certainly the case during the 1970's, exchange rates adjust immediately while commodity prices do not. Exchange rates reflect expectations about *future* circumstances while prices reflect more *present* and *past* circumstances as they are embedded in existing contracts. This difference implies that large fluctuations of exchange rates are likely to be associated with large deviations from purchasing power parities and these large deviations reflect the intrinsic difference between commodity and asset prices.[4] With this perspective the recent volatility of exchange rates and the associated departures from the predictions of the PPP doctrine are much less of a mystery; they reflect the volatile character of the 1970's which witnessed great turbulence in the world economy and large volumes of real shocks like the oil embargo, supply shocks, commodity booms and shortages, shifts in the demands for money and differential productivity growth. In addition, the 1970's witnessed great uncertainty about the future course of political and economic events which induced sharp and frequent changes in expectations.

6. Conclusions and policy implications[5]

This paper analyzed the collapse of PPP during the 1970's. One of the points made in this paper was that there are circumstances during which large deviations from PPP are to be expected and that the 1970's presented an example of such circumstances. Given the expected large deviations what is left of the purchasing power parity theory and what role should it play in guiding policy? It is clear that it should not be viewed as a theory of exchange rate determination since it specifies a relationship between two endogenous variables without providing the details about the processes which bring it about. It is also clear that it does not provide a guide for day-to-day or month-to-month fluctuations of exchange rates. Further, when the economy experiences real structural changes which require adjustments of relative prices, purchasing power parities may not be satisfied even in the long run. Its usefulness is in providing a guide as to the general trend of exchange rates in particular in circumstances where the main shocks underlying the trend are of a monetary origin. As for the conduct of macroeconomic policy, it serves as an important reminder that the exchange rate and the price level cannot be divorced from each other and that policies which affect the trend of domestic (relative to foreign) prices are likely to affect the exchange rate in a similar manner.

---

[4]For further analysis of the role of expectations and 'news' in exchange rate analysis, see Dornbusch (1978), Mussa (1976, 1979), Frenkel (1981a) and Frenkel and Mussa (1980).
[5]The discussion in this section draws on Frenkel (1981b).

Emphasis on the fact that exchange rates and prices are both endogenous variables is important in view of the recent allegations that flexible exchange rates have been inflationary. Both exchange rates and prices respond to the same set of shocks and both can be influenced by a similar set of policies. The fact that exchange rates adjust faster than commodity prices reflect the known phenomenon that asset markets clear relatively quickly. This fact does not imply that as an economic matter the chain of causality runs from exchange rates to prices.

The recognition that exchange rate fluctuations reflect the underlying circumstances rather than creating them is fundamental. It implies that, for a given conduct of macroeconomic policy the basic choice is not between costly turbulence and free tranquility but rather between alternative outlets to the underlying turbulence. If the source of evil was the variability of exchange rates, then pegging the rate would have been the simple and the feasible solution. The experience with the Bretton–Woods system indicates that this is not the case. One could argue, however, that the obligation to peg the rate would alter the conduct of policy by introducing discipline. Experience suggests, however, that national governments are unlikely to be disciplined by the exchange rate regime; rather, the exchange rate regime is more likely to adjust to whatever discipline national governments choose to have.

One of the relevant questions that remains is whether exchange rate fluctuations during the 1970's have been excessive. It should be obvious that in order to answer this question we need a standard for comparison. If a relevant yardstick is the extent of variation of national price levels, then indeed exchange rates have fluctuated excessively. For example, from June 1973 through July 1979, the average absolute monthly percentage change of the Dollar/Pound, the Dollar/French Franc and the Dollar/DM exchange rates exceeded two percent per month. In comparison the average absolute monthly percentage change for wholesale and consumer price indices and for the ratios of national price levels were only about half that of the corresponding exchange rates. As a result, adherence to a narrow interpretation of the purchasing power parity theory results in the conclusion that exchange rate variations were excessive. The asset market approach suggests, however, that a relevant yardstick should be the variations of other asset prices rather than commodity prices. During the same period the average absolute percentage change in the various stock market indices has been about twice the corresponding changes in exchange rates. By this standard exchange rates have not fluctuated excessively.

With this interpretation it seems that intervention in the foreign exchange market which ensures that exchange rates conform with purchasing power parities would be a mistaken course of policy. If commodity prices do not adjust fully in response to exogenous shocks, it seems that a large adjustment of exchange rates serves a useful role since it provides the outlet for the pressure which otherwise would have been reflected in commodity prices.

Government policy can, however, make a positive contribution to reducing costly and unnecessary variations of exchange rates by adopting more stable and predictable patterns of policies. This is particularly relevant in the case of exchange rates since as was argued before, current exchange rates reflect expectations concerning future events and future policies. Current policy instability may induce expectations for future policy instability and, thereby, have a magnified effect on current exchange rates. When policies are erratic and unpredictable, monetary policy exerts real side effects. Put differently, money is felt when it is out of order; when it is in order it only serves as a veil over the real equilibrium of the economy. This unique property of money is best summarized by the following quotation from John Stuart Mill:

> There cannot, in short, be intrinsically a more insignificant thing, in the economy of society, than money; except in the character of a contrivance for sparing time and labour. It is a machine for doing quickly and commodiously, what would be done, though less quickly and commodiously, without it: and like many other kinds of machinery, it only exerts a distinct and independent influence of its own when it gets out of order.
>
> *Principles of Political Economy*
> 5th edition, 1962, Book III, Ch. VII, §3

The role of policy is to ensure that money is in order and this can be achieved by following a predictable stable course of policy. Following such a course will not eliminate variations of exchange rates nor will it ensure that exchange rates conform with the predictions of the purchasing power parity theory. It will, however, reduce some of the unnecessary and costly fluctuations which are induced by unstable and erratic policies.

Data appendix

A.1. Exchange rates

The spot exchange rates are end of month rates obtained from the IMF tape (May 1979 version, updated to July 1979 using the November 1979 issue of the *International Financial Statistics*) obtained from the International Monetary Fund. Sources for the 1920's are indicated in Frenkel (1980).

A.2. Prices

The wholesale and cost of living price indices are period averages obtained from the IMF tape, lines 63 and 64, respectively. Sources for the 1920's are indicated in Frenkel (1980).

A.3. Stock markets

The stock market indices correspond to the last trading day of the month. The sources are *Capital International Perspective*, Geneva, Switzerland, monthly issues.

References

Bilson, John F.O., 1980, Permanent and transitory changes in international competitiveness (University of Chicago, Chicago, IL) in process.

Dornbusch, Rudiger, 1978, Monetary policy under exchange rate flexibility, in: Managed exchange rate flexibility: The recent experience, Federal Reserve Bank of Boston Conference Series no. 20.

Frenkel, Jacob A., 1978, Purchasing power parity: Doctrinal perspective and evidence from the 1920's, Journal of International Economics 8, no. 2, May, 169–191.

Frenkel, Jacob A., 1980, Exchange rates, prices and money: Lessons from the 1920's, American Economic Review 70, no. 2, May, 235–242.

Frenkel, Jacob A., 1981a, Flexible exchange rates, prices and the role of 'news': Lessons from the 1970's, Journal of Political Economy 89, no. 4, Aug., forthcoming.

Frenkel, Jacob A., 1981b, Comments on exchange rates volatility and purchasing power parities, in: J. Dreyer, G. Haberler and T. Willett, eds., The international monetary system under stress (American Enterprise Institute, Washington, DC).

Frenkel, Jacob A. and Harry G. Johnson, eds., 1978, The economics of exchange rates: Selected studies (Addison-Wesley, Reading, MA).

Frenkel, Jacob A. and Michael L. Mussa, 1980, The efficiency of foreign exchange markets and measures of turbulence, American Economic Review 70, no. 2, May, 374–381.

Gordon, Robert J., 1976, Recent developments in the theory of inflation and unemployment, Journal of Monetary Economics 2, 185–219.

Gordon, Robert J., 1977, Can the inflation of the 1970s be explained?, Brookings Papers on Economic Activity, no. 1, 253–277.

Katseli-Papaefstratiou, Louka T., 1979, The re-emergence of the purchasing power parity doctrine in the 1970's, Special Papers in International Economics no. 13 (Princeton University, Princeton, NJ).

Mill, John S., 1862, Principles of political economy, 5th ed. (Parker & Co., London).

Mussa, Michael L., 1976, Our recent experience with fixed and flexible exchange rates: A comment, in: K. Brunner and A.H. Meltzer, eds., Institutional arrangements and the inflation problem, Carnegie–Rochester Conference Series on Public Policy, Vol. 3, A supplementary series to the Journal of Monetary Economics, 123–141.

Mussa, Michael L., 1979, Empirical regularities in the behavior of exchange rates and theories of the foreign exchange market, in: K. Brunner and A.H. Meltzer, eds., Policies for employment, prices and exchange rates, Carnegie–Rochester Conference Series on Public Policy, Vol. 11, A supplementary series to the Journal of Monetary Economics, 9–57.

Officer, Lawrence H., 1976, The purchasing-power-parity theory of exchange rates: A review article, International Monetary Fund Staff Papers 23, March, 1–16.

European Economic Review 18 (1982) . North-Holland

REAL EXCHANGE RATE OVERSHOOTING AND THE OUTPUT COST OF BRINGING DOWN INFLATION*

Willem H. BUITER

University of Bristol, Bristol BS8 1HY, UK, and NBER

Marcus MILLER

University of Warwick, Coventry CV4 7AL, UK

1. Introduction

The proposition that under a floating exchange rate regime restrictive monetary policy can lead to substantial 'overshooting' of the nominal and real exchange rate is now accepted fairly widely. The fundamental reason is the presence of nominal stickiness or inertia in domestic factor and product markets combined with a freely flexible nominal exchange rate. Current and anticipated future monetary policy actions are reflected immediately in the nominal exchange rate, set as it is in a forward-looking efficient auction market while they are reflected only gradually and with a lag in domestic nominal labour costs and/or goods prices. Nominal appreciation of the currency therefore amounts to real appreciation — a loss of competitiveness. Since in most of the simple analytical models used to analyse the overshooting propositions there is no long-run effect of monetary policy on the real exchange rate, any short-run real appreciation implies an overshooting of the long-run equilibrium. The transitory (but potentially quite persistent) loss of competitiveness is associated with a decline in output below its capacity level. This excess capacity is one of the channels through which restrictive monetary policy brings down the rate of domestic cost and price inflation.

One of the virtues claimed for the sharp initial appreciation of the nominal and real exchange rate in response to a previously unanticipated tightening of the stance of monetary policy is its immediate effect on the domestic price level. The domestic currency prices of those internationally traded goods whose foreign currency prices can be treated as exogenous will decline by the same proportion as the increase in the value of the domestic currency. To a greater or lesser extent

*The authors have benefitted from discussions with Avinash Dixit. Financial support from the Leverhulme Trust is gratefully acknowledged. Opinions expressed are those of the authors and not of the National Bureau of Economic Research nor of the Leverhulme Trust.

the same holds even for those internationally traded goods where the home country is large in relation to the world market. Both through its effect on the prices of internationally traded final goods and through its effect on the price of imported raw materials and intermediate inputs, a sudden step appreciation of the exchange rate will immediately bring down the domestic price level. In this paper we shall argue that the effect of such exchange rate jumps is merely to redistribute the cost of reducing inflation over time: early gains have to be 'handed back' later as the equilibrium level of competitiveness is restored. Crucial to this argument is the assumption of stickiness of some nominal domestic cost component. In our model this is built in by our assumption of a predetermined nominal money wage and through our specification of the behaviour of the 'core' or underlying rate of inflation, π, the augmentation term in the wage Phillips curve. Subject to one quite significant qualification, the core rate of inflation is viewed as predetermined with its behaviour over time governed by a first-order partial adjustment mechanism. It can be thought of as an adaptive expectations mechanism for the labour market although we do not favour that interpretation. In our view the core rate of inflation, which is a distributed lag on past rates of inflation, stands for all the factors in the economy that give inertia to built-in trends in wages and prices. Also, whereas the level of the money wage is always treated as predetermined, π, while determined by a 'backward-looking' process, can make discrete jumps at a point in time. This will happen whenever there is a discrete jump in the general price level. In our model this can occur either if the exchange rate jumps or if there is a change in indirect taxes. Since the exchange rate is a forward-looking price which responds to 'news' about current and future shocks, the underlying rate of inflation indirectly and to a limited extent also responds to such shocks.

To put the present paper in perspective it is useful to relate our current approach to that of an earlier paper [Buiter and Miller (1981)]. This is done in section 2 where a simple model of real exchange rate overshooting is discussed. Section 3 contains some modifications of the simple model. It is here that we discuss the implications of assuming flexibility of domestic nominal wage costs. While we do not believe that such a 'neo-classical' specification is appropriate for the analysis of an advanced industrial economy like the U.K., the discussion of this case helps bring out the crucial nature of the assumption of nominal inertia in the behaviour of domestic costs. Section 4 analyzes in some detail the behaviour of the model with sluggish 'core' inflation.

2. A simple model of real exchange rate overshooting

A slightly simplified version of the model in Buiter and Miller (1981) is given in eqs. (1)–(5), all variables except for r, r_d, r^*, π, θ and τ being in logs,

$$m - p - \theta = ky - \lambda(r - r_d), \qquad k, \lambda > 0, \qquad (1)$$

$$y = -\gamma(r - Dp - D\theta) + \delta(e + p^* - p), \qquad \gamma, \delta > 0, \tag{2}$$

$$Dp = \phi y + \pi, \qquad\qquad\qquad \phi > 0, \tag{3}$$

$$\pi = D^+ m, \tag{4}$$

$$De = r - r^* - \tau. \tag{5}$$

The notation is as follows:

m = nominal money stock (exogenous),
p = domestic price level 'at factor cost', i.e., excluding indirect taxes (predetermined),
p^* = foreign price level (exogenous),
y = real output (endogenous),
r = domestic nominal interest rate on non-money assets (endogenous),
r_d = nominal interest rate paid on domestic money (exogenous),
r^* = foreign nominal interest paid on non-money assets (exogenous),
θ = rate of indirect tax (exogenous),
e = exchange rate (domestic currency price of foreign currency) (endogenous),
π = trend or core rate of inflation (endogenous),
τ = rate of tax on capital inflows or subsidy on outflows (exogenous),
D = differential operator, i.e., $Dx(t) \equiv (d/dt)x(t)$,
D^+ = right-hand-side differential operator, i.e., $D^+ x(t) = \lim_{\substack{T \to t \\ T > t}} (x(T) - x(t))/(T - t)$,

Eq. (1) is the LM curve: m denotes a fairly wide monetary aggregate such as £M3 which consists to a significant extent (50–60%) of interest-bearing deposits. We therefore measure the opportunity cost of holding money by the interest differential between the loan rate, r, and the own rate on time deposits (r_d). Eq. (2) is the IS curve. Demand for domestic output depends on the short real interest rate and on the relative price of foreign and domestic goods. A fiscal policy variable could be added without difficulty. Preferable alternative specifications include replacing the short real interest rate by the long real interest rate and modelling output as predetermined, with its rate of change depending on the excess of *ex ante* effective demand over the level of real output. This would preclude the unrealistic immediate jumps in real output in response to e.g. a loss of competitiveness which are a feature of the current model. This country is small in the world market for its importables so that it takes p^* as given. It is large in the world market for its exportables. No explicit distinction is made between traded and non-traded goods. Eq. (3) is the augmented Phillips curve. By choice of units (the logarithm of) capacity output is set equal to zero. The augmentation term π is identified, in (4) with the right-hand-side time derivative of the money supply. Thus even if m were to make a discrete jump, the price level would not jump. This is one way of imposing the crucial property of nominal inertia, stickiness or sluggishness. Eq. (5) reflects the assumption of perfect capital mobility and perfect substitutability between domestic and foreign bonds. Risk-neutral speculators equate the uncovered interest differential in favour of the domestic country, net of any tax on capital imports, to the expected rated of depreciation of the domestic currency. The country is small in the world financial markets and r^* is treated as given. The assumption of rational expectations, employed in Dornbusch (1976), Liviatan (1980) and Buiter and Miller (1981), is equivalent to perfect foresight in out deterministic model. It is used in eqs. (2) and (5). For simplicity the foreign price level, p^*, is assumed to be constant. Choice of units sets it equal to zero, so competitiveness is measured by $e - p$.

The own rate of interest on money is assumed exogenous. In a competitive banking system with a binding required reserve ratio h $(0 < h < 1)$ on all bank deposits, the loan rate r and the deposit rate r_d are linked by $r_d = (1 - h)r(TD + DD)TD^{-1}$. TD is the volume of interest-bearing time deposits and DD the volume of non-interest-bearing demand deposits. If demand deposits are only a small fraction of the total, then $r_d \simeq (1 - h)r$. This can be used to eliminate r_d from the model. The main consequence is to reduce the interest sensitivity of money demand. We prefer treating r_d as exogenous so that discretionary changes in r_d can be used to describe policy actions to alter the degree of competitiveness of the banking system. The dynamics of the system is conveniently summarized in terms of the two state variables l and c,

$$l \equiv m - p, \tag{6a}$$

$$c \equiv e - p. \tag{6b}$$

Real liquidity, l, is a backward-looking or predetermined variable. It only makes discrete jumps when the policy instrument m changes discontinuously. Real competitiveness c is a forward-looking or jump variable. It jumps whenever e jumps. The state–space representation of the model of eqs. (1)–(6) is

$$
\begin{bmatrix} Dl \\ Dc \end{bmatrix} = \frac{1}{\gamma(\phi\lambda - k) - \lambda} \begin{bmatrix} \phi\gamma & \phi\lambda\delta \\ 1 & \delta(\phi\lambda - k) \end{bmatrix} \begin{bmatrix} l \\ c \end{bmatrix}
$$

$$
+ \frac{1}{\gamma(\phi\lambda - k) - \lambda} \begin{bmatrix} \phi\lambda\gamma & 0 & -\phi\gamma & -\phi\gamma\lambda \\ \lambda & -\gamma(\phi\lambda - k) + \lambda & -1 & -\lambda \end{bmatrix}
$$

$$
\times \begin{bmatrix} Dm \\ r^* + \tau \\ \theta \\ r_d \end{bmatrix} .^1 \tag{7}
$$

---

[1] For simplicity, the term $D\theta$ in eq. (2) has been ignored. We consider it in section 4.

A necessary and sufficient condition for the stationary equilibrium of this model to be a saddlepoint is $\gamma(\phi\lambda - k) - \lambda < 0$.[2] This is equivalent to the condition that, at a given real exchange rate, an exogenous increase in aggregate demand raises output.

Assuming that the conditions for the existence of a saddlepoint equilibrium are satisfied, it is easily checked that the long-run equilibrium has the following properties. Output is equal to its full employment value, 0. The steady-state real interest rate, $r - Dp$ equals $r^* - Dp^* + \tau = r^* + \tau$ since we assume that the foreign rate of inflation is zero. The nominal interest rate r equals $r^* + \tau + De = r^* + \tau + Dp - Dp^* = r^* + \tau + Dm - Dp^*$. Long-run competitiveness is independent of Dm, θ and r_d but improves when $r^* + \tau$ increases. The steady-state stock of real money balances l decreases when Dm or $r^* + \tau$ increase but increases when θ or r_d increase.

We now briefly summarize the effects on competitiveness and output of a number of policy actions similar to the ones implemented by the Thatcher government.

2.1. An unanticipated and immediately implemented reduction in the rate of monetary growth

There is no long-run effect on competitiveness associated with a reduction in the monetary growth rate. The steady-state stock of real money balances increases owing to the lower nominal interest rate associated with the lower steady-state rate of inflation. The dynamics are described in fig. 1. The reduction in Dm is implemented as soon as it is first anticipated. The initial long-run equilibrium is at E_1, the new one at E_2. For convenience we assume that the initial position is also at E_1. To achieve convergence to the new equilibrium the nominal exchange rate jumps so as to put the system on the saddlepath SS' through E_2. With p predetermined, a jump in e corresponds to a jump in c. This jump-appreciation of the real exchange rate to E_{12} in response to an unanticipated reduction in the rate of monetary growth is associated with a decline in output and a fall in the nominal interest rate. Note from eqs. (3) and (4) that 'on impact' the reduction in Dm lowers the rate of inflation by more than the change in the rate of growth of the money supply: *ceteris paribus* there is a one-for-one relationship between Dp and Dm^+. The induced decline in output further lowers the rate of inflation. This somewhat implausible feature of the model will be removed below in section 4.

From the LM equation (1) it can be seen that with r_d and θ exogenous and l predetermined, r and y have to move in the same direction in response to any exogenous shock. The nominal interest falls in response to the monetary growth deceleration, reflecting the current and anticipated future success of the anti-

---

[2]The equilibrium is a saddlepoint if the state matrix has one stable and one unstable characteristic root. A necessary and sufficient condition for this is that the determinant of the state matrix be negative.

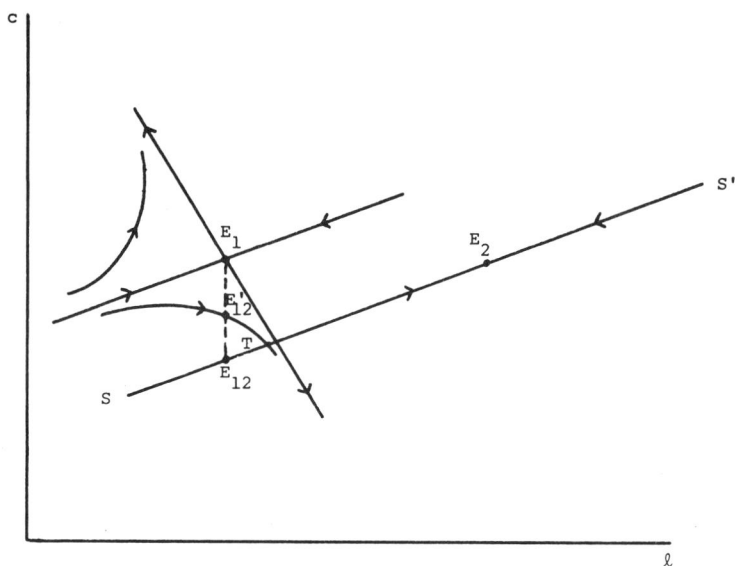

Fig. 1. Reductions in monetary growth.

inflationary strategy. To equate the demand for money to its predetermined real supply, output falls. The reduction in output is achieved both through appreciation of the real exchange rate and through the increase in the real interest rate.[3] To avoid the conclusion of our model that a reduction in the rate of growth of the money stock lowers the nominal interest rate, the money demand function would have to be modified. Possible modifications are the following. The inclusion of a long rate of interest in the money demand function. Even if the nominal interest rate on long-term debt declines in response to the anti-inflationary strategy, the short rate may rise in the short run. Similar conclusions for the behaviour of the short rate would follow if the (expected) rate of inflation were to have a negative effect on the demand for money. Finally, wealth effects on the demand for money could be included. A fall in the long-term nominal interest rate means an upward revaluation of private sector holdings of long-dated public debt. This would raise the demand for money, thus rendering a decline in output consistent with an increase in the short nominal interest rate.

2.2. A previously unanticipated future reduction in the rate of monetary growth

If the unanticipated reduction in monetary growth does not occur until an interval of length T has lapsed after the announcement, the behaviour of c and l in

[3]It is easily checked that r declines less than Dp. Note also that we can use (2) and (5) to obtain $y = -\gamma Dc + \delta c - \gamma(r^* + \tau)$. Immediately following the unanticipated reduction in Dm, c is lower and Dc becomes positive. This causes y to fall.

fig. 1 follows the path $E_1 - E'_{12} - T - E_2$. When the 'news' breaks there is a jump appreciation of the real exchange rate to E'_{12}. This places the system on that unique unstable trajectory, drawn with reference to the initial equilibrium, which will cause it to arrive on the unique convergent path SS' through E_2 after an interval of duration T. In the absence of further 'news' no other discrete jumps in e and c occur, reflecting the assumption that the behaviour of risk-neutral speculators will eliminate anticipated future jumps in e, as these would be associated with infinite anticipated rates of capital gain or loss.

2.3. The medium-term financial strategy

The medium-term financial strategy (MTFS) of the Thatcher government had as its centrepiece an announced sequence of four annual one-point reductions in the target range of monetary growth. Approximating the range by its central value, the response of the system to the unanticipated and immediate introduction of the MTFS can be depicted as in fig. 2.[4] If there were only a single unanticipated one-point reduction in the rate of monetary growth, c would jump immediately to E_{12} on $S_1 S_1$. If the entire four point reduction in Dm were to be implemented immediately, the system would jump to E'_{12} on $S_4 S_4$.

The actual effect is intermediate between these two extremes. The initial jump in c takes it beyond E_{12} to a point such as T_0 because the magnitude of the initial jump in c is a function of the announced future reductions in monetary growth. Under rational expectations the system must follow a path which will, without future jumps in competitiveness, put it on $S_4 S_4$ when the fourth and final year of the MTFS dawns. We assume that no further reductions in monetary growth are planned after the fourth year. If a non-inflationary rate of monetary growth is the long-term target and if the MTFS is likely to be extended to achieve this purpose, a further five or six years of successive one-percentage-point reductions in Dm should be added to the picture of fig. 2. The initial jump in c would be correspondingly greater. All this assumes of course that the inflationary mechanism, and more specifically the degree of nominal inertia in the level of p, remains unchanged, regardless of how far in advance monetary growth reductions are announced and irrespective of the degree of belief attached to these announcements. The four-year MTFS leads in fig. 2 to an immediate loss of competitiveness, which places the system at T_0 below E_{12}. After this there is a sequence of connected one-year-long paths $(T_0 - T_1, T_1 - T_2, T_2 - T_3)$ which will place the system on the convergent path $S_4 S_4$ through E_4 at the beginning of the fourth and final year of the MTFS. Each one-year-long path $T_{i-1} - T_i (i = 1, 2, 3)$ follows a divergent trajectory, drawn with reference to the long-run equilibrium E_i because during the ith year the system is 'driven' by the values of the forcing variables for that year.

[4]We assume that the policy announcement was unanticipated and credible — perhaps a doubtful assumption.

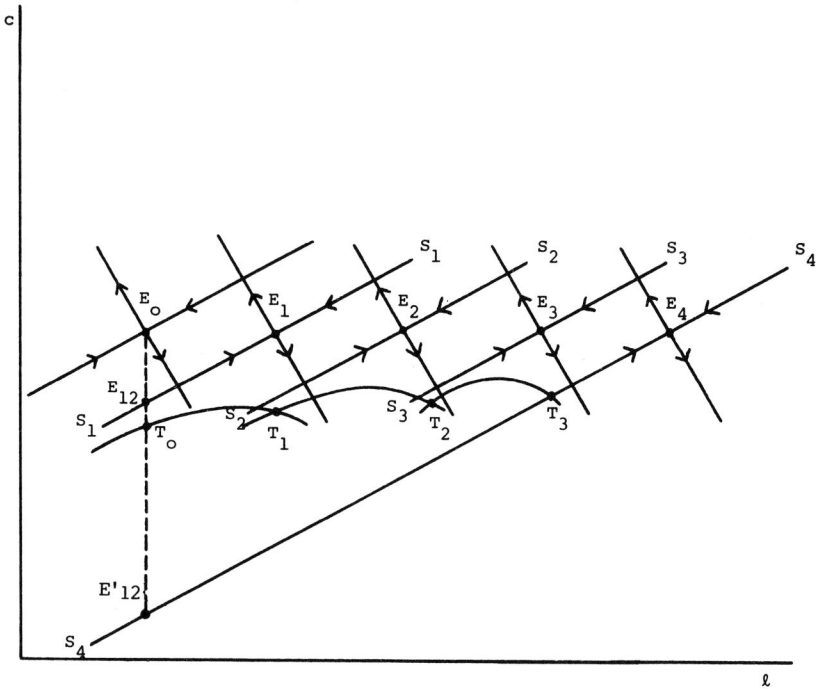

Fig. 2. The medium-term financial strategy.

2.4. An unanticipated increase in direct taxes

To model the important monetary aspects of the Conservative government's fiscal policy, we consider a fiscally neutral increase in the rate of indirect taxation, θ. There is assumed to be no direct effect on aggregate demand because the increase in indirect taxes is matched by a reduction in direct taxes. The price equation 'at factor cost' is assumed unaffected by the reduction in direct taxes. To justify this assumption for the wage component of factor costs, one could plausibly postulate a labour supply schedule that is perfectly inelastic with respect to the after-tax real wage. The long-run effect of an increase in θ is an increase in $l = m - p$ by the same amount as the increase in θ.[5] With the path of m exogenous, prices net of indirect tax decline so that market prices follow their previous path and $m - p - \theta$ is unchanged in the steady state. The dynamic behaviour of the economy is described in fig. 3. It is qualitatively the same as that following a reduction in Dm. The exchange rate jump-appreciates and output declines. Fig. 3 also describes the consequences of an unanticipated immediate increase in r_d. The abolition of the 'corset', which we model (crudely) as an increase in r_d, is estimated to have increased money demand by about 4%.

---

[5]The Thatcher government's 8% increase in VAT has been estimated to be equivalent to a 4 percentage point increase in the average rate of indirect taxation, θ.

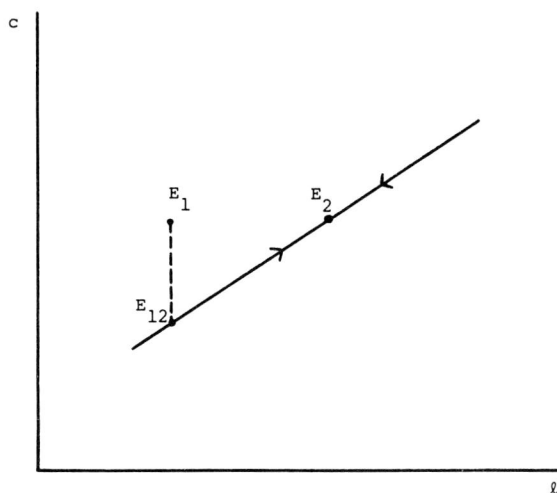

Fig. 3. Unanticipated increase in indirect taxes.

2.5. An unanticipated increase in the level of the money stock

An unanticipated and immediately implemented once-and-for-all increase in m does not alter the long-run equilibrium real money stock or level of competitiveness. With p predetermined, an increase in m is an increase in l. The behaviour of the economy when subjected to such a shock is described in fig. 4. The initial and final equilibrium are both at E_1. The initial real money stock is l_1 $= m_1 - p_1$. The unanticipated increase in m raises the real money stock to $l_2 = m_2 - p_1$, $m_2 > m_1$. The real exchange rate jump-depreciates to E_{12} to place the system on the convergent saddlepath SS' through E_1. Output expands and the nominal interest rate falls on impact. Note the difference between an increase in m and an increase in Dm. Both are expansionary in the short-run, but while an increase in Dm raises the nominal interest rate, an increase in m lowers it. Neither policy action affects long-run competitiveness, but while a once-and-for-all increase in the level of the nominal money stock leaves long-run real balances unchanged, an increase in the rate of growth of the nominal money stock will, by raising inflation and the nominal interest rate, reduce the long-run stock of real money balances.

Comparing fig. 4 with figs. 1 and 3 suggests a way of avoiding the excess capacity and the loss of competitiveness associated with policies to reduce the rate of inflation by reducing the rate of monetary growth and with switches from direct to indirect taxation. Consider an initial equilibrium at E_1 in fig. 5. An unanticipated immediate reduction in Dm (or increase in θ or r_d) would, by itself, move the economy to E_{12}, with real exchange rate appreciation and excess capacity resulting during the transition to the new long-run equilibrium E_2. The reason for this costly disequilibrium adjustment is stickiness of the real money

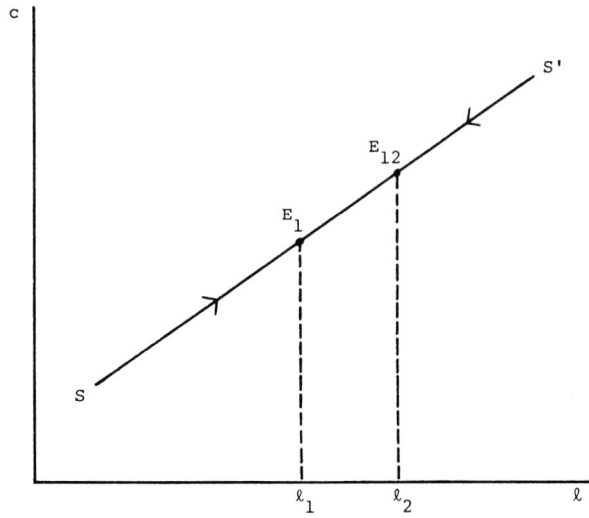

Fig. 4. Unanticipated increase in the level of the money stock.

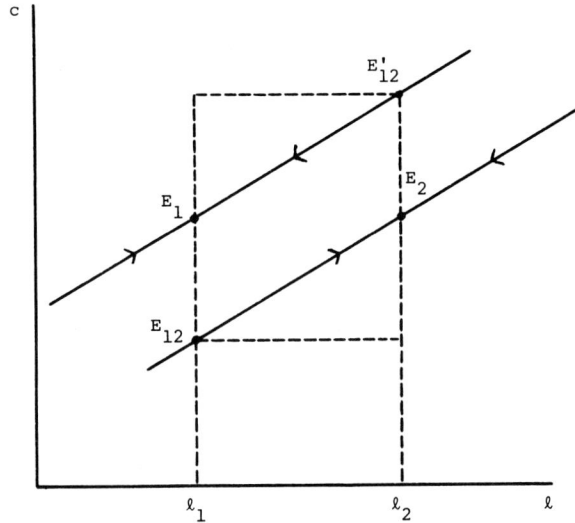

Fig. 5. A reduction in the growth of the money supply combined with a jump in the level.

supply. This is the result of the combination of price level stickiness, an assumed feature of the private economy, and stickiness in the level of the nominal money stock, the result of a deliberate policy choice. It is easy in the present model to calculate the increase in the level of the nominal money stock that would immediately achieve the required long-run increase in real balances without any need for the price level path to be adjusted downward. Without a 'jump' in the level of the nominal money stock the price equation $Dp = \phi v + D^+ m$ tells us that the only way of lowering p relative to m is through excess capacity. The required nominal money stock jump is simply $l_2 - l_1$. By itself, an increase in m by that amount would move the system to E'_{12}. A combination of a reduction in Dm (or an increase in θ or in r_d) and an increase in m of the right magnitude will immediately and without transitional loss of competitiveness and output, place the economy at E_2. The jump appreciation associated with the reduction in the rate of monetary growth, the increase in indirect taxation or the increased competitiveness of the banking system, and the jump depreciation associated with the increase in the level of the money stock cancel each other out exactly. It can be argued that the government's decision not to try to recoup the large overshoot during the second half of 1980 of the £M3 target amounts to an (involuntary) m-jump of the kind advocated here. Whatever the motivation, it has prevented a further massive deflationary jolt to an economy already going through the worst recession since the 1930's.

3. Real exchange rate overshooting and the wage–price process

A crucial component of all models exhibiting disequilibrium overshooting of the real exchange rate is the wage–price process. The price equation used in the paper so far, as in many others [e.g. Buiter and Miller (1981), Dornbusch (1976)], has a number of weaknesses. It is important to perform a 'sensitivity analysis' of the specification of this equation in order to establish the robustness of the overshooting proposition.

3.1. A direct effect of the exchange rate on the domestic price level

Even if domestic wage costs are sticky in nominal terms, so that the money wage rate, w, can be treated as predetermined, the domestic price level might in an open economy still be capable of making discrete jumps at a point in time. This will be the case if the domestic currency price of internationally traded goods is a function of the exchange rate. A convenient way of representing this notion is to express the domestic price level, p, as a weighted average of the sticky domestic money wage and the domestic currency value of an appropriate (trade-weighted) index of world prices, p^*. Making the small country assumption that p^* is given and choosing units such that $p^* = 0$, we have

$$p = \alpha w + (1 - \alpha)e, \qquad 0 \leq \alpha \leq 1.^6 \tag{8}$$

Eq. (3) is then replaced by

$$Dw = \phi y + \pi. \tag{9}$$

For the time being we still assume that

$$\pi = D^+ m.$$

With $\alpha < 1$, the domestic price level is no longer predetermined. The jump appreciation of the nominal (and real) exchange rate in response to e.g. an unanticipated reduction in the rate of monetary growth will have the immediate effect of lowering the price level. However, as long as $\alpha > 0$, the earlier analysis is not affected qualitatively. We redefine our state variables as follows:

$$l = m - w, \tag{10a}$$

$$c = e - w. \tag{10b}$$

As before, l is predetermined (except when m jumps) and c is a jump variable. The state space representation of the model given in eqs. (1), (2), (8), (9), (4) and (5) is

$$\begin{bmatrix} Dl \\ Dc \end{bmatrix} = \frac{1}{\alpha\gamma(\lambda\phi - k) - \lambda} \begin{bmatrix} \phi\alpha\gamma & \phi\alpha(\lambda\delta - \gamma(1-\alpha)) \\ 1 & \alpha\delta(\phi\lambda - k) + \alpha - 1 \end{bmatrix} \begin{bmatrix} l \\ c \end{bmatrix}$$

$$+ \frac{1}{\alpha\gamma(\lambda\phi - k) - \lambda}$$

$$\begin{bmatrix} \alpha\gamma\lambda\phi & -\phi\lambda\gamma(1-\alpha) & -\phi\alpha\gamma & -\phi\alpha\gamma\lambda \\ \lambda & \lambda + \gamma(k - \phi\lambda) & -1 & -\lambda \end{bmatrix} \begin{bmatrix} Dm \\ r^* + \tau \\ \theta \\ r_d \end{bmatrix}$$

$$\tag{11}$$

---

[6]A more general approach is the following. Let p_H be the price of domestically produced goods. It is a weighted average of unit labour costs, w, and unit imported intermediate input costs: $e + p^{*I}$, i.e.,

$$p_H = \beta_1 w + (1 - \beta_1)(e + p^{*I}), \qquad 0 \leq \beta_1 \leq 1. \tag{12'}$$

It is easily seen that (7) is the special case of (11) with $\alpha = 1$. A necessary and sufficient condition for the existence of a unique saddle-point equilibrium is

$$\alpha\gamma(\lambda\phi - k) - \lambda < 0, \tag{12}$$

which again has the interpretation that, at a given level of competitiveness, an increase in aggregate demand increases output. The single convergent path is again upward-sloping and the real exchange rate overshooting results of section 2 carry over to the more plausible model under consideration here. The main change from the previous analysis with $\alpha = 1$, is that the exchange rate appreciation consequent upon restrictive monetary policy actions (or increases in θ or r_d) now has an immediate beneficial effect on the price level although as long as $\alpha > 0$, a given percentage appreciation of e will be associated with a smaller percentage reduction in p.

The special case $\alpha = 0$ represents the 'law of one price' for all goods or instantaneous purchasing power parity (P.P.P.). Although few propositions in economics have been rejected more convincingly by the data than P.P.P. [Kravis and Lipsey (1978), Frenkel (1981), Isard (1977)] it is mentioned briefly for completeness. With the domestic price level moving perfectly in line with the exchange rate, the wage equation (9) which still incorporates stickiness in the level of the money wage, ceases to be relevant to the rest of the model. The relative price of domestic and foreign goods is constant. Real output is a function of the exogenous real interest rate. Unless we impose the requirement that steady-state real wages are constant, output need not be at its full employment level. Alternatively we could add an equation making output a (decreasing) function of the real wage. As this model has little to recommend it, we shall not pursue it any further here.

3.2. Money wage flexibility and real wage flexbility

We now consider the case where both the money wage and the real wage are perfectly flexible, and output is always at its equilibrium or capacity value, 0. We can view this as the case where the core rate of wage inflation, π, equals the expected (and actual) rate of wage inflation, i.e.,

$$\pi = Dw. \tag{4'}$$

The domestic price level or c.p.i. is a weighted average of the price of domestically produced goods and the price of imported final goods $e + p^{*F}$, i.e.,

$$p = \beta_2 p_H + (1 - \beta_2)(e + p^{*F}), \qquad 0 \leq \beta_2 \leq 1. \tag{12''}$$

For our purposes not much is lost by using the simpler formulation in (12). An alternative interpretation in terms of traded and untraded goods is also possible.

The model of eqs. (1), (2), (8), (9), (4′) and (5) has the following very simple state-space representation:

$$
\begin{bmatrix} Dl \\ Dc \end{bmatrix} = \begin{bmatrix} \lambda^{-1} & \gamma^{-1}\delta - (1-\alpha)\lambda^{-1} \\ 0 & \gamma^{-1}\delta \end{bmatrix} \begin{bmatrix} l \\ c \end{bmatrix}
$$

$$
+ \begin{bmatrix} 1 & -\alpha^{-1}(1-\alpha) & -\lambda^{-1} & -1 \\ 0 & -\alpha^{-1} & 0 & 0 \end{bmatrix} \begin{bmatrix} Dm \\ r^* + \tau \\ \theta \\ r_d \end{bmatrix}. \tag{13}
$$

With both e and w freely flexible, neither of the two state variables l and c is predetermined. A unique convergent solution trajectory exists because there are now two unstable characteristic roots (λ^{-1} and $\gamma^{-1}\delta$). The system is also recursive, with Dc independent of l and also of the policy instruments Dm, r_f and θ. Only a real shock (such as a change in the foreign real interest rate $r^* + \tau$) will affect the dynamics and steady state behaviour of c.

The diagrammatic representation of the system is given in fig. 6. Without loss of generality we assume that the $Dl = 0$ locus is downward-sloping. Consider an unexpected, immediately-implemented reduction in Dm. The initial equilibrium is at E_1, the new equilibrium at E_2. Note that these equilibria are completely unstable. Since the cut in the monetary growth rate is immediately implemented, l jumps immediately from E_1 to E_2 with no change in c. Monetary disinflation is costless. If we consider a previously unanticipated future reduction in Dm, l will jump to an intermediate position like E_{12} between E_1 and E_2 at the moment the

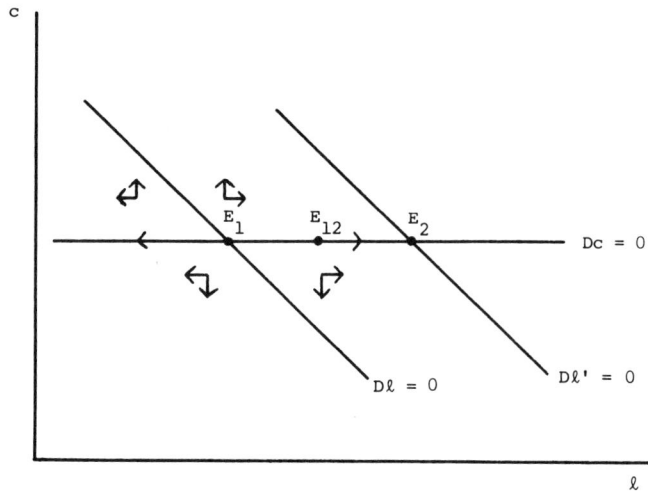

Fig. 6. Money disturbances (with money and real wage flexibility).

future policy change is announced. After that it moves gradually in a straight line from E_{12} to E_2 where the system arrives at the moment that Dm is actually reduced. Again there is no effect on competitiveness in the short run or in the long run.

It is instructive to contrast monetary disturbances with a real shock such as an increase in $r^* + \tau$, analysed in fig. 7. The steady-state effect is to alter the long-run equilibrium from E_1 to E_2, lowering l and raising c. If the increase in $r^* + \tau$ occurs immediately both c and l jump to E_2 without delay. If we have a future increase in $r^* + \tau$, the system jumps to an intermediate position such as E_{12} after which it proceeds gradually to E_2 where it arrives when $r^* + \tau$ is actually raised. Note that this adjustment of the real exchange rate is an equilibrium phenomenon, taking place at a constant level of output.

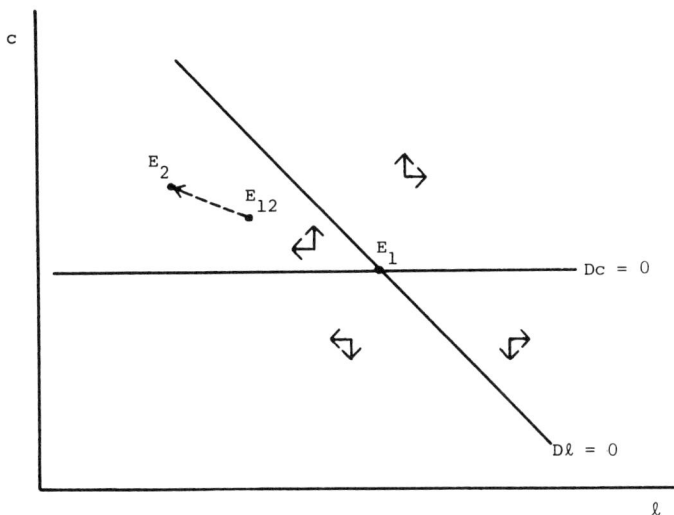

Fig. 7. Real disturbances (with money and real wage flexibility).

3.3. Money wage flexbility and real wage rigidity

Some recent work on wage and price behaviour can be interpreted as combining the assumption of perfectly flexible money wages with the assumption of sluggish adjustment in the real wage. The latter is treated as predetermined because of (generally unspecified) transactions and adjustment costs.

Consider e.g. the following specification for π:

$$\pi = Dp - \eta(w - p), \qquad \eta \geq 0. \tag{4''}$$

Eq. (4″), in combination with (9), yields

$$Dw = \phi y + Dp - \eta(w - p), \tag{14}$$

or

$$D(w - p) = \phi y - \eta(w - p). \tag{14'}$$

Eq. (14) can be viewed as a rational expectations version of the kind of equation proposed by Sargan (1980). It is also very close to an equation found in Minford (1980) although his equation incorporates nominal stickiness. The state-space representation of the model with nominal flexibility and real stickiness is given in eq. (15) below:

$$
\begin{bmatrix} Dl \\ Dc \end{bmatrix} =
$$

$$
\begin{bmatrix} \lambda^{-1} & -\dfrac{(1-\alpha)[\eta\lambda + k\alpha\gamma\eta + 1 - \alpha(1+\gamma\phi) + \alpha\delta k] + \alpha\delta\phi\lambda}{\lambda(1-\alpha(1+\gamma\phi))} \\[2ex] 0 & -\dfrac{[\eta(1-\alpha) + \phi\alpha\delta]}{1 - \alpha(1+\gamma\phi)} \end{bmatrix} \begin{bmatrix} l \\ c \end{bmatrix}
$$

$$
+ \begin{bmatrix} 1 & \dfrac{\lambda[1-\alpha(1+\gamma\phi)] + \lambda\phi\gamma + k\gamma(1-\alpha)}{\lambda[1-\alpha(1+\gamma\phi)]} & -\lambda^{-1} & -1 \\[2ex] 0 & \dfrac{\phi\gamma}{1-\alpha(1+\gamma\phi)} & 0 & 0 \end{bmatrix} \begin{bmatrix} Dm \\ r^* + \tau \\ \theta \\ r_d \end{bmatrix}. \tag{15}
$$

Note that real wage rigidity implies real exchange rate rigidity as $w - p = (\alpha - 1)c$. With a flexible money wage, l now is a jump variable. The roles of l and c as predetermined and jump variables is the exact reverse of what it is in the model with sticky money wages (and flexible real wages) of section 2. The two characteristic roots of eq. (15) are λ^{-1} and $-[\eta(1-\alpha) + \phi\alpha\delta]/[1 - \alpha(1+\gamma\phi)]$. The sign of the second root — the one governing the behaviour of c — depends on the sign of $1 - \alpha(1+\gamma\phi)$. This has the following interpretation. Add an exogenous demand shock f to the IS equation (2). This yields $y = -\gamma(r - Dp) + \delta(e - p) + f$. It is readily checked that

$$e - p = \alpha c, \tag{16a}$$

$$r - Dp = r^* + \tau + \alpha Dc, \tag{16b}$$

$$Dc = (\phi/(\alpha - 1))y - \eta c. \tag{16c}$$

The IS curve can therefore be written as

$$y = -\frac{\gamma(1-\alpha)}{1 - \alpha(1 + \gamma\phi)}(r^* + \tau) + \frac{\alpha(1 - \alpha)(\gamma\eta + \delta)}{1 - \alpha(1 + \gamma\phi)}c$$

$$+ \frac{(1 - \alpha)}{1 - \alpha(1 + \gamma\phi)}f. \tag{16d}$$

For $0 \leq \alpha < 1$, $1 - \alpha(1 + \gamma\phi)$ must be positive if an exogenous increase in demand is to raise output at a given level of competitiveness. We shall make this assumption. It implies that the root governing c is negative. Note that with eq. (14′) governing the behaviour of the real wage, there is no automatic tendency for the level of output to converge to its capacity level 0. In long-run equilibrium we have [setting $D(w - p) = 0$],

$$y = \frac{\eta}{\phi}(w - p) = (\alpha - 1)\frac{\eta}{\phi}c. \tag{17}$$

The system is still dichotomized, and the behaviour of c, $w - p$, y and $r - Dp$ is independent of monetary shocks, but even if we start at full employment, real shocks will not necessarily be followed by a return to full employment. Only if η (− the coefficient on the lagged real wage in the wage equation) is zero will the system tend to full employment. This can be shown as follows. In long-run equilibrium the IS equation is

$$y = -\gamma(r^* + \tau) + \delta\alpha c + f. \tag{18}$$

Combining (17) and (18) gives

$$y = \frac{(\alpha - 1)\eta\gamma}{\phi\delta\alpha - (1 - \alpha)\eta}(r^* + \tau) - \frac{(\alpha - 1)\eta\delta\alpha}{\phi\delta\alpha - (1 - \alpha)\eta}f. \tag{19}$$

Apart from the absence of an automatic return to full employment the behaviour of the flexible money wage — sticky real wage model is qualitatively the same when $\eta = 0$ and when $\eta > 0$. The response to an unanticipated reduction in Dm is shown in fig. 8. An unanticipated immediately-implemented reduction in Dm instantaneously moves the system to the new stationary equilibrium E_2 without any change in c, y or $r - Dp$. An announced future reduction in Dm instantaneously moves the system to an intermediate position such as E_{12}, between E_1 and E_2 from where it moves gradually to E_2 where it arrives at the

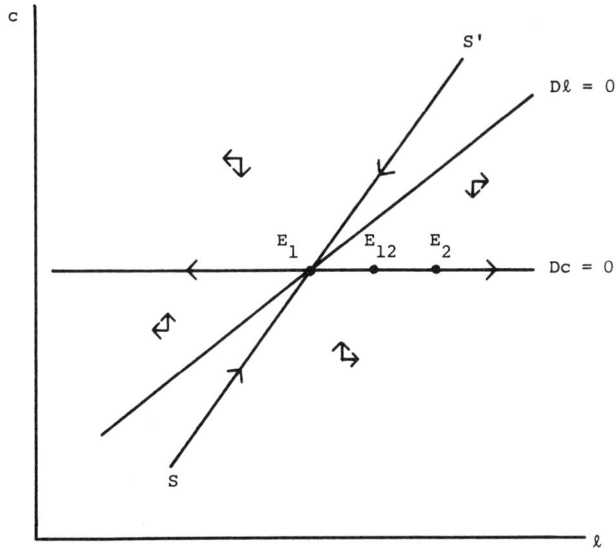

Fig. 8. Money disturbances (with money wage flexibility and real wage rigidity).

moment that the reduction in Dm actually occurs. This whole process again takes place without any changes in c, y or $r - Dp$.

Now consider the effect of an increase in $r^* + \tau$ in this model, which changes the long-run equilibrium in fig. 9 from E_1 to a point such as E_2. With c predetermined, an immediate unanticipated increase in $r^* + \tau$ causes an equal jump increase in e and w, lowering l to E_{12}. From there c and l converge gradually to the new long-run equilibrium E_2 along the unique convergent trajectory $S'S'$. A previously unanticipated future increase in $r^* + \tau$ leads to an immediate jump in l down to a point intermediate between E_1 and E_{12}, such as E_{12}'. From there l declines gradually to E_{12} where it arrives when $r^* + \tau$ is actually raised. c and l then increase gradually along SS' towards E_2.

It is interesting to see what happens to the wage equation (14') when the exchange rate has no effect on the price level, i.e., when $\alpha = 1$. In that case the price equation (8) becomes

$$p = w, \tag{20a}$$

while the wage equation reduces to

$$\phi y = \eta(w - p). \tag{20b}$$

Eqs. (20a) and (20b) imply that $y = 0$ at each instant. The model now is in many ways the same as the model with money wage and real wage flexibility discussed in section 3.2 and summarized in eq. (13). The link between the real wage and the

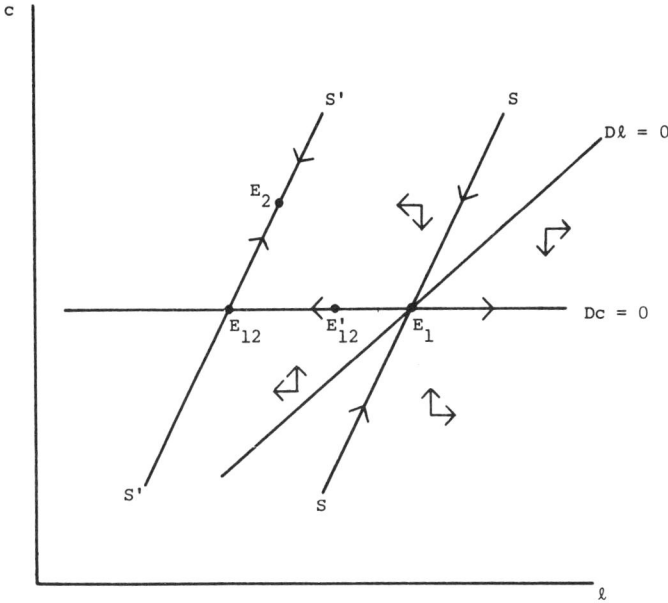

Fig. 9. Real disturbances (with money wage flexibility and real wage rigidity).

real exchange rate, given by $w - p = (\alpha - 1)c$ in the general model, disappears. Even though the real wage is still predetermined (and indeed remains constant throughout at 0), the real exchange rate again becomes a jump variable. Because w still is a jump variable, l also stays that way. The state-space representation of this version of the model is given in

$$
\begin{bmatrix} Dl \\ Dc \end{bmatrix} = \begin{bmatrix} \lambda^{-1} & \gamma^{-1}\delta \\ 0 & \gamma^{-1}\delta \end{bmatrix} \begin{bmatrix} l \\ c \end{bmatrix} + \begin{bmatrix} 1 & 0 & -\lambda^{-1} & -1 \\ 0 & 0 & 0 & 0 \end{bmatrix} \begin{bmatrix} Dm \\ r^* + \tau \\ \theta \\ r_d \end{bmatrix} \tag{21}
$$

The response of this sytem to nominal and real shocks is qualitative similar to that described in section 3.2 and figs. 6 and 7.

3.4. Rational expectations in the labour market with money wage stickiness

Without changing the equation for the core rate of inflation (4″) and the associated wage equation (14) of the previous section, a single change of assumption concerning the behaviour of the money wage destroys the classical policy implications of that model. The crucial change in assumption is to rule out discrete jumps in w, that is to require w to be a continuous function of time. The exchange rate, however, is still free to make discrete jumps at a point in time. This change in assumption does not rule out a rational expectations interpretation of (14). This is particularly obvious if we assume that $\eta = 0$. The behaviour of this rational expectations model of the labour market is, however, very different from the classical behaviour of the models of sections 3.2 and 3.3. Instead it resembles the behaviour of the sticky money wage model of section 2 and 3.1. Monetary shocks lead to real exchange rate overshooting and departures of actual from capacity output. Note that this kind of behaviour is ruled out when $\alpha = 1$. This 'closed economy' representation means that rational expectations automatically rule out departures of output from capacity output.[7] With the assumed asymmetry in the behaviour of c and w, and with a direct effect of e on p, monetary shocks will alter the real wage and the real exchange rate and cause departures from full employment.

With the sticky money wage interpretation of eq. (14), l and c again assume the roles of section 2. l is predetermined while c (via e) can jump in response to 'news'.

The response of the system to an unanticipated reduction in Dm is sketched in fig. 10.

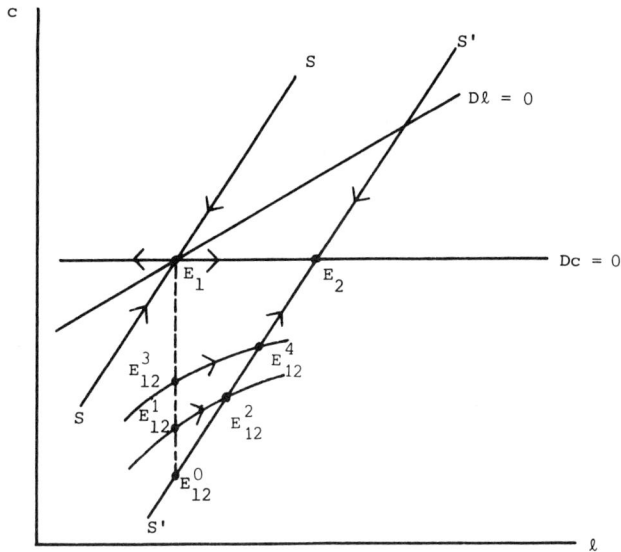

Fig. 10. Reduction of money growth (with money wage stickiness).

If the reduction in Dm takes place immediately c jump appreciates to E_{12}^0. After that it moves gradually to E_2 along $S'S'$. From eq. (16d) we see that this jump-appreciation of c will be associated with a fall in output. An anticipated future reduction in Dm will be associated with a smaller immediate jump-appreciation of c when the news arrives, to E_{12}^1 say. This jump places c and l

[7]These issues are discussed for the fixed exchange rate case in Buiter (1978, 1979).

on the divergent path, driven by the values of the forcing variables determining E_1 that will put it on the convergent path through E_2 ($S'S'$) when the cut in Dm is actually implemented. An equal reduction in Dm at a more distant future time will again be associated with smaller initial jump-appreciation of c (to E_{12}^3 say) after which c and l follow the unstable trajectory (drawn with reference to E_1) that will put it on $S'S'$ when Dm is actually cut. There always will be a finite initial jump in c when the news of a future reduction in Dm arrives, except in the limiting case when the announced monetary growth reduction is infinitely far in the future. One implication is that if a monetary deceleration is planned, the loss of output and competitiveness is smaller the further in advance the proposed policy action is announced.

From eq. (16c) with $\eta = 0$, we obtain

$$y = ((\alpha - 1)/\phi)Dc. \tag{22}$$

Assume the system starts in long-run equilibrium at $t = 0$. The net cumulative loss of output[8] following a monetary deceleration is

$$\int_0^\infty y(t)\,dt = ((\alpha - 1)/\phi)[c(\infty) - c(0)]. \tag{23}$$

$c(\infty)$ is the steady-state real exchange rate which is the same in the initial and the final long-run equilibrium. $c(\infty) - c(0)$ is therefore just the initial jump in the real exchange rate. The cumulative loss of output is minimized by minimizing the initial jump in c. This is achieved, for a given proposed reduction in Dm by announcing the reduction as early as possible.

The assumption made so far, that $w(t)$ is a continuous function of time, can be derived from two more basic assumptions. The first is that $w(t)$ cannot jump instantaneously in response to new information. In principle this would still permit discrete jumps in $w(t)$ at some $t > t_0$, where t_0 is the instant at which new information becomes available. The second assumption is an arbitrage condition for the labour market, which asserts that efficient speculative behaviour in the labour market eliminates all profit opportunities associated with anticipated future jumps in w. This assumption is analogous to the arbitrage condition we have used to rule out anticipated future jumps in e, although its application to the labour market is rather less convincing than its use in the foreign exchange market.

3.5. Gradual adjustment of core inflation with occasional jumps

The final specification of the equation for the core rate of inflation that we shall

---

[8]Since the adjustment path of output is monotonic in all our examples, y does not change sign during the transition. The net output loss therefore also equals the gross output loss.

consider is given in

$$D\pi = \xi(Dp + D\theta - \pi), \qquad \xi > 0. \tag{4'''}$$

This adaptive process for π does not rule out discrete jumps in π, although it is consistent with our assumption that the *level* of the money wage is predetermined. Eq. (4''') defines π as a backward-looking weighted average of past rates of inflation with exponentially declining weights.

$$\pi(t) = \xi \int_{-\infty}^{t} e^{-\xi(t-s)}(Dp(s) + D\theta(s))\,ds.$$

Because $\pi(t)$ is backward-looking it will be associated with a stable eigenvalue. It is, however, not predetermined. $\pi(t)$ depends also on current $Dp(t)$ and $D\theta(s)$. If $p + \theta$ makes a discontinuous jump at $t = \bar{t}$, $Dp + D\theta$ becomes unbounded and so does $D\pi$. π therefore jumps. This characteristic of π as a 'dependent' jump variable — it jumps at $t = \bar{t}$ if and only if $p + \theta$ jumps at $t = \bar{t}$ — will be important when we come to consider the specification of the boundary conditions of this model — our preferred model.

It is easily checked that the following relation holds for π:

$$\pi(t) = \pi(t^-) + \xi[p(t) - p(t^-) + \theta(t) - \theta(t^-)], \tag{24}$$

where

$$\pi(t^-) = \lim_{\substack{\tau \to t \\ \tau < t}} \pi(\tau) \quad \text{etc.}$$

The jump in π is ξ times the sum of the jumps in p and θ. Rewriting (24) in terms of the state variables we get

$$\pi(t) - \pi(t^-) = \xi[(1-\alpha)(c(t) - c(t^-)) + \theta(t) - \theta(t^-)$$

$$+ l(t) - l(t^-) - (m(t) - m(t^-))]. \tag{24'}$$

If there are no level jumps in m this becomes

$$\pi(t) - \pi(t^-) = \xi((1-\alpha)(c(t) - c(t^-)) + \theta(t) - \theta(t^-)). \tag{24''}$$

For convenience we reproduce the complete model (to be used in section 4) below [eqs. (1), (2), (8), (9), (4'''), (5), (10a) and (10b)]:

$$m - p - \theta = ky - \lambda(r - rd),$$

$$y = -\gamma(r - Dp - D\theta) + \delta(e - p),$$

$$p = \alpha w + (1 - \alpha)e,$$

$$Dw = \phi y + \pi,$$

$$D\pi = \xi(Dp + D\theta - \pi),$$

$$De = r - r^* - \tau,$$

$$l = m - w,$$

$$c = e - w.$$

Its state-space representation is given in eqs. (25) and (26),[9]

$$
\begin{bmatrix} Dl \\ D\pi \\ Dc \end{bmatrix} = \Delta^{-1} \begin{bmatrix} \phi\alpha\gamma & \lambda + \alpha\gamma k \\ \xi(1 - \alpha(1 + \gamma\phi)) & \xi\lambda(1 - \alpha(1 + \gamma\phi)) \\ 1 & \lambda \end{bmatrix}
$$

$$
\begin{bmatrix} \phi\alpha(\lambda\delta - \gamma(1 - \alpha)) \\ \xi[\alpha\phi(\gamma(1 - \alpha) - \alpha\delta\lambda) - (1 - \alpha)(1 - \alpha(1 - \delta k))] \\ \alpha\delta(\phi\lambda - k) - (1 - \alpha) \end{bmatrix} \begin{bmatrix} l \\ \pi \\ c \end{bmatrix}
$$

$$
+ \Delta^{-1} \begin{bmatrix} \Delta & -\phi\lambda\gamma(1 - \alpha) & -\phi\alpha\gamma \\ 0 & \xi(1 - \alpha)(\lambda + \gamma k) & -\xi(1 - \alpha(1 + \gamma\phi)) \\ 0 & \lambda + \gamma(k - \phi\lambda) & -1 \end{bmatrix}
$$

$$
\begin{bmatrix} -\phi\alpha\gamma\lambda \\ -\xi\lambda(1 - \alpha(1 + \gamma\phi)) \\ -\lambda \end{bmatrix} \begin{bmatrix} Dm \\ r^* + \tau \\ \theta \\ r_d \end{bmatrix}, \tag{25}
$$

[9]The $D\theta$ term is again omitted. It will be discussed in section 4.

where $\Delta = \alpha\gamma(\phi\lambda - k) - \lambda < 0$, and

$$
\begin{bmatrix} r \\ y \\ Dw \\ Dp \\ De \end{bmatrix} = \Delta^{-1}
\begin{bmatrix}
1 - \alpha\gamma\phi & -k\alpha\gamma \\
-\alpha\gamma & -\alpha\lambda\gamma \\
-\alpha\gamma\phi & -(\lambda + \alpha\gamma k) \\
1 - \alpha(1 + \gamma\phi) & -\alpha(\lambda + \gamma k) \\
1 - \alpha\gamma\phi & -k\alpha\gamma
\end{bmatrix}
$$

$$
\begin{bmatrix}
-[k\alpha\delta + (1 - \alpha\gamma\phi)(1 - \alpha)] \\
-\alpha(\lambda\delta - \gamma(1 - \alpha)) \\
-\alpha\phi(\lambda\delta - \gamma(1 - \alpha)) \\
\alpha\phi(\gamma(1 - \alpha) - \alpha\delta\lambda) - (1 - \alpha)(1 - \alpha(1 - \delta k)) \\
-[k\alpha\delta + (1 - \alpha\gamma\phi)(1 - \alpha)]
\end{bmatrix}
\begin{bmatrix} l \\ \pi \\ c \end{bmatrix}
$$

$$
+ \Delta^{-1}
\begin{bmatrix}
0 & k\gamma(1 - \alpha) & -(1 - \alpha\gamma\phi) \\
0 & \lambda\gamma(1 - \alpha) & \alpha\gamma \\
0 & \phi\lambda\gamma(1 - \alpha) & \phi\alpha\gamma \\
0 & (1 - \alpha)(\lambda + k\gamma) & -(1 - \alpha(1 + \gamma\phi)) \\
0 & \lambda + \gamma(k - \alpha\lambda\phi) & -(1 - \alpha\gamma\phi)
\end{bmatrix}
$$

$$
\begin{bmatrix}
-(1 - \alpha\gamma\phi)\lambda \\
\alpha\gamma\lambda \\
\phi\alpha\gamma\lambda \\
-\lambda(1 - \alpha(1 + \gamma\phi)) \\
-\lambda(1 - \alpha\gamma\phi)
\end{bmatrix}
\begin{bmatrix} Dm \\ r^* + \tau \\ \theta \\ r_d \end{bmatrix}. \tag{26}
$$

We now turn to a more detailed study of the behaviour of the model of eqs. (25) and (26) in section 4.

4. The real exchange rate and the output cost of monetary disinflation in a model with sluggish 'core' inflation

In this section we solve the model of eqs. (25) and (26) for the time paths of selected variables, using a particular set of 'plausible' parameter values. The numerical example is designed to focus on the role of the real and nominal exchange rate in monetary disinflation. Two common channels of the monetary transmission mechanism are intentionally closed off. Thus 'core' inflation in the labour market is backward looking (although π will jump iff e jumps) and, in addition, it is assumed that aggregate demand is interest inelastic: the IS curve is vertical. The real exchange rate continues to function as an effective channel of monetary policy, which is successful in bringing down steady-state inflation. We refer to this as policy A.

We examine the mechanism through which inflation is reduced and calculate the costs, in terms of lost output, incurred in the process. We also examine an alternative policy, referred to as policy B, which reduces the long-run rate of inflation by the same extent *without* varying the real exchange rate, but following the same path of output. We note that these policies differ in their effects on the price *level*, even in the long run. In the short run, the recession induced by an overvalued exchange rate will show a sharper fall in the rate of inflation than the recession of equal magnitude induced by the alternative policy that keeps the real exchange rate constant. In the former case, there will also be an immediate fall in the price *level*, which is absent in the latter. Since the long-run real exchange rate is independent of the rate of monetary growth, the initial jump decline in $c = e - w$ under policy A will be followed by a gradual increase in $e - w$ back to its initial level. On balance, during the adjustment process, De exceeds Dw. While $e - w$ is unchanged in the long run, the new steady-state paths of both e and w under policy A lie below the initial steady-state paths and are also lower relative to the path of the nominal money stock, since the lower steady-state rate of inflation is associated with a higher stock of real money balances. It is possible (but not necessary) for e to overshoot its new steady-state path.[10] In that case De will not only exceed Dw on balance during the adjustment process, it will also on balance exceed the new, lower, rate of monetary growth. [See Buiter and Miller (1981).] The alternative policy has the same real long-run equilibrium, including the same stock of real money balances but its long-run price level path lies above the price level path of policy A. Its endogenously determined long-run nominal money stock path also lies above the exogenously determined nominal money stock path of policy A.

We noted that, under policy A on balance after the initial jump appreciation, $De > Dw$, while with the alternative policy of model B, $De = Dw$. This does not mean that De will typically be larger with policy A than with policy B because the levels of the new steady state paths of e and w are lower in the former case than in the latter.

We also briefly consider another policy designed to attain the same reduction in the rate of inflation as with policy A, but without any loss of output. This policy involves a cut in indirect taxes and (in general) a change in the level of the nominal stock of money.

As long as w is predetermined, the output cost of achieving a given reduction in the steady-state rate of inflation (defined as the cumulative net amount of excess capacity) is entirely independent of the exchange rate. While it may be possible to

---

[10]The slope of this path equals the new rate of monetary growth.

bring forward the anti-inflationary gains, it is not possible to reduce the net output cost of bringing down inflation by engineering an early appreciation of the real exchange rate.

4.1. Parameter values

To illustrate the operation of the model we consider the results of choosing particular values for the parameters as follows:

$$\lambda = 2, \quad k = 1, \quad \alpha = \tfrac{3}{4}, \quad \phi = \xi = \delta = \tfrac{1}{2}, \quad \gamma = 0.$$

Without loss of generality let $r^* + \tau = \theta = r_d = 0$.
With these values substituted into eq. (25) the system becomes

$$
\begin{bmatrix} Dl \\ D\pi \\ Dc \end{bmatrix}
=
\begin{bmatrix}
0 & -1 & -3/16 \\
-1/16 & -1/8 & 7/64 \\
-1/2 & -1 & 1/8
\end{bmatrix}
\begin{bmatrix} l \\ \pi \\ c \end{bmatrix}
+
\begin{bmatrix} \mu \\ 0 \\ r^* \end{bmatrix}.
\tag{27}
$$

The characteristic equation is $\rho^3 - \rho/16 - 3/64 = 0$ and the determinant is $3/64$ (see appendix), $u = Dm$.
The roots are 0.418 and $-0.209 \pm 0.2618i$ and the row eigenvector associated with the positive root $\hat{\rho}$ is found to be

$$[\hat{v}_1, \hat{v}_2, -1] = [1.271, -0.499, -1].$$

4.2. The impact effects of an unanticipated change in monetary growth ($d\mu$)

Using these values for $\hat{\rho}$, $\hat{v}_1$, $\hat{v}_2$ we find (see appendix) the initial jump in competitiveness is $dc = 2.8624 \, d\mu$, that is, the initial percentage change in competitiveness will be just under three times the percentage change in monetary growth announced by the monetary authorities. The immediate effect that this has on the 'core' rate of inflation is

$$d\pi = \xi(1 - \alpha) \, dc = dc/8 \approx 0.36 \, d\mu.$$

Given the simple structure of the model, the change in competitiveness will be associated with an immediate change in output,

$$dy = \delta\alpha \, dc = 3 \, dc/8 \approx 1.1 \, d\mu,$$

so output will change by roughly the change in the rate of monetary growth.

The rate of wage settlements will jump on impact as a result of both the shift in π and of the recession as follows:

$$d(Dw) = \phi \, dy + d\pi = (\phi\delta\alpha + \xi(1-\alpha)) \, dc = 5dc/16 \approx 0.9 \, d\mu.$$

4.3. The long-run equilibrium

In a system which is superneutral, one would not expect a change in monetary growth to affect the equilibrium real interest rate or the real exchange rate, though nominal interest rates will reflect the monetary slowdown. By setting the left-hand side of eq. (27) at zero and differentiating with respect to μ, we can confirm that a change in μ has no long-run effect on c, but changes π one-for-one. As the equilibrium nominal rate of interest will also move in line with μ, the impact on real balances in the long run is $-\lambda \, d\mu$.

4.4. The dynamic behaviour of the system

The dynamic behaviour of the variables in the system is summarised in table 1. In the first column of panel (a) are shown the 'starting values' for l, π and c discussed above, measured as deviations from their new equilibrium values after a one point slowdown in monetary growth at $t = 0$. (All variables are scaled by 100, so a one-point slowdown in monetary growth will appear as $d\mu = -1.0$.) The second column shows Dl, $D\pi$, Dc at time zero calculated from eq. (27) and from the first column.

Table 1

		Starting values[a]		Dynamic characteristics[b]			
		$x(0)$	$Dx(0)$	B_1	B_2	B	ε
(a)	l	-2.0	-0.1055	-2.0	-2.0	-2.8284	0.7854
	π	0.6422	-0.2684	0.6422	-0.5126	-0.8217	2.4680
	c	-2.8624	0	-2.8625	-2.2862	-3.6634	0.6739
(b)	y	-1.0734	0	-1.0734	-0.8573	-1.3738	0.6739
	Dw	0.1055	-0.2684	0.1055	-0.9413	-0.9472	1.6824
	Dc	0	0.3213	0	1.2272	1.2272	1.5708
	Dp	0.1055	-0.2019	0.1055	-0.6345	-0.6432	1.7356
Alternative policy[c]							
(c)	y	-1.0734	0	-1.0734	-0.8573	-1.3738	0.6739
	Dp	0.4633	-0.2684	0.4633	-0.6553	-0.8026	2.1862

[a]See text for derivation of $x(0)$ for l, π, c; $Dx(0)$ can be obtained by multiplying matrix shown in (27) into $x(0)$.
[b]Damping factor $\rho = -0.2090$, frequency $\omega = 0.2618$.
[c]For which $\pi(0) = 1.0$, and y follows same path as above (see text).

These starting values are chosen so as to place the system on the two-dimensional stable manifold, on which the stable path of l, π, and c can be described by

$$x(t) = e^{\rho t}(B_1 \cos \omega t + B_2 \sin \omega t) = B\, e^{\rho t} \cos(\omega t - \varepsilon),$$

where the values for B_1, B_2, B and ε are calculated from the initial conditions in the first two columns.

The same parameters, calculated in the same manner, are shown for y, Dw, Dc and Dp in the second panel of table 1. These variables are also measured as deviations from their new equilibrium values. For output (y) this is zero, by construction, but for wage and price inflation (Dp and Dw) the new steady state will correspond to the new rate of monetary growth ($\bar{\mu}$). For convenience, in what follows, we will assume that the newly chosen rate of monetary growth is zero, so that there is *no* inflation in the new equilibrium.

A check on the calculations contained in the table, and some indication of how the policy works, is obtained by integrating the paths shown there for Dw and Dp. The formula[11] which gives the required integral is

$$\int_0^\infty x(t)\,dt = (-\rho B_1 + \omega B_2)/(\rho^2 + \omega^2),$$

where B_1 and B_2 are shown in the body of the table and the values for ρ and ω are given in note b to the table. Applying this we find

$$\int_0^\infty Dw(t)\,dt = -2.0 \quad \text{and} \quad \int_0^\infty Dp(t)\,dt = -1.2843.$$

The discrepancy is accounted for by the fact that the price level shows an instantaneous discrete fall at time zero, which is not picked up in the integration. The fall will be simply $(1-\alpha)\,dc$, where dc measures the initial impact of the monetary policy on competitiveness. The initial loss of competitiveness is -2.864 (see the first entry in the third row of the table), and $1-\alpha$ is 0.25, which provides a figure of -0.7156 for the initial fall in the price level. Together with the integral reported above, this gives a total of -2.0 for the long-run effect on the price level. Thus the real wage is unchanged in the long-run, as one would expected from a model which is 'superneutral'. (The 2% fall in the price level is required to increase real balances to satisfy the higher demand for liquidity at the lower nominal interest prevailing when prices are stable.)

The cyclical path towards this long-run value is sketched in fig. 11. In the top panel of the figure, by choice of units, both the price level and the money stock can

[11]Kindly provided by Peter Burridge and Avinash Dixit.

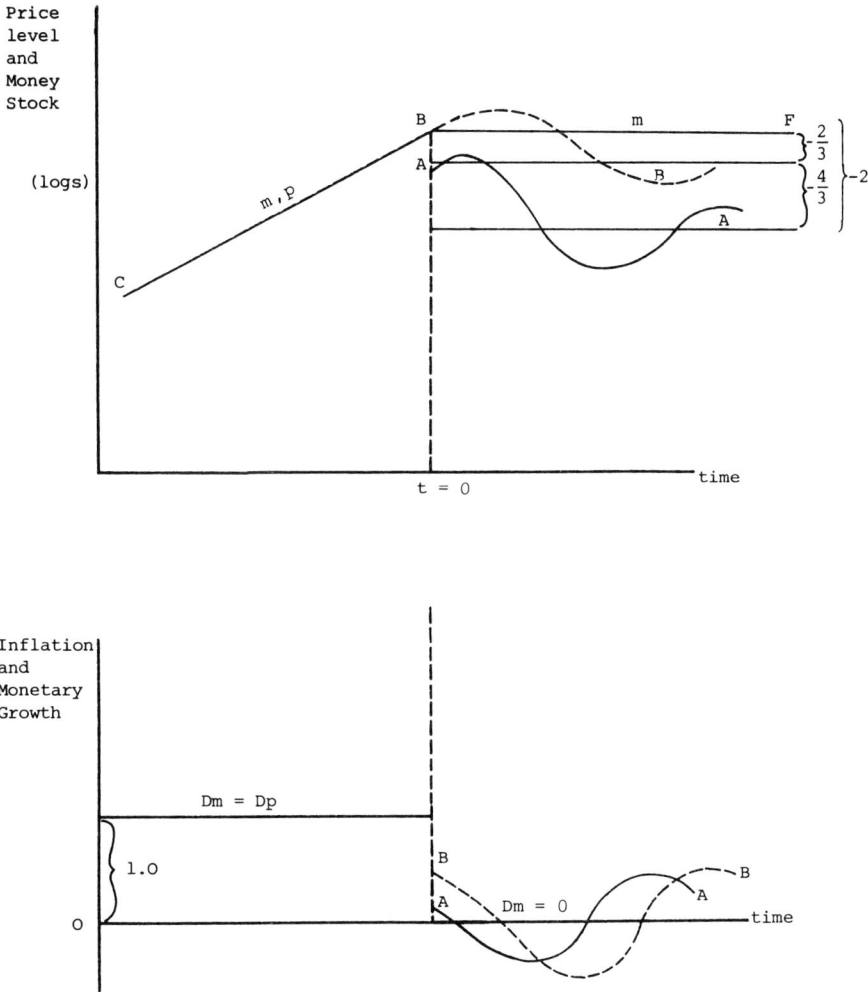

Fig. 11. Money and prices.

be represented by the same line, CB, until the time $t=0$ of the monetary slowdown. The money stock levels off at point B, and the price level jumps down (because of the jump-appreciation of e) and then rises for a while as shown by the path labelled AA. In the lower panel of fig. 11, the paths after $t=0$ for monetary growth (the axis and the rate of price inflation (AA) are shown. It is evident from the fact that the initial rate is only a little above zero that this policy has a prompt effect upon inflation. This effect is due to two factors; the immediate fall in core inflation (by about $\frac{1}{3}$ from 1.0 to 0.6422; see table 1, column 1, row 2) and the recession in output (of just over 1.0; see table 1, column 1, row 4).

This rapid fall in inflation might lead one to be optimistic about the costs of eliminating inflation as measured by the size and duration of the recession. But if we measure the output costs of checking inflation simply by the unweighted integral of y (which means that some of the recession is cancelled out by subsequent boom as output cycles towards equilibrium) the following expression for the cumulative net loss of output can be obtained:

$$\int_0^\infty y(t)\,\mathrm{d}t = (\bar{\bar{\mu}} - \bar{\mu})/\xi\phi.$$

With $\bar{\bar{\mu}} - \bar{\mu} = -1.0$ and $\xi\phi = 0.25$, the cumulative net output cost required to bring down the steady-state inflation rate by 1 percentage point is four 'point-years' loss of output.[12]

Our model ignores possible benefits from bringing down inflation slowly due to non-linearities in the Phillips curve which might cause two years with 5% excess capacity to have a stronger counterinflationary effect than 1 year with 10% excess capacity. The evidence on this is, however, by no means clear.

We now consider alternative policies which specifically avoid any fluctuations in competitiveness. We see how they compare with what we have just seen for policy A in terms of the speed with which inflation is reduced and the cost in terms of lost output.

4.5. Alternative policies

In order to see how much the initial loss of competitiveness contributes to the speed with which inflation is reduced and to cutting the cost of reducing inflation we consider alternative policies which keep competitiveness constant at its long-run equilibrium value throughout. If competitiveness is thus kept constant and $c = e - w = 0$, the price level and the wage rate will move together, as can be seen from eq. (8). As a consequence the inflation process in the model reduces to the familiar augmented Phillips curve commonly used to characterize closed economies. We get

$$Dp = \phi y + \pi, \tag{28}$$

$$D\pi = \xi(Dp - \pi). \tag{4''''}$$

The stabilization of the real exchange rate precludes both the discrete adjustment to the core rate of inflation π, which was a feature of the previous policy, as well as any discrete jumps in the price level. Both π and p are predetermined. Given the

---

[12]As a measure of economic waste, $\int_0^\infty y(t)\,\mathrm{d}t$ is only really useful if $y(t)$ does not change sign on the interval $|0, \infty)$. Zero net output loss is consistent with periods of prolonged and large excess supply followed by periods of prolonged and large excess demand. A more appropriate index of economic waste might be $\int_0^\infty |y(t)|\,\mathrm{d}t$, which penalizes all deviations of output from capacity output in the same way.

initial level of core inflation $\pi(0) = \bar{\mu} = 1.0$, the initial value of the price level $p(0)$ and a path for real output, eqs. (28) and (4'''') will by themselves generate the entire path to be followed by the price level. Note that, by construction, money has become a complete 'side-show'. Two of the transmission mechanisms, the real balance effect and an interest rate effect in the goods market, have been ruled out from the start. Now that the real exchange rate is also kept constant, there is no feedback from money on real output. Since the model has the standard homogeneity properties, it will of course still be true that in the long run the rate of inflation equals the rate of growth of the money supply. As will become clear, however, the truism that 'inflation is always and everywhere a monetary phenomenon' should in the current example be turned around: money here is an inflation phenomenon.

The first alternative policy (called B) takes the path of output to be *precisely the same* as that generated by the monetary contraction just described with policy A. This can be achieved e.g. by adding a fiscal instrument g to the IS curve so that

$$y = \delta \alpha c + \eta g, \qquad \eta > 0. \tag{29}$$

With c kept constant at 0, we can duplicate policy A's real output path by making ηg follow the exact path of $\delta \alpha c$ under policy A. The real exchange rate could e.g. be stabilized by adopting the exchange rate management rule that $De = Dw$. This then implies of course that $De = Dp$. With the exchange rate thus managed, the nominal money stock is endogenously determined. When $De = Dw = Dp$, the nominal interest rate is given by $r = r^* + De = r^* + Dp$. The LM equation (1) then becomes

$$m = p - \lambda(r^* + Dp) + ky = p - \lambda r^* + (k - \lambda \phi) y - \lambda \pi. \tag{30}$$

With p and π predetermined and y determined by (29) with $c = 0$, eq. (30) determines the nominal money stock. Other ways of stabilizing the real exchange rate such as a variable tax on capital inflows (subsidy on outflows) can be thought of. In the present example the inflation generated by eqs. (28), (4'''') and (29) (with $c = 0$) is the dog wagging the money supply tail through eq. (30). Given eqs. (28) and (4''''), it will of course always be the case that the path of inflation is determined once a path for output is specified. If other transmission mechanisms of monetary policy, such as an interest rate effect and a real balance effect in the output market, are included in the model, however, it is less straightforward (although possible) to specify an output path without reference to the money supply.

The results of the alternative policy for inflation are shown in the bottom row of table 1. Inflation starts at a significantly higher level than before with policy A because the starting value for core inflation π is now $\bar{\mu} = 1.0$. The path followed by inflation has the same damping factor ρ and frequency ω as the output path but the amplitude is smaller and the inflation cycle leads the output cycle. The rate of inflation will, as before, be reduced to zero at a net cost of 4 point-years of output.

The price *level* towards which the system converges under the alternative policy is, however, higher than the long-run price level of policy A. This can be seen from the coefficients in table 1. While $\int_0^\infty Dp_A(t)\,d(t) = -2$ for model A, as we have already discussed, integrating the path for inflation under model B yields a smaller fall,

$$\int_0^\infty Dp_B(t)\,dt = \frac{-\rho 0.4633 - 0.6553\omega}{\rho^2 + \omega^2} = -\frac{2}{3}.$$

These results are illustrated in fig. 11 where the path followed by the price level and the rate of inflation under policy B are plotted alongside those already described for policy A. In the top panel the price level under the alternative policy proceeds from point *B* without any 'jump' along a path (*BB*) which cycles around a steady state level which is 4/3 of a point above the steady state price level for policy A.

In the bottom panel the rate of inflation is shown starting at point *B* and cycling towards zero along the path *BB*. Thus inflation starts at a higher level under the alternative policy than under the floating exchange rate case. The determination of those 'starting values' and the subsequent comparison of inflation can be seen from fig. 12. There, labelled $SRPC_B$, is the 'short-run Phillips curve' which determines initial inflation under policy B where $\pi_B(0) = \bar{\mu}$. This value of π determines the intercept of $SRPC_B$, and the value of $y(0)$ determines the values of inflation shown as $Dp_B(0)$. From this point inflation and output cycle towards the origin as shown by the path labelled *BB*.

By contrast the relationship determining inflation under policy A (*after the initial jump at time zero*),

$$Dp_A(0) = \phi y(0) + \pi_A(0) + \frac{(1-\alpha)}{\alpha\delta} Dy(0) = \phi y(0) + \pi_A(0)$$

$$\text{as} \quad Dy(0) = 0,$$

yields the Phillips curve shown as $SRPC_A$ which has an intercept of $\pi_A(0)$ which is lower than $\pi_B(0)$ because of the jump induced by the revaluation of the currency at the inception of the monetary slowdown under floating rates. Thereafter inflation falls away following the path shown as AA.

The *gap* between the two paths in fig. 12, $D\tilde{p}$, can be plotted against time. Its dynamic characteristics (*after* the jump in p_A) are obtained from table 1 where

$$D\tilde{p} \equiv Dp_A - Dp_B = e^{\rho t}(-0.3578 \cos \omega t + 0.0208 \sin \omega t)$$

$$= 0.3583\, e^{\rho t} \cos(\omega t - 3.0855).$$

The path of $D\tilde{p}$ is therefore sinusoidal and its integral is -0.6183, which together with the initial jump in the price level, gives the figure of $-4/3$ as the long-run difference in the price level resulting from the two policies.

What is apparent from the above is that the policy of fighting inflation by cycles in output *and in the real exchange rate* (with an initial recession associated with an overvalued exchange rate) does not lead to any change in long-run inflation, compared to the same output cycle and a stable real exchange rate. The loss of competitiveness does however reduce inflation more quickly early on, as shown in fig. 12; the early lead established by this policy over the alternative is whittled away later when competitiveness is regained in the boom, but we are left with the conclusion that inflation *is* brought down more quickly with policy A, as shown by the solid line in fig. 12. (Inflation under the alternative policy is shown by the dotted line.)

The fluctuations of the real exchange rate can therefore be seen to have effects on inflation not unlike those attributed to temporary incomes policies by those who argue that the latter hold down inflation in the short run, but have *no* effect on the inflation rate in the long run. If that is true, then a temporary bout of

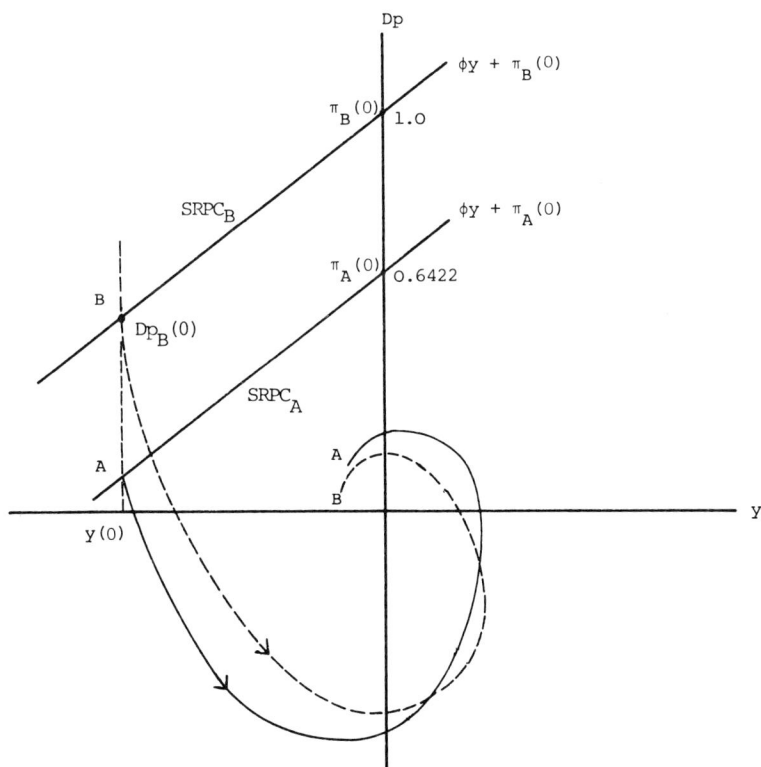

Fig. 12. Inflation under the two policies.

incomes policy would change only the long-run price level without changing the long-run growth of prices, which is what we have found to be characteristic of the policy of permitting the real exchange rate to vary.

4.6. 'Efficient disinflationary policies'[13]

Once we permit changes in the indirect tax rate, θ, we have a way of costlessly reducing inflation. Consider the money demand function and the wage equation,

$$m - p - \theta = -\lambda r + ky,$$

$$Dw = \phi y + \pi.$$

Given a reduction in the rate of monetary growth by $d\mu = \bar{\bar{\mu}} - \bar{\mu}$, we can easily calculate the change in θ required to jump π to its new long-run equilibrium value, $\bar{\bar{\mu}}$. Holding p constant, eq. (24) shows that $d\pi(t) = -\xi \, d\theta(t)$. The required change in θ is therefore given by

$$d\theta = \xi^{-1} \, d\pi = \xi^{-1} \, d\mu.$$

From the money market equilibrium condition we obtain that, since the long-run interest rate changes in line with μ,

$$d(m - p - \theta) = -\lambda \, dr = -\lambda \, d\mu.$$

Holding p constant this yields

$$dm - d\theta = -\lambda \, d\mu \quad \text{or} \quad dm = (-\lambda + \xi^{-1}) \, d\mu.$$

Therefore a change in the rate of monetary growth by $d\mu$, accompanied by a change in indirect taxes by $\xi^{-1} \, d\mu$ and a change in the *level* of the nominal money stock of $(-\lambda + \xi^{-1}) \, d\mu$ will immediately move the system to the new steady-state equilibrium with the lower rate of inflation. Output and the real exchange rate are unaffected. With our choice of parameter values ($\lambda = 2$ and $\xi = 0.5$), $d\theta = 2 \, d\mu$ and $dm = 0$.

The mechanism permitting the required reduction in inflation to be brought about without loss of output is the following. First, the cut in θ (in general together with the change in m) permits the long-run change in the stock of real money balances to be brought about immediately without any need for a jump in nominal prices, including the exchange rate. Second, the cut in θ achieves the

---

[13]Okun (1978).

immediate change in the core rate of inflation to its new long-run value. The use of indirect taxes to facilitate the process of bringing down inflation has been advocated frequently by Okun (1978).

Alternatively, incomes policy can be used to jump π. If *incomes policy* can be identified with a once-and-for-all reduction in π, without any other 'overwriting' of the behavioural equations of the model, then it will lower the cost of disinflation. If *monetary policy* changes or announcements themselves directly change π, as is the case in the model of section 2, then disinflationary monetary policies will also be 'efficient' in the sense we are using that term here.

5. Conclusion

After a summary of various approaches to the modelling of the inflationary process in an open economy with a floating exchange rate, we have studied the way in which a monetary slowdown might be expected to work in an economy where core inflation is sluggish, and adjusts to actual inflation with a significant (mean) lag.

Despite such sluggishness we found that core inflation can be reduced quickly by jumps in the price level induced by jumps in the exchange rate. In the simple model used to focus on this particular aspect of the monetary transmission mechanism we found that, even *without* any direct real balance and real interest rate effects on aggregate demand, a monetary slowdown might nevertheless cut inflation promptly via its impact on the nominal and the real exchange rate. Indeed our numerical example has the property that the inflation responds *immediately* by almost the full extent of the monetary slowdown! This reduction of inflation follows, in our example, from the effects of announced monetary policy on the exchange rate. The appreciation of the exchange rate cuts the inflation rate in two ways, first by reducing core inflation and second by cutting the level of output. Both of these effects involve sharp changes in the real exchange rate.

Since the model is 'superneutral', however, such changes in the real exchange rate and in real output must ultimately be reversed. Pursuit of a constant growth rate of money generates a cyclical convergence for these variables. The net output costs associated with a steady state reduction in inflation are found to be given by a simple formula, $d\mu/\xi\phi$ where $d\mu$ shows the change in steady state inflation, ϕ is the slope of the short-run Phillips curve and ξ measures the speed of adjustment of core inflation. Thus for $\xi = \phi = \frac{1}{2}$ the net output loss associated with reducing monetary growth and steady state inflation by 1% is 4 point-years of GNP.

For comparison we considered an alternative where the real exchange was held constant but output was constrained to follow the same path as before. Such an alternative, whose net output loss is of course identical, was found to achieve the same effect on steady state inflation, but the path taken by inflation was different.

The prompt anti-inflation success due to the loss of competitiveness being absent, inflation starts from a higher level under this alternative. The early lead achieved by the policy of 'overvaluing' the currency is never entirely lost, so that the long-run price level is lower than is true for the alternative policy.

In a superneutral model, with core inflation modelled in the way we have, it turns out that *any* path for output which exhibits a cumulative 4 point-years loss of output will (if $\xi\phi = \frac{1}{4}$) reduce steady state inflation by 1%, irrespective of the path taken by the real exchange rate (provided it starts and finishes at the same level). Thus the freedom to vary the real exchange rate in order to reduce inflation does *not* succeed in reducing the output costs of changing steady state inflation; it does however change the time path of inflation, relative to other policies which exhibit the same output path.

While the numerical model makes no claim to being a realistic model of the U.K., we would point out that the sort of output costs associated with reductions in medium term inflation in Treasury evidence to the Treasury Committee suggested a figure of 4 point-years of output for each 1 point of medium-term inflation. A more detailed analysis of simulations on an earlier version of the Treasury model, when the slope of the Phillips curve was flatter and the mean lag of core inflation longer, showed even higher costs [see Miller (1979)].

In considering 'efficient' disinflationary policies, we noted that a cut in indirect taxes could reduce the output costs of curing inflation by securing an immediate jump reduction in the price index at market prices and in the core rate of inflation. In our model a reduction in the rate of growth of money by $d\mu$ accompanied by a cut in indirect taxes of $\xi^{-1} d\mu$ will immediately and costlessly achieve a reduction in steady state inflation of $d\mu$. (In general a change in the *level* of the money stock will also be required.)

In the U.K., a one point cut in VAT is reckoned to cut the rate of indirect taxation by a half a point. A 4 point reduction in VAT would therefore avoid the four point-years of output loss otherwise associated with a point reduction in monetary growth. The present administration's decision to raise VAT by 8 points early in their term of office, at the same time that a programme of successive reductions in monetary growth was announced, would in our model increase the cost of bringing down inflation. In the short run, however, the adverse consequences of the VAT increase on the price level are countered by the appreciation of the exchange rate.

Those who argue that incomes policies can secure a step reduction in core inflation, would of course advocate their use as a way of cutting the output costs of reducing inflation [see, for example, Tobin (1977)]. We have not examined this case in detail in this paper. We have however, considered the possibility that announced *monetary* policy could immediately and directly reduce core inflation in just such a fashion. If announced monetary policy has this sort of direct expectational effect, then it will save output costs, just as a similarly successful incomes policy would. If, however, monetary targets only secure immediate effects on core inflation by a sudden loss of competitiveness, this will not constitute an 'efficient' way of reducing inflation.

Appendix: Derivation of the initial conditions

First, we note that when aggregate demand is completely interest inelastic (i.e., $\gamma = 0$), the term Δ in (25) and (26) becomes $-\lambda$ and, omitting θ, $r^* + \tau$ and r_d, eq. (25) simplifies to

$$
\begin{bmatrix} Dl \\ D\pi \\ Dc \end{bmatrix} = \begin{bmatrix} 0 & -1 \\ -\xi(1-\alpha)\lambda^{-1} & -\xi(1-\alpha) \\ -\lambda^{-1} & -1 \end{bmatrix}
$$

$$
\left. \begin{matrix} -\phi\delta\alpha \\ \xi(1-\alpha)\lambda^{-1}(1-\alpha+k\delta\alpha)+\phi\delta\alpha^2 \\ \lambda^{-1}(1-\alpha+k\delta\alpha)-\phi\delta\alpha \end{matrix} \right] \begin{bmatrix} l \\ \pi \\ c \end{bmatrix} + \begin{bmatrix} Dm \\ 0 \\ 0 \end{bmatrix}, \quad \text{(A.1)}
$$

where the determinant of the coefficient matrix A in (27) is given by $\Omega = \xi\lambda^{-1}\delta\alpha > 0$ and the characteristic equation, $f(\rho) = 0$ where ρ is a root, is

$$
\rho^3 - [(\lambda^{-1}-\xi)(1-\alpha)+(k\lambda^{-1}-\phi)\delta\alpha]\rho^2
$$

$$
- [(\lambda^{-1}-\xi)\phi\delta\alpha + \xi(1-\alpha)\lambda^{-1}]\rho - \Omega = 0. \quad \text{(A.2)}
$$

As can be seen from the characteristic equation, $f(0) < 0$ as $\Omega > 0$, but $f(\rho)$ tends to infinity when ρ tends to infinity; hence there exists one positive root, which is not surprising given the presence of the forward looking variable, c. The other two roots must be stable for the model to make sense. (For most plausible values of the parameters these other roots will turn out to be complex, as we see below.)

The row eigenvector v' associated with any root must satisfy the condition that $v'[\rho I - A] = Z'$ where Z' denotes the zero vector. Normalizing the eigenvector appropriately, this means

$$
\begin{bmatrix} v_1 & v_2 & -1 \end{bmatrix} \begin{bmatrix} \rho & 1 & -a_{13} \\ \xi(1-\alpha)\lambda^{-1} & \rho+\xi(1-\alpha) & -a_{23} \\ \lambda^{-1} & 1 & \rho-a_{33} \end{bmatrix} = \begin{bmatrix} 0 & 0 & 0 \end{bmatrix},
$$

$$
\text{(A.3)}
$$

where the last column is not given in full for simplicity. This implies

$$v_1 = 1 - v_2(\rho + \xi(1 - \alpha)),$$

$$v_2 = 1/(\xi(1 - \alpha) - \rho^2(\lambda^{-1} - \rho)^{-1}).$$

To ensure stability, the path to be followed by the system must not depend on the eigenvector associated with the positive (unstable) root. Dixit (1980) has shown that for a previously unanticipated immediately implemented shock this can be achieved by ensuring that the product of this eigenvector with the initial values of the variables (measured as deviations from the new long-run equilibrium) equals zero, i.e.,

$$\hat{v}_1(l(0) - \bar{l}) + \hat{v}_2(\pi(0) - \bar{\pi}) - (c(0) - \bar{c}) = 0. \tag{A.4}$$

$\bar{l}, \bar{\pi}$ and $\bar{c}$ are the new long-run equilibrium values of l, π and c and $\hat{v}_1$ and $\hat{v}_2$ are elements associated with the unstable root.

Let $Dm \equiv \mu$. The terms measuring initial disequilibrium following an unanticipated change in μ, denoted $d\mu$, can be evaluated as follows:

$$l(0) - \bar{l} = \lambda \, d\mu,$$

$$\pi(0) - \bar{\bar{\pi}} = \pi(0) - \bar{\bar{\mu}}, \tag{A.5}$$

$$c(0) - \bar{\bar{c}} = dc, \quad \text{the jump in competitiveness,}$$

where $\bar{\bar{\mu}}$ denotes the *new* value of μ.

From eq. (24″) we know that

$$d\pi = \xi(1 - \alpha) \, dc,$$

and so the initial disequilibrium in π becomes

$$\pi(0) - \bar{\bar{\pi}} = \xi(1 - \alpha) \, dc - d\mu.$$

Hence eq. (A.4) can be rewritten as

$$\hat{v}_1 \lambda \, d\mu + \hat{v}_2(\xi(1 - \alpha) \, dc - d\mu) - dc = 0,$$

and so the initial change in competitiveness found to be

$$dc = \frac{\hat{v}_1 \lambda - \hat{v}_2}{1 - \hat{v}_2 \xi(1 - \alpha)} \, d\mu.$$

References

Buiter, W.H., 1978, Short-run and long-run effects of external disturbances under a floating exchange rate, Economica 45, 251–272.

Buiter, W.H., 1979, Unemployment–inflation trade-offs with rational expectations in an open economy, Journal of Economic Dynamics and Control 1, June, 117–141.

Buiter, Willem H. and Marcus Miller, 1981, Monetary policy and international competitiveness, Oxford Economic Papers, Sept.

Dixit, Avinash, 1980, A solution technique for rational expectations models with applications to exchange rate and interest rate determination, Mimeo., Nov. (University of Warwick, Coventry).

Dornbusch, Rudiger, 1976, Expectations and exchange rate dynamics, Journal of Political Economy 84, Dec., 1161–1176.

Frenkel, J., 1980, The collapse of purchasing power parities in the 1970's, Working paper (University of Chicago, Chicago, IL).

Isard, P., 1977, How far can we push the law of one price, American Economic Review 67, 942–949.

Kravis, I. and R. Lipsey, 1978, Price behaviour in the light of balance of payment theories, Journal of International Economics 8, 193–247.

Liviatan, N., 1980, Anti-inflationary monetary policy and the capital import tax, Warwick Economic Research Paper no. 171 (University of Warwick, Coventry).

Miller, M., 1979, The unemployment costs of curing steady state inflation, Mimeo. (University of Warwick, Coventry).

Minford, P., 1980, A rational expectations model of the U.K. under fixed and floating exchange rates, Carnegie–Rochester Conference Series on Public Policy 12, 293–355.

Okun, Arthur M., 1978, Efficient disinflationary policy, American Economic Review 68, May, 353–357.

Sargan, J.D., 1980, A model of wage–price inflation, Review of Economic Studies 47, Jan., 97–112.

Tobin, James, 1977, How dead is Keynes?, Economic Enquiry 15, Oct., 459–468.

European Economic Review 32 (1988). North-Holland

THE INTERNATIONAL MONETARY SYSTEM

An Analysis of Alternative Regimes

Marcus H. MILLER*

University of Warwick, Coventry CV4 7AL and CEPR, UK

John WILLIAMSON*

Institute for International Economics, Washington, DC 20036, USA

This is an exercise in the positive economics of alternative monetary regimes. The behavior of output and prices is compared using a stochastic specification which allows asymptotic variances to be obtained without difficulty. Free floating of exchange rates together with national money supply targets is analyzed first, with and without the presence of 'fads' in the exchange rate. Two alternatives for monetary coordination are then considered. First is McKinnon's proposal to fix nominal exchange rates and stabilize aggregate monetary growth (or average inflation); second is Williamson's system of target zones for stable real exchange rates, complemented by nominal income targets for fiscal policy.

1. Introduction

At the beginning of the 1970s the OECD countries were on a de facto Dollar Standard, in which the U.S. selected its monetary policy with a view to domestic stability and other countries pegged to the dollar, with the right to change the peg at their unilateral discretion. By 1973, however, the Dollar Standard had collapsed, giving way to a regime of floating exchange rates coupled with national money supply targets, a regime long advocated by Milton Friedman [see for example, his influential papers on flexible exchange rates (1953) and monetary targets (1968)].

Since the Plaza Agreement of September 1985, however, the U.S.A. has made the external value of the dollar an explicit target of policy. The coordination of international macroeconomic policies has been sought in order to help secure a reduction of its external deficit. These developments prompt two questions – first, is a change in the international monetary

*Thanks are due to David Currie and his colleagues for use of the PRISM programme and to M. Emadi-Moghadam for his expertise in running it. The paper has benefitted considerably from comments made at the International Seminar on Macroeconomics, particularly those of Stan Fischer. Financial support from the ESRC is gratefully acknowledged.

system really called for rather than simply a change in, for example, U.S. fiscal policy; and, second, if so, what are the alternatives?

It is not the purpose of the present paper to debate the first question with those who maintain 'if it ain't broke, don't fix it', as the case for reform of the system has been developed in some detail elsewhere [see Williamson (1985)]. What we offer instead, on the second question, is a simple exercise in positive economics in which the floating rate regime of 1973–85 is compared with alternatives.

The alternatives considered are indicated in table 1, which classifies monetary systems on two criteria, whether they are hegemonic or not, and how exchange rates are determined. Thus the international system prevailing from 1973 to 1985 appearing in the first column is classified as 'symmetric', in contrast to the hegemony under the Dollar Standard, which appears in the second row of the second column.

The focus of this paper is on regimes *without* hegemony. The alternatives to floating with monetary targets that are considered are, first, McKinnon's proposals for fixed exchange rates, and, second, Williamson's system of target zones for real exchange rates.

McKinnon's proposal of 1984 was designed both to ensure symmetry in the operation of the international monetary system and to put the control of inflation on an explicitly monetarist footing. The plan was to have three key-currency members (U.S.A., Germany and Japan) agree a target for their *combined* monetary growth, which was to be pursued under fixed exchange rates by national DCE targets and symmetrical non-sterilised intervention. McKinnon's confidence that the variations of velocity observed at the national level were due to currency substitution and so would cancel out at the global level (and be adequately neutralised by the intervention policy) was challenged ex ante [Dornbusch (1983)] and has also been eroded by subsequent experience. As a result McKinnon has, in a later version of his proposal (1986), shifted to the 'classical' position that monetary policy at the global level should aim directly at price stability, rather than at the control

Table 1
International monetary systems compared.

	Floating rates with national money supply targets	Fixed exchange rates	Managed exchange rates
Symmetry	OECD 1973–85	McKinnon's proposals	Williamson's target zones
Hegemony	—	Dollar standard 1968–73	EMS 1979–

of a monetary aggregate. McKinnon has thus addressed two issues arising under fixed exchange rates, how to make the determination of monetary policy more symmetric and subsequently how to cope with the observed instability in the demand for money.

Under neither of McKinnon's proposals do the mechanisms which keep inflation at bay at a national level involve control of a *domestic* monetary aggregate. In the absence of portfolio shocks monetary policy will require keeping interest rates in line with those elsewhere (and controlling domestic credit expansion in the first case). The mechanisms are rather the longer run effect on expectations of belonging to such a currency union, together with the immediate impact of union wide interest rates, and more directly the impact on trade and employment of allowing prices to rise relative to those in partner countries. With nominal exchange rates fixed, inflation differentials will change real exchange rates in ways which shift demand from inflationary countries towards non-inflationary countries (while the level of the 'global' interest rate will act so as to stabilise inflation in the union as a whole).

Under the regime of floating-with-money-supply-targets the experience of the U.S. and the U.K. was not that the nominal exchange rate simply adjusted to offset inflationary differentials so as to keep real exchange rates fairly stable (as Friedman had implied would be the case) but that real exchange rates showed prolonged deviations frrom equilibrium ('misalignments'). It is this feature that *Williamson's target zones* are designed to remedy: on the assumption that fiscal policy is not allowed to crowd out the desired (high employment) balance of payments, domestic interest rates (and foreign currency intervention) are to be aimed at keeping the real exchange rate within a band of $\pm 10\%$ of the equilibrium level implied by the balance of payments target.

Williamson's plan resembles McKinnon's proposal in assigning domestic monetary policy to an external objective; in this case, however, the requirement to stabilise the real exchange rate will in the absence of portfolio shocks require *real* interest rates to be kept reasonably in line with those in partner countries. This policy assignment has been severely criticised by Adams and Gros (1986) for leaving domestic inflation out of control. As we show below, however, the combination of assigning monetary policy to this external objective and fiscal policy to a domestic money income target is not open to this criticism – indeed, at a formal level, the mechanism for checking domestic inflation resembles that which operates under the McKinnon plan.

At a global level there is a good deal in common between the Williamson and McKinnon plans. Whereas McKinnon proposed that 'global' interest rates be set so as to stabilise aggregate money or aggregate prices, the proposal in Edison, Miller and Williamson (1987) is that nominal income be the target.

Since 1979 Germany, Italy, France, the Benelux countries and Denmark have created a regional monetary system (EMS) with agreed nominal parities, which have, however, been adjusted ex post to accommodate most of the inflation differentials emerging between them. It has recently been argued by Giavazzi and Giovannini (1987) that the EMS is in effect a regional currency standard, a hegemony led by Germany, with limited independence permitted by extensive capital controls in France and Italy, so it is entered in the second row of table 1. The EMS, as such, is not analysed in this paper, because it is not symmetric.

2. The framework of analysis

The formal framework used to assess alternative proposals is a simple two bloc model with goods prices which adjust more slowly than the exchange rate which is determined by rational expectations in the foreign exchange market [cf. Dornbusch (1976)]. Inflation expectations are captured simply by augmenting the Phillips curve by terms measuring long-run inflation under the regime in question [cf. Buiter and Miller (1981)]. The formal analysis of the two country, floating rate case is essentially that developed in Miller (1982) to which 'fads', as Poterba and Summers (1987) describe them, have been added, while treatment of the fixed rate case is derived from Buiter (1986). The stochastic specification closely follows recent contributions by Fukuda and Hamada (1986) and Aoki (1987), and we are grateful to have had access to the PRISM package developed by David Currie and his colleagues for the stochastic analysis.

In this paper we make use of asymptotic or steady-state variances (obtained under the assumption of rational expectations) to study the performance of monetary and fiscal policy rules without falling foul of the Lucas critique, as advocated by John Taylor (1985) in an earlier issue of this *Review*. For a comprehensive stochastic treatment of various monetary policy rules – chosen optimally but subject to a 'time consistency' constraint – the reader is referred to McKibbin and Sachs (1986).

The equations which constitute the model are listed in detail in table 2, and the notation is given in table 3. The structure is doubtless familiar so it can be quickly summarised. First comes the condition for money market equilibrium (the LM curves) which are subject to stochastic serially uncorrelated disturbances $\varepsilon_m, \varepsilon_m^*$ (asterisks are used to denote variables involving the foreign country). Output in each country depends on the ex ante real interest rate, the real exchange rate, fiscal stance, output overseas and a stochastic shock $(\varepsilon_g, \varepsilon_g^*)$. As shown in the third line, inflation reflects domestic demand pressure and also long run inflation expectations under the regime in question (represented by the term π). The inflation process is also subject to white noise $\varepsilon_p, \varepsilon_p^*$.

The specification of the foreign currency arbitrage condition contains a novelty as the usual assumption of 'uncovered interest parity' is modified so

Table 2

Model equations.[a]

Home country		Foreign country
Money $\quad m-p=ky-\lambda i+\varepsilon_m$		$m^*-p^*=ky^*-\lambda i^*+\varepsilon_m^*$
Goods $\quad y=-\gamma E[r]+\delta c+s+\eta y^*+\varepsilon_g$		$y^*=-\gamma E[r^*]-\delta c+s^*+\eta y+\varepsilon_g^*$
Prices $\quad Dp=\phi y+\pi+\varepsilon_p$		$Dp^*=\phi y^*+\pi^*+\varepsilon_p^*$
Currency arbitrage	$E[De]=i-i^*+E[Df]$	
Poterba/Summers fad	$Df=-\psi f+\omega,\qquad$ where	
	$r=i-Dp$	$r^*=i^*-Dp^*$
	$E[r]=i-\phi y-\pi$	$E[r^*]=i^*-\phi y^*-\pi^*$
	$c=e+p^*-p$	

[a]Strictly speaking solutions of stochastic differential equations have no derivatives so the use of the differential operators is inadmissable. Nevertheless for linear
systems with constant coefficients, asymptotic moments can be obtained by
treating the system as if it were continuously differentiable [see, for example,
Jazwinsky (1970, Chapter 4)].

that expected changes in the nominal exchange rate are set equal to the
interest differential plus the change in an exogenous, autoregressive 'fad'. The
idea comes fromn Poterba and Summers (1987) who show that the existence
of such 'fads' is consistent with the behaviour of U.S. stock prices. Adding
such a 'coloured noise' process to the arbitrage equation violates the usual
assumption of market efficiency – but, as Poterba and Summers also show,
the tests used (successfully) to establish market efficiency have very low
power against such fads.

Since the parameters in each country are identical, the dynamic (and
stochastic) analysis can be conducted separately in terms of 'averages' and
'differences' [cf. Aoki (1981)]. The global economy (averages) looks like a
closed economy, see table 3(a), and does not involve the exchange rate. The
latter is determined only by the system of differences given in table 3(b).
While it may seem rather contrived to work in terms of these artificial
variables, the gain in analytical simplification makes it worthwhile. We look
first at the global economy (in the next section) before going on to examine
the determination of exchange rates, inflation, etc. under the three alternative
regimes.

3. The global economy

Thanks to the assumption of symmetry, the analysis of global aggregates is
very straightforward. The focus here is on the different nominal targets

Table 3

(a) Global economy

Money	$m_a - p_a = ky_a - \lambda i_a + \bar{\varepsilon}_m$
	$\Rightarrow i_a = \lambda^{-1}(p_a + k_{ya} + \bar{\varepsilon}_m - m_a)$
Goods	$y_a = -\gamma(i_a - \phi y_a - \pi_a) + s_a + \eta y_a + \bar{\varepsilon}_g$
Prices	$Dp_a = \phi y_a + \pi_a + \bar{\varepsilon}_p$
with notation	$y_a \equiv \dfrac{y + y^*}{2}$ for variables and $\bar{\varepsilon}_m \equiv \dfrac{\varepsilon_m + \varepsilon_m^*}{2}$ for stochastic shocks

(b) International differences

Money	$m_d - p_d = ky_d - \lambda i_d + \hat{\varepsilon}_m$
Goods	$y_d = -\gamma E[r_d] + 2\delta c + sd - \eta y_d + \hat{\varepsilon}_g$
Prices	$Dp_d = \phi y_d + \pi_d + \hat{\varepsilon}_p$
Arbitrage	$E[De] = i_d - \psi f$
Fad	$Df = -\psi f + \omega$
where	$E[r_d] = i_d - E[Dp_d] = i_d - \phi y_d - \pi_d$
	$c = e - p_d$
with notation	$y_d \equiv y - y^*$ for variables and $\hat{\varepsilon}_m = \varepsilon_m - \varepsilon_m^*$ for stochastic shocks.

Notation

y	real output, measured relative to capacity (in logs)
i	short term nominal interest rate
$E[r]$	ex ante short term real interest rate, $i - E[Dp]$
r	ex post real interest rate, $i - Dp$
c	real exchange rate in logs, $(e + p^* - p)$: increase indicates higher competitiveness for home country
s	index of fiscal stance, scaled to have unit effect on log output
p	domestic price index, in logs
m	money supply, in logs
n	nominal income target, in logs
π	'augmentation' term systematically affecting price changes
f	'fad' [see Poterba and Summers (1987)]
ε, ω	white Gaussian noise process; $N(O, \sigma_\varepsilon^2)$, $N(O, \sigma_\omega^2)$ respectively
Dp	inflation
D	differential operator

proposed as guidelines for world monetary policy, starting with the world *money supply target* m_a, growing at the rate μ_a (McKinnon).

Substituting world interest rates i_a from the first line of table 3(a) into the world IS curve of line two we obtain

$$y_a = \frac{1}{\Delta_a}(-\gamma\lambda^{-1}p_a + \gamma\lambda^{-1}m_a + \gamma\mu_a + s_a - \gamma\lambda^{-1}\bar{\varepsilon}_m + \bar{\varepsilon}_g), \tag{1}$$

where $\Delta_a = 1 + \gamma\lambda^{-1}k - \phi\lambda - \eta$, and π_a has been set equal to μ_a as in Buiter and Miller (1981), i.e., the inflation process is

$$Dp_a = \phi y_a + \mu_a + \bar{\varepsilon}_p. \tag{2}$$

To simplify matters a little we set $m_a = \mu_a = s_a = 0$, i.e., the world money stock is fixed and fiscal policy 'neutral', so output is determined only by prices and aggregate shocks to velocity and demand, as shown in the top row of table 4. On combining this with the inflation process (2), the asymptotic or unconditional variance of price is determined (see annex 1) as,

$$\sigma_{p_a}^2 = \frac{1}{2|\rho_s|}\left\{\rho_s^2\sigma_{\bar{\varepsilon}_m}^2 + \left(\frac{\phi}{\Delta_a}\right)^2\sigma_{\bar{\varepsilon}_g}^2 + \sigma_{\bar{\varepsilon}_p}^2\right\}, \tag{3}$$

given that the shocks are independent. The speed of adjustment, ρ_s, appearing here is found from table 4, column 2. Note that the variance of price includes the variance of velocity multiplied by half this speed of adjustment.

The results so obtained for a money supply target are easily modified to reflect a change of target variable. For convenience we assume that the McKinnon price level target is for *stable* prices and Williamson's is for *stable* nominal income – and take the growth of potential GNP to be zero. Now the rules for interest rate setting involved in pursuing these targets can be written as simplified versions of the inverted LM curve used above; specifically McKinnon II: $i_a = \beta_M p_a$, i.e., $k = 0$, $\lambda^{-1} = \beta_M$ and $\sigma_{\bar{\varepsilon}_m}^2$ is omitted, and Williamson: $i_a = \beta_w(p_a + y_a)$, i.e., $k = 1$, $\lambda^{-1} = \beta_w$ and $\sigma_{\bar{\varepsilon}_m}^2$ is omitted.

These parameter substitutions will alter the speed of adjustment and the term Δ_a appearing in eq. (3), but one can see that both these rules, like McKinnon's monetarist rule, involve a feedback of interest rates on the price level (the integral of past inflation). But they omit the 'noise' caused by using money supply targets to achieve this feedback (as $\sigma_{\bar{\varepsilon}_m}^2$ is omitted).

Table 4

Determinants of output (y) and the speed of adjustment (ρ_s).[a]

	Output	Speed of adjustment
Averages Global economy	$y_a = \frac{1}{\Delta_a}(-\gamma\lambda^{-1}p_a - \gamma\lambda^{-1}\bar{\varepsilon}_m + \bar{\varepsilon}_g)$	$\rho_s = -\phi\gamma\lambda^{-1}/\Delta_a$ $\Delta_a = 1 + \gamma\lambda^{-1}k - \phi\gamma - \eta$
Differences 1. Floating with money targets	$y_d = \frac{1}{\Delta_1}(-(\gamma\lambda^{-1} + 2\delta\theta)p_d - \gamma\lambda^{-1}\hat{\varepsilon}_m + \hat{\varepsilon}_g)$	$\rho_s = \phi(\gamma\lambda^{-1} + 2\delta\theta)/\Delta_1$ $\Delta_1 = 1 + \gamma\lambda^{-1}k - \phi\gamma + \eta$
2. McKinnon	$y_d = \frac{1}{\Delta_2}(-2\delta p_d + \hat{\varepsilon}_g)$	$\rho_s = -\phi 2\delta/\Delta$ $\Delta_2 = 1 - \phi\gamma + \eta$
2a. McKinnon with fiscal activism	$y_d = \frac{1}{\Delta_{2a}}(-(2\delta + \xi\alpha)p_d + \hat{\varepsilon}_g)$	$\rho_s = -\phi(2\delta + \xi\alpha)/\Delta_{2a}$ $\Delta_{2a} = 1 - \phi\gamma + \eta + \xi\beta$
3. Williamson	$y_d = \frac{1}{\Delta_3}(-\sigma p_d + \hat{\varepsilon}_g)$	$\rho_s = -\phi\sigma/\Delta_3$ $\Delta_3 = 1 + \sigma + \eta$

[a]The denominators (indicated by $\Delta_a, \Delta_1, \ldots$) in the first column are given in detail in the second column. The 'speed of adjustment' refers to ρ_s, the stable root characteristic of the system averages or differences for the regime in question.

4. Floating with national monetary targets

In this section we analyse the behaviour of the real exchange rate when each country adopts a fixed target growth rate for its money supply (not necessarily the same) and allows its currency to float freely. With identical coefficients in the separate national economies, the exchange rate depends only on 'differences', including the differences of shocks (denoted $\hat{\varepsilon}_m, \hat{\varepsilon}_g, \hat{\varepsilon}_p$ where $\hat{\varepsilon}_m = \varepsilon_m - \varepsilon_m^*$), together with the fad process

On the assumption that the 'augmentation' term in the price equation is the domestic rate of monetary growth, i.e.,

$$Dp = \phi y + \mu + \varepsilon_p \quad \text{and} \quad Dp^* = \phi y^* + \mu^* + \varepsilon_p^*, \quad \text{then}$$

$$Dp_d = \phi y_d + \mu_d + \hat{\varepsilon}_p \quad \text{and} \quad E[Dp_d] = \phi y_d + \mu_d. \tag{4}$$

Since inflation (and the inflation differential) may persist, it is convenient to deflate each nominal money stock by the domestic price level, so $l = m - p$, $l^* = m^* - p^*$ and $l_d = l - l^*$. As the evolution of real balances depends on the rate of inflation relative to the rate of monetary growth, so, using eq. (4), we note that

$$Dl_d = -\phi y_d - \hat{\varepsilon}_p. \tag{5}$$

The behaviour of the *real* exchange rate reflects both the inflation differential and the determinants of the *nominal* exchange rate. So, using eq. (4) again, we find (on taking expectations of both sides) that as

$$Dc = De + Dp^* - Dp \quad \text{so} \quad E[Dc] = E[i_d] - \psi f - \phi E[y_d] - \mu_d. \tag{6}$$

Eqs. (5) and (6) show the evolution of real balances (l_d) and the real exchange rate (c) depend on both income and interest differentials. Solving for the latter (using the goods and money market relationships from table 3(b)) and adding the autoregressive fad process

$$Df = -\psi f + \omega \tag{7}$$

yields the stochastic differential equations for this regime, as follows:

$$
\begin{bmatrix} Dl_d \\ E[Dc] \\ Df \end{bmatrix} = \frac{1}{\Delta} \begin{bmatrix} \phi\gamma & 2\phi\lambda\delta & 0 \\ 1+\eta & 2\delta(\phi\lambda-k) & -\Delta\psi \\ 0 & 0 & -\Delta\psi \end{bmatrix} \begin{bmatrix} l_d \\ c \\ f \end{bmatrix}
$$

$$
+ \frac{1}{\Delta} \begin{bmatrix} -\phi\gamma & \phi\lambda & \phi\gamma\lambda & -\Delta & 0 \\ 0 & 0 & \lambda(1+\eta) & 0 & 0 \\ 0 & 0 & 0 & 0 & \Delta \end{bmatrix} \begin{bmatrix} \hat{\varepsilon}_m \\ \hat{\varepsilon}_g \\ \mu_d \\ \hat{\varepsilon}_p \\ \omega \end{bmatrix}
$$

where $\Delta = -k\gamma - \lambda(1 - \phi\gamma + \eta)$ and is assumed to be negative, and $s_d = 0$.

Since the nominal exchange rate is a forward looking variable, stable behaviour is observed only on the stable manifold (i.e., the subspace of this system associated wth the stable roots which we denote as ρ_s and $-\psi$). The stable dynamics of this system and the role played by the serially correlated fads in changing the more orthodox account is most easily seen from fig. 1. In the absence of fads, the dynamics of adjustment in this Dornbusch-style model would lie on the line marked SS in this figure. Where there is 'overshooting', the slope of this line will be greater than one – since a shock to the money stock will have a greater than unit effect on the exchange rate [cf. Dornbusch (1976, Appendix)].

However, the serial correlation of the fad process adds another stable root, and (in the diagrammatically convenient case where $-\psi = \rho_s$) the stable trajectories leading to equilibrium have the shape shown in the line TT.

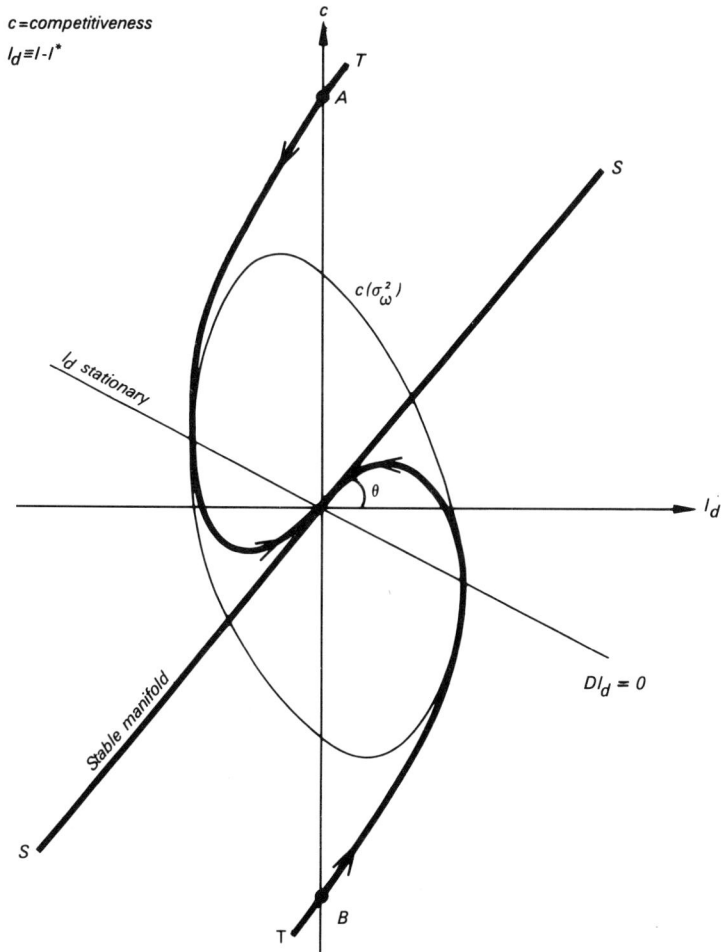

Fig. 1. 'Fads', dynamics and asymptotic probability contours.

These trajectories are symmetric around the origin but not around SS. The reason is that a fad which by raising the value of the domestic currency cuts competitiveness (so that c lies beneath SS) *slows down* the adjustment of real balances towards the origin, while a fad which increases competitiveness (putting c above SS) gives rise to forces which *speed up* the adjustment of l_d towards equilibrium.

Also shown in the figure is an (asymptotic) probability contour, showing points of equal probability in the long run. As the orientation of the ellipse demonstrates, the pattern of correlation between l_d and c arising from such fads is negative. The reason is made clear by observing that from a point such as A a large part of the subsequent expected trajectory is in the North West quadrant, and conversely for movements from point B; which orients the ellipse in the fashion shown. (This negative correlation appears to be independent of the respective sizes of $|\rho_s|$ and $|\psi|$.)

In the absence of fads, the probability distribution of outcomes for c and l_d lies along the stable manifold (and the isoprobability 'contours' become two points on SS). Under the convenient assumption that the rates of monetary growth are the *same* (so we can write $\mu_d = m_d = 0$) then $l_d = -p_d$ and on the stable manifold, $c = \theta l_d = -\theta p_d$, i.e., competitiveness is simply relative prices multiplied by the coefficient θ (which measures the degree of overshooting). Under these assumptions the determination of output is shown in line 2 of table 4 and the formulae of annex 1 may be used to calculate asymptotic moments.

As was observed earlier the regime of floating with money supply targets led to much greater fluctuations in real exchange rates than many economists had expected. The above account is inevitably something of a caricature, but it suffices to show how the combination of sluggish prices, shocks to the economy and inefficiency in the foreign exchange market is in principle capable of generating substantial fluctuations in the real exchange rates.

5. Fixed exchange rates

The combination of a fixed exchange rate regime wth perfect capital mobility is usually taken to ensure that nominal interest rates are equalised across countries, which would mean *eliminating* the fad process included earlier to characterise the behaviour of the floating exchange rate. Of course, if the fad were to be treated as a phenomenon which has nothing to do with the exchange rate regime per se – but is for example a 'safe-haven' portfolio shift – then it would be perfectly possible to incorporate the effects of such fads on interest differentials under fixed exchange rates. For present purposes, however, we assume that the fad *is* eliminated by the change of regime.

Under a fixed rate regime, 'competitiveness' is measured by the ratio of nominal prices, $c \equiv p^* - p = -p_d$, and its evolution reflects differential inflation. Under the assumption, which seems reasonable in this context, that the augmentation term π_d will also go to zero the inflation differential is as in eq. (4) above, except that $\pi_d = 0$ [cf. Buiter (1986)].

The determination of output differences (after substitutions reflecting the assumption of zero interest differentials, constant nominal exchange rate and the inflation process) is given in the line labelled for McKinnon in table 4. Using the values for Δ_2 and ρ_s shown there, the asymptotic variance of the real exchange rate may be calculated as

$$\sigma_c^2 = \sigma_{p_d}^2 = \frac{1}{2|\rho_s|}((\phi^2/\Delta_2)\sigma_{\hat{\varepsilon}_g}^2 + \sigma_{\hat{\varepsilon}_p}^2).$$

assuming for convenience that $\hat{\varepsilon}_g$ and $\hat{\varepsilon}_p$ are independent and $s_d = 0$.

Thus the real exchange rate depends on shocks to the goods market and on differential inflation shocks, but not on the money market disturbances represented by $\hat{\varepsilon}_m$, which are accommodated so as to keep interest rates equalised. What keeps relative prices in line in the long run – and so keeps the asymptotic variance of the real rate from diverging – is the negative *feedback* effect of past inflation differentials on the current output and inflation differentials; the country which has had more inflation is less competitive and loses demand for that reason.

It is of course possible to include in addition a fiscal policy response to external developments. Thus if

$$s_d = -\xi B = -\xi(-\alpha p_d - \beta y_d),$$

where B is the balance of trade, the parameters are modified as shown on the next line of table 4, labelled 'McKinnon with fiscal activism'.

6. Stable real exchange rates with domestic nominal income targets

Finally we turn to the case where real exchange rates are stabilised, and fiscal policy used to support the anti-inflationary stance of policy. For reasons discussed earlier, we treat the fad as a characteristic of free floating which disappears with the change of regime. (Once again, however, behaviour of this sort which reflects portfolio shifts can if necessary be included). We consider in detail a regime where the real exchange rate is kept constant; this is, of course, a limiting case since Williamson's target zones are 20% wide. Nevertheless it is of interest in view of the argument that limiting movements in the real rate will necesarily destabilise inflation [see Adams and Gros (1986)].

Assume first that nominal interest differentials are set equal to the anticipated inflation differential (reducing to zero the ex ante real interest differential), i.e.,

$$i_d = \phi y_d + \pi d. \tag{10}$$

Let fiscal policy be used to pursue a nominal income target (n, n^*) with fiscal stance being adjusted in *proportion* to the deviation from target, i.e, $s = -\sigma(p + y - n)$, $s^* = -\sigma(p^* + y^* - n^*)$, so

$$s_d = -\sigma(p_d + y_d - n_d). \tag{11}$$

The nominal income targets are designed to accommodate non-inflationary potential income growth; as we are, for simplicity, ignoring the growth of potential output in this paper, the two targets n and n^* will be constant (and their difference n_d can be set to zero by choice of units). For the same reason, the term π_d appearing in (10) can be set to zero, just as in McKinnon's monetary union – except here it is the commitment to nominal income targets that is to achieve this result. Relative output demand is usually affected by the (ex ante) real interest differential and the real exchange rate. But the former is zero (by assumption); and the latter will also be constant (as a corollary). The argument is simply that the real rate differs from equilibrium by the integral of expected future real interest differentials, which are set to zero by policy.

So relative output depends only on relative prices and demand shocks as shown in the last row of table 4, which is formally very similar to the preceding calculations for the fixed *nominal* exchange rate, the main difference being that here only relative fiscal stance and not the real exchange responds to past inflation differentials (represented in integral form by p_d). Since the inflation process is unchanged, the formula for the unconditional variance of inflation will be as for (9) above, except that now $\rho_s = -\phi\sigma/\Delta_3$ and $\Delta_3 = 1 + \sigma + \eta$.

How can one square the striking correspondence between the output and inflation behaviour and that derived for McKinnon's monetary union (where surely inflation was under control) with the basic conclusion of Adams and Gros (that assigning monetary policy to real things destabilises inflation)? The answer lies in the fact that, in the extended target zone system being analysed here, a fiscal policy rule is used in conjunction with the monetary policy assignment. If this is deleted, so σ goes to zero, then indeed the asymptotic variance will go to infinity – the Adams and Gros point.

7. Summary and conclusions

When the Dollar Standard came to an end, macroeconomic policy became ipso facto more decentralised, and by and large policy-makers adopted national monetary targets to fight inflation and floated exchange rates to offset inflation differentials. But the velocity of money has proved highly variable; and deviations from purchasing power parity have been both pronounced and prolonged. The alternative systems examined here attempt to cope with these developments.

In seeking to stabilise exchange rates, they seek to coordinate monetary policy across countries, but without returning to a Dollar Standard. In the belief that variations in velocity were due to 'currency substitution' McKinnon initially proposed that the world interest rate be set so as to attain an aggregate money supply target. Even in aggregate, however, velocity has proved too fickle. Both McKinnon's revised plan to use the *price level* as a target and Williamson's choice of *nominal income* are ways of avoiding shocks to velocity while retaining the crucial monetarist principle that monetary stringency be progressively increased in response to inflation.

At the national level McKinnon proposes to fix nominal exchange rates while Williamson seeks to stabilise real exchange rates within a relatively wide band: in neither case are monetary targets recommended. The adoption of such policy rules may avoid the 'fads' which appear to characterise floating exchange rates, although this is still an open question. Even aside from this important issue, there are crucial differences between the regimes, as illustrated for example in table 5, where the long-run variances of prices and output – in the face of supply and demand disturbances – are shown for various regimes. For brevity, we consider only the variances arising from supply-side shocks, shown in columns (4) and (5) of the table. It is apparent that, for the illustrative parameters used here, the product of price and output variances is a constant in the face of supply-side shocks: the regimes are 'trading off' variations in prices and output.

In row 1, one can see that for both a world money supply target as originally proposed by McKinnon and for a global nominal income target (pursued with an equally active use of interest rates), the variance of prices exceeds that of output. (If one were to include shocks to the velocity of money as well, they would increase the variances associated with the money supply rule, leaving those for the nominal income target unchanged). However, targeting the price level directly, as McKinnon has more recently recommended, does, even without fiscal activism, reduce price variance (see row 2) – at the cost of higher output variance.

Turning now to the country-specific inflation shocks, one sees, in rows and 3 and 4, that the fluctuations in relative prices and of relative output levels are much closer together. The reason is that, in an open economy, the movement of the real exchange rate adds an extra channel to monetary policy. In addition to the direct effect of real interest rates on aggregate demand, the real interest rate will influence the trade balance via its effect on the real exchange rate. Interestingly, however, the 'gold standard' results appearing in row 4 – where the country with high inflation sticks to a fixed exchange rate and suffers a loss in competitiveness – are much the same as those for free floating with money supply targets (in row 3). The intuitive reason for this is that if, as here, the exchange rate does not significantly 'overshoot' under floating, and if the money target is constant, then the floating nominal exchange rate will be pretty stable too – absent the 'fads'. (In practice the variance of exchange rates seems to have exceeded what can be explained in terms of variation in economic fundamentals: this is why we have included 'fads' in the foreign exchange market, which affect the behaviour of the floating exchange rate but disappear when the rate is fixed or managed.)

Under both these two regimes international competitiveness will fluctuate as relative prices move but the nominal exchange rate remains stable. As can be seen from the last row, moving nominal rates so as to keep competitive-

Table 5

Asymptotic variances of price and output under various regimes: Supply and demand shocks only.[a]

	Key parameters values			Asymptotic variances			
				Supply side shocks		Demand shocks	
	a	Δ	ρ_s $\dfrac{-\phi a}{\Delta}$	σ_p^2 $\dfrac{1}{2\lvert\rho_s\rvert}$	σ_y^2 $\dfrac{a}{2\phi\Delta}$	σ_p^2 $\dfrac{\phi}{2a\Delta}$	σ_y^2 $\dfrac{1}{\Delta^2}\!\left(\dfrac{a\phi}{2\Delta}+1\right)$
	See table 4	See table 4					
	(1)	(2)	(3)	(4)	(5)	(6)	(7)
Averages							
(1) Money or nominal income target	0.25	0.9	−0.139	3.60	0.28	1.11	1.32
(2) Price level target (with $\beta=\lambda^{-1}$)	0.25	0.65	−0.192	2.60	0.38	1.54	2.59
Differences							
(3) Floating with money target	1.18	1.1	−0.536	0.93	1.07	0.19	1.05
(4) McKinnon's proposal	1.0	0.85	−0.588	0.85	1.18	0.29	1.79
(5) Williamson's target zones	0.5	1.6	−0.156	3.2	0.31	0.31	0.42

[a]Supply side shocks are disturbances to the inflation equation. Demand side shocks are disturbances to the demand equation. a is the parameter appearing in eq. (1) of Annex 1. Asymptotic variances are given as a multiple of the variances of the shock indicated. Parameter values: $\eta=0.1$, $\gamma=\phi=\delta=\sigma=0.5$, $\theta=0.93$, $k=1$, $\lambda=2$.

ness constant does stabilize output, but it means that prices become more volatile. Indeed, the outcomes begin to look more like those for the closed economy – which makes sense as the monetary authorities are acting so as to prevent real exchange rates from moving as they have in the previous two cases.

In the remainder of the table the variances arising from demand shocks are also shown for the several regimes. A more complete treatment would of course include other shocks and a consideration of their joint distribution. But this illustration gives some idea of the way in which the different exchange rate regimes seek to spread the burden of checking supply side inflation. [See also Frankel, 1983)].

The options with regard to exchange rate policy are no longer simply of whether to use monetary policy so as to fix the exchange rate or to let it float freely. This paper has shown that schemes to manage the exchange rate, involving both monetary and fiscal policy, give distinct and equally coherent answers to the issues involved in the choosing of an exchange regime.

Annex 1

Deriving the asymptotic moments for price and output

Given (1) $y = \dfrac{1}{\Delta}(-ap - b\varepsilon_m + \varepsilon_g),$

(2) $Dp = \phi y + \varepsilon_p = -\dfrac{\phi}{\Delta}ap - \dfrac{\phi}{\Delta}b\varepsilon_m + \dfrac{\phi}{\Delta}\varepsilon_g + \varepsilon_p,$

so $\rho_s = -\phi a/\Delta$, then the asymptotic variance of price is

(3) $\sigma_p^2 = \dfrac{1}{2|\rho_s|}\left\{\dfrac{\phi^2}{\Delta^2}(b^2\sigma_{\varepsilon_m}^2 + \sigma_{\varepsilon_g}^2) + \sigma_{\varepsilon_p}^2\right\}$

$\qquad = \dfrac{\phi}{2a\Delta}(b^2\sigma_{\varepsilon_m}^2 + \sigma_{\varepsilon_g}^2) + \dfrac{\Delta}{2\phi a}\sigma_{\varepsilon_p}^2,$

assuming that the disturbances are independently distributed. From (1) and (3), the asymptotic variance of output is

(4) $\sigma_y^2 = \dfrac{1}{\Delta^2}(a^2\sigma_{\varepsilon_p}^2 + b^2\sigma_{\varepsilon_m}^2 + \sigma_{\varepsilon_g}^2)$

$\qquad = \dfrac{1}{\Delta^2}\left\{\dfrac{a\phi}{2\Delta}b^2\sigma_{\varepsilon_m}^2 + \left(\dfrac{a\phi}{2\Delta}+1\right)\sigma_{\varepsilon_g}^2 + \dfrac{a\Delta}{2\phi}\sigma_{\varepsilon_p}^2\right\}.$

The asymptotic covariance of price and output is simply

$$(5) \quad \sigma_{py} = -\frac{a}{\Delta}\sigma_p^2.$$

Footnote

Where the balance of trade is governed by $B = -\alpha p_d - \beta y_d$, then the unconditional covariance of B is

$$\sigma_B^2 = \alpha^2 \sigma_{p_d}^2 + \beta^2 \sigma_{y_d}^2 + 2\alpha\beta\sigma_{p_d y_d}.$$

References

Adams, Charles and Daniel Gros, 1986, The consequences of real exchange rate rules for inflation: Some illustrative examples, IMF Staff Papers 33, no. 3, Sept., 439–476.

Al-Nowaihi, Ali, Paul Levine and Andrew Fontenelle, 1985, The PRISM computer package for the simulation of continuous and discrete time stochastic rational expectations models: A users guide, Mimeo. (Queen Mary College, London).

Aoki, Masanao, 1981, Dynamic analysis of open economies (Academic Press, New York).

Aoki, Masanao, 1987, Decentralized monetary rules in a three country model and time series evidence of structural dependence, Mimeo., Prepared for Conference of Money and Banking, Aix-en-Provence (University of California, Los Angeles, CA).

Buiter, Willem H., 1986, Macroeconomic policy design in an interdependent world economy, IMF Staff Papers 33, no. 3, Sept., 541–582.

Buiter, Willem H. and Marcus H. Miller, 1981, Monetary policy and international competitiveness: The problems of adjustment, Oxford Economic Papers 33 (suppl.) July.

Buiter, Willem H. and Marcus H. Miller, 1982, Real exchange path overshooting and the output cost of bringing down inflation, European Economic Review 18, 85–123.

Dornbusch, Rudiger, 1976, Expectations and exchange rate dynamics, Journal of Political Economy 84, Dec., 1161–1176.

Dornbusch, Rudiger, 1983, Flexible exchange rates and interdependence, IMF Staff Papers 30, no. 1, March.

Edison, Hali J., Marcus H. Miller and John Williamson, 1987, On evaluating and extending the target zone proposal, Journal of Policy Modeling 9, no. 1, 199–227.

Frankel, Jeffrey A., 1983, The desirability of a dollar appreciation, given a contractionary U.S. monetary policy, Working paper, no. 1110 (NBER, Boston, MA).

Friedman, Milton, 1953, The case for flexible exchange rates, in: M. Friedman, ed., Essays in positive economics (University of Chicago Press, Chicago, IL).

Friedman, Milton, 1968, The role of monetary policy, American Economic Review 58, no. 1, March.

Fukuda, Shin-Ichi and Koichi Hamada, 1986, Towards the implementation of desirable rules of monetary coordination and intervention, Growth Center Discussion Paper (Yale University, New Haven, CT).

Giavazzi, Francesco and Alberto Giovannini, 1987, Models of the EMS: Is Europe a greater deutsche-mark area, forthcoming in R. Bryant and R. Portes, eds., Global macroeconomics (Macmillan, London).

Jazwinsky, A.H., 1970, Stochastic processes and filtering theory (Academic Press, London).

Levine, Paul and David Currie, 1985, Optimal feedback rules in an open economy macromodel with rational expectations, European Economic Review 27, 141–163.

McKibbin, Warwick J. and Jeffrey D. Sachs, 1986, Comparing the global performance of alternative exchange rate arrangements, Brookings Discussion Papers, no. 49, Aug.

McKinnon, Ronald I., 1984, An international standard for monetary stabilisation (Institute for International Economics, Washington, DC).

Miller, Marcus H., 1982, Differences in the policy mix and consequences for the real exchange rate, Mimeo., University of Warwick, to appear in: S. Honkapohja, ed., Money, inflation and economic policy (Y. Jahnsson Foundation, Helsinki), forthcoming.

Poterba, James M. and Lawrence H. Summers, 1987, Mean reversion in stock returns: Evidence and implications, Mimeo. (NBER, Boston, MA).

Taylor, John B., 1985, International coordination in the design of macroeconomic policy rules: European Economic Review 28, 53–81.

Williamson, John, 1985, The exchange rate system (revised) (Institute for International Economics, Washington, DC).

COMMENTS

'The International Monetary System: An Analysis of Alternative Proposals' by Marcus H. Miller and John Williamson

Stanley FISCHER

This paper presents a formal model designed to analyze the two leading alternative proposals to the current international monetary system, the McKinnon proposal to return to fixed nominal rates, and the more subtle and elusive Williamson proposal for target zones. The conclusions are regrettably not crystal clear.

1. The proposals

McKinnon's proposal is the more conventional. In its original form it proposed fixing the exchange rates among the U.S., Japan and Germany, and fixing the growth rate of their combined money stock. The proposal reflected his view that currency substitution was the main cause of exchange rate changes.

McKinnon has moved away from the currency substitution emphasis in more recent versions of the proposal. He now expects the three largest countries basically to follow gold standard rules, manipulating short term interest rates to defend the exchange rate. Presumably it would be the deficit countries that would come under more pressure to pursue active monetary policies. Money growth would be treated as an intermediate run target, consistency with interest rate manipulation being attained by movements of the average level of the nominal interest rate in the three countries.

Two other features should be noted: first, McKinnon's belief that appropriate exchange rates are provided by purchasing power parity calculations and not by the need to attain current account balance; and second, his view that the current account is essentially unaffected by the exchange rate.

Accordingly, fiscal policy would have to be used to bring about current account balance.

By contrast, Williamson's target zone proposal envisages setting exchange rates to bring about current account balance. Central exchange rates, which may crawl, are set by agreement. These rates adjust one for one with relative inflation rates, and thus may be construed as real exchange rates. Wide, $\pm 10\%$, bands around the central rate retain most of the virtues of the floating rate system. But when the rate approaches the limits of the band, action has to be taken. This may involve either monetary or fiscal policy, though Williamson also leaves open the soft option of adjusting the target zone. The benefits and disadvantages of this scheme have been extensively discussed, in the 1986 *Brookings Papers* and elsewhere.[1]

Because the central rates can be viewed as fixed in real terms, the Williamson proposal is vulnerable to the charge, made by Adams and Gros, that price levels become indeterminate. The paper implies that it is for this reason Williamson has recently appended the assumption that fiscal policy should be directed at a nominal income target. This is logically impeccable, but in practice ensures that the proposal will not be accepted – for reasons that I will discuss below. The problem of price-level indeterminacy should not be regarded with as much solemnity as it evidently is by the authors – it goes away if the target exchange rate is adjusted only by 0.99% for every 1% change in relative price levels.

However, there is a more serious reason to worry about fiscal policy. The prime objection to the original Williamson target zone proposal was that divergent fiscal policies (with the difference between the U.S. and the rest of OECD in the early eighties in mind) could overwhelm the defenses of any target zones. The modification of the proposal to include co-ordinated fiscal policies deals appropriately with that difficulty, even if it does reduce the likelihood of its adoption.

2. The analysis

One way of analyzing the alternative proposals is by simulation of a large-scale econometric model. This was done in the paper by Edison, Miller and Williamson. A difficulty in an exercise of this sort is modelling expectations, particularly of the very non-linear Williamson proposal.

The alternative adopted here is to use as simple a stochastic open economy model as possible. The model consists of the IS–LM apparatus, plus an aggregate supply function and asset market relations determined by the perfect mobility of capital plus an assumption about the existence of a fad.

[1]See 'Symposium on Exchange Rates, Trade, and Capital Flows', Brookings Papers on Economic Activity, 1986:1.

The determinisic component of the IS–LM curves is standard. It is not obvious though that the errors in those equations should be treated as white noise – certainly velocity changes appear in practice to be quite persistent. Such serially correlated shocks should be modelled, since they are certainly relevant to the behavior of the system under money targeting. The aggregate supply relationship omits any exchange rate effects on costs: these could be incorporated with little additional complexity. The aggregate supply function includes a term in p that represents a core inflation rate, but that ends up in some versions of the model as the growth rate of money. Although this assumption has been made by Buiter and Miller in earlier work, it is hardly persuasive; expectations are not well handled in this theoretical model.

The authors are obviously pleased with the inclusion of the fad components in the interest rate equalization equation. It serves to complicate the analysis of the floating rate regime, and is interesting. However, the authors fail to make clear its contribution to the comparison among the different policies.

Although the Williamson proposal focuses on the current account, there is no current account equation in this model. Similarly, there is no accounting for reserves, implying that the treatment of the McKinnon proposal is biased in its favor.

The authors use the sum and difference method of Aoki to carry out the analysis. By making the two countries identical they abstract from divergent productivity trends, divergent inflation preferences, and differences in wage and price flexibility in the countries. All these are an important part of the case for flexible exchange rates. Their inclusion would strengthen the case for the existing system or the Williamson proposal over the McKinnon proposal.

The authors take the view that the fads would not be present in the Williamson and McKinnon worlds. I certainly believe that something like the fads of this paper are partly a result of uncertainty of market participants about the exchange rate intentions of governments, but it is doubtful that such movements would disappear if there was a shift to exchange rate targeting or fixing. Rather the fads would be reflected in attacks on the fixed exchange rate or on the edges of the target zones.

The results of the analysis simply do not emerge clearly. It appears that McKinnon and Williamson emerge more or less tied. Table 5 at the end gives comparisons for one set of parameter values, but regrettably no indication of the robustness of the results.

3. General comments

All economists have suffered through the joke about the physicist, engineer and economist marooned on a desert island with a can of food but no can opener. The economist's solution to the problem begins 'Assume a can-opener'. This paper has a can-opener of that type in it, namely the assumption in the Williamson proposal that fiscal policy is operated to target nominal income.

The main cause of exchange rate movements in the last five years has been U.S. fiscal policy. If fiscal policy had been directed to a nominal income target over the last five years, the Williamson proposal would not now be receiving the serious attention it is.

The key question about the McKinnon and Williamson proposals is whether the choice of the exchange rate system will constrain domestic policy choices. The answer for some European countries evident from the EMS is yes. It still seems unlikely though that the U.S. Congress or Administraton will allow itself to be constrained. It was the failure of the U.S. to constrain its policies in the late sixties that led to the failure of the Bretton Woods system. There has been no indication subsequently that the U.S. is prepared to modify its behavior in a way that would make either fixed exchange rates or greater exchange rate fixity more likely. That is so despite the Plaza and Louvre agreements – for there has been no evidence that the Administration as opposed to the Secretary of the Treasury plans to adjust fiscal policy. Perhaps all that will change in 1989, but don't bet on it.

This paper has one other failing. It represents the Williamson proposal as one that uses monetary policy to fix the real exchange rate while fiscal policy targets nominal income. None of the subtlety of the proposal's combination of fixed and flexible rates appears here. That is undoubtedly very difficult. But in justice to Williamson the authors should make the attempt, perhaps through simulation of a theoretical model.

COMMENTS

'The International Monetary System: An Analysis of Alternative Regimes' by Marcus H. Miller and John Williamson

Gilles OUDIZ

Marcus Miller and John Williamson have written an attractive paper which applies up to date macroeconomic analysis to the discussion of International Monetary Coordination. The author's objective is to study within a single formal framework the proposals of R. McKinnon and J. Williamson for monetary reform.

We will briefly discuss here the 'technical' aspects of the paper: the model and the policy coordination framework, before commenting on the conclusions of the authors.

1. The model of a two country world

The basic equations of the world economy model follow closely the 'standard' literature in open economy macroeconomics and do not need much comment.

However the authors introduce a more original specification of exchange rate determination. The introduction of 'fads', modelled as a 'coloured noise' process, within the traditional arbitrage equation aims at taking into account the actual working of exchange markets.

The authors are unfortunately quite short on the motivations of their choice which seems largely ad-hoc. Further in the paper this technicality is assumed away partly because it complicates the formal analysis, partly because the introduction of monetary coordination is supposed to eliminate these fads.

2. The policy framework

Using a technique developed by Aoki (1981) the authors analyze separately the behavior of average and differential economic variables.

Far from being strictly technical this choice has in fact an interesting econonomic interpretation. The model of averages – i.e., the global economy – behaves like a closed economy without any exchange rate problem whereas the model of differences focuses on the problem of exchange rate management.

Let us consider a very simple two country model of the world economy to make this point clearer.

Let the model of the home country be:

$$M(m, y, p, m^*, p^*, e) = 0,$$

with the notations of the authors.

Let us further consider that the authorities of the home country choose their monetary policy so as to minimize the following loss function:

$$L = y^2 + \phi p^2.$$

The foreign country's behavior is assumed to be determined by a symmetrical model and loss function:

$$M^*(m^*, y^*, p^*, m, y, p, -e) = 0,$$

$$L^* = y^{*2} + \phi p^{*2}.$$

A supranational authority would thus be faced wih the following optimization problem:

$$\begin{cases} \underset{m,\, m^*}{\text{Min}}\ 0.5L + 0.5L^*, \\[2mm] M = 0, \\[2mm] M^* = 0. \end{cases}$$

Taking into account the fact that

$$0.5L + 0.5L^* = L_a + L_d,$$

where

$$L_a = y_a^2 + \phi p_a^2,$$

$$L_d = y_d^2 + \phi p_d^2,$$

and the symmetry of the models, this problem is separable in two sub-problems:

$$\begin{cases} \underset{m_a}{\text{Min}}\ L_a, \\[2mm] M_a(m_a, y_a, p_a) = 0, \end{cases}$$

$$\begin{cases} \underset{m_d}{\text{Min}}\ L_d, \\[2mm] M_d(m_d, y_d, p_d, e) = 0. \end{cases}$$

The problem of a supranational authority having to determine an optimal coordinated monetary policy is thus twofold: the determination of the global level of output and prices through the management of the world money supply, m_a, and the management of international differences through exchange rate policy, m_d.

This separability of the world economy model is thus meaningful under two quite restrictive assumptions:

- the world economy is symmetrical,
- economic policy is controlled by a supranational authority (or jointly by the two national authorities through policy coordination) which allows for

the separate management of average and differential levels of policy instruments.

The first assumption is clearly not granted at the world level if one considers the three major groups of industrialized economies: U.S.A., Japan and Europe. As the authors acknowledge, it is not granted among European economies either.

The second assumption is more fundamental for it raises the question of the strategic framework within which the world economic policy is set.

A major weakness of Miller and Williamson's paper is the absence of a properly specified welfare analysis. We have no way of knowing whether the two countries are worse off or better off with either monetary coordination proposals. Nor does the formal analysis explicitly specify how the average and differential levels of policy instruments are set.

To put it in less technical terms, it does not suffice to state that the exchange rate is fixed. The policy framework is essential in this respect. A fully developed welfare analysis will yield different results depending on whether this fixed exchange rate level is set by a single dominant country or jointly through policy coordination.

The collapse of the Bretton Woods system of fixed exchange rates and recent European experience show that this is far from being a merely academic consideration.

3. Concluding remarks

The idea of applying recent developments in international macroeconomics literature to the discussion of exchange rate reform is by all means appealing to specialists in both fields.

Following a previous paper which emphasized empirical simulations, the authors have attempted to derive analytically some meaningful conclusions on the advantages of McKinnon's and Williamson's proposals.

However the discussion which they provide falls short of being really convincing. Their sophisticated dynamic analysis remains ad hoc. It does not provide easily understandable conclusions and the strategic interaction of the two countries – conflict or cooperation? – remains unclear.

In short this paper is welcome as a much needed attempt at sorting out formally the arguments in favour of international monetary reform proposals, but further research will be needed along the lines pioneered by the authors.

European Economic Review 32 (1988) · North-Holland

THE ADVANTAGE OF TYING ONE'S HANDS*

EMS Discipline and Central Bank Credibility

Francesco GIAVAZZI

Universita' di Venezia and CEPR, 30123 Venice, Italy

Marco PAGANO

Universita' di Napoli and CEPR, 80138 Naples, Italy

It is often argued that the EMS is an effective disciplinary device for inflation-prone countries in Europe, since it forces the respective policy-makers to pursue more restrictive monetary policies than they would otherwise. It is not clear, however, why these countries should submit themselves to such discipline. This paper argues that, to answer this question appropriately, one must consider that EMS membership brings potentially large credibility gains to policy-makers in inflation-prone countries: the reason is that not only it attaches an extra penalty to inflation (in terms of real appreciation), but makes the public aware that the policy-maker is faced with such penalty, and thus helps to overcome the inefficiency stemming from the public's mistrust of the authorities.

1. Introduction

So far, in the EMS experience, countries with above-average inflation have lost competitiveness relative to the low inflation countries of the system. This loss originates from two distinct factors. First, between successive realignments, excess inflation (combining with the fixity of the nominal exchange rate) results in a one-for-one appreciation of the real exchange rate. Second, at realignment dates, excess inflation countries obtain devaluations which are generally insufficient to make-up for the real appreciation experienced since the previous realignment.

If each realignment were to compensate high inflation countries for their entire real appreciation – i.e., if the first factor were to operate in isolation – their real exchange rate would fluctuate between realignments, but would exhibit no long-run trend (and, for an appropriate choice of the initial level, could in fact fluctuate around PPP). What the second factor instead does is to introduce a trend of real appreciation in the exchange rates of high inflation countries: for instance, between 1978 and 1986 Denmark and Italy

*First draft October 1986; revised July 1987. We thank Franco Bruni, Alberto Giovannini, Guido Tabellini and the ISOM seminar participants for valuable comments. Financial support from Consiglio Nazionale delle Ricerche is gratefully acknowledged.

have experienced real appreciations relative to Germany of 9 and 11 percent respectively.[1]

The obvious question that arises is then: why should a high inflation country ever want to belong to an agreement such as the EMS? Credibility of central banks' commitments to low inflation is often advanced as the rationale for participation of these countries in the EMS:[2]

> 'The EMS is currently an arrangement for France and Italy to purchase a commitment to low inflation by accepting German monetary policy'. [Fischer (1987)].

Even perspective members of the EMS see the main advantage of membership as arising from gains in credibility:

> 'If sterling does join, the biggest change will be the transfer of responsibility for Britain's monetary policy from the Bank of England to Germany's Bundesbank which, as the central bank keenest on sound money, sets the pace for others to follow. This would be a blessing: Tory governments may like appointing City gents as governors of the Bank, but Mr. Karl Otto Poehl would do a better job'. (*The Economist*, September 21, 1985).

The argument behind these statements presumably runs as follows. The EMS countries where inflation is above-average are presumably those that have the highest incentive to use inflation surprises and the level of inflation as tools of monetary policy: the incentive to use inflation surprises is strong when the response of output and employment to unanticipated inflation is large, and when the government has a high outstanding stock of nominal liabilities; the incentive to produce a high level of inflation (even if perfectly anticipated) is strong when money demand is inelastic, and thus the potential revenue from the inflation tax is high.[3] However, when the monetary authority has an incentive to raise output and to reduce the value of the public debt via unanticipated inflation, the public will rationally discount such incentive in forming their forecast of inflation, so that the equilibrium has the two following features: (a) the policy-maker does not succeed in surprising the public systematically (and thereby permanently increase

---

[1]Real appreciation is measured in terms of relative unit labor costs, accounting for competition on third markets. Source: *EEC*.

[2]Thygesen (1979) makes the point that this incentive is what kept the European 'snake' together between 1972 and 1978.

[3]This incentive is particularly strong in countries like Italy, Spain, Portugal and Greece, where the ratio of base money to GDP is much higher than in the rest of Europe, despite the fact that these countries are also characterized by inflation rates above the European average [see Fischer (1982) for cross-country evidence on the revenue from seignorage].

employment and government revenue); (b) the expected, and actual, rate of inflation is higher than the inflation rate that would prevail if the policy-maker could credibly precommit.[4] In other words, the set of incentives is such that the result of the non-cooperative game between the monetary authority and the public is an excessively high equilibrium inflation rate. In this setup, if the monetary authority is able to reduce its incentive to produce inflation surprises, it will be able to induce the public to expect lower inflation, so that the solution to the game will get closer to the cooperative outcome.

Joining the EMS can be seen precisely as a way of changing the set of incentives faced by the monetary authority: as explained above, all inflation in excess of the EMS average translates into (possibly permanent) real exchange rate appreciation. This, by reducing the policy maker's incentive to inflate, leads to lower inflation in the non-cooperative equilibrium, and eliminates part of the inefficiency that arises from the lack of credibility of the monetary authority. The result parallels that in Rogoff [1985], who shows that the non-cooperative rate of inflation can be reduced 'through a system of rewards and punishments which alters the incentives of the central bank', for example by placing 'some direct weight on achieving a lower rate of growth for a nominal variable, such as the price level, nominal GNP or the money supply'. In the case of EMS membership the relevant nominal variable is the exchange rate, that the system constrains to zero growth except at realignments dates.

Below we offer a formal statement of this argument and we investigate the conditions under which the gains in credibility delivered by membership in the EMS outweigh the implied losses (choosing as benchmark an idealized flexible exchange rate system where the monetary authority cannot affect the real exchange rate). It should be stressed that the central issue is not whether the EMS is an effective *disciplinary* device for inflation-prone countries, but whether it is a *welfare-improving* arrangement from the viewpoint of the monetary authority of those countries. It is obvious that their inflation rate will be lower inside than outside the EMS – what is less obvious is whether, after paying the implied cost the monetary authorities will be better off, so that they will be happy to tie their hands. This is in fact the only guarantee that they will feel committed to the system – and, in turn, only if their commitment can be expected to last, the system will enhance their current credibility. This point – the welfare issue – is obviously the relevant one both for current members and for countries which are now weighing the costs and benefits of joining the EMS.

---

[4]The inefficiency associated with the incentive to create surprise inflation is discussed in Barro and Gordon (1983); see also Fischer (1986). Barro (1983) and Grossman and Van Huyck (1984) discuss the inefficiency that arises from the incentive to generate revenue from seignorage.

2. The basic model

Consider a country that produces two goods: one is sold at home; the other is exported. On the domestic market, prices are set with a fixed mark-up over wages, whereas on the foreign market firms are price-takers, so that, for given exchange rate and foreign prices, an increase in domestic wages reduces the profits of exporters (equivalently, one could assume that the country produces a single good and that firms are able to sell at different prices at home and abroad). Let π_i denote the rate of price inflation on the domestic market – by assumption equal to the rate of wage inflation. Let q_t be the (log of the) real exchange rate, defined as the price on foreign markets, in units of domestic currency, relative to the price of goods sold at home. Since we assume wages to be uniform across the economy, it is clear that the profitability of the exporting firms is an increasing function of q_t (i.e., it is raised by a real depreciation).

One of the concerns of the domestic policy-maker is the profitability of the export sector: we thus assume that the real exchange rate q_t enters with a positive weight in the authorities' objective function. On the other hand, the authorities have an incentive to create inflation surprises $(\pi_t - \pi_t^e)$ in order to reduce the product wage faced by firms selling to the home market, thereby raising their output.[5] The interaction between the monetary authority and the workers' unions therefore takes the form of a non-cooperative game (as for example in Fischer [1986]).[6] The new twist here is that the wage and domestic price inflation resulting from this interaction affects the profits of exporters (for a given nominal exchange rate): since the authorities care about the profitability of the export sector, their behaviour in the game with the union takes into account this side effect of domestic inflation.[7] Finally the authorities dislike price instability, and this is captured by a quadratic term in inflation (π_t^2) in their objective function. This can thus be written as[8]

$$V = \int_0^\infty e^{-\rho t}[hq_t + c(\pi_t - \pi_t^e) - (a/2)\pi_t^2]\,dt, \qquad h, a, c > 0, \tag{1}$$

[5]This incentive to raise domestic output can be motivated by the fact that distortions keeps its equilibrium level below the optimal level.

[6]In its simplest form this game can be described assuming that workers contract nominal wages before prices are set, according to $w_t = p_t^e + \beta y_t$, where the last term captures the sensitivity of wages to demand, and p_t^e is the expectation of domestic prices at the time the contract is signed. Domestic prices are set as a mark-up over wages $(p_t = w_t)$. Aggregate demand is simply $y_t = m_t - p_t$, neglecting the spillover effect from the profits of the exporting sector. In a rational expectations equilibrium $y_t = (1/\beta)(p_t - p_t^e)$, and $p_t = (\beta m_t + p_t^e)/(1 + \beta)$. The last equation shows how the moves of the two players interact in determining the price level in a non-cooperative (Nash) equilibrium: the union plays its expectation $p_t^e = p_t$; the policy-maker plays the nominal money supply m_t so as to maximize its objective function.

[7]An additional incentive to produce surprise inflation comes from the fact that inflation reduces the real value of the nominal liabilities issued by the government, thus replacing distortionary taxes with a non-distortionary capital levy.

[8]Most of the results in the paper do not depend upon the specific form of the objective function in eq. (1). See footnote 16.

where ρ is the authorities' rate of time preference. The objective function (1) neglects the constraints imposed upon the monetary authorities by the financial behaviour of the private sector in a system characterized by periodic exchange rate realignments. It is thus only consistent with an economy that operates prohibitive exchange controls. We analyze the case of perfect capital mobility in section 5.

In the EMS regime the (log of the) real exchange rate at time t, q_t, is equal to the (log of the) real exchange rate established at the time of the last realignment minus the cumulated inflation differential. We shall suppose that: (i) the length between realignments is exogenously fixed at T periods;[9] (ii) at each realignment the real exchange rate is set back to a pre-assigned level q_0. The expression for q_t is thus

$$q_t = q_0 - \int_{kT}^{t} \pi_s \, ds, \qquad t \in (kT, KT+T), \quad k = 1, 2, 3, \ldots, \tag{2}$$

which can be substituted in eq. (1), yielding the following expression for the objective function:

$$V = \sum_{k=0}^{\infty} \int_{kT}^{(k+1)T} e^{-\rho t} [h(q_0 - \int_{kT}^{t} \pi_s \, ds) + c(\pi_t - \pi_t^e) - (a/2)\pi_t^2] \, dt. \tag{3}$$

The policy-maker's problem is to maximize V. His control variable is the rate of money creation, and thus inflation π_t: the solution is an optimal rule for π_t, to be denoted π_t^*. For this rule to be time-consistent, the policy-maker must regard expected inflation π_t^e to be independent of its own actions, treating it as exogenous in the maximization problem [see Barro and Gordon (1983, pp. 595–596), and Cohen and Michel (1985, pp. 10–14)]. Clearly, in a rational expectations equilibrium, $\pi_t^e = \pi_t$, so that no gain will accrue to the government from unanticipated inflation. The authorities' incentive to create surprises is thus merely a source of inefficiency, and it is precisely this inefficiency that EMS membership is supposed to correct.

The time interval between realignments, T, and the initial level of the real exchange rate, q_0, are also outside the control of the domestic policy-maker: they are parameters of the EMS regime. However, we shall see below that if the country's membership in the EMS is to be sustainable in the long run these two parameters cannot be chosen independently from each other. (The issue of sustainability is extensively dealt with in section 3.) For the time being, let us assume that q_0 is equal to zero, i.e., that at each realignment the exchange rate is set back to PPP.

[9]See Giavazzi and Pagano (1985) for a model where realignment dates are endogenously determined.

Maximization of (3) yields the following path for inflation:[10]

$$\pi_t^* = (1/a)\left[c - \frac{h}{\rho}(1 - e^{-\rho(T-t)}) \right] \quad \text{for} \quad t \in (0, T). \tag{4}$$

Eq. (4) immediately brings out the fact that the optimal inflation path has precisely the same shape between any two realignments: inflation rises monotonically from the date following one realignment until the date of the next, when it reaches its maximum – before falling once again, back to the initial level. Thus, over an extended period of time, inflation displays a sawtooth pattern. The reason why it rises smoothly between realignments is that it is best to concentrate inflation at the end of the interval, so as to carry over for a shorter period the implied loss of competitiveness. The slope of the time-profile of inflation is steeper the smaller is ρ, and flattens out for $\rho \to \infty$, as the authorities give less and less weight to the effect of current inflation on the future level of competitiveness.

The optimal level of inflation, on the other hand, is decreasing in T, the length of the interval between realignments, since more infrequent opportunities to devalue increase the time period for which a given increase in inflation remains embodied in the real exchange rate, and thus reinforce the disciplinary role of the system. Moreover, as T increases, the profile of inflation between realignments flattens out, and for $T \to \infty$ it settles at a constant value (to be denoted π_∞^* hereafter). The role of the other parameters of the problem also accords with intuition: inflation is increasing in c (the incentive to produce inflation surprises); it is decreasing in h (the marginal value of a real depreciation) and in a (the marginal cost of price instability).

What would inflation be if the country were not a member of the EMS? The answer to this question depends on what the exchange rate regime would be outside the EMS. We assume that the alternative is an idealized system of flexible exchange rates in which the real exchange rate cannot be systematically affected by domestic monetary policy, and PPP continuously prevails. Incidentally, this is giving more than a fair chance to flexible rates in the welfare comparison with the EMS, since it overlooks what many people regard as one of the main drawbacks of flexible rates – namely the experience of large and unpredictable fluctuations in real exchange rates stemming from 'overshooting' or speculative bubbles in the behaviour of nominal exchange rates.

Thus, to derive the optimal inflation path in the alternative regime we solve the policy-maker's problem under the assumption that q_t is exogenous.

---

[10]Differentiation of the objective function makes use of the fact that

$$d\pi_t^d \int_0^T \int_0^t \pi_s \, ds e^{-\rho t} \, dt = \int_t^T e^{-\rho s} \, ds = (1/\rho)(e^{-\rho t} - e^{-\rho T}).$$

The result is the constant inflation rate:

$$\tilde{\pi}_t^* = c/a, \tag{5}$$

where the twiddle (˜) denotes values associated with the flexible exchange rate regime. Clearly $\pi_t^* < \tilde{\pi}_t^*$, for all $t < T$, and $\pi_T^* = \tilde{\pi}_T^*$: inflation is always lower in the EMS regime, except at realignments dates – when it reaches the same level that would prevail under flexible rates. The average inflation rate is thus strictly smaller when the country belongs to the EMS, witness to the fact that the system's discipline is effective.

The result $\pi_t^* \leq \tilde{\pi}_t^*$ is quite obvious; what is less intuitive is whether participation to the EMS is also superior from a normative standpoint. To perform this comparison, we need to compute the difference between the equilibrium value of the policy-maker's welfare inside the EMS (V^*) and outside the EMS ($\tilde{V}^*$), respectively, substituting the inflation rates computed in (4) and in (5) in the objective function. The equilibrium welfare in the flexible rates regime is $\tilde{V}^* = -c^2/2a\rho$: it is a decreasing function of (c/a), the incentive to generate unanticipated inflation, relative to the cost of inflation, because in a time-consistent equilibrium that incentive is perfectly under-stood and acted upon by the public, and therefore is only a source of inefficiency. As shown in the appendix, the difference between the equilibrium welfare in the two regimes, $V^* - \tilde{V}^*$, is

$$\Delta = V^* - \tilde{V}^* = \frac{h^2}{a\rho^3}\left[(1/2)(1 - e^{-\rho T}) - \frac{\rho T e^{-\rho T}}{1 - e^{-\rho T}}\right]. \tag{6}$$

Δ measures the discounted welfare gain of EMS membership. For $T \to 0$ the EMS regime coincides with flexible rates so that Δ vanishes. We show in the appendix that Δ is positive, uniformly increasing in T, and has a finite asymptote

$$\lim_{T \to \infty} \Delta = \frac{a}{2\rho}(\pi_\infty^* - \tilde{\pi}^*)^2 = \frac{1}{2a\rho}(h/p)^2, \qquad \text{where}$$

$$\pi_\infty^* = \lim_{T \to \infty} \pi_T^* = \frac{1}{a}(c - h/\rho).$$

Thus, as T becomes large, and the discipline imposed by the system tightens, the welfare gain increases. The lowest possible level of the inflation rate in the EMS regime is π_∞^*, which obtains when $T \to \infty$ and the EMS regime coincides with fixed exchange rates; the reduction in inflation $(\tilde{\pi}^* - \pi_\infty^*)$ is then equal to a constant, $h/a\rho$, and the welfare gain from EMS membership (that is then at its maximum) is simply proportional to the square of the reduction in inflation.

The intuition for this result runs as follows. In this economy inflation is only a source of inefficiency. By attaching an extra penalty to inflation, the EMS reduces the incentive to inflate; since this disincentive scheme is public knowledge, a low inflation policy will be credible, and the EMS will partly overcome the inefficiency deriving from the public's mistrust for the authorities. Moreover, as T increases, the incremental efficiency gain exceeds the corresponding cost, so that the appeal of EMS membership increases the less frequently the country is allowed to realign its parity with the EMS average.

A difficulty is that the penalty that the system attaches to inflation makes the EMS regime unsustainable in the long-run: the credibility gains stemming from indefinite membership are thus not really available. The reason is that our assumption that $q_0 = 0$ implies that the real exchange rate fluctuates *below* PPP: it is set back at PPP at each realignment, and gradually falls between one realignment and the next, thus shifting domestic demand towards foreign goods and worsening the trade balance: with no capital mobility, foreign exchange reserves will be gradually depleted (or an unbounded stock of foreign debt accumulated). Eventually the country will have to drop out of the system.[11] There are two ways to deal with this problem: the first is to allow the real exchange rate to fluctuate *around* PPP, rather than *below* PPP, thus making the system sustainable in the long run; the second is to ask whether, if *permanent* membership is ruled out, *temporary* membership can still yield a benefit.

3. Welfare gains from permanent EMS membership

The way to make EMS membership sustainable in the long run is to design the system so that the real exchange rate fluctuates around PPP, rather than below PPP. This implies granting high-inflation countries a sufficiently large real depreciation at each realignment, so that they will initially run trade surpluses large enough as to compensate subsequent deficits.[12] If we assume that the trade balance (and thus the change in reserves) is a linear function of the (log of the) real exchange rate, the sustainability condition imposes the following relationship between q_0 and T:[13]

---

[11]The welfare gain Δ should thus be computed over a finite horizon, rather than over an infinite horizon, as in eq. (6).

[12]We overlook the complications that arise from any lag in the response of the trade balance to changes in the real exchange rate.

[13]In the absence of capital mobility, we assume that the current account is identically equal to the trade balance. We also assume that the latter is a linear function of the real exchange rate, q_t, and that the authorities' rate of time preference, ρ, equals the fixed rate of interest at which the central bank can borrow or lend in the world financial market. The accumulation of foreign reserves, R, is therefore described by $\dot{R}_t = \rho R_t - CA_t = \rho R_t - \alpha q_t$, and the path of foreign reserves is $R_t = R_0 e^{\rho t} + e^{\rho t} \int_0^t e^{-\rho s} (-\alpha q(s)) \, ds$. Assuming $R_0 = 0$, the condition for the stock of reserves to go back to zero at each realignment is $R_T = e^{\rho t} \int_0^T e^{-\rho s} \dot{R}_s \, ds = 0$.

$$q_0^* = (1/T) \int_0^T \int_0^t \pi_s^* \, ds \, dt, \tag{7}$$

i.e., on the date of the realignment the real exchange must be above PPP by an amount exactly equal the average loss of competitiveness that the country incurs between one realignment and the next.

It is apparent from (7) that the competitiveness 'bonus' granted to the country at each realignment is an increasing function of the level of inflation at each point in time. If the policy-maker could exploit the sustainability condition (7) in choosing the optimal path π_t^*, any credibility gain arising from membership in the EMS would vanish, since he could set q_0 high enough as to cancel, on average, all losses due to real appreciation.[14] Thus, a crucial condition for EMS membership to be sustainable and still yield credibility gains is that the policy-maker does not regard the choice of q_0 as something he can affect. This, for example, could be enforced by letting the country know that q_0 will not be changed if it deviates from the path π_t^* chosen assuming q_0 exogenous, i.e., the path shown in eq. (4). For that inflation path, and with q_0^* given by eq. (7), the welfare gain from permanent membershhip is equal to

$$\Delta' = (h/\rho)q_0^* + \Delta, \tag{6'}$$

where Δ is the gain calculated assuming $q_0 = 0$ and shown in eq. (6) above. Δ' is higher than Δ because the country is now granted a competitiveness 'bonus' at each realignment. For $c > h/\rho$, i.e., when the policy-maker's incentive to create inflation surprises exceeds the discounted penalty, the EMS regime is unambiguously superior.[15] The welfare gain is still uniformly increasing in T and has a finite symptote

$$\lim_{T \to \infty} \Delta' = \lim_{T \to \infty} \Delta + \frac{h}{a\rho^2}(c - h/\rho),$$

where the second term is the discounted value of the initial competitiveness bonus – because $\lim_{T \to \infty} q_0^* = (1/a\rho)(c - h/\rho)$.

If however the discounted penalty exceeds the incentive to create inflation surprises ($c < h/\rho$), the EMS regime is no longer unambiguously superior. In particular, for $c < h/2\rho$ the EMS regime is inferior to flexible rates for all T;

[14]One can see this by substituting the value of q_0^* from eq. (7) into the objective function (3), thus assuming that the policy-maker is able to exploit the relationship between q_0^* and T. For the value of q_0^* given by (7) $\int_0^T e^{-\rho t}(q_0^* - \int_0^t \pi_s \, ds) \, dt = 0$ and the real exchange rate drops out of the objective function. Any disciplinary effect arising from membership in the EMS vanishes because the real exchange rate is independent of the actions of the domestic policy-maker.

[15]The discount factor appears in this comparison because an inflationary impulse translates into a temporary increase in government revenue but into a lasting loss of competitiveness.

for $(h/2\rho) < c < h/\rho$ the EMS regime is superior only if its discipline is sufficiently strict – i.e., if T is sufficiently large. (The different cases are summarized in fig. 1; derivations are shown in the appendix.) Equilibrium inflation is increasing in $(c - h/\rho)$, that describes the incentive to produce inflation in the EMS (net of the discounted penalty). As the net incentive becomes smaller, the equilibrium level of inflation falls. But with lower inflation, the competitiveness bonus that the country must be granted at each realignment is also smaller. This reduces welfare.[16]

3.1. Seignorage as a further incentive to inflate

The temptation to reduce the real value of its nominal liabilities creating inflation surprises is not the only incentive that a government has to produce inflation: even perfectly anticipated inflation yields a benefit generating a revenue from seignorage. It is often argued, in this respect, that EMS membership, by raising the cost of inflation, and thereby reducing the equilibrium level of inflation, is not beneficial for a government that needs to

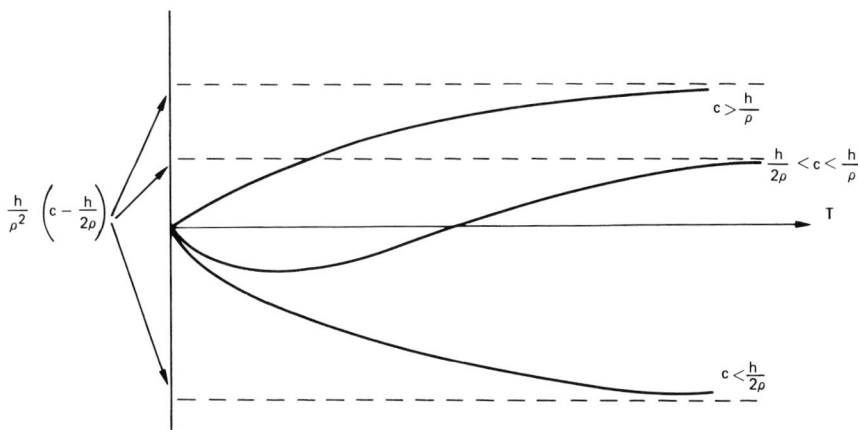

Fig. 1. Welfare gain from permanent EMS membership.

[16]Consider for example the limiting case as $T \to \infty$. In this case, as we have seen, the optimal inflation path is the constant inflation rate $\pi_\infty^* = (c - h/\rho)/a$. If the discounted cost of a real appreciation is higher than the incentive to generate unanticipated inflation $(c < h/\rho)$, the optimal inflation rate is negative. Sustainability now requires that the country starts off with a real *appreciation* equal to $(1/a\rho)|c - h/\rho|$. Rather than a competitiveness bonus, sustainability now requires that the country starts off with a penalty. If the cost associated with this penalty exceeds the benefit that arises from the reduction in the inflation inefficiency, the EMS regime may be inferior to flexible rates; the condition is $(h/\rho^2)|c - h/\rho| > h^2/(2a\rho^3)$, or $c < h/2\rho$. A similar argument applies for T finite. The particular form of the objective function – linear in q_t – may be responsible for this ambiguity. Giavazzi and Giovannini (1987) using an objective function quadratic in q_t show that for small values of T a sustainable EMS regime is *unambiguously* superior.

tap the inflation tax. We investigate this issue by adding a linear term in inflation to the instantaneous objective function of the government

$$V' = \int_0^\infty e^{-\rho t}[hq_t + c(\pi_t - \pi_t^e) - (a/2)\pi_t^2 + b\pi_t]\,dt, \qquad b > 0, \tag{1'}$$

where the term $b\pi_t$ describes the authorities' incentive to collect revenue from seignorage. Maximization of (1') now yields the following path for inflation:

$$\pi_t^{*'} = \pi_t^* + \frac{b}{a} \quad \text{for} \quad t \in (0, T), \tag{4'}$$

where π_t^* is the optimal inflation rate when $b = 0$, shown in eq. (4). The shape of the inflation path between realignments remains unchanged, relative to the case when $b = 0$, but at each point in time the level of inflation is higher by an amount equal to the value that the central bank attaches to seignorage, relative to the cost of inflation.

Assuming that q_0 is again chosen so as to allow the country to remain in the system in the long run, the welfare gain from *permanent* membership is now

$$\Delta'' = (h/\rho)q_0^{*'} + \Delta - (hb/a\rho^2)[1 - \rho T/(1 - e^{-\rho T})], \tag{6''}$$

where Δ is the welfare gain computed assuming $q_0 = 0$ and $b = 0$, shown in eq. (6), and $q_0^{*'}$ is the level of q_0 which guarantees that the EMS regime is sustainable, now equal to

$$q_0^{*'} = q_0^* + (b/a\rho)[1 - \rho T/(1 - e^{-\rho T})]. \tag{7'}$$

One can see immediately that substituting $q_0^{*'}$ in (6'') all terms in b cancel out and $\Delta'' = \Delta'$: the welfare gain is identical to that which obtains when seignorage has no value in the government's objective function. The reason is that the value of the seignorage loss [arising from the fact inflation is lower inside than outside the EMS, and appearing as the last term in eq. (6'')] is exactly compensated by a higher value of the competitiveness bonus that the country must be granted at each realignment to sustain its permanent membership.[17,18]

[17]In (1') we overlook the fact that the revenue from seignorage is really a non-linear function of π_t: the linear term is an approximation to the rising portion of the revenue schedule. If non-linearity were important, it could easily be accommodated in the analysis by approximating the revenue function with a linear-quadratic form in π_t: this would simply increase the coefficient (a) on π_t^2 in (1'). Since all welfare comparisons are proportional to $(1/a)$, this would reduce Δ'': the condition for the EMS to be a superior regime remains unaffected, but the size of the welfare gain is uniformly lower.

[18]This is most clearly seen considering again the limiting case as $T \to \infty$. In this case $\Delta'' = (h\pi_\infty/\rho^2) + (1/2\rho)(\Delta\pi)^2 - (b/\rho)\Delta\pi = (1/a\rho)[(h/\rho)(c + b - h/\rho) + (h^2/2a\rho^2) - (hb/\rho)]$, where and

3.2. Permanent membership: Summing up

We conclude this section summing up the two main points that have been made: (i) the first is that an EMS designed to be sustainable in the long run, not only is an effective disciplinary device – in the sense that it keeps inflation lower than in a regime of flexible exchange rates – but may also be a welfare improving device. To improve welfare, however, the system must satisfy two conditions: (a) the competitiveness 'bonus' that the country must be granted at each realignment, and which is necessary to make the system sustainable, must be kept outside the control of the domestic monetary authorities – otherwise all credibility gains vanish; (b) the central bank's incentive to produce inflation surprises, net of the discounted cost of real appreciation, must be relatively high; (ii) if the EMS regime is designed to be sustainable in the long run, the welfare comparison with flexible exchange rates is unaffected by the incentive to produce a high anticipated level of inflation.

4. Temporary EMS membership

As we have shown in the last section, sustainability requires that the real exchange rate fluctuates around PPP. This conclusion, however, is at odds with the EMS experience so far: as a matter of fact EMS members with above-average inflation have never succeeded in securing realignments so large as to bring their real exchange rate above PPP [see, e.g., Collins (1987)] and it may well be that the system, as currently designed, is not indefinitely sustainable. In principle, however, it could still be the case that *temporary* participation to the EMS makes excess-inflation countries better off.

To check this conjecture, we now assume that each realignment brings back to PPP, so that $q_0 = 0$, and let $T\bar{K}$ be the length of time for which the EMS regime can be sustained: $T\bar{K}$ could correspond to the time when foreign exchange reserve vanish, or when the central bank thinks it cannot cumulate more foreign debt. We assume that at time $T\bar{K}$ the authorities abandon the EMS and return to flexible rates: provided that their decision is public knowledge, at time $T\bar{K}$ the economy moves from a time-consistent equilibrium where the inflation rate is given by eq. (4), to a different time-consistent equilibrium where the inflation rate is equal to c/a.[19] Temporary

---

$\Delta\pi = (\tilde{\pi}^* - \pi_\infty^*) = h/a\rho$ is the difference between the equilibrium inflation rate outside and inside the EMS. The last term on the right-hand-side of the expression for Δ'' is the discounted value of the seignorage loss; the first term is the discounted value of the competitiveness bonus. The value of the seignorage loss is exactly compensated by the competitiveness bonus.

[19]Notice that we rule out the possibility that at any time before $T\bar{K}$ (say, towards the end, right before $T\bar{K}$) the central bank may suddenly decide – with a *surprise* move – to abandon the EMS, inflating wildly without having to bear the competitiveness cost of the this decision. Allowing for such a possibility would add a new dimension to the time-consistency problem faced by the central bank. The reason for ruling it out is that the decision to abandon the EMS cannot be treated on the same grounds as the decision to change the money supply: it is unlikely that the government could abandon the EMS with a surprise move.

membership in an EMS regime that would be unsustainable in the long run may thus be beneficial so long as the country remains in the system. What is crucial for temporary membership to yield credibility is that the authorities' commitment to stay in the system for $T\bar{K}$ periods is credible. It will be credible if the decision to join the system for $T\bar{K}$ periods improves the authorities' welfare function.

Assuming $q_0 = 0$ and EMS membership for $\bar{K}$ periods, the welfare gain relative to flexible rates is

$$\Delta(\bar{K}) = (1 - \exp(-\rho T \bar{K}))\Delta, \tag{7}$$

where Δ is the gain calculated over an infinite horizon, assuming $q_0 = 0$, and shown in eq. (6). $\Delta(\bar{K})$ is a monotone transformation of Δ: it is thus always positive, provided of course that the country can afford to stay in the system at least for one interval of length T. Thus, despite the fact that EMS membership now implies a real appreciation, temporary participation in the system may still be beneficial.

It could be objected that this conclusion overlooks the fact that in this case the country pays an additional cost in terms of the foreign exchange reserves that it burns throughout the period of membership in the system. This, however, can easily be captured by the analysis, assuming that the cost of burning foreign exchange reserves raises the value of h, the shadow cost of a real appreciation (having assumed that the trade balance is a linear function of the real exchange rate, the loss of foreign exchange reserves is also linearly related to the real exchange rate). It will be recalled that Δ is increasing in h: thus also $\Delta(\bar{K})$, the welfare gain from temporary membership is higher, if h is larger. Therefore, the fact that now a real appreciation not only lowers output, but also burns foreign exchange reserves, increases (rather than lowering) the attraction of EMS membership: the higher the penalty attached to inflation, the more effective is the system at correcting the inflation inefficiency.[20]

4.1. Persistent real appreciation as a further disincentive to inflate

Above we have assumed that, at each realignment, excess-inflation countries are granted devaluations that bring them back to the same level of the real exchange rate (q_0, that in particular we have assumed to be the PPP level $q_0 = 0$ in the previous paragraph). What happens if instead they are granted devaluations which are *insufficient* to make up for the entire loss of competitiveness cumulated since the previous realignment? Essentially, at each realignment they move to a lower value of q_0 and their real exchange

---

[20]Notice that while in the sustainable case the welfare gain depends on the difference between the efficiency gain and the penalty paid to secure that gain, here a higher penalty unambiguously improves welfare. The reason is that here, as in the basic model of sec. 2, q_0 is unaffected by the equilibrium path of inflation, and thus by the penalty attached to inflation.

rate, rather than fluctuating around a stable level (as in all the cases studied so far) fluctuates around a trend of real appreciation. As mentioned in the introduction, there are reasons to believe that this is a closer approximation to how realignments actually take place in the EMS.

To study the effects of persistent real appreciation, we introduce a single additional feature in the model: we assume that at each realignment countries with excess inflation are only allowed to devalue their nominal exchange rate by a proportion $1-\lambda$ of the competitiveness they have lost since the previous realignment. In other words, a proportion λ of the cumulated inflation differential intervened between any two successive re-alignments remains embodied in the level of the real exchange rate so long as the country remains in the system. This apparently small change in assumptions alters the formal structure of the model considerably, since now the policy-maker will have to consider that a proportion λ of the competi-tiveness lost at each date is going to be lost forever: intervals between successive realignments are thus no longer independent in the maximization problem.

The policy-maker's instantaneous objective function remains that described in eq. (1). The difference is rather the real-exchange-rate-term that now becomes

$$
\int_0^{T\bar{K}} e^{-\rho T} q_t \, dt = \sum_{k=0}^{\bar{K}} \int_{kT}^{(k+1)T} \left(q_0 - \int_{kT}^{t} \pi_s \, ds \right) e^{-\rho t} \, dt
$$

$$
-\lambda \sum_{k=1}^{\bar{K}} \int_{kT}^{(k+1)T} e^{-\rho t} \int_0^{kT} \pi_s \, ds \, dt. \tag{8}
$$

$T\bar{K}$ is the horizon of the policy-maker and corresponds to the time beyond which EMS membership is no longer sustainable. The last term in (8) represents the memory of the system, i.e., the discounted loss associated with the portion of real appreciation that the country is never allowed to recover (in fact it vanishes for $\lambda=0$).

To keep things simple, and without loss of generality, assume that the system can only be sustained for two periods (i.e., $\bar{K}=2$). The optimal inflation path is

$$
\pi_t^{*''} = \pi_t^*, \qquad\qquad\qquad T \le t \le 2T
$$

$$
= \pi_t^* - (\lambda h/a\rho)e^{-\rho(T-t)}(1-e^{-\rho T}), \qquad 0 \le t \le T, \tag{4''}
$$

where π_t^* is the optimal inflation path when the real exchange rate has no trend, as shown in eq. (4). The optimal inflation path no longer has the same shape between any two realignments: as time goes by, and the date when the system will have to be abandoned approaches, the average inflation rate rises, since the implied losses of competitiveness will have to be borne for a shorter period of time. The welfare gain relative to the flexible exchange rate regime, computed over the horizon $0 \leq t \leq 2T$, is now

$$\Delta(\bar{K}=2, \lambda > 0) = \Delta(\bar{K}=2) + (\lambda h^2/a\rho^3)e^{-\rho T}(1-e^{-\rho T})[\rho T-(1-e^{-eT})$$

$$+(\lambda/2)(1-e^{-\rho T})^2], \tag{7'}$$

where $\Delta(\bar{K}=2)$ is the welfare gain when the real exchange rate reverts to PPP at each realignment, i.e., the expression in eq. (7), calculated over two periods. For $\lambda > 0$, $\Delta(\bar{K}=2, \lambda > 0) > \Delta(\bar{K}=2)$: the penalty of persistent real appreciation raises the cost of inflation and unambiguously improves welfare.[21]

4.2. Temporary membership: Summing up

The examples discussed in this section suggest that even when EMS membership is unsustainable in the long run, it may still yield temporary benefits. So long as the country can afford to stay in the system the authorities' welfare function improves. Their commitment to temporary membership is thus credible.

5. Credibility gains in an EMS without capital controls

Up to this point we have assumed that prohibitive capital controls insulate the domestic financial market from the international financial market. This assumption is not inconsistent with the facts: the two largest excess-inflation-countries in the EMS – France and Italy – have operated strict exchange controls for many years; among the small countries, Belgium has a dual exchange market that also serves the purpose of separating the domestic from the international financial market.

Capital controls have played an important role in the EMS: in fact the very success of the system is often attributed to the presence of exchange controls in countries where inflation is above the European average. The argument is that a regime of fixed but adjustable parities is bound to collapse under the impact of speculative attacks on central bank reserves in the anticipation of a realignment, unless the volume of speculative capital flows is limited by exchange controls [see, e.g., Wyplosz (1985)]. This argument however overestimates the need for exchange controls because it overlooks the role of interest rate differentials as an equilibrating mechanism

---

[21]Notice that the term in square brackets on the right-hand-side is always positive because $(-1+\rho T+\exp(-\rho T))$ tends to 1/2 for $T \to 0$ and to $+\infty$ for $T \to \infty$.

in the wake of a parity realignment. If the central bank does not attempt to peg domestic interest rates, these will move so as to compensate holders of interest-bearing assets for the anticipated capital loss (or gain) arising from a prospective realignment. The adjustment of domestic interest rates strongly dampens the speculative attack, and can make a system of fixed exchange rates with periodic realignments viable even in the absence of capital controls.[22] The resulting fluctuation of domestic interest rates may however be very large, so that any gain from free capital mobility should be weighed against the costs associated with the higher volatility of interest rates. The higher volatility, however, is concentrated on short rates, and tends to die-out as the maturity of the asset lengthens – the obvious reason being that long rates are less affected than short rates by a realignment of given magnitude. The costs of free capital mobility, in a system such as the EMS, are thus really the costs associated with a high volatility of short term interest rates.[23] There are good reasons why monetary authorities should worry about the volatility of short term rates. For example, in countries – such as Italy – where public debt is high and the liabilities of the government are mostly short term bills, an increase in the volatility of short term rates induces fluctuations in the budget deficit, and these, presumably, are undesirable.[24]

In this section we investigate whether, in the absence of exchange controls, the EMS may still yield credibility gains that exceed the cost of membership. We modify the basic model developed in section 2 in two ways: (i) domestic nominal rates are now linked to interest rates on the international financial market through the condition of uncovered interest rate parity; (ii) the policy-maker assigns a negative weight also to the volatility of nominal interest rates.[25] The objective function becomes:

[22]The adjustment of domestic interest rates eliminates the possibility of an unbounded speculative attack: this is thus confined to the size of the monetary base. Since the domestic interest rate on deposits of instantaneous maturity shoots up to ∞ at the moment of a (perfectly anticipated) realignment, one could suppose that at that time money demand falls to zero, thus depleting all central bank reserves. In reality however, there exist no assets of instantaneous maturity, so that interest rates remain unbounded. Furthermore, the transaction motive suggests that money demand remains positive even for very high values of the rate of interest.

[23]Giavazzi and Pagano (1985) compare the variability of 3-month 'on-shore' and 'off-shore' interest rates in France and Italy over the period November 1980–August 1984. We find that in both countries capital controls have significantly reduced the variability of domestic rates: from (a standard deviation of) 5.2 to 0.5 in France; from 4.8 to 1.8 in Italy.

[24]Another reason why fluctuations in short term rates may be undesirable is an optimal tax argument: in a model where agents derive utility from holding money balances, the optimal level of the opportunity cost of holding money is zero. In the presence of taxes, however, the marginal cost of holding money has to equal the social marginal benefit of the revenue from seignorage: in this case the optimal level of the opportunity cost of holding money is positive. Moreover, the solution to the optimal tax problem requires that this opportunity cost be smooth over time: large fluctuations of short term nominal rates are thus sub-optimal.

[25]As discussed above, there are good reasons why the government may care about the volatility of *nominal* interest rates. The volatility of nominal rates is here also an approximation

$$V' = \int_0^T e^{-\rho t}[hq_t + c(\pi_t - \pi_t^e) - (a/2)\pi_t^2 - (f/2)(i_t^\tau - i^{-\tau})^2]\,dt, \tag{9}$$

with $f > 0$ and q_t defined as in eq. (2). i_t^τ is the interest rate on a deposit issued at time t and that will mature at time $t + \tau$; $\bar{i}^\tau$ is the mean of i_t^τ over an interval of length T. We treat τ as a parameter of the problem because the welfare gain depends on the value of τ, i.e., on the maturity of the asset that the authorities care about.[26] We assume that the foreign nominal interest rate on deposits of maturity τ is fixed and equal to zero for convenience; realignments take place every T periods, and bring the real exchange rate back to PPP (we thus concentrate on the case where the real exchange rate fluctuates below PPP, with no long run trend, i.e., $q_0 = 0$). The path of domestic interest rates is given by

$$i_t^\tau = 0, \qquad\qquad 0 \le t \le T - \tau$$

$$= \tau^{-1} \int_0^T \pi(t)\,dt, \qquad T - \tau \le t \le T. \tag{10}$$

The nominal interest rate is zero on all deposits maturing before the date of the realignment because we assume interest rates to be zero abroad; it jumps to compensate for the capital loss incurred on the day of the realignment at time $T - \tau$, and stays at that level until the realignment date, when it goes back to zero. The same path repeats in between any two successive realignments. Notice that $\bar{i}^\tau = (1/T)\int_0^T \pi(s)\,ds$, so that the average *real* rate of interest is zero and is unaffected by the fluctuations of the nominal rate.

The optimal inflation path is now

$$\hat{\pi}_t^* = \pi_t^* - (f/\rho)(1/\tau - 1/T)^2 e^{-\rho(T-t)}(e^{\rho\tau} - 1)\left(\int_0^T \hat{\pi}_t^*\,dt\right), \tag{11}$$

where π_t^* is the inflation path reported in eq. (4). The welfare gain *relative to an EMS with capital controls* (assuming $q_0 = 0$ in both cases) is (see appendix for derivation):

$$(e^{\rho\tau} - 1)(1/\tau - 1/T)^2 F(T) > 0 \quad \text{for all} \quad T, \tag{12}$$

---

to the volatility of real rates because, in between realignments, nominal interest rates fluctuate much more than the rate of inflation.

[26]In writing eq. (9) we also implicitly assume that the interest rate elasticity of money demand is zero, and that output demand does not respond to fluctuations in interest rates. These assumptions seem reasonable in view of the fact that the interest rate fluctuations we are considering are short-run phenomena, concentrated around realignment dates.

The expression (12) is positive: thus, in this setup, the assumption of perfect mobility improves welfare in the EMS regime. The welfare improvement is *decreasing* in τ, the maturity of the deposits whose interest rate enters the objective function. The intuition for the latter result is that for a given path of inflation the volatility of interest rates is increasing in $1/\tau$ and is unbounded for $\tau \to 0$ (the interest rate on an asset of instantaneous maturity shoots up to infinity at the date of realignment, if we suppose that this is perfectly anticipated, as we do here). Since now the policy-maker is also concerned about the volatility of interest rates, he will have to be all the more cautious about generating inflation, the more he cares about short-term (as opposed to long-term) rates: higher inflation translates into a larger devaluation at the time of the following realignment, and this will then require a larger rise in interest rates, particularly towards the short-end of the maturity structure. This is why the shorter the maturity τ, the lower the equilibrium path of inflation, and the larger the credibility and the welfare gain relative to the flexible rate regime.

Appendix

1. Derivation of Δ, Δ' and Δ'' (eqs. (6), (6') and (6'') in the text)

The value of the objective function [eq. (3) in the text] along the optimal path in the EMS regime is

$$V^* = \sum_{k=0}^{\infty} e^{-\rho T k} \left\{ \int_0^T \left[hq_0 - h \int_0^t \frac{1}{a} [c - (h/\rho) \right. \right.$$

$$\left. \left. + (h/\rho) e^{-\rho(T-s)}] \, ds - \frac{1}{2a} [c - (h/\rho) + (h/\rho) e^{-\rho(T-t)}]^2 \right] dt \right\}, \qquad \text{(A.1)}$$

which, noticing that $\sum_{k=0}^{\infty} e^{-\rho T k} = (1 - e^{-\rho T})^{-1}$, can be written as

$$V^* = (1/\rho) \left[hq_0 - \frac{c^2}{2a} + \frac{h^2}{a\rho^2} \left[\frac{1}{2} - e^{-\rho T} \left(\frac{\rho T}{1 - e^{-\rho T}} - \frac{1}{2} \right) \right] \right]. \qquad \text{(A.2)}$$

The correspondence expression in the flexible exchange rates regime is instead simply

$$\tilde{V}^* = -\frac{c^2}{2a} \int_0^{\infty} e^{-\rho t} \, dt = -\frac{c^2}{2a\rho}. \qquad \text{(A.3)}$$

For $q_0 = 0$ the differences $V^* - \tilde{V}^*$ yields the value Δ reported in eq. (6). At the limits, when the EMS regime coincides with fixed and flexible exchange rates respectively, we have

$$\lim_{T \to \infty} \Delta = \frac{h^2}{2a\rho^3} \quad \text{and} \quad \lim_{T \to \infty} \Delta = 0.$$

Δ is uniformly increasing in T, as can be seen noticing that

$$\frac{\partial \Delta}{\partial T} = -\frac{h^2}{a\rho^2} e^{-\rho T} \left[\frac{1}{2} + \frac{1 - e^{-\rho T} - \rho T}{(1 - e^{-\rho T})^2} \right], \tag{A.4}$$

where the last term inside the square brackets $(1 - e^{-\rho T} - \rho T)/(1 - e^{-\rho T})^2$ tends to $-(1/2)$ for $T \to 0$, and to $-\infty$ for $T \to \infty$.

For $0 < T < \infty$, this term is monotonically decreasing in T since

$$\frac{\partial}{\partial T} \left[\frac{1 - e^{-\rho T} - \rho T}{(1 - e^{-\rho T})^2} \right] = \frac{\rho T e^{-\rho T}}{(1 - e^{-\rho T})^3} (e^{-\rho T} - e^{\rho T} + 2\rho T)$$

$$= \frac{\rho e^{-\rho T}}{(1 - e^{-\rho T})^3} (\rho T - \sinh(\rho T)) < 0, \tag{A.5}$$

recalling that $x - \sinh(x) = -[(x^3/3!) + (x^5/5!) + (x^7/7!) + \cdots]$.

The welfare gain in the sustainable case, Δ' in eq. (6') is obtained substituting in the expression for V^* in (A.2) the value of q_0^* obtained from eq. (7), and equal to

$$q_0^* = (c - h/\rho)/(a\rho) - (1/a\rho)e^{-\rho T} \left[(c - h/\rho) \frac{\rho T}{1 - e^{-\rho T}} + (h/\rho)(1 - \rho T - e^{-\rho T}) \right].$$

It is straightforward to show that $\lim_{T \to 0} q_0^* = 0$, $\lim_{T \to \infty} q_0^* = (c - h/\rho)/a\rho$ and $\lim_{T \to 0} \partial q_0^*/\partial T = (1/2a)/(c - h/\rho)$. Using these results, together with the results shown above for the case $q_0 = 0$, we obtain $\lim_{T \to 0} \Delta' = 0$; $\lim_{T \to \infty} \Delta' = (h/a\rho^2)(c - h/2\rho)$; and $\lim_{T \to 0} \partial \Delta'/\partial T = (h/2a\rho)(c - h/\rho)$. Δ' is uniformly increasing in T for $c > h/\rho$, and uniformly decreasing in T for $c < h/2\rho$. For $h/2\rho < c < h/\rho$, Δ' is negative for small values of T (because $\partial \Delta'/\partial T$ is negative around $T = 0$), but eventually turns positive and has a positive asymptote.

Finally, when seignorage enters the authorities' objective function, as in eq. (1'), the value of V along the optimal path in the EMS regime and in the flexible rates regime are, respectively

$$V^* = (1/\rho) \left\{ hq_0 - \frac{(c+b)^2}{2a} + \frac{h^2}{a\rho^2} \left[\frac{1}{2} - e^{-\rho T} \left(\frac{\rho T}{1 - e^{-\rho T}} - \frac{1}{2} \right) \right] \right\}$$

$$+(b/a)\left[c+b-(h/\rho)\left(1-\frac{\rho T e^{-\rho T}}{1-e^{-\rho T}}\right)\right]. \qquad (A.6)$$

$$\tilde{V}^* = -\frac{c^2-b^2}{2a}\int_0^\infty e^{-\rho t}\,dt = -\frac{c^2-b^2}{2a\rho}. \qquad (A.7)$$

The difference $V^* - \tilde{V}^*$ is the value of Δ'' reported in eq. (6'').

2. Derivation of the welfare gain with perfect capital mobility [eq. (12)]

Substituting the expression for i_t^τ from eq. (10) into the objective function (9) we obtain

$$V'' = V - f(1/\tau - 1/T)^2\left[\int_0^T \pi_t\,dt\right]^2 \frac{e^{-\rho T}(e^{\rho T}-1)}{2\rho},$$

where V is the objective function in eq. (1).

Eq. (12) is obtained calculating V'' along the optimal inflation path shown in eq. (11), and subtractiong the welfare gain Δ [eq. (6)]. The value of $F(T)$ in eq. (12) is

$$F(T) = \frac{f e^{-\rho T}}{2a\rho^2}\left[c\frac{\rho T}{1-e^{-\rho T}} - \frac{h(1-\rho T - e^{-\rho T})}{\rho^2(1-e^{-\rho T})^2}\right].$$

References

Barro, Robert J., 1983, Inflationary finance under discretion and rules, Canadian Journal of Economics 16, Feb., 1–16.

Barro, Robert, J. and David B. Gordon, 1985, Rules, discretion and reputation in a model of monetary policy, Journal of Political Economy 12, July, 101–121.

Cohen, Daniel and Philippe Michel, 1985, Dynamic consistency of government's behaviour: A user guide (1), Mimeo.

Collins, Susan M., 1987, PPP and the peso problem: Exchange rates in the EMS, Mimeo.

Fischer, Stanley, 1982, Seignorage and the case for a national money, Journal of Political Economy 90, no. 2, April, 295–313.

Fischer, Stanley, 1986, Time consistent monetary and fiscal policies: A survey, Mimeo.

Fischer, Stanely, 1987, British monetary policy, in: R. Dornbusch and R. Layard, eds., The performance of the British economy (Oxford University Press, Oxford).

Giavazzi, Francesco and Alberto Giovannini, 1987, Models of the EMS: Is Europe a greater Deutsche Mark area?, in: R. Bryant and R. Portes, eds., Global macroeconomics: Policy conflict and cooperation (Macmillan, London).

Giavazzi, Francesco and Marco Pagano, 1985, Capital controls and the European monetary system, in: Capital controls and foreign exchange legislation, Euromobiliare occasional papers no. 1.

Grossman, H.I. and J.B. Van Hujck, 1984, Seignorage, inflation and reputation, Working paper no, 1505 (NBER, New York).

Rogoff, Kenneth, 1985, The optimal degree of commitment to an intermediate monetary target, Quarterly Journal of Economics 100, no. 4, Nov., 1169–1190.
Thygesen, Niels, 1979, The emerging European monetary system: Precursors, first steps and policy options, in: R. Triffin, ed., EMS – The emerging European monetary system, off-print bulletin of the National Bank of Belgium, Vol. I, no. 4, April.
Wyplosz, Charles, 1985, Capital controls and balance of payments crises, Journal of International Money and Finance, Dec.

COMMENTS

'The Advantage of Tying One's Hands: EMS Discipline and Central Bank Credibility'
by Francesco Giavazzi and Marco Pagano

David K.H. BEGG

Giavazzi and Pagano have given us an interesting and elegant paper. Their starting point is a small country with a credibility problem. Its central bank faces a temptation to resort to surprise inflation to secure higher output. As first explained in Barro and Gordon (1985) the private sector will anticipate such behaviour and the resulting equilibrium has an inefficiently high rate of inflation. One solution, suggested in Rogoff (1985), is the appointment of an unduly conservative central banker. Giavazzi and Pagano do not explain why this solution is unattractive or infeasible; rather they explore whether a similar precommitment can be achieved by joining the EMS. Clearly what they have in mind is that inflation prone countries such as France and Italy effectively delegate monetary policy to the Bundesbank when they join the EMS.

Before discussing the analysis in detail, it is worth noting which aspects of the EMS this approach can and cannot explain. First, although the interpretation of the EMS as a device for securing inflation discipline has become increasingly popular during the 1980s, it should be remembered that such considerations may have been less important at the outset when a major goal of the EMS was to reduce exchange rate volatility. Second, to the extent the authors' analysis is about whether a small country should join a system with given rules of the game, the analysis explains neither the initial bargain to establish the EMS nor the continuing conflicts within it.

With these preliminary comments, let me turn to the substance of the paper. In a world of flexible prices, the policy maker chooses monetary growth and inflation knowing that the period between EMS realignments is exogenous (and for simplicity constant) and that the real exchange rate reverts to a given point (PPP) after each realignment. Against the apparent benefits of surprise inflation the policy maker trades off two costs – a dislike of inflation and the knowledge that it is making the economy less competitive until another realignment can occur. Since there is no more (sluggish) inflation and since the economy reverts to the same real exchange rate after each realignment, the optimal policy has a saw tooth shape. Each subperiod is identical to any other, and within each subperiod the optimal inflation rate rises monotonically since the cost of misalignment is smaller the closer the next realignment. On the one hand, this set up is very neat, since the repetitive nature of the decision problem greatly simplifies the analysis and the solution. On the other hand, I cannot help feeling it throws away too much. Specifically, it cannot explain a gradual process by which high inflation EMS countries converge to the EMS average. The latter seems to me much more like the actual EMS experience in the early 1980s. To model that, the authors would require sluggish prices, which would complicate both the model and the solution procedure.

I turn now to my central reservation about the paper. By the end of section 2 the authors have obtained the EMS solution and shown that it yields higher welfare for the small country that the 'outside option' of floating. EMS discipline offsets the inflationary bias which is present when policy makers cannot otherwise precommit themselves. But the authors get worried about the implications of their model. If real exchange rates begin each subperiod at the PPP level, and the optimal policy for inflation prone countries remains to have some additional inflation throughout the subperiod, then on average such countries are insufficiently competitive, have trade deficits, and experience capital outflows. Most of the rest of the paper is about trying to solve this sustainability issue.

I do not find either of the claimed solutions appealing. One solution is to allow high inflation countries to devalue to a real exchange rate more competitive than PPP at the start of the subperiod, a competitive advantage which is gradually eroded by excess inflation until the next realignment, such that on average the real exchange rate is at the correct level. Not only does this not accord with the facts – the authors note that high inflation countries if anything have been allowed devaluations insufficient not oversufficient to restore PPP – but it has little theoretical appeal as a rule of the game. Either individual countries believe that their chosen inflation rates affect the *real* realignments they will subsequently be allowed, in which case as the authors observe the disciplining mechanism and credibility are destroyed, or it is simply hard to believe that the concerted EMS decision on realignments will happen to provide the realignment which indeed yields different partners the right real exchange rate on average. The second solution is even less attractive: if countries cannot afford to stay in the EMS forever, simply analyse the temporary periods in which it will be possible for them to stay in until foreign exchange reserves are exhausted.

There is no need for such contortions. Imagine a household which ignores its intertemporal budget constraint and finds it is overspending its income.

Would anyone argue that this unsustainability should be resolved either by imagining that the household just happens to receive additional transfer payments sufficient to restore its solvency, or that we only study this household 'for a while' before its assets run out or its borrowing is exhausted? I hope we should prefer to reanalyse the problem making the intertemporal budget constraint part of the analysis. In the same way, the natural way to treat the authors unsustainability problem is to make the policy maker take full account of it in the optimisation problem. Crudely speaking this means that periods of above average inflation (uncompetitiveness and capital outflows) must be balanced by periods of below average inflation (supercompetitiveness and capital inflows) except to the extent the policy maker is prepared to let the net asset position change over time. Thinking about it in this way highlights the EMS issue of *when* a country should disinflate relative to its partners, rather than *whether* it should disinflate.

As with my earlier remarks about price sluggishness, the consequence of such an amendment to the analysis would be to convert a repeated game into a dynamic game: the net asset stock would be the state variable. Although it would complicate the analysis, it would, like core inflation, provide a possible mechanism in which to explain and interpret the gradual-convergence of EMS members' monetary policies.

These are rich questions. Although I have sought to indicate how this line of research might be extended, Giavazzi and Pagano are to be congratulated for making considerable progress within the simpler model of this paper.

References

Barro, Robert J. and David B. Gordon, 1985, Rules, discretion and reputation in a model of monetary policy, Journal of Political Economy 12, July, 101–121.
Rogoff, Kenneth, 1985, The optimal degree of commitment to an intermediate monetary target, Quarterly Journal of Economics 100, no. 4, Nov., 1169–1190.

COMMENTS

'The Advantage of Tying One's Hands: EMS Discipline and Central Bank Credibility' by Francesco Giavazzi and Marco Pagano

Maurice OBSTFELD

In this interesting paper, Giavazzi and Pagano suggest that a government that cannot otherwise precommit to low inflation can 'tie its hands' by pegging to a low-inflation currency. The authors assume a setup in which domestic inflation is suboptimally high before pegging [perhaps for reasons explored by Barro and Gordon (1983)]. Pegging can make inflation more costly for the policymaker because external competitivenesss suffers more between exchange-rate realignments. If this is the case, pegging leads to an equilibrium with lower domestic inflation. Indeed, the inflation gain may be so great that the government prefers to have its hands tied. The conclusion is that high-inflation European countries such as Italy may have gained from pegging to the Deutschemark (and periodically realigning) as part of the EMS exchange-rate mechanism.

As the authors point out, the analysis is a variant of Rogoff's (1985a) point that countries can sometimes achieve socially preferable macroeconomic outcomes by modifying policymaker preferences relative to the 'true' preferences of society. Giavazzi and Pagano pursue the implications of modifying constraints rather than preferences.

My comments on the paper are related to four broad questions:

(1) How does the model match up with reality?
(2) What incentives does the low-inflation country (Germany) have to participate in the system?
(3) Is the model specification persuasive?
(4) Can a system of periodically devaluing to restore external competitiveness cause problems of self-fulfilling inflation-devaluation spirals and speculative attacks?

1. The model and reality

The major stylized fact motivating the authors' analysis is that EMS realignments have not fully offset losses in competitiveness by high-inflation members. The resulting real appreciation may represent a cost of inflation that has deterred policymakers from pursuing more expansionary policies. Data such as those presented by Ungerer et al. (1986) show that this pattern of competitiveness loss applies most easily to Italy (and perhaps Ireland), but not clearly to France. When CPIs are used to compute real exchange rates, the lira's real appreciation against other EMS currencies between 1979 and 1986 (first quarter) amounts to 23 percent; the figure is 11 percent when based on unit labor costs.

Even in the Italian case, however, the currency has not recently been at the limit of its wide fluctuation band: the Italian government could have had less real appreciation within the constraints of its exchange-rate obligations. Further, Italy's current account has been trendless over the EMS period, improving sharply in 1986. One wonders if these facts are consistent with the Giavazzi–Pagano story, and whether some lira appreciation may have resulted from real demand shifts toward Italian products.

France shows less conformity with the authors' account. From 1979 to 1986 (first quarter), the franc experienced only a 2 percent real appreciation in terms of CPIs, or a 4 percent real appreciation in terms of unit labor costs. In terms of CPIs, the currency was *more* competitive in 1983–1984 than in 1979. Perhaps a plausible story for France is that President Giscard d'Estaing wished to tie the hands of *future* French governments by imposing a high cost of exiting from the EMS. In this regard the system seems to have been successful.

It is certainly true that other EMS members have voluntarily surrendered some monetary sovereignty to the German Bundesbank. Article 15 of the EMS agreement permits member central banks to hold only 'working balances' of participating currencies – but the Bundesbank has not objected as other central banks have added DM assets to their foreign reserves and expanded their inframarginal intervention operations in DM. Thus, the position of Germany within the EMS has become much like that of the United States within the Bretton Woods system. This evolution calls to mind Rogoff's (1985a) parable of surrendering one's monetary policy to a 'conservative' central banker.

2. What does Germany gain?

The Giavazzi–Pagano analysis takes the low-inflation center country as an exogenous player, but it is natural to ask what that country gains from the system, and how policy interactions between it and the peripheral countries can affect outcomes.

Henderson and Canzoneri (1988) offer an interesting example in which it is definitely *not* in Germany's interest to have foreign countries peg to the DM and use their DM exchange rates, rather than their money supplies, as policy instruments. Assume that Germany, like other countries, also faces a Barro–Gordon credibility problem (though perhaps to a lesser degree). *Given* other countries' exchange-rate choices, monetary expansion by the Bundesbank causes no currency depreciation, and thus has a lower perceived inflation cost than if other countries targeted money supplies and allowed DM exchange rates to float. In a multi-country Nash equilibrium, Germany ends up with higher inflation under pegged than under floating rates. Clearly, Germany would prefer that other countries set money supplies rather than DM exchange rates. Another troublesome possibility is raised by Rogoff (1985b), who shows how all countries that join the fixed-exchange-rate system can end up with higher inflation if they do not resolve their domestic credibility problems first.

These examples may not apply to actual EMS experience – in part because it is not clear that a noncooperative paradigm applies. But the examples do show that the Giavazzi–Pagano conclusions could be overturned by a more complete modelling of Germany's incentives and the resulting policy game. Future research should examine more carefully the purely economic benefits Germany derives from its unique position in the EMS.

3. Model specification

In describing complex situations, model builders inevitably face a trade-off between tractability and theoretical consistency. Several of the modelling choices made by Giavazzi and Pagano appear to me to sacrifice too much in the interest of analytical convenience. Although most of these choices could probably be modified without altering the model's main message, the approach followed makes the authors' conclusions less compelling than they might otherwise be.

The model departs sharply from reality in assuming a fixed period, T, between currency realignments. Presumably this feature of the model could be relaxed, as the authors have done elsewhere. As the model stands, though, we are left with the uncomfortable implication that the optimal value of T is infinity – the value that maximizes anti-inflationary discipline. Thus, an optimal EMS based on the author' principles would outlaw realignments altogether. A motivation for realignments requires some additions to the model, such as output-market shocks or imperfect government control over inflation.

Central to the paper's model is the assumption that, all else equal, real currency appreciation lowers the value of the policymaker's objective function. The justification for this assumption is official concern for the export sector's profitability. While export profitability is undoubtedly an important consideration for policy, other equally plausible considerations would seem to *favor* real appreciation. For example, real appreciation can benefit the economy by stimulating employment when wages are indexed to the CPI, by lowering the cost of imported intermediate goods, and, more generally, by giving consumers improved terms of trade. A superior specification might be one in which the policy objective function penalizes absolute deviations from a target real exchange rate.

Also controversial is the assumption that purchasing power parity (PPP) always holds when the exchange rate floats. It is hard to imagine assumptions consistent with the paper's models such that PPP would hold under a floating rate, but not a fixed rate.

A related puzzling aspect of the model is the treatment of inflation choice under conditions of capital mobility. By pegging to the DM and allowing free capital movements, the home country gives up its ability to affect its money supply through domestic-credit measures. How, then, is inflation controlled under these circumstances if the exchange rate is fixed? Presumably through fiscal policy – though this policy tool is not explicitly analyzed.

The introduction of fiscal considerations suggests a final issue that is raised by the authors but not, in my opinion, given a satisfactory resolution. That issue is sustainability. To analyze the sustainability of different exchange rate paths, the model treats the current account as a function of the real exchange rate alone and analyzes sustainability in terms of reserve changes. It would be preferable to assess sustainability in a framework that takes account of the full range of official borrowing opportunities and the intertemporal constraints on borrowing. Such a framework would allow one to address at the same time the role of fiscal policies and the sustainability of external deficits.

The authors' modelling of current-account imbalances is far too simple. In particular, *anticipated* realignments, central to the current story, can have crucial effects on the covariation between the current account and the real exchange rate.

4. Devaluation cycles and crises

Anticipation of future realignment have several other effects on the economy that deserve more complete analysis. These effects show up in the behavior of asset prices and spending, in the wage-setting and inflation processes, and in the private capital account. The authors' assumption that the government can choose the inflation rate sidesteps the possibility that anticipatory inflation can itself fuel a devaluation cycle. Balance-of-payments crises that disrupt the fixed-rate system may be part of that cycle.

The simplest case to consider is one with capital immobility, in which sharp foreign-reserve losses can be minimized. Suppose that the public expects a devaluation to restore competitiveness as soon as the domestic price level reaches value, p^*. Then the economy's equilibrium can occur along any one of a multiplicity of paths in which asset and output prices rise in anticipation of a devaluation, pushing up interest rates and depleting reserves. Once the price level reaches p^* devaluation occurs, after which central-bank reserves increase as the economy returns to a new long-run position characterized by a higher price level. Public awareness that the government will devalue to restore competitiveness can thus lead to a cycle of inflation and accommodation, of a type seen in several countries.

The same cycle can occur with capital mobility but it is complicated by the possibility that speculators will attack the central bank's foreign-exchange reserves and force the temporary suspension of fixed exchange rates. Assume first that the home central bank can borrow an essentially unlimited volume of foreign reserves from partner banks – at least enough to repurchase the *entire* domestic monetary base. In this setting, anticipations alone can again drive up prices, with a sharp rise in interest rates and a fall in reserves maintaining money-market equilibrium the period before the devaluation. (In continuous time the money supply drops to zero for an instant and the interest rate shoots up to infinity.) If reserves are inadequate to preserve monetary equilibrium just before the devaluation, however, an attack by speculators will force the central bank off fixed exchange rates at some earlier point. After the attack, the currency will depreciate to its new peg as the price level continues to rise to the trigger level p^*.

These scenarios – analyzed in greater detail in Obstfeld (1987) – suggest that the realignment mechanism described by Giavazzi and Pagano has adverse side effects not captured in their model. Another suggestion is that the realignment process on which the EMS has so far relied will become increasingly disruptive as France and Italy open their financial sectors to the rest of the world.

5. Conclusion

Formal models of exchange-rate union are essential to understanding the normative and positive implications of currency arrangements such as the EMS. The approach taken by Giavazzi and Pagano views exchange-rate union as a mechanism that enhances the pegging government's credibility by raising the cost of inflationary policies. At a fundamental level, this approach must explain why governments can make binding commitments to EMS rules when they cannot precommit to macroeconomic rules outside the system. Recent experience suggests that individual members of the EMS exchange-rate mechanism do attach significant costs to the option of dropping out. Since these costs may given EMS undertakings a credibility that other policy announcements do not have, an important aim of future research should be to model them. My hunch is that the costs are related to the gains from macroeconomic cooperation that member countries would forgo by going it alone.

References

Barro, Robert J. and David B. Gordon, 1983, A positive theory of monetary policy in a natural rate model, Journal of Political Economy 91, 589–610.
Canzoneri, Matthew B. and Dale W. Henderson, 1988, Is sovereign policymaking bad?, Carnegie–Rochester Conference Series on Public Policy, Vol. 28 (North-Holland, Amsterdam) forthcoming.
Obstfeld, Maurice, 1987, Competitiveness, realignment and speculation: The role of financial markets, Paper presented at the conference on the European Monetary System, Perugia, Oct., 16–17.
Rogoff, Kenneth, 1985a, The optimal degree of commitment to an intermediate monetary target, Quarterly Journal of Economics 100, 1169–1190.
Rogoff, Kenneth, 1985b, Can international monetary policy cooperation be counterproductive?, Journal of International Economics 18, 199–217.
Ungerer, Horst, et al., 1986, The European Monetary System: Recent development, Occasional paper no. 48 (International Monetary Fund, Washington, DC).

European Economic Review 21 (1983) . North-Holland

DOMESTIC SAVING AND INTERNATIONAL CAPITAL MOVEMENTS IN THE LONG RUN AND THE SHORT RUN*

Martin FELDSTEIN

NBER, and Harvard University, Cambridge, MA 02138, USA

1. Introduction

A nearly universal assumption in international economic analysis is that capital flows freely among countries to keep the return to capital equal in all places. The implications of this assumption of perfect capital mobility are not only extremely important but are also contrary to most economists' beliefs about the behavior of national economies. Perfect capital mobility implies, for example, that the burden of corporate income taxes falls primarily on labor, that government deficits do not crowd out private investment, that increases in saving do not raise domestic investment, and that monetary and tax policies cannot alter the real net rate of return on domestic capital. To avoid such intellectual schizophrenia, we must either modify the assumption of perfect capital mobility or abandon the view that national monetary and fiscal policies that alter domestic saving can thereby influence the process of domestic capital formation.

An alternative view of the international economy recognizes that capital mobility is less perfect. Capital tends to flow in the direction of higher returns but risk considerations, institutional barriers and government policies impede that flow. For private lenders and portfolio investors, foreign stocks and bond are a very imperfect substitute for domestic securities. The profitability of foreign direct investment reflects not only the factor proportions in the host country but also firm-specific considerations of marketing, tariff barriers, tax rules, etc. Foreign direct investment also involves political risks that are fundamentally different from investing in the home country. Further, government policies may seek to encourage or prevent capital inflows or outflows during long periods of time. These restrictions on perfect capital mobility imply that national economic policies that affect domestic saving can also influence domestic capital formation.

In an earlier paper, Charles Horioka and I presented a direct test of the

*The research is part of the Bureau's project on Productivity and Industrial Change in the World Economy. I am grateful to Glenn Hubbard for assistance with this work and the several colleagues, especially Jeffrey Sachs, for discussions.

perfect capital mobility assumption [Feldstein and Horioka (1980)]. We reasoned that with perfect capital mobility there should be no relation between a country's domestic saving rate and its domestic rate of investment. Instead, a sustained increase in saving in any one country should add funds to the world capital market. These funds would then be divided among countries in a way that depends on the relative size of each country's initial capital stock and the elasticity of its marginal efficiency of capital schedule, but that does not depend on which country did the additional saving.

We used data for the industrial countries that are members of the Organization for Economic Cooperation and Development (OECD) to test this implication of perfect capital mobility. We showed first that there are substantial differences in domestic saving rates among these countries and that these differences remain stable over a long period of time. We then estimated regression equations relating the ratio of domestic investment to gross domestic product as the dependent variable to the ratio of domestic saving to GDP as the independent variable. To reduce the impact of cyclical variations and random shocks, both variables were averaged over a minimum of five years.

The evidence overwhelmingly rejected the implication of perfect capital mobility. The relation between the investment ratio and the savings ratio is significantly different from zero in every period that we examined at significance levels that were always less than 0.001. Indeed, the coefficients were always greater than 0.85 and within two standard errors of 1.0. The conclusion was unavoidable that, contrary to the implication of the perfect capital mobility assumption, a sustained increase in the domestic saving ratio caused an almost equal increase in the domestic investment ratio.

The Feldstein–Horioka analysis explicitly assumed that intercountry differences in savings rates are caused by differences in demographic structure, population growth rates and social security retirement income programs. This specification, based on earlier work by Modigliani (1970) and Feldstein (1977), permitted using a simultaneous equations approach to estimating the investment equation with the savings ratio treated as endogenous. These estimates confirmed the ordinary least squares results.[1]

The findings of the Feldstein–Horioka study should not however be overinterpreted. They do not imply that there is no capital mobility nor that there is no tendency of capital to shift toward countries where it can earn a high after-tax rate of return.[2] Strictly interpreted, the Feldstein–Horioka paper only claims to be a test of the extreme hypothesis of perfect capital mobility. More generally, however, it is reasonable to interpret the Feldstein–

[1] The Feldstein–Horioka paper also reported several other tests that will not be repeated here, e.g., adding variables measuring country size and openess to the investment equation. Section 4 of the present paper returns to the problem of simultaneity.

[2] Frisch (1981) and Hartman (1981) present some evidence that investment flows are sensitive to after-tax rates of return.

Horioka findings as evidence that there are substantial imperfections in the international capital market and that a very large share of domestic savings tends to remain in the home country. This implies further that sustained government deficits do reduce domestic capital formation and that corporate income taxes can reduce the net return to capital.[3]

The Feldstein–Horioka study used data for the fifteen year period from 1960 through 1974. The sample period ended just as the dramatic 1973 OPEC price increase had begun to alter substantially the current account deficits of the industrial nations and therefore the international flow of capital. Government interference with international capital movements was also reduced in some countries in the 1970s; the United States, for example, ended its interest equalization tax on foreign borrowing in the United States in 1974, and reduced the pressure on U.S. multinationals to finance overseas investment by borrowing abroad.

One major purpose of the present study is to extend the sample period to the end of the 1970s. The evidence presented in section 2 confirms that the second half of the 1970s was a period of substantially greater international capital flows. Nevertheless, the earlier finding that international differences in saving rates are associated with nearly equal differences in investment rates is reconfirmed. There is no more support for the perfect capital mobility hypothesis in the regression estimates for 1974 through 1979 than there was in the previous fifteen years.

Since net foreign investment is equal to the difference between domestic savings and domestic investment, the strong association between domestic investment and domestic savings implies that there is only a weak association between net foreign investment and domestic savings. The empirical analysis presented in section 3 decomposes net foreign investment and examines the relation between each of the major components of net foreign investment and the domestic saving rate. A different type of decomposition is suggested by the essential equality of net foreign investment and the current account surplus. Section 3 also examines the relation between the components of the current account balance and the domestic

---

[3]I interpret Harberger (1980) as essentially accepting this interpretation. In an earlier paper [Harberger (1978)], he argued that international capital markets were essentially perfect and therefore that rates of returns are equalized internationally just as 'water seeks its own level'. But by his 1980 paper, Harberger concludes: 'My own intuition does not want to accept the notion that increments of investment activity are in all or nearly all countries effectively 100 percent 'financed' by funds flowing in from abroad, and that increments in saving simply spill out into the world capital markets. I find the analogy to a hydraulic system with perhaps a viscous fluid, in which the pipes are partially clogged, and in which some vessels are separated by semipermeable membranes, to be more consonant with my image of the world than the alternative analogy to a hydraulic system where the water flows freely through the system and, essentially instantaneously, finds the same level everywhere' (p. 336). If that flow is slow enough, so that the tendency toward equalization must be measured in decades rather than months or even years, any relevant analysis must regard the capital movements as incomplete and rates of return as potentially unequal.

saving rate. Neither of these analyses suggests any change in the basic conclusion about the long-run independence of international capital flows from domestic savings rates.

Since domestic savings and domestic investment are parts of an interdependent economic system, the regression of investment ratios on savings ratios raises problems of estimation and interpretation. Section 4 discusses the issues of identification and estimation with the help of a minimal theoretical model of investment, savings and international capital flows. The analysis indicates why cross-country data averaged over substantial periods are likely to be a much more reliable basis for testing the hypothesis of perfect capital mobility and for estimating structural paramenters than time series data for individual countries.

Section 5 then examines an explicit model of portfolio choice that shows why sustained changes in domestic savings may have only a small effect on net foreign investment in the long run and yet may also have a more substantial effect on capital flows in the short run.

There is a brief concluding section that comments on some of the limitations of the current paper and that suggests direction for future research.

2. The effect of saving on domestic investment

The basic data for the present analysis are the ratios of investment to GDP and savings to GDP for seventeen OECD countries.[4] These ratios are calculated using the current dollar magnitudes published by the OECD (1981) and therefore adjusted by the OECD to a common set of statistical definitions.

Table 1 presents the values of the saving and investment ratios and of the differences between them. All of the figures refer to gross investment and saving. The first three columns show the mean values of these ratios for each country in the 15-year period from 1960 through 1974.[5] The comparable ratios for the post-OPEC years 1975 through 1979 are shown in the next three columns.

These figures show a striking increase in the absolute differences between the domestic savings rate and the domestic investment rate. In the fifteen years ending in 1974, the difference between the average savings ratio and the average investment ratio ranged from −0.030 (in Greece) to 0.018 (in the Netherlands) with a mean of 0.007 and a standard deviation of 0.016. in contrast, in the second half of the 1970s the range was from −0.042 (in

[4]The other seven OECD countries had to be excluded from the sample because consistent data are not available for the entire period.
[5]These ratios differ from the ratios presented in table 1 of Feldstein and Horioka (1980) only because of data revisions.

Table 1

Savings and investment ratios in OECD countries.[a]

	Mean values, 1960–1974			Mean values, 1975–1979		
	S/Y	I/Y	$S/Y-I/Y$	S/Y	I/Y	$S/Y-I/Y$
Australia	0.245	0.267	−0.022	0.217	0.231	−0.014
Austria	0.287	0.284	0.003	0.250	0.267	−0.017
Belgium	0.233	0.224	0.009	0.201	0.215	−0.014
Canada	0.218	0.231	−0.013	0.209	0.235	−0.026
Denmark	0.220	0.248	−0.028	0.194	0.228	−0.034
Finland	0.288	0.306	−0.024	0.276	0.318	−0.042
France	0.251	0.250	0.001	0.229	0.232	−0.003
Germany	0.270	0.262	0.008	0.229	0.222	0.007
Greece	0.222	0.252	−0.030	0.247	0.276	−0.029
Ireland	0.197	0.225	−0.028	0.234	0.272	−0.038
Italy	0.237	0.227	0.010	0.221	0.214	0.007
Japan	0.366	0.358	0.008	0.305	0.317	−0.012
Netherlands	0.284	0.266	0.018	0.269	0.215	0.054
New Zealand	0.230	0.255	−0.025	0.205	0.275	−0.070
Sweden	0.243	0.241	0.002	0.195	0.211	−0.016
United Kingdom	0.189	0.193	−0.004	0.177	0.190	−0.013
United States	0.188	0.188	0.000	0.171	0.179	−0.008

[a]*Source*: 'National accounts of the OECD countries: 1950–1979' (OECD, Paris, 1981). S/Y is gross domestic savings divided by GDP. I/Y is gross domestic investment divided by GDP.

Finland) to 0.054 (in the Netherlands) with a mean of −0.016 and a standard deviation of 0.025.

For virtually every industrial country, the second half of the 1970s represented a time when domestic investment exceeded domestic savings. This in turn implied that net foreign investment was negative and therefore that the current account was in deficit. The negative net foreign investment for the industrial countries as a whole in these years was largely a reflection of the higher prices being paid for imported oil and the resulting surpluses of the OPEC countries.

Despite the substantial increase in the size and variability of international capital flows, the second half of the 1970s showed the same strong tendency for countries with high domestic savings rates to have high rates of domestic investment. Table 2 presents estimates of the basic investment equation,

$$I_i/Y_i = \alpha + \beta[S_i/Y_i] + \varepsilon_i, \tag{1}$$

where I_i is domestic investment in country i, S_i is domestic savings, Y_i is GDP, and ε_i is a random disturbance. The equation is estimated with the sample of seventeen countries listed in table 1 and with the investment and savings ratios averaged over several different subperiods as well as for the entire 20-year period from 1960 through 1979.

The estimate for the second half of the 1970s indicates that an additional 'dollar' (pound, franc, mark, etc.) of domestic saving raised domestic investment by 0.865 dollars with a standard error of 0.185.[6] Comparison with the other subperiods indicates that the response of investment to savings was at least as high in this final period as in any of the earlier periods. This was true even though, as the lower $\bar{R}^2$ implies, there was more 'unpredictable' variation in domestic investment during this period.[7]

For the 20-year period as a whole, each extra 'dollar' of saving was associated with 0.796 additional dollars of investment. With a standard error of 0.112, this is clearly significantly different from zero at any relevant probability level. The alternative null hypothesis, i.e., that the coefficient of S/Y is 1.0, can be rejected at a probability level of 10 percent, implying that capital does tend to flow to countries with low savings rates although certainly much less than perfect capital mobility would imply.

The first five equations reported in table 2 refer to gross saving and gross investment. Since capital accumulation depends on net investment, it is interesting to consider also the relation between net investment and net saving. Since this requires subtracting an estimate of depreciation from both variables, any error in measuring depreciation will tend to bias the estimated coefficient toward one. This potential bias is consistent with the result presented in the sixth equation of table 2 that shows a coefficient of 0.99 for the regression of the net investment ratio on the net savings rate.

If there were no problems of measuring savings, investment and international transactions, the difference between gross domestic savings and gross domestic investment would be equal to the balance on current account (CA). This suggests that, instead of using the conventional national income account measure of domestic savings, the value of gross domestic savings could be defined as the sum of gross domestic investment and the current account balance: $\hat{S} = I + CA$.[8] The basic equation is reestimated for the decade of the 1970s with this derived measure of savings and presented in the final line of table 2. The coefficient of 0.886 is only slightly higher than the previous estimate of 0.843 for this decade and show that this source of measurement error does not influence the basic result.

The estimation of eq. (1) with a cross-section of country averages implicitly assumes that each country's disturbance is purely random and uncorrelated

---

[6]If the equation is estimated in level form rather than ratio form, the coefficient is very close to one but this reflects the pure scale effect. Only ratio equations are therefore presented in this paper.

[7]These differences in domestic investment reflected such things as differences in the response of profitability and of capacity utilization to the 1973 OPEC shock and to the rising rates of inflation.

[8]This is the procedure used by Sachs (1981a).

Table 2

The relation between domestic savings ratios and domestic investment ratios.[a]

Equation	Sample period	Definition	Const.	S/Y	$\bar{R}^2$
1	1975–1979	gross	0.046 (0.042)	0.865 (0.185)	0.57
2	1970–1974	gross	0.048 (0.033)	0.826 (0.125)	0.73
3	1970–1979	gross	0.047 (0.036)	0.843 (0.146)	0.67
4	1960–1969	gross	0.059 (0.022)	0.779 (0.090)	0.82
5	1960–1979	gross	0.057 (0.028)	0.796 (0.112)	0.75
6	1960–1979	net	0.011 (0.016)	0.993 (0.111)	0.83
7	1970–1979	gross; derived	0.039 (0.027)	0.886 (0.112)	0.79

[a]The coefficients refer to eq. (1) in the text. Standard errors are shown in parentheses. The 'gross' equations relate gross investment and saving while the 'net' equation relates net investment and saving.

with the savings ratio. If country investment rates do differ systematically for some reason that is not directly related to the savings ratio, eq. (1) should be replaced by an equation in which the constant term is allowed to differ among countries,

$$I_i/Y_i = \alpha_i + \beta(S_i/Y_i) + \varepsilon_i. \tag{2}$$

If eq. (2) is the correct specification but eq. (1) is estimated, the coefficient of β will be biased if α_i is correlated with the savings ratio.

This potential source of bias can be eliminated by extending the analysis to two observations for each country so that the constant values of the α_i's can be eliminated. If eq. (2) is generalized by assuming that all investment ratios may shift by a constant amount δ between times t and t', the new specification may be written as[9]

$$I_{it}/Y_{it} - I_{it'}/Y_{it'} = \delta + \beta[S_{it}/Y_{it} - S_{it'}/Y_{it'}] + \varepsilon_{it} - \varepsilon_{it'}. \tag{3}$$

[9]Although the α_i's are eliminated by first differencing in this way, they can be estimated in a second step once β and δ are estimated. The procedure is exactly equivalent to estimations with individual constant terms and two observations for each country.

Defining the latter period as 1973 through 1979 (i.e., the years affected by the OPEC price shock) and the earlier period as the previous seven 'pre-OPEC' years implies an estimate of β of 1.024 with a standard error of 0.227, and an estimate of δ of 0.013 with a standard error of 0.005. The $\bar{R}^2$ for this equation is 0.55. Thus countries that increased their saving between the earlier period and the later period found that their investment increased on average by an equal amount between the two dates. There is certainly no support in this estimate for the view that increases in saving merely augmented the total world supply of funds and that such capital was allocated among countries in unconstrained pursuit of the highest rate of return.[10]

An alternative method of estimating eq. (2) is to use each of the annual observations in a pooled cross-section of time series. Using data for the entire 20-year period[11] implies an estimate of 0.771 for β with a standard error of 0.046, very similar to the estimate of 0.796 shown in table 2 and obtained when the annual data are averaged to produce a single value for each country.

The similarity of the estimates with individual constant terms and with averaged data suggests that including the individual constant terms has little effect on the estimate of β. This is confirmed when eq. (1) is re-estimated with individual annual observations for all countries for the 20-year period. The estimate of β is 0.797 with a standard error of 0.031, virtually identical to the estimates in table 2.

The use of individual annual observations makes it possible to estimate a more general dynamic relation between savings and investment. When a lagged value of the savings ratio is added to the basic specification, its coefficient is relatively small and negative,

$$I_{it}/Y_{it} = 0.074 + 0.832(S_{it} - Y_{it}) - 0.109(S_{i,t-1}/Y_{i,t-1}), \qquad R^2 = 0.68. \qquad (4)$$
$$\phantom{I_{it}/Y_{it} = 0.074 + 0.}(0.033)\phantom{(S_{it} - Y_{it}) - 0.}(0.033)$$

The negative coefficient of the lagged savings variable suggests that investment does not adjust to savings gradually but overadjusts at first. The coefficients of further lagged values are smaller and not statistically significant. Finally, using the annual observations to estimate the average effect of year to year changes in saving among all countries indicates that

$$I_{it}/Y_{it} - I_{i,t-1}/Y_{i,t-1} = -0.0001 + 0.863[S_{it}/Y_{it} - S_{i,t-1}/Y_{i,t-1}], \qquad (5)$$
$$\phantom{I_{it}/Y_{it} - I_{i,t-1}/Y_{i,t-1} = -0.0001 + }(0.040)$$

$$\bar{R}^2 = 0.60.$$

[10]The use of differences in saving and investment ratios may cause simultaneous equations bias that is not present in the estimates of table 2. This is discussed in section 4.

[11]Some individual annual observations are missing, reducing the sample to 320 observations.

Thus, even year to year increases in saving tend on average to be associated with increases in domestic investment in the saving country by approximately equal amounts.[12]

3. Domestic savings and the components of international capital flows

The basic investment equation can be rewritten in terms of net foreign investment and then used to analyze the relation between saving and the components of international capital flows. More specifically, subtracting the savings ratio from both sides of eq. (1) and multiplying by minus one yields

$$(S_i - I_i)/Y_i = -\alpha + (1-\beta)(S_i/Y_i) - \varepsilon_i. \tag{6}$$

The national income accounts divide the excess of domestic saving over domestic investment into net foreign investment (NFI) plus the statistical discrepancy in the savings–investment account (SDS).[13] Substituting this into eq. (6) implies

$$NFI_i/Y_i = -\alpha + (1-\beta)(S_i/Y_i) - SDS_i/Y_i + \varepsilon_i. \tag{7}$$

If SDS/Y were uncorrelated with the savings ratio, the estimate of β obtained from eq. (7) would be exactly the same as the estimate obtained from eq. (1). In fact, there is a small positive association between the statistical discrepency ratio and the saving ratio in the sample, implying that the estimate of β implied by estimating eq. (7) with the decade averages of NFI/Y and S/Y for 1970 through 1979 yields

$$NFI_i/Y_i = 0.019 + 0.092(S_i/Y_i).$$
$$\quad\quad (0.002)\ (0.785) \tag{8}$$

The implied value of β is 0.908 and therefore slightly higher than the estimate presented in table 2. The coefficient of 0.092 implies that each extra 'dollar' of domestic saving causes a capital export of approximately 9 cents, but the very large standard error indicates that there is no statistically significant relation at all between net foreign investment and the domestic savings rate.[14]

Net foreign investment can itself be decomposed into the four major components of the international capital account (direct investment; portfolio

[12]Sections 4 and 5 show that the similarity of the coefficients based on long-term averages and annual changes may be subject to different interpretations.

[13]The net foreign investment of the United States thus represents the net investment abroad financed by savings in the United States.

[14]The much larger standard error in eq. (8) than in table 2 reflects the importance of the statistical discrepancy.

investment; other long-term capital flows; and short-term capital flows) plus the total change in official reserves, the net errors and omissions, and a remaining minor category of the official settlements balance. The lack of a significant or substantial relation between domestic savings and net foreign investment as a whole could in principal reflect a balancing of positive and negative relationships among different components. For example, portfolio investment outflows might respond positively to the domestic savings rate only to be offset by changes in official reserves.

In fact, in each of the separate regressions, the coefficient of the savings ratio is always less than its standard error. There is no indication of a relation between sustained differences among countries in savings rates and any of the components of net foreign investment.

Net foreign investment is conceptually equal to the balance on current account.[15] This suggests another decomposition that might be useful in analyzing the effect of intercountry savings differences.[16] The relation between the current account balance and the savings ratio can be decomposed into the separate effects of savings on: merchandise exports; merchandise imports; other credits for goods, services and investment income; other debits for goods, services and investment income; private unrequited transfers; and public unrequited transfers. None of the six regression coefficients relating a current account component as a fraction of GDP to savings as a fraction of GDP had an absolute value as large as 0.1 and none was as large as its standard error. The lack of a significant relationship between the current account balance and savings reflects a lack of relation between each of its components and savings.

In short, the two decompositions that have been examined confirm the finding of section 2 that there is no relation between sustained differences in domestic savings rates and the external position of the country.

4. Parameter identification and estimation with cross-country and time-series data

The regression of the domestic investment ratio on the domestic savings ratio is an intuitively appealing test of the hypothesis of perfect capital mobility. Nevertheless, there are fundamental problems of identification and estimation that should be considered when it is recognized that both savings and investment are endogenous variables in an economic system. Feldstein and Horioka (1980) discussed the problem of simultaneous equations bias briefly and suggested that this was likely to be much less serious in estimates based on cross-country data averaged over long periods of time than in

---

[15]In practice, the two numbers differ because of such things as the allocation of special drawing rights and the statistical treatment of gold, extraordinary military transactions, etc.

[16]This analysis was suggested to me by Douglas Purvis.

estimates based on annual time series for individual countries. As I noted in the introduction to the present paper, instrumental variable estimates suggested by a simultaneous equations model confirmed the ordinary least squares results.

The current section presents an explicit model and uses it to assess the regression of domestic investment on domestic saving as a test of the perfect capital mobility hypothesis and, when international capital mobility is less than perfect, as an estimate of the effect on domestic investment of endogenous shifts in domestic saving.

The simplest model that is adequate for this purpose requires a domestic investment function, a domestic savings function, a net foreign investment function, and a savings–investment equilibrium condition. I shall assume that all investment is financed by issuing bonds and that the demand for gross domestic investment (I) can be written as a function of the domestic real interest rate (r) plus a random shock (u),

$$I = \phi(r) + u, \tag{9}$$

with $\phi' < 0$. A similar specification of the domestic savings function,

$$S = \psi(r) + v, \tag{10}$$

provides that the supply of saving is a non-decreasing function of the real interest rate ($\psi' \geq 0$) plus a random shock.

Writing N for net foreign investment (i.e., the net outflow of capital from the home country), the net capital outflow in response to a higher interest rate can be written as

$$N = \eta(r) + e, \tag{11}$$

where $\eta'(r) \leq 0$ implies that a higher real domestic interest rate reduces (or leaves unchanged if $\eta' = 0$) net foreign investment (or causes a greater net inflow from abroad, i.e., a negative net foreign investment), and e is a random shock. Perfect capital mobility implies that $\eta' = -\infty$. More generally, η' could differ between the short run and the long run and could vary among countries or time periods. Some reasons for such differences are discussed below.

Equilibrium in the goods market requires that domestic saving equal domestic investment plus net foreign investment,[17]

$$S = I + N. \tag{12}$$

---

[17]In a simple theoretical model, this is equivalent to the equilibrium condition $S = I + X - M$, where X is exports and M is imports, since net foreign investment equals the current account surplus.

These four equations determine values for the four endogenous variables I, S N and r as functions of the three random distributions u, v and e.

Substituting (9), (10) and (11) in (12) yields

$$\psi(r) + v = \phi(r) + u + \eta(r) + e. \tag{13}$$

Differentiating and solving for the change in the real interest rate implies:

$$dr = (du - dv + de)/(\psi' - \phi' - \eta'). \tag{14}$$

Since $\psi' \geq 0$, $\phi' < 0$ and $\eta' \leq 0$, the denominator is unambiguously positive. Thus the interest rate rises when there is a positive shock to domestic investment demand ($du > 0$) or to the domestic demand for net foreign investment ($de > 0$).

The effect of investment and savings shocks on net foreign investment can be obtained by combining eqs. (11) and (14),

$$dN = \eta' \, dr + de = \eta'[du - dv + de]/(\psi' - \phi' - \eta') + de. \tag{15}$$

To interpret eq. (15), recall that $dN > 0$ means an increased capital outflow and that $\eta' \leq 0$. Thus an increase in domestic savings ($dv > 0$) causes an increase in net foreign investment and, therefore, both a capital outflow and a current account surplus. With perfect capital mobility, $\eta' = -\infty$ and $dN/dv = 1$; in this case, all of the additional domestic saving goes abroad. Similarly, even with a finite value of η', an increase in domestic investment ($du > 0$) causes a decrease in net foreign investment and therefore both a capital inflow and a current account deficit.[18]

This brief description of the international effects of shifts in domestic savings and investment has ignored the exchange rate movements that are likely to occur as part of the process of change. An autonomous increase in domestic investment demand (or decrease in savings) will raise the domestic interest rate and cause a real appreciation of the home currency. With this increase in the exchange rate there is a current account deficit that accommodates the capital inflow. The model is consistent with this exchange rate behavior even though the exchange rate is not explicitly modelled.

Combining eqs. (9) and (14) shows the relation between domestic investment and a shift in domestic savings,

$$dI = \phi'[du - dv + de]/(\psi' - \phi' - \eta') + du, \tag{16}$$

which implies

[18]This is the case discussed by Sachs (1981a, b). I will return to his empirical results later in this section.

$$dI/dv = \phi'/(\phi' + \eta' - \psi').$$ (17)

With perfect capital mobility, $\eta' = -\infty$ and $dI/dv = 0$. At the other extreme, if international capital movements do not respond to the interest rate, $\eta' = 0$ and

$$dI/dv = \phi'/(\phi' - \psi').$$ (18)

Since $\phi' < 0$ and $\psi' \geq 0$, in this case $dI/dv \leq 1$. If ψ' is 'small' relative to $-\phi'$, i.e., if the interest elasticity of savings is small relative to the interest elasticity of investment, dI/dv will be close to 1.

Now that the theoretical relation between domestic saving and investment has been clarified it is possible to examine more explicitly the interpretation of the regression coefficient estimated by regressing the investment ratio on the savings ratio, i.e., the coefficient of eq. (1) estimated to be approximately one in the cross-country regressions reported in table 2. The regression coefficient of eq. (1) is the ratio of the covariance between investment and saving divided by the variance of saving. The variance of savings can be approximated in terms of the current model in the following way. First, differentiate eq. (10) and eliminate dr with the help of eq. (14) to obtain

$$dS = \psi'[du - dv + de]/(\psi' - \phi' - \eta') + dv.$$ (19)

Now evaluate each of the derivatives at the mean value of the corresponding variable, square both sides, and take expectations. Since the expected value of the squared deviation from the mean is the variance.,

$$\sigma_{SS} = E(dS)^2$$

$$= [(\phi' + \eta')^2 \sigma_{vv} + (\psi')^2(\sigma_{uu} + \sigma_{ee} + 2\sigma_{ue})$$

$$- 2\psi'(\phi' + \eta')(\sigma_{uv} + \sigma_{ev})]/(\psi' - \phi' - \eta')^2.$$ (20)

Similarly, combining eqs. (16) and (19) yields an approximation for the covariance between S and I.

$$\sigma_{SI} = E(dS \cdot dI)$$

$$= E[-(\phi' + \eta')dv + \psi'(du + de)]$$

$$\times [(\psi' - \eta')du - \phi'(dv - de)]/(\psi' - \phi' - \eta')^2$$

$$= [-(\phi' + \eta')(\psi' - \eta')\sigma_{uv} + \phi'(\phi' + \eta')(\sigma_{vv} - \sigma_{ev})$$

$$+ \psi'(\psi' - \eta')(\sigma_{uu} + \sigma_{ue}) - \psi'\phi'(\sigma_{uv} - \sigma_{ue} + \sigma_{ve} - \sigma_{ee})]/(\psi' - \phi' - \eta')^2.$$ (21)

The regression of I on S can be approximated by the ratio of σ_{SI} to σ_{SS} or

$$\hat{\beta} = [-(\phi' + \eta')(\psi' - \eta')\sigma_{uv} + \phi'(\phi' + \eta')(\sigma_{vv} - \sigma_{ev})$$

$$+ \psi'(\psi' - \eta')(\sigma_{uu} + \sigma_{ue}) - \psi'\phi'(\sigma_{uv} - \sigma_{ue} + \sigma_{ve} - \sigma_{ee})]$$

$$/[(\phi' + \eta')^2 \sigma_{vv} + (\psi')^2(\sigma_{uu} + \sigma_{ee} + 2\sigma_{ue}) - 2\psi'(\phi' + \eta')(\sigma_{uv} + \sigma_{ev})]. \quad (22)$$

With the help of eq. (22), we can now consider two questions. First, what is the implication of perfect capital mobility for the estimated coefficient $\hat{\beta}$? Second, what is the relation between the estimated coefficient $\hat{\beta}$ and the effect on domestic investment of a shift in domestic saving (dI/dv)?

4.1. Testing the perfect capital mobility hypothesis

With perfect capital mobility, $\eta' = -\infty$ and eq. (22) implies that

$$\hat{\beta} = \sigma_{uv}/\sigma_{vv}. \quad (23)$$

Thus perfect capital mobility is consistent with a positive parameter estimate only to the extent that the exogenous shifts in saving and investment are positively correlated. The likely magnitude of the correlation between savings and investment shifts depends on the nature of the data.

With time-series observations for an individual country, demand shocks could well make $\sigma_{uv} > 0$. A downturn in economic activity might cause savings to be relatively low (because consumption depends on permanent income) and might also cause investment to be relatively low (because of low capacity utilization). Similarly, a supply shock that lowers income and profitability might also reduce both saving and investment. In either of these cases, the regression coefficient $\hat{\beta}$ could be positive and substantial even if there is perfect capital mobility. Conversely time-series data for an individual country could also have $\sigma_{uv} < 0$; an exogenous temporary increase in the propensity to save ($dv > 0$) could reduce aggregate output and thereby induce a decline in investment ($du < 0$). Estimates of β based on time-series data for a single country are thus an unreliable basis for evaluating the hypothesis of perfect international capital mobility.[19]

In contrast, when the sample is a cross-section of countries and the observations for each country are averaged over a long period of time, there is no reason to expect any correlations between intercountry differences in

[19]Feldstein and Horioka estimated time-series regressions for individual countries and presented the results in NBER Working Paper No. 310, but did not include these time-series estimates in the published version [Feldstein and Horioka (1980)] because we concluded that the problem of simultaneous-equations bias meant that these individual country coefficients could not be interpreted as estimates of the effect on investment of exogenous changes in saving.

the exogenous component of saving and in the exogenous component of investment. These intercountry saving differences reflect such things as the demographic structure of the population, the extent to which unfunded social security substitutes for private saving, the average level of government deficits, consumer credit and mortgage arrangements, and the long-term rise in income since current retirees were working and saving. Sustained differences in investment rates that are not just a reflection of savings differences (through the effect of saving on the cost of capital) reflect such things as business tax rules and the effects of unions on profitability. The intercountry variance in exogenous investment shifts is thus likely to be smaller than the intercountry variance in exogenous saving shifts ($\sigma_{uu} < \sigma_{vv}$), and the covariance between the two is likely to be small or zero. If there is a non-zero covariance, there appears to be no presumption about its sign.

Eq. (23) shows that the estimated values of β presented in table 2 are not consistent with perfect capital mobility if σ_{uv} is zero or negative. Moreover, even if there is a positive covariance between exogenous savings differences and exogenous investment differences, the high values of the estimated β's are not consistent with perfect capital mobility if the variance of the savings shifts (σ_{vv}) is large relative to the variance of the investment shifts (σ_{uu}). To see this, note that eq. (23) can be rewritten as

$$\hat{\beta} = \sigma_{uv}/\sigma_{vv}$$

$$= \rho_{uv}(\sigma_{uu}\sigma_{vv})^{\frac{1}{2}}/\sigma_{vv}$$

$$= \rho_{uv}[\sigma_{uu}/\sigma_{vv}]^{\frac{1}{2}}, \tag{24}$$

where ρ is the correlation between u and v. Since $\rho \leq 1$, with perfect capital mobility $\hat{\beta}$ is at most equal to the ratio of the standard deviation of the investment shifts to the standard deviation of the savings shifts. Since the observed estimates of β are approximately one, eq. (24) shows that the evidence is not consistent with both perfect capital mobility and a low ratio of σ_{uu}/σ_{vv}.

It is easily shown that with perfect capital mobility the correlation between savings and investment is the same as the correlation between u and v.[20] The observed correlations between saving and investment (i.e., the square root of the R^2 values reported in table 2) imply implausibily high correlations between the exogenous components of saving and investment.

In short, the identifying restriction in cross-country data that $\sigma_{uv} \leq 0$ or

---

[20]With perfect capital mobility, the regression of saving on investment produces a coefficient equal to $\beta_{SI} = \sigma_{uv}/\sigma_{uu}$. Multiply this by $\beta_{IS} = \sigma_{uv}/\sigma_{vv}$ from eq. (23) and note that $\beta_{IS}\beta_{SI} = \sigma_{uv}^2/\sigma_{uu}\sigma_{vv} = \rho_{uv}^2$. But the product of a regression coefficient and the coefficient for the reverse regression is equal to the squared correlation; i.e. $\beta_{IS}\beta_{SI} = \rho_{SI}^2$. Thus $\rho_{IS}^2 = \rho_{uv}^2$.

that σ_{uu}/σ_{vv} is small, is sufficient to permit interpreting the observed regressions of investment on savings presented in table 2 as strong evidence against perfect capital mobility. Alternatively, the restriction that the correlation between exogenous saving and investment differences is not greater than 0.5 also implies rejection of the perfect capital mobility hypothesis.

Estimates of β based on a cross-country sample of *changes* in investment and saving provides a different type of evidence against the hypothesis of perfect capital mobility. In such a regression, any association between the *levels* of exogenous saving and investment effects is irrelevant. Instead, σ_{uv} in eq. (23) must be interpreted as a relation between shifts in saving and shifts in investment. If countries in which the exogenous component of saving has increased between two dates (or two periods) tend to be those countries in which the exogenous component of investment has also increased, $\sigma_{uv} > 0$ and the estimate of β can be high even if there is perfect capital mobility. The danger of this covariance being large is greatest when the data can reflect changes from one phase of a business cycle to the next. It is therefore reassuring that the estimate of $\beta = 1.04$ based on the changes in saving and investment reflected a comparison of two periods of six years (1968–1973 and 1974–1980) and that similar results were obtained by Feldstein and Horioka for a different set of years ($\beta = 0.724$ with a standard error of 0.158 based on the changes for 1960–1969 to 1970–1974).[21]

4.2. Estimating dI/dv

Under what plausible conditions does the estimate of β based on eq. (1) represent the effect on domestic investment of a shift in the exogenous factors influencing saving? Equivalently, when does the value of $\hat{\beta}$ given in eq. (22) equal the value of dI/dv shown in eq. (17)? And, more generally, even when exact identification is not achieved, does $\hat{\beta}$ tend to dI/dv as certain limiting conditions are achieved?

Consider first the case in which saving rates are not sensitive to the interest rate ($\psi' = 0$) and in which the exogenous differences in saving among countries are not correlated with exogenous differences in the domestic investment function or the net foreign investment function ($\sigma_{vu} = \sigma_{ve} = 0$). In this case, eqs. (22) and (17) imply that $\hat{\beta} = \phi'/(\phi' + \eta') = dI/dv$ and there is no simultaneous equation bias.[22]

Although these assumptions may not hold exactly, they may be a reasonable approximation for cross-country data based on averages over extended periods. In this context, the interest elasticities of domestic

---

[21]Although the 1968–1973 to 1971–1980 comparison is influenced by the OPEC-induced slowdown, the comparison based on the earlier pair of periods is not biased by a supply shock.

[22]The assumptions of $\psi' = 0$ and $\sigma_{ve} = \sigma_{vu} = 0$ make the model recursive with respect to S and, therefore, make ordinary least squares an unbiased estimator.

investment may be high relative to the interest elasticity of domestic savings. Similarly, the variance of domestic savings may be large relative to the covariance between exogenous savings differences and exogenous differences in investment and net foreign capital. The value of $\hat{\beta}$ in eq. (22) tends to dI/dv as ψ'/ϕ', σ_{uv}/σ_{vv} and σ_{ve}/σ_{vv} all tend to zero.

An alternative specification places no restriction on the interest sensitivity of domestic savings but posits that the exogenous differences among countries in saving rates are large relative to the exogenous differences in domestic and foreign investment: thus σ_{uu}/σ_{vv} and σ_{ee}/σ_{vv} are both small and, therefore, σ_{uv}/σ_{vv}, $\sigma_{ev}\sigma_{vv}$ and σ_{ue}/σ_{vv} are also small. Taking the limit as σ_{vv} grows relative to the other variances and covariances implies that $\hat{\beta}$ tends to $\phi'/(\phi'+\eta')$. Since the true value of dI/dv is $\phi'/(\phi'+\eta'-\psi)$, the estimate overstates the true value. More specifically, the ratio of the sample estimate ($\hat{\beta}$) to the true value of dI/dv is $(\phi'+\eta'-\psi')/(\phi'+\eta')=1-\psi'/(\phi'+\eta')$. To express these as elasticities, let $\varepsilon_{Sr}=\psi'r/S$ be the saving elasticity, $\varepsilon_{Ir}=-\phi'r/I$ be the investment elasticity, and $\varepsilon_{Nr}=-\eta'r/N$ be the elasticity of net foreign investment. Thus

$$\hat{\beta}/(ds/dv)=1+S\varepsilon_{Sr}/(I\varepsilon_{Ir}+N\varepsilon_{Nr})$$
$$=1+(S/I)\varepsilon_{Sr}/(\varepsilon_{Ir}+(N/I)\varepsilon_{Nr}). \qquad (25)$$

Since S/I is approximately one and N/I is very close to zero, $\hat{\beta}/(dI/dv)$ is approximately one plus the ratio of ε_{Sr} to ε_{Ir}. Most empirical research indicates that this ratio is low and, therefore, that the relative bias in $\hat{\beta}$ is small.

4.3. The regression of savings on investment

In an interesting pair of papers, Sachs (1981a, b) emphasized the response of international capital flows to temporary shifts in domestic propensities to invest. Sachs showed that countries that increased their share of investment in GDP between 1968–1973 and 1974–1979 also experienced substantial increases in net capital inflows, i.e., substantial decreases in net foreign investment. As a leading example of this, Sachs pointed to the major flow of capital into Norway that accompanied the Norwegian investment boom caused by Norway's discovery of North Sea oil.

Eq. (26) is typical of the type of results reported by Sachs,[23]

$$\Delta[NFI/Y]_i=-0.227-0.561\,\Delta[I/Y]_i, \qquad (26)$$
$$\quad\;\;(0.039)\;\;(0.148)$$

$$\bar{R}^2=0.46,$$

[23]The dependent variable in Sachs' equation is actually the current account balance, but results for the current account and for NFI are very similar.

where $\Delta(NFI/Y)$ denotes the average NFI/Y ratio in country i in 1974–1979 minus that ratio in 1968–1973, and $\Delta(I/Y)$ denotes the corresponding change in the investment ratio. The paramenter estimate implies that one 'dollar' increase in domestic investment is associated with a net capital inflow of 0.56 dollars. Thus, treating I/Y as the independent variable appears to imply that net capital flows play a much more significant role.

It would be wrong, however, to interpret -0.56 as an estimate of dN/du. Unless the model is recursive with investment having no interest elasticity ($\phi' = 0$) and no covariance between shifts in domestic investment and shifts in either saving or foreign investment ($\sigma_{uv} = \sigma_{ue} = 0$), the regression coefficient will not be an unbiased estimate of dN/du. Since the equation is based on changes in domestic investment and changes in capital flows, such lack of covariance is unlikely. If, for example, a change in economic conditions between the two periods caused not only an exogenous increase in domestic investment but also a shift from foreign investment to domestic investment ($\sigma_{ue} > 0$), the absolute value of the estimated coefficient will overstate the induced capital inflow.

The ambiguity that results from using the change form of the regression can be avoided by examining the relation between the level of net foreign investment and the level of domestic investment. Since net foreign investment is essentially equal to the excess of domestic saving over domestic investment, an alternative specification is the regression of the domestic saving ratio on the domestic investment ratio, i.e., just reversing the left- and right-hand variables of eq. (1). The finding of a regression coefficient significantly less than one implies that intercountry differences in investment are associated with international capital flows to finance that investment.[24]

For the final five years of the data (1974–1979), the results with such a specification support Sachs' view. The regression coefficient in the regression of S/Y on I/Y is 0.66 with a standard error of 0.14. Taken at face value, this implies that each extra dollar of exogenous domestic investment induces a capital inflow of 34 cents.[25]

The most recent five years are, however, an unusual subperiod. For the entire 20-year period, the regression of S/Y on I/Y is 0.94 with a standard error of 0.13. The point estimate thus implies that each dollar of additional domestic investment is associated with a net capital inflow of only 6 cents; with a standard error of 13 cents, this is clearly not significantly different from zero. Similarly, for the decade of the 1960s the regression of S/Y on I/Y is 1.05 with a standard error of 0.12, while for the first half of the 1970s the regression coefficient is 0.088 with a standard error of 0.13.

---

[24]There are of course still identification problems in interpreting the regression coefficient as an estimate of dS/du [and therefore making inferences about $d(S-I)/du$] but these are similar to the ones discussed in sections 4.1 and 4.2.

[25]See the previous footnote.

One possible interpretation is that conditions have changed in the mid-1970s to make international capital flows more sensitive to differences in yields. To support this one might point to the end of the U.S. interest equalization tax in 1974, to the growth of the Eurodollar market and of the OPEC balances, and to the relaxation of restrictions on portfolio investment that were occurring in a variety of OECD countries [OECD (1980)]. Nevertheless, there is also the alternative possibility that the regression coefficient for this brief period provides a biased estimate of dS/du because of a temporary covariance among the 'exogenous' saving and investment factors during this unusual period. Only further time will tell.

It is clear, however, that for the previous fifteen years, the regressions of S/Y on I/Y as well as the regressions of I/Y on S/Y support the conclusion that higher levels of domestic investment do not induce foreign capital inflows but can only be financed by domestic saving.

5. Portfolio adjustment and capital flows in the long run and the short run

The analysis of section 4 indicates that the regression estimates are more relevant as a guide to the long-run response of international capital movements to changes in domestic savings and investment than to their short-run response. Coefficient estimates based on annual variations in savings and investment are subject to potentially severe simultaneous equation bias that is not present when annual observations are averaged over a decade or more, and the regression is estimated with a cross-country sample of these averages. The empirical estimates based on such data that were presented in sections 2 and 3 imply that, for the 1960s and 1970s as a whole, higher savings rates induce higher rates of domestic investment but virtually no increase in net foreign investment.

The behavior of capital flows in the short run may be quite different. Although the empirical analysis of sections 2 and 3 is not directly relevant, theoretical considerations suggest that the short run response of international capital flows to changes in domestic saving may be much greater than the long-run response. The essential reason for this is that the short-run capital flow is part of a once-for-all adjustment of the international portfolio. When the adjustment is complete, the rate of capital flow returns to a lower level governed by the rate of growth of the world capital stock and the share of international assets in the equilibrium portfolio.[26]

To make these ideas more precise, consider an investor who divides his portfolio between domestic and foreign assets. Domestic assets earn an

---

[26]Although early models of Mundell (1968) and others did not distinguish between the adjustment phase and the steady state flow, the importance of distinguishing a temporary capital flow as part of a once-for-all capital stock adjustment has been recognized at least since Branson (1970). See also Branson (1979), Cumby and Obstfeld (1982), Girton and Henderson (1977) and Obstfeld (1981).

uncertain return r, with subjective mean μ and subjective variance σ_{oo}. Foreign assets earn an uncertain return, r^*, with subjective mean μ^* and variance σ_{**}. The covariance between the returns is σ_{*o}. If the investor's preferences can be summarized by a utility function that is a quadratic function of the portfolio return, the investor will maximize

$$Eu[pr^* + (1-p)r)] = p\mu^* + (1-p)\mu$$

$$-\tfrac{1}{2}\gamma[p^2\sigma_{**} + (1-p)^2\sigma_{oo} + 2p(1-p)\sigma_{o*}], \qquad (27)$$

where E is the expectations operator, p is the proportion of the portfolio invested abroad, and $\gamma > 0$ is a measure of risk aversion.

The first-order maximization condition implies that the optimal proportion invested abroad (p^*) is

$$p^* = [\mu^* - \mu - \gamma(\sigma_{o*} - \sigma_{oo})]/\gamma(\sigma_{oo} + \sigma_{**} - 2\sigma_{o*}), \qquad (28)$$

the denominator is γ times the variance of $r - r^*$ and is therefore unambiguously positive. The numerator is easier to discuss if we replace σ_{o*} by $\rho\lambda\sigma_{oo}$ where ρ is the correlation between r and r^* and $\lambda^2 = \sigma_{**}/\sigma_{oo}$, the ratio of the foreign variance to the domestic variance. Thus

$$p^* = [\mu^* - \mu - \gamma(\rho\lambda - 1)\sigma_{oo}]/\gamma(\sigma_{oo} + \sigma_{**} - 2\sigma_{o*}). \qquad (29)$$

It is clear that even if the foreign expected return exceeds the domestic return ($\mu^* > \mu$), the investor may not wish to invest abroad, i.e., $p^* \leq 0$. This can happen only if (1) there is a positive correlation between domestic and foreign rates of return (reflecting, for example, the international business cycle or common long-term trends in productivity and profitability) and (2) the subjective variance on the foreign return exceeds the subjective variance on the domestic return. The subjective variance on the foreign return may be very large because investors lack information about the foreign economy, its individual firms, accounting practices, etc.[27] If $p^* < 0$, the investor may be constrained to a corner solution with no foreign investment. It is clear that since λ reflects *subjective* variances, investors in two countries may both decide not to invest in the other's securities.

Conversely, eq. (29) implies that p^* may be greater than zero even if $\mu^* < \mu$ if foreign investing provides a useful diversification, i.e., if $\rho\lambda < 1$. Thus

[27]A recent story in the Wall Street Journal reporting from Tokyo summarized the difficulty that foreign investors have in getting information on Japanese securities: 'A foreigner here once asked a Japanese securities salesman where to get investment advice, and this is what he was told: "We have a saying: the better the English, the worse the analysis".' [Marcom (1982)]. European investors may do more portfolio investment in the United States than *vice versa* because of the greater ease with which detailed information can be obtained about U.S. firms.

investors in two countries may both decide to invest in the other's securities even if they have accurate assessments of the expected rates of return.

A sustained increase in the domestic saving rate raises capital intensity at home and thereby depresses the expected rate of return, μ. This unambiguously raises p^*, implying that some of the additional capital should be invested abroad.[28] If the initial p^* is negative, however, the increase in p^* may still leave the actual p at a constrained corner solution of $p^* = 0$. In this case, domestic investors do not seek to transfer any of the additional saving abroad. The increased domestic saving may nevertheless lead to an increase in net foreign investment if foreign investors respond to the lower expected return by reducing their oversease investment. In terms of eq. (29), from the point of view of foreign investors μ^* has fallen, causing an unambiguous reduction in p^*. Again, however, if foreign investors were originally not investing abroad, the reduction in the expected return would have no effect. Thus portfolio considerations alone could explain why a change in domestic saving in one country would have no effect on its net foreign investment.

Ignoring the possibility of corner solutions, a sustained exogenous increase in domestic saving will, by reducing the expected domestic rate of return, raise p^* and cause a capital outflow. This will be reinforced by foreign investors who respond to the lower expected return by reducing their overseas investment. The response of p^* to the change in μ is inversely proportional to $\gamma(\sigma_{oo} + \sigma_{**} - 2\sigma_{o*})$. The greater the risk aversion (γ) or the uncertainty about domestic and foreign rates of return (σ_{oo} and σ_{**}), the smaller will be the change in p^*. Thus, even for countries that do have overseas portfolio investments, the effect of a change in the expected return on domestic or foreign investment may be a relatively small change in the optimal allocation of assets between home and abroad.[29]

It is useful, however, to divide the response of international investment into two components. First, a sustained increase in the domestic saving rate alters $\mu^* - \mu$ and, therefore, changes p^* for both domestic and foreign investors. There is then a relatively brief period during which portfolios are readjusted to the new optimal mix.[30] During this readjustment there is a relatively large increase in the rate of net foreign investment. The shorter the time period during which the adjustment occurs, the greater will be the rate of net foreign investment per unit of time. Once the adjustment is complete, p^* remains unchanged. As the national capital stocks at home and abroad grow over time with the economies, the fraction p^* will flow abroad. Net foreign investment during this steady state growth will be the difference

---

[28]This is unambiguous only because I assume that the increase in domestic capital has no effect on the variance of the return or the risk aversion parameter.

[29]Hartman (1980) presents evidence that international capital flows are large enough to affect rates of return on U.S. securities but not enough to equalize returns here and abroad.

[30]Although such a reallocation should in principle occur instantly, institutional reasons may cause the adjustment to take a year or more.

between the steady state outflow of funds by domestic investment and the steady state inflow of funds from foreign investors. Although the evidence of sections 2 and 3 indicates that this long-run response to a sustained shift in domestic saving is quite small, the short-run response during a brief period of transition could be quite substantial.

6. Concluding comments

The evidence and analysis in this paper support the earlier findings of Feldstein and Horioka (1980) that sustained increases in domestic savings rates induce approximately equal increase in domestic investment rates. Although this limited extent of international capital mobility is consistent with the portfolio model developed in section 5, there are clearly other aspects of both international portfolio investment and international direct investment that should be taken into account in explaining the observed mobility.

Government policies establish the framework for private international investing. Governments of OECD countries have sought to restrict both capital inflows and capital outflows, including both direct and portfolio investment. Even the United States, perhaps the most liberal of the OECD countries in its attitude to capital movements, restricts the class of institutions that can invest abroad and thereby reduces the total volume and sensitivity of foreign investment. It would be useful to examine the capital restriction policies in detail, to evaluate their effectiveness and to understand the reasons why governments may choose to restrict international capital movements.[31]

More generally, although net capital flows do not appear to be sensitive to domestic saving rates, a stable pattern of net capital flows exists. It would be desirable to examine the reasons for this stable pattern and, in particular, to resolve the puzzling fact that substantial gross capital flows produces relatively small net capital flows.

---

[31]One such reason, the ability of foreign governments to capture the tax revenue of foreign investment, is discussed in Feldstein (1982).

References

Branson, W.H., 1970, Monetary policy and the new view of international capital movements, Brookings Papers on Economic Activity, 235–270.

Branson, W.H., 1979, Exchange rate dynamics and monetary policy, in: A. Lindbeck, ed., Inflation and unemployment in open economics (North-Holland, Amsterdam).

Cumby, R.E. and M. Obstfeld, 1982, International interest-rate and price-level linkages under 'flexible exchange rates: A review of recent evidence', Lecture given at the NBER conference on exchange rate theory and practice, Bellagio, Italy.

Feldstein, M., 1977, Social security and private savings: International evidence in an extended life-cycle model, in: M. Feldstein and R. Inman, eds., The economics of public services, An International Economic Association conference volume.

Feldstein, M., 1982, International tax rules, restrictions on capital mobility and domestic savings policies, forthcoming.

Feldstein, M. and C. Horioka, 1980, Domestic savings and international capital flows, The Economic Journal 90, 314–329.

Frisch, D., 1981, Issues in the taxation of foreign source income, NBER working paper no. 798 (NBER, Cambridge, MA).

Ginton, L. and D.W. Henderson, 1977, Central bank operations in foreign and domestic assets under fixed and flexible exchange rates, in: P.B. Clark, D. Logue and R. Sweeney, eds., The effects of exchange rate adjustments (U.S. Government Printing Office, Washington, DC).

Harberger, A.C., 1978, Perspectives on capital and technology in less developed countries, in: M.J. Artis and A.R. Nobay, eds., Contemporary economic analysis (London).

Harberger, A.C., 1980, Vignettes on the world capital market, American Economic Review, 331–337.

Hartman, D., 1980, International effects on the U.S. capital market, NBER working paper no. 581 (NBER, Cambridge, MA).

Hartman, D., 1981, Domestic tax policy and foreign investment: Some evidence, NBER working paper no. 784 (NBER, Cambridge, MA).

Marcom, J. Jr., 1982, Brokers intensify stock studies in Tokyo as more foreign investors look to Japan, Wall Street Journal, May 7.

Modigliani, F., 1970, The life cycle hypothesis of saving and intercountry differences in the saving ratio, in: W.A. Eltis et al., eds., Induction, growth and trade, Essays in honor of Sir Roy Harrod (Clarendon Press, Oxford).

Mundell, R.A., 1960, The monetary dynamics of international adjustment under fixed and flexible exchange rates, Quarterly Journal of Economics 74, 227–257.

Obstfeld, M., 1980, Imperfect asset substitutability and monetary policy under fixed exchange rates, NBER working paper no. 485 (NBER, Cambridge, MA).

OECD, 1980, Experience with controls on international portfolio operations in shares and bonds (OECD, Paris).

OECD, 1981, National accounts of the OECD countries: 1950–1979, Vols. 1 and 2 (OECD, Paris).

Sachs, J., 1981a, The current account and macroeconomic and macroeconomic adjustment in the 1970s, Brookings Papers on Economic Activity, 201—282.

Sachs, J.D., 1981b, Aspects of the current account behavior of OECD economies, NBER working paper no. 859 (NBER, Cambridge, MA).

III. INTERNAL AND EXTERNAL DEBT

Introduction to Part III

Along with structural maladjustment and exchange rate volatility (the themes of the previous two parts of this volume), the ballooning of internal and external debt can be viewed as the final member of the 'terrible trio' of economic maladies in the 1980s. And these themes interact. The sharp increase in the U.S. internal and external debt in the first half of the 1980s was often singled out as the most important cause of the real appreciation of the dollar, and in turn of the internal imbalance between the U.S. manufacturing and services sectors. In less-developed countries the links between external debt, exchange rate adjustment, and structural problems have been even more direct. In some countries heavy external debt burdens lead governments to distort exchange rates, fix domestic prices, inhibit imports, and other combinations of structural and exchange rate remedies.

This final part of the volume contains papers which emphasize theoretical aspects of internal and external debt. In each case, they provide examples of the way in which economic events stimulate economic ideas. The emergence in the United States of a large structural fiscal deficit (i.e., corrected for the business cycle) stimulated a substantial amount of new theoretical work on the long-run sustainability of fiscal deficits, and the implications of fiscal deficits for external borrowing and for the interaction of monetary and fiscal policy. One of these theoretical contributions appears as the first paper in this part of the volume, 'Current and Anticipated Deficits, Interest Rates, and Economic Activity', by Olivier J. Blanchard. The paper takes as its point of departure a 'new view' that fiscal deficits hurt rather than help an economic recovery after a recession; it examines the relationships among anticipated future internal government deficits, current real interest rates, and real output.

Starting from first principles, Blanchard begins by constructing a formal model in which outstanding government debt influences consumption and saving decisions and thus interest rates, despite the fact that individuals treat government as transparent and thus discount fully all future tax payments (this is the assumption of Barro–Ricardian equivalence). In his model, uncertainty regarding life expectancy makes individuals require interest in excess of pure time discount as an inducement to hold bonds. The resulting non-neutrality implies a positive relationship between the size of the current government debt and the contemporary short-term interest rate.

The main conclusions follow directly. Progressively increasing deficits create expectations of higher future debt and thus higher future short-term interest rates. These expectations in turn raise the current long-term interest rate and thus depress real activity. Whether or not this depressive rate effect is large enough to offset the traditional Keynesian stimulus to demand (as would be necessary to confirm the 'new view') depends on the quantitative importance of the relative effects. The object of the model is to demonstrate that a perverse effect is possible and plausible.

A qualification of the Blanchard paper, recognized by the author, is that he deals only with the effects of deficits within closed economies. If deficits are anticipated to be much larger in the U.S. than in other countries, then in open economies with international capital mobility there would be large movements in exchange rates. Indeed, the large appreciation of the dollar that peaked in 1985 is widely believed to have been caused in large part by the emergence of the U.S. structural fiscal deficit.

The emergence of an international 'debt crisis' was a continuing feature of the 1980s and generally refers not to the growing external debt of the U.S. but rather that of the developing countries. The problem suddenly emerged into the consciousness of academicians in August, 1982, at the time of the Mexican debt crisis, when Mexico became unable to pay the interest and principal due on its ballooning debt, and when lenders refused to advance it any additional funds. In one interpretation, the huge debt of the developing countries was a side-effect of the supply shocks of the mid and late 1970's, and of the role of banks in the developed countries in 'recycling' the surplusses of oil-producing nations to the poorer oil-using nations. Some of the developing countries, e.g., Mexico and Venezuela, were themselves oil producers, borrowed to support a consumption boom under conditions of an overvalued currency and capital flight, and then found that they could not roll over short-term debt when the price of oil began to drop after 1981.

The last two papers in this volume deal not with the specific events that led to the debt crisis of the 1980s, nor with the details of its resolution (which is not yet complete), but rather with first principles essential to understand the nature and effects of international lending for any country in any era. The first of these is 'The Pure Theory of Country Risk' by Jonathan Eaton, Mark Gersovitz, and Joseph E. Stiglitz. Their analysis helps to clarify a number of central issues. They distinguish among default, insolvency, and illiquidity in the context of a multi-period model in which default has future consequences. They stress that internal debt is a legal obligation, enforceable in courts, and thus differs from external debt for which repayment is largely voluntary with only indirect penalties possible. Collateral plays little role in external debt, because there is little that a creditor can do to seize it.

The authors use several simple models to focus on a key issue in international lending, the need for creditors to devise penalties that provide incentives for debtors to avoid default, and to maintain credibility in applying the penalties. They discuss two models, in one of which lenders do cut off credit from those who are in default (as part of a reputational equilibrium), but in the other they do not, and the market ceases to function. They also draw a parallel between the incentive problems of external lenders and the traditional problem of domestic bank runs. The paper contains no empirical analysis but rather provides a number of comments and guidelines on how econometric studies of external debt should be carried out. The authors conclude by stressing the central role played by the enforcement problem and the absence of collateral, both of which make the international credit market differ fundamentally from domestic financial markets. They emerge surprised that there was so much lending to developing countries, in light of the evident risks for creditors. They do not believe that their analysis allows predictions to be made about future repayment behavior by debtors, or future extensions of new loans by creditors.

The final paper in the volume is 'Growth and External Debt under Risk of Debt Repudiation' by Daniel Cohen and Jeffrey D. Sachs. They take as given the theoretical insights of the previous paper and examine their implications for the growth patters of developing countries. Their paper is an abstract analysis of the pattern of growth of a nation which borrows abroad and which has the option of repudiating its foreign debt. The authors show that the equilibrium strategy of competitive lenders is to make the growth of the foreign debt contingent on the growth of the borrowing country.

The result is a two-stage pattern of growth. During the first stage, the debt grows more rapidly than the economy. During the second stage, both the debt and the economy grow at the same rate, and more slowly than in the first stage. During this second stage, the total interest falling due on the debt is never entirely repaid. Only an amount equal to the difference between the rate of interest and the rate of growth of the economy, multiplied by the level of the debt, should be repaid each period. This permanent refinancing of part of the interest is the only way for a country to reach the optimum pattern of growth consistent with no default.

European Economic Review 25 (1984) . North-Holland

CURRENT AND ANTICIPATED DEFICITS, INTEREST RATES AND ECONOMIC ACTIVITY

Olivier J. BLANCHARD*

Massachusetts Institute of Technology, Cambridge, MA 02139, USA

There is a widespread feeling that current deficits, in Europe and the U.S., may hurt rather than help the recovery. This paper examines some of the issues involved, through a sequence of three models. The first model focuses on sustainability and characterizes its determinants. It suggests that the issue of sustainability may indeed be relevant in some countries. The second model focuses on the effects of fiscal policy on real interest rates, and in particular on the relative importance of the level of deficits and the level of debt in determining interest rates. The third model focuses on the effects of fiscal policy on the speed of the recovery. It shows how a sharply increasing fiscal expansion might be initially contractionary rather than expansionary.

1. Introduction

The size of fiscal deficits is becoming a major source of concern. In Europe and Japan, the large current deficits are inhibiting the use of further, even temporary, fiscal expansion; indeed at the bottom of a recession, most governments are attempting to reduce spending and increase tax revenues. In the United States on the other hand, where current deficits are large and anticipated deficits much larger, there is widespread concern that they may slow or even prevent a complete recovery.

The perception that deficits may hurt rather than help the recovery is clearly at odds with the traditional view that deficits, although they will in general increase interest rates, will nevertheless increase demand and economic activity. Although no unified or well articulated 'new view' has emerged, challengers of the traditional view insist on the abnormally large size of current deficits. Such deficits, they argue, may be simply unsustainable, a possibility never considered by the traditional view. They may be so large and so prolonged that the increase in real interest rates may more than offset their direct expansionary effect. The purpose of this paper is to see whether this new view has some validity, and more generally to reexamine the relation between debt, deficits, interest rates, and economic activity.

The first issue taken up in the paper is that of sustainability. Is it the case that some countries are running unsustainable deficits and may be forced, at

*I thank Eliana Cardoso, Rudiger Dornbusch, Benjamin Friedman, and my discussants, Edmond Malinvaud and Stephen Marris, for useful suggestions and discussions. I also thank the Sloan Foundation for financial support.

some time in the future, to repudiate the debt either explicitly or through inflation depreciation? If this was the case, the increased uncertainty generated by deficits might well offset their expansionary effect. The purpose of the first model is thus to clarify the notion of sustainability and to think about its determinants. A casual examination of the evidence suggests that sustainability may indeed have become a relevant issue in some European countries.

The second issue taken up is that of the relation between real rates, debt, and deficits. Even if deficits are sustainable, they will affect interest rates. Do interest rates, however, depend on the level of debt, or on the level of deficits, or on both? These are the questions addressed in the second model of the paper. Central to this set of issues is the question of the horizon of agents, as we know that if agents have infinite horizons, interest rates may depend neither on debt nor on deficits. The main element of the model is thus the derivation of an aggregate consumption function which does not satisfy Ricardo–Barro equivalence. The model shows that long real rates depend on the anticipated sequence of debt, or equivalently on the current level of debt and the anticipated sequence of deficits.

The third and last issue is that of potentially perverse effects of deficits on output. Can deficits increase real rates by so much as to decrease aggregate demand and output? The third model builds on the previous one but allows for an effect of aggregate demand on output. Its main conclusion is that, although current deficits are expansionary, the anticipation of growing deficits may well reduce economic activity. This suggests that the fiscal program of the current U.S. administration could be currently contractionary rather than expansionary.

The paper has four sections. Section 2 presents briefly the basic facts about debt, current and anticipated deficits, and spending levels. Section 3 focuses on sustainability. Section 4 and 5 characterize the relation between debt, deficits, interest rates, and output.

2. Basic statistics

The relevant basic statistics are presented for the U.S. and eight EEC countries in table 1.

Focusing first on debt, we find that the average ratio of debt to GDP is relatively low by historical standards. There are, however, wide variations of this ratio across countries, from 16% in Denmark to 98% in Ireland. (These inter-country variations are no wider than intra-country variations over time: the ratio fell in the U.S. from 100% in 1947 to 25% in the mid 70's.)

Turning to deficits, we see that they are large by historical standards; this is true for both 1982 and projected 1983 deficits and still holds after inflation correction of nominal interest payments on government debt, as shown in

Table 1

Debt, deficits, and spending (percentages).[a]

	(1) 1981 (end) Debt/GDP	(2) 1982 Surplus/GDP	(3) 1983 Surplus/GDP (forecast)	(4) 1982 Surplus/GDP Inflation adjusted	(5) 1982 Surplus/GDP Full employment inflation adjusted	(6) 1982 Receipts/GDP	(7) 1982 Disbursements/GDP
Belgium	88	−12.8	−12.1	−5.8	−2.0	47.2	59.9
Denmark	16	−9.5	−9.6	−9.0	−6.3	51.5	60.9
Germany	35	−3.9	−4.1	−2.3	−0.5	45.6	49.5
France	17	−3.0	−3.0	−1.5	+2.2	48.1	51.2
Ireland	98	−14.7	−14.4	−3.2	−0.1	44.1	58.8
Italy	64	−11.6	−11.0	−5.4	−2.1	40.7	52.3
Netherlands	47	−5.7	−5.5	−2.5	+3.5	54.8	60.5
United Kingdom	58	−2.0	−0.5	−0.1	+3.4	44.7	45.6
EEC total	42	−3.9	−4.9	−2.2	+0.9	45.8	50.8
U.S.	29	−4.8	−6.5	−3.9	−1.1	32.1	36.0

[a]Sources: Columns (1) to (3): EEC: EEC, Annual Economic Report, tables 6.1, 6.4; U.S.: budget of the U.S. Government, fiscal year 1984. Columns (4), (5): calculations by author. Columns (6), (7): EEC: EEC, Annual Economic Report, table 6.1; U.S.: Economic report of the President, 1983.

column (4). Column (5) shows, however, that with some exceptions, the current deficits are largely cyclical: if there was no change in fiscal policy, they would disappear as the world economy returned to full employment. As return to full employment is still far in the future, these full employment surpluses would still correspond to actual deficits until at least the mid 80's.

Most countries, therefore, do not currently have structural deficits. There is, however, evidence in the U.S. of looming structural deficits starting in 1983 and, in the absence of further changes in fiscal policy, averaging 6% of GNP for the rest of the decade.[1] Two of the proximate causes, the income tax cuts voted in 1981 and the increase in defense spending, are clearly specific to the U.S. The third, the increase in real interest rates, is common to all countries, affecting them in proportion to their debt to GDP ratios. The stance of discretionary fiscal policy is quite different outside of the U.S.: cyclically adjusted budget deficits have been and are expected to be reduced by 0.5% in 1981, 0.8% in 1982, and 1.2% in 1983 in Japan, and 0.9% in 1981, 1.4% in 1982, and 1.2% in 1983 for the EEC as a whole.[2]

Finally, although the focus of the paper is on deficits, that is, on decreases in taxes given spending, it is important to remember what has happened to government spending. Except in the U.S., the level of spending has steadily gone up over time. The ratio of government outlays to GDP for the EEC as a whole has increased by 10% since 1970, by 15% since 1960. Columns (6) and (7) show how high the levels are. It is not unlikely that some of the problems attributed to deficits come in fact from the levels of government spending and that some arguments against deficits are really arguments against the level of spending.

3. Sustainability of deficits

What does it mean to say that a given combination of debt and deficits is unsustainable? To answer that, we can start with the government budget constraint

$$\dot{D} = rD + G - T.$$

D is government debt and the deficit is assumed to be entirely debt financed. r is the real interest rate, G and T spending and taxes, respectively. Let's further define $\overline{T}$ as the maximum amount of taxes which can be collected by the government and $\underline{G}$ as the minimum socially acceptable amount of government outlays. Both, and especially the second one, are admittedly fuzzy and would be difficult to determine empirically. Consider the level of debt $\overline{D} = r^{-1}(\overline{T} - \underline{G})$: if debt ever exceeds $\overline{D}$, the level of debt will

---

[1] Budget of the U.S. Government, fiscal year 1984, section 3–31.
[2] Sources: *OECD Economic Outlook*, December 1982, table 9, and *Annual Economic Report*, EEC, November 1982.

be forever increasing. The government will be in effect running a Ponzi scheme and will ultimately have to repudiate its debt. The implication is that the government cannot sell debt beyond $\bar{D}$, which is therefore the maximum sustainable level of debt.[3] If, for example, $\bar{T}-\underline{G}$ is equal to 10% of the GNP and r to 5%, $\bar{D}$ is 2 times GNP. This shows why the issue of sustainability has arisen in parallel with increases in real interest rates. Sustainable levels of debt are very large at the historical level of real rates of 1–2%, much smaller at the current 3–6%.

This computation is too simple for many reasons. It is too pessimistic in that it does not take into account GNP growth which increases the sustainable ratio of debt to GNP, and does not allow for possible monetization and the use of the inflation tax.[4] It is also too optimistic for at least two reasons: The first is that, unless Ricardo–Barro equivalence holds, r itself is likely to be an increasing function of the level of debt. The second is that increases in the tax burden or decreases in spending can only happen gradually. It is this element which is currently used to argue against a temporary fiscal expansion; many doubt that the new spending programs can indeed be only temporary. It is this last argument that we now formalize. Let

$$\dot{D}=rD-X, \qquad X \equiv T-G, \tag{1}$$

$$\dot{X} \leq \alpha(\bar{X}-X), \qquad \bar{X} \equiv \bar{T}-\underline{G} > 0. \tag{2}$$

X is the budget surplus (deficit if negative) before interest payments. Eq. (2) says that the gap between $\bar{X}$, the maximum surplus, and X can only be reduced at rate α.[5] We now want to know whether a given pair (X_0, D_0) [or equivalently $(\dot{D}_0, D_0)$] is sustainable or not. We can draw the phase diagram of the system, with the inequality in (2) replaced by an equality. This is done in fig. 1. The equilibrium is a saddle point, with stable arm AA'. Consider point C. Point C is not sustainable as, even if the deficit is reduced as fast as feasible, i.e., if (2) holds with equality, the maximum level of debt $\bar{D}$ is reached before deficits are eliminated. Point B on the other hand is sustainable as deficits can be eliminated before D reaches $\bar{D}$. BF represents the fastest feasible path of reduction of deficits. When F is reached, X need not be increased further and (2) holds as an inequality.

The critical locus is therefore the locus AE. Pairs (X, D) below it are not

---

[3]For the argument to be complete, it should show why the government cannot issue more and more debt forever and therefore has to repudiate the debt. Dealing with these issues would lead us too far astray.

[4]The maximum inflation tax is relatively small. Unanticipated inflation may, however, if debt is in the form of long term bonds with nominal coupons, substantially reduce the real value of the debt.

[5]An interesting attempt to estimate OECD fiscal reaction functions in this light and to study implications for structural deficits is described in Hubbard (1983).

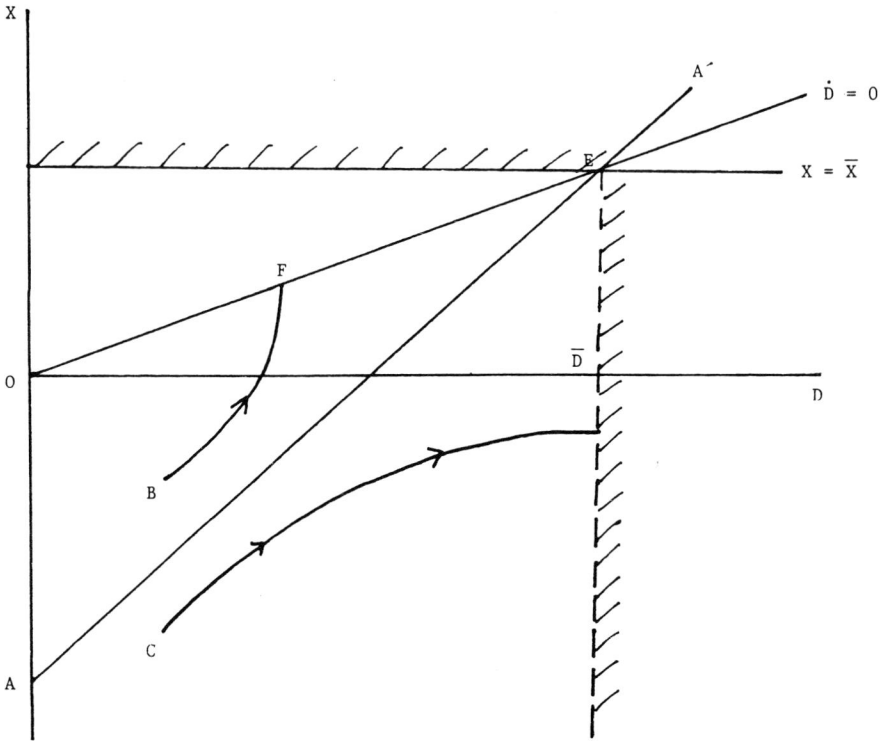

Fig. 1. Sustainable deficit debt pairs.

sustainable and pairs above it are. It is given by[6]

$$(r+\alpha)(D-\bar{D})-(X-\bar{X})=0, \qquad \bar{D}=r^{-1}\bar{X}.$$

The sustainability condition for a given (X_0, D_0) is therefore

$$(r+\alpha)(D_0-\bar{D})-(X_0-\bar{X})\leq 0. \qquad (3)$$

If $\alpha=\infty$, so that there are no restrictions on changes in X, the condition is again that D_0 be less than $\bar{D}$. If $\alpha=0$, the condition reduces to $\dot{D}\leq 0$: there cannot be a positive deficit.

Eq. (3) shows the role of the speed of adjustment α, the interest rate, the level of debt, the actual deficit, and the maximum potential surplus. Returning to table 1, Ireland and Belgium with their large debt, deficits, and

----

[6]The roots of the system (1), (2) (with equality) are r and $-\alpha$. The characteristic vector associated with α, (x_1,x_2), is such that $x_1/x_2=(r+\alpha)^{-1}$. Thus $D-\bar{D}=c_1(r+\alpha)^{-1}e^{-\alpha t}$ and $X-\bar{X}=c_1e^{-\alpha t}$. Taking the ratio gives the equation in the text.

level of spending seem to be the countries most likely to violate (3). We can attempt some crude computations for Belgium, for example. Using the implied values from table 1 for D, X^7 together with $r = 5\%$ and $\alpha = 20\%$ implies that $\bar{X}$ be at least equal to 7.5% for the inequality (3) to be satisfied. At the current level of spending, this would imply a ratio of receipts to GDP of close to 60%, which appears very high.[8] Thus sustainability might indeed be an issue; it appears to be less so in other countries.

The model does not tell us what happens when a current fiscal program appears unsustainable. It is likely that a program does not suddenly become unsustainable but rather that agents start taking the possibility of repudiation into account. What happens depends on the type of repudiation that agents anticipate. If they anticipate attempts to depreciate the debt through inflation at some point in the future, they will require higher nominal interest rates on new issues of public and private bonds. Only if public debt is of sufficiently long maturity can the government successfully use inflation to repudiate part of the debt. If agents anticipate repudiation of government debt only — a less likely case — they will require a higher real rate on government debt than on private debt so as to be compensated for the risk of repudiation. In both cases, a shift in demand towards short maturity debt is likely.

4. Interest rates, debt, and deficits at full employment

This section focuses on the effects of debt and deficits on the equilibrium sequence of interest rates in a full employment economy. This is needed to understand their effects in an economy which may not be at full employment; it is also of more than academic interest as some of the larger anticipated U.S. deficits are expected to take place in an economy which should be by then at full employment.

The first step is to construct a consumption function consistent with non-neutrality of debt; the second is to close the model to derive equilibrium interest rates.

4.1. Aggregate consumption

Aggregate consumption functions derived from individual life cycle behavior are usually intractable, for individuals differ in two respects, making

---

[7]Interest payments were equal to 7.8% of GDP in 1982, and have to be deducted from disbursements to get G.

[8]The medium term budgetary objectives, as of fiscal year 1982, for Belgium are of a reduction of the general government deficit from 12.8% in 1982 to 7% in 1985. This is to be achieved partly through a reduction in spending. (Source: OECD, *Public Sector Deficits: Problems and Policy Implications*, Occasional Papers, June 1983). The June 1983 EEC projections of deficits in Belgium are, however, 11.7% for 1983 and 12.1% for 1984 (Source: *European Economy*, Supplement A, no. 6, June 1983, table 9).

exact aggregation difficult: they have different horizons and thus different propensities to consume out of wealth, as well as different levels of wealth. There is, however, one set of assumptions (and I believe only one) which preserves the assumption of finite horizons, essential to the analysis of debt and deficits but leads to a tractable aggregate consumption function; we now explore it.

Time is continuous. At any instant, a new cohort, composed of many agents, is born, its size normalized to be unity. Agents face, during their lifetime, a constant instantaneous probability of death p, so that their expected life is p^{-1}. Because of the large number of agents in each cohort, the probability p is also the percentage of agents in each cohort which die at any instant. The size of a cohort born at time zero as of time t is therefore e^{-pt} and the size of the population at any time t is $\int_{-\infty}^{t} e^{-p(t-s)} ds = p^{-1}$. The main implication of this set of assumptions is that, although agents are of different ages, they all have at any time the same expected remaining life, p^{-1}, and thus the same marginal propensity to consume out of wealth.

Two additional assumptions, about income distribution and financial markets, considerably simplify the analysis. The first is that all agents alive work and thus share labor income equally.[9] The second is that agents can save or dissave by buying or selling actuarial bonds rather than regular bonds, i.e., bonds which are cancelled by death. Because of the large number of agents, intermediation between lenders and borrowers can be done risklessly. Lenders lend to intermediaries; these claims are cancelled by death of the lenders. Borrowers borrow from intermediaries; these claims are cancelled by death of the borrower. If the rate of interest on regular bonds is r then arbitrage and the zero profit condition in intermediation imply a rate of interest on actuarial bonds of $(r+p)$. As by assumption agents have no bequest motive, they prefer to borrow and save only through these actuarial bonds. As a result, they leave no bequest [this clever device was introduced by Yaari (1965)].[10]

The aggregate consumption can now be derived intuitively as follows: (A derivation is given in the appendix.) Assume each agent is an expected utility maximizer, with instantaneous logarithmic utility and subjective discount rate θ. Then, denoting individual variables by lower case letters, his consumption is characterized by

$$c = (p+\theta)(w+h), \qquad h = \int_{t}^{\infty} y_s \exp\left\{\int_{t}^{s}(r_v+p)\,dv\right\}ds, \qquad (4)$$

[9]Although the model captures the idea that agents do not have infinite horizons, agents in the model do not go through a life cycle. Thus the model cannot be used to examine issues for which the life cycle is essential, such as, for example, saving for retirement or social security.

[10]In the absence of actuarial bonds, agents would not only leave unanticipated bequests but might also go bankrupt. Actuarial bonds allow agents to insure themselves against such contingencies. Their presence simplifies the analysis considerably but is in no way the source of the non-neutrality of deficits or debt.

$$\dot{w} = (r+p)w + y - c. \tag{5}$$

c is consumption, y is non-interest income, w and h are non-human and human wealth respectively. The presence of uncertainty about death modifies the standard formulation in two ways: The relevant interest rate is $(r+p)$ rather than r; at the same time the marginal propensity to consume out of wealth is $(p+\theta)$ rather than θ.

Aggregate consumption is obtained by aggregating (4) and (5) over all agents alive at time t. Denoting aggregate variables by upper case letters, this gives

$$C = (p+\theta)(W+H), \qquad H = \int_t^\infty Y_s \exp\left\{\int_t^s (r_v + p)\, dv\right\} ds, \tag{6}$$

$$\dot{W} = rW + Y - C. \tag{7}$$

Those two equations are similar to the individual equations with one — major — difference. Whereas the rate of interest used to discount non-interest income is $(r+p)$, aggregate non-human wealth accumulates at rate r, not $(r+p)$. This is because, although the interest on actuarial bonds is $(r+p)W$, a portion, pW, is extinguished with the death of wealth holders. Thus, the discount rate for aggregate human wealth $(r+p)$ is higher than the discount rate for aggregate non-human wealth (r). The simple form of the result is due to the existence of actuarial bonds. The qualitative nature of the result, namely the use of a higher discount rate for human than for non-human wealth does not depend on the existence of actuarial bonds but on the positive probability of death faced by agents. It is this difference in discount rates which implies non-neutrality of debt and deficits.

4.2. Debt and interest rates in steady state

Let us introduce now a government which collects lump sum taxes T on non-interest income, spends G on goods, and has debt oustanding in amount D. Debt is in the form of actuarial bonds, so that the budget constraint is

$$\dot{D} = (r+p)D + G - T - pD = rD + G - T. \tag{8}$$

The term $-pD$ again represents the portion of the debt which is extinguished with the death of debt holders. To see why deficits matter, we can integrate eq. (8) forward, subject to the condition that debt reaches some steady state level,

$$D_t + \int_t^\infty G_s \exp\left\{-\int_t^s r_v\, dv\right\} ds = \int_t^\infty T_s \exp\left\{-\int_t^s r_v\, dv\right\} ds. \tag{9}$$

From eq. (6), now that non-interest income net of taxes is given by $Y - T$, human wealth is given by

$$H_t = \int_t^\infty Y_s \exp\left\{-\int_t^s (r_v + p)\,dv\right\}ds - \int_t^\infty T_s \exp\left\{-\int_t^s (r_v + p)\,dv\right\}ds. \qquad (10)$$

In the absence of changes in government spending, changes in taxes must leave the right-hand side of (9) unchanged. This will, however, change the value of the second term in (10). In effect the government 'discounts' taxes at r, agents at $r + p$. Current deficits, that is, lower taxes today and higher taxes later, will, unless $p = 0$, increase H_t and C_t at given interest rates.

To close the model, we simply assume that the economy is an exchange economy, with exogenous output Y. Thus in equilibrium, private non-human wealth W is equal to government debt D. Equilibrium is, therefore, characterized by

$$Y = C + G = (p + \theta)(D + H) + G, \qquad (11)$$

$$\dot{D} = rD + G - T, \qquad (12)$$

$$\dot{H} = (r + p)H - Y + T. \qquad (13)$$

Eq. (11) is the condition for equilibrium in the goods market. Eqs. (12) and (13) give the dynamic behavior of debt and of human wealth; (13) follows from time differentiation of (10).[11]

In steady state, $\dot{D} = \dot{H} = 0$ and this, with some manipulation, implies

$$rD = T - G, \qquad (14)$$

$$r = \theta + (p + \theta)\,p(D/(Y - G)). \qquad (15)$$

Eq. (14) is the steady state government budget constraint. Eq. (15) characterizes the steady state interest rate (on regular bonds).

If $p = 0$, then the interest rate equals the subjective discount rate and is independent of debt and spending. If p is positive, however, the interest rate is an increasing function of both debt and spending; the larger p — the shorter the expected life — the stronger the effect. In order to induce agents to hold the debt, the government must make agents save more; it does so by increasing the interest rate over the subjective discount rate. The formula suggests relatively small effects of debt on interest rates. For example, if we take reasonable upper bounds, say $D/Y = 1$, $G = 0.5Y$, $\theta = 10\%$, and $p = 5\%$, $r - \theta$ is equal to 1.5%. The strength of this model is, however, not in its quantitative answers and these numbers should be looked at with caution.[12]

[11]In this section, no notational distinction is made between actual and expected values. $\dot{H}$, for example, is the expected change in H.

[12]Tobin (1967) developed a realistic model of life cycle to look at steady state savings. He did not look, however, at the effects of debt.

4.3. Dynamic effects of deficits

Starting from steady state and keeping government spending constant, we now consider changes in the sequence of taxes which satisfy the intertemporal government budget constraint. From goods market equilibrium, given output and government spending, interest rates must be such as to leave consumption and thus the sum of debt and human wealth constant. If $D + H = $ constant, $\dot{D} = -\dot{H}$ and from (12), (13)

$$rD + (r+p)H = Y - G.$$

Combining this with (11) gives

$$r = \theta + p(p+\theta)(D/(Y-G)). \tag{16}$$

Thus the relation between interest rates, debt, and government spending holds at any point of time and not only in steady state. The short-term interest rate depends on the current level of debt and does not depend on the current level of deficits: a decrease in taxes, given spending, has no effect on r. Deficits will, however, affect anticipated future real rates. To illustrate the effects of deficits on the whole term structure, consider now the sequence of deficits implied by

$$\dot{D} = rD + G - T(D, x), \qquad T_D > 0, \quad T_x > 0. \tag{17}$$

Taxes are now a function of a shift parameter x and an increasing function of debt. We want to consider only sustainable deficits and thus impose

$$d\dot{D}/dD = Ddr/dD + r - T_D = 2r - \theta - T_D < 0.$$

This requires that taxes increase sufficiently fast as debt increases thus closing the deficit. Let's further define the long term interest rate as the yield on consols paying a constant coupon flow of unity. Let R be their yield and thus $1/R$ be their price. The instantaneous rate of return on consols is

$$(1 + d(1/R)/dt)/(1/R) = R - \dot{R}/R.$$

It is the sum of the yield and of the expected capital gain, which is negative if yields increase, or equivalently, if prices decrease. By arbitrage between short and long bonds,

$$R - \dot{R}/R = r. \tag{18}$$

We may now consider the system composed of (16), (17), and (18), which determines the dynamic behavior of debt, short and long rates.[13] Eliminating

---

[13]The system is in fact recursive. R depends on D, but D does not depend on R. Consols may actually not be traded at all in the economy. R is introduced to get a convenient characterisation of the term structure, and because it will play an important role in the next section.

r using (16) gives a system in debt and the long rate,

$$\dot{D} = \left(\theta + p(p+\theta)\frac{D}{Y-G}\right)D + G - T(D, x),$$

$$\frac{\dot{R}}{R} = \left(R - \theta - p(p+\theta)\frac{D}{Y-G}\right).$$

This system has a saddle point equilibrium. Its local dynamics around equilibrium are characterized in fig. 2. The stable arm AA is upward sloping.

A decrease in x, i.e., a decrease in taxes at any level of debt, shifts the $\dot{D}=0$ locus to the right. The dynamics of adjustment to an unanticipated permanent decrease in x are characterized in fig. 3. Starting from point E, R jumps to point C, and R and D move over time along CE'. The economic interpretation is straightforward: A decrease in x decreases taxes, creating a deficit. This deficit increases debt over time and thus short-term rates. As debt increases, taxes increase reducing the size of the deficit. In the new steady state, debt and interest rates are higher. The initial deficits twist the term structure as short-term rates do not move but long rates move in anticipation of higher short rates later. The term structure flattens over time, until R and r are again equal in the new steady state.

The effects of anticipated deficits can also be characterized using fig. 3. A decrease in x, anticipated at t to take place at time t' leads to a jump from E to B at t, a movement from B to C from t to t' and a movement along CE' after t'. Although the short-term rate does not move until t', the long rate

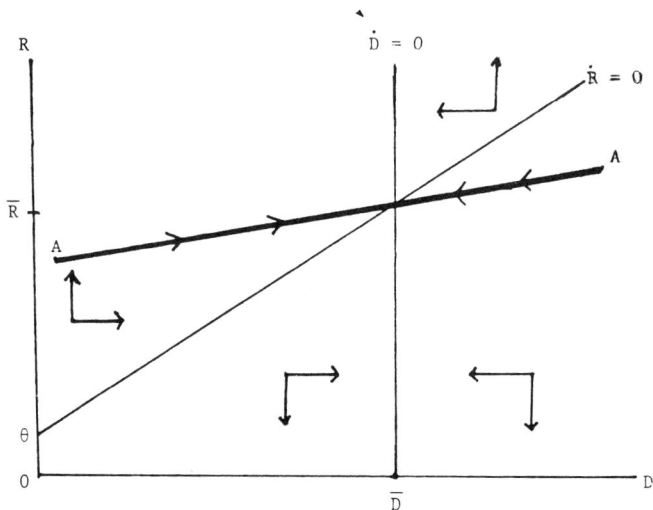

Fig. 2. Debt, deficits and interest rates in full employment.

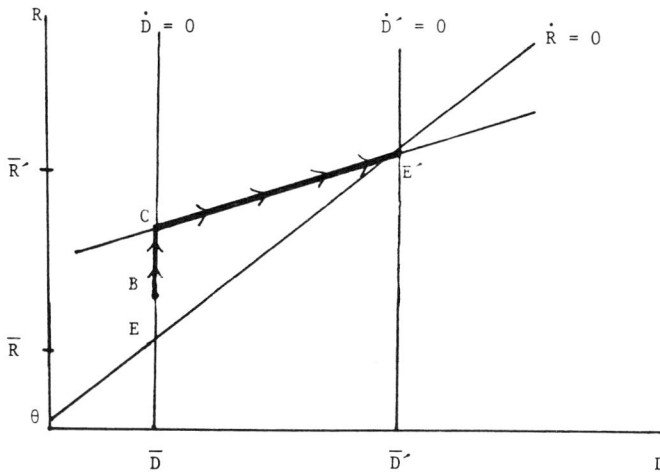

Fig. 3. Anticipated deficits, short and long rates.

increases at time t to cancel the effects of anticipated lower taxes on human wealth.

To summarize, short rates depend in this full employment exchange economy on the current level of debt. Thus long rates depend on the sequence of anticipated debt, or equivalently, on the initial level of debt and the anticipated sequence of deficits. A sequence of higher deficits will initially increase long rates over short rates, leading over time to higher short and long rates. This analysis suggests that the current focus on deficits rather than on debt is possibly misdirected. It is true that the anticipated sequence of U.S. deficits is exceptional in peacetime and implies a large increase in the level of debt. The current level of debt as well as the anticipated levels of debt for the medium run are still much lower than at many times in the past.

5 Deficits, interest rates, and output

The focus is now on the potentially perverse effect of deficits on aggregate demand and on output. The strategy has been to remain close to the traditional Phillips curve augmented IS–LM, extending it only to introduce the distinction between short and long rates.[14, 15] The model is the following:

[14]An alternative strategy would have been to imbed the aggregate consumption function of the previous section in an otherwise Keynesian model. It would, however, be slightly more cumbersome analytically.

[15]This is a simplified and modified version of Blanchard (1981). It is very similar to a model developed by Cardoso (1983). It is related to a recent model by Turnovsky and Miller (1982) which treats the government budget constraint explicitly but maintains the fixed price assumption.

IS: $Y = Y(R, g)$. $Y_R < 0$, $Y_g > 0$,

LM: $i = L(Y, m/p)$, $L_Y > 0$, $L_{m/p} < 0$,

$$r^* = i - \dot{p}^*/p,\tag{19}$$

$$\dot{R}^*/R = R - r^*,\tag{20}$$

PC: $\dot{p}^*/p = \dot{p}/p = \theta(Y)$, $\theta_Y > 0$, $\bar{Y} | \theta(\bar{Y}) = 0$.

Aggregate demand is assumed to depend on the long term rate, current income, and an index of fiscal expansion g. Behind this specification is one important assumption and a technical short cut. The important assumption is that, although financial markets look forward, agents themselves do not; there is no direct effect of future income or future taxes on current aggregate demand (there will be an indirect effect through long real rates). We shall return to this assumption later. The short cut is that fiscal policy is summarized by a single index g. We know from the previous section that aggregate demand depends on each of the components of fiscal policy, taxes, spending, and debt. Thus a permanent increase in g may correspond to a balanced budget increase in spending or, more interestingly, to initially higher deficits which resorb themselves as debt accumulates to reach a new higher steady state.[16]

The LM relation determines the short-term nominal rate as a function of income and real money balances m/p. The next two equations provide the links between this short-term nominal rate and the long real rate which appears in the IS. (19) defines the short real rate; asterisks denote expectations. (20), which was derived previously, relates short and long real rates. The last equation is a Phillips curve, relating inflation to the level of output.

The long-run equilibrium of this model is similar to that of the previous section:

---

[16]In the case where consumption is given by the consumption function derived in the previous section, and where consumers have static expectations, we can derive g explicitly. In that case,

$$C + G = (\theta + p)\left(D + \frac{Y - T}{r + p}\right) + G. \quad \text{Thus,}$$

$$g = (\theta + p)\left(D - \frac{T}{r + p}\right) + G.$$

Rearranging and using the government budget constraint gives

$$g = (\theta + p - r)D + \dot{D} + \frac{\theta - r}{r + p} T.$$

If r is close to θ, this simplifies to

$$g \doteq pD + \dot{D}.$$

If

$$\dot{p} = \dot{p}^* = \dot{R} = 0,$$

$$\bar{Y}|\theta(\bar{Y}) = 0, \quad \bar{r}, \bar{R}|\bar{Y} = Y(\bar{R}, \bar{g}), \quad \bar{r} = \bar{R},$$

$$\bar{p}|\bar{r} = L(\bar{Y}, m/\bar{p}).$$

Fiscal expansion has no long-run effect on output but increases the steady state rate of interest. Prices adjust so that real money balances are consistent with the new rate of interest.

To characterize the dynamics of output and interest rates to a fiscal stimulus, we can reduce the system to a system in R and p. Replacing the IS, the LM and the Phillips curve in the interest rate equations (19) and (20),

$$\dot{R}^*/R = (R - r), \tag{21}$$

where r is given by

$$r = L(Y(R, g), m/p) - \theta(Y(R, g)).$$

The effect of output on the short-term rate is a priori ambiguous: an increase in output increases both the short term nominal rate and expected inflation. We shall assume that the nominal rate effect dominates, i.e., that $L_Y - \theta_Y > 0$, so that an increase in output increases the short real rate.[17] In this case, fiscal expansion increases short real rates; an increase in the long real rate decreases output and decreases short real rates. Finally, an increase in prices decreases real money balances, increasing the short real rate.

The other relation follows from the IS and the Phillips curve,

$$\dot{p}/p = \theta(Y(R, g)). \tag{22}$$

Fiscal expansion increases output and inflation, while an increase in long real rates decreases output and inflation.

The analysis can again be carried out most easily with a phase diagram. The system has a saddle point equilibrium so that given p, there is a unique value of R consistent with convergence to steady state. The local dynamics around equilibrium are characterized in fig. 4. The stable arm AA is upward sloping.

The dynamic effects of a fiscal expansion, that is, of an increase in g, are characterized in fig. 5. We first characterize the dynamics technically: The system jumps from E to C and converges to E' over time. From the Phillips curve, as $\dot{p}$ is positive, output initially increases. From the IS, as R increases along CE', output decreases along CE'. Finally, from the arbitrage equation, as $\dot{R}$ is positive, R is larger than r along CE'. Thus a fiscal expansion leads

[17](Saddle point) stability of the system does not depend on this assumption.

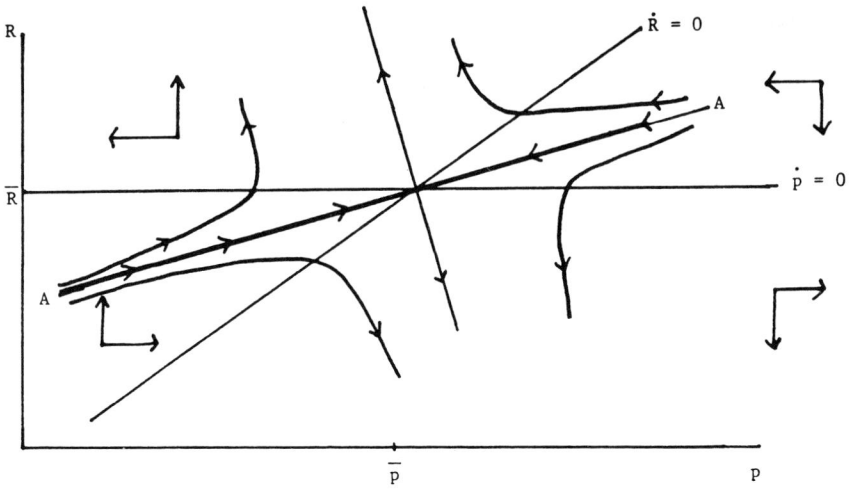

Fig. 4. Dynamics of interest rates and prices.

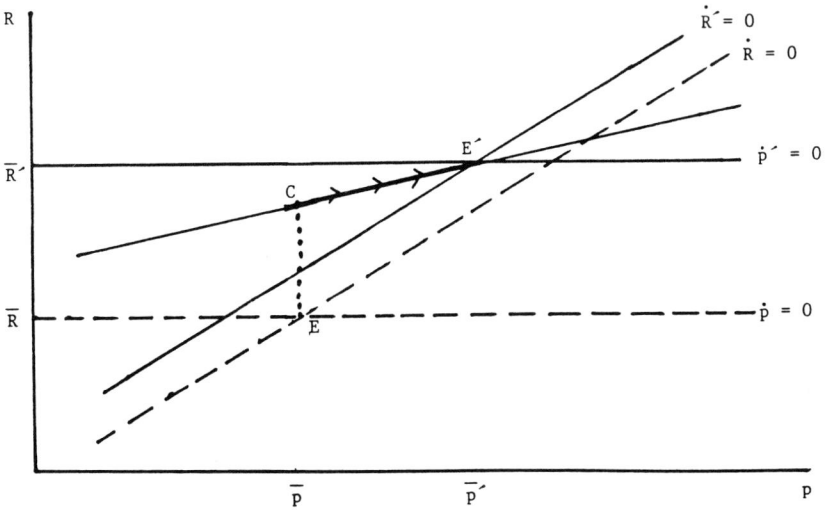

Fig. 5. Effects of a fiscal expansion.

initially to an increase in short real rates and output; over time, output goes back to normal and short real rates increase further. It is this increasing sequence of short rates which explains the initial jump in long rates. Fiscal expansion, therefore, twists the term structure, increasing long rates over short rates. This leads to more crowding out than would be predicted by models which do not distinguish between short and long rates. It does not, however, lead to perverse effects of a fiscal expansion on output.

Consider however a more realistic experiment, in which deficits instead of being suddenly larger, increase slowly through time. Instead of a jump of g from $\bar{g}$ to $\bar{g}'$ as before, consider instead the following fiscal expansion: until time t, g is equal to, and expected to remain equal to $\bar{g}$. At t, anticipations change and the new actual and anticipated path of g is

$$\dot{g} = \Psi(\bar{g}' - g), \qquad \Psi' > 0.$$

Such a path for g corresponds, for example, to deficits which initially grow over time before resorbing themselves as debt accumulates to a new, higher, steady state level. The path of adjustment is characterized in fig. 6. R jumps from E to C; R and p then adjust along CDE' over time. The behavior of R, r, and Y is given below the phase diagram; whether r further decreases after its initial decrease is ambiguous.[18]

Thus this type of fiscal expansion has temporarily perverse effects on output. The reason is simple. The initial current fiscal stimulus is small. It is, however, anticipated to be large and thus to lead to high short real rates later. As a result, long real rates increase, leading to a decrease in aggregate demand which more than offsets the fiscal expansion, at least initially. Thus, the model tells us, the U.S. fiscal program and its growing projected deficits could well be initially contractionary. The model also suggests a way in which fiscal policy could be improved. As current deficits are expansionary and anticipated deficits contractionary, shifting of government spending towards the present would, by increasing current deficits and decreasing future deficits, increase aggregate demand and help the recovery.

It is, however time to return to the specification of aggregate demand. What if agents are forward looking and take into account the anticipated sequence of taxes and income, as in the previous section? First, if they take into account the anticipated sequence of taxes, a slow increase in deficits is not equivalent to a slow effect of fiscal expansion on aggregate demand, to a slow increase in g: agents will realize that the present value of their tax burden has decreased and this will increase aggregate demand even if current deficits are still small. Second, if they take into account future income, the anticipation of temporarily higher output and income may also increase aggregate demand initially.[19] This effect will be stronger, the smaller the effect of liquidity constraints, the larger the effect of fiscal expansion on output — if, for example, the economy is expected to have substantial unemployed resources for many years to come. Whether these effects more than offset the interest rate effects is theoretically ambiguous. If these income effects dominate, the large U.S. anticipated deficits are expansionary in spite of their effect on current long-term real rates.

---

[18]The algebraic derivation of these paths is straightforward but extremely tedious. The method is identical to that used in appendix B in Blanchard (1981).

[19]This possibility is partially explored in Blanchard (1981) by the introduction of a stock market which affects aggregate demand.

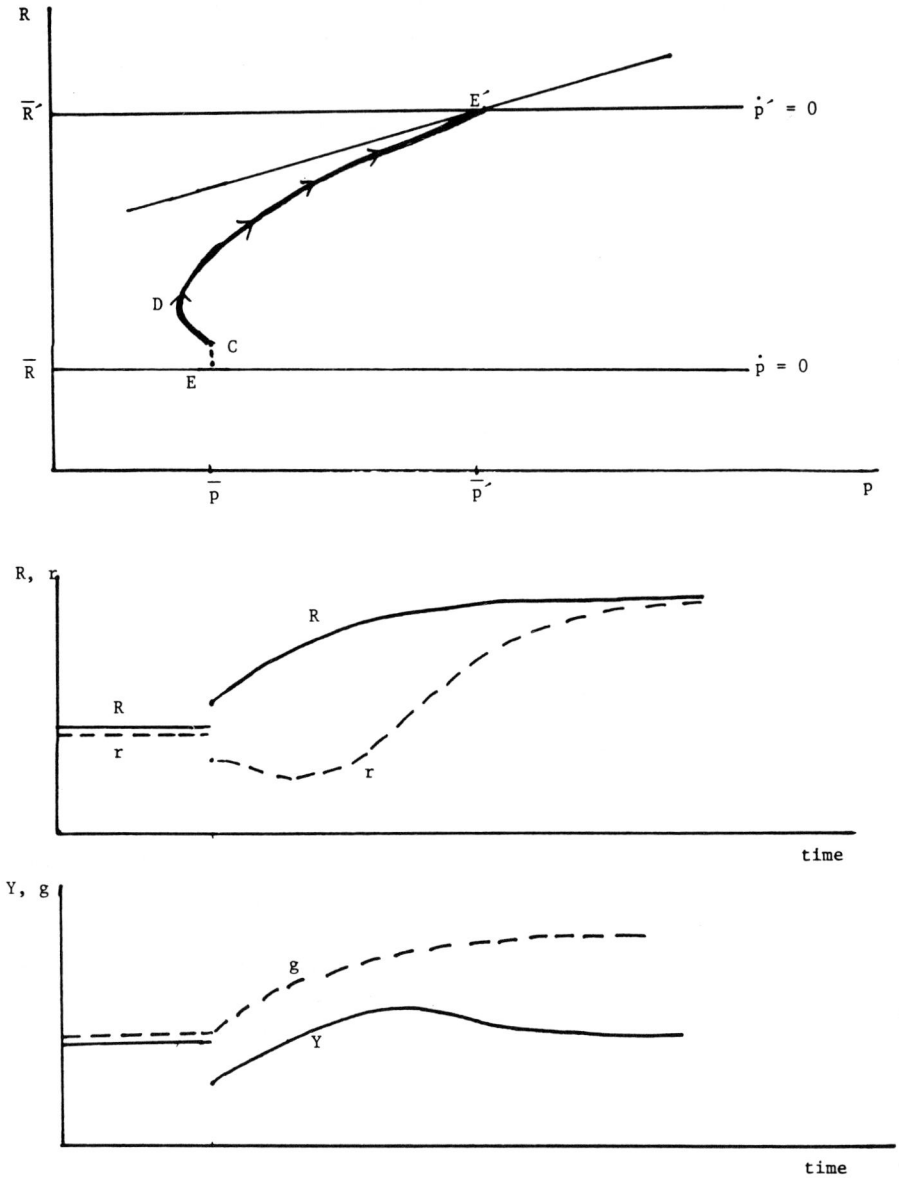

Fig. 6. Effects of an anticipated fiscal expansion.

6. Conclusion

What do we make then of the new view that fiscal deficits hurt rather than help the recovery? We have found that the issue of sustainability has indeed, because of the increase in real rates, become a relevant issue although probably not yet a pressing one. We have found that in turn, at full employment, short real rates increase with the level of debt; as a result, prolonged deficits lead to increasing real rates, thus to long rates being higher than short rates. We have finally found that, if output responds to aggregate demand, anticipations of growing deficits may be initially contractionary.

The three models presented in this paper are simple enough that they can withstand added complexity and realism without loosing analytical tractability. In particular integrating the first and the second, and the second and third, would probably be quite useful.

Finally, this paper has focused on the effects of deficits in closed economies. One major issue is, however, that deficits are anticipated to be much larger in the U.S. than in the other countries. This would lead in closed economies to large differences in real rates. It is likely to lead, in open economies with capital mobility, to large movements in exchange rates. I believe that a two-country extension of the second model will prove useful to analyze this issue.

Appendix: Derivation of the aggregate consumption function

Individual consumption. Denote by $c(t,s)$, $y(t,s)$, $w(t,s)$, $h(t,s)$ consumption, non-interest income, non-human wealth, and human wealth of an agent born at time t, as of time s.

At time s, the agent maximizes

$$E_s \int_s^\infty \log c(t,v) e^{(s-v)\theta} \, dv.$$

Under the assumption of a constant instantaneous probability of death p, and of subjective certainty about $c(t,v)$, $v \geq t$, this is equivalent to

$$\max \int_s^\infty \log c(t,v) e^{(s-v)(\theta+p)} \, dv. \tag{A.1}$$

The 'budget constraint' faced by the agent at time s is, if the rate on actuarial notes is $r(\mu)+p$ at time μ [the discussion and justification of the implicit transversality condition is given in Yaari (1965, p. 146)],

$$\int_s^\infty c(t,v) \exp\left\{-\int_s^v (r(\mu)+p)\, d\mu\right\} dv$$

$$= w(t,s) + \int_s^\infty y(t,v) \exp\left\{-\int_s^v (r(\mu)+p)\, d\mu\right\} dv. \tag{A.2}$$

The solution to this maximization problem is

$$c(t,s) = (p+\theta)\left(w(t,s) + \int_s^\infty y(t,v)\exp\left\{-\int_s^v (r(\mu)+p)\, d\mu\right\} dv\right), \tag{A.3}$$

$$dw(t,s)/ds = (r(s)+p)w(t,s) + y(t,s) - c(t,s). \tag{A.4}$$

Aggregate consumption. Denote aggregate consumption, aggregate non-interest income, aggregate non-human wealth and aggregate human wealth at time s by $C(s)$, $Y(s)$, $W(s)$ and $H(s)$. Then,

$$C(s) = \int_{-\infty}^s c(t,s)\, e^{(t-s)p}\, dt \Rightarrow$$

$$C(s) = (\theta+p)\left[W(s) + \int_{-\infty}^s e^{(t-s)p}\left(\int_s^\infty y(t,v)\exp\left\{-\int_s^v (r(\mu)+p)\, d\mu\right\} dv\right) dt\right], \tag{A.5}$$

where

$$W(s) = \int_{-\infty}^s w(t,s)\, e^{(t-s)p}\, dt.$$

Under the assumption that non-interest income is the same for all agents alive, $y(t,v) = pY(v)\ \forall\, t$ and all agents alive have the same human wealth. Thus (A.5) can be rewritten as

$$C(s) = (\theta+p)[W(s) + H(s)], \tag{A.6}$$

$$H(s) = \int_s^\infty Y(v)\exp\left\{-\int_s^v (r(\mu)+p)\, d\mu\right\} dv,$$

Differentiating $W(s)$ with respect to time gives

$$dW(s)/ds = w(s,s) - pW(s) + \int_{-\infty}^s \frac{dw(t,s)}{ds} e^{(t-s)p}\, dt.$$

Using (A.4) and $w(s, s) = 0$ gives

$$dW(s)/ds = r(s)W(s) + Y(s) - C(s). \tag{A.7}$$

Eqs. (A.3) and (A.4) are eqs. (4) and (5) in the text, eqs. (A.6) and (A.7) are eqs. (6) and (7) in the text.

References

Barro, Robert J., 1974, Are government bonds net wealth?, Journal of Political Economy 82, no. 6, 1095–1117.

Blanchard, Olivier J., 1981, Output, the stock market and interest rates American Economic Review 71, no. 1, 132–143.

Cardoso, Eliana, 1983, Fiscal policy and asset prices, Mimeo.

Hubbard, G., 1983, 'Structural' government budget deficits: Reappraisal and implications, Mimeo.

Tobin, James, 1967, Life cycle saving and balanced growth, in: Ten studies in the tradition of Irving Fisher (Wiley, New York).

Turnovsky, Steven and M. Miller, 1982, Bond market efficiency and macroeconomic policy in a simple dynamic model, Mimeo.

Yaari, Menahem E., 1965, Uncertain lifetime, life insurance and the theory of the consumer, Review of Economic Studies 32, 137–150.

COMMENTS

'Current and Anticipated Deficits, Interest Rates and Economic Activity'

by Olivier Blanchard

E. MALINVAUD

INSEE, 75675 Paris, France

To which extent should we revise our ideas on the impact of fiscal policy when its anticipated consequences are taken into account by the markets? This is indeed a quite important question for the progress of our macroeconomic theory. Before anything else, we must thank Olivier Blanchard for giving us an opportunity of discussing this important issue.

We know that the question was raised about ten years ago, as part of the critiques that attacked previous conceptions on the efficiency of Keynesian policies. We also know the answer given by Robert Barro in his famous article entitled 'Are government bonds net wealth?', claiming that there is no persuasive case for treating government debt as increasing perceived household wealth. This conclusion was said to imply the inefficiency of an expansionary fiscal policy financed by the issue of such bonds.

One should never have drawn this conclusion from Barro's model since it assumed full employment whereas the problem is precisely to know whether fiscal policy can reduce disequilibrium on the labor market. But on the one hand the question was worth raising, on the other hand Barro's model is stimulating for thinking about some aspects of the relationship between government debt and private saving.

A fully convincing theory of the impact of fiscal policy under perfect foresight is clearly quite difficult to build. It should indeed combine three features, each one of them taken alone already making modelling delicate: a proper representation of rational behavior by agents, an adequate formalization of market disequilibria, a long term perspective with in particular a correct treatment of stock–flow relationships. It is, therefore, not surprising that such a theory does not yet exist.

In order to make progress toward it, a good strategy consists in dealing at this stage with models that still neglect some important complications, but also in trying such a variety of models that we may hope to grasp all relevant aspects of the subject, although not yet within an integrated framework. This is precisely the strategy adopted by Blanchard since the three theoretical sections of his paper adopt three different approaches. He explicitly recognizes that these three sections are not integrated with one another. He tells us in his conclusion that 'integrating the first and the second (models), and the second and third, would probably be quite useful', but he does not dwell on this somewhat puzzling and not committing statement (would not integrating the first and third models be useful?).

The third model is the most interesting one for answering my main queries. But before considering it, I must say a few words about the second one.

Section 4, presenting this second model, is a quite neat and interesting piece of theoretical work. Adopting admittedly heroic simplifications proposed by M. Yaari, it succeeds in dealing with a dynamic equilibrium under rational expectations, while starting from individual life cycle behavior of consumers. It shows that, when consumers have a non-zero probability of dying, Barro's equivalence does not hold and an increase of government debt leads to an increase of long term interest rates, which changes the resulting equilibrium.

I am not surprised by the result, which fits well within the many cases that were considered by Barro in his article, not all of which implying neutrality of government debt. I even wonder whether one should not try to change the assumptions of the present model in one respect, so as to make them more realistic while keeping most of its simplicity. If consumers were subject to two risks instead of one, that of becoming inactive and not only that of dying, an important inducement for saving would be recognized in the model whereas it does not appear in the present form.

But the model of this section 4 assumes market clearing, aggregate demand exactly exhausting at any time the exogenously given supply. As I said at the beginning, this cannot be the proper framework for dealing with the impact of fiscal policy on output and unemployment.

I am, therefore, turning to section 5 which considers fiscal policy within an almost traditional IS–LM model augmented with a Phillips curve. The novelty of the model is the distinction between the long term real interest rate occuring in the IS equation and the short-term nominal interest rate of the LM equation; the relationship between the two is ruled by perfect foresight market equilibrium equations given by (19) and (20) on page 20. In the same way as in the models used in the early sixties, the long-term equilibrium output is given by the Phillips curve; namely, it is this output level that is consistent with a constant price level.

The conclusion drawn from the model is that current government deficits are expansionary but growing deficits are initially contractionary. More precisely:

— A sudden unanticipated increase of government spending g to a higher permanent level leads to a jump of long term interest rate and to a progressive increase of the price level up to a new equilibrium, while there is a temporary expansion of output; there will be more crowding out than would be predicted by models which do not distinguish between short and long interest rates, but no perverse effect of a fiscal expansion on output.

— On the other hand, if the decision is suddenly taken that government spending will from now on progressively grow to a higher level according to the equation of page 23, then the long term interest rate will immediately jump to a higher level on the way to its new equilibrium level; this will have a depressing effect on demand and will initially dominate the stimulating impact of increasing government spending.

Discussing this section, I must first stress the great pedagogical value of the model. It is excellent for exhibiting in a simple way one aspect of the role of anticipations on the short term equilibrium. In this respect, I find it more convenient than the model presented by Blanchard in his 1981 *American Economic Review* paper, in which stock prices were added to interest rates as market variables. The extra complication that this implied does not seem to me to be worth it.

With respect to the object of the paper the model is, however, subject to two limitations that should be noted. In the first place, its Phillips curve and the implied determination of equilibrium output are subject to criticism. I do not need to remind you of all the arguments showing why the Phillips curve may shift when anticipations are revised. I do not consider this comment as being devastating, since I know that, at the present time and for decades to come, macroeconomic theory has to be eclectic. But the limitation should be kept in mind; it means that the conclusions are well founded only when expectations about the long-term trend of inflation are insensitive to short term fluctuations of prices, as long as expectations on the money supply do not change (strictly speaking the paper assumes that long term expectations imply no inflation and a constant money supply).

The second limitation is made explicit on page 18: although financial markets look forward, agents themselves do not, in the sense that aggregate private demand does not directly react to future income and future taxes, but only to future prices and interest rates. The result would have been different if the framework of section 4 had been applied to the determination of aggregate demand and this is precisely why integration of sections 4 and 5 would be illuminating.

Blanchard speculates in section 5 about what changes would then be brought to his results. He convincingly argues that expectation of higher output and incomes will raise aggregate demand initially and that this income effect may dominate the interest effect, which was shown to be initially perverse in the case of a progressively increasing government deficit.

From this interesting section 5 I draw the conclusion that the approach of the paper is quite appropriate for dealing with the important issue of knowing how anticipations react on policy changes and how this reaction affects the impact of such changes. But there is still a good deal of work to be done, in order to apply the approach to various models exhibiting other relevant aspects of macroeconomic realities.

I shall be very brief in my comments on section 3 that considers the question of knowing how a present government deficit will be sustainable in the long run. Sustainability fails if future payments of interest on government debt will have to grow indefinitely as a result of present deficit. This notion of a possible lack of sustainability relates to another one, namely that taxes cannot be too high and government spending too low. The paper formalizes the idea in two simple alternative ways, taking as given, and constant through time, the maximum aggregate value of taxes that can be collected and the minimum value of non-interest government spending that has to be made.

It should be clear that other formalizations of the issue could be explored, concerning, for instance, the case of a growing economy, or the case in which the maximum concerns not the value of the flow of taxes but the rate of taxation, which would make a difference if the long-run value of output depends on present deficit.

How persuasive are such theoretical models for changing the views of people concerned with the present increase of interest charges in government budgets? I do not know. But the models are worthy of discussions in much larger circles than the present one.

COMMENTS

'Current and Anticipated Deficits, Interest Rates and Economic Activity'

by Olivier Blanchard

Stephen MARRIS

Washington, DC 20036, USA

It is obviously no accident that this paper addresses some issues at the heart of recent policy debate. All the discussions on macroeconomic policy in the OECD over the past two years have been bedevilled by the fact that about half of the people have been arguing that the best way to get out of a recession is to increase budget deficits, while the other half has been arguing that the best way is to reduce them. Actually, half of them have also been arguing that the best way to get out of a recession is to speed up the growth of the money supply, while the other half wants to slow it down — but this is a different story to which I will return only briefly.

As the author himself points out, the analysis of the sustainability of deficits in section 3 is rather static and oversimplified. On the one hand, allowing for positive GNP growth would provide most countries with significantly more room than suggested by eq. (3) before they found themselves caught in a Ponzi game. On the other hand, many countries could already be in a position where it might not be politically feasible to cut back deficits fast enough to match the cyclical reduction in the excess of savings in the private sector as we move into a recovery phase. If so, these deficits are not 'sustainable' in the sense that they will inevitably lead, either to crowding out with inadequate investment, or to monetisation with accelerating inflation.

This is where Blanchard's α term comes in — *the maximum politically feasible rate* at which today's deficit can be reduced. This is a very useful construct which deserves further thought and elaboration by both economists and political scientists.

A first suggestion would be to divide α into αG and αT, the maximum politically feasible rates of reducing public expenditure or increasing taxes. In most countries αG is probably more severely constrained than αT. Increases in expenditure are often deeply embedded in the legislation and administration of social programmes; and indexation and demography add

0014-2921/84/$3.00 © 1984, Elsevier Science Publishers B.V. (North-Holland)

to the momentum. It is generally politically easier, at least in the short term, to reduce deficits by raising taxation, partly because the pain is spread out more thinly through the electorate. There are, of course, economic constraints on the tax side, e.g., if higher taxes generate 'tax push' inflation or squeeze profits and depress investment, but these take some time to make themselves felt.

A second thought is that α no doubt varies quite a lot between countries. In parliamentary democracies with a clear majority the government can increase taxes almost at will. Indeed in a centralised country like France the authorities have a remarkably strong grip on both revenues and expenditure. In the United States, however, recent events have vividly illustrated the old adage that 'the Administration proposes, but Congress disposes'.

A third comment is that α should be engraved on the gravestone of Reagonomics. The basic idea was that the only way to reduce public expenditure is to reduce taxes. In certain circumstances this may be correct in terms of political realities. But anyone trying this experiment should be sure to get their sums right. If you knock $70 billion off your tax revenues, you may well be able to use the threat of large deficits to push through some cuts in expenditure. But if you are overambitious you will run head on into αG. If so, you will not be able to convince the financial markets that there is any politically feasible way of bringing the large budget deficit under control — and this, of course, is what has happened.

Blanchard tries to model the consequences of this for interest rates and economic activity in sections 4 and 5. Put very simply, eqs. (21) and (22) yield a world in which if action is taken which will lead to large deficits in the future, this creates the expectation of a *future* rise in short-term real interest rates which pushes up the long-term real rate *now*. If, in addition, the initial fiscal stimulus is small, its positive effects on activity could be more than swamped by the negative effect of these higher long-term rates. This model is not only elegant, it fits suspiciously well with what many commentators felt was happening to the United States economy at the time Blanchard was writing his paper.

One attractive feature of this model is that it calmly assumes that: 'although financial markets look forward, agents do not'. This seems to me to be a very sensible way to put some realism back into the wreckage created in the world of theoretical economics by the rational expectations school. It should be obvious that the man in the street does *not* spend all his time trying to work out with great ingenuity the ultimate consequences of every government action; but financial markets (and exchange markets) do.[1]

It is important to note that Blanchard's model does not seem to be able to explain why real *short-term* rates have remained so high during this

[1]For a similar approach to current macro-economic problems, see Andrea Boltho, 'Is Europe Caught in an Expectations Trap?', *Lloyds Bank Review*, April 1983.

recession. In other words, it leaves open the other half of the macro-policy debate: was US monetary policy unduly tight because of a failure to anticipate the magnitude of the recession-induced drop in velocity? What is interesting, however, is that it tackles directly the other much disputed question of why nominal long-term rates have not fallen more given the sharp drop in inflation. The answer suggested is that it is not (only) because of the downward stickiness of inflationary expectations, but also because of the emergence of high *interest rate* expectations related to the prospect of large and growing structural budget deficits.[2]

If this model is correct, what are the policy implications? In terms of *economics* it is simple: what is needed is action *now* to reduce budget deficits later. Various ideas have been put forward along these lines. The Institute for International Economics '26 economists' suggested 'front-loading' inevitable expenditure increases, while 'back-loading' the corresponding tax increases.[3] The Chairman of the Council of Economic Advisors has proposed a contingency plan to trigger the necessary tax increases if, as he assumes, the deficit problem does not solve itself as the supply-siders would like to believe.

But this is where we run into the politics of the α-factor with a vengeance. Nobody really believes that the US Congress is prepared to commit itself firmly to doing something nasty to its electors at some point in what is, in political terms, the dim and distant future. Indeed, more fundamentally, political realists are inclined to dismiss such ideas as pie in the sky on the grounds that if we cannot summon the political will to get public expenditure under control now, when deep recession and massive deficits create a strong sense of crisis, then we never will. 'Father, please let me stop sinning, but not just yet' may be good economics, but it is lousy politics. This is a real dilemma, and both sides clearly have a good case.[4]

A final comment: could these models explain why other countries have had abnormally high interest rates? Apparently not, because as Blanchard points out in section 2, when adjusted for inflation and low levels of activity, the structural budget position of most of the other major countries looks much better than that of the United States, and the prospects are that it will improve rather than deteriorate over the recovery period.

But an alternative 'closed economy' explanation is often given for a postulated negative effect of large deficits on interest rates, namely the consequences of the rapid accumulation of debt from *past* deficits. The

---

[2]The opening of financial future markets provides some indication of what has been happening to expected future rates of interest. It would be interesting to compare this with, e.g., Michigan survey data on what has been happening to inflationary expectations, to see whether this provides any empirical confirmation for this thesis.

[3]*Promoting World Recovery*. A statement on global economic strategy by 26 economists from 14 countries, Institute for International Economics, Washington, DC, December 1982.

[4]The 1983 Canadian budget, which combined a short-term stimulus with quite strong action to reduce expenditure and raise revenue two and three years out, was an interesting attempt to resolve this dilemma. Although it got quite a good reception, it may well not get a fair trial because of events in the United States.

argument is essentially that the higher the ratio of public debt to GNP, the higher the interest rate needed to finance a given budget deficit.

It is true that the ratio of government debt to GNP has increased strongly in some countries since the first oil crisis. Taking figures from a recent article by Robert Price and Jean-Claude Chouraqui,[5] which sets out a fascinating cross-country quantitative analysis of several of the issues dealt with in the Blanchard paper, we get:

	Japan	Germany	UK
Ratio of central government debt to GNP (percent): ·			
1973	11	7	44
1982	43	19	42
Change in percentage points	+32	+12	−2
Of which due to:			
Net new borrowing excluding interest payments	+37	+12	+28
'Inflation tax'[6]	−1	+2	−23
Other[7]	−4	−2	−7

It is interesting to note that the size of current budget deficits was not the only important factor. The debt ratio *fell* in the United Kingdom even though it was running deficits much larger than in Germany and three-quarters as large as in Japan over this period, the main factor being the heavy 'inflation tax' on holders of government debt.

Whatever the reasons, does the sharp rise in the ratio of government debt to GNP in Japan and Germany over this period help to explain the abnormally high levels of interest rates during the 1981–82 recession? Basically I am skeptical. In part this is because the historical record shows that different countries — and the same countries at different times — have been able to live with remarkably different ratios of debt to GNP. It is also because an alternative explanation lies readily to hand. The high level of interest rates outside the United States can be explained, not in terms of the size of budget deficits outside the United States, but rather in terms of the size of the actual and potential budget deficit in the United States, working its way out via a non-accommodating monetary policy to high interest rates, a strong dollar, and very large potential capital inflows.

Indeed, the question of how excesses or deficiencies in the balance of *ex ante* private savings versus public dissaving get transmitted from country to country has become central to international economic policy making. As Blanchard suggests at the end of his paper, it would be interesting to try to model it. But given the key role that exchange rates and exchange-rate expectations play in this process, and the weakness of virtually all attempts to model exchange-rate behaviour, this is likely to be a difficult task.

[5]Robert Price and Jean-Claude Chouraqui, 'Public Sector Deficits: Problems and Policy Implications', *OECD Economic Outlook, Occasional Studies*, Paris, June 1983.
[6]Interest payments less the reduction in the real value of government debt due to inflation.
[7]Effect of real GNP growth and relative price changes.

European Economic Review 30 (1986) . North-Holland

THE PURE THEORY OF COUNTRY RISK

Jonathan EATON*

University of Virginia, Charlottseville, VA 22901, USA

NBER, Cambridge, MA 02138, USA

Mark GERSOVITZ*

Princeton University, Princeton, NJ 08544, USA

Joseph E. STIGLITZ*

Princeton University, Princeton, NJ 08544, USA

NBER, Cambridge, MA 02138, USA

This paper attempts to survey, and to put into perspective, recent literature that has analyzed the nature of credit relations between developed and developing countries. This analysis has made use of recent advances in the economics of information and strategic interaction. Traditional concepts of solvency and liquidity are of little help in understanding problems of sovereign debt. Creditors do not have the means to seize the assets of a borrower in default. Hence the borrower's net worth is not relevant in determining the amount of a loan that can be recovered. A borrower who is expected eventually to repay his debts should be able to borrow to meet any current debt-service obligations. A problem that is essential to a theory of international lending is that of enforcement. The difficulty is one of ensuring that the two sides of a loan contract adhere to it, in particular that the borrower repays the lender and the lenders can commit themselves to penalize the borrower if he does not.

1. Introduction

In the early 1980's, several LDC's with very large debts to foreign banks did not meet the payments schedules to which they had originally agreed. Various participants in, and observers of, these markets began to speak of a crisis, one which they feared might shake the banking system of the developed countries. So far there has been no dramatic event to resolve the status of these loans. The absence of overt clues to what will happen to those involved with these debts generates a widespread interest in a conceptual framework useful in interpreting the current situation.

In this paper, we seek to articulate very general principles for looking at the most essential problems posed by international lending, ones that will be common to the relationships of most sovereign debtors and their creditors.

*Eaton and Stiglitz acknowledge the support of the National Science Foundation. We would like to thank Roger Guesnerie and Martin F. Hellwig for valuable comments.

This set of concepts is a necessary, although admittedly not a sufficient, tool kit for understanding current events and prescribing public policy.

Our concern, then, is with the pure theory of sovereign lending or country risk. We discuss the roles of borrowers, of lenders and of the various public authorities who mediate between the two groups, or regulate the lenders, or insure deposits in the banks. We make use of the literature on LDC indebtedness, which is related to recent advances in the general theory of credit markets. This work, in turn, incorporates recent advances in the general theory of the economics of information and the theory of games.

Loans are a particular contractual arrangement between suppliers of capital and the users of capital. The borrower promises to pay the lender certain amounts at certain times. A paramount concern in designing the contract is that the borrower may not be able to or may not wish to make payments under certain circumstances. The possibility that the lender will not recover his money is reflected not only in a high interest rate, but in the covenants of the loan contract. The purpose of these covenants is to protect the lender by precluding the borrower from engaging in certain activities, and ensuring that he engages in others. The loan contract also stipulates conditions under which the lender can intervene, e.g., in the event of a default on another loan.

Credit markets, like labor markets, are characterized by implicit as well as explicit contracts. For example, it is frequently the case that a lender makes a short-term loan for a long-term investment. There is an understanding that the loan will be renewed, except under unusual circumstances. The advantage of the short-term contract is that the lender can insist on additional restrictions on the borrower to renew the loan. To stipulate all of these restrictions on a conditional basis beforehand, at the time of the original loan, would have been virtually impossible. What prevents the lender from taking unfair advantage of the borrower are, as usual, reputation and competition from other lenders.

Consequently, the distinction between equity and debt, that the borrower is required to repay the principal plus interest on the latter and not on the former, becomes somewhat blurred. Though indeed the borrower is required to service a debt, there is no way that, in general, the borrower can be forced to do so under all contingencies. Debt and equity are both contingent claims, although they clearly differ in the nature of the contingencies involved. What factors are observable, and therefore can be used to condition contractual obligations, is an important determinant of the relationship between debtors and creditors.

1.1. Defining default

We have not, so far, said what we mean by default. In a two-period model of the economy, default may easily be defined: Whenever the borrower gives resources to the lender that are less than the fixed amount that he is committed to pay the lender, then there is a default.

In multi-period models, however, the concept is somewhat more elusive. A default occurs whenever the lender formally declares that the borrower has violated a certain condition of the loan.[1] A loan may be declared in default when a borrower refuses (or is unable) to pay another loan. The lender does not have to declare a loan in default, however; the contract only provides him the right to do so.

Thus, in most situations, a default is a result of a set of decisions, not the mechanical realization of some outcome. The proximate cause is generally the result of the borrower's decision not to make all or part of a loan payment that is due. But that decision, in turn, is frequently the result of the lender's decision not to extend further credit.

When the relationship between debtor and creditor can, in principle, last beyond the period in question, a violation of the repayment schedule, with or without a default, is neither necessary nor sufficient for the lender to realize less than the (present-discounted) value of the loan. A failure to make current payments does not necessarily imply that future payments will not be made, and conversely. This is one reason why observers of, and participants in, the market cannot expect any very overt sign of the status of these loans.

There is therefore an important difference between two-period and finite horizon, but multi-period, models. Furthermore, as we shall show, finite-horizon and infinite-horizon models can have qualitatively quite different properties when lenders can only ensure repayment through exclusion from future borrowing.

Much of the recent literature has failed to recognize these aspects of default. Thus, some writers attempt to relate default to insolvency, which arises in the case of unsecured loans when the borrower's debt exceeds his net worth (presumably inclusive of the debt). This is neither necessary nor sufficient for the declaration of a default. The declaration of a default usually has a large cost associated with it; an ongoing firm is almost always worth more than the value of its assets sold in a bankruptcy sale.[2] And in

---

[1]We only use default in this restricted sense.

[2]Consider a firm for which it has suddenly become apparent that there is a large probability that output will be zero. The expected present discounted value of its future income stream is less than the value of its outstanding obligations. The firm is (by standard definitions) insolvent. But a rational lender would not declare the firm in default if there were no moral hazard problem. For doing so would simply waste away some of the value which the lender might otherwise be able to appropriate. Consider, by contrast, a similar firm for which a new investment opportunity suddenly becomes available. The new investment is very risky. The expected present discounted value of the firm is very positive. If the firm undertakes the project, however, the expected return of the bank will be substantially decreased. The bank only obtains a return when the firm does not go bankrupt; it does not share in the bonanza which accrues if the risky investment project is successful. The bank would like to stop the project, but its loan contract does not have any provision enabling it to do so. If, however, there is a provision in the loan contract which enables it to declare the loan in default, it would be in the interests of the lender to do so, even though the firm is not insolvent.

international banking, declarations of default may trigger certain actions of bank regulators that are costly to lenders, in the first instance, and possibly to debtors as a consequence. What is at stake is more than the distribution of claims between debtors and creditors. More importantly, in a formal sense, insolvency is not really an issue in lending to foreign governments. The debt of a country in almost all instances is less than the value of the assets owned by nationals and the government of the country. There may be limits on the extent to which governments can appropriate the assets, but these limits themselves are, in general, not hard and fast constraints, but involve trade-offs.[3]

While some writers have linked default to insolvency, others have linked it to illiquidity. A borrower with a positive net worth who cannot convert the required portion of his net worth into a means of payment is said to be illiquid. The question is: why would no supplier of capital be willing to supply credit if it were unambiguously clear what the net worth of the asset were? Frequently, it is the withdrawal of credit that leads to the borrower's illiquidity; but it is precisely this withdrawal of credit that the theory should explain.

1.2. Domestic versus international lending

The ambiguity in the notion of default is relevant to both domestic and international lending. But there are also very important differences between the two, with consequences for the applicability of various concepts. We review briefly three problems traditionally addressed in theories of credit markets: Enforcement, moral hazard and adverse selection.

One problem in all lending is enforcement, the difficulty in ensuring that both sides of a contract adhere to its terms. Here, the particular concern is the difficulty of ensuring that the borrower pays the lender. The major difference between domestic and international debt is that the former are legal obligations, enforceable in courts. Another difference is that, domestically, debtors who cannot meet their obligations have the option of filing for bankruptcy. Repayment of international debt, however, is largely voluntary; the penalties to be imposed on a country that does not honor a contract are, at best, indirect. On the other hand, there is no systematic procedure, corresponding to bankruptcy, by which a country that has undertaken an excessive amount of debt can discharge its obligations and proceed on its way.

For similar reasons, collateral, which can be important domestically, plays little role in international lending.[4] If the collateral is retained in the

---

[3]We emphasize our dissatisfaction with models that simply take critical parameters of the economy as exogenous and, by so doing, create a problem.

[4]Note that the losses to the borrower often exceed the gains to the lender. This suggests that, at least in some circumstances, the incentive effects of collateral are more important than its guarantee effects.

borrowing country, there is no mechanism by which the creditor can seize it. If the collateral is moved outside the country, where the creditor can seize it, the borrower will usually lose fully the use of it, so that the value of the loan is reduced by the value of the collateral.[5] A fully and effectively collateralized loan would then be of no value to the borrower. As we shall see, the inability to provide collateral may significantly exacerbate the problems facing credit market participants.

When making loans to borrowers within the developed countries, lenders need to pay relatively little attention to enforcement problems, but instead must worry about problems of moral hazard. These arise because it is difficult for the lender to monitor actions of the borrower to ensure that they do not affect adversely the prospects for debt service. For instance, a firm may have an investment opportunity with low expected return, but with the possibility of a high return under some circumstances. In the good states, the firm pays its creditors and reaps large net benefits; otherwise, the firm goes bankrupt, and the creditor loses. Such a project may be quite attractive to the firm, although quite undesirable from the creditor's viewpoint.

In international loans, such problems are much less prominent in the relationship between country borrowers and their creditors. As we have argued, the resources of the debtor are likely to be adequate to repay the loans regardless. In a sense, it is the very importance of the enforcement problem that, as we shall explain, keeps creditors from ever lending so much that moral hazard problems involving choice among risky investments become central. On the other hand, moral hazard problems may arise if (1) borrowers can affect their susceptibility to penalties that enforce payment, or (2) they can affect the likelihood that creditors will impose penalties (if creditors cannot precommit fully), or (3) the total amount that they have borrowed cannot be observed by individual lenders. In each of these situations, borrowers' actions affect the probability of payment.

Moral hazard issues also arise in the relationship between banks and the governmental insurers of bank deposits. This insurance obviates the need for depositors to monitor adequately bank portfolios. There is a consequent incentive for banks to lend in a risky fashion, hoping for big profits but able to transfer large losses to their insurers. The traditional role for bank regulators is to prevent these actions by rules on portfolio composition, but these have been loosely designed, and have not prevented the lending of multiples of bank capital to LDC's.

A third set of problems facing lenders are ones of adverse selection. Here the difficulty is one of ascertaining the characteristics of a borrower, both transitory and permanent, relevant to designing a repayment schedule and judging whether a borrower will adhere to it. Without this ability, the lender

---

[5]There may, of course, be some exceptions such as the opportunity to seize airplanes owned by a national airline in default that tries to use them in international service.

is vulnerable to attracting only those borrowers who know that their repayment prospects are poor or who claim that they cannot pay when they can. In many cases, however, outside lenders are as fully informed as domestic politicians about the country's economic situation, and so adverse selection may be less important internationally than domestically.

In our view, then, the problems of moral hazard and adverse selection deserve attention, but really central to our understanding of credit relations between developed and developing countries is identifying the incentives for borrowers to repay, and for suppliers of capital to continue supplying capital. As we shall show, actions of the borrower (or lender) may affect these incentives. To the extent that borrowers can take actions that increase the likelihood that they will repay their loans, they will be better off. By doing so, they can increase the willingness of lenders to lend. Similarly, to the extent that lenders take actions that increase the likelihood that they will continue to renew the loans, borrowers may be more willing to borrow and repay.

2. The willingness-to-pay of borrowers

In the introduction, we sketched our basic view that, in most situations, what happens to a loan is a result of a series of decisions, not the mechanical realization of some outcome. Thus, the analysis of international credit markets must focus on how borrowers and lenders make their decisions. Surprisingly, a few simple notions can help to delimit the possible relationships between debtors and creditors. For instance, the fact that loans are voluntary rules out situations in which all future net transfers as of any date are always from the lender to the borrower. Later on, we show that in an important class of models, also net transfers cannot always be from the borrower to the lender.

In this section, we focus on the behavior of borrowers, and in the next section, we turn to the lenders. In a fundamental sense, the dichotomy is artificial: A borrower's willingness to pay depends critically on his beliefs about (1) the lender's resolve to penalize a recalcitrant borrower, and (2) the lender's willingness to lend in the future. For now, we assume that the potential penalties we discuss will always be imposed.

2.1. The general structure of models with penalties

We begin with an extremely simple two-period model. A loan of amount L is made in the first period with an obligation to repay $r(L)$ in the second period. The model ends after the second period, so that there are no further considerations that affect the participants.

If the borrower does not discharge this obligation, he suffers a penalty, $\bar{P}$

expressed in the same units as $r(L)$. The borrower's welfare is a function $U[L, x]$ which increases with the amount borrowed, L, and decreases in the obligation imposed by the loan, x, where

$$x = r(L) \quad \text{if he repays,}$$
$$= \bar{P} \qquad \text{if he defaults.}$$

(1)

The borrower who defaults receives total utility of

$$U_d = U[L, \bar{P}]$$

(2)

in the second period. If he does service the debt as agreed, his utility is

$$U_p = U[L, r(L)].$$

(3)

The borrower chooses to pay if

$$U_p \geq U_d.$$

(4)

This comparison of alternatives is at the heart of a willingness-to-pay approach.

Under the assumptions that lenders are competitive and face an opportunity cost of funds of i, the repayment lenders require is

$$r(L) = (1 + i)L.$$

(5)

Substituting (1), (2), (3), and (5) into (4) implies that repayment occurs for

$$L \leq \bar{P}/(1 + i).$$

(6)

As long as lenders understand the borrower's situation some central conclusions follow:

(1) Borrowers may be credit constrained. If the borrower wishes to borrow a little more than $\bar{P}/(1 + i)$ at rate i, he cannot. On the other hand, the borrower need not wish to borrow as much as he can.
(2) There is never any inconsistency between a loan contract that says the loan must be repaid with interest at rate i and what happens.
(3) Penalties are never imposed.
(4) If the borrower wants to borrow more, he benefits from an increase in the penalty $\bar{P}$.
(5) If there is no penalty, one observes no lending rather than a rash of loan-

contract violations. At its simplest, willingness-to-pay is a theory of rationing, not one of lender losses.

We use the simple model and its conclusions as a mechanism to organize other formulations of the willingness-to-pay approach.

For instance, one modification that undermines the fourth conclusion on the welfare effects of enhanced penalties, while maintaining the others, can occur if the borrower is large, or if we consider simultaneous increases in the penalties applied to a large number of borrowers. An increase in $\bar{P}$ may then raise the world interest rate, to the borrowers' detriment. In the extreme, if funds available for this kind of lending are fixed, an increase in $\bar{P}$ raises i without raising L.

2.2. Models with uncertainty

Next, we begin to introduce uncertainty into the model, otherwise returning to all the assumptions of eqs. (1)–(5). For simplicity, assume that the penalty depends on the state of nature, s,

$$P = P(s). \tag{1a}$$

Utility of the borrower if he defaults is

$$U_d = U[L, P, s], \tag{2a}$$

and if he does not

$$U_p = U[L, r(L), s], \tag{3a}$$

where the argument s indicates that utility may depend on s in other ways than through P. Note, however, that $r(L)$, the amount of payment, does not depend on s.

The debtor pays off his obligations in all states s in S for which

$$U_p \geq U_d \tag{4a}$$

and otherwise not, for s in S'. The borrower's expected utility is

$$\int_S U_p f(s)\, ds + \int_{S'} U_d f(s)\, ds,$$

where $f(s)$ is the probability of state s. If lenders are competitive, risk-neutral and face a constant cost of funds i then

$$\pi r(L) = (1 + i)L, \tag{5a}$$

where the probability of repayment is

$$\pi = \int_S f(s)\, \mathrm{d}s. \tag{7}$$

The existence of uncertainty means that payment may not be made, and the penalty may be imposed. An increase in the penalty need not increase a borrower's expected utility. While it will normally increase the amount lent, to the borrower's benefit, in those states when the country does not pay it may be worse off.[6]

On the other hand, uncertainty need not imply $\pi < 1$ if the repayment schedule can also be made contingent on the state of nature. In this case, the state contingent repayment, $r(L, s)$, is chosen so that $U_p \geq U_d$ for all s. This is the approach taken by Grossman and Van Huyck (1985). The explicit legal contract, however, conventionally specifies a single interest rate (or a single spread above the market rate). Lenders do not have the scope to revise the contractual interest rate upward, unless the borrower violates the contract. The contractually specified payment must therefore be the maximum of payments in all possible states, $r^+(L) = \max_s r(L, s)$. Any state s with $r(L, s) < r^+$ could then be called a situation of excusable default, in the Grossman–Van Huyck terminology. Penalties are only imposed if the country pays less than $r(L, s)$, not less than r^+. This is one interpretation of the current reschedulings. It presupposes that the state s can be observed by both parties after the fact, and that disputes over what has happened do not arise. The issue therefore remains of what situations can be used to condition contracts.

A further set of complications arises if the actions by the borrower can affect the burden of the penalty. Actions that lenders perceive as increasing the burden may improve the terms of loans. To do so such actions must be observable by the lender and costly to reverse. Actions that are unobservable but still raise the burden of the penalty give rise to a whole range of moral hazard issues [Stiglitz and Weiss (1981) and (1983)].

2.3. The nature of penalties

The simple models just discussed do not show how the penalty originates; its size is exogenously given and does not depend on the characteristics of debtors or creditors. In fact, however, we believe that the penalties available to creditors are rather indirect, and that identifying their ultimate implications for debtors is one of the basic issues in the pure theory of

---

[6]For instance, Sachs and Cohen (1985) point out that the opportunity not to pay may substitute for insurance, allowing a risk-averse borrower to offset bad shocks elsewhere. See also Eaton and Gersovitz (1984) on penalties under uncertainty.

country risk. Only by modeling the penalty realistically can one tell which countries are most susceptible to them.

Eaton and Gersovitz (1981b) discuss some of the legislation that potentially provides for penalties imposed by the U.S. government, while Kaletsky (1985) provides a comprehensive review of the relevant legal, institutional and political issues. What concerns us here are two types of exclusions that creditors can potentially impose on debtors: (1) an embargo of future borrowing, and (2) various forms of interference with the debtors' international transactions and transfers.

Eaton and Gersovitz (1981a) consider what it means to a borrower to be excluded from future loans. Some very simple situations in which such a penalty has no force can be mentioned. First, such a penalty only makes sense in a model with an infinite horizon. If there were a last period, no loans would be repaid in that period since there would be no future exclusion to worry about. Lenders knowing this would never make a loan coming due in this period. But, this in turn would render a threat of exclusion meaningless from the viewpoint of the penultimate period, so no loan coming due in this period would be possible. And so on, by backward induction, the penalty would be unable to support any lending. Second, even in an infinite-horizon world, such a penalty would be ineffective if the model ever predicts that a point will be reached after which the flow will always be from debtor to creditor, via arguments similar to those just made.

It is only when the future always holds some possibility of transfers in *both* directions that this penalty becomes operative. It is for this reason that Eaton and Gersovitz focus on a model in which the income of the borrower alternates between low and high values, either in a deterministic or stochastic way. If borrowers are risk averse, the demand for loans derives from a desire for consumption smoothing. The cost of the denial of credit is that the country must resort to other methods for consumption smoothing (e.g., building up stockpiles), or it must accept a greater fluctuation in its consumption pattern.

If lenders are risk neutral and borrowers risk averse, the lenders can smooth borrowers' consumption at no cost to themselves. In effect, the penalty is the loss of consumers' surplus on being excluded from the market; it is inframarginal from the borrower's viewpoint. The penalty (and hence the supply of credit) is higher the greater the cost to the borrower of exclusion, which in turn is higher: (1) the greater the borrower's elasticity of marginal utility, (2) the more variable its income, (3) the lower the cost of smoothing via the international capital market, i.e., the lower the world interest rate; and (4) the more limited are domestically available options for smoothing consumption. A country with limited risk aversion may still want to make great use of the possibilities for consumption smoothing afforded by international lending if its income is highly variable. The cost of losing this option may not be large, however, so that the current demand for the facility is not necessarily related to the penalty occasioned by the loss.

Uncertainty, or at least income variation, seems crucial for the penalty of exclusion to have force. By contrast, the argument is sometimes made informally that countries that need funds for development are likely to suffer if denied loans. It is true that they may benefit greatly from being able to borrow, but this is not the same as saying that the penalty of exclusion can assure the lender that he will be repaid. Borrowing for capital accumulation or productive investment implies that a point will be reached beyond which the debtor will begin making transfers to his creditor. Once the marginal product of capital equals the interest rate, there will be no further gain to moving capital to the debtor. At this point, the debtor will lose nothing by being denied access to credit markets, and will refuse to service his debts. And, by backward induction as before, it will never be possible to lend with prospects of payment.

Owners of capital can entrust it to others who have the opportunity for profitable investment, and obtain payment by threatening exclusion from future access to capital, but in situations that do not seem relevant to financial lenders. Allen (1983) discusses how landowners may be able to ensure that they are paid even if those who use their land could, in principle, abscond without paying their rents. In his model, the land must be left behind, and those who do not pay landlords cannot get land to farm in the future. As a result, they may have diminished income opportunities in the future, in which case the penalty has deterrent value.

Eaton and Gersovitz (1983) discuss a model of direct foreign investment. In this case, capital depreciates and cannot be replaced without the help of foreign investors. If they are expropriated, foreign investors refuse to cooperate, and exclude the country from the market for physical capital in the future. Here again, financial lenders do not seem able to impose such a penalty package.

International lending appears to play an important role in financing international trade. Borrowing does not simply finance the current account deficit, but is associated with the level of international purchases. In principle, a country could trade on the basis of barter, but to do so is likely to be costly. Kraft (1984) reports that Mexican officials perceived the disruption of trade as the primary cost of default. Iran, when faced with a temporary credit embargo, found trade difficult, even though the country was a net creditor.

When countries can anticipate problems in effecting transactions, however, they can act to shield themselves. Waiting to impose penalties may diminish their efficacy. Countries may accumulate foreign reserves to finance post-default trade, rather than use income to pay debts. Trading partners that gain from trade with debtors may help to facilitate transactions; it is hard to know what potential institutions will try to substitute for banks, thereby undermining the sanctions available to banks.

Gersovitz (1983) develops a model in which the penalty associated with default depends positively on the importance to a debtor of its opportunity to trade. An implication is that a borrower's commitment to increase investment raises the credit ceiling if it increases the value of the option to trade. In the factor endowment model this is not always the case. If the investment is in import-competing industries, then the country may be better able to withstand a credit embargo. If the investment is in export industries, requiring at the same time large imports of certain key materials, then the country may be in a much worse position to withstand a credit embargo.

In a series of papers Sachs (1984), Cooper and Sachs (1985), and Sachs and Cohen (1985) assume that the penalty is proportional to income. This assumption is useful in illustrating certain basic aspects of creditor–debtor relationships, as is the model of subsection 2.1, but the penalty is clearly not a plausible one in the same way as an exclusion from future borrowing or trade transactions. As a consequence, some of their conclusions seem questionable, such as their emphasis on the benefits obtained by a credit-constrained borrower who can precommit to investment rather than consumption; see Gersovitz (1985).

3. The resolve of lenders

So far, we have assumed that lenders always penalize debtors who do not adhere to loan agreements. But will lenders do so? There is no obvious way that lenders can commit themselves at the time the loan is made to punish a country that refuses to pay. Depending on the situation, it may be costly to penalize recalcitrant debtors. Moreover, punishment may not affect the prospect of a resumption of debt service. If it is not in the interest of lenders to punish, then the threat of punishment will not be credible to borrowers. An equilibrium with positive lending will be infeasible.

In some cases the penalties may be fairly automatic. For instance, if a country that refuses to pay banks tries to transact with the help of these same banks, it may find that its transactions balances are offset by the banks against its outstanding obligations. The country will then have to seek alternative means of effecting transactions, presumably at higher cost, to avoid this threat. In fact, a promise by the banks not to seize the country's balance may itself not be credible. This mechanism is part of the justification behind the trade–cost model in Gersovitz (1983).

There is more doubt, however, about the resolve of lenders to exclude debtors from future loans. Below, we discuss two models. In one, lenders do cut off credit from those who are in default (as part of a reputational equilibrium), but in the other they do not, and the loan market ceases to function.

3.1. Penalties in reputation-based models

Contracts that are unenforceable through the legal system may still be enforced by some kind of reputational mechanism. The threat of losing one's reputation (credit rating) is what induces so-called good behavior (repayment of the loan). There are two classes of reputational models. In one there are markets in which there are inherently good and bad borrowers. Lenders make an inference concerning individuals according to their past behavior. Thus it is the fear of being classified as a bad borrower that induces good behavior. But even if there is only one type of borrower, reputational mechanisms may be effective. To construct a reputational equilibrium one must show that, if a borrower does not service a loan, it will not pay the lender (or any other lender) to extend credit to him. Thus reputational models entail the simultaneous analysis of borrower and lender behavior.

In Eaton and Gersovitz (1981a), lenders are competitive, and each occupies a small share of the market, earning zero profit on any loan. It therefore costs the lender nothing to refrain from future lending. Moreover, in their model, the borrowers and lenders interact over a potentially infinite horizon. [In a finite horizon, a loss of reputation means nothing in the last period, and therefore cannot justify any last-period lending. By backward induction, reputation is meaningless, as in the chain-store paradox discussed by Selten (1978).[7]]

If there is no finite upper bound on the number of times players expect to play a game, however, and their identity is remembered by their opponents, then the players' reputation as cooperative players can succeed in enforcing some degree of cooperation. A player who fails to cooperate at any single play will not find cooperative partners for subsequent plays. If players' discount rates are zero then full cooperation is ensured, while infinite discount rates leads to no cooperation. With a finite but positive discount rate, some cooperation emerges, and in Eaton and Gersovitz (1981a) this is embodied in the credit ceiling that sets the maximum loan that lenders will extend to countries that have paid in the past.

For the threat of withdrawal of credit to be a credible sanction, it must not only be in the interests of the current creditors to withdraw credit, but it also must be in the interests of potential creditors not to extend credit. The relatively small number of international banks may be able to sustain the cooperative outcome (in which they all punish defaulters) within a non-cooperative context. Since they deal with each other repeatedly, those who fail to cooperate will themselves be punished. Moreover, the country's current bankers are likely to be more informed concerning the country than other potential lenders. Hence, the refusal of the current lenders to continue

---

[7]Kreps and Wilson (1982) suggest how imperfect information of a particular kind can sustain a reputational equilibrium even in a finite-horizon game.

extending credit may lead others to refuse as well; see Greenwald, Stiglitz and Weiss (1984). Indeed, the current lender usually has more to gain from the continuation of credit than do others, for it stands to recover earlier loans as well.

Finally, seniority clauses in international loan contracts could be enforced by earlier lenders against subsequent lenders in the courts of developed countries, thereby dissuading other potential lenders. Such clauses are attractive because they do not require a suit or enforcement of a judgement against the sovereign debtor. Stiglitz and Weiss (1983) show that if there are seniority provisions in outstanding loans, then if the current lender refused to lend, others will as well.

Because individuals are finite lived, they may lack incentives to impose penalties, so lending among individuals may not be sustainable. Infinitely-lived institutions, such as banks, can emerge, however, that can credibly threaten to punish debtors in order to maintain their reputation as lenders. Maintaining the value of their equity investments in a bank provides the incentive to the owners of the bank to punish default. The failure to do so would cause the value of a bank's equity to fall to zero.

For this mechanism to work, the value of bank equity must exceed the cost of imposing the penalty. If it is costly to punish, a bank must earn a profit strictly in excess of zero. The interest rate on loans consequently exceeds that on deposits. Even though in equilibrium the penalty is never imposed, the cost of implementing the penalty causes the equilibrium allocation to differ from what would emerge if loan repayment were automatic, see Eaton (1985).

3.2. Information and the lender's problem

Lenders need information to make sure that they can prevent the debtor from getting into situations in which debt is not serviced. In subsection 2.2, we discussed a model in which debtors did not pay in some states of nature, but debtors and lenders had the same information about the likelihood of these states of nature. Borrowers may, however, have more information than lenders about their own attributes that determine their susceptibility to penalties, and even about the total amount of debt they have undertaken which, with the penalty, determines the set of states when the borrower does not pay as he contracted.

Kletzer (1984) analyzes some of the problems that arise under these circumstances in a model similar to that of Eaton and Gersovitz (1981a). He focuses on knowledge about the amount lent, a crucial determinant of borrower behavior. [See also Arnott and Stiglitz (1982) for the basic structure of such moral hazard problems.]

If lenders *can* observe the total quantity lent, competition will assure a loan-interest-rate combination that maximizes borrower utility subject to the zero-profit condition. The equilibrium is consequently determined by a tangency of a borrower's indifference curve to the supply curve. The borrower will be constrained in that, given the interest rate, he would prefer to borrow more.

On the other hand, the total amount lent may be unobserved by lenders. *If* an equilibrium with positive debt exists under these circumstances, it will be characterized by both a higher debt and a higher interest rate than if debt is observable. The borrower is better off when debt is observable, however; the lower rate of interest more than compensates for the rationing of credit. Kletzer interprets lending through syndicates and the importance of short-term debt as institutional arrangements in international financial markets that facilitate lenders' monitoring and control of the borrower's total debt.

As we noted in section 2, borrowers may be able to take actions that affect penalties, and thereby undermine their willingness to pay. To the extent that these actions are observable, and lenders can deter them by credibly threatening sanctions, no moral hazard problems arise. But when the action is unobservable, moral hazard problems are a concern [Stiglitz and Weiss, (1981, 1983)]. Furthermore, if different borrowers have different unobservable susceptibilities to penalties, creditors will have an incentive to design contracts that improve the quality of their borrowers, or that sort borrowers. As a result market equilibria may be characterized by credit rationing and/or a non-linear relationship between interest payments and loan size [see Jaffee and Russell (1976) and Stiglitz and Weiss (1981, 1983)]. For instance, in the context of international loans, whether debtors are prepared to adopt an IMF program or not may serve to distinguish between countries that do and do not intend to service their debts.

3.3. The breakdown of lending

So far, we have looked at models in which lenders may manage to deal with problems of asymmetric information and credibility, at least sufficiently to justify some lending. Hellwig (1977) provides a model that stresses the inability of lenders to cope with enforcement problems, and their consequent inability to lend.

In this model, the breakdown of lending results from the lender's inability to precommit himself to a ceiling on indebtedness. The borrower is an agent with zero current income. At some unknown future date the borrower's income is expected to jump to a permanently higher level. If by that time the borrower has not defaulted then any debt up to some maximum is repaid. In the meantime, the borrower finances his consumption from loans. The lender extends a line of credit which the borrower draws down as he consumes. If the line is depleted before income rises, the loan goes into default unless more credit is forthcoming. If default occurs, the borrower's utility from that moment onward is specified exogenously as a decreasing function of indebtedness.

A particular consumption profile corresponds to each amount of total credit that the borrower believes available. The lender wants the borrower to draw on credit slowly, minimizing the probability of default before income rises. If the lender could precommit to providing a particular amount of credit then a loan to the borrower can provide a non-negative expected yield. The problem is that if the borrower exhausts the initial line of credit before his income rises, the lender has an incentive to provide more. Cutting the borrower off ensures default; extending credit maintains a hope of repayment. Part of the return on additional funds committed to the borrower is the possibility of salvaging some of what has already been lent. The lender will consequently make loans that would not yield a profitable expected return on their own. It pays him at that point to throw good money after bad.[8]

The borrower perceives that when he exhausts the initial loan the lender will provide more. He consequently draws down the initial loan more quickly. This raises the probability of his incurring the maximum amount of debt that will be repaid before income rises, at which point credit is cut off.

By initially extending credit, then, the lender places himself in a situation in which the commitment of additional funds may be profitable even though the expected return on all funds committed is negative. To avoid this imbroglio he desists from lending in the first place. He suffers from his inability to control the borrower's consumption once the loan has been made, and from his inability to control his own future lending behavior. While some features of Hellwig's model may seem special, the point raised is more general, as shown by Stiglitz and Weiss (1981).

3.4. Panics by lenders

The previous section explained why enforcement and commitment problems may constrain lending in some circumstances, even though additional lending may be mutually beneficial in the absence of these problems. We now examine situations in which banks that have been lending suddenly cut off credit. There is some similarity between such credit runs and the traditional problem of bank runs.

While bank runs have long been a source of concern, only recently have researchers developed simple models to analyze them [see Diamond and Dybvig (1983) and Nakamura (1985)]. Diamond and Dybvig analyze runs using game theory. All lenders are better off if none withdraws his funds. But

---

[8]Note that the current lender's incentives for extending credit are thus greater than the incentives of other potential lenders [recall our earlier discussion and Stiglitz–Weiss (1983)].

if some depositors run, the others are better off if they simultaneously withdraw their funds, or, indeed, anticipate the others' action and withdraw first. There exist perfect equilibria in which all try to withdraw and others in which none do.

Nakamura observes that the expected rate of return on deposits is a function of the number of depositors withdrawing their funds; while at the same time, the number of depositors withdrawing their funds is a function of the expected rate of return. There may be multiple solutions to this pair of equations, in one of which many depositors withdraw funds (a run), and in the other of which few do. The existence of multiple equilibria raises questions about which equilibrium prevails, and why and how the economy moves among them.

Depositors are, of course, the bank's creditors; the phenomenon of runs can arise whenever a borrower has many creditors and there are short-term liabilities. Each creditor wishes to protect himself; in doing so, he may actually increase the likelihood that others will be unable to recoup what they have lent. This is a potentially important externality.

The occurrence of runs depends critically on the form of the debt instrument. For instance, in the Diamond–Dybvig model, the bank must allow any customer to withdraw his entire deposit at the posted yield on a first-come-first-served basis. Other contract arrangements avoid this problem; for instance, if there is a well-defined seniority structure, runs will not occur. Runs do not occur against mutual funds, since the asset value is continuously redefined. To the extent that the runs problem is important, one needs to explain why a contractual form that leads to runs is employed.

Sachs (1984) and Krugman (1985) present models similar to Diamond and Dybvig with respect to syndicated bank loans to developing countries, only with the borrowing country assuming the role of the banks and the lending banks that of the individual depositors. In period one the borrower owes debt to a large number of bank lenders, an amount that exceeds current income.

The central problem in explaining credit runs is why it does not pay other banks to step in when one lender withdraws credit. Sachs resolves this difficulty by assuming that each bank faces a rising marginal cost of loans, an assumption that can be justified by bank exposure regulations or by managerial risk aversion. Because individual banks face an increasing marginal cost of lending, it may not pay any single bank to extend a loan to avoid a default in the first period. It is in the collective interest of all creditors to extend further credit in concert, guaranteeing themselves the necessary return. The reason for this in Sachs' model is that a failure to renew any loan in the first period brings about a situation in which no loan is repaid in either period. More generally, this will be true if the return on one loan increases with the amount lent by others. This hypothesis can be contrasted with that of Kletzer (and moral hazard analysis, in general) where the return on one loan decreases with the amount lent by others.

The assumption of an increasing marginal cost to each bank of lending may be questioned. The senior debtor knows that if he refuses to renew credit others will do so as well [see also Stiglitz and Weiss (1981)]. Even if the cost of capital increases with exposure, once some amount has been extended, a bank may be willing to commit further funds to prevent the loss of the original commitment even if, standing alone, the yield would be inadequate. Consequently, it is a bank with an initially large exposure that will find the value of extending further credit the greatest.

The criticisms levied earlier at the Diamond–Dybvig model apply here as well. In particular, to the extent that this is a serious problem, it should have been anticipated. To the extent that it was anticipated, the problem could have been forestalled, e.g., by each bank lending for two periods, and only on the condition that other banks lent for a similar period. There is, moreover, one important difference between bank behavior and the behavior of depositors. Because banks are engaged in economic relations with each other repeatedly over an extended period of time, there may exist a cooperative equilibrium that sustains the efficient outcome (no-runs).

As Gersovitz (1985) has pointed out, there is a basic difference between a situation in which the debtor would like to obtain a new net flow of funds and one in which he merely wants to postpone debt service. It is the latter situation that most debtors have confronted who have recently engaged in reschedulings. They are making net payments to their creditors, but less than would be required by the original loan contracts in the absence of new loans. In this case, the debtor can deal with reluctant creditors by declaring a unilateral, partial moratorium on debt service. If all creditors have the same upward-sloping cost of funds, the debtor will minimize their losses by making proportional (although partial) payments. By contrast, the upward-sloping cost of funds and the associated externality means that it may not be possible for the debtor first to pay all creditors and then to ask them for further funds. It is this difference between a pro-rated moratorium or rescheduling and a refinancing after payment that the Sachs and Krugman models explain. On this interpretation current problems are more ones of form than substance, assuming, of course, that there is no fundamental reason, such as willingness-to-pay, why debt service will not be resumed.

It would be quite another thing if debtors needed positive flows. For instance, a debtor may have an investment project already underway that will become valueless without a further infusion of funds to allow its completion. In this case, the debtor could not unilaterally initiate a solution and the prospects for success under the Sachs and Krugman assumptions would be very much reduced. The problem would then be closer to that originally postulated by Diamond and Dybvig who assume that two-period investments are inherently more productive.

4. A re-examination of the solvency issue

Earlier, we remarked that it seems implausible that lending to developing countries is constrained by their ability to pay, or solvency. Debt levels do not seem so high, and, we argue, for a good reason: Long before a country's ability-to-pay would become relevant, its willingness-to-pay constrains its access to credit.

An earlier literature did analyze the sovereign debt problems from a solvency viewpoint, however, and in this section we briefly re-examine this literature using the framework we have just presented. Although primary reliance on ability-to-pay models is dangerous, some important insights can be gained from this approach. Indeed, as noted, some of the models of lenders' resolve we reviewed use solvency concepts in determining when payment occurs.

A useful way of understanding the problems that arise in evaluating the ability of the borrower to repay a loan is to look at the basic balance of trade identities. If D is total debt, ΔD repayment of debt, r the interest rate, and B the trade balance then in any period

$$\Delta D + rD \equiv B. \tag{8}$$

If S is private savings, I domestic investment, T tax revenue and G government spending, another identity is that

$$\Delta D \equiv (S - I) + (T - G). \tag{9}$$

Thus debt service is related both to the trade surplus and to private and government savings. If domestic product Y is independent of T, an unconstrained government could in theory set $T = Y$, and $G = I = 0$, in which case $S = -rD$ and $\Delta D + rD = Y$. Though eqs. (8) and (9) are nothing more than identities, they provide a framework for understanding possible sources of problems in a country's meeting its foreign debt obligations.

An early paper by Domar (1950) made the point that a lender country could perpetually run a current account surplus only if the growth rate of loanable funds permanently exceeded the interest rate. Avramovic et al. (1964) applies an analysis somewhat like Domar's to a borrowing country. There are fixed savings, tax and import parameters. In this context a borrower eventually cannot repay his debt unless his growth rate permanently exceeds the interest rate.

Such models suffer from two problems. First, the variables that they take as exogenous, such as the growth rate, are endogenous. Second, if they were exogenous, a variety of conundrums would arise. If the borrower's growth rate remains permanently above the interest rate, there would be the problem of matching loanable funds to the implied loan demand. On the other hand, how is repayment to occur if and when the growth falls below the interest rate?

Since sovereign loans are owed by the governments of countries, repayment is not constrained by the net worth of the country, but by that component of net worth that the government can (or is willing to) appropriate. For a government that can impose lump-sum taxation at no administrative cost, national wealth and maximal government revenue do coincide. Taxes typically impose excess burdens and are costly to raise, however, so that the maximal amount that the government can extract from an economy falls short of the net worth of the economy. Nonetheless, it seems implausible that governments are anywhere near making the maximum feasible debt service.

Kharas (1984) and Sachs (1984) model solvency in terms of a constraint on government revenue. The first is a variant of the Domar (1944) and Avramovic et al. (1964) models with an exogenous, fixed proportional tax rate, as well as an exogenous saving rate. Sachs (1984) considers a two-period optimizing framework in which a government faces a revenue constraint only in the repayment period. He emphasizes that such a government should borrow less than the amount that equates the world interest rate to the domestic marginal product of capital. The reason is that the binding resource constraint implies a higher marginal cost of government revenue in the repayment period than in the borrowing period.

The argument that a binding government budget constraint reduces optimal borrowing does not, however, generalize much beyond this example. If the government were constrained in total resources from domestic sources in the initial, rather than the repayment, period then the marginal cost of funds in that period would exceed that in the repayment period. Efficiency would demand borrowing *more* than the amount that, if invested, would equate the domestic marginal product of capital to the world interest rate. The argument also assumes that the revenue from investments financed by the loan does not accrue to the government, but must be taxed from the private sector. Otherwise the standard condition for optimality would apply.

More generally, there is not a rigid constraint on raising taxes in any period. Efficient borrowing-cum-tax policy will take into account three factors: (1) the marginal (social) cost of raising revenue increases with the amount raised in any period, (2) additional investment at one date may affect the marginal cost of raising funds at a later date, and (3) borrowing costs may increase as a country borrows more within any period. Plausible models may be constructed that imply a country should borrow more than the amount that would, if invested, equate the domestic marginal product of capital to the world interest rate.

A second reason why national net worth may overstate resources available for repayment to lenders abroad is the difficulty in transferring national assets to foreigners. Simonsen (1985) provides an extreme version of this view which postulates an autonomous trade balance. A country's net worth, from a lender's perspective, is consequently the discounted present value of its trade account. For a solvent borrower this amount exceeds the value of debt. The value of resources within the country is irrelevant since there is no way to transfer them to foreigners except through the trade account. A less extreme version of this view models the trade account as a function of a set of variables that are partially responsive to policy. Repayment then requires that the government pursue policies that yield the necessary trade account surplus. This view precludes the possibility of repayment by a direct sale of domestic assets to foreigners without their contemporaneous export.

One argument why the trade balance constrains a debtor's ability to repay is the traditional transfer problem, an issue raised by Diaz-Alejandro (1984). Repayment could worsen the terms of trade of a debtor, consequently reducing his capacity to service debt. But the transfer of purchasing power (as represented by the repayment of loans) from a small debtor to a larger creditor probably will not have a significantly adverse effect on the terms of trade.[9]

These solvency models emphasize how borrowers can come up against a net-worth constraint and become unable to pay. A more complete picture is given by other models that incorporate the behavior of lenders, who only lend if there is a reasonable probability that this situation can be prevented. In these models credit crises never arise since no bank lends more than the borrower can repay. If repayment capacity is stochastic the bank will in general lend so much that in some contingencies repayment is impossible, at least without rescheduling (recall section 2.2).

Jaffee and Modigliani (1969) present a model of a borrower with limited resources next period to repay a loan. They make the point that if the resources available to repay a loan are limited, then there is clearly an upper bound on the amount that a lender will be willing to lend.

The models of solvency that we have discussed up to this point have treated the value of the borrower's resources available for repayment as an exogenous variable, and have assumed that borrowers and lenders share the same subjective probability distribution about that value. In fact, borrowers are more likely to have better information about their worth in the repayment period than lenders, and borrowers' actions affect what that distribution will be. Consequently lenders face problems of adverse selection and moral hazard.

The terms of the contract affect both the mix of applicants and the actions undertaken by those who get loans. Thus, increasing the rate of interest may

---

[9]It is worth noting, however, that the initial extension of the loan must have been accompanied by a terms-of-trade gain to the borrower, if repayment implies a loss.

actually lower the bank's expected return, both because the best risks (from the lender's perspective) decide not to apply and because the higher interest charges induce borrowers to undertake greater risks. The consequence of this is that banks may find it profitable to charge an interest rate below the market clearing level. This results in credit rationing [see Keeton (1979) and Stiglitz and Weiss (1981)].

Stiglitz and Weiss (1983) also show how a bank involved repeatedly in lending to a particular borrower can use the terms of subsequent loans to modify the selection of borrowers or decisions of borrowers to its own advantage. They assume that the bank credibly commit itself to the terms of subsequent loans when the initial loan is extended. In particular they show that a bank may exclude a borrower in default from subsequent loans to discourage (ex ante) risky investments.[10] They also have analyzed the role of collateral, showing that its absence exacerbates problems, although credit rationing may still exist with collateral. Thus credit rationing may be more important in country loans, where collateral is not feasible, than in domestic loans.

The Modigliani–Jaffee and Stiglitz–Weiss papers show how credit rationing can arise when the borrower's insolvency threatens a loan. An implication of the Stiglitz and Weiss papers is that solvency itself cannot be defined independently of the actions of borrowers and lenders. Even though, ex post, the lender receives all the borrower's assets if a default occurs, the borrower can affect the probability of being able to pay. Ex ante the lender's return is affected by the borrower's actions. Even when the solvency constraint is binding ex post, the borrower's willingness-to-pay is important in this ex ante sense.

5. Operationalizing and testing the theories

Economists have investigated a fairly large number of theoretical notions in their discussion of international lending. While many of the models complement each other, we have remarked upon important conceptual differences among them. In this section and the next we are motivated by a set of very general questions about the empirical relevance of these models: How can these theories help to interpret recent developments in international lending? How can they be used to identify future topics of importance and to make predictions? How can experience in the markets be used to distinguish which theories are relevant? What are the priorities for further theoretical research? In short, what are the connections between the theories, empirical research and what is happening in these markets?

---

[10]Their analysis thus provides part of the explanation of why lenders wish to cut bad borrowers off from credit.

Specific empirical questions facing the researcher range from knowing the facts to understanding the actual behavior of borrowers and lenders. Some examples are: How much has been lent and what determines the amount lenders wish to lend, borrowers wish to borrow, and the actual amount of debt outstanding? What are the terms of the loans, and what determines them? What types of ruptures occur between lenders and borrowers, and why? Do lenders maintain unity in confrontations with debtors, and under what circumstances? What are the terms of the reschedulings? of IMF agreements?

Some of these questions are informational, and knowledge of particular facts can answer them. No econometric analysis is needed. Others involve evidence on the motivations of borrowers and lenders, and involve inferences about behavior. In principle, econometric analysis is appropriate; in practice, there are limitations to the application of econometric methods. One obstacle to econometric work arises because the informational questions are logically prior to econometric analysis, and when they cannot be answered in a satisfactory manner, there may be little point to pressing on with econometric analysis.

One basic problem confronting all econometric studies of sovereign debt is that the unit of analysis is unavoidably the country. Consequently, it is very difficult to identify exogenous variables that vary by the unit of analysis. The interpretation of many results in the literature is clouded by the inclusion in the estimated relationships of many endogenous variables as explanatory variables. The terms of trade, however, is one important source of external shocks that may be roughly exogenous for many developing countries, which tend to be relatively small in world markets. Similarly, it may be possible to introduce climatological variables to measure an important set of domestic shocks when agriculture is an important source of income, exports and government revenues.

Existing studies fall into two groups corresponding to an earlier and a later stage in the relationship between borrowers and lenders. One group focuses on an environment of voluntary lending, and seeks to identify the determinants of the quantity of debt, and the terms at which it is contracted. The second type of study focuses on when debt problems arise. So far there are no studies that address the prospects for a resumption of voluntary lending to countries that have experienced problems.

Estimating the determinants of debt outstanding is quite difficult. Even in the absence of problem cases, it is necessary to allow for the possibility that observed debt is the minimum of the credit ceiling and desired debt. This implies two regimes. An appropriate econometric technique produces not only coefficient values but also a probabilistic separation of the sample into the two regimes. The existence of problem debtors whose debt exceeds the level desired by creditors means that three or more regimes are required in empirical work if both cases of voluntary and involuntary lending are to be treated in a unified analysis.

At present, only the two-regime model has been estimated [Eaton and Gersovitz (1980, 1981a)]. In these studies the observations on individual countries were from 1970 and 1974, so that there was no need to account for problem debtors. By the same token, however, these results apply to only a very early period in the evolution of lending to developing countries. Bank lending was much less important before 1973–1974. The results of these studies indicate that two regimes rather than only one are justified; the credit-constrained regime was relatively more prevalent.[11] In 1974 relatively more countries were credit-constrained. Some of the oil exporters that were included in the sample for both years moved against this trend, however, as one would expect. The analysis of Eaton and Gersovitz (1980), which considers determinants of foreign reserve holdings as well as international indebtedness, suggests that debt was a substitute for reserves.

In the analysis of debt levels and debt problems, an important distinction is between the long-run characteristics of countries (for instance, the standard deviation of the terms of trade about trend) and transitory shocks that they may experience (the actual deviation of the terms of trade from trend in any one year). For instance, Eaton and Gersovitz (1981a) present a model in which an increase in the permanent variability of a debtor's income can increase the debt ceiling it faces, although a failure to repay, if it occurs at all, will occur in a period of relatively low income. Existing studies use some constructed measures for long-run country characteristics such as the variability of exports. They do not, however, incorporate variables capturing transitory factors into the estimation. Under reasonable distributional assumptions, the omission of these variables (and their implicit inclusion in the error term) need not bias the estimated coefficients. Of course, their omission does mean that these models do not reflect the role of shocks in determining indebtedness.

Gersovitz (1985) presents graphical evidence that debt has tended to increase most markedly when the terms of trade would seem to have been temporarily high. Thus, debt does not seem to have helped countries to smooth their absorption, despite the theoretical presumption that debtors would want this pattern, and that creditors should want to accommodate them to the extent that debt is below the borrower's credit ceiling. It may be that when shock variables are included in the formal econometric work, this casual impression will be reversed. If it is not, however, it may be possible to

---

[11]Identification of the regimes is difficult because theory suggests that almost all variables influencing the desired debt should also influence the credit ceiling, and conversely. Eaton and Gersovitz use restrictions on the signs of coefficients as well as the fact that when the credit ceiling is binding it affects desired reserves. A further possibility is to assign certain countries to different regimes with probability one based on prior knowledge, something that may be attractive now that cases of apparently intractable debtors have emerged.

determine whether this pattern reflects behavior of lenders, borrowers, or both groups.

Finally, there is scope for improving these models by using data available since the earlier studies and variables that could be constructed from unpublished data sources. The Eaton–Gersovitz studies use the World Bank's *World Debt Tables* series on debt to private creditors. It is important to add short-term debt guaranteed by the debtor country to the World Bank figures to produce a dependent variable that is more comprehensive. Cline (1984, pp. 291–292) discusses one way this can be done. It would also be useful to integrate debt owed by the private sector that is not guaranteed by the debtor's government. This leads to questions of model specification as well as of data because such debt is subject to sovereign risk in rather special ways, as well as subject to conventional risks of corporate failure. At the same time, a significant part of debt owed to private creditors is guaranteed by the governments of these creditors, and these debts must be treated more like debt to public creditors.

Bank loans to sovereign borrowers typically specify an interest rate that is the sum of two components, a reference rate from an OECD financial market, usually the London Inter Bank Offer Rate, and a spread. The reference rate component is adjusted at fixed intervals to its current market value, so that the loans are at floating rates. The spread is set for the duration of the loan, and is the component specific to the loan.

There are several econometric investigations of these spreads. McDonald (1982) provides references and some description of individual studies. These studies focus on an interpretation of the spread as a risk premium, and attempt to infer the lenders' perception of loss from the size of the spread. The type of loan problem leading to the spread is not, however, explicitly specified, nor could it be, given the methodology and information. Insofar as a probability of loss is inferred, it seems to correspond to a probability (π) of total loss of present value, via the condition $(1 - \pi)(1 + r + s) = (1 + r)$ where r is the safe, base rate and s is the spread.

In fact, however, the spreads may reflect other factors. There may be higher costs of originating loans in certain countries. Tax treatment of interest income earned by foreigners in the borrowing countries may have implications for spreads. For instance, in Mexico, the Mexican withholding tax may be paid by the borrower but still generates U.S. tax credits for the lender. Other components of the loan contract, such as the front-end fees, affect the total return to the lender.

In general, these studies use an eclectic list of explanatory variables that are not derived from a clearly stated model of sovereign lending and borrowing. Because they share this characteristic with models of debt problems, we postpone a discussion of individual variables.

One problem that is specific to these models, however, is the inclusion of other conditions of the loan agreement as explanatory variables, and these are most probably endogenous. The motivation for their inclusion is that these factors are known to be related to interest rates even in markets without a risk of repayment. For instance, there is a term structure relationship between rate and maturity on U.S. government bonds. On the other hand, such loan characteristics can play a special role in the context of sovereign lending. For instance, we have already noted that loans of short maturity allow for more frequent and effective monitoring of the sovereign debtor, the so-called short leash. On the other hand, very short-term debt is often poorly recorded and it is often feared that debtors who anticipate debt problems and credit constraints may surreptitiously run up their short-term indebtedness, the problem modeled by Kletzer (1984). Thus these econometric studies have included explanatory variables that are themselves endogenously determined by lenders and borrowers with reference to considerations of sovereign risk.

By far the largest number of econometric studies of sovereign lending attempt to explain instances of so-called problem debtors. McDonald (1982) and Saini and Bates (1984) provide extensive surveys of variables used, estimation methods, coefficient estimates and success in predicting the events studied. Edwards (1984) and McFadden et al. (1985) are recent studies in this tradition.

All these investigations try to understand the determinants shifting a country from being a good to a bad borrower. The fundamental difficulty with these models is defining appropriately the dependent variable, the occurrence of a debt problem. The earliest study, Frank and Cline (1971), asked when multilateral reschedulings of debt owed to official creditors occur in Paris-Club type arrangements. This type of question is well posed, and has some obvious policy interest. But it is not the question that seems central to the current debate over sovereign lending; namely, will banks regret having made loans to developing countries? None of the observable events (arrears, reschedulings, or IMF programs) that these econometric studies analyze answer this question. Within the group of countries experiencing each of these events are presumably good credit risks and bad. It is just not possible to say based on an event analysis what the prospects for ultimately realizing the present value of loans are. Even in the case of an explicit repudiation, the rupture between debtors and creditors is never irrevocable. Furthermore, even in very bad situations from the banks' viewpoint, there may be reason for the banks to avoid calling a default and for the country to demur from an explicit repudiation. Such actions may trigger intervention by bank regulators that is unwelcome to creditors, and consequently to debtors. Debt problems are therefore hard to define. We have come full circle to our opening comments about the difficulties of ascertaining loan status inherent in situations in which the relationship between debtors and creditors potentially stretches over an indefinite future.

As an alternative to the study of such events as arrears, reschedulings or IMF problems with their hazy implications for market participants, it is probably better to focus on flows of funds between creditors and debtors. In other words, the critical question is: When will a country with certain characteristics owing a certain amount of debt under certain contractual arrangements pay or receive funds from creditors with certain characteristics? One could then, in principle, make an estimate of the present value that creditors will realize on their original loan, as well as whether countries can expect to receive more funds. This strategy means a return to the estimation of debt supply and demand equations, as in Eaton and Gersovitz (1980, 1981a) but with potentially more regimes. McFadden et al. (1985) introduce a multi-regime model of sovereign debt, but it focuses on arrears and reschedulings, and therefore analyzes events rather than the flow of funds.

Another shortcoming of these econometric models is their incorporation of many variables on a rather ad hoc basis [see Eaton and Gersovitz (1981b) for a further discussion]. For instance, some studies have used the ratio of capital inflow to debt service, a variable that is likely to be simultaneous with default. Others use variables like the inflation rate with little obvious theoretical justification. If the notion is that a government short of revenue will resort to the inflation tax as well as run arrears, then the variables are endogenous.

While econometric analysis of international lending faces severe difficulties, there are other types of empirical approaches that have been tried in an attempt to forecast the prospects of debtors and creditors. Kaletsky (1985) reviews the prospects for sanctions of various types and their costs to debtors. This type of analysis is potentially prescriptive; it provides the type of information that banks and debtors may use in making decisions. By contrast, the econometric analysis assumes that the participants know what they should do, and are doing it.

A second type of exercise used to determine repayment prospects is represented by Cline's (1984) projection of exports, imports and other balance of payments entries. He argues that if the credit entries grow relative to the debit entries excluding debt service, the prospects for debt service are enhanced. This approach neglects that the magnitudes of all these variables are jointly determined. A country may decide that its creditors will neither extend it new funds nor be able to deploy effective sanctions. It can then choose to increase its imports or reserves or decrease its exports relative to the levels projected by reference to past trends and OECD variables.

6. Conclusions

The rash of debt reschedulings led to a widespread view that banks had lent too much. Though bankers may now regret having made some of these loans, the relevant question is whether there was some market failure leading to inappropriate lending behavior. We have already noted that the unenforceability of contracts can imply that credit is rationed, and that lending is probably too low relative to what would be optimal if contracts were enforceable, and that borrowers would prefer this latter situation. Now we turn to a related set of questions: (1) Are there factors motivating bankers to lend more than what is likely to be repaid? (2) What is the role of bank regulation in this context? and (3) What is the interpretation of rescheduling?

These questions are inherently very difficult to answer because there is a one-shot aspect about the debt situation. The players do not make repetitive choices in similar situations. There is the comparative behavior of many countries, but they all borrow from more or less the same group of banks. Analysts can refer, therefore, to only a rather limited experience.

6.1. Potential inefficiencies in international lending

One potentially important inefficiency results when lenders cannot observe the magnitude of outstanding loans. In this case, the lending of an additional dollar has an externality since it increases the likelihood of default. As Kletzer (1984) shows, this factor can increase the amount lent and the probability of default, as well as the initial interest rate. This type of problem may be more relevant to international lending than domestic lending to individual firms. In sovereign lending, seniority clauses are less important, and a number of lenders make loans to a multitude of government ministries, agencies and public enterprises.

There is another informational externality of potential importance: The fact that one lender is willing to lend funds conveys information about the creditworthiness of the borrower. Similarly, the refusal of a bank to lend funds conveys information to other suppliers of capital. This externality may contribute to the occurrence of runs. In our earlier discussion, we noted that one might view a lending crisis as a run. Each creditor wishes to protect himself; in doing so, he may actually increase the likelihood that others will be unable to recoup what they have lent.

It is not only that the forced liquidation of assets consequent upon an unexpected withdrawal of credit has a deleterious effect on the net worth of the borrower. The withdrawal of credit by some creditors induces a revision in others' estimates of the likelihood of a default, and this by itself can lead to a run.

Lenders must make inferences about the likelihood of a default on the basis of partial information. Some of the risks facing one borrower are similar to those facing another borrower. Withdrawal of credit against one borrower may even cause a re-evaluation of credit extended to other similarly situated borrowers. Thus, there are informational externalities extending across borrowers as well as across lenders. But in general, our conclusion is that if a runs externality were the sole cause of debt problems, it can be handled by a lender-initiated moratorium since new funds net of interest payments do not seem to be required.

Banks are limited liability institutions. Thus, when a bank undertakes a risk, it may be imposing some costs on its creditors which it does not fully take into account, just as firms or countries to which it lent money did not fully take into account the costs that their actions had on the bank.

Many governments of developed countries insure deposits by their citizens in the banks that lend to developing countries. This insurance obviates the need for depositors to supervise bank portfolios, a presumably costly activity for small depositors that provides the rationale for the insurance. In addition, there may be a role for insurance in removing the incentive for bank panics, as discussed by Diamond and Dybvig (1983).

To ensure that this insurance does not lead to moral hazard on the part of banks, various regulations have been adopted to circumscribe their behavior. In the United States, loans to individual borrowers are not to exceed a fraction of bank capital, but all loans to a single country or even to all agencies of a single government were never classified as being to an individual borrower, in this sense. This provision has therefore not prevented the aggregate of loans to entities in individual developing countries from becoming a significant fraction of bank capital.

One important policy that regulators can take is to force banks to increase their net worth. This is particularly important in a situation of involuntary lending (rescheduled loans that otherwise would be in default). Banks are induced to make these loans because they can pay dividends based on interest income that is only paid to them because they extend new loans. Unless these regulators prevent banks from paying these dividends, their loans to developing countries will continuously rise relative to their capital. This process will increase the contingent claim on the insurance schemes, potentially without bound. In fact U.S. regulators have required two major banks to increase their capital. There is really very little cost to extending this program since it requires no judgment on the ultimate worth of the loans.

A related policy that regulators should adopt is to require full disclosure of loans made to individual countries. Increased reporting requirements have been promulgated by U.S. regulators. This information can help uninsured depositors and shareholders to monitor the portfolio decisions of bank managements and thereby to deter moral hazard.

Insurance agencies can also deter the undesirable risk-taking consequences of insurance by adopting differentiated premia that increase with the riskiness of loans and with their proportion in an individual bank's portfolio. This has not been a general feature of insurance programs, but would deter banks from undertaking correlated loans that yield expected returns net of insurance payments below those on a safe loan, but expected profits to the banks above those on a safe loan. Similarly, the categorization of loans as requiring loss reserves can also be further differentiated.

The moral hazard problems caused by deposit insurance are reinforced by typical (implicit) managerial compensation schemes in which judgments concerning performance are based on relative performance. This too may lead to excessive correlation of risks undertaken across banks. Assume most banks are undertaking higher yielding loans to LDC's. If all loans go into default, then it is unlikely that all (or possibly any) bank managers will be punished; each manager's judgment is confirmed by the actions of the others. On the other hand, if any one refuses to lend, and there is no default, the lower return earned by the bank will count against the manager. Thus, as emphasized elsewhere in the New Theory of the Firm, one must take into account the incentives of the managers; risks faced by the firm and risks faced by the manager are not necessarily the same. It may be possible to deter moral hazard if regulators directly penalize managers, as happened to some extent in the Continental–Illinois case.

6.2. Interpreting the reschedulings

In terms of the models discussed so far, rescheduling has a number of interpretations. One is simply that it is a device to extend the term of the loans in question; rescheduling a short-term loan is simply another means of issuing a long-term loan.

As we have noted, the option for certain types of unspecified interventions that a short-term loan contract allows provides it with certain advantages over long-term contracts. In particular, rescheduling a short-term loan gives creditors more control over the borrower's indebtedness. That is why short-term loans may be employed, even when it is correctly anticipated that there will be a high probability of a rescheduling.[12]

Still other explanations are that rescheduling is an action by creditors to bring a solvent, willing-to-pay debtor through a liquidity crisis or that it is an attempt by an insolvent or unwilling-to-pay borrower to postpone the inevitable sanctions it will suffer when repayment ultimately is not made. Creditors go along in the latter instance because they hope: (1) that the problem is really one of liquidity; (2) that, by waiting, they may find other,

---

[12]Several recent papers have attempted to model this idea formally. See, in particular, Kletzer (1984) and Sachs and Cohen (1985) who provide models in which rescheduling agreements prohibit the borrower from tapping sources of credit other than the initial lenders. The likelihood of the ultimate repayment of the initial loan amount is consequently enhanced. What is not clear in the analysis is why a long-term loan agreement could not attain the same objective by prohibiting the borrower from borrowing from other sources during the term of the loan.

more gullible lenders or a public institution to assume the debt; or (3) that the moment of public realization of the worthlessness of the loan can be postponed until the bank personnel responsible for it have left. Hellwig's (1977) model suggests another rationale, that rescheduling is the lender's throwing of good money after bad to keep alive some prospect of the debtor's repaying.

In most cases, rescheduling reflects a failure to contract completely against all possible contingencies.[13] Ozler (1984) has developed a model analyzing the consequences of this when, after the initial loan, the two parties confront each other as bilateral monopolists (even though initially the loan market is competitive). From the perspective of the initial period two magnitudes are in doubt, the borrower's income in the second period and the penalty of default. The borrower is ultimately solvent, however. The initial loan is extended for one period. Three outcomes are possible. First, the borrower's income and the default penalty both exceed the repayment obligation; the loan is repaid on schedule. Second, the borrower's income falls short of the repayment obligations. A liquidity problem forces the borrower to reschedule at terms more favorable to the lenders than the initial loan, since lenders are now monopolists vis-à-vis the borrower. Third, the penalty of default falls below the borrower's debt service obligation. The borrower uses the threat of nonpayment to negotiate a rescheduling of the loan on terms more favorable to himself.

Two features of the model may have particular relevance to actual lending in international capital markets. First, even though default never actually occurs, borrowers can use the threat of default to extract better loan terms. Kraft's (1984) description of Mexico's debt rescheduling indicates that Mexican negotiators raised the specter of default for exactly this purpose. Second, reschedulings may take place for different reasons, with different implications for borrowers and lenders. Ozler studies the effect of rescheduling announcements on the value of the equity of banks involved. She finds that during the late 1970's reschedulings typically raised equity, suggesting a liquidity explanation. The opposite is the case for the early 1980's, which she interprets as reflecting a decline in the perceived cost of default to the debtor. This view also seems consistent with the pattern of interest-rate spreads on rescheduled loans, which were first higher and then lower than those on so-called voluntary loans.

6.3. Final remarks

The central role played by the enforcement problem and the absence of

[13]With complete contracting, repayments would be a function of the state, just as they are with incomplete contracting, but the dependence would be specified ex ante. The following discussion notes some of the differences that arise in the nature of the relationship between debtors and creditors with incomplete contracting.

collateral make the international loan market fundamentally different from domestic credit markets. In a sense, our analysis leads to a view that it is perhaps more surprising that there has been as much lending to developing countries than that there is not more. It is hard to interpret events to ascertain the future course of payments by debtors to creditors and by creditors to debtors. But we believe that our framework can help to organize thinking about the topics raised by sovereign lending and country risk, and to point up inconsistencies that could otherwise plague analysis in this area.

References

Allen, Franklin, 1983, Credit rationing and payment incentives, Review of Economic Studies 50, 639–646.

Arnott, Richard J. and Joseph E. Stiglitz, 1982, Equilibrium in competitive insurance markets: The welfare economics of moral hazard, Queen's University Institute of Economic Research, Discussion paper no. 465.

Avramovic, Dragoslav et al., 1964, Economic growth and external debt (Johns Hopkins University Press, Baltimore, MD).

Cline, William R., 1984, International debt: Systematic risk and policy response (Institute for International Economics, Washington, DC).

Cooper, Richard N. and Jeffrey D. Sachs, 1985, Borrowing abroad: The debtor's perspective, in: Gordon W. Smith and John T. Cuddington, eds., International debt and the developing countries (IBRD, Washington, DC) 21–60.

Diamond, Douglas and Philip E. Dybvig, 1983, Bank runs, deposit insurance, and liquidity, Journal of Political Economy 91, 401–409.

Diaz-Alejandro, Carlos F., 1984, Latin American debt: I don't think we are in Kansas anymore, Brookings Papers on Economic Activity, no. 2, 335–403.

Domar, Evsey, 1944, The 'burden of debt' and national income, American Economic Review 34, 798–827.

Domar, Evsey, 1950, The effects of investment on the balance of payments, American Economic Review 40, 805–826.

Eaton, Jonathan, 1985, Lending with costly enforcement of repayment and potential fraud, Journal of Banking and Finance, forthcoming.

Eaton, Jonathan and Mark Gersovitz, 1980, LDC participation in international financial markets: Debt and reserves, Journal of Development Economics 7, 3–21.

Eaton, Jonathan and Mark Gersovitz, 1981a, Debt with potential repudiation: Theoretical and empirical analysis, Review of Economic Studies 48, 289–309.

Eaton, Jonathan and Mark Gersovitz, 1981b, Poor country borrowing and the repudiation issue, Princeton Studies in International Finance no. 4, Princeton, NJ.

Eaton, Jonathan and Mark Gersovitz, 1983, Country risk: Economic aspects, in: Richard Herring, ed., Managing international risk (Cambridge University Press, New York) 75–108.

Eaton, Jonathan and Mark Gersovitz, 1984, A theory of expropriation and deviations from perfect capital mobility, Economic Journal 94, 16–40.

Edwards, Sebastian, 1984, LDC foreign borrowing and default risk: An empirical investigation, 1976–80, American Economic Review 74, 726–734.

Frank, Charles R. and William R. Cline, 1971, Measurement of debt servicing capacity: An application of discriminant analysis, Journal of International Economics 1, 327–344.

Gersovitz, Mark, 1983, Trade, capital mobility and sovereign immunity, Research Program in Development Studies Discussion paper no. 108 (Princeton University, Princeton, NJ).

Gersovitz, Mark, 1985, Banks' international lending decisions: What we know and implications for future research, in: Gordon W. Smith and John T. Cuddington, eds., International debt and the developing countries (IBRD, Washington, DC) 61–78.

Greenwald, Bruce, Joseph E. Stiglitz and Andrew Weiss, 1984, Informational imperfections in the capital market and macroeconomic fluctuations, American Economic Review 74, 194–199.

Grossman, Herschel I. and John B. Van Huyck, 1985, Sovereign debt as a contingent claim: Excusable default, repudiation and reputation, Mimeo (Brown University, Providence, RI).

Hellwig, Martin F., 1977, A model of borrowing and lending with bankruptcy, Econometrica 45, 1879–1906.

Jaffee, Dwight M. and Franco Modigliani, 1969, A theory and test of credit rationing, American Economic Review 59, 850–872.

Jaffee, Dwight M. and Thomas Russell, 1976, Imperfect information, uncertainty and credit rationing, Quarterly Journal of Economics 90, 651–666.

Kaletsky, Anatole, 1985, The costs of default (Priority Press, New York).

Keeton, William R., 1979, Equilibrium credit rationing (Garland Publishing, New York).

Kharas, Homi, 1984, The long-run creditworthiness of developing countries: Theory and practice, Quarterly Journal of Economics 99, 415–439.

Kletzer, Kenneth M., 1984, Asymmetries of information and LDC borrowing with sovereign risk, Economic Journal 94, 287–307.

Kraft, Joseph, 1984, The Mexican Rescue (Group of Thirty, New York).

Kreps, David M. and Robert Wilson, 1982, Reputation and imperfect information, Journal of Economic Theory 27, 253–279.

Krugman, Paul, 1985, International debt problems in an uncertain world, in: Gordon W. Smith and John T. Cuddington, eds., International debt and the developing countries (IBRD, Washington, DC) 79–100.

McDonald, C. Donagh, (1982), Debt capacity and developing country borrowing: A survey of the literature, IMF Staff Papers 29, 603–646.

McFadden, Daniel et al., 1985, Is there life after debt? An econometric analysis of the creditworthiness of developing countries, in: Gordon W. Smith and John T. Cuddington, eds., International debt and the developing countries (IBRD, Washington, DC) 179–209.

Nakamura, Leonard I., 1985, Checking accounts, borrowing and bank runs, Mimeo (Princeton University, Princeton, NJ).

Ozler, Sule, 1984, Rescheduling of sovereign government bank debt, Mimeo (Stanford University, Stanford, CA).

Sachs, Jeffrey, 1984, . Theoretical issues in international borrowing, Princeton Studies in International Finance 54 (Princeton, NJ).

Sachs, Jeffrey and Daniel Cohen, 1985, LDC borrowing with default risk, Kredit und Kapital, forthcoming.

Saini, Krishan G. and Philip S. Bates, 1984, A survey of the quantitative approaches to country risk analysis, Journal of Banking and Finance 8, 341–356.

Selten, Reinhard, 1978, The chain-store paradox, Theory and Decision 9, 127–159.

Simonsen, Mario Henrique, 1985, The developing-country debt problem, in: Gordon W. Smith and John T. Cuddington, eds., International debt and the developing countries (IBRD, Washington, DC) 101–126.

Stiglitz, Joseph E. and Andrew Weiss, 1981, Credit rationing in markets with imperfect information, American Economic Review 71, 393–411.

Stiglitz, Joseph E. and Andrew Weiss, 1983, Incentive effects of terminations, American Economic Review 73, 912–927.

European Economic Review 30 (1986) 515–519. North-Holland

COMMENTS

'The Pure Theory of Country Risk'
by J. Eaton, M. Gersovitz and J. Stiglitz

R. GUESNERIE

Ecole des Hautes Etudes en Sciences Sociales, 75006 Paris, France

Commenting on a long and impressive survey is not a straightforward task and one may hesitate between different solutions. The first one would consist in focusing attention on some selected models of the paper. Actually, a number of articles described in the survey would justify detailed reflections. The second option, somewhat utopian however, is to summarize the ideas contained in the paper in a way which gives justice to the broad coverage of the subject which is provided by the authors. I will take here a somewhat intermediate path, since the subject I consider is neither very specific nor very broad; but it is, I hope, transverse to the topics of the survey. Precisely, my discussion concentrates on the adequacy of the general theory of contracts to the actual understanding of contracts in the field of international credit.

First, the relevance of some of the standard concepts of contract theory for the economics of international credit will be assessed (A). The non-commitment hypothesis – which is standard in the theory of international credit contracts – will be compared to the commitment hypothesis and the specific difficulties of the former will be evoked (B). Finally it will be argued that some unsolved questions of the economics of international debt raise more general challenges to the general theory of contracts (C).

(*A*) Modern contract theory emphasizes that contracts in general, credit arrangements in particular, should be designed to alleviate both moral hazard and adverse selection problems.

In the survey by Eaton–Gersovitz–Stiglitz the moral hazard problem is often evoked but there are apparently few formal models supporting the unformal argument which is made. This is not surprising. Many models of moral hazard, even if they are formulated in a general principal–agent framework, reflect the situations from which they are most often inspired, i.e., situations in which the agent is a firm. This specific inspiration may be very explicit; for example, the study of incidence of moral hazard on the financial structures (debt–equity ratio) of the firm, has no clear counterpart for the understanding of international debt. I wonder how frequent is the fact that the agent of the 'general' theory has, implicitly to be interpreted as a firm. In any case an assessment of the specific aspects of moral hazard in international credit contract would be welcome.

My next and more substantive comment concerns adverse selection; I argue that it is likely to be a less sensitive issue for the understanding of the specific aspects of international credit than it is for standard credit contract. Adverse selection obtains when the borrower has more information on the project (or set of projects) which has to be financed than the lender has. There is little doubt that, for example, a firm, when compared to its banker, has superior ability in assessing the riskiness of the investment it undertakes. However, when debtors are countries, the asymmetry of information is more debatable. Is it clear that a government – say a South American government – has better information on the returns of a set of projects than the bankers – say the foreign bankers – financing the projects? The question is particularly relevant for those projects the evaluation of which is made under the supervision of international bodies. These bodies generally rely on a strong group of experts; they have developed their own methodology of project evaluation and have direct connections with lenders. They are able to provide reliable assessments either on the returns of specific projects or on the general economic situation of a country. The question then arises whether adverse selection is crucial for the modelling of the conditions of international credit. More exactly, I wonder to which extent the specific explanations to credit rationing drawn from adverse selection models 'à la Stiglitz–Weiss' are valid for international debt.

(*B*) Another specific and more central aspect of international credit contracts, when compared to standard credit contracts, originates in the legal situation of the lender. In international credit, the lender is a country exerting sovereignty within its border and not a private body subject to the penalty of (national) law. It follows that the enforcement mechanisms for a contract involving a country are much less powerful than the corresponding mechanisms in the absence of sovereignty considerations. In other words, a debtor can more easily default when he is a sovereign country than when he is a private agent. The possibility of easier repudiation of debt is then one issue which has to be taken seriously; it has indeed been taken seriously both in the literature surveyed by Eaton–Gersovitz–Stiglitz and in this present conference (where it is the subject of two papers).

The opposition of the commitment hypothesis versus the non-commitment hypothesis divides the general literature on contracts. Under the commitment hypothesis, contracts are binding agreements between the two parties. There are different possible explanations for the emergence of binding agreements.[1] The existence of a third neutral party observing at low cost all the contractual variables is a favourable factor.[2] This situation is particularly favourable when the third party is a Court. Then agreements are legally enforceable, the breach of contract is subject to the penalty of law. Also, in the absence of a third party, both parties may take ex ante actions which will make very costly the breach of contract (this is what the strategy of burning its vessels is about). Finally, in a repeated relationship, reputation will act as a (partial) substitute for penalties to enforce the realization of the contract.

The commitment hypothesis has been more explored in contract theory than the alternative one; however the present theory does not shed full light on all the issues. For example, if we understand in depth the static adverse selection problem with one dimensional one-sided asymmetry (when a principal faces an agent having private information)[3] much less is known on the structure of optimal contracts with multidimensional information and two-sided asymmetries; also, the optimal incorporation of the flow of new information in an intertemporal contract to which both parties are fully committed only starts to be understood, even in the simplest case where the static model is fully grasped.

The commitment hypothesis implies that contracts are binding for the duration of the relationship between the partners. At contrary, the non-commitment hypothesis covers cases either where no commitment at all is possible, or when only short-term commitment (short-term with respect to the duration of the relationship) is feasible. The theory of contracts is usually recognized as more difficult under the non-commitment hypothesis than under the commitment hypothesis. Without going into the details of the problem, one can note that non-commitment is associated with truly dynamic stories and involves a more sophisticated game theoretic structure. Indeed the choice of adequate game theoretical equilibrium concepts raises a number of delicate questions on the so-called 'out of equilibrium beliefs' of the players.[4]

Real contractual conditions seldom exactly fall in the polar cases sketched above. (Commitment may be limited to some variables; reputation can partially act as a substitute.) However, the preceding analysis of the case of international credit suggests that it stands closer to the polar case of non-

---

[1]To be binding, contracts have obviously to be detailed enough to be adapted to any contingency.

[2]The neutrality of the third party being the main source of problems.

[3]See Guesnerie–Laffont (1985) for an analysis of a general model of this type, a model which includes as particular cases the standard adverse selection model of credit contracts.

[4]It has induced a technical literature originating in the work of Selten, see also Kreps–Wilson (1983), Kreps (1984), etc....

commitment than to the other and better explored case of commitment. The considerations of sovereignty of the borrower pushed at their limits leads to view the credit contract between the lender and the borrower as a non-commitment arrangement. Before stressing some of the modelling problems associated with non-commitment, let me open a parenthesis. Commitment is always in a sense preferable to non-commitment. This is even a 'theorem' following from the fact that the non-commitment optimal contract can (at least) be mimicked under commitment. Why is then non-commitment so frequent in real contracts? A number of answers can be given which I do not want to discuss. Note, however, that the argument of beneficial commitment is not irrelevant for the organization of international relationship between nations.[5]

(C)   How to model the international credit relationship under the polar assumption that enforcement mechanisms are very costly or equivalently that repudiation is a decision with no direct cost for the borrower?

The simpler option rules out uncertainty from the picture; the lender and borrower have known utility functions; the lender proposes a contract, the borrower can repudiate it without direct cost. Indirect costs follow first from the exclusion of the capital market after the time of default; the exact exclusion cost may reflect different considerations. [It depends upon the volume of international trade in Gersovitz (1983), on the fluctuations of unsmoothed consumption in Eaton–Gersovitz (1981), on the restriction to capital accumulation in Allen (1983) or Cohen–Sachs (1985).] Also, exclusion generates an inefficiency in the rise of the stock of capital in Cohen–Sachs (1985). Whatever the given set of assumptions, the contract must be taken from the set of self enforceable contracts, i.e., from the set of contracts for which it is in the interest of both parties to respect it. The optimal contract naturally reflects the specific exclusion costs which are assumed. Let me now suggest some extensions of the above basic frame and then evoke different objections to this basic frame.

Directions of extensions are obvious but may involve significant technical difficulties. First, the contract could be made contingent to exogenous events,[6] so that circumstances in which rescheduling occurs are agreed upon at the outset. Second, although I previously expressed doubts on the relevance of adverse selection arguments bearing on the efficiency of the borrower, one might like to introduce adverse selection arguments bearing

---

[5]As argued unformally at the Conference, it is because one can go to jail in case of default that somebody can possibly borrow the money to buy the Château de Ragny. No definitive conclusion for the organisation of international trade should however be drawn from this remark!

[6]In the literature on wage contracts, there are models in which the wage contract, supposed to be self enforceable, is made contingent to the exogenous fluctuations of the spot wage; see Thomas–Worrall (1984).

on other of the borrower's characteristics. The complexity of the analysis, which would then have to rely on concepts such as sequential equilibria, perfect Nash–Bayesian equilibria, would increase significantly.[7]

To finish, let me come to some difficulties with the basic frame. Rather than attempting a more synthetical assessment of these difficulties, let us approach them through a sample of two questions. First question: Why is it the case that after default the country is assumed to be excluded for ever from the credit market? Second question. Often the self enforceable contract will be such that at several times the borrower is almost indifferent between defaulting and continuing the relationship. At these times the loss caused by default to the lender may be very high. Why is it not the case that the lender cannot take advantage of his bargaining power at such times?

I understand that one can give answers to each of these questions. I only wonder whether coherent answers are actually given. In other words, I am asking myself whether the assumptions on competition and cooperation (number of lenders and borrowers, nature and degree of cooperation between them) which are needed to justify each one of the above mentioned features are both compatible between them and coherent with the assumed form of the contract. In still other words, I found it difficult to understand in some of the models of international credit contract surveyed here the precise nature of competition which is assumed. This may reflect my limited knowledge of the models under consideration. This may also not be so surprising since the theory has not built at the present stage a satisfactory theory of competition when complex contracts are involved. The questions raised by the economics of international debt could hence be relevant and challenging for the general theory of contracts.

---

[7]For an example of the analysis of an optimal contract under adverse selection and non-commitment, see Freixas–Guesnerie–Tirole (1985).

References

Allen, F., 1983, Credit rationing and payment incentives, Review of Economic Studies.

Cohen, D. and J. Sachs, 1985, Growth and external debt under risk of debt repudiation.

Eaton, J. and M. Gersovitz, 1981, Debt with potential repudiation: Theoretical and empirical analysis, Review of Economic Studies 48.

Freixas, X., R. Guesnerie and J. Tirole, 1985, Planning under uncertainty and the ratchet effect, Review of Economic Studies.

Gersotitz, M. 1983, Trade capital mobility and sovereign immunity (Princeton University Press, Princeton, NJ).

Grossman, H. and J. Van Huyck, Sovereign debt as a contingent claim. Excusable default repudiation and reputation.

Guesnerie R. and J.J. Laffont, 1985, A complete solution to a class of principal agent problem with an application to a self managed firm, Journal of Public Economics.

Kreps, D., 1984, Signalling games and stable equilibria, Discussion paper.

Kreps, D. and R. Wilson, 1983, Sequential equilibria, Econometrics discussion paper.

Thomas-Worrall, 1984, Self enforceable contracts, Mimeo.

European Economic Review 30 (1986) . North-Holland

COMMENTS

'The Pure Theory of Country Risk'
by J. Eaton, M. Gersovitz and J. Stiglitz

Martin HELLWIG

University of Bonn, 53 Bonn, FRG

I agree with the authors that the problems of international borrowing and lending must be analysed in terms of strategic behaviour rather than mechanical concepts of 'insolvency' or 'illiquidity'. In this comment, I shall briefly try to give my own perspective on some of the underlying issues.

1. Debt contracts and the allocation of risks

First I want to pose the question why most international finance is based on the instrument of the *debt contract*. In its traditional form, the debt contract imposes a fixed repayment obligation on the borrower. He must meet this obligation or else default and incur a set of more or less severe sanctions.

In an uncertain world, this type of contract usually involves an inefficient allocation of risks. Efficiency would require that financiers and borrowers share all risks in proportion to their respective degrees of risk tolerance. Unless a borrower is risk neutral, at least some risk should be born by his financiers.

However, the debt contract provides for hardly any risk sharing at all and imposes most risks on the borrower. Unless the borrower defaults, the financier gets his fixed repayment and bears none of the risks surrounding the borrower's financial situation. This one-sided imposition of risks upon the borrower is exacerbated by the more recent form of debt contracts which specify the borrower's repayment obligation with reference to the London interbank offered rate (LIBOR). In addition to the risks surrounding his own financial situation, the borrower now also bears the risks involving the financier's opportunity cost of funds as measured by LIBOR. Since I do not believe that borrowers are risk neutral, I find this one-sided imposition of risks hard to explain.

The absence of risk sharing is usually explained by considerations of moral hazard or other types of information asymmetry. For example, Douglas Gale and I have shown that the standard debt contract with a fixed repayment obligation actually is the optimal incentive compatible contract for a private firm and a risk neutral (!) lender, if (a) only the firm's returns are risky, and (b) except in the event of bankruptcy, the lender cannot directly observe the realizations of the firm's random returns [Gale and Hellwig (1985)]. Under this information asymmetry, the firm's payment to the creditor must be independent of its return realization – at least outside the event of bankruptcy – because the firm can always 'lie' and report that return realization which minimizes its repayment obligation to the lender. Similarly, debt finance may be desirable if the firm's returns depend on, e.g., the manager's effort and if the level of effort cannot be observed by the financiers [see, e.g., Jensen and Meckling (1976)].

Considerations of this type also apply in the case of lending to countries rather then firms. Many of the factors determining a country's financial and economic situation are country specific and cannot be observed by outside financiers. Therefore, the underlying potential for sharing the risks surrounding these factors cannot be exploited. Any attempt to share these risks would provide the borrowing country with incentives to reduce its payments to its financiers either by reducing its own economic effort or by simply misreporting its actual financial and economic situation. In contrast, the debt contract is much less vulnerable to moral hazard. As long as default is not an issue, the financier does not get involved in the borrower's affairs at all. The fixed interest obligation does not depend on the borrower's activities. Whatever incentive problems arise must, therefore, be limited to the case of default.

However, the preceding argument applies only to risks that involve an information asymmetry between the borrower and the financier. The moral hazard argument does *not* apply to risks whose incidence is unaffected by either party's actions and which can be observed by both parties alike. In particular, the moral hazard argument does not apply to risks arising (i) from fluctuations in the exchange rate of the dollar, and (ii) from fluctuations in international interest rates, such as LIBOR. Both, the dollar exchange rate and the London interbank offered rate are universally observable and are hardly affected by the actions of any particular borrower or lender in the market. Therefore, it should be possible to share the risks arising from these variables efficiently between international borrowers and lenders. To the extent that the lenders seem to be better qualified to bear these risks, such efficient risk sharing would have left most of the exchange and interest rate risk with the lenders rather than the borrowers. The debt contracts that have been concluded have done the opposite and have imposed practically all exchange and interest rate risks on the borrowers rather than the lenders.

From this perspective, the international debt crisis of recent years seems to be the consequence of (i) an inefficient prior allocation of exchange and interest rate risks in international borrowing and lending, and (ii) an exceptionally unfavourable realization of these very risks. The unanticipated combination of high dollar exchange rates and high interest rates in recent years entails an exceptionally high real value for the borrowing countries' contractual repayment obligations to the lenders. Under an ex ante efficient risk sharing agreement, at least some of the consequences of the high dollar exchange rates and the high interest rates would have been borne by the lenders.

At this point, one is tempted to follow Grossman and Van Huyck (1985) and to regard the current reschedulings as a substitute for the risk sharing arrangements that were absent from the original contracts. However, the reschedulings do not seem to distinguish between the incidence of exchange and interest risks that are immune from moral hazard and the incidence of other risks that are subject to moral hazard. In order to assess the reschedulings, we must, therefore, take a closer look at the strategic issues connected with default and, in particular, with default on country debt.

2. Sovereign debt and the problem of default

To the extent that the borrower may default on his obligation, the debt contract is vulnerable to moral hazard just like any other contract. Default may occur because the debtor is unwilling to pay or because he is unable to pay. Even if he is unable to pay, this inability may be due to his own careless behaviour as well as to circumstances outside his control.

In the given context of lending to countries, Eaton, Gersovitz and Stiglitz stress the problems arising from a debtor's *unwillingness to pay*. I have no quarrel with their analysis of these problems, but I believe that they underrate the role played by the debtor countries' *inability to pay*.

As Eaton, Gersovitz and Stiglitz note, a government's ability to pay its debts to its foreign creditors depends on (a) its ability to raise funds through taxation, and (b) its ability to transfer there funds abroad. On both accounts I believe that a government's objective ability to pay is significantly less than Eaton, Gersovitz and Stiglitz suggest.

First, any assessment of a government's ability to raise revenues through taxation must take account of social and political constraints as well as the deadweight cost of taxation. Taxation will be considered excessive and will lead to an overthrow of the government long before tax receipts reach the Eaton–Gersovitz–Stiglitz measure of national net worth minus deadweight costs. If we look at eighteenth century France, the mere observation of 'the poor state in the rich country' [Gaxotte (1928)] might suggest that, in the words of Eaton, Gersovitz and Stiglitz, the government was not 'anywhere near making the maximum feasible debt service'. Yet in the 1780's, the government's attempt to avoid a debt crisis by increasing taxes played a major role in the developments leading to the French Revolution.

Secondly, I believe that Eaton, Gersovitz and Stiglitz underrate the traditional transfer problem. I do not see why the effect of the transfer upon the terms of trade should be negligible (in relation to the transfer itself) if the paying country is small relative to the receiving country. The terms of trade effect should depend on the difference between the paying and the receiving countries' marginal propensities to consume different goods. Unless these marginal propensities are taken to differ according to a country's size, I do not see why relative size should matter. Moreover, any adverse terms of trade effect that does occur can be quite large if demand for the debtor country's export goods is sufficiently price-inelastic.

In summary, we cannot dismiss the possibility that the current international debt crisis is due to the debtor countries' objective inability to pay. However, by the very nature of the underlying incentive problems, the creditors and the international monetary and financial institutions will find it impossible to determine whether a given default is due to unwillingness or inability to pay. Any debtor who is merely unwilling to pay will claim that he is actually unable to pay, e.g., that any tightening of fiscal poling would risk a social revolution. The validity of such a claim can hardly be assessed from the outside. The reparations that were owed by Weimar Germany after the Treaty of Versailles provide a good example: Even now, the historians find it difficult to decide whether 'the Germany could have paid (the) reparations ... if they had loyally tried to' [Kindleberger (1984, p. 306)].

In the context of sovereign debt, this information asymmetry is significantly more serious than for private debt. In our analysis of private borrowing and lending with asymmetric information, Douglas Gale and I assume (i) that a default imposes real costs on the debtor, e.g., because of non-monetary sanctions, and (ii) that in the event of a default, a receiver is put in to observe the debtor's true ability to pay and to force him to pay. Under these assumptions, the borrower never wants to default on his repayment obligation if he can avoid it.

In the case of sovereign debt, such disciplining devices are much less effective. By today's legal standards, the imposition of a receivership on a country represents an intolerable violation of national sovereignty. Moreover, it is of some interest to note that such receiverships have been unsuccessful even where they were tried in the past. In the case of Weimar Germany, the Reparation Agent-General under the Dawes Plan performed some of the functions of a receiver. This Reparation Agent-General himself felt that he had so little impact on German fiscal policy that he did not want to take any responsibility, and in 1928 he himself took the initiative to restore the German government's fiscal autonomy [Fischer (1968, p. 36)].

Respect for national sovereignty also limits the sanctions on default by a country. A country that defaults on its debts need not fear any analogue of the criminal proceedings to which a private debtor may be subjected. Eaton, Gersovitz and Stiglitz rightly observe that an inability to obtain loans in the future may be the severest sanction altogether that creditors have available.

Even this sanction may be quite ineffective. For consider the decision of a debtor who must choose whether to honour a repayment obligation $x > 0$ or to default and thereby lose all access to future borrowing. Presumably this debtor will default unless the present value to him of having access to the market in the future is at least x. The present value to him of having access to the market in the future is *not* given by the size of future loans – which will have to be repaid – but by the size of the *surpluses* on future loans after deducting future repayments. For the repayment x to be worthwhile, the present value of the sum of surpluses on future loan contracts must exceed x. Assuming that discount rates are non-negligible, I expect that this condition can only be met if the debtor anticipates substantial growth so that future surpluses are quite large.

From this perspective, the international debt crisis of recent years may be seen as a consequence of reduced growth expectations in international capital markets and in the world economy. The downward revision of growth estimates in the recession of the 1980s reduced the present value of the debtor countries' future access to international capital markets. The one sanction that creditors have thereby lost some of its bite. Therefore the debtor countries began to feel that default might be preferable and asserted that they were unable to fulfil their obligations. By the very nature of the information asymmetry, this moral hazard interpretation of the debt crisis is empirically indistinguishable from an inability-to-pay explanation based on the movements in exchange and interest rates.

3. Rescheduling and the problem of time inconsistency

So far I have assumed that the threat of sanctions on default is credible. However, this is not generally the case. Once we look at repeated credit relations, we realize that the creditor's behaviour is subject to a fundamental *time consistency*: Ex ante, when the contract is concluded, he wishes to threaten the most severe sanctions in order to provide the debtor with an incentive to manage his affairs as carefully as he can and to default on his obligation only if he is truly unable to pay. However, ex post, after the debtor has defaulted, the creditor usually does not want to carry out his threat. If he forces the debtor into immediate bankruptcy, he may as well write his claims off. On the other hand, if he extends a further loan, success on whatever project the debtor pursues next will ensure the profitability of previous loans as well as the next loan.

The current renegotiations and reschedulings provide ample evidence of this time inconsistency. In fact, the lenders who do not wish to write off their country loans seem to be more eager to avoid an open default than the borrowers. In fear for their balance sheets, they 'reschedule' payments in order to avoid having to recognize a default as such.

In the ex post situation when a debtor claims that he cannot pay, rescheduling may actually be the best alternative given that an open default would entail considerable private risks for some of the lender banks as well as social risks for the international financial and monetary system.

However, we must realize that from the ex ante point of view these renegotiations impose considerable costs on future loans. In the future any borrowing country will know that the sanctions on default are small and will behave accordingly. For the currently outstanding loans, the incentive effects of sanctions may be irrelevant because they concern only bygones. For future loans, these incentive effects are anything but irrelevant. If a lack of credible sanctions induces a high risk of negligent or fraudulent default, then the volume of borrowing and lending is likely to be substantially reduced.

This 'breakdown of lending', as Eaton, Gersovitz and Stiglitz call it, was the main subject of my earlier paper [Hellwig (1977)]. The problem can be avoided if the creditor takes account of reputation effects whereby the renegotiation of an outstanding loan has a negative impact on the anticipations and behaviours of other borrowers. However, such reputation effects are implausible if no two borrowers are alike so that there is no inherent reason why the lender's treatment of current borrowers should give any indication of his likely treatment of future borrowers. In the case of lending to countries, this problem is particularly bothersome since, of course, Poland is different from Iran, which in turn is different from Mexico, which in turn is different from....

As far as I can see, the only way to avoid the problems caused by time inconsistency is for the creditor to obtain some direct control over the debtor's net cash flows. If there is no such control and if the debtor anticipates that the creditor will not give him up, then the debtor is never forced to be careful about how he manages his resources.

To see the point, consider the example of New York City. In the early seventies, the New York City banks found it necessary to repeatedly renegotiate their loans to the city. Whatever promises of fiscal discipline accompanied these renegotiations were not kept, and the banks had to provide *additional* loans at an ever increasing rate. The problem was that New York City's cash flows were under the effective control of the unions who did not see the need for fiscal discipline because the banks were always willing to renegotiate and to provide more money. The situation only changed when the Municipal Assistance Corporation took over and imposed fiscal discipline through its control of New York City's finances.

The question is whether something like this can be achieved by, e.g., the International Monetary Fund's imposition of austerity measures during loan renegotiations. In this context it is important that whatever agency imposes fiscal discipline should not appear as a receiver who merely liquidates past claims. As in the case of New York City, such an agency must actually provide the debtors with a positive incentive for cooperation by providing a promise of additional loans – and hence of some hope for the future – which will be mutually beneficial if the required discipline is kept. However, the arguments of the preceding section suggest that in a climate of pessimism about the world economy the scope for such promises is rather narrow.

References

Fischer, W., 1968, Deutsche Wirtschaftspolitik 1918–1945 (Opladen).

Gale, D. and M. Hellwig, 1985, Incentive-compatible debt contracts: The one-period problem, Review of Economic Studies 52, 647–663.

Gaxotte, P., 1928, La Révolution Française (Paris).

Grossman, H. and J.B. Van Huyck, 1985, Sovereign debt as a contingent claim: Excusable default, repudiation, and reputation, Mimeo. (Brown University, Providence, RI).

Hellwig, M., 1977, A model of borrowing and lending with bankruptcy, Econometrica 45, 1879–1906.

Jensen, M.C. and W.H. Meckling, 1976, Theory of the firm: Managerial behavior, agency costs and ownership structure, Journal of Financial Economics 3, 305–360.

Kindleberger, D.P., 1984, A financial history of Western Europe (London).

European Economic Review 30 (1986) . North-Holland

GROWTH AND EXTERNAL DEBT UNDER RISK
OF DEBT REPUDIATION*

Daniel COHEN

CEPREMAP, Paris, France

Jeffrey SACHS

*Harvard University and National Bureau of Economic Research,
Cambridge, MA 02138, USA*

We analyze the pattern of growth of a nation which borrows abroad and which has the option
of repudiating its foreign debt. We show that the equilibrium strategy of competitive lenders is
to make the growth of the foreign debt contingent on the growth of the borrowing country. We
give a closed-form solution to a linear version of our model. The economy, in that case, follows
a two-stage pattern of growth. During the first stage, the debt grows more rapidly than the
economy. During the second stage, both the debt and the economy grow at the same rate, and
more slowly than in the first stage. During this second stage, the total interest falling due on the
debt is never entirely repaid; only an amount proportional to the difference of the rate of interest
and the rate of growth of the economy is repaid each period.

1. Introduction

When borrowers have an option to repudiate their debts, the interactions
of borrowers and lenders over time presents a strategic situation of enormous
complexity. Consider the case of a sovereign borrowing country, raising
loans from the world capital market. Following Eaton and Gersovitz (1981),
suppose that repudiation of the debt results in financial autarky and a loss of
productive efficiency of the defaulting country. An indebted country must
balance these costs with the direct costs of debt repayment, in considering
the option of repudiation. In turn, credit rationing will emerge from the
lenders' decision to limit their exposure to a level low enough to render debt
repudiation an inferior option to the borrowing country.

It turns out that the lenders' strategy is not easy to compute. The simple
maxim is to lend freely to the point where the country is indifferent between

---

*Paper presented at the International Seminar on Macroeconomics, Chateau de Ragny,
France, June 1985. The authors would like to thank Atish Ghosh, who designed and
implemented the numerical dynamic programming algorithm used in section 4 of the paper.

debt repayment and repudiation. But what point is that? One of the incentives for debt repayment is the option to borrow again in the future. But the value of that option depends on how much lenders will lend in the *future*. That in turn will depend on the future lenders' assessment of the point of indifference of the country between repayment and repudiation, which in turn will depend on the capacity of the country to borrow in the still further distant future. Thus we have a problem of infinite regress, and the method of dynamic programming is needed to solve the lenders' problem.

In this paper, we examine a growth model in which sufficiently many linearities allow us to give a closed form solution to the lender's and borrower's strategies. We also describe an algorithm and a suitable numerical technique to solve for borrower and lender behavior in more complex, non-linear settings. In the analytical version of the model, the borrowing country goes through two borrowing stages: (1) a stage with unconstrained borrowing and a rising external-debt-to-*GDP* ratio, with the rate of *GDP* growth falling progressively; and (2) a stage with a constant, low rate of *GDP* growth and constrained (rationed) borrowing. During the second stage (which always occurs after a finite time), the country never repays the full amount of interest falling due but only the fraction which is necessary to make the debt grow at the same rate as the *GDP* of the country.

Section 2 sets out the model. Section 3 analyzes the optimal lending strategy when default is an available alternative to the borrower, and presents analytical results in the linear version of the model. Section 4 briefly discusses the use of numerical techniques for more general models. Finally, section 5 examines the sensitivity of the equilibrium to alternative lending strategies. A conclusion summarizes the paper. All technical derivations are presented in four appendices.

2. The model

We study a discrete-time growth model of a small country which has access to an international capital market. We assume that the consumption, investment and borrowing decisions are made by a social planner maximizing an intertemporal utility function. The numeraire (both national and international) is a good which serves for both consumption and investment. The international rate of interest is assumed to be a constant, r. In this paper we do not deal with the important distinction between traded and non-traded goods. This will enable us to use *GDP* as a measure of the potential foreign-exchange revenues of the country. In a more general framework, one should be careful to use the production of traded goods as the measure of the revenues which enable the country to repay its debt [see Cooper and Sachs (1984) and Dornbusch (1983)].

2.1. Technology and capital installation

The technology available to the country is described by a linear production function with only one input, capital,

$$Q_t = aK_t. \tag{1}$$

Q_t is GDP at time t, and K_t installed capital. (In section 4, we briefly examine the case of more general technologies.) Installed capital depreciates at rate d, so that the net increment to installed capital is

$$K_{t+1} = I_t + (1-d)K_t, \tag{2}$$

where I_t is the flow of newly installed capital. If there were no installation costs, a social planner able to borrow at a world interest rate r would choose either to invest or disinvest at an infinite rate depending on whether r is less than or greater than $a - d$. In what follows, we shall assume the inequality

$$r < a - d, \tag{3}$$

so that the planner would choose to invest at an infinite rate. In fact, we shall also assume that installation of capital is costly. Following Abel and Hayashi, we let J_t, total investment expenditure, and I_t, the flow of new installed capital, be related by the functional form

$$J_t = [1 + (1/2)\phi(I_t/K_t)]I_t. \tag{4}$$

The unit cost to install capital is therefore $(1/2)\phi(I_t/K_t)$, which increases with the rate of capital accumulation. With this formulation, the planner will always choose to invest at a finite rate.

2.2. The wealth of the country

We shall define the productive wealth W of the country as the discounted value of current and future production net of the investment expenditure, using the world interest rate as the discount factor

$$W_t = \sum_{i=t}^{\infty} (1+r)^{-(i-t)}(aK_i - J_i). \tag{5}$$

It is easy to show [see Appendix 2, eqs. (A2.5) to (A2.10)] that the wealth so defined is maximized by selecting a fixed rate of capital accumulation

$$x^* = I_t/K_t. \tag{6}$$

Capital stock growth is then given by

$$K_{t+1}/K_t - 1 = g^* \equiv x^* - d. \tag{7}$$

From now on, we shall assume that the value of g^* satisfies $g^* < r$ so that the infinite sum in (5) is meaningful. We show in Appendix 2 (A2.9) that the value x^* maximizing W_t and satisfying (3) is

$$x^* = (r+d)[1 - \sqrt{1 - (2/\phi)(a-d-r)/(r+d)}]. \tag{8}$$

This value of x^* exists under the condition

$$\phi > 2(a-d-r)/(r+d). \tag{9}$$

(9) says that installation cost must be sufficiently large so as to make the maximum rate of capital accumulation lower than the rate of interest. We henceforth assume that (9) holds.

2.3. Optimizing behavior of the country

We shall assume that the country is governed by a social planner maximizing a time-separable utility function of the form

$$U = \sum_{t=0}^{\infty} \beta^t \log C_t. \tag{10}$$

The choice of logarithmic utility helps to preserve key linearities necessary for a closed-form solution.

When the constraint on foreign borrowing is not binding, the optimal consumption path will satisfy

$$C_{t+1}/C_t = \beta(1+r). \tag{11}$$

From now on we shall assume

$$\beta(1+r) < 1 + g^*, \tag{12}$$

which guarantees that the planner discounts the future sufficiently to desire to be a net borrower.

2.4. Foreign borrowing

The international capital market is assumed to be competitive, and to supply loans at a fixed interest rate r (though in a rationed quantity, yet to be determined). All loans are for one period, with D_t denoting the principal repayments due at time t, and rD_t the interest payments due at time t. The balance of payments equation is

$$D_{t+1} = (1+r)D_t + C_t + I_t[1 + (\phi/2)(I_t/K_t)] - Q_t. \tag{13}$$

In general, as described in section 3, new borrowing will be limited by a constraint of the form $D_{t+1} \le h(K_{t+1})$. The goal is to characterize the $h(K_{t+1})$ function, and to study optimal borrowing under that constraint.

2.5. The threat of repudiation

We shall assume that the planner has the option of repudiating the country's external debt. If it does so, it suffers two penalties. First, the country permanently loses its access to international capital markets so that it is forced into financial autarky. Second, there is a direct penalty on production following debt repudiation (due, for example, to a loss of efficiency following increased difficulties in foreign trade) so that the productivity of capital becomes $a(1-\lambda)$ for some $\lambda \in [0,1]$. GDP hence becomes

$$Q_t = a(1-\lambda)K_t. \tag{14}$$

Given these constraints, a defaulting country can reach an autarkic intertemporal utility level, which we name $V^D(K_t)$. Note that this utility level is a function of the stock of capital in place when the decision to default is taken. We show in Appendix 1, eq. (A1.8), that $V^D(K_t)$ is of the form

$$V^D(K_t) = \log(K_t)/(1-\beta) + \text{constant}. \tag{15}$$

The constant term is a decreasing function of λ. We shall assume full information of both creditors and debtors of the value of λ, as well as of the level of the capital stock. Given this absence of uncertainty, default will never happen: the lenders will select a supply of credit such that the borrower will never find it profitable to repudiate its debt. The main purpose of section 3 will be to find this loan supply and to derive its consequences for the growth of the country.

3. Equilibrium with repudiation

We now examine the consequences of a threat of debt repudiation on the strategies available to the lenders, and on the rate of growth of the borrowing economy. At each point of time, the country has built up both external debt and productive capital. In order to decide whether to default or to repay the debt coming due, the country has to compare the autarkic utility level $V^D(K)$, which is a function of installed capital only, with the utility it can derive by servicing the debt and at least postponing the decision to default. The subtlety of the problem is that the country's decision depends in part on the future credit lines it expects from the lenders, who must relate their lending decisions to the country's present and future choices. Technically, the solution must be obtained by backward recursion. Given the constraints on lending that the country is expected to face in the future, present lenders must keep their exposure to a level which keeps the country from defaulting on its current debt.

Solving the problem in its full generality is a hard task and simplifications are needed to find a closed form solution. An example is solved in Eaton and Gersowitz by assuming a fixed cyclical pattern to the country's output, and no capital accumulation. In our previous work (1984, 1985), a three-period horizon allowed us to solve a model with uncertainty via backward recursion. In the model here, the many linearities which we imposed on consumer tastes and on production technology enable us to give a closed-form solution to the problem in an infinite-horizon model with capital accumulation. Before we solve our specific model, we first set the problem in its general form.

3.1. Finitely-lived economy

In order to show how backward recursion is used to find the optimal decision rule of the lenders, we first assume that the horizon of the country ends at some finite time T.

Let us assume that the country has not defaulted before the last period and that it has accumulated by then a capital stock K_T and an external debt D_T (with debt D_T, the country owes $(1+r)D_t$ in the last period). During the last period, the decision to repay or to default is straightforward since the country has only to compare the costs and benefits of defaulting in one period. We define [following Eaton and Gersovitz (1981)]

$$V_T(K_T, D_T) = \max\{V_T^R(K_T, D_T), V_T^D(K_T)\}, \quad \text{with} \tag{16}$$

$$V_T^R(K_T, D_T) = \log[aK_T - (1+r)D_T], \quad \text{and} \tag{17}$$

$$V_T^D(K_T, D_T) = \log[(1-\lambda)aK_T], \tag{18}$$

where V_T^R denotes the utility that the country can reach by repaying its debt at time T, and V_T^D the utility it can reach by defaulting at T. V_T is the maximum of V_T^R and V_T^D, and is thus the maximum utility achievable at time T. We assume that when repudiation and repayment yield exactly the same utility (i.e., $V^D = V^R$), the country repays the debt. Let us call $h_T(\ )$ the lending limit which keeps the country from defaulting at T. h_T is defined implicitly by the condition

$$D_T \leqq h_T(K_T) \Leftrightarrow V_T^R(K_T, D_T) \geqq V_T^D(K_T).$$

From (17) and (18), h_T is simply

$$h_T(K_T) = \lambda a K_T / (1 + r). \tag{19}$$

Thus, the country will repay D_T if and only if $D_T \leqq h_T(K_T) = \lambda a K_T / (1 + r)$.

Let us now analyze the problem at time $T - 1$. We define $V_{T-1}^R(D_{T-1}, K_{T-1})$ as

$$V_{T-1}^R(D_{T-1}, K_{T-1}) = \max_{C_{T-1}, I_{T-1}, D_T} \{\log C_{T-1} + \beta V_T(K_T, D_T)\}, \tag{20}$$

subject to

$$K_T = I_{T-1} + (1 - d) K_{T-1}, \tag{2}$$

$$J_T = [1 + (1/2)\phi(I_{T-1}/K_{T-1})] I_{T-1}, \tag{4}$$

$$D_T = (1 + r) D_{T-1} + C_{T-1} + I_{T-1}[1 + (\phi/2)(I_{T-1}/K_{T-1})] - Q_{T-1}, \tag{13}$$

and

$$D_T \leqq h_T(K_T).$$

$V_{T-1}^R(K_{T-1}, D_{T-1})$ is the utility that the country can reach by repaying the debt, D_{T-1}, *when it faces a new supply of credit which is constrained by* $D_T \leqq h_T(K_T)$.

Let us finally define

$$V_{T-1}(D_{T-1}, K_{T-1}) = \max\{V_{T-1}^R(K_{T-1}, D_{T-1}), V^D(K_{T-1})\}, \tag{21}$$

with $V_{T-1}^D(K_{T-1})$ the utility level that the country can reach by defaulting on the debt D_{T-1}. V_{T-1} is the best outcome that the country can reach at time t given its ability to repudiate the debt. We now define $h_{T-1}(\ )$ as the rule which will keep the country from defaulting at time $T - 1$. We want

$$D_{T-1} \leqq h_{T-1}(K_{T-1}) \Leftrightarrow V_{T-1}^R(K_{T-1}, D_{T-1}) \geqq V_{T-1}^D(K_{T-1}). \tag{22}$$

By backward recursion, we can clearly define a sequence of lending rules $\{h_T(\ ), h_{T-1}(\ ), \ldots, h_0(\ )\}$ such that (22) holds for all $t \geqq 1$, and V_t^R, V_t^D and V_t defined analogously to the expressions in (20) and (21). Eq. (22), when generalized for all t, is the condition for the country to repay its debt D_t

falling due at time t when it expects at time $t, \ldots, T$, the lending rules $h_t, \ldots, h_T$ to apply.

It is interesting to consider the case when $\lambda = 1$, i.e., when all output is lost in the event of default. In this case, a default at time t results in $C_{t+i} = 0$ for all $i \geq 0$. Thus, $\lambda = 1$ is tantamount to assuming that the country has no option to repudiate. It is easy to see that the planner will always choose to service the debt as long as it is *feasible* to pay $(1+r)D_t$ out of net exports at time t plus new borrowing. At $T-1$, therefore, lenders limit loans D_T such that $(1+r)D_T \leq aK_T$ (clearly, for $(1+r)D_T > aK_t$, repayment in period T is not feasible, as there is no lending in $T+1$). At $T-2$, lenders require that $(1+r)D_{T-1} \leq \max(aK_{T-1} - J_{T-1} + D_T)$, such that $D_T \leq aK_T/(1+r)$. Thus, $(1+r)D_{T-1} \leq \max[aK_{T-1} - J_{T-1} + aK_T/(1+r)]$. In other words, $(1+r)D_{T-1}$ will be kept less than or equal to the maximum productive wealth at time $T-1$. By induction, it is easy to prove this result for all $t \leq T$

$$(1+r)D_t \leq \max \sum_{i=t}^{T} (aK_i - J_i)(1+r)^{-(i-t)} \quad \text{subject to (2), (4),} \tag{23}$$

or, using earlier notation

$$(1+r)D_t \leq \max W_t. \tag{24}$$

To sum up, when $\lambda = 1$, borrowing is limited only by the maximum productive wealth of the economy.

3.2. A digression on the precommitment of capital installation

In the maximization problem which we set in (20), we implicitly assumed that the investment and borrowing decisions are made simultaneously, since the lenders at time t can condition their loans on the investment decision of the country. The loan at time t, D_{t+1}, is therefore made a function of the capital stock that will be in place at time $t+1$. If the lending decision must be made before I_t is observed, there is a moral hazard problem. The country, even if it wishes to precommit itself to investing a certain amount I_t in light of the borrowing constraint $D_{t+1} \leq h_{t+1}(K_{t+1})$, may find it profitable not to do so *after* the loan has been granted. In such situations, the lending strategy by the banks should be written

$$D_t \leq h_t(K_{t-1}),$$

and the borrower will typically reach a lower level of utility because of this lagged relationship. In all that follows, we shall ignore this problem by assuming that the loan can be predicated on the investment decision each period. We refer the reader to our previous work (1984) for further discussion.

3.3. Infinite-horizon economies

When one lets the time horizon of the economy go to infinity, the definition of the lending rule remains the same except that the time subscript may be dropped, since $h_t(K_t)$ will be the same for all t. An equilibrium will be defined by the four functions $V^D(K_t)$, $V^R(K_t, D_t)$, $V(K_t, D_t)$ and $h(K_t)$, such that

$$V^R(D_t, K_t, h(\ )) = \max_{C_t, I_t, D_{t+1}} [\log C_t + \beta V(D_{t+1}, K_{t+1}, h(\ ))], \qquad (25)$$

subject to (2), (4), (13) and

$$D_{t+1} \leq h(K_{t+1}), \qquad V(D_t, K_t) = \max\{V^R(\ ), V^D(\ )\},$$

$$D_t \leq h(K_t) \Leftrightarrow V^R(K_t, D_t, h(\ )) \geq V^D(K_t).$$

$h(\ )$ is therefore a stationary rule such that if future lenders are to apply it as a criterion for future lending, it will also be used as a criterion for current lending.

Before proceeding to the specific solution for V^D, V^R, and h in the case of $\lambda < 1$, it is useful to make one small amendment to (25). Though V^R equals $\log C_t + \beta V_{t+1}$, and $V_{t+1} = \max(V^R_{t+1}, V^D_{t+1})$, the lending constraint $D_{t+1} \leq h(K_{t+1})$ guarantees that $V^R_{t+1} \geq V^D_{t+1}$ as long as the debt is repaid at time t. In other words, as long as the debt is repaid once, borrowing constraints will guarantee that all future debts will also be repaid (this is true only in a model without uncertainty). Therefore, V^R in (25) will also satisfy

$$V^R(D_t, K_t) = \max[\log C_t + \beta V^R(D_{t+1}, K_{t+1})], \qquad (25')$$

where V^R replaces V on the right-hand side.

One case of (25) is easily solved: for $\lambda = 1$. As noted earlier, $(1+r)D_t$ will always be repaid as long as repayment is feasible out of net exports $aK_t - J_t$ and new borrowing D_{t+1}, i.e., as long as $(1+r)D_t \leq \max(aK_t - J_t + D_{t+1})$. Of course, D_{t+1} is limited by $D_{t+1} \leq h(K_{t+1})$. Thus, the borrowing constraint is defined by a stationary h function, such that $h(K_t) = [\max(aK_t - J_t + D_{t+1})]/(1+r)$, with $D_{t+1} \leq h(K_{t+1})$. Upon substitution, for D_{t+1} we have $h(K_t) = \max[aK_t - J_t + h(K_{t+1})]/(1+r)$. The solution to this functional equation is

$$h(K_t) = \max\left[\sum_{i=t}^{\infty} (1+r)^{-(i-t)}(aK_i - J_i)\right]\Big/(1+r) = \max W_t/(1+r). \qquad (26)$$

Thus, as in the case of finite T, the borrowing constraint when $\lambda = 1$ is simply that $D_t(1+r)$ must be less than or equal to the maximum value of national productive wealth.

For $\lambda = 1$, the problem in (24) reduces to the standard borrowing problem without repudiation risk

$$\max \sum_{t=0}^{\infty} \beta^t \log C_t, \tag{27}$$

subject to (2), (4), (13), $D_0 = 0$, K_0 given and, for all t,

$$D_t(1+r) \leq \max \sum_{i=t}^{\infty} (aK_i - J_i)(1+r)^{-(i-t)}.$$

It is a standard exercise to show under these circumstances that the optimal production decision and the consumption choice can be separated. Given the international rate of interest, investment is chosen to maximize the productive wealth of the country. Given the path of productive wealth, the planner then selects an optimal pattern of consumption, subject only to the constraint that $D_t(1+r) \leq \max W_t$ is satisfied. We show in Appendix 3 that the equilibrium will be characterized by the two following conditions:

Proposition 1. When $\lambda = 1$ (i.e., the country can never profitably repudiate its debt)

(1) *GDP grows at the fixed rate g^* [eq. (8)] which maximizes productive wealth,*
(2) *consumption grows at a rate $\theta = \beta(1+r) - 1$.*

The initial value of consumption is defined so that the discounted value of the infinite sequence of consumption is equal to the wealth of the country.

Under the assumption (12), consumption over *GDP* tends to zero in the stationary state. This says that in the long run all *GDP* goes to repayment of the debt. When the country has the option to repudiate its debt, even at a substantial loss, a path in which consumption asymptotically approaches zero, as a fraction of *GDP*, can never be an equilibrium since the option to repudiate would eventually be exercised. Lenders will restrain their lending so that in the limit only a fraction of *GDP* goes to the repayment of the debt, and so that consumption does not tend to zero in the long run.

One additional feature of the equilibrium is the following. The productive wealth of the economy W_t is maximized by the investment path, and it grows at the same rate as *GDP*, i.e., at the rate g^*. Since $g^* < r$ (by our earlier assumptions on the technology parameters), and since $(1+r)D_t \leq W_t$ by the lending rule, we see that D_t must grow less rapidly than rate r in the long run. Therefore, the path of $(1+r)D_t$ satisfies the so-called 'transversality condition'

$$\lim_{t \to \infty} D_t/(1+r)^t = 0. \tag{28}$$

Let us define RP_t as the net repayment of debt each period, given by the difference of $(1+r)D_t$ and new borrowing D_{t+1}

$$RP_t = (1+r)D_t - D_{t+1}. \tag{29}$$

Since (29) implies $D_{t+1} = (1+r)^{t+1}D_0 - \sum_{i=0}^{t}(1+r)^{(t-i)}RP_i$, we have $D_{t+1}/(1+r)^t = (1+r)D_0 - \sum_{i=0}^{t}(1+r)^{-i}RP_i$. Then, taking limits and applying the transversality condition, we have

$$(1+r)D_0 = \sum_{i=0}^{\infty} (1+r)^{-i}RP_i. \tag{30}$$

In effect, the transversality condition is a zero-profit condition for the sequence of loans: it guarantees that the discounted value of repayments equals the outstanding debt payment due at time t, $(1+r)D_t$.

We have found the transversality condition to be implied by the market equilibrium. If lenders expect $(1+r)D_{t+i} \leq W_{t+i}$ for all $i > 0$, they will impose $(1+r)D_{t+1} \leq W_{t+1}$ in period t. In some models, the transversality condition need not be an implication of market equilibrium [see Cohen and Sachs (1985) as an example]. Later in this paper, in section 4, we will need to impose the zero-profit condition (30) directly, rather than finding it as an implication of the model.

3.4. Market equilibrium with repudiation risk

We now turn to the case of $\lambda < 1$, and show that the lending rule $h(K_t)$ is linear in K_t. The equilibrium path, when $\lambda < 1$ is described by the following proposition:

Proposition 2. Lending in each period is governed by a linear credit constraint

$$D_t \leq h^* K_t, \tag{31}$$

where h^* is a constant which depends both on the technology of production and on the taste parameters of the intertemporal utility function. Given this constraint, a country with no initial debt selects a path with two stages

Stage 1.   *The constraint (31) on the debt is not binding. The rate of growth of the economy is high initially, and declines progressively, and the debt-to-GDP and debt-to-capital ratios increase.*

Stage 2.   *The constraint on the debt is binding. The economy and the debt grow at a same rate n, which is lower than the growth rates in Stage 1 and below the rate of growth, g*, which maximizes productive wealth.*

According to Proposition 2, the threat of repudiation forces the economy into an equilibrium with productive inefficiency, since the rate of growth in Stage 2 is below the level g^* which maximizes productive wealth. With debt growing at rate n, we have $D_{t+1} = (1+n)D_t$. Also, $D_{t+1} = (1+r)D_t - RP_t$, where RP_t is the amount of repayment at time t. Thus, $RP_t = (r-n)D_t$, or

$$RP_t = \theta Q_t \quad \text{with} \quad \theta = (r-n)h^*/a. \tag{32}$$

One sees that the repayment is always less than the amount of interest falling due, rD_t, so that the lenders always refinance some interest payments. Despite this property, the discounted value of debt repayments equals $(1+r)D_t$, i.e., the zero profit condition in (3) holds. [We know this to be true, since with debt growing at rate $n < r$, the transversality condition in (28) is satisfied.]

Once the binding debt-to-capital ratio, h^*, has been reached, the only way the lenders can keep the country from defaulting is to continue to lend according to the same rule. If they cease to do so, and demand, for example, the repayment of all interest falling due, then the country will default. (*Proof.* The rule $D^* \leq h^*K$, when it is binding, leads by construction to $V^D = V^R$. Any *tighter* lending rule will then have $V^D > V^R$, and the country will default.)

The proof of Proposition 2 is given in Appendix 3. Here we sketch the main steps of the proof. First, we guess a function for $\tilde{h}(K)$ and solve the optimal borrowing problem under the constraint $D_t \leq \tilde{h}(K_t)$, assuming no debt repudiation. The optimal borrowing problem yields an optimal consumption plan, $\{C_t^{\tilde{h}}\}$, where the superscript $\tilde{h}$ stresses the dependence of the optimal plan on the assumed borrowing constraint. We then define the value of the optimal program (under $\tilde{h}$) as $V^{\tilde{h}}(K_t, D_t) = \sum_{i=0}^{\infty} \beta^{t+i} \log(C_{t+i}^{\tilde{h}})$. By construction, $V^{\tilde{h}}$ satisfies the eq. (25′): $V^{\tilde{h}}(K_t, D_t) = \max(\log(C_t) + \beta V^{\tilde{h}}(K_{t+1}, D_{t+1}))$ such that $D_{t+1} \leq \tilde{h}(K_{t+1})$. Then, we prove for our choice $\tilde{h}$ that $D_{t+1} \leq \tilde{h}(K_{t+1})$ if and only if $V^{\tilde{h}}(K_t, D_t) \geq V^D(K_t)$. Thus, we have found a solution to (25), with $V^R = V^{\tilde{h}}$, $h = \tilde{h}$, and $V^D = V^D$. Using $C_t^{\tilde{h}}$, we then prove the part of the proposition concerning the two-stage growth path.

Specifically, we prove that the *linear* credit rule in (31) satisfies the market equilibrium in (25). The properties of the borrowing equilibrium under $D_t \leq h^*K_t$ are easy to calculate, as shown in Appendix 3. We solve the optimal control problem for foreign borrowing subject to the constraint that

$D_t \leq h^* K_t$. The result is the two-stage growth process described in Proposition 2. Starting $D_0 = 0$, there is an initial period of rapid but declining growth, with D/K rising to h^*. Once the constraint is binding, D/K remains equal to h^*, and growth remains equal to x^{h^*}, where x^{h^*} is the root of eq. (A3.8) in Appendix 3. The growth rate is less than g^*, the growth rate that maximizes W_t. (Remember that g^* is achieved when $\lambda = 1$, i.e., when there is no viable threat of repudiation.)

In Appendix 3, we present the non-linear eq. (A3.12) that defines h^*. It is straightforward to show that h^* is: increasing in a, β, and λ; and is decreasing in r. In words, the sustainable debt per unit of capital rises with capital productivity, the discount factor, and the penalty for default, while it falls with the world interest rate. By a simple transformation, the maximum debt–GNP ratio is a similar function of these variables, since $D/GNP = D/[aK - rD)$, which must be less than or equal to $h/(a - rh)$ when $D \leq hK$. In table 1, we calculate the maximum debt–GNP ratios for alternative values of a, β, λ, and r.

Table 1a

Maximum debt–GNP ratios: Alternative values of capital productivity, a, and subjective discount rate, β (for $r = 0.1$, $\lambda = 0.4$).[a]

| | β | | | |
a	0.6	0.7	0.8	0.9
0.15	2.31	2.48	2.82	3.75
0.20	2.44	2.68	3.15	4.55
0.25	2.61	2.92	3.60	5.89
0.30	2.81	3.23	4.24	9.28

[a]The other parameter values are $d = 0.05$, $\phi = 10$.

Table 1b

Maximum debt–GNP ratios: Alternative values of world interest rate, r, and default penalty rate, λ (for $a = 0.2$, $\beta = 0.9$).[a]

| | λ | | | |
r	0.1	0.2	0.3	0.4
0.10	0.95	2.02	3.22	4.55
0.15	0.67	1.42	2.28	3.26
0.20	0.51	1.10	1.78	2.58
0.25	0.41	0.90	1.46	2.14

[a]The other parameter values are $d = 0.05$, $\phi = 10$.

It is also instructive to compare the equilibrium growth paths for *GDP* under alternative borrowing assumptions, as is done in fig. 1. The dashed line, which increases most rapidly, is for *GDP* in the absence of repudiation risk (i.e., for $\lambda = 1$); the solid line, which shows intermediate growth, is for *GDP* with repudiation risk (specifically, $\lambda = 0.4$), with D/K initially below h^*; the dotted line, with the slowest growth, represents the case without foreign borrowing (either a closed economy, or open economy with $\lambda = 0$). There are two notable aspects of the figure. First, it is apparent that productive wealth is reduced by the option to repudiate. Second, we see the point of inflection (in period 17) in the intermediate growth path, which according to Proposition 2 is reached when the constraint $D_t \leq h^* K_t$ begins to bind.

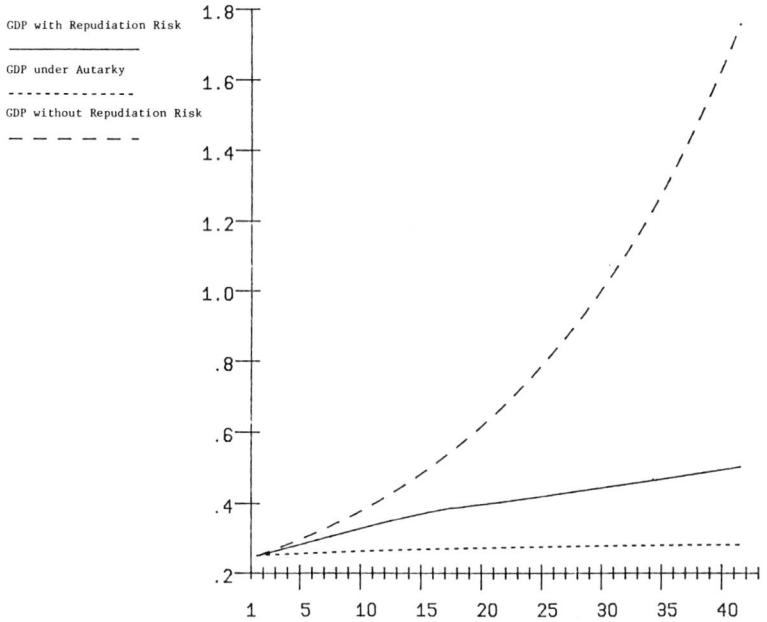

Fig. 1. GDP under alternative borrowing assumptions.

4. Equilibrium with repudiation in non-linear models

We have been able to derive a closed-form solution for the growth path in the case $Q_t = aK_t$ because the value function V^R is separable in K and D (see Appendix 3). This separability arises because two economies with the same D_t/K_t but different K_t will differ only in scale. With $D_t^1/K_t^1 = D_t^2/K_t^2$ and $K_t^2 = K_t^1$, economy 2 will simply follow a path in which all variables (C_t^2, D_t^2, K_t^2, GDP_t^2) are equal to D_t^2/D_t^1 times the values in economy 1 (C_t^1, D_t^1, K_t^1, GDP_t^1).

Once the linear production technology is abandoned, an analytical solution appears out of reach. Now, a rise in K is more than a scale change, since output does not (by assumption) rise in the same proportion. For a standard neoclassical production technology, $Q_t = F(K_t)$, with $F' > 0$, $F'' < 0$, a rise in K_t lowers the marginal product of capital and reduces the incentive to invest. It is not surprising, therefore, that the maximum D_t associated with K_t will not rise in equiproportion with K_t. In other words, the h function giving D_t, $h(K_t)$ will be less than unit elastic in K_t.

In order to investigate this case, we resort to numerical dynamic programming methods (designed by Mr. Atish Ghosh in conjunction with the authors). Specifically, the value function $V^D(K_t)$ is calculated numerically for a grid on K_t varying between 0 and 10.0, with steps of 0.1. Then, $V^R(K_t, D_t)$ is calculated using the backward recursion methodology outlined in section 3. The V^R function is analyzed on a grid of 0 to 10.0 for K_t, and 0 to 2.0 for D_t, both with step sizes of 0.1. Once V^D_{T-t} and V^R_{T-t} are calculated for a period of $T-t$, as in section 3, the optimization in (20) is carried out by a numerical search procedure over I and C, using step sizes of 0.05 for these variables. The backward recursion procedure is repeated until V^D and V^R converge to steady-state functions within the specified tolerance.

An example of this numerical exercise is shown in figs. 2 and 3. We adopt a Cobb–Douglas production technology $Q_t = 3K_t^{0.3}$. Fig. 2 plots the maximum debt/GDP ratio as a function of GDP. (Note that the jagged nature of the curve results only from the discrete step-sizes used in the programming algorithm. These minor blips are unimportant quantitatively. A smoother curve could be achieved by a finer grid size, but at the cost of much higher computing time.)[1] In the linear case, of course, this maximum ratio is a constant (h^*/a), independent of the level of GDP. In the case of Cobb–Douglas technology, however, the maximum ratio *declines* as GDP increases. This is for a straightforward, yet illuminating reason. At low levels of GDP, the marginal productivity of capital is very high and the investment incentives are consequently strong. The returns to borrowing abroad are large, as are the costs of debt repudiation (which would freeze out new borrowing to finance further increases in K). As the capital stock deepens, the incremental returns to investment fall, and the costs of debt repudiation as a fraction of GDP are reduced pari passu. Thus, a capital-poor country will be allowed a wide latitude in foreign borrowing, while a capital-abundant economy will be much more restricted (as a proportion of GDP). The allowable debt rises as GDP rises but less than proportionately.

---

[1] With the grid selected, there are two thousand points in the domain of $V^R_t(K_t, D_t)$. An optimization must be performed at *each* of these points for *each* period in which V^R_t is evaluated. Even with the coarse grid that has been used, the evaluation of V^R and V^D requires substantial computer time.

h '(K)/GDP

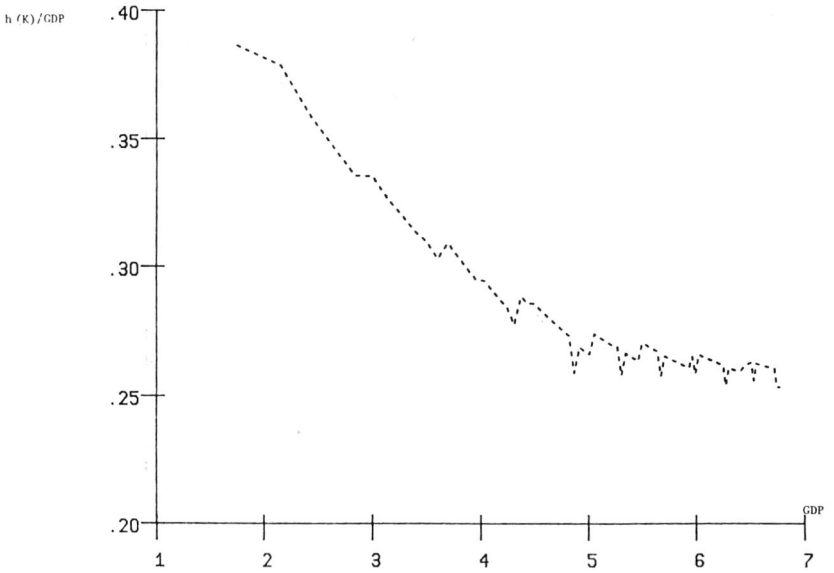

Fig. 2. Maximum debt-to-GDP ratio.

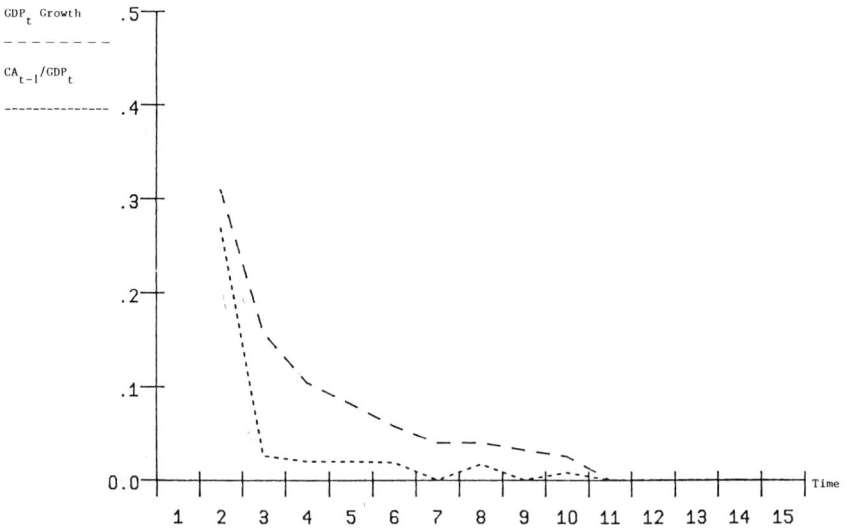

Fig. 3. GDP growth and current account deficits (GDP$_t$ growth is $(Q_t - Q_{t-1})/Q_{t-1}$; CA$_{t-1}$/GDP$_t$ is $(D_t - D_{t-1})/Q_t$).

As shown in figs. 3 and 4, this feature of the $h(\;)$ function has important implications for the growth path and for foreign borrowing. As in the linear model, growth and foreign borrowing start out high and then fall sharply as the debt constraint is hit (in this case as of period 2). Fig. 3 shows the *GDP* growth rate and the current account deficit as a percentage of *GDP*. Fig. 4 shows the actual and maximum debt–*GDP* ratios for periods 1 through 15. In each period, the maximum rate is calculated as $h(K_t)/GDP_t$ where K_t is the level of K_t on the equilibrium growth path. In the first period, actual $D_t/GDP_t < h(K_t)/GDP_t$. In periods 2 through 15, the debt constraint is binding as shown. Note that the debt–*GDP* ratio jumps sharply between periods 1 and 2, and then *declines* over, as the country becomes wealthier (i.e., as the capital stock deepens). The decline reflects the already observed fact that $h(K_t)/GDP_t$ is a declining function of K_t.

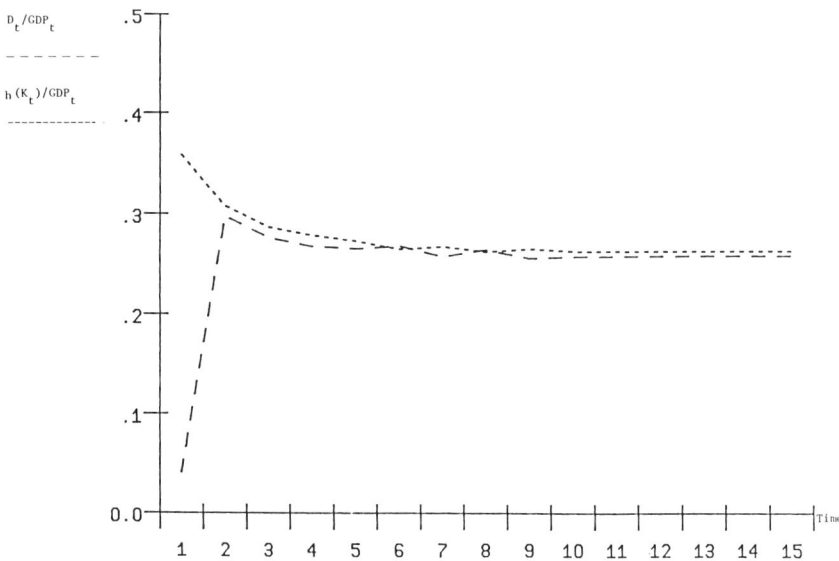

Fig. 4. Actual and maximum debt-GDP ratios.

5. Alternative lending strategies

In this section we return to the linear version of the model in order to examine lending and repayment strategies which differ from the market equilibrium described above. In the first subsection, we assume that the lenders and the borrower can act cooperatively to decide upon a path of future debt, consumption and investment, subject only to the zero profit condition in (3) and to the condition that the country keep its sovereign right to repudiate the debt at any time and to suffer the penalty thereafter. (If the country can also credibly promise never to repudiate, it reaches the equilibrium of Proposition 1.) Is there any contractual scheme between the lenders and the borrower that can dominate the market equilibrium and still keep the country from defaulting? The answer is no, as we show in the proof of Proposition 3.

In the second subsection, we analyze a repayment scheme which has been suggested by some analysts. We have seen that when $D_t = h^* K_t$, in Stage 2 of the market equilibrium, the country repays every period a fixed fraction θ of GDP, as in (32). What if the lenders simply demand that $RP_t = \theta Q_t$, rather than sticking to the rule $D_t = h^* K_t$? It turns out that when the borrower expects to face the rule $RP_t = \theta Q_t$ rather than the rule $D_t = h^* K_t$, the incentives for growth are changed in a way that undermines this alternative lending rule.

5.1. Contractual agreements between the lenders and the borrower

In this subsection, we assume that the borrowing country and its lenders can design a path of future debt, investment and consumption such that (i) the loan satisfies the zero-profit condition (30), and (ii) the country never finds it profitable to repudiate its debt. The path is set once and for all at $t = 0$. Surprisingly, such a contractual arrangement cannot dominate the market equilibrium.

Proposition 3. The market equilibrium yields the optimal pattern of growth that a country can reach, subject to the constraint that it never prefers to default.

The proposition says, among other things, that there is no way to avoid the slowdown of growth described in Proposition 2. This slowdown is an inherent implication of the option of repudiation; there is no way that the country can credibly promise to grow at g^* forever.

To prove Proposition 3, we first define new utility function Ω which would be attained if the country can design in advance its path of consumption and investment subject to (3) and the constraint that it never prefer to default.

$$\Omega[D_0, K_0] = \max_{\{C_t, I_t, D_t\}} \sum_{t=0}^{\infty} \beta^t \log C_t, \tag{33}$$

subject to (2), (4). (13), (30), transversality condition (16), and

$$\sum_{(t=s)}^{\infty} \beta^{(t-s)} \log C_t \geq V^D(K_s). \tag{34}$$

Note that (34) guarantees that the country will never choose to repudiate the debt. A priori, Ω does not coincide with the utility V achieved in the market equilibrium. V was defined as the fixed point of problem (25). Ω is defined directly by an optimizing problem. They in fact are equal, as we show in Appendix 4. The crux of the argument is to show that inequality (34) can be written $D_t \leq h^*K_t$, as in the market equilibrium case.

5.2. Repayment of a fixed fraction of the revenues each period

Let us assume that the country has already entered Stage 2 of its pattern of growth. Each period, it repays a fixed fraction of its revenues to the lenders in order to equalize the growth of debt and the growth of GDP. These repayments can be written $RP_t = [(r-n)h^*/a]Q_t$, with $n = x^{h^*} - d$, where x^{h^*} is the investment rate in Stage 2.

Now, let us assume that the lenders ask to be repaid some fraction $\tilde{\Theta}$ of GDP, instead of sticking to the original rule of lending $D \leq h^*K$. $\tilde{\Theta}$ may or may not equal $(r-n)h^*/a$. We prove the following:

Proposition 4. When a country has reached the Stage 2 of its pattern of growth, the lenders cannot get repayment of their loans by abandoning the rule $D_t \leq h^*K_t$ and by asking instead to be repaid a fixed fraction of the country's GDP each period. By doing so, they would either induce the country to default, or they would get repayment of only a portion of the outstanding debt [i.e., the zero profit condition in (3) would not hold].

The proposition stresses the importance to the creditors of stating correctly the rule governing their lending. In the market equilibrium, the lenders are ready to increase their exposure at the rate of GDP growth. By doing so, they create an incentive for the country to grow. Any slight modification of the rule which reduces this incentive to grow yields a sub-optimal result. A repayment scheme as in Proposition 4 creates an incentive that is adverse to growth, since debt repayments are made an *increasing* function of the output of the economy.

To prove Proposition 4, assume that the country is asked to repay a fixed fraction $\tilde{\Theta}$ of its GDP. It will select an optimal rate of growth by solving

$$V_{\tilde{\Theta}} = \max_x \{\log[a(1-\tilde{\Theta}) - x(1+\phi x/2)]/(1-\beta)$$

$$+ \beta[\log(1+x-d)]/(1-\beta)^2 + \log K_0/(1-\beta)\}. \tag{35}$$

[See eq. (A1.8) where $a\tilde{\Theta}$ is substituted for λ.]

Let $x_{\tilde{\Theta}}$ be the solution to (35). We can compute the value of this repayment stream by noting that $RP_{t+1} = \tilde{\Theta}GDP_{t+i} = \tilde{\Theta}aK_{t+i} = \tilde{\Theta}a(1+x_{\tilde{\Theta}}-d)^iK_t$.

Thus, the discounted value of repayments, which we denote by P_t, is given as

$$P_t = \sum_{i=t}^{\infty} RP_t/(1+r)^i = [aK_t\tilde{\Theta}(1+r)]/r - d - x_{\hat{\theta}}]. \tag{36}$$

Now, suppose $\tilde{\Theta}$ is selected so that $P_t = (1+r)D_t$, i.e., so that the debt is repaid in present value terms. Call the selected value $\hat{\Theta}$. Since $D_t = h^*K_t$ by assumption, we must have $P_t = h^*(1+r)K_t$. Thus, from (36) we must have the equality $h^* = a\hat{\Theta}/[r+d-x_{\hat{\theta}}]$. From (35) we then see that

$$V_{\hat{\theta}} = \log[a - h^*(r+d-x_{\hat{\theta}}) - x_{\hat{\theta}}(1+\phi x_{\hat{\theta}}/2)]/(1-\beta)$$

$$+ \beta[\log(1+x_{\hat{\theta}}-d)]/(1-\beta)^2 + \log K_t/(1-\beta). \tag{37}$$

Now we prove that $V_{\hat{\theta}} < V^D$, as asserted in Proposition 4. That is, we prove that the country would default if required to pay ΘGDP, for Θ high enough to yield $P_t = (1+r)D_t$. By definition of x^{h^*} and h^* (at which the country is at autarky utility in the market equilibrium), we can use (37) to write

$$V^D = \log[a - h^*(r+d-x^{h^*}) - x^{h^*}(1+\phi x^{h^*}/2)]/(1-\beta)$$

$$+ \beta[\log(1+x^{h^*}-d)]/(1-\beta)^2 + \log K_t/(1-\beta). \tag{38}$$

Note that the right-hand side of (38) is the same as the right-hand side of (37) but with x^{h^*} replacing $x_{\hat{\theta}}$. But x^{h^*} maximizes the right-hand side of (37) for given h^*, so it must be $V^D > V_{\hat{\theta}}$. If the creditors are to be repaid, the borrower is driven below the autarky level.

6. Conclusion

We have constructed a model with endogenous growth and endogenous credit ceilings, We have shown that the equilibrium path for the country is one with initially rapid growth followed by a permanent slowdown. The equilibrium strategy of the lenders makes the growth of debt contingent on the growth of the borrowing country. In the linear version of our model, under the equilibrium lending rule, the evolution of the debt follows two stages, a first stage in which debt grows faster than the economy, and a second stage where both the economy and the debt grow more slowly, and at the same rate. Along this path, the interest due, rD, is never repaid in full; only an amount equal to the difference between the interest due and g^*D (the growth rate times the debt) should be repaid. This permanent refinancing of part of the interest is the only way to reach the optimum pattern of growth consistent with no default by the borrowing country.

Appendix 1: Optimal growth under autarky

The optimal growth problem under autarky is

$$V_t(K_0) = \max \sum_{t=0}^{\infty} \beta^t \log(C_t), \tag{A1.1}$$

such that $K_{t+1} = K_t(1-d) + I_t$, $aK_t = C_t + I_t[1 + (\phi/2)(I_t/K_t)]$ and K_0 is given.

To solve this problem, we define $c_t = C_t/K_t$, $x_t = I_t/K_t$. Note that $K_{t+1} = K_t(1-d+x_t)$, so that

$$K_t = K_0 \prod_{i=0}^{t-1} (1-d+x_i),$$

and

$$\log K_t = \log K_0 + \sum_{i=0}^{t-1} \log(1-d+x_i).$$

Since $c_t = C_t/K_t$, $\log C_t = \log c_t + \log K_t$. Hence,

$$\sum_0^{\infty} \beta^t \log(C_t) = \sum_0^{\infty} \beta^t \log c_t + \sum_0^{\infty} \beta^t \log K_t$$

$$= \sum_0^{\infty} \beta^t \log c_t + \sum_0^{\infty} \beta^t \log K_0 + \sum_0^{\infty} \beta^t \left[\sum_{i=1}^{t-1} \log(1-d+x_i) \right].$$

After a bit of manipulation,

$$\sum_0^{\infty} \beta^t \left[\sum_{i=0}^{t-1} \log(1-d+x_i) \right]$$

can be rewritten as

$$\sum_{t=0}^{\infty} [\beta^{t+1}/(1-\beta)] \log(1-d+x_t).$$

Thus, the original problem (A1.1) can be rewritten as

$$V^A(K_0) = \max \sum_{t=0}^{\infty} \beta^t \{\log c_t + \log K_0 + [\beta/(1-\beta)] \log(1-d+x_t)\}, \tag{A1.2}$$

such that $a = c_t + x_t[1 + (\phi/2)x_t]$.

Note that we have solved out for K_t in the objective function, so we no longer need to include $K_{t+1} = K_t(1-d+x_t)$ among the constraints. Now there are no longer any real dynamic constraints in the problem, so that we need only to maximize $\{\log c_t + [\beta/(1-\beta)] \log(1-d+x_t)\}$ each period, subject to $a = c_t + x_t(1 + \phi x_t/2)$. This maximization leads to a fixed c^A and x^A (i.e., optimal c and x under autarky) for all t, with x^A given by the largest root of

$$(1-\beta)(1+\phi x)(1-d+x) - \beta a + \beta x(1+\phi x/2) = 0. \tag{A1.3}$$

c^A is then given as

$$c^A = a - x^A[1 - \phi x^A/2]. \tag{A1.4}$$

Note that since c^A and x^A are invariant to K_0, we have from (A1.2) that $V^A(\lambda K_0) - V^A(K_0) = \sum_{t=0}^{\infty} \beta^t \log(\lambda K_0) - \sum_{t=0}^{\infty} \beta^t \log K_0 = \log \lambda/(1-\beta)$. Thus,

$$V^A(\lambda K_0) = V^D(K_0) + \log \lambda/(1-\beta). \tag{A1.5}$$

By substitution of (A1.4) into (A1.2), we find the explicit solution for $V^A(K_0)$

$$V^A(K_0) = \sum_{t=0}^{\infty} \beta^t \{\log[a - x^A(1 + \phi x^A/2] + \log K_0$$

$$+ [\beta/(1-\beta)] \log(1-d+x^A)\}$$

$$= \log[a - x^A(1 + \phi x^A/2)]/(1-\beta) + \beta \log(1-d+x^A)/(1-\beta)^2$$

$$+ \log K_0/(1-\beta). \tag{A1.6}$$

The solution for the default utility $V^D(K_0)$ is the same as for $V^A(K_0)$ except that $a(1-\lambda)$ replaces a in the equation for the growth rate (A1.3). That is, x^D is the largest root of the equation

$$(1-\beta)(1+\phi x)(1-d+x) - \beta a(1-\lambda) + \beta x(1+\phi x/2) = 0. \tag{A1.7}$$

Then, as in (A1.6), we may write

$$V^D(K_0) = \log[a(1-\lambda) - x^D(1 + \phi x^D/2)]/(1-\beta)$$

$$+ \beta \log(1-d+x^D)/(1-\beta)^2 + \log K_0/(1-\beta). \tag{A1.8}$$

It is easy to show that $x^D < x^A$, and $V^D(K_0) < V^A(K_0)$.

Appendix 2: Optimal growth without repudiation

The planner solves

$$\max \sum_{t=0}^{\infty} \beta^t \log C_t, \tag{A2.1}$$

subject to

$$\sum_{t=0}^{\infty} (1+r)^{-t} C_t = NW_0, \tag{A2.2}$$

where NW_0 is consumer wealth. The solution to (A2.1) is

$$C_t = C_0 \beta^t (1+r)^t, \tag{A2.3}$$

$$C_0 = (1-\beta) NW_0. \tag{A2.4}$$

Productive wealth W_0 is maximized by solving

$$\max W_0 = \sum_{t=0}^{\infty} (1+r)^{-t} \{ aK_t - I_t[1 + (1/2)\phi(I_t/K_t)] \}, \tag{A2.5}$$

subject to

$$K_{t+1} = K_t(1-d) + I_t. \tag{A2.6}$$

If one calls q_t the Lagrange multiplier associated with (A2.6), one finds

$$x_t \equiv I_t/K_t = (q_t - 1)/\phi, \quad \text{and} \tag{A2.7}$$

$$q_{t-1}(1+r) = q_t(1-d) + a + \phi x_t^2/2. \tag{A2.8}$$

The optimal path is obtained by selecting the unique value value of q_0 which satisfies the transversality condition. Here, q_0 is such that all q_t will stay constant, so that x_t is also a constant, x^*, which solves

$$(1/2)x^2 - x(r+d) + (a-d-r)/\phi = 0. \tag{A2.9}$$

The solution, x^*, which we look for is the smaller root of (A2.9) (the other solution can be ruled out by the second-order conditions of the optimization problem). The solution is shown in eq. (8) in the text. We let $1+g^* \equiv 1+x^*-d$. K_t is now defined by

$$K_t = K_0(1+g^*)^t. \tag{A2.10}$$

The productive wealth of the country is now defined by

$$W_0 = [a - x^*(1 + \phi x^*/2)][(1 + r)/(r - g^*)]K_0.$$

Net wealth (subtracting foreign debt D) is defined by NW_t

$$NW_t = W_t - (1 + r)D_t. \tag{A2.11}$$

At initial time, $D_0 = 0$, so that NW_0 and W_0 coincide.
The law of motion of the debt is given by

$$D_{t+1} = (1 + r)D_t + C_t - [a - x^*(1 + \phi x^*/2)]K_t. \tag{A2.12}$$

Since $C_t = (1 - \beta)NW_t = (1 - \beta)[W_t - (1 + r)D_t]$, we have

$$D_{t+1} = (1 + r)D_t + (1 - \beta)[a - x^*(1 + \phi x^*/2)][(1 + r)/(r - g^*)]K_t$$

$$- (1 - \beta)(1 + r)D_t - [a - x^*(1 + \phi x^*/2)]K_t. \tag{A2.13}$$

Now, define $d_t = D_t/K_t$. Note that $D_{t+1}/K_t = d_{t+1}(K_{t+1}/K_t) = (1 + g^*)d_{t+1}$. Then, by dividing both sides of (A2.13) by K_t we can write

$$d_{t+1} = [\beta(1 + r)/(1 + g^*)]d_t$$

$$+ [(1 + g) - \beta(1 + r)][a - x^*(1 + \phi x^*/2)]/(r - g^*)K_t. \tag{A2.14}$$

We begin with $d_0 = 0$. The country becomes and remains a net debtor as long as $\beta(1 + r) < (1 + g^*)$. This condition, which we assume, is more likely to hold when: the world interest rate r is low, the future is heavily discounted (β small), investment is highly productive (a large), and the adjustment costs in investment, ϕ, are small.

By solving (A2.14), starting from $d_0 = 0$, we find

$$d_t = \{1 - [\beta(1 + r)/(1 + g^*)]^t\}[a - x^*(1 + \phi x^*/2)]/(r - g^*). \tag{A2.15}$$

Note that as $t \to \infty$, d_t asymptotically approaches $\bar{d} = [a - x^*(1 + \phi x^*/2)]/(r - g^*)$. When $d_t = \bar{d}$, we have $(1 + r)(D/W) = 1$. Thus, consumption over *GDP* asymptotically approaches zero.

Appendix 3: Borrowing equilibrium with risk of debt repudiation

Lenders' strategies

Consider the following optimization problem:

$$V^h(K_0, D_0) = \max \sum_{t=0}^{\infty} \beta^t \log C_t, \tag{A3.1}$$

such that

$$D_{t+1} = D_t(1+r) + C_t + I_t[1 + (\phi/2)(I_t/K_t)] - aK_t,$$

$$K_{t+1} = K_t(1-d) + I_t,$$

$$D_{t+1} \leqq hK_{t+1},$$

with $D_0 \leqq hK_0$ and D_0, K_0 given.

Define the following variables:

$$c_t \equiv C_t/K_t, \qquad d_t \equiv D_t/K_t, \qquad x_t \equiv I_t/K_t.$$

Then, the problem in (A3.1) can be rewritten as

$$V^h(K_0, D_0) = \max \sum_{t=0}^{\infty} \beta^t \log c_t + \sum_{t=0}^{\infty} \beta^t \log K_t, \tag{A3.2}$$

such that

$$(1 - d + x_t)d_{t+1} = (1+r)d_t + c_t + x_t[1 + (\phi/2)x_t] - a,$$

$$K_{t+1} = K_t(1 - d + x_t),$$

$$d_{t+1} \leqq h,$$

with d_0, K_0 given, and $d_0 \leqq h$.

Using the same method as in Appendix 1, (A3.2) may be rewritten again as

$$V^h(K_0, D_0) = \max \sum_{t=0}^{\infty} \beta^t \log c_t + (\log K_0)/(1 - \beta)$$

$$+ \sum_{t=0}^{\infty} [\beta^{t+1}/(1 - \beta)] \log(1 + d + x_t), \tag{A3.3}$$

such that $(1 - d + x_t)d_{t+1} = (1+r)d_t + c_t + x_t[1 + (\phi/2)x_t] - a$, and $d_{t+1} \leqq h$.

Note that we no longer need the equation of motion for K_t, since K_t is no longer part of the objective function.

The optimal policy for c_t, x_t in (A3.3) is clearly independent of K_0, for a given d_0 ($=D_0/K_0$), since the objective function is additively separable in K_0, and the dynamic constraints do not depend on K_0. Thus, $V^h(\lambda K_0, \lambda D_0) - (V^h(K_0, D_0) = (\log \lambda K_0)/(1-\beta) - (\log K_0)/(1-\beta) = \log \lambda/(1-\beta)$.

Rearranging, we have

$$V^h(\lambda K_0, \lambda D_0) = V^h(K_0, D_0) + \log \lambda/(1-\beta) \tag{A3.4}$$

as asserted in Lemma 1.

Now, choose $\lambda = 1/K_0$, so that we find $V^h(1, D_0/K_0) = V^h(K_0, D_0) - (\log K_0)/1 - \beta)$. Since we already know from Appendix 1 that $V^D(K_0) = V^D(1) + \log(K_0)/(1-\beta)$, we see that

$$V^h(K_0, D_0)(\gtreqless)V^D(K_0) \quad \text{if and only if} \quad V^h(1, D_0/K_0)(\gtreqless)V^D(1). \tag{A3.5}$$

It is easy to show that V is strictly decreasing in its second argument (more debt is strictly worse than less debt). Thus there is at most one value $\hat{h} = D_0/K_0 \leq h$ such that $V^h(1, \hat{h}) = V^D(1)$, and if such $\hat{h}$ exists, then $V^h(1, D_0/K_0)(\gtreqless)V^D(1)$ as $D_0/K_0(\lesseqgtr)\hat{h}$. From (A3.5), the same $\hat{h}$ is such that $V^h(K_0, D_0)(\gtreqless)V^D(K_0)$ as $D_0(\lesseqgtr)\hat{h}K_0$.

Now, suppose we find an h^* such that $V^{h*}(1, h^*) = V^D(1)$. Then, $V^{h*}(K_0, D_0)(\gtreqless)V^D(K_0)$ as D_0 $(\lesseqgtr)h^*K_0$. V^{h*}, V^D, and h^* then constitute an equilibrium of the capital market, as defined by (24) in the text with $V^R = V^{h*}$. We now derive the equilibrium h^*.

Let us first derive $V^{h*}(1, h^*)$. This is the solution to

$$\max \sum_{t=0}^{\infty} \beta^t \log c_t + \sum_{t=0}^{\infty} [\beta^{t+1}/(1-\beta)] \log(1-d+x_t), \tag{A3.6}$$

such that

$$(1-d+x_t)d_{t+1} = (1+r)d_t + c_t + x_t[1+\phi x_t/2] - a,$$

$$d_{t+1} \leq h \quad \text{and} \quad d_0 = h^*.$$

We set up the Lagrangian for the problem as

$$\mathcal{L} = \sum_{t=0}^{\infty} \beta^t \{\log c_t + [\beta/(1-\beta)] \log(1-d+x_t) + \beta^t \lambda_t \{(1-d+x_t)d_{t+1}$$

$$- (1+r)d_t - c_t - x_t[1+\phi x_t/2] + a\}\beta^t \mu_{t+1}[d_{t+1} - h]\}. \tag{A3.7}$$

(a) $1/c_t = \lambda_t$ $(\partial \mathcal{L}/\partial c_t = 0)$.

(b) $[\beta/(1-\beta)]/(1-d+x_t) + \lambda_t d_{t+1} - \lambda_t(1+\phi x_t) = 0$ $(\partial \mathcal{L}/\partial x_t = 0)$,

(c) $(1-d+x_t)\lambda_{t-1}/\beta - \lambda_t(1+r)\mu_t/\beta = 0$ $(\partial \mathcal{L}/\partial d_t = 0)$.

To these first-order conditions we add the budget constraint from (A3.6)

(d) $(1-d+x_t)d_{t+1} = (1+r)d_t + c_t + x_t[1+\phi x_t/2] - a$.

Solutions to (a) through (d) are given by constant values of c, λ, x, and μ, with $d_t = h$ for all t. Using (a), (b), and (d) we find the optimal x^h as the positive root to the following equation:

$$[(2-\beta)\phi]x^2 + 2[(1-d)(1-\beta)\phi - (h-1)]x$$

$$+ 2[-\beta a + \beta h(r+d) - (1-d)(1-\beta)(h-1)].   \tag{A3.8}$$

Now, we rewrite the budget constraint $d_{t+1}(1-d+x_t) = (1+r)d_t + c_t + x_t[1+(\phi/2)x_t] - a$ to give c_t as a function of x^h. Since $d_t = d_{t+1} = h$, we have

$$c^h = (x^h - r - d)h + a - x^h[1 + \phi x^h/2].   \tag{A3.9}$$

Note that c^h is written without a time subscript, now since consumption per unit capital is a constant along the optimal path. We now plug c and x^h back into the utility function in (A3.6) to get

$$V^h(1,h) = \sum_{t=0}^{\infty} \log \beta^t c^{\bar{h}} + \sum_{t=0}^{\infty} [\beta^{t+1}/(1-\beta)] \log(1-d+x^h),   \text{ or }   \tag{A3.10}$$

$$V^h(1,h) = \log[(x^h - r - d)h + a - x^h(1+\phi x^h/2)]/(1-\beta) + [\beta/(1-\beta)^2]$$

$$\times \log(1-d+x^h).   \tag{A3.11}$$

The last equation is found by substituting (A3.10) into (A3.11). Note that $d[V^h(1,h)]/dh = \partial V^h/\partial h + (\partial V^h/\partial x^h)\,\partial x^h/\partial h = \partial V^h/\partial h$, where the last inequality follows from the envelope theorem (i.e., from the fact that with an optimal choice of x, $\partial V^h/\partial x = 0$). Thus, $\text{sign}(dV^h/dh) = \text{sign}(x^h - r - d) < 0$, so that $V^h(1,h)$ is *strictly decreasing* in h.

Now, it is easy to prove that there exists a unique h^* such that $V^{h^*}(1,h^*) = V^D(1)$. First, $V^0(1,0) = V^A(1)$, since $h=0$ implies no borrowing at all. But $V^A(1) > V^D(1)$, so that $V^h(1,h) > V^D(1)$ for $h=0$. Now, consider $V^{\bar{d}}(1,\bar{d})$, where $\bar{d}$ is the limit of D_t/K_t in the no-repudiation case of Appendix 1. Since c equals zero in the limit in that case, $V^{\bar{d}}(1,\bar{d}) = -\infty < V^D(1)$. Thus, since $V^0(1,0) > V^D(1) > V^{\bar{d}}(1,\bar{d})$, and since $V^h(1,h)$ is strictly decreasing in h, there must exist an h^* between 0 and $\bar{d}$, such that $V^{h^*}(1,h^*) = V^D(1)$. In particular

h^* is the unique root of the equation

$$\log\{(x^h - r - d)h + a - x^h[1 + (\phi/2)x^h]\} + [\beta/(1-\beta)]\log(1-d+x^h)$$

$$= \log\{a(1-\lambda) - x^D[1 + (\phi/2)x^D]\} + [\beta/(1-\beta)]\log(1-d+x^D),$$
(A3.12)

where x^h is the positive root of (A3.8) and x^D is the positive root of (A1.7).

We can readily establish various properties of h^*. By total differentiation of (A3.12), we have

$$dh^*/da = [\xi_2 - \xi_1(1-\lambda)]/\xi_2(r+d-x^h)] > 0,$$

$$dh^*/d\lambda = -a\xi_1/[\xi_2(x^h - r - d)] > 0,$$
(A3.13)

$$dh^*/d\beta = \log[(1-d+x^h)/(1-d+x^d)]/[(1-\beta)^2\xi_2(r+d-x^h)] > 0,$$

$$dh^*/dr = h\xi_2/[\xi_2(x^h - r - d)] < 0,$$

where

$$\xi_1 = [a(1-\lambda) - x^d(1+\phi x^d/2)]^{-1} > 0,$$

$$\xi_2 = [(x^h - r - d)h + a - x^h(1+\phi x^h/2)]^{-1} > 0.$$

Finally, let us show that

$$h < 1 + \phi x^h.$$
(A3.14)

This inequality can be derived directly from eq. (A3.8). Another way is as follows. Eq. (A3.8) can be derived from

$$\max_x V^h(1, h).$$
(A3.15)

(A3.15) says that x^h maximizes the utility which is reached when the constraint on the debt is binding. The first-order condition [using the definition of V^h in eq. (A3.11)] yields

$$(1+\phi x - h)(1+x-d)(1-\beta) = \beta[h(x-r-d)+a-x(1+\phi x/2)]. \quad (A3.16)$$

The right-hand side is positive (it measures consumption per unit of capital). Therefore, $(1+\phi x - h)(1+x-d)(1-\beta)$ is positive, so that (A3.14) follows. (A3.16), when developed, yields (A3.8).

Two-staged growth

Now that we have characterized the lending strategy by $D_t \leq h^* K_t$, we can describe explicitly the optimal pattern of growth. From eq. (A3.7), we can write

$$(1 + \phi x_{t-1})(1 + r) = [a + \phi x_t^2 / 2 + (1 - d)(1 + \phi x_t)][1 - \gamma_{t-1}]$$

$$+ d_t (1 + r) \gamma_{t-1} \tag{A3.17}$$

with $\gamma_{t-1} = \mu_t / [\lambda_{t-1}(1 + x_{t-1} - d)]$, when the constraint $D_t \leq h K_t$ is not binding, the shadow price γ_{t-1} is zero, so that the dynamics of the system can simply be written

$$(1 + \phi x_{t-1})(1 + r) = [a + \phi x_t^2 / 2 + (1 - d)(1 + \phi x_t)]. \tag{A3.18}$$

Let us call T the time when the constraint on the debt is first binding (i.e., the first period for which $D_t = h K_t$). For $t \leq T - 2$, we have $\gamma_t = 0$, while for $t \geq T - 1$, $\gamma_t > 0$. After time T, the value of x_t will be constantly held to x_h. All that we need in order to find the entire sequence $\{x_t\}$ is the value x_{T-1} and to define the sequence $\{x_t\}_{t \leq T-2}$ by backward application to eq. (A3.18).

At time $T - 1$, eq. (A3.17) can be written

$$(1 + \phi x_{T-1})(1 + r) = [a + \phi x_h^2 / 2 + (1 + \phi x_h)(1 - d)][1 - \gamma_{T-1}]$$

$$+ h \gamma_{T-1}(1 + r). \tag{A3.19}$$

(Note that we have substituted $x_h = x_T$.) In order to find the equilibrium value of x_{T-1} and γ_{T-1}, we need only to consider one more equation in x_{T-1} and γ_{T-1}. From the system (A3.7), we can derive

$$[c_h(1 - \gamma_{T-1})]/[\beta(1 + r)] = h - [(1 + r)d_{T-1} + x_{T-1}(1 + \phi x_{T-1}) - a] \Big/$$

$$[1 + x_{t-1} - d]. \tag{A3.20}$$

Eq. (A3.20) can be shown to be an upward sloping line for the values of x_{T-1} which are above x^h. When $d_{t-1} = h$, eq. (A3.20) is a modified version of the current account equation when the constraint on the debt is binding: the line would pass through (x^h, γ_h), with γ_h the stationary state value of γ_t when the constraint is binding. One can also check that a lower value of d_{t-1} yields a higher value of x_{t-1}.

The system (A3.19), (A3.20) defines the equilibrium value of (x_{T-1}, γ_{T-1}). Here, we shall prove that (A3.19) defines a downward sloping line. To see this, one need only to check that

$$h(1+r)<(1-d)(1+\phi x^h)+a+\phi x_h^2. \tag{A3.21}$$

We already know that

$$h<1+\phi x^h, \tag{A3.22}$$

so that we only need check that

$$(1+r)(1+\phi x^h)<(1-d)(1+\phi x^h)+a+\phi x_h^2/2,$$

or, equivalently, that

$$\phi x_h^2/2-(r+d)\phi x^h+a-r-d\geq 0. \tag{A3.23}$$

To see this, it is enough to write eq. (A3.17) when $t=T+1$. Both values x_T and x_{T+1} are equal to the stationary state value x^h. Since $h<1+\phi x^h$, eq. (A3.17) can be rewritten to yield the inequality in (A3.23).

We can now represent eq. (A3.19) as a downward sloping line. Its intersection with the upward sloping line defines the equilibrium value of (x_{T-1},γ_{T-1}). Since the upward sloping line is below H_h (defined by $d_{t-1}=h$), this shows that x_{T-1} is greater than x^h.

We can now see the full dynamics of the system. First, note that eq. (A3.18) shows that x^h is lower than x^*, the optimal rate of capital accumulation. Second, note that x_{T-1} is below x^* [from eq. (A3.19)], and eq. (A3.21): $(1+\phi x_{T-1})(1+r)<a+\phi x_h^2/2+(1+\phi x^h)(1-d)<a+\phi x^{*2}/2+(1+\phi x^*)$ $(1-h)=(1+\phi x^*)(1+r)$, so that $x_{T-1}<x^*$. x_{T-1} takes therefore some intermediate value between x^h and x^* and the dynamics are clear.

Appendix 4: Proof of Proposition 3

Let us prove that Ω coincides with V in 5 steps.

Step 1. First, we show

$$\Omega(\lambda D_0, \lambda K_0)=\Omega(D_0, K_0)+\log \lambda/(1-\beta). \tag{A4.1}$$

The argument is as in Appendix 3. If $\{C_t, I_t\}$ is an optimal solution to $\Omega(D_0, K_0)$, $\{\lambda C_t, \lambda I_t\}$ is an optimal solution to $\Omega(\lambda D_0, \lambda K_0)$.

Step 2. In the constraint (34), we can write $\Omega(D_s, K_s)$ in place of $\sum_{t=s}^{\infty}\beta^{(t-s)}\log C_t$. The proof uses a standard argument of dynamic programming. If the right-hand side did not coincide with Ω (which is the maximum one can reach at time s), then one could increase $\Omega(D_0, K_0)$ by changing $\{C_t, I_t\}_{t \geq s}$, to the solution $\{C_t', I_t'\}_{t \leq s}$, which maximizes $\Omega(D_s, K_s)$. Clearly this change would not violate inequality (34). Thus, (33) can be rewritten as

$$\Omega\{D_0, K_0\} = \max_{\{C_t, I_t, D_t\}} \sum_{t=0}^{\infty} \beta^t \log C_t, \tag{A4.2}$$

subject to $\Omega[D_s, K_s] \geq V^D(K_s)$, and (2), (4), (13), (16) and (30).

Step 3. There exists an h_Ω such that $\Omega(D_0, K_0) \geq V^D(K_0) \Leftrightarrow D \leq h_\Omega K_0$. The argument is as in Appendix 3 when (A4.1) is acknowledged.

Step 4. From Steps 2 and 3, $\Omega(D_0, K_0)$ can be written $\Omega(D_0, K_0)$ $= \max \sum_{t=0}^{\infty} \beta^t \log C_t$ subject to $D \leq h_\Omega H$.

Step 5.

$$h_\Omega = h^*.$$

$h_\Omega \geq h^*$, since Ω defines the optimum optimorum. But $h^* \geq h_\Omega$, since h^* defines the largest D/K retio which keeps the country from defaulting.

References

Bardhan, Pranab, 1967. Optimum foreign borrowing, in: Karl Shell, ed., Essays on the theory of optimal economic growth (MIT Press, Cambridge, MA).

Borchard, Edwin, 1951, State insolvency and foreign bondholders, vol. 1, General principles (Yale University Press, New Haven, CT).

Bulow, Jeremy I. and John B. Shoven, 1978, The bankruptcy decision, Bell Journal of Economics, 437–456.

Cohen, Daniel and Jeffrey Sachs, 1984, LDC borrowing with default risk, Kredit und Kapital, special issue on international banking.

Cohen, Daniel and Jeffrey Sachs, 1985, The debt of nations (Harvard University, Cambridge, MA) forthcoming.

D'Autume, A. and P. Michel, 1983, Epargue et investissement et monnaie dans une perspective intertemporelle (INSEE, Paris).

Eaton, Jonathan and Mark Gersovitz, 1981a, Poor country borrowing in private financial markets and the repudiation issue (International Finance Section, Princeton, NJ).

Eaton, Jonathan and Mark Gersovitz, 1981b, Debt with potential repudiation: Theoretical and empirical analysis, Review of Economic Studies 48.

Eaton, Jonathan and Mark Gersovitz, 1981c, Country risk: Economic aspects (Yale University, New Haven, CT) unpublished manuscript.

Feis, Herbert, 1930, Europe: The World's Banker, 1870–1914 (Yale University Press, New Haven, CT).

Foley, Duncan K. and Martin Hellwig, 1975, A note on the budget constraint in a model of borrowing, Journal of Economic Theory 11, 305–314.

Grossman, Sanford J. and Oliver D. Hart, 1980, Corporate financial structure and managerial incentives, Conference paper no. 48, May.

Guitian, Manuel, 1981, Policies on access to fund resources – An overview of conditionality (International Monetary Fund, Washington, DC) manuscript.

International Monetary Fund, 1980, International capital markets, Occasional paper no. 1, Sept. (IMF, Washington, DC).

International Monetary Fund, 1981, External indebtedness of developing countries, Occasional paper no. 3, May (IMF, Washington, DC).

Jensen, Michael and William Meckling, 1976, Theory of the firm: Managerial behavior, agency costs, and capital structure, Journal of Financial Economics 3, 305–360.

Madden, John T., Marcus Nadler and Harry C. Sauvain, 1937, America's experience as a creditor nation (Prentice-Hall, New York).

Myers, Stewart C., 1977, Determinants of corporate borrowing, Journal of Finance 5, 147–155.

Sachs, Jeffrey D., 1981, The current account and macroeconomic adjustment in the 1970s, Brookings Papers on Economic Activity 2.

Sachs, Jeffrey D., 1982a, The current account in the macroeconomic adjustment process, Scandinavian Journal of Economics 84 (2).

Sachs, Jeffrey D., 1982b, Aspects of the current account behavior of OECD economics, NBER Working paper no. 859, Feb. (NBER, Cambridge, MA).

Sachs, Jeffrey D., 1982c, Problems and prospects, in: P. Wachtel, ed., Crises in the economic and financial structure Lexington, MA).

Sachs, Jeffrey D., 1984, Theoretical issues in international borrowing, Princeton Studies in International Finance, no. 54.

Smith, Clifford and J. Warner, 1979, On financial contracting: An analysis of bond covenants, Journal of Financial Economics 7, 117–161.

Stiglitz, J. and A. Weiss, 1981, Credit rationing in markets with imperfect information: I, American Economic Review.

Winkler, Max, 1933, Foreign bonds: An autopsy (Swain, Philadelphia, PA).

Wynne, William H., 1951, State insolvency and foreign bondholders, vol. 11, Case histories (Yale University Press, New Haven, CT).

European Economic Review 30 (1986) . North-Holland

COMMENT

'A Geometrical Analysis of the Incentives for Default and Credit Rationing' by Daniel Cohen and Jeffrey Sachs

William D. NORDHAUS

Yale University, New Haven, CT 06520, USA

The paper by Cohen and Sachs forms part of a growing literature attempting to understand and explain the enormously complex set of phenomena surrounding the international debt issue. Its strength is that it places the discussion of lenders and sovereign borrowers into an explicit intertemporal framework and derives therein an explicit description of debt dynamics. Its weakness is mainly that, as a purely theoretical exercise, we are left unsure about whether it describes wordly phenomena or whether, like a growing part of economic literature, it is self-referential. In my comments I will undertake both to explain the Cohen–Sachs results and to place them in the context of behavior in the trenches of economic life.

Fig. 1 describes the apparatus concisely in a static framework. A country contracts debt D. With this debt it is able to produce *gross wealth* (equal to the present value of income) shown as $W(D)$. With no debt, the country is at autarky point, N. But, at least in the more realistic model of part 4, the marginal product of debt (equal to the marginal product of capital times the

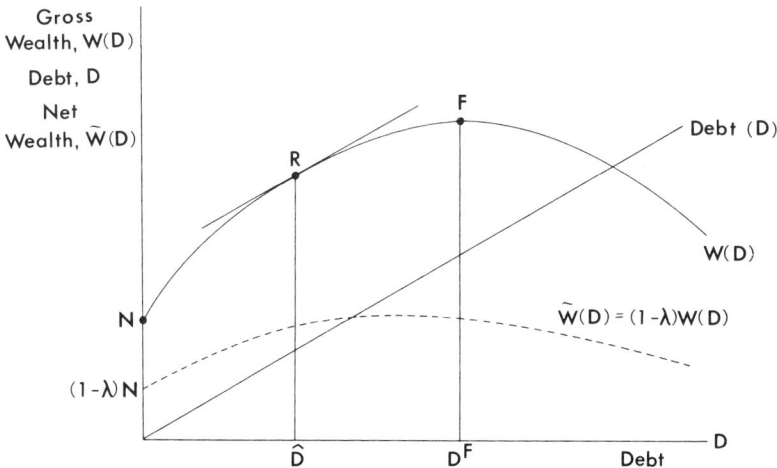

Fig. 1. Wealth and net wealth without default.

fraction of debt going into capital) is higher than the interest rate on the debt – hence the $W(D)$ curve rises rapidly at first. Then the country gradually becomes saturated with capital and debt, so $W'(D)=0$ at D^F. A country wishes to maximize its *net wealth* (or discounted value of income after either paying off debt or defaulting). If a country undertakes to repay its debt, then its wealth is equal to gross wealth less debt, shown as the solid line in fig. 2.

To understand a country's incentive to repay its debt, we consider curves showing the effect of repudiation. In fig. 1, repudiation lowers *net wealth* to $\tilde{W}(D)=(1-\lambda)W(D)$, shown as the dashed line. According to Cohen–Sachs, the $\tilde{W}(D)$ line lies exactly $(1-\lambda)$ below the $W(D)$ line, reflecting the assumption that the fraction λ of output, and hence of the present value of output, is lost because of loss of access to capital markets as well as because of other forms of economic retaliation.

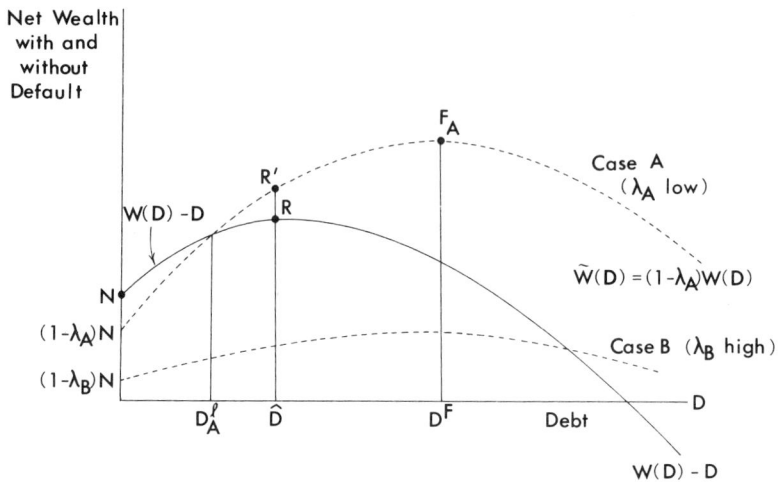

Fig. 2. Net wealth with and without default; lending limits at D_A^l.

Fig. 2 lays out a country's choices. If a country plays the repayment game, it stays on the solid line; as long as it knows it will always play the repayment game, its best policy is to borrow only up to point $\hat{D}$, the *honest optimum*.

If a country is contemplating repudiation, it must consider dashed lines in fig. 2, which represent net wealth after repudiation. If λ is high (as in case B of fig. 2), then it will never pay for a country to repudiate its debts. Lenders know that repudiation doesn't pay, so they need not constrain lending. Cohen and Sachs' Proposition 1 concerns the corner solution of $\lambda=1$, but there must also be a whole range of relatively high λ's where repudiation does not pay so banks need not restrain lending.

The more interesting situation in case A, where losses from repudiation are low. Note that for any debt level greater than D_A^l, a country is better off repudiating its debt than repaying its debt. At the honest optimal debt level $\hat{D}$, a country's wealth rises from R to R' after repudiation.

Enter the lenders. As Cohen and Sachs show, because lenders understand borrowers' options, they will never lend more than D_A^l in fig. 2. For debt levels up to D_A^l, lenders prefer not to default. Cohen and Sachs show that until debt is accumulated up to D_A^l, there will be no credit rationing. But once borrowers reach D_A^l, lenders will lend no more for fear of leading borrowers into temptation.

Using this informal graphical apparatus, we can perhpas shed some light on realistic aspects of international indebtedness.

(*1*) To begin with, it is apparent that there is a threshold λ^*, which is given by $(1-\lambda^*)W(D^F) = W(\hat{D}) - \hat{D}$. For λ is greater than λ^*, credit rationing is necessary. For λ less than λ^*, the painful consequences of default make credit rationing unnecessary.

(*2*) This insight leads to a second and paradoxical conclusion. If we can make the consequences of default sufficiently automatic and painful, then borrowers will exercise the necessary restraint on themselves. Conversely, the more humane and generous become the institutions of national bankruptcy and IMF lending, the more will lenders have to protect their portfolios. Hence, it is in the interest of *debtors* to make the rules of default more draconian. By raising the cost of default, default becomes less attractive and lenders will thereby raise their lending limits. (I might add that I have yet to find a constrained country that espoused draconian consequences of default or debt rescheduling – just as I have yet to find a lender who advocated repeal of usury legislation or a homeless person lobbying for decontrol of apartment rents. The inability of people to perceive subtle self-interests is troubling here as in other places.)

(*3*) A third point about the approach concerns the nature of the equilibrium. They propose that banks simply calculate the indifference point at D^l in fig. 2 and then ration their lending. Alas, this would be a very poor policy because behavior at that point – and the payoffs – is violently asymmetrical. Start out in an equilibrium where a country – call it Mañanaland – has borrowed up to the limit, $D^l < \hat{D}$. Everyone is solvent; everyone is happy. Then a foolish go-go bank – Penn Square, if you will – lends a bit more, so Mañanaland decides to default. Mañanaland doesn't much care whether it defaults or not, but banks care a lot as they lose their entire portfolio of D^l-plus.

Or do they? Won't everyone be better off is the banks 're-schedule' the debt, effectively reducing Mañanaland's debt below the default threshold? Such a solution makes everyone better off – everyone except future lenders. But if lenders blink in the face of disaster (as they have every time to date), doesn't this give borrowers tremendous power to threaten default? Won't the whole process break down because default is so wasteful? If default never occurs, because default is never the solution of the relevant game, then the analysis becomes curiously irrelevant?

(4) Although the authors do not relate their paper to recent events, they might use their results to explain the dramatic decline in lending during the early 1980's. According to their theory, what occurred was that major Latin American countries were suddenly at the point where a default was economically attractive relative to repayment. Banks were reining in countries to keep them in the corral of responsible financial behavior.

While this explanation is ingenious, it is flying against a very powerful fact – that no non-communist country has defaulted since World War II. If all the big Latin American countries were really near the threshold, then one would certainly have tipped over the threshold and declared default after 1980. My hunch is that default is so undesirable that countries will go to any lengths to avoid it. If this hunch is correct, then countries are in case B of fig. 2 – they are not tempted to default and in fact are not being credit rationed to avoid default.

Surely, you will say, *something* was happening to debtor countries and to banks. What was happening was that countries were forcing banks to reschedule at the same time countries were being visited by the IMF. Perhaps this is the set of events to which the Cohen–Sachs paper applies. If a debt rescheduling is a partial default under another name, then banks will ration credit to Mañanaland as long as rescheduling is not unpleasant enough to make countries restrain themselves. So perhaps the Cohen–Sachs model really will apply to events of the 1980's, where the analyzed event is the complex set of events involving IMF negotiations and debt rescheduling.

The curious factor here, however, is that the events surrounding an IMF visit are not well described by a high λ. Indeed, most orthodox economists would say that an IMF visit allows a country to undertake policies that improve future prospects, or have a negative λ! By the Cohen–Sachs logic, won't every country desire rescheduling? Perhaps not. For an IMF visit is an interesting arrangement – somewhat like making convicted felons pick up garbage – which is immediately unpleasant to *decisionmakers* even though it is ultimately healthy to the *country*. It has a high *psychic* λ and a negative *real* λ. Surely as an institution such an arrangement is far improved over the horribly inefficient mechanism of default – indeed from the point of view of institutional arrangements to combat self-selection and moral hazard, the arrangement is remarkable.